Third Edition

Population Change in Canada

Don Kerr
Roderic Beaujot

OXFORD
UNIVERSITY PRESS

OXFORD
UNIVERSITY PRESS

Oxford University Press is a department of the University of Oxford.
It furthers the University's objective of excellence in research, scholarship,
and education by publishing worldwide. Oxford is a registered trade mark of
Oxford University Press in the UK and in certain other countries.

Published in Canada by
Oxford University Press
8 Sampson Mews, Suite 204,
Don Mills, Ontario M3C 0H5 Canada

www.oupcanada.com

Copyright © Oxford University Press Canada 2016

Library and Archives Canada Cataloguing in Publication
Beaujot, Roderic P., 1946-, author
Population change in Canada / Don Kerr and Roderic Beaujot.
– Third edition.

Revision of: Beaujot, Roderic P. Population change in Canada.
Includes bibliographical references and index.
ISBN 978-0-19-900262-7 (paperback)

1. Canada–Population. 2. Canada–Population policy.
I. Kerr, Donald W., 1959-, author II. Title.

HB3529.B43 2015   363.90971   C2015-904555-X

Cover image: © iStock/tonivaver

Population Change
in Canada

Contents

Tables

Figures

Boxes

Preface

Fully a decade has passed since the previous edition of *Population Change in Canada*, and for this reason, this book is a complete revision and update of the earlier work. Our book attempts to cover the full range of areas relevant to the study of Canadian demography: the science of population. It has been designed primarily for use as a supplemental text for a course on population studies, yet can be considered of general interest to the student of sociology, history, geography, economics, and public policy. Of particular interest throughout the text are ongoing references to the *consequences* of population change, or, more specifically, what might be the appropriate policy response when we consider the impact of demographic change on fundamental aspects of Canadian society.

Demography can be defined as "the study of population in terms of processes (fertility, mortality, and migration) and states (population size, distribution, and composition)." This third edition of *Population Change in Canada* begins by providing some historical context, including a separate chapter on Canada's pre-Confederation population. We then move on to devote three chapters to these demographic processes (mortality, fertility, and migration), prior to providing three chapters on the consequences of population change (regional distribution, population growth, and age structure). From here, we consider changes in population composition, including a separate chapter on change in the Canadian family and household units as well as a chapter on Canada's sociocultural and socioeconomic characteristics. Given the importance of First Nations people in Canada's history and development, we also offer an entire chapter on Aboriginal demography.

In this third edition of the text, we offer a new penultimate chapter on population and environment, including efforts to link developments in Canada with what has been happening elsewhere on the environment front. With only half of 1 per cent of the global population living in Canada, we can't help but remind ourselves that what happens elsewhere in the world really matters, particularly when we think about population growth and the environment. Global population surpassed the 7 billion mark in 2011, and it is expected to easily top 9 billion, and possibly even 10 billion, well within the lifetime of most of our students. We take the position here that demographic developments occurring in Canada should not be observed in isolation.

We owe debts of thanks to many people, but most of all to Statistics Canada, where we each worked at earlier stages of our careers. Most of the data come directly or indirectly from Statistics Canada, not only from the Census, but also from its surveys, ranging from the Labour Force Survey and the National Household Survey, to various general social surveys. We also borrowed heavily from Statistics Canada's Population Estimates and Projections, as well as many of its flagship publications, particularly the *Report on the Demographic Situation in Canada*, but also *Health Reports*, *Canadian Social Trends*, *Perspectives on Labour and Income*, *Canadian Economic Observer*, and *Education Quarterly Review*. We could not do better than to encourage students to read further in these publications and to learn from their methods of analyzing and writing about the Canadian population. We strongly encourage students to subscribe to the free email version of *The Daily*, from Statistics Canada. If they check their email and read *The Daily* when they get up in the morning, students will be ahead of the media and possibly ahead of their professor, who is likely busy preparing for the lecture.

We also owe debts of thanks to Canadian demographers whose research and insight we have used liberally in this volume. It is our hope that we have not done any injustice to their work, and we take full responsibility for any errors or misinterpretations.

Some pieces of Chapter 4 are taken from "Family Policies in Quebec and the Rest of Canada" in *Canadian Public Policy* (co-authored with C. Du and Z. Ravanera), as well as "Low Fertility in Canada: The Nordic Model in Quebec versus the U.S. Model in Alberta" in *Canadian Studies in Population* (co-authored with J. Wang). Parts of Chapter 5 come from a chapter on immigration (co-authored with M. Raza) in *Canadian Studies in the New Millennium*, published by University of Toronto Press. Portions of Chapter 9 come from "Family Diversity and Inequality" (co-authored with Z. Ravanera and J. Liu), a discussion paper published by the Population Change and Life Course Cluster. Chapter 11 here borrows from our chapter on Aboriginal demography in *Visions from the Heart* (Oxford University Press), and parts of Chapter 12 come from "Energy, Population, and the Environment" (co-authored with H. Mellon) in the journal *Population and the Environment*. Other parts of this book have migrated through *Earning and Caring in Canadian Families* (Broadview Press, 2000), which won the Porter Award of the Canadian Sociology Association.

We would also like to thank our respective institutions, the University of Western Ontario and Kings University College at Western, which have supported us throughout this work. In addition, Donna Maynard has helped us with her work on tables, graphs, and bibliographies, as well as a careful proofreading of the text. We cannot say enough to thank Oxford University Press's reviewers for their most supportive comments and thoughtful suggestions. We are also indebted to Phyllis Wilson, managing editor at Oxford, Michelle Welsh, senior production coordinator, as well as Joe Zingrone, who has done an exceptional job of careful and insightful editing.

—Don Kerr and Roderic Beaujot
May 2015

1 The Study of Population Change

The Chapter at a Glance

- Demography involves the study of population—its size, growth, distribution, composition, fertility, mortality, and migration.
- Demography distinguishes between population states (size, distribution over space, and composition by various characteristics) and population processes (fertility, mortality, and migration); it analyzes how processes influence states and vice versa.
- Population processes are mostly studied through rates, and population states through proportions and distributions.
- Thomas Malthus argued that populations have a tendency to grow more rapidly than other resources but that people can control the growth of the population by reducing the number of children they have. In contrast, Karl Marx argued that economic and social conditions determine the rate of population growth and that proper social arrangements should be able to accommodate population growth.
- The demographic-transition theory summarizes the history of population growth through three stages: from high birth and death rates, to a stage where mortality declines faster than fertility, and eventually to a new equilibrium of low birth and death rates. Economic and cultural factors are involved in fertility change.

Introduction

The release of the 2011 Census helped to increase our awareness of important changes occurring in the Canadian population. Counter to earlier expectations, Canada's growth rate in the first decade of the twenty-first century was actually slightly greater than the demographic growth during the 1990s. The first release on population size not only showed a continuation of growth—up by almost 6 per cent over the 2006–2011 period—but also that this demographic growth outpaced all other G8 countries. This was largely due to the influx of new Canadians, as immigration was shown to be responsible for over two thirds of the nation's overall demographic growth.

With immigration and internal migration unevenly distributed geographically, Canada's growth across provinces and regions continues to be uneven. Partially due to the strength of Canada's resource sector—and specifically, the strength of economic activity in Canada's western provinces—population growth in Alberta, Saskatchewan, and British Columbia all outpaced that of other provinces from 2006 to 2011. Over the same period of time, Ontario's population growth slipped below the national average for the first time in over 25 years. For the first time, the population share of all provinces west of Ontario (the Prairie provinces and British Columbia) surpassed that of all provinces to east of Ontario (the Atlantic provinces and Quebec) at 30.7 per cent relative to 30.6 per cent. *The Globe and Mail*'s editorial "Go West, Young Canadians" reflected this ongoing shift in the distribution of population westward (Wente, 2012). In addition, demographic growth continued to be concentrated in Canada's large urban centres, whereas most other regions of Canada grew very little or even declined.

When the age and sex data were released from the 2011 Census we were made aware of how quickly the population was aging. While Canada's birth rate had risen slightly from 2000's historic low of 1.49 births per woman to 1.61 births per woman in 2011, the greying of Canada's baby boom generation continued to dominate the country's age structure. For the first time, the census showed that there were more persons aged 55–64, typically the ages when people exit the workforce, than people aged 15–24, typically around the time persons start working. Questions were raised about immigration as a means of ensuring the growth of the labour force. The 2011 Census release on language data also showed that the strongest growth was taking place among people whose first language was neither English nor French, and that outside Quebec, only about one in ten of the population was bilingual in the official languages.

The projections of population expect these overall trends to continue. In 1951, for instance, there were 7 people between the ages of 20 and 64 for every person 65 and over, but this ratio had been reduced to about 4.5 to 1 by 2011. It is expected that by 2031, there will be fewer than three people of working age for every person of retirement ages. Besides the higher proportion of retirees and associated problems concerning pension plans, the anticipated future aging of the population raises questions about economic growth when the population and the labour force are growing more slowly. The particularly rapid growth of the population aged 80 and above can be expected to make more demands on the health-care system. The uneven distribution of population, accentuated by immigration, may intensify regional disparity. The relative growth of populations with native languages other than English and French may undermine the very definition of Canada as a bilingual country.

These examples illustrate the importance of demographic questions. Our purpose here is to take a systematic look at population change in Canada. This includes interpreting past change, anticipating possible future changes and their implications. After a chapter on the history of the population before Confederation, we will take a close look at each of mortality, fertility, immigration, and internal migration. In the following chapters, we will then look at the overall growth of the population, with a separate chapter on its changing age structure. There follow three chapters on population composition: by

household and family units, by sociocultural and socioeconomic characteristics, and by Aboriginal status. In addition, we have added a chapter in which we consider the environmental impact of continued population growth.

The Reasons for Studying Population

Two of the most important features of any society are the number of people and the relative size of the various subgroups. When populations grow or shrink and when subgroups change in relative size, various repercussions may follow.

Consider English–French relations in Canada. For a long time, the French constituted about a third of the population. In response to heavy English immigration, French-Canadian society emphasized the importance of births for maintaining the relative power of the French element in the country. A Catholic priest called for *la revanche du berceau*— that is, for maintaining a high francophone birth rate as a means of securing the status of the French in the country. When Quebec fertility fell in the 1960s and the French-speaking population of Canada dropped to nearly a quarter of the total, the long-term relationship between the country's two charter groups was threatened.

Particularly problematic for Quebec was the eagerness of various immigrant groups to associate themselves with the English minority of the province. In the early 1970s, it was even feared that French would no longer be the working language in the province. Various measures have been taken over the years in response to this demographic change, such as the Official Languages Act, the policy on multiculturalism, the granting to Quebec the right to have a voice in the selection of immigrants, and the Quebec Charter of the French Language (Bill 101). The constitutional crises of the 1980s and '90s, particularly as they pertain to the concept of Quebec as a distinct society, show that Canada is still looking for ways to accommodate its changing demographics.

Aging is another crucial feature of the changing relative size of various subgroups of the population. Although aging is a long-term phenomenon, different stages have different consequences. At first, population aging took place in Canada because there were fewer children. Between 1966 and 1981, for instance, the population grew by 22 per cent but the number of people under the age of 15 declined by 17 per cent. These *early stages of aging* were relatively easy to accommodate. Although changes in the sizes of different age groups caused difficulties in the school system, in a broad sense, adults were freer because they had fewer children to care for. These changes both enlarged the proportion of the population that was at an employable age and freed women from family responsibilities, thereby encouraging them to join the labour force. These trends permitted an expansion of the social programs that depend on revenues from the taxation of employed persons (particularly health, education, social security, and pension programs).

At *later stages of aging*, however, it is no longer the relative size of the population of labour-force age that is growing, but rather the numbers of seniors. From 1986 to 2011, although the population grew by 31.5 per cent, the number of people aged 65 and over grew by about 80 per cent. In 1986, the population aged 65 and over constituted 10.7 per cent of the total, compared to 14.8 per cent according to the 2011 Census; and by 2036, when the baby boomers are all retired, it could make up a quarter of the population. In effect, our social programs were set up when the demographic and economic circumstances were very different. When the population of labour-force age is growing and real incomes are increasing, it is not hard to enrich our social programs, including those, such as health and pensions that benefit the elderly. But policy debates surrounding taxation and social programs show that accommodations in the later stages of aging may not be as easy as in the earlier stages. Some observers have come to question whether we will be able to afford all our social programs. Others call for different forms of accommodation, such as greater individual responsibility for personal health, greater repayment for the economic benefits of government-subsidized education, a longer work life, lower pension benefits, and even the promotion of higher birth rates and increased immigration.

Another phenomenon that can be studied from the point of view of population change is health. A comparison of the relative health of various sectors of the population shows differences across groups—these differences point to the dynamics of well-being as a major concern. For instance, men have always had a lower life expectancy than women, but the longer lifespan of women has shrunk over time from seven to four years. Besides the purely biological factors in this difference, there are important differences between men and women regarding risk factors in health, including smoking, drinking, diet, and exercise. Although the gender differences in smoking for young people have largely disappeared, the mortality of older persons is still affected by past differences in their behaviour. Similarly, the higher life expectancy of married persons can partly be attributed to the "protective role of marriage." That is, married people benefit from having someone to help them when they are ill or if they fall on hard times. Married men, in particular, have historically benefited from keeping better diets than single men—and they engage in fewer risky activities (Trovato, 1998).

We can also look at the consequences of population change at the level of the total human population. Some scholars have proposed that, in biological terms, the rapid growth of the human species is a catastrophic event for the planet, comparable to an ice age or a collision with a substantial meteor. Biologists measure change over millions of years and, from that point of view, the human presence, which was once insignificant, can be seen as changing the very environment of the planet. Many call for sustainable development, and various world meetings sponsored by the United Nations are attempting to find ways to ensure that the sheer size of the human population does not endanger our viability on the planet.

The Study of Population

Demography is the study of populations, their size, distribution, and composition, and the immediate causes of population change—births, deaths, and migration. We are interested in the stock and flow of population. The stock, or the population state, is a picture of the population at one point in time, including its size, its geographical distribution, and its composition among a variety of characteristics, including age, sex, marital status, education, language spoken at home, occupation, income, and so on. The flow, or the population processes, changes population from one point in time to another. People are born, they move around, and they die. Demographically, these processes are called fertility, migration, and mortality. Population states and processes are inter-related: for instance, fewer births (process) produce an older population (state), and also an older popula-tion tends to have a lower birth rate.

The links between population processes and states are most easily studied through the change in population size (see also Appendix D, "Population Estimates and Demographic Accounts"). A change in population size—that is, a change from one state to a second state—is clearly a function of intervening births, deaths, immigration, and emigration. Births minus deaths is called *natural increase* and immigra-tion minus emigration is called *net migration*. Thus, the basic equation for population at a given time is as follows:

$$P_2 = P_1 + B - D + I - E$$

where P_2 is the population at a given time, P_1 is the population at an earlier time (normally the time at which a census is taken), B is the number of births in the interval, D is the number of deaths in the interval, I is the number of immigrants who arrived in the interval, and E is the number of emigrants who departed in the interval.

When we consider the distribution of the popu-lation over space, the analysis becomes more com-plex. For one thing, international immigrants tend to settle in certain parts of the country more than in oth-ers. For another, internal immigration is not evenly distributed throughout the country, either in terms of the migrants' destinations or their places of origin. Finally, regions may differ in fertility and mortality rates. Changes in a society's age structure can also be affected by births, deaths, and migration. Other analy-ses of changes in population states follow the same pattern. Recall that a population stock, or state, is the picture of a population at one time in terms of size,

distribution, or composition. For instance, we could analyze the change in composition by marital status, educational attainment, or labour-force status. Health may be studied in terms of the transitions from good to poor health, and vice versa, along with the factors that help predict these transitions.

We have been considering how the population processes of fertility, mortality, and migration affect the population states of size, distribution, and com-position. We could also consider how population *states* affect population *processes*. One of the reasons for the decrease in the number of births in Canada, for instance, is that at present, the composition of the population by marital status is characterized by a lower proportion of young adults living in marital or cohabiting unions. As another example, the number of deaths in Canada is increasing, not because death rates in any age groups are increasing, but because there is now a greater proportion of people at ages at which deaths are more common—that is, we have an older population.

Besides the relationship between population states and processes, we are interested in the rel-evance of demographics to our changing society. Births, migrations, and deaths mark an individual's life course. While these events are clearly experienced by people, added together they also demarcate the development of societies over time. At the group level, fertility and immigration are the basic mech-anisms through which populations, countries, soci-eties, and communities are regenerated. Not only do these regenerative processes add numbers to the population, ensuring demographic continuity in the face of departures through death and emigration, but they also change the character of the population and, consequently, the society. The character of the popu-lation is changed in terms of age and sex structure, socioeconomic composition, cultural makeup, and regional distribution.

When we try to understand how a society changes and how it compares to other societies, it is natural to start by describing its demographic profile. In effect, the study of population is closely inter-twined with the study of society. One looks to the broader society in attempting to understand both the causes and the consequences of demographic phenomena. You would, for example, consider various social factors when analyzing the causes of variations in fertility, mortality, and migration. A demographer also takes into account that certain population trends, like the rate of growth, the distribution over space, and the composition by language, have consequences for the society.

The study of population also has practical importance. To plan public services, it is important to know the nature of the population groups that need these services. How many people are at retirement age, and how will this change in the future? How many single-parent families are there? What proportion of the unemployed are secondary wage earners in their families? These are among a host of questions that are important to the structuring of social programs.

Population and Policy

Given that demographic processes are fundamental to societies and their regeneration, society has a vested interest in ensuring that population dynamics operate to produce an overall net benefit (Demeny, 1986). All societies attempt to shape the decisions made by individuals in such a way as to promote this common benefit. Behaviour that promotes reproduction will sometimes be encouraged and sometimes discouraged. Behaviour that will prolong a person's life in the society will be encouraged, and the society will often take some responsibility for the health and safety of its citizens. And with respect to immigration, the society as a whole will establish structures, policies, and rules through which entry (and sometimes exit) are controlled in order to produce a social benefit.

There are a number of questions that interest the society as a whole. How many new members are to be added and by what means (through births or immigration)? How are the costs of these additions to be paid, and who receives the benefits? How should the costs and benefits of children be absorbed by the families into which they are born, the extended family, the community, and society as a whole? How are the costs and benefits of immigration to be distributed between, on the one hand, the immigrants themselves and their sponsoring families and, on the other hand,

the receiving country, province, city, and community? To what extent are health and safety the responsibility of the individual or the surrounding society? How does society accommodate an aging population in terms of pensions, health care, and regenerating the labour force while ensuring that the young are not disadvantaged? These are among the policy questions that all societies must address.

Public policy on changing demographics can take two forms: it can attempt to influence the course of demographic events, or it can ensure that society makes the adjustments necessary to accommodate the population change. Some policies are aimed directly at influencing population processes, while others have unintended effects on population. Demographic trends also need to be considered in the analysis of such policy issues as support services for the aged, health, education, the labour force, and social security. Especially in a welfare state—that is, where the state takes some responsibility for the welfare of individuals—detailed knowledge about the population is important for those who make policy.

Such policy considerations underline the importance of gathering accurate information. Censuses were first taken to enable rulers to tax their citizens and to determine the number of men available for military service. With the advent of the welfare state, it is particularly important for governments to have accurate and up-to-date information on the populace, whose welfare they are trying to enhance. It is crucial for governments to know how various groups would benefit or suffer from a given policy.

Data and Methods

The data used for demographic analyses come largely from the censuses, registries of vital statistics, and other administrative files. In Canada, censuses are taken every five years, and births and deaths are registered through various provincial and territorial departments. Immigration is regulated, and information is collected about every landed immigrant. That leaves only emigration and illegal immigration to be estimated. Using Canadian data recorded over the period 1971–2011, Appendix D shows the basic equation by which population change can be studied over time.

The methods used in the study of population start with proportions and rates. Proportions show how a population is distributed into subparts, by geography (generally called *population distribution*), age and sex (*population structure*), and other characteristics (*population composition*). In the study of population states, much use is made of proportions—that is, considering how a total population is divided into various subparts, each representing a certain proportion of the total. Rates represent the frequency of events occurring in a given population at a given time. Population processes are studied through rates, which are numbers of events (e.g., births and deaths) per population exposed to the risk of that event (see also Appendix C, "2014 World Population Data Sheet"). The Glossary at the end of this book further defines crude rates and various specific rates that are used in the study of population. Appendix B, "Crude Rates, the Total Fertility Rate, and Standardization," illustrates further how rates and probabilities of death can be analyzed through life tables.

An important technique used for demographic analysis is called *standardization*. This takes advantage of the observation that rates of a given phenomenon may be different in various parts of a population, and, thus, the change in the relative size of these parts, or the population composition, may influence the overall predominance of the event in the population (see Appendix B). For instance, in order to see if crime rates are really changing, one should standardize for the changing age structure of the population, since there are different crime rates at different ages (i.e., young adults are far more likely to commit certain types of crimes). The standardization method can also be used to decompose the prevalence of events. Demographers are trying to determine the extent to which the changed prevalence of events in the total population is due to (1) changes in the composition of the population and/or (2) rate changes in subparts of the population. A change in a given phenomenon, then, is analyzed in terms of rates in subparts of the population and the relative size of these subparts of the population.

Demographic analyses often use a cohort approach. A cohort is a group of people who all experienced a particular event in the same period of time. For instance, people who were all born in a particular period (i.e., a birth cohort) can be followed over their lives in terms of marrying, having children, and dying. Similarly, everyone who finished school in a given year can be followed in terms of their entry into the labour force, career progression, and retirement. The cohort approach can be a very useful way of studying various social and economic phenomena.

The Canadian Census and the 2011 Long-Form-Census Controversy

In the summer of 2010, less than a year before the 2011 Census date, the federal government effectively cancelled the 2011 mandatory long-form census. Prior to this decision, Statistics Canada had relied upon data provided by both the short-form census (which remained in place in 2011) and an accompanying long-form census, this latter document completed by one in five households, once every five years. All Canadians (citizens, landed immigrants, and non-permanent residents) were required by law to complete their census forms. In combination, this methodology allowed for the collection of high-quality information on Canada's population structure and composition, with past censuses reporting response rates hovering at about 95 per cent. Past censuses, in particular, had provided detailed information on the population composition of Canada, not only at the national and provincial/territorial levels, but also at the more granular levels of smaller geographies—including smaller cities, towns, and even neighbourhoods.

This information was not only invaluable to demographers, but also to a wide range of users, such as academics, industry analysts, government planners, school boards, NGOs, among many others. Protesting the decision to end the long-form census, then chief statistician of Canada, Munir Sheikh, emphasized its utility to the federal government, as "decisions based on evidence, rather than ideology, enhance the well-being of citizens both at the personal and public policy levels" (Sheikh, 2013). As a replacement for the long form, the Harper government directed Statistics Canada to undertake a "voluntary" survey to supplement the short-form census: the National Household Survey (NHS). The justification was that the government should not be "forcing" Canadians to provide personal information via a mandatory census. The new NHS would include the original 59 questions of the long-form census and be sent out to 30 per cent of households.

The initial reaction among users of Canadian data was near uniform. The fear was that the cancellation of the long form would lead to lower-quality data at a higher price tag. The reason people worried about lower quality related to the fact that voluntary surveys must address the biases associated with *non-response* (i.e., people who do not complete an optional survey typically differ from those who do). When conducting social research, the higher the non-response, typically the higher the resultant bias. It is well understood among social scientists that non-response tends to be "selective"—for example, selective in terms of the socioeconomic characteristics of the population. Boudarbat and Grenon have recently demonstrated with Canadian data that low-income groups tend to be less likely to participate in voluntary surveys than middle-income groups (Boudarbat and Grenon, 2013). In addition, the NHS was expected to cost more, as not only would it require greater initial follow-up, but also it targeted a larger proportion of households (e.g., 30 per cent compared to 20 per cent with the long form).

Particularly troubling in this context was the federal government's complete disregard for the views of senior scientists at Statistics Canada, ultimately leading to the resignation of the then Chief Statistician, Munir Sheikh. The government also ignored the vocal opposition of social scientists from across the country, including academics, but also analysts working at other levels of government and within industry; public health officials; urban planners; as well as the other political parties in Parliament. The academic associations opposed to this decision included the Canadian Federation of Demographers, the Canadian Sociology Association, the Canadian Association of Geographers, the Canadian Economics Association, and the Canadian Federation of Social Sciences and Humanities. Among non-academic associations, the Canadian Medical Association was vocal in its opposition, as this move was seen as a threat to the quality

of data available in epidemiological research and health-care planning. The Federation of Canadian Municipalities was vocal in its critique, as cities are reliant upon census data, often at the neighbourhood level, in the planning for and evaluation of urban services.

The opposition to this decision was eventually shown to be well founded. The Auditor General of Canada reported in 2014 that the voluntary NHS in 2011 had cost taxpayers an additional $22 million while producing less reliable data (Ferguson, 2014). Despite all of Statistics Canada's expertise going into the NHS, the preliminary response level in the NHS was at 69 per cent (Michalowski, 2013). Even though the response was quite high by the standards of a voluntary survey, it was markedly lower than the 93.5 per cent response rate of the 2006 Census's mandatory long form. While Statistics Canada did an exceptional job in the adjustment of the NHS in light of identifiable biases, the quality of information available in 2011 was decidedly below that of the 2006 Census. The NHS suffered from a suppression of data for approximately 25 per cent of Canada's *census subdivisions* (CSDs), as only geographies with global response rates of greater than 50 per cent were released—of the 4,567 CSDs across the country, Statistics Canada released data for 3,439 of them.

Overall, Statistics Canada can be credited for its implementation of the NHS, as it was the largest voluntary survey of its kind in Canadian history and StatsCan was asked to conduct the NHS with only a few months' notice. The agency has always been transparent in its data evaluation, warning users of possible biases, particularly for smaller municipalities with populations under 25,000. This includes issues regarding data comparability over time on First Nations populations, ethnicity, mobility, education, housing, income, and language (Houle, 2013; Michaud, 2014). Michaud points out that there was likely an overstatement in the number of Canadians reporting some university education and that the low-income estimates from the NHS were markedly different from what is suggested by the Canada Revenue Agency's tax files and StatsCan's Survey of Labour and Income Dynamics. In other words, lower-income Canadians in many regions appear to have been under-reported in the 2011 NHS—leaving for difficulties in comparing the 2011 NHS with the 2006 long-form census.

This third edition of *Population Change in Canada* is selective in its use of NHS data, as there are limits in terms of what we consider trustworthy. Since the demographic data on place of residence, age, sex, marital status, household and family composition, and language were collected in the 2011 short-form census, these data are of high quality and comparable to earlier censuses. Also, the statistics published at the national and provincial/territorial levels appear to be of decent quality, largely due to StatsCan's skill in making adjustments for known biases in non-response. Yet this edition of our book does not use information from the NHS on income

characteristics; fortunately, there are other sources within Statistics Canada for high-quality income data at the national and provincial/territorial levels. The likelihood of bias increases when a study focuses on smaller areas (e.g., towns, neighbourhoods, census tracts)—that is not what we emphasize here. At the time of writing, the plan for 2016 is to again rely upon the NHS rather than the long form, and the next federal election is expected in the fall of 2015. Two former chief statisticians of StatsCan, Ivan Fellegi (1985–2008) and Munir Sheikh (2008–2010), are on the record in arguing that Canada's Statistics Act be reformed to give Statistics Canada greater autonomy in fulfilling its mandate, particularly with regard to technical and methodological matters (Fellegi, 2010; Sheikh, 2010).

Box 1.1 ▣ Privacy Rights and the Statistics Act

Part of the justification behind the federal government's long-form census decision relates to alleged privacy concerns expressed by Canadians. In 2010, for example, then industry minister Tony Clement said that he received many complaints from citizens about the intrusive nature of the long-form census; one of his predecessors, Maxime Bernier, also claimed that he was inundated with complaints in the months leading up to the 2006 Census (Brennan, 2010). Yet critics have since argued that the politicians were misleading the public and that the decision made by Stephen Harper's government was driven more by ideology than by any real threat to the privacy of Canadians (Simpson, 2010). Support for this position later came from a report of Canada's privacy commissioner, which published a formal and independent investigation of this matter. In so doing, it documented just 3 complaints about the 2006 Census and only 50 complaints about the census over the previous 20 years (Office of the Privacy Commissioner of Canada, 2011).

In a sarcastic manner, the political scientist Saurette (2010) writes, "Just in case you're won-

dering, in statistical terms that's 0.0000067 per cent of all Canadians complaining or something close to 0.000015 per cent of households." The federal government has yet to provide any direct evidence to contradict this report—Maxime Bernier merely stated in 2006 that the emails he referred to were obtained exclusively by his constituency office (since deleted) and not by Statistics Canada, the Ministry of Industry, or the Office of the Privacy Commissioner. Thompson (2010) situates this controversy into a wider international context by noting that the census has also been the subject of partisan politics in both the United States and the United Kingdom. As she points out, "The record of political interference in censuses elsewhere and the recent events in Canada point to the need for an informed discussion over the desirability and feasibility of strengthening the institutional autonomy of Statistics Canada."

Perhaps part of the problem relates to a simple misunderstanding of the privacy rights of Canadians—for example, many Canadians are not fully aware of how the information as collected in the census is protected under the Statistics Act. As a result, some might worry about the potential misuse of this information. Yet, while the Statistics Act has granted StatsCan the authority to enact a mandatory census every five years, in order to balance these extensive powers, the Act also establishes safeguards for privacy protection and confidentiality. The Statistics Act, for example, legally requires StatsCan to never release information in a form that allows for the identification of individuals without their authorization. The agency is forbidden by law from releasing information that could identify individuals, even if the request comes from another arm of government, such as the Canada Revenue Agency, the RCMP, and the courts. Furthermore, in publishing information, StatsCan always carefully screens final results to ensure confidentiality, releasing aggregated information only. In other words, all information as collected by Canada's statistical agency is kept under the strictest of confidentiality and is used exclusively for statistical purposes. We are not aware of any example whereby StatsCan has violated the Statistics Act and released compromising information from the census or any of its surveys. Proper safeguards have been in place both before and after the 2010 controversy over the long-form census.

Theories on the Causes and Consequences of Population Change

A useful starting point from which to study the causes and consequences of population change is the contrast between Thomas Malthus and Karl Marx. *Demographic-transition theory* will then be discussed in order to understand changes in mortality and fertility, with associated implications, especially in population growth and age structure.

Thomas Malthus

The political economist Thomas Malthus (1766–1834) was the first to develop a systematic theory of population change and its relation to economic conditions (Malthus, [1798] 1965). He considered the causes of population growth to be grounded in human nature. On the one hand, because of the natural attraction between the sexes, along with what he called an "urge to reproduce," Malthus thought there was a natural tendency for the population to grow—and so rapidly as to outgrow the food supply. On the other hand, he saw two checks on population growth. One, which he called "positive," occurred through mortality, from causes such as famine, epidemics, wars, and plagues. The other, which he called "preventive," occurred through fertility; it could take the form of "moral restraint,"—that is, the postponement of marriage or abstinence within marriage—or "vice," which included the prevention of births in marriage through abortion, infanticide, and other unacceptable methods of contraception.

Today, infanticide is universally condemned, and there are ongoing disagreements about abortion. Some people disagree with specific methods of contraception on ethical grounds, and others are concerned about the health risks of certain methods. It is perhaps not surprising, then, that Malthus, a nineteenth-century Anglican clergyman, argued both for abstinence and that marriages be postponed until a young person was sufficiently established to support children.

While Malthus's moral values seem somewhat antiquated by contemporary standards, some debate continues about what are acceptable and unacceptable means of reducing births. The dominant view at the 1994 United Nations conference on population and development was that the unacceptable means include a top-down population-control approach while reproductive health was promoted as the acceptable means for controlling births (United Nations, 1995).

Malthus also had a clear view of the basis for population change. Populations grow if births outnumber deaths—if this growth strains the available resources, there are likely to be more deaths or fewer births or both. If most births take place in marriage, the postponement of marriage or the use of contraception by married couples could be relied upon to produce fewer births.

Malthus thought that the consequences of population growth were serious. He argued that, left unchecked, population growth would proceed in a geometric progression (2, 4, 8, 16), whereas resources would grow only arithmetically (2, 4, 6, 8). What is important here is not whether there is precisely a geometric versus an arithmetic progression, but his conclusion that population has a tendency to grow more rapidly than available resources, particularly the supply of food. As a consequence, population growth could be expected to eventually bring about poverty and misery.

Particularly in his early writings, Malthus did not hold out much hope of finding a solution to this problem. If for some reason the food supply increased more than the population did, people would probably marry earlier and have more children, so there would eventually be even more people living in poverty. He felt strongly that people had to accept the consequences of their own actions, and he preached "responsible procreation" or "moral restraint" as a way of avoiding excessive growth.

Today, we often refer to Malthus's theory as the *Malthusian trap.* Advocates of Malthus argue that population is limited by the means of subsistence, and, consequently, continuous growth is not possible in a limited world. The Malthusian solution is to encourage a reduction in births, both through delayed marriages and, especially, through the use of contraception, in order to avoid an increase in deaths. Malthus's contribution to demography lay in his view of population growth as a serious problem that causes poverty, strains resources, and undermines efforts to improve society.

We shall return to Malthus in Chapter 12, "Population and the Environment," where we'll see that present-day neo-Malthusian thinking is less concerned with questions of food supply and more

concerned with the impact of population growth on the environment. Today, neo-Malthusian concerns have less to do with the number of people who can be fed and more to do with the consequences for the health and sustainability of a changing environment. Paul and Anne Ehrlich (1990) advanced this thinking by observing that the environment can be greatly affected by both rapid population growth and the unsavoury by-products of our affluent society: polluted water and air, the concentration of carbon dioxide in the atmosphere and its impact on climate change, as well as ozone depletion and the resulting exposure of people to ultraviolet light. It is not only a matter of population size and growth that is of concern, but also technological change and the associated consumption patterns. All of these sorts of variables are interrelated and their interaction can have negative effects. A shrinking and aging population, for instance, may not be well placed to change technology in an environmentally friendly direction.

Karl Marx

Karl Marx (1818–1883) wrote extensively on economic, political, and social relations in society, but his writing on population was mostly in opposition to Malthus (Marx [1890] 1906; Meek, 1971). Marx thought that there were several stages in human history—slavery, feudalism, capitalism, and socialism—and that in each, the vested interests of the various groups in society were different. Each stage had a unique "mode of production," or a way in which economic production was organized, and specific "relations of production," or relations among classes of people with different stakes in the production process. He also thought that each stage of human history had its own "laws of population," whereby the dynamics of population growth were derived from the mode of production and the relations of production as these worked themselves out in specific stages of human history.

Although Marx did not specify the laws of population for each stage of history, he did write about the population dynamics under capitalism specifically. He argued that the capitalist elite class had a tendency not only to become more powerful as it acquired increasing control over the means of production, but also to become smaller. In contrast, the working class, as it lost control over the product of its labour, would have a tendency to get larger. He argued that workers were not paid the full value of their labour and that the "surplus value" they generated was appropriated by the capitalist elite class, who would often invest this surplus value in technologies that displaced labour.

Marx observed that the capitalist economy tends to experience periods of strong growth and periods of recession. More workers are needed during growth periods; during periods of recession, those who are not needed are let go. As argued, surplus labour would ensure that wages be kept low in order to maximize the amount of surplus value that is extracted. Thus, the capitalist system depends on a "reserve army of labour." Since capitalism has become a world economic system, some of these dynamics have become evident at the global level. In particular, the argument follows that populations of the richer countries are becoming relatively smaller and the system is becoming more dependent on cheap labour and raw materials from the rapidly growing populations of developing nations.

Marx concluded that problems of excess population were specific to the capitalist system. According to him, the problem was not that there were too many people (overpopulation), but that there were too many poor people and that they were impoverished as a result of the exploitation of workers. He proposed that in a more equitable society, the problem would disappear. Contrary to Malthus, Marx felt that with the proper economic and social arrangements—which he called *socialism* and *communism*—people would be able to produce all the food and other resources necessary to accommodate population growth. He saw the populace not so much as consumers but as a labour force; more workers, he reasoned, should be able to create more wealth and more food.

Even if we do not agree with the specific stages of human history that Marx wrote about, and even if we question some of his conclusions regarding the "laws of population under capitalism," we cannot ignore his conclusion that, given certain economic and social arrangements, particular population dynamics will follow. According to Marx, if population dynamics

are to be changed, it is first necessary to change basic economic and social arrangements. In his view, rapid population growth is not a cause of social problems, as Malthus argued, but a consequence of specific socioeconomic conditions.

This sort of thinking regarding current population problems places these issues in the broader context of development. Today, many argue that development in poorer countries would reduce the numbers of impoverished people and, consequently, the growth of the population. Social development—i.e., improvements in health, education, and security, and a reduction in inequality—is more important than economic development in reducing fertility. However, these forms of development are dependent on establishing a new economic order with significant redistribution of wealth from the richer to the poorer countries.

The Contemporary Debate

While nineteenth-century thinking on population remains relevant today, the contemporary debate as to the determinants and consequences of population growth takes on various forms. Ehrlich and Ehrlich (2012) continue to argue that, given limited resources, rapid population growth will tear our world apart. As an opposite extreme, the US economist Julian Simon (1996) has argued the exact opposite position: that people constitute the ultimate resource, and that population growth, in fact, stimulates economic growth and innovation. Clearly, the Ehrlichs have been inspired by Malthus's thinking, whereas Simon explicitly attacks the neo-Malthusian argument. For Simon, population, or human capital, is the ultimate resource (i.e., human ingenuity and creativity), and greater population size implies an enhanced ability to solve basic problems. Ehrlich and Ehrlich have argued that such thinking is irresponsible, and that rapid population growth, particularly at the world level and in poorer countries, is creating misery and poverty. Moore and Simon (2000) respond that technological innovation in the context of scarcity drives human progress and that the whole notion of a Malthusian trap is a falsehood.

In the Canadian context, some commentators have argued that the dangers of population growth are not only the strain it places on limited resources, but also its deleterious effects on the environment, including the possibility of global climate change (Suzuki, 2011). Others have argued that population growth is good for Canada because its population is small compared to other industrialized nations and a larger population would create more markets and more economic development (Saunders, 2012). In short, some arguments point to the disadvantages of population size and growth, whereas others point to their advantages.

From Malthus, we learn that society needs to be concerned about its population, whether because growth is too rapid or because it is not rapid enough. Questions of population are important to the welfare of societies, and it makes sense to promote the evolution of the population in a way that benefits society. From Marx, we learn that population dynamics are largely a function of socioeconomic arrangements, particularly of broadly defined economic structures. As society changes, population dynamics also change. In order to understand population trends, it is essential to understand the underlying economic and social dynamics.

The Demographic Transition

A major theory in the field, *the demographic transition* has been used to summarize the historical demographic experience of societies of European origin over the past two centuries, as well as the more recent experience of less developed regions. The basic elements of the theory are presented in Figure 1.1. Births and deaths per 1,000 population are represented on the vertical axis; time is shown along the horizontal axis. Although the rates and dates vary by country, the basic pattern is a movement from an equilibrium of high birth rates and high death rates, through a transitional disequilibrium in which death rates decline more than birth rates, to a second equilibrium of low birth rates and low death rates. In the pre- and post-transition states of equilibrium, there is little change in population size. The transition period, however, is characterized by a large increase in population—sometimes as large as sevenfold.

Stage 1 of the demographic transition is one of high but fluctuating mortality and high fertility. Mortality is high because of poor nutrition, low standards of living, poor sanitation, and poor control over disease. Several reasons can be given for high fertility. The demographic argument proposes that when mortality is high (among infants and children, in particular), fertility needs to be high in order for the group to survive. The economic argument suggests that because the family was the main economic unit in pre-industrial societies, children were important to their parents both as producers and as a source of security for the future. The cultural argument

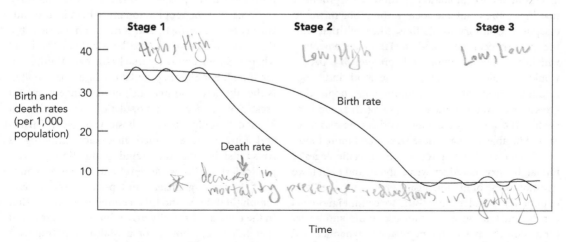

Figure 1.1 ▣ The Demographic Transition in Three Stages

focuses on ideas, and values, suggesting that pre-industrial societies did not consider deliberate family limitation to be acceptable.

In stage 2, mortality declines as a result of various agricultural, industrial, sanitation, and health innovations. There are two interpretations of the fertility decline that have received the most attention: one economic and the other cultural. The economic interpretation notes that the transformation of society during the Industrial Revolution changed the role of the family, as most economic production came to be organized outside the household. Consequently, children became less valuable in family production, and the costs of raising them increased as they came to spend a larger portion of their lives in school. Later, social security replaced the family as the basic welfare net in the face of economic hardship, incapacity, and old age. With the expansion of the role of the state, the economic rationale for having children was reduced and families became less important as guarantees of economic security. The cultural interpretation of fertility decline suggests that the idea of limiting births within marriage, along with the use of contraception, gradually gained legitimacy. From this perspective, fertility changed as a result of new attitudes toward the family and new ideas of what was acceptable behaviour. The deliberate regulation of births within marriage was a new practice that spread across societies through cultural contact, first in Europe and eventually around the world.

The spread of new family-planning practices, however, was sometimes impeded by cultural barriers. In Belgium, for instance, fertility declined faster in the French-speaking population than in the Flemish population. Similarly, for a long time, fertility remained higher among French Canadians than among English Canadians. In support of this cultural explanation, Van de Walle and Knodel (1980) noted that the beginning of the decline in fertility has occurred in a variety of different socioeconomic conditions, and that, once the decline starts, it appears to be irreversible, as if people have adopted a new form of behaviour.

Stage 3, as shown in Figure 1.1, involves persistent low mortality with low but fluctuating fertility. Mortality is now under control, with fertility varying slightly depending on economic and cultural conditions. Depending on the economic and social climate, it may be considered more or less economically feasible and more or less culturally desirable to have children.

The essence of the demographic-transition theory is that decreases in mortality precede reductions in fertility, and that populations move from relatively high and stable vital rates to relatively low and stable vital rates. During the transition, the gap between births and deaths causes the population to expand considerably.

Debates about this theory do abound, however. Some scholars have noted that fertility reductions can occur when standards of living are threatened. The early fertility declines in France may not have been a function of economic improvements and mortality decline, but rather of economic stagnation in a rural society. While there is general agreement that the effect of improving economic circumstances for families usually leads to lower fertility, there have been exceptions. Cases have been found in less developed nations where economic reversals appear to have accelerated fertility decline (Sinding, 1993; 2009).

Other discussions focus on the third stage, suggesting that a number of rich countries may have gone beyond stable, low birth and death rates to a fourth stage. This stage involves considerable population aging and the threat of eventual population decline (Van de Kaa, 1987; 2008). Some have called this fourth stage a second demographic transition, where there is much change in family behaviour (Lesthaeghe, 1995; 2010). In particular, relationships become less permanent and more flexible, evidenced by the prevalence of cohabitation and divorce, child-bearing is postponed, and there are fewer births (Beaujot and Bélanger, 2001).

The liveliest debate about the demographic-transition model pertains to the relative importance of economic and cultural considerations. This discussion can be traced back to the Malthusian–Marxist debate. In some ways, the demographic-transition model brings into question both the Malthusian and the Marxist perspectives. Malthus would have to admit that, historically, improvements in standards of living and increases in the food supply did not induce people to have more children; on the contrary, fertility declined. Marx, for his part, would have to admit that demographic dynamics changed without a movement from capitalism to a new socialist stage of human history.

If, however, they focused on different aspects of the demographic transition, both Marx and Malthus could argue that history also supports their views. Marx would note, in particular, that fertility declined as a result of major economic and industrial transformations. Although it was not a revolution from capitalism to socialism, industrialization involved a significant change in the economic structure of society. Thus, as the economic circumstances of people's lives changed, fertility declined. Malthus, on the other hand, might argue that his emphasis on ideas such as "moral restraint" and "responsible parenthood" helped to instill new moral values, prompting people to take control of their reproduction and to deliberately limit the size of their families. In other words, Malthus would subscribe to the cultural argument, noting that the spread of modern contraception has not only given people the means to limit the size of their families but also promoted new values. According to these new values, it is proper to control conception, and small families are best.

The experience of various countries suggests that the fertility transition requires that people be ready, willing, and able to control the size of their families (Coale, 1973; Lesthaeghe and Vanderhoeft, 1997). The changed economic climate makes people ready to have fewer children because they do not need the children to produce or work for the family unit, the prevalent norms make them willing to use contraception, and the availability of contraceptives enables them to control the number of children they have.

Summary

In subsequent chapters, we will raise other theoretical ideas about population. The epidemiological transition that we discuss in Chapter 3, "Mortality, Health, and Health Care," is useful for studying long-term changes in mortality. In Chapter 4, "Fertility and the Reproduction of Society," we will elaborate further on Canada's fertility transition and the second demographic transition. We will frequently discuss questions of the advantages and disadvantages of larger populations, as seen in the Malthus–Marx debate. Chapter 13, "Conclusions," will return to issues related to demographic change and human capital. In the next chapter, we turn to an overview of Canada's population history until the turn of the twentieth century.

Critical Thinking Questions

1. Specify the processes to consider when analyzing how the Canadian population size and structure changes from one year to the next.
2. Using the frameworks of the Malthusian and Marxist theories, discuss the relationship between population and economic development in Canada.
3. For the Canadian demographic transition, do you think that economic or cultural arguments are more relevant?
4. Canada has the second-largest land mass in the world (after Russia), but currently has only about 0.5 per cent of the global population. Do you think Canada is underpopulated?

Recommended Readings

Population Reference Bureau. 2011. *Population Handbook*. Washington, DC: Population Reference Bureau. A quick guide to population dynamics for non-specialists, focusing on definitions, methods of calculating various rates, and interpretive examples.

Statistics Canada. 2014. *Report on the Demographic Situation in Canada*. Ottawa: Statistics Canada cat. no. 91-209-X. The 2014 issue provides highly up-to-date data on the changing demographic situation in Canada and provides an analysis of some of the major observations. Past issues have focused on topics of special interest.

Trovato, Frank. 2009. *Canada's Population in a Global Context: An Introduction to Social Demography*. Don Mills, ON: Oxford University Press. An exhaustive and balanced overview of most of the core issues of concern to the discipline of demography in both Canadian and global contexts.

Weeks, John R. 2012. *Population: An Introduction to Concepts and Issues*, 11th edition. Belmont, MA: Wadsworth. This introductory text is well designed to familiarize students with the study of population.

Related Websites

www.census.gov/population/international. This is the website of the International Programs Center at the US Bureau of the Census. It is very well maintained and includes a downloadable international database of population information.

www.prb.org. The Population Reference Bureau's website is a comprehensive source for population-related issues—by region, country, or topic.

www.statcan.gc.ca. At Statistics Canada's site, the user can browse by subject or do automated searches on a wide assortment of statistical data collected on Canada's population and economy. This includes data from the 2011 Census as well as community profiles of Canadian municipalities. A free email subscription to *The Daily* is also available.

www.un.org/en/development/desa/population. This is the website of the United Nations' Population Division.

2 The Population of Canada before the Twentieth Century

The Chapter at a Glance

- From the sixteenth century onward, the First Nations population in Canada experienced almost 3 centuries of population decline.
- Mortality was very high in Canada until the end of the nineteenth century. In New France, for example, life expectancy at birth has been estimated to have been somewhere between 30 and 35 years.
- Whereas immigration from France was brought to a near standstill in the late eighteenth century because of the British conquest of New France, immigration from both the United States and the British Isles continued to be particularly important to Canada's demographic development.
- The fertility of Canadians in the eighteenth and nineteenth centuries has been described as being very high, with little evidence of voluntary control over reproduction. In studying Canada's demographic transition, mortality decline predated fertility decline, which augmented the rate of natural increase.

Introduction

Most accounts of Canada's demographic history begin with European contact (Gemery, 2000; Charbonneau et al., 2000). History has often been described as a document-bound discipline, and for this reason there have been large obstacles to research on the early history of the peoples of the Americas. Nonetheless, the research of archaeologists, physical anthropologists, and ethno-historians provide some information on the demography of North America prior to European contact. Physical anthropologists make estimates of the living conditions, diet, fertility, morbidity, and mortality of pre-contact peoples through the systematic study of skeletal remains and burial sites. Archaeologists can inform demographers on settlement patterns and technology use prior to contact. Ethno-historians attempt to make sense of the scattered and incomplete documents left behind by the first Europeans who came into contact with the Aboriginal population in North America. In combination, a number of inferences are possible on the demography of the original inhabitants of Canada, prior to and following contact with Europeans.

Pre-contact Demography

As the Portuguese, the Basques, and the French were first navigating the waters off Newfoundland, about 50 distinct languages were being spoken within the boundaries of modern-day Canada. This has been characterized as a conservative estimate on the number of pre-contact languages, and includes exclusively those that have been relatively well documented and classified on the basis of usable information (Goddard, 1996; Sturtevant, 2006). As a result of decades of exhaustive historical study, historians and linguists have approximated the locations and distributions of these languages at the time of contact, while also identifying their structural variety. As distinct languages, rather than dialects, linguists have classified them as belonging to 11 major linguistic families, suggestive of a high level of linguistic diversity (see Figure 2.1). In fact, most languages would

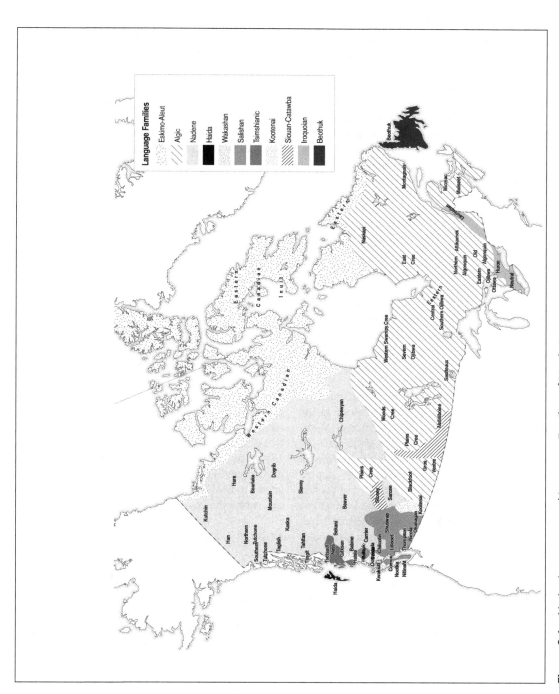

Figure 2.1 ▣ Native Languages and Language Families of North America

Source: Based on Goddard (1996).

have had less in common with each other than did the European languages that were establishing themselves on the eastern coast of North America at this time, all belonging to the same major Indo-European linguistic family (Gordon, 2005; Grimes, 2000).

While there are certainly limitations in reconstructing historical population distributions, it is well established that the most densely populated region in the country at this time was at the other end of the continent, along the coast of British Columbia. Of the 50 languages spoken in Canada, approximately half were located within present-day British Columbia. Due to the relative richness in the resources in this part of Canada, as well as the comparatively mild climate, population densities were higher there than in any other region of the country, including relatively highly populated Iroquoian territories of southern Ontario and Quebec. It is also well established that the West Coast pre-contact peoples largely depended on the sea for subsistence. Successful as whalers and fishers, they also exploited the abundant salmon runs that once characterized this part of North America (Muckle, 2007).

Given the potential for more permanent settlement, the peoples of the West Coast of Canada were among the most densely populated "non-agricultural" peoples ever documented by anthropologists (Boyd, 1990). The only other region of Canada with comparable (albeit lower) population densities prior to the arrival of Europeans includes the territories of the Saint Lawrence River and Great Lakes Iroquoians. Yet unlike the peoples of British Columbia, slash and burn (swidden) agriculture was relatively widely adopted by these farmer-hunters. The typical pre-contact Iroquoian village was occupied year-round, only to be relocated every few decades, owing to resource depletion (Saunders et al., 1992). Consequently, archaeologists and historians have been left with physical evidence as to the various settlement patterns that characterized this part of the continent during the pre-contact period, as well as evidence on early regional trade routes and likely socioeconomic and political alliances (Waldram et al., 2006).

In more northern areas, population densities declined, given the climatic and physical characteristics of Canada's North. For example, in northern Quebec and Ontario, population densities were relatively low with little evidence of permanent settlement. In the absence of agriculture, the Algonquin, Montagnais, Ojibwa, and Cree had adapted to an often difficult environment by developing an intimate knowledge of the resources of the boreal forest (Dickason and Newbigging, 2010). In this context, resources were obviously used extensively rather than intensively, such that the available physical resources were likely a constraining factor in regard to population densities. Demographers and physical anthropologists have used the concept of *carrying capacity* to study non-agricultural populations—that is, the number of people who can be supported in an area, given the available physical resources and the way that people use those resources (Boserup, 1965; Harris and Ross, 1987). Obviously, the carrying capacity of these northern regions would have been lower than in the south, and just as is the case now in modern-day Canada, population was concentrated in the most habitable southern regions.

In the western provinces, the northern plains were relatively thinly populated with smaller communities, primary subsistence being obtained from the communal hunting of bison and other game. In Canada's Arctic, the Inuit were extremely sparsely populated across an enormous land mass, from Greenland all the way to present-day Alaska. Due to their remote locations, there are examples of isolated bands of Copper and Netsilik Inuit who were unknown to the Canadian government until the 1920s (Morrison, 1984). Whereas the Beothuk of Newfoundland encountered Europeans in the sixteenth century, isolated bands of Inuit encountered people of European descent for the first time some 400 years later.

Mortality Conditions in Pre-contact North America

While some historians have portrayed pre-contact North America as a "disease free paradise" (Stewart, 1973; Dobyns, 1983), more recent research on the part of physical anthropologists and epidemiologists contradict this conclusion (Waldram et al., 2006; Williamson and Pfeiffer, 2003). Archaeological research on pre-contact North American settlement and subsistence patterns along with a careful analysis of the many skeletal remains located at these sites suggest that mortality was high (by modern standards), particularly among the young. Evidence has been gathered suggestive of various contagious diseases, gastrointestinal illnesses, and anemia (at least partially related to meat-borne parasitic infection), deaths due to trauma and accidents (fractures and broken bones), respiratory illnesses, and evidence of some populations experiencing malnutrition and periodic starvation (Ubelaker, 2000).

These hardships among pre-contact North American societies can be placed into a broader historical context, as such situations were by no means unique. First, these high levels of mortality paralleled those in Europe at the same time—and such levels could be found in all major world regions. It is relatively well known that throughout most of the world, and throughout most of human history, life expectancy probably fluctuated somewhere between 25 and 35 years (Weiss, 1973; Angel, 1984), and there is no good reason to believe that this would not have also characterized the Americas at this time. Second, the epidemiological patterns of North America prior to contact can be characterized by their diversity—populations adapted to a variety of social and environmental circumstances, as associated with differences in diet and subsistence patterns. Some populations were obviously healthier than others, and there were significant fluctuations associated with climate and conflict. Also the level of mortality was significantly worsened through European contact. Mortality increased in a major way particularly due to pandemic conditions, with new lethal diseases introduced from Europe that had a devastating demographic impact.

Comparative Context

As we discussed in Chapter 1, the classic formulation of the demographic transition describes first the gradual decline in mortality across European populations that largely began in the nineteenth century, followed eventually by a corresponding decline in fertility. Both of these changes accompanied the Industrial Revolution in Europe, as climbing affluence and advances in medicine and public health allowed for a dramatic reduction in mortality. These advances resulted in a dramatic reduction in mortality from infectious, parasitic, and contagious disease. The gradual transition over a period of several hundred years involved a shift away from this earlier disease profile through to the present-day situation whereby chronic and degenerative disease act as the primary causes of death (e.g., cancer and heart disease). Yet with additional historical research, including studies conducted by archaeologists and physical anthropologists, our understanding of the health history of humanity has been expanded to also consider what was characteristic of non-agricultural societies (in the Americas and elsewhere).

Paleoepidemiology is a branch of epidemiology that attempts to explain how certain diseases might have been distributed in pre-modern times, using predominantly archaeological methods, with a careful analysis of bones, teeth, stomach contents, and coprolites, among other scattered evidence found in thousands of archaeological sites (Waldram et al., 2006). As Wells (2010) has suggested, after taking a closer look at this archaeological data, there is far greater uncertainty as to the health conditions experienced by hunting and foraging populations than was previously believed. It is likely a myth that population health has progressively improved in moving from hunting and foraging populations to agricultural societies (following the logic that the latter societies allowed for a more regular food supply, and, hence, improved population health). The Hobbesian notion that hunter-gatherers had lives that were uniformly "solitary, poor, nasty, brutish, and short" is increasingly being challenged in light of more careful empirical research.

While all pre-modern populations had high mortality, different populations had distinct disease profiles and causes of death—something that was true in comparing the Americas with Europe as well as different populations in pre-contact North America itself. It is quite likely that there were many populations in pre-contact Canada that were, in fact, healthier than their contemporaries in Europe, although others may have also been less healthy. The hunters and foragers of coastal British Columbia, for example, can be contrasted with the populations of Europe in the fifteenth century, in recognition of

major differences in diet and day-to-day living conditions. Much of Europe's population at the time was deeply impoverished, with many living on a low-protein diet, based almost exclusively on carbohydrates: wheat, rye, oats, and barley (Singman, 1999). Contrast this with the wealth of resources in British Columbia, including the availability of a rich diet of fish, sea and land mammals, and seaweed and plant foods, suggestive of a diversity of nutrients and protein. The archaeological evidence available suggests that coastal populations in the Americas at that time had less nutritional stress, and, in fact, were likely well favoured relative to an impoverished European peasantry (Cybulski, 1994). The historical record has carefully documented recurrent famine throughout medieval Europe, made even more difficult by several major pandemics and warfare. In addition, mortality rates appear to have been particularly high in some of Europe's largest and most densely populated cities.

With increasingly sedentary settlement patterns as well as population growth and higher population densities, the potential for disease also increases. Permanent settlements of larger size are conducive to crowding and greater potential for contagions. Common water sources can have greater potential for contamination, with the accumulation of human and other forms of waste, along with a greater exposure to the pathogens of domesticated animals. In focusing exclusively on North America, Steckle and Rose (2002), drawing from a database of more than 12,500 skeletal remains, have provided evidence to suggest that some of the agriculture-based, larger, and more densely populated communities in North America (e.g., Mesoamerica in modern-day Mexico) had populations that were actually less healthy than many of the farther-north hunting-and-foraging societies. The introduction of maize into the Great Lakes region of southern Ontario had its impact on population health, as documented through evaluations of the chemical constituents and trace elements in bone and teeth, providing evidence as to diet and nutritional stress. While pre-contact Iroquoian populations relied upon a variety of food sources, including horticulture, hunting, fishing, and foraging, there is evidence to suggest that climbing population densities and an increased reliance upon maize may have brought higher pathogen levels and possibly lesser dietary variation.

Archaeologists have found that bone lesions from infections were highest when maize consumption was highest, as one might expect with more crowded conditions and greater population densities (Katzenberg, 1992; Waldram et al., 2006). In contrast, populations that were less sedentary, and nomadically searching out game, would also have high mortality, but due to other reasons. The stresses associated with continuous relocation as part of the nomadic lifestyle were likely substantial, particularly in the context of often difficult environmental and climatic conditions. The likelihood of dying accidentally through trauma seems to have been quite high, as a fracture or wound obtained while hunting or in warfare could have often led to a serious infection and/or permanent disability. The climatic conditions particularly in Canada's North can be severe, with long and cold winters. The Inuit, while they were well equipped to handle life in the Far North, dealt with an extremely harsh environment—stresses stemming from such a difficult life likely took their toll. The Inuit of Baffin Island, for example, lived with an extremely cold climate (the average annual temperature was about −10°C), with severe winters and foggy, short summers, plus continuous snow, even heavy snow, that could fall at almost any time of the year.

Infant and Maternal Mortality in a Context of High Fertility

In populations with high mortality, the risk of death is typically highest among those who are most vulnerable, including infants and young children. At such a high level of mortality, the likelihood of dying before one's first birthday was about 1 in 4, with at least 40 per cent of all offspring not surviving childhood, although, again, this likely varied across populations and across historical periods. Childbirth was always a difficult event in pre-modern populations, with an elevated risk for both infant and mother. Considering what we currently know of potential complications in childbirth (in the absence of medical intervention), it is very likely that maternal mortality in pre-contact North America would have been quite high, particularly when mothers suffered from nutritional or environmental stress. Van Lerberghe and de Brouwere (2001) have estimated that in a high-fertility context, child-bearing women would have at least a 1 in 10 lifetime chance of maternal death, without modern medical interventions, due to such factors as exhaustion, dehydration, infection, hemorrhage, and convulsions. The excavation efforts of physical anthropologists have demonstrated that both maternal and childhood mortality had always been quite high (Ubelaker, 2000), although, again, this varied considerably across populations (e.g., the likelihood of infection would have been higher in more settled populations).

In this context, female life expectancy was shorter than male life expectancy, a situation that has been reversed in the modern era. This sex difference was likely true of the many populations that inhabited Canada, just as it would have been true of the first settlers in the Americas. Mintz (2012) has estimated that among the earliest European populations to settle in the Americas, maternal mortality over a lifetime was likely as high as 1 in 8, as greater population densities were associated with elevated risks of infection. In this context, population numbers could have been maintained from one generation to the next only through relatively high fertility.

Prior to European contact in Canada, the scattered evidence available suggests that child-bearing started relatively early in a woman's life and continued through to menopause (Charbonneau, 1984). Involuntary sterility was more common than in contemporary populations, due to the impact of untreated disease as well as the nutritional constraints imposed by often-difficult ecological conditions (Romaniuc, 2000). Fertility was also affected by long durations of breastfeeding. While this reduced fertility, the spacing of births enhanced child survival and, thus, effective reproduction. Especially in harsh conditions, new mothers would have a respite from the risk of conception after the birth of a baby—this was achieved through long periods of breastfeeding lengthening the intervals between pregnancies, resulting in lower rates of fertility (Jain and Bongaarts, 1981).

From a Quasi-stationary State to Three Centuries of Aboriginal Population Decline

Romaniuc (2000) has stated what he considers the main demographic stages in the historical evolution of Aboriginal peoples in Canada. Prior to contact with Europe, he described what was, in the long run, most likely a quasi-stationary demographic state characterized by high mortality offset by moderately high fertility. Due to the aforementioned constraints (including involuntary sterility and lactational infecundity), fertility was not exceptionally high, but it was high enough to assure continuity from one generation to the next. In all likelihood, Aboriginal population increase characterized certain regions of the country during certain historical periods, whereas disease and natural disasters periodically reduced numbers considerably. With contact, the Aboriginal population of Canada underwent an almost three-centuries-long depopulation, a tragic situation that characterized all of the Americas with few parallels in modern demographic history.

A recurrent theme for historical demography in the study of pre-modern populations is the so called *crises de mortalité*, meant to designate a sudden and pronounced rise in the death rate, with devastating consequences for local or even national populations (Meuvret, 1965; Charbonneau and Larose, 1979). Throughout much of human history, famine and epidemic mortality would periodically have a devastating impact on populations, with perhaps the best documented example being the Black Death (bubonic plague) of fourteenth-century Europe, thought to have been responsible for the deaths of 25 million people, or as much as a quarter of Europe's total population at the time. By most accounts, the impact of European contact on the Americas was even greater than the Black Death, with new lethal diseases having a devastating demographic effect. The extent of this depopulation is certainly open to debate, but there is no doubt that the arrival of Europeans was an enormous disaster in human and cultural terms. With the European colonization of Canada, the mortality of Aboriginal peoples climbed, often dramatically, first in the East, and then in a piecemeal fashion across Canada's vast territory. It was not until the late-nineteenth century that population numbers among the Aboriginal population finally stabilized and began to recover, albeit slowly (Charbonneau, 1984).

A variety of factors were responsible for three centuries of population decline among First Nations, although the most important was the introduction of disease from Europe. With no previous exposure to many European and African diseases, the original inhabitants of Canada lacked acquired immunity. As described by Thornton (2000), new diseases introduced into North America often resulted in what are termed "virgin soil epidemics," whereby a new disease could spread to virtually all members of a population. The diseases that had a devastating impact on the First Nations peoples of North America include smallpox, measles, cholera, typhoid, diphtheria, scarlet fever, whooping cough, pneumonia, malaria and yellow fever (Thornton, 2000:14). Compiled by priests, soldiers, traders, and early settlers, over a span of several hundred years, historical records contain innumerable examples of disease taking on epidemic proportions and decimating entire peoples (Jenness, 1932 [1977]; Dickason and Newbigging, 2010).

Boyd (1992) describes a well-documented example of Aboriginals being afflicted with devastating disease: a smallpox epidemic that hit the Queen Charlotte Islands of British Columbia in the 1860s. Smallpox was not completely new to the northwest coast of North America, as it was first introduced almost one hundred years earlier when initial contact took place. While the first few outbreaks are of unknown magnitude, with limited descriptions of empty villages and a few oral reports from early inhabitants, the latter epidemics are described in detail through Indian censuses, as compiled by the Hudson's Bay Company and early government officials (Belshaw, 2009). In working with reliable records, Boyd describes how in 1862 a ship infected with smallpox docked at Victoria and the disease spread quickly to the crowded First Nations encampment on the city's outskirts. Instead of quarantining all those infected, the authorities evicted the encampment, sending Kwakiutl, Haida, Tlingit, and Tsimshian traders back to their villages. Consequently, over a two-year period, records from the Hudson's Bay Company indicate a 60 per cent decline in the Aboriginal population in this coastal region of British Columbia. This was not an isolated event, but rather the fifth known outbreak of smallpox to hit this region since initial contact—Aboriginal depopulation continued for decades, into the twentieth century.

In addition to the impact of disease, other factors contributed to depopulation, including the intensification of warfare and fighting that resulted from the efforts of the British and French to establish control over contested territory in their colonies. Romaniuc (2000) emphasizes that in addition to fostering the spread of disease, European colonialism in North America introduced wars, forced widespread removals of people, and accelerated the destruction of traditional economic bases. Through the early accounts of Europeans, it is possible to piece together what far too often appeared to be a situation of total social disorganization due to colonization and high mortality. In nineteenth-century Newfoundland, the Beothuk (an indigenous people) disappeared completely—the tragic result of spreading disease and continuing feuds with early settlers. Open conflict with the British and Iroquois led to the near disappearance of the Huron along the St Lawrence River, who had been left particularly vulnerable and weakened due to the combined impact of disease and armed conflict. The opening of the West and the Prairies to settlement and farming led to forced removals and the destruction of the traditional economic base of these regions—as well as the near extinction of bison. Over time, depopulation has significantly affected First Nations populations in all areas of present-day Canada.

Population Size

While one cannot dispute three centuries of population decline among the First Nations, there is less consensus as to the magnitude of this decline. The obvious reason for a lack of consensus is the absence of direct information on the size of Canada's pre-contact population. According to the estimates currently available, a wide range of population figures come to light, largely due to differences in opinion as to the accuracy and completeness of the earliest population figures of colonial administrators (Daniels, 1992). Because much of the information first compiled by priests, soldiers, traders, and government officials was compiled many years after initial contact, historians disagree over the extent to which depopulation might have already occurred in the context of "virgin soil conditions" (Thornton, 2000; Ubelaker, 2000).

The obvious difficulty that ethno-historians have in efforts to piece together North American pre-contact history is that in many of the earliest accounts, communities were already in a state of social disorganization and epidemic, whereas in other communities, groups had hitherto remained intact and largely isolated from European influence. In examining scattered historical evidence over three centuries, it is virtually impossible to determine the extent to which depopulation may have occurred—all efforts at demographic reconstruction become highly speculative and open to debate. Such accuracy problems were made worse by probable gross inaccuracies in the population figures compiled several centuries ago by authorities who were not trained census takers. Even today, in enacting the modern census in Canada, it is noteworthy that the level of undercount has been estimated to be particularly high among First Nations persons, several times higher than for the population in general (AFN, 2008).

In this context, Dickason (1992: 63) states that for pre-contact Canada, "the most widely accepted estimate is about 500,000," a figure that was adapted by the Royal Commission on Aboriginal Peoples (1995) in its brief appraisal of the demographic history of Canada. It is unclear why the RCAP decided to rely upon Dickason's figure, as absolutely no evidence or references are provided in support of it. Earlier estimates have placed the pre-contact population at less than one half of this number; for example, Mooney (1928) provides a very conservative estimate of just under 200,000. This latter figure was based on a systematic review of the earliest available written accounts, which were typically very partial or imprecise, with virtually no adjustments. The physical

anthropologist Ubelaker (1976) estimates that Canada's pre-contact population was about 270,000. This estimate was obtained by compiling and adding together regional estimates of specialists affiliated with the Smithsonian Institution. The Canadian historical demographer Charbonneau (1984) estimates the pre-contact population at about 300,000 by upwardly adjusting the earlier work of Mooney and others, taking into account the most serious of omissions or understatements. At the opposite extreme, there are a limited number of estimates published that suggest the pre-contact population may have been many times higher than Dickason's figure, based on the assumption of major depopulation that could not possibly be detected through early colonial records (Dobyns, 1983; Thornton, 1987).

If we accept Dickason's figure of a pre-contact population of about 500,000, it would take almost three centuries after Jacques Cartier first sailed into the Gulf of Saint Lawrence in the 1530s for the European population in Canada to reach the half million mark. As emphasized by Charbonneau (1984: 24), this basic observation is far too often overlooked in historical accounts of the demography of Canada—that is, early European settlement was accompanied by major depopulation of the First Nations population.

Early European Settlement

Although the historical record is very sketchy, the first contact between First Nations peoples of Canada and Europeans likely occurred long before the establishment of any permanent European settlement in the Americas. Archaeological evidence and carbon dating techniques, for example, have decisively established that Norse voyagers lived temporarily at L'Anse-aux-Meadows area of the Northern Peninsula of Newfoundland, circa 1000 CE (Ingstad, 2001). In addition, given a natural abundance of resources off the Grand Banks of Newfoundland, there is evidence to suggest that fishers, including the Basques and Portuguese, had visited the waters off Canada's East Coast and built temporary settlements, perhaps as early as the fifteenth century (Barkham, 1989). As to whether these early visitors made direct contact with the Beothuk of Newfoundland, or the Montagnais and Naskapi of Labrador, one can only speculate in the absence of written records and direct archaeological evidence.

While we know relatively little about these early contacts, one thing is virtually certain: even though temporary European settlements were established with increased frequency throughout the sixteenth century, in both Atlantic Canada and Quebec, it was not until the beginning of the seventeenth century that permanent settlements began to develop. In 1605, the French established a base at Port Royal, off Nova Scotia's Bay of Fundy (Clark, 1968); in 1608, New France was established at the site of modern-day Quebec City (Charbonneau et al., 1987). A few decades later, the first Scottish migrants arrived in Nova Scotia, both at the Port Royal area and on Cape Breton Island. As their numbers were originally quite small, these early settlements struggled throughout much of the seventeenth century in establishing a permanent presence in the Americas, often receiving very little help from their respective European homelands.

Historical Demography of New France

While the earliest demographic history of northeastern North America includes much uncertainty, the situation is very different if we turn our attention to the establishment of New France. In fact, historical demographers are relatively privileged in Quebec, having access to remarkably accurate and detailed records. From its origin, New France continued a practice first established in France in the fifteenth century, with relatively complete birth, marriage, and burial registers, largely owing to the diligence of the colonial clergy and authorities. In combination with several censuses of the population of New France, this information on the dynamics of population change for this colony is among the most complete currently available for any seventeenth- or eighteenth-century society.

As documented in the *Registre de la population du Québec ancien*, New France recorded approximately 700,000 baptisms, marriages, and burials from its founding in 1608 through to 1800 (Charbonneau et al., 2000). With such information, the demographic growth of New France has been exhaustively researched to carefully document the pace and underlying dynamics of population growth. From a handful of settlers in the early seventeenth century, the population of New France increased to about 70,000 at the time of the British conquest in 1760, and over 200,000 by the end of the eighteenth century. As to the contribution of immigration from France to this growth, the best estimates currently available indicate that only about 14,000 French immigrants settled in the colony, from its origin through to the British conquest (Henripin and Péron, 1972). After the most important immigration years of 1663–1673, natural increase (or births minus deaths) became the main factor of growth for the population of New France (Charbonneau et al., 2000).

The society that established itself along the Saint Lawrence River had much in common with eighteenth-century France, with the direct transferral across the Atlantic of many of its most fundamental institutions. While initially interested almost exclusively in the fur trade, the colony gradually established a foothold in North America, with the distribution of land to a growing number of settlers and their descendants. As an example of France's influence on the organization of life in the colony, land was distributed according to the seigniorial system, an essentially feudal form of territorial management inherited from France. With its own class of landowners (seigniors), early censuses of New France describe a population of agricultural workers, tradespeople, indentured servants, soldiers, as well as many others involved directly or indirectly in the fur trade. From its earliest years, the Catholic Church was omnipresent in the life of the colony, with religious authorities holding considerable influence on both the overall administration and day-to-day lives of its earliest inhabitants. While settlers were drawn from all over France, the colony appeared to be relatively homogeneous, at least in terms of language, religion, and ethnicity.

Fertility in New France

For a colony that experienced little immigration, New France grew at a relatively rapid pace. As total population growth corresponds to both natural increase and net international migration, New France compensated for its low rate of net migration from France through a particularly high level of fertility. In fact, few societies have ever exhibited, for as extended a period, the particularly high fertility rates that characterized French Canada, both before and after the British conquest. As living conditions were particularly difficult, a very high level of fertility more than offset steep mortality. Charbonneau and colleagues (2000), for example, indicate that the average family in New France had between seven and eight children, a remarkably high level given the fact that premature death often disrupted family life. The fertility of French Canadians was consistently higher than in France over this same period, with levels of child-bearing that can be described as prolific.

With detailed information available on all marriages and baptisms, demographers have managed to highlight some of the more striking features of family life in New France, including traits that may have been responsible for its high fertility (Charbonneau, 1980, 1981; Landry, 1993). For example, the average age at which women married in New France has been documented as particularly young—women often married in their teens or early twenties (Dillon, 2005). As a determinant of fertility, the age at which people enter into marriage is often highlighted as crucial, particularly when there is little evidence of intentional fertility control in marriage (Coale and Watkins, 1986). Conversely, the longer couples delay marriage, the lower the resultant fertility, as couples are exposed to a shorter period at risk to bearing children. In comparison with France in the seventeenth and eighteenth centuries, marriage and child-bearing began relatively early on in the life cycle of French Canadian women. Completed fertility was typically higher, merely due to the simple fact that child-bearing began at a younger age and was spread out over a more extended period of time.

Following the same logic, fertility tends to be higher in societies with lower levels of celibacy, and in the event of widowhood, in societies where remarriage is common. Relative to France, not only did Quebec women marry at younger ages, but also the proportion of the adult population that didn't marry

was relatively low (even after including the significant numbers of young men and women who entered religious orders). Similarly, in the event of widowhood (a relatively frequent event in a high-mortality society), a significant proportion of adults who lost a spouse ultimately ended up remarried, perhaps to a greater extent than elsewhere (Charbonneau, 1981). The relative effect of remarriage on fertility is not of trivial consequence, given that life expectancy was probably somewhere between 30 and 35 years. Under such conditions, it can be estimated that probably about one third of women aged 20 in New France died before reaching age 45, making it imperative that child-bearing begin as soon as possible. Not surprisingly, a comparable proportion of men would not have made it through to what we currently label middle age. With child-bearing occurring across the full range of a woman's potential reproductive period, orphanhood was obviously far more common than it is today, as was the likelihood of an infant or young child losing at least one parent.

In accounting for the distinctive marriage patterns that characterized New France, Roy and Charbonneau (1978) have foregrounded the highly imbalanced sex ratio that characterized the early life of the colony, which, in turn, likely exerted considerable pressure on women to marry, to do so at a young age, and, if widowed, to remarry. While the sex ratio of this colony eventually corrected itself (once the bulk of its population came to be Canadian born), the first several decades of New France had a major surplus of men, including many soldiers and indentured servants. Yet even with the establishment of a more balanced sex ratio, the aforementioned nuptiality patterns lingered. Whereas the average age at marriage increased somewhat in moving into the eighteenth century, the women of New France continued to marry young, with relatively few remaining single.

Regarding New France's high fertility, Charbonneau and colleagues (2000) refer to the "natural fertility conditions" of New France, a situation that was to continue largely unabated well into the nineteenth century. The concept of *natural fertility*, first introduced by Henry (1961), is meant to designate the marital fertility of a population that is not involved in any form of intentional fertility regulation. Under such conditions, couples do not alter their reproductive behaviour according to the number of children already born. No effort is made to reduce fertility at older ages, with age apparently having little relationship with marital fertility. Beyond the simple fact that fecundity declines sharply as women move into their forties (or, in other words, the biological potential to bear children declines), fertility remained relatively high from marriage through to the end of a woman's fertile period. This is precisely the situation documented in New France, with child-bearing starting early and with fertility consistently high across the full range of reproductive years. As documented by Charbonneau (1975), fertility was almost as high among married women in their later thirties as among married women in their early twenties. This is consistent with the idea of no voluntary regulation of fertility, as middle-aged women who have already born a number of children would normally be among the first to limit their fertility.

Mortality

Once the earliest European inhabitants learned to adapt to the particularly harsh winters of Quebec, this colony apparently benefited from an abundant fauna, a fertile environment for farming, a ready supply of clean water, and reasonable levels of public sanitation (at least relative to the many European cities from which many came). As evidence of improved health, mortality rates have been documented as slightly lower than in Europe, albeit still extremely high by today's standards. Over the history of New France, life expectancy at birth has been approximated as averaging 35 years (Charbonneau, 1975), which is some years longer than what has been estimated for eighteenth-century France (Blayo, 1975). With modest gains made in terms of nutrition and the avoidance of disease, it is likely that modest gains were made in terms of reduced fetal mortality (stillbirths and miscarriages) and sterility (including premature sterility)—two additional reasons why fertility was relatively high. The principal control that a woman has over her fecundity (or biological potential to successfully have children) is to achieve a good diet with proper physical care, something that was likely easier to obtain in New France than in most of the home

cities and regions of France. Fertility was higher and mortality was lower, contributing to higher rates of both natural increase and population growth in a predominantly rural and sparsely populated eighteenth-century colony of France.

Since we currently take for granted a life expectancy of about 75–80 years, it is certainly difficult for us to imagine what life must have been like in such a high-mortality society. True of all populations that had yet to experience what demographers label the *epidemiological transition* (Omran, 1971; Olshansky and Ault, 1986), mortality was very high, taking a particularly heavy toll on the young. In considering the demographic history of French Canada, it was really not until the nineteenth century that the epidemiological transition began to take on some momentum, with the eventual shift in health and disease patterns, away from very high mortality, as associated with communicable disease—through to the very low mortality, as associated with degenerative disease.

Under the mortality conditions of New France, infant mortality was extremely high, such that one in four births did not survive the first year of life, and as many as four in ten children did not make it through to adulthood. As throughout most of human history, death in childhood was a common event and surviving through to old age the exception rather than the rule. This can be contrasted with the current situation, whereby fewer than 1 per cent of all births die in the first year of life (6 per 1,000 births) and over 98 per cent make it to age 20, with most mortality concentrated among the elderly (Trovato, 2009).

With remarkably complete records of deaths, it is possible to make further insights into the mortality experience of this pre-modern population. Particularly striking in this regard is the degree to which the total number of deaths registered in New France tended to vary from year to year. Such fluctuations are consistent with expectations for a population whereby communicable disease was responsible for the majority of deaths (Bengtsson and Gagnon, 2011). In contrast, most modern populations experience relatively modest shifts in mortality from one year to the next. But epidemics and pandemics in the eighteenth century continued to wreak havoc on populations. In 1687, for example, the number of deaths in

New France more than doubled relative to neighbouring years, pushing the colony temporarily into a state of negative natural increase. People suffered greatly, as unsanitary conditions and problems with the drinking water of the colony led to the outbreak of a major typhoid epidemic that took a particularly deadly toll. Similarly, a particularly rampant strain of smallpox led to a major jump in mortality in 1703, one of several epidemics to characterize the eighteenth century.

Population Increase

Throughout much of the history of New France, crude death rates ranged between 20 deaths per 1,000 through to 40 deaths per 1,000, with little stability and no clear trend over time. Nonetheless, natural increase remained relatively high, with the population of New France growing about fivefold throughout the

eighteenth century. The primary reason for this was the high fertility, with a crude birth rate that averaged at about 50 births per 1,000 over this extended period. Unknown here is the exact degree to which there was intermarriage involving Aboriginal Canadians, as the available records are incomplete in this regard. Tremblay and Vézina (2010) have estimated that the admixture between the two populations was relatively limited, with parish registers and genealogical data indicating that less than 1 per cent of maternal and paternal lineages involved this type of intermarriage. As we mentioned, rapid population expansion in New France was accompanied by a period of dramatic population decline among First Nations people, with an uncertain contribution of the latter populations to the eventual gene pool of the Quebec and other colonial populations (Moreau et al., 2009).

Box 2.1 ▣ *Naissance d'une Population*

As a result of several decades of effort, experts affiliated with the Department of Demography at the Université de Montréal have produced a large volume of historical research on New France. Due to the abundance and quality of information available in Quebec's parish registers, a computerized population register was created in the 1980s that reconstitutes the population of New France (Légaré, 1988). One of the first publications to fully benefit from this register was the important book *Naissance d'une Population: Les Français établis au Canada au XVIIᵉ siècle* (Charbonneau et al., 1987). *Naissance* chronicles in some detail the characteristics and experiences of the earliest pioneers to establish themselves in Canada. The book also demonstrates the degree to which most French Canadians can draw a direct line of descent back to this original pioneer population of the seventeenth century.

Due to the quality of parish records, it can be convincingly argued that no other pioneer population in the Americas (in New England, Latin America, or elsewhere in Canada) has ever undergone

such a careful examination, at least not for such a long-ago time period. In this case, the pioneer population is composed of persons born outside the St Lawrence lowlands (Canada at this time) who had managed to establish themselves in families by 1680. In identifying what Charbonneau and colleagues (1987) denote as the "true pioneers of the French Canadian lineage," considerable information is available on who exactly these first settlers were; their marital status on arrival; their occupations; their social status; and how they behaved once in New France in terms of marriage, living arrangements, fertility, and mortality. As an example of the detail available in this register, it is even possible to identify the exact French city, village, or region from which the vast majority of immigrants originated (see Figure 2.2). Immigrants were predominantly young adults, with over one half of women originating from the cities of France, whereas the overwhelming majority of the men were from rural regions. Over three quarters of all immigrants were single on arrival, and the overwhelming majority of women quickly married.

Continued

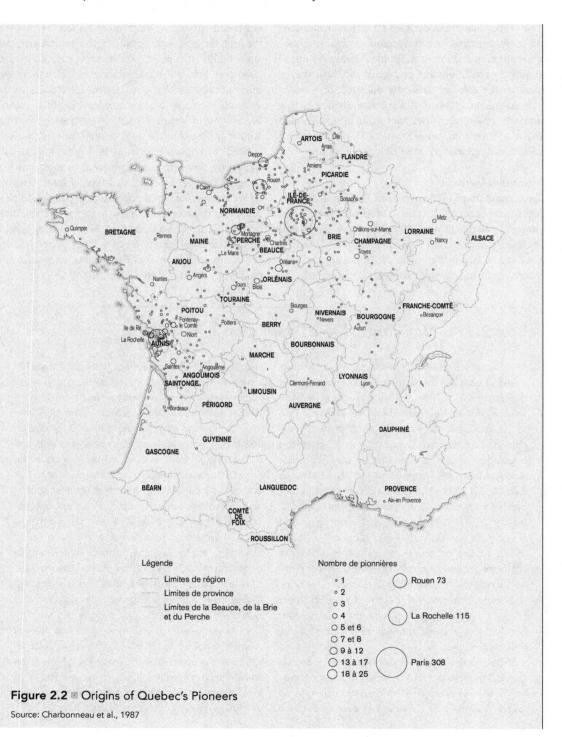

Figure 2.2 ▣ Origins of Quebec's Pioneers

Source: Charbonneau et al., 1987

A particularly important facet to Quebec's demographic history is the extent to which this colony evolved, closed to international migration. Whereas about 14,000 immigrants settled permanently in New France prior to 1760, only about 10,000 of these immigrants married within the colony—and fewer still are known to have surviving descendants. With the British conquest in 1760, immigration was virtually cut off from France, as French Canadians came to rely almost exclusively on natural increase for population growth. While there was some integration of Irish Catholics and First Nations peoples into the French-speaking population of North America through the eighteenth and nineteenth centuries, this contribution to overall population growth is generally understood as being relatively unimportant. These features make it possible for historical demographers to study the evolution of a population that was largely closed to immigration over a very long period of time. All told, Canada's French-speaking population grew at a remarkably rapid pace.

Human populations have the capacity for exponential increase, and this was clearly what was documented in the population register of New France. A common way that is often employed in measuring the growth potential of a population is to calculate its *doubling time*, defined simply as the period necessary for a population to double in size, given a specific growth rate. As a shorthand technique for estimating doubling time, demographers refer to what is labelled the *rule of 69*, whereby the doubling time can be easily obtained as 69 divided by the annual growth rate. In this context, it is noted that the annual growth rate of New France averaged at about 3 per cent throughout the seventeenth century and about 2.5 per cent throughout the eighteenth. While such growth rates might not appear to be that high at first glance, growth rates of 2.5 per cent and 3 per cent can be translated into doubling time of only 27.6 years and 23 years, respectively.

As the French Canadian population experienced very high growth through to the twentieth century, a population of about 6 million can now draw a direct line of descent back to a few thousand immigrants who made their way across the Atlantic from France three centuries ago. As Charbonneau and colleagues (1993:161) write, "Thirteen or fourteen generations later the genes of these descending prolific pioneers are still part of all new-borns descending from these lines." In working with a computerized population register, Charbonneau and colleagues estimated that these initial seventeenth-century pioneers accounted for over two thirds of the 1980 makeup of the French-speaking population of Quebec (Charbonneau et al., 1987). Besides the French of Quebec, these original pioneers have descendants in the French Canadian population who moved to other parts of Canada and New England in the nineteenth and early twentieth centuries.

Population Growth in Early Canada outside New France

While the demographic history of New France has been carefully documented, the same cannot be said for the other parts of Canada. The primary reason for this is relatively simple: there is a scarcity of sources available to undertake this research. Proper records have been lost, destroyed, or were never collected in the first place. Under British rule, there appears to have been a lack of interest in extending to non-Catholic populations the data-collection activities characteristic of New France. As a result, the historical literature on the demography of early Canada outside New France is much less detailed, particularly for the years prior to the mid-nineteenth century.

In the study of this early European settlement, there is relatively little beyond an array of population estimates produced for specific settlements and colonies (see Clark, 1968; Lachapelle and Henripin, 1982; Wells, 1975; Maloney et al., 1973; McInnis, 1969; Stavely, 1977; Beaujot and McQuillan, 1982; McVey and Kalbach, 1995). One common assertion made in all these estimates is that the European population outside Quebec in Canada was very small, at least until the beginning of the nineteenth century. Lachapelle and Henripin (1982) estimate for 1760 a population of about 70,000 in New France, roughly 10,000 British in Newfoundland, perhaps 9,000 in the remainder of Atlantic Canada, and probably no more than 12,000 French-speaking setters in Acadia. In other words, at the time of the British conquest of New France in 1760, probably less than one third of the European population in Canada lived outside New France, for a total European population in Canada of some 100,000 people. West of New France, there were few Europeans, with very limited efforts at establishing permanent settlements.

Whereas European settlement in Canada was relatively sparse at this point in history, the same was certainly not the case in the colonial United States. Most of the migration from Britain to North America during the seventeenth and eighteenth centuries went to colonies such as in New England, Virginia, and Pennsylvania. With literally hundreds of thousands of people migrating to these American colonies, the population of the colonial United States grew at a very rapid rate. By 1760, the population of European origin in the American colonies is estimated as having grown to over 1,260,000 (Gemery, 2000), supplemented by several hundred thousand people of African ancestry (Walsh, 2000). This figure clearly dwarfs the aforementioned population estimate of about 100,000 for all of Canada. From a relatively early point on in the demographic development of North America, the United States had already established its demographic weight—Canada has always had a much smaller population.

British North America

It has been estimated that about 160,000 people from Britain migrated to the colonial United States in the seventeenth century, and perhaps as many as 600,000 in the following century (Gemery, 2000). In direct contrast, early Canada likely received about 10,000 migrants in the seventeenth century, and roughly 50,000 in the eighteenth. In discussing this disparity, Lachapelle and Henripin (1982) speculate as to what might have happened if France, early on, had

followed a policy of populating its North American colonies in a manner comparable to Britain. As the authors observed, if France (which had a population about three times that of England at the time) had sent perhaps a few thousand colonists a year (comparable to Britain) rather than a few hundred (as indicated in their historical record), the demographic and linguistic balance of North America would clearly be very different from what we have today. During the seventeenth century, the French had control over the St Lawrence, Missouri, and Mississippi River systems, giving them potential control over more than half of the North American continent. Despite this geopolitical advantage, no effort was forthcoming on the part of France to exploit this situation by introducing settlers on a scale anywhere close to the British numbers.

The Deportation of the Acadians

Through most of the seventeenth and eighteenth centuries, France and England competed for control over much of Eastern Canada, as boundaries and territories were continuously being redrawn. The civilian population of Canada was often drawn directly into this conflict, frequently with tragic consequences. The best-known example was the forced expulsion of Acadians from Atlantic Canada in 1756, following the outbreak of the Seven Years' War in Europe. The Acadians were the descendants of original French settlers who landed in Atlantic Canada, predominantly in what is now New Brunswick, Nova Scotia, and Prince Edward Island. Whereas the Acadians first established themselves in Atlantic Canada in the early seventeenth century, they came under British rule in 1713. The outbreak of hostilities in Europe was used as an excuse for local authorities to force this community into exile, a situation that in today's language might be called *ethnic cleansing*. This action was taken by the British to radically alter the demographic base of the Maritimes, with about one third of the population of Acadia forced into permanent exile, and comparable numbers relocated elsewhere in Atlantic Canada (Lachapelle and Henripin, 1982). Thousands lost the land they had previously cleared and farmed, in some cases for generations.

The United Empire Loyalists

While the Acadian deportation temporarily slowed population growth in the Maritimes, it did not take long for the numbers to rebound. In fact, Canada's population was to expand relatively rapidly toward the end of the eighteenth century. Particularly important in this regard was the American War of Independence, which quite unintentionally contributed to Canada's settlement through the forced migration of tens of thousands of refugees from the American Revolution. Beginning largely in 1784, an estimated 40,000 United Empire Loyalists, who opposed the revolution, moved from New England northward into areas still controlled by the British (MacDonald, 1939). Of this migration, roughly three quarters settled in the Maritimes, with the remainder moving to what is currently eastern Ontario and western Quebec.

The influx of migrants made the population of the Maritime provinces more than double, providing the founding population of New Brunswick and the earliest pioneers to eastern Ontario. For the first time, British settlement in Canada expanded westward from Quebec, following along the St Lawrence River toward the lands adjacent to Lake Ontario and Lake Erie. Closely following the Loyalists into Ontario, many more migrants entered Canada from the United States, drawn largely by the availability of quality agricultural land. In many respects, the movement of Americans into Ontario resulted from an ongoing population expansion westward from New England, involving a series of both "push" and "pull" factors. While many were pushed as political refugees from the American War of Independence, others were pulled by economic considerations, in a context where political boundaries and allegiances were often of secondary importance. The availability of quality land on affordable terms must have been a very attractive draw for many eighteenth- and early-nineteenth-century farmers and pioneers setting out to establish farms in a context of rapid population expansion.

With this movement of population, Ontario, which had been inhabited almost exclusively by Aboriginal peoples prior to the American War of Independence, reached a population of over 100,000 anglophones by the second decade of the nineteenth century (Beaujot and McQuillan, 1982). With this influx of migrants from the United States, the population of English Canada was to quickly catch up with and surpass the population of New France. It is estimated that by 1805, the French population of Canada was outnumbered by the English (Lachapelle and Henripin, 1982: 10–11). By 1810, it has been estimated that Canada's population surpassed the 500,000 mark, with about one half of this population outside Quebec (Lachapelle and Henripin, 1982). With the outbreak of war between the United States and Britain in 1812, migration from south of the border was understandably brought to a halt. Since American settlers were viewed as a potential threat, England turned to other sources of immigration in populating its North American colonies and imposed restrictive measures to curtail immigration from south of the Canadian border.

Nineteenth-Century Population Growth

In the decades immediately following the War of 1812, British North America continued to grow quite rapidly, with a relatively high rate of natural increase supplemented by an unprecedented number of immigrants. Yet in contrast to recent decades, the bulk of these migrants were now coming from Ireland, England, and Scotland. While significant numbers of Irish, English, and Scottish people migrated to Canada, a precise accounting by ethnic stream is largely not possible. For example, Northern Irish Protestants and Scottish immigrants were often very difficult to distinguish, as were second-generation Scots or Irish emigrating from England. The ships that departed from England typically included not only English emigrants but also many emigrants from both Scotland and Ireland, a fact that was rarely obvious in available records. Irrespective of such difficulties, Cowan (1968) has roughly approximated that probably just over one half of the emigrants originated in Ireland, with the remainder equally distributed among the English and Scottish. As the historical record suggests, several hundred thousand emigrant embarkations originated in the British Isles during the first half of the nineteenth century, which subsequently contributed to the establishment of a society characterized for its heterogeneity—in terms of its ethnic or cultural heritage.

According to records maintained by the British, total emigration from Britain to North America fluctuated considerably from year to year, from not more than a few thousand emigrants leaving Britain in the years immediately following the War of 1812 to a high of over 100,000 in 1847—the latter year being not particularly representative, as it was one of the worst years of the potato famine in Ireland and western Scotland. The hardships among the rural poor throughout much of Britain at this point in history understandably drove tens of thousands to emigrate to North America, where agricultural and economic conditions were far more favourable. Disregarding this outlier, total emigration from Britain typically fluctuated between about 10,000 and 40,000 emigrants annually throughout most of the period 1817–1860. In reviewing what is probably the most reliable information on this migration, it is noted that in the nineteenth century the British collected information on the total number of "embarkations" from British ports, which was certainly not the same thing as the actual numbers of "retained immigrants" to eventually settle in Canada.

As the cumulative number of migrants increased, so too did shortages in terms of quality agricultural land in Eastern Canada, pushing settlement further west into Ontario. Throughout this period, much of Canada's Atlantic region was populated and settled, with unprecedented high growth rates (not since observed in that part of the country). Despite the enticements in Canada, a significant yet unknown number of migrants either immediately or eventually moved on to the United States. In addition, many other overseas embarkations were never to settle in Canada due to the excessive mortality that frequently characterized the transatlantic voyage. In the early to mid-nineteenth century, thousands of prospective immigrants succumbed to *emigrant fever*, or the combined risks of cholera, smallpox, and typhoid, among other infectious diseases. As migrants were often seriously weakened by near-starvation conditions in their home countries, many did not survive the trip to North America, or they died shortly thereafter. Contagious disease often ran rampant under the very crowded and unsanitary conditions that characterized the holds of ships sailing from British ports.

While the historical record lacks detail on the actual number of "retained immigrants" who eventually settled in Canada, McInnis (2000a) suggests that the main contours of Canada's demographic development can be identified. The time-series of emigrant embarkations is revised downward with some rough approximations as to the impact of both emigration and mortality (see Table 2.1). It would appear that many historians of the nineteenth century may have overstated the importance of immigration to Canada's population growth during this period.

McInnis (2000a) presents the results from a simulation, whereby Canada's population growth in the nineteenth century is estimated with and without immigration. From a population of slightly greater than 500,000 at the outset of the War of 1812, Canada's population would have risen to roughly 2.2 million by 1861 in the absence of international migration, compared with the documented population of about 3.2 million. In other words, over two thirds of Canada's population growth for this period was due to natural increase—this high level of natural increase strongly suggests very high levels of fertility during the nineteenth century. In particular, the natural fertility conditions of French Canada were likely also true of Atlantic Canada and Ontario.

Canadian Fertility and Mortality in the Nineteenth Century

In contrast to current conditions, the fertility and mortality of British North America in the early nineteenth century meant that families were often large and usually suffered frequent deaths when children were in infancy and childhood. In many ways, the mortality and fertility situation in Canada at that time was very similar to Europe and the United States, or, for that matter, any society that was yet to experience what demographers broadly label the *demographic transition*. It is useful to separate demographic transition into an *epidemiological transition* (a shift from high to low mortality) and a *fertility transition* (a shift from natural fertility to fertility limitation and low fertility). Historical demographers have noted a number of socioeconomic and cultural changes accompanying these transitions, typically (yet not always) involving industrialization and urbanization. In

Table 2.1 ▣ Emigration from the United Kingdom to Canada and Immigration to Canada, 1815–1860

Year	Emigration, United Kingdom to Canada[1]	Immigrant Arrivals in Quebec[2]	Revised, Retained Immigrants[3]
1815	680	n.a.	n.a.
1816	3,370	n.a.	n.a.
1817	9,979	n.a.	n.a.
1818	15,136	n.a.	n.a.
1819	23,534	n.a.	n.a.
1820	17,921	n.a.	n.a.
1821	12,995	n.a.	n.a.
1822	16,018	n.a.	n.a.
1823	11,355	n.a.	n.a.
1824	8,774	n.a.	n.a.
1825	8,741	n.a.	n.a.
1826	12,818	n.a.	n.a.
1827	12,648	n.a.	n.a.
1828	12,084	n.a.	n.a.
1829	13,307	15,822	15,822
1830	30,574	27,549	24,189
1831	58,067	49,830	43,226
1832	66,339	51,200	44,654
1833	28,808	21,407	19,776
1834	40,060	30,596	28,311
1835	15,573	12,302	11,905
1836	34,226	27,487	25,499
1837	29,884	21,627	18,342
1838	4,577	2,993	2,993
1839	12,658	7,184	5,389
1840	32,293	22,002	18,482
1841	38,164	27,846	22,846
1842	54,123	43,818	37,903
1843	23,518	21,233	19,233
1844	22,924	19,925	17,925
1845	31,803	25,215	21,181
1846	43,439	32,753	25,153
1847	109,860	89,562	54,562
1848	31,065	27,097	19,742
1849	41,367	37,526	28,749
1850	32,961	31,591	18,224
1851	42,605	39,970	21,409
1852	32,873	37,992	24,695
1853	34,522	36,203	23,532
1854	43,761	52,326	32,442
1855	17,966	20,583	15,083
1856	16,378	22,178	12,826
1857	21,001	32,073	22,748
1858	9,704	12,596	11,371
1859	6,689	8,778	4,643
1860	9,786	6,276	6,276

Note: "n.a." means cannot be calculated.
1 Emigrant embarkations destined for British North America from UK ports (Cowan, British Immigration to North America).
2 Immigrant arrivals in Quebec, net of arrivals from the Maritime colonies (Cowan, British Immigration to North America).
3 Revised series of immigrant arrivals in Canada, net of immigration agent Buchanan's estimate of immediate departures to the United States.

Source: McInnis, 2000a.

studying the specific timing of these transitions, experts have noted that mortality decline typically predated fertility decline, augmenting the rate of natural increase over the transitional period.

Epidemiological Transition

According to the classic formulation of the theory of epidemiological transition, populations experience three stages in the pattern of disease dominance (Omran, 1971). Pre-modern societies are described as being in an *age of pestilence and famine*, dominated by infectious/parasitic disease and frequent famine. This is followed by a stage referred to as *the age of receding pandemics*, featuring a progressive decline in the risk of premature death. In the third phase, the stage of *human-made and degenerative diseases*, the predominant causes of death shift from the lethal viral and parasitic diseases of the past toward the chronic and degenerative diseases that are predominant in the present (disease as experienced in old age). Whereas the timing of this transition is difficult to date with precision, and the progression from one stage to the next has varied widely across populations, Riley (1989) has suggested that perhaps the earliest evidence of the second stage be situated in the seventeenth century, whereas it was not until the twentieth century that Western societies fully entered into the third stage. Overall, the eighteenth and nineteenth centuries in both North America and Europe are noted for some modest gains in terms of reduced mortality and increased longevity. In the Canadian context, it was not until the latter nineteenth and early twentieth centuries that some of the most dramatic changes were observed: a systematic reduction in the risk of premature death.

The first stage of the epidemiological transition applies to the pre-contact period as well as the period of early European settlement. As already observed, the mortality of Aboriginal peoples included a significant increase in the seventeenth and eighteenth centuries, while the mortality of the population of European origin neither increased nor declined dramatically. Bourbeau and colleagues (1997), for example, have estimated that by the early nineteenth century, Canadians born in 1801 had a life expectancy at birth of just under 40 (applying to both English and French Canada). This is only slightly different from the life expectancy at birth of about 35 years said to characterize New France throughout much of the eighteenth century. Among children born at mid-century (e.g., 1850 or 1851), Bourbeau and colleagues estimate a life expectancy at birth of about 43 years, as indicative of the gradual pace of mortality decline in Canada over this period.

While mortality continued to decline throughout the nineteenth century, serious setbacks were common, with the ongoing threat of epidemic diseases. In taking a closer look at this epidemiological transition, perhaps Canada's mortality history can be better described in terms of several different transitions, as the pace of this mortality decline has been known to vary considerably. For example, just as the mortality history of First Nations peoples was very different from other Canadians, the mortality of selected regions or cities also differed noticeably. The pace of this transition was influenced by various environmental conditions, the state of public health, sanitation, and nutrition. Noteworthy in this regard is the fact that mortality rates appear to have been particularly high in nineteenth-century "urban" Canada (Pelletier et al., 1997; Thornton and Olson, 2011), a situation that was also found to exist in several other countries at this point in history (Preston and van de Walle, 1978; Haines, 2001).

Toward the mid-nineteenth century, Montreal was easily Canada's largest city, with a population of about 100,000 and a disproportionate share of the colony's emerging industry and commerce. Yet, as demonstrated in Table 2.2, throughout most of the century, mortality was much higher in Montreal than elsewhere in Quebec (Pelletier et al., 1997). By the 1841–1850 period, for example, the city's crude death rate was estimated at 51.1 deaths per 1,000 inhabitants, more than twice as high as the 22.9 deaths per 1,000 estimated for Quebec as a whole. This level of mortality was likely significantly higher than practically anywhere else in Canada at this time (McInnis, 2000a), or, for that matter, practically anywhere else in North America (Preston and Haines, 1991). The rapid industrialization and urbanization that characterized Montreal in the mid-nineteenth century appears to have imposed very severe strains

Table 2.2 ▣ Crude Death Rates per 1,000, Nineteenth-Century Quebec

Period	Lower Canada/ Quebec	Montreal
1801–10	26.43	–
1811–20	25.61	–
1821–30	25.28	44.30
1831–40	25.86	53.80
1841–50	22.99	51.10
1851–60	20.97	38.35
1861–70	21.91	40.35
1871–80	24.41	33.34
1885–90	22.43	29.23 / 32.98
1891–1900	20.89	23.99

Source: Pelletier et al., 1997: 98.

on the living conditions of its inhabitants, as the crude death rate of the city steadily increased over this period.

Consistent with what is known of the epidemiological transition in a nineteenth-century context, most of the important gains owed relatively little to medical progress, but much more so to improvements in living conditions, personal hygiene, nutrition, housing standards, and the introduction of some simple public health measures. Because mortality was higher in urban Canada, we are alerted to the simple fact that improvements in sanitation and hygiene did not occur during the early stages of urbanization. In Montreal, industrialization promoted an increase in population size and density, with a greater level of crowding, an increased likelihood of epidemic and contagious disease and a higher probability of contaminated food and water supply. In explaining the considerable mortality decline in Montreal toward the end of the century (as shown in Table 2.2), Pelletier and colleagues (1997) point to some basic changes in terms of the public sanitation and in the quality of the city's water supply. The construction of a large-scale aqueduct system dramatically reduced, almost overnight, the incidence of cholera, typhoid, and a variety of digestive and diarrheal afflictions (diseases easily spread through parasites in contaminated food and water).

A fundamental feature of high-mortality societies is that an infant's chances of surviving through to adulthood are not very good. Olson and Thornton (2011), for example, have estimated for mid-nineteenth-century Montreal what were exceptionally high infant and child mortality rates, at levels suggestive of deterioration in living conditions rather than progress relative to the situation as documented in Canada during the seventeenth and eighteenth centuries.

The Fertility Transition

With such a high risk of premature death in a society, demographers have long pointed out that high fertility is a rational response to such circumstances (Davis, 1949). To maintain a positive rate of natural increase in a context of high mortality, high fertility is obviously necessary. Pre-modern societies developed social institutions that were *pro-natalist* in orientation, encouraging both marriage and parenthood.

In early-nineteenth-century Canada, all available information suggests that fertility continued to remain quite high, at levels that were perhaps even higher than in most of Europe and the United States at the same time (McInnis, 2000a; Henripin and Péron, 1972). Particularly relevant in this context was evidence to suggest that the proportion of women of child-bearing age who married continued to remain quite high, a generalization that seemed to apply equally well to both French and English Canada at this time. As nuptiality is a particularly important *proximate determinant* of fertility, particularly among societies that practise little control of fertility within marriage, the high proportion of married people translated into a relatively high level of fertility. With high fertility more than compensating for high mortality, the rate of natural increase in Canada remained high throughout the nineteenth century. That is, it would not be until the late 1800s that the more substantial transitional changes would take place.

It is not always the case that lower mortality in a society is directly accompanied by a corresponding reduction in the number of births as individuals and societal institutions often take considerable time to adjust to this new situation. As we will see in subsequent chapters, the combination of several concurrent changes was ultimately responsible for the fertility transition in Canada. Particularly important were the shift in the nature of work (from the home and farm to industrial production and the factory floor); shifts in values, including the decline in the influence of religion on family life; and the development of far more efficient means of birth control. A widespread explanation of fertility decline has focused on both industrialization and urbanization. Lower fertility, so the explanation goes, tends to happen in a society when children become more expensive and less able to contribute to family income—and parents become more receptive to the idea of family planning and limitation.

Conclusion

In this chapter, we have focused on Canada's early demographic history, beginning with the pre-contact period, and broadly sketched Canada's demographic experience through to the end of the nineteenth century. Although we do not have direct information on the size of Canada's population during the pre-contact period, it is probably safe to generalize that the First Nations population experienced at least three centuries of population decline—prior to reaching its nadir of about 100,000 toward the year 1900 (Thornton, 1987; Waldram et al., 2006). At the same time, Canada's non-Aboriginal or European-origin population experienced continued strong growth, as many scattered settlements were to eventually establish a solid foothold throughout much of what is now Quebec, Ontario, and Atlantic Canada. The nineteenth century can be described as a period of considerable demographic growth in Canada, starting with a population of only about 350,000 persons in 1800 (excluding the First Nations population) and increasing roughly tenfold to 3,500,000 by the time of Confederation in 1867 (McVey and Kalbach, 1995; McInnis, 2000b; Simmons, 2010).

While population growth accelerated in the nineteenth century, clearly not all regions of Canada experienced this growth equally. Prior to Confederation, for example, very little of this growth occurred west of Ontario, as the largest proportion of Canada's land mass continued to be populated almost

exclusively by First Nations peoples. While there were a few exceptions, with some small-scale settlements in both Manitoba and on the Pacific Coast, British efforts at settling Western Canada were very limited overall. While the West played a minor role in the early demographic development of Canada, this was to change in a pronounced manner in the decades following Confederation. In the last few decades of the nineteenth century and the first two decades of the twentieth, hundreds of thousands of migrants (from both overseas and Eastern Canada) were drawn to the grasslands of the Prairies and to the newly forming lumber towns of the Pacific Coast (Belshaw, 2009). The western provinces at the time of Confederation were on the verge of a period of dramatic change and population settlement, such that the internal distribution of Canada's population was to shift in a permanent and pronounced manner.

Just as the western provinces were about to experience dramatic changes, the same could be said for Canada's demographic development overall. The late nineteenth century was a particularly crucial period for the country's demographic transition, as both fertility and mortality declined substantially. With an ongoing high rate of natural increase, this time period was noted for substantial emigration to the United States, whereas the early twentieth century was a period of major immigration. Canada had encouraged immigration from Britain throughout the latter nineteenth century, but the source countries of immigration were to diversify in the twentieth century, with hundreds of thousands of newcomers of German, Hungarian, Ukrainian, Polish, Scandinavian, and Italian background. Canada's internal distribution of population was also to shift, in light of its urban transition, as a predominantly rural society was to eventually become one of the more highly urbanized countries in the world. Canada's population continued to remain relatively small in comparison with the United States, but both continued to grow quite rapidly. For the First Nations peoples of Canada, the late nineteenth century was transitional in the sense that after 300 years of population decline, a demographic recovery brought about considerable population growth in the twentieth century.

Critical Thinking Questions

1. What were some of the factors responsible for population decline among Canada's First Nations population, beginning in the sixteenth century?
2. How was the demographic experience of the original inhabitants of New France different from the experience of France's population?
3. How do you think North America's current demographic makeup would have differed if France had pursued a similar strategy to Britain in populating its North American colonies?
4. Describe the early stages of Canada's demographic transition.
5. Why is it useful to think of Canada's mortality history as involving several different transitions?

Recommended Readings

Beaujot, Roderic, and Kevin McQuillan. 1982. *Growth and Dualism: The Demographic Development of Canadian Society.* Toronto: Gage Publishing. This book explores the sociological and historical dimensions of the population and language issues in Canada from the seventeenth century through to the twentieth.

Belshaw, J.D. 2009. *Becoming British Columbia: A Population History.* Vancouver: University of British Columbia Press. This is a well-written, comprehensive demographic history of Canada's westernmost province from pre-contact through to the present.

Charbonneau, H., A. Guillemette, J. Légaré, B. Desjardins, Y. Landry, and F. Nault. 1987. *Naissance d'une population: Les Français établis au Canada au XVIIe siècle.* Montréal: Les Presses de l'Université de Montréal. The beginnings of the French population in Canada are explored through an analysis of records of people who settled in this country in the seventeenth century.

Haines, Michael, and Richard Steckel. 2000. *A Population History of North America.* Cambridge, UK: Cambridge University Press. This large edited collection includes two chapters on the history of First Nations populations, a chapter on Quebec population history, and two chapters covering Canada in the eighteenth and nineteenth centuries.

Livi-Bacci, Massimo. 2012. *A Concise History of World Population*, Fifth Edition. Cambridge, UK: Blackwell. This book considers population throughout human history, and it reviews the issues facing the world population into the early twenty-first century.

Related Websites

www.genealogy.umontreal.ca/en/home. The main objective of this website, as maintained by the *Programme de recherche en démographie historique* is to make genealogical information on New France available on the internet. This site is hosted by the Department of Demography at the Université de Montréal.

http://web.uvic.ca/hrd/cfp. The Canadian Families Project is an interdisciplinary research group based at the University of Victoria. The project team is studying families in Canada and has completed a national sample of the 1901 Canadian Census.

www2.h-net.msu.edu/~demog. H-Demog is an international scholarly online discussion list on demographic history, sponsored by the National Endowment for the Humanities and Michigan State University.

https://familysearch.org. Interested in a bit of family history? On this site you can choose the 1881 Canadian census, the 1880 United States Census or the 1881 British Isles Census and do a systematic search on ancestors. Enter your ancestor's first or last name and then click *Search*.

www.prdh.umontreal.ca/census/en/main.aspx.html. The 1852 and 1881 Canadian Censuses Project is based at the Département de Démography/CIED, Université de Montréal, to enhance samples of the 1852 and 1881 Canadian Census for academic historical, demographic, and genealogical research.

The Population Processes

In Chapter 1, we defined the study of population in terms of processes (fertility, mortality, and migration) and states (size, distribution, and composition). We also made the case for the importance of studying demographic questions as a means of studying societies, and we introduced the theories and methods for studying populations. In Chapter 2, we considered the evidence of all aspects of population for the period before Confederation. Here in Part I, we consider mortality, fertility, and immigration in Chapters 3, 4, and 5; in Part II, Chapters 6, 7, and 8, we examine the consequences of demographic processes for regional distribution, population growth, and the age structure.

Mortality is studied here in relation to health and health care. Through the phases of the epidemiological transition, the causes of death have shifted to degenerative diseases (i.e., heart disease and cancer) and accidents. A further analysis of the causes of death leads to a consideration of risk factors (biological, behavioural, and environmental) and treatment factors for those who are subject to particular risks. There are also significant differences in mortality by sex, by socioeconomic status, and marital status, but the regional differences have declined. Both risk factors and treatment factors are associated with these differences, but it would appear preventive approaches that would reduce risks would have the largest impact. The increased awareness of risks and the interest in achieving good health point to the potential to make further gains in life expectancy.

Fertility is analyzed here in terms of maintaining society's population. The long-term trends are placed within the context of the demographic transition. The decline in fertility was interrupted through the period of the baby boom, but it has since continued through a second demographic transition. Fertility trends and differences are further analyzed through the consideration of proximate factors (especially union formation, union dissolution, and contraception), along with micro-level considerations (economic and cultural values and costs of children to parents) and macro-level considerations (that is, the interplay of production and reproduction). In 2011, the total fertility rate was 1.61 births per woman. This can be placed in the context that globalization creates risks for individuals; these risks can be reduced through investments in human resources and delayed child-bearing. Most people want to have children, but they face constraints, especially opportunity costs. These costs rise with women's relative income, but they may be reduced through arrangements that allow a better interface of family and work.

PART I

Chapter 5, "Immigration and the Population of Canada," is the longest in the book, pointing to the importance of migration in the Canadian case. Over the previous century, net international migration accounted for a quarter of our population growth. From 2001 to 2011, it accounted for about 64 per cent of growth. Whereas immigration has a strong influence on the size and growth of the population, it has less influence on its age structure, and it tends to accentuate the unequal distribution of the population. Immigration increases the cultural diversity of Canada, and especially the relative size of the visible-minority population. It also reduces the relative size of the French population of Canada. Studies of the macroeconomic consequences of immigration suggest that the impact is minor but positive.

A comparison of cohorts shows that the economic well-being of immigrants of the postwar period (especially 1946–1975) has been greater than that of immigrants of the last few decades (especially 1986–2011). It can be argued that, rather than making the case for immigration in demographic or economic terms, it needs to be made in sociopolitical terms, as a means of increasing cultural diversity and pluralism in a globalizing world.

3 Mortality, Health, and Health Care

The Chapter at a Glance

- Life expectancy in Canada increased from 39 years in 1831 to 81.5 years in 2009–2011. These long-term changes can be attributed to higher standards of living, improvements in sanitation, and advances in medicine.
- Degenerative diseases have replaced infectious diseases as the major causes of death.
- Mortality can be analyzed through causes of death, risk factors, and treatment factors. The risk factors are biological, behavioural, and environmental. The treatment factors consider

the extent to which the health system can alleviate the problems for people subject to these risks.

- Mortality differentials can be analyzed by age, sex, marital status, socioeconomic status, and sociocultural factors.
- Canadians give high priority to health policy, which needs to consider future health-care needs, preventative as opposed to curative approaches, as well as corresponding costs and ethical issues.

Introduction

10% = 80
Confederation = 42 = e°

We have witnessed remarkable changes in longevity and health care over the course of Canadian history. At the time of Confederation, the average life expectancy at birth was 42 years, and the leading causes of death, especially among infants and children, were infectious diseases. Fewer than 10 per cent of the population reached the eighth decade of life. Health care was largely the responsibility of individuals and charities. For the 2009–2011 period, life expectancy surpassed 81.5 years, while the leading causes of death had become the chronic diseases that mainly affect older people (Statistics Canada, 2013a; Martel, 2013), and unprecedented numbers of people are reaching these later decades; in fact, among the fastest-growing age groups are persons in their eighth and ninth decades of life, up by almost 25 per cent during the 2006–2011 intercensal period (Statistics Canada, 2012a). Because of the greying of the population, health and health care have become even more important government priorities.

The changes and adaptations that will be necessary for the future are uncertain, at least partially driven by the extent to which mortality continues to decline. In a review of mortality changes in developed countries, Oeppen and Vaupel (2002; 2004) see no reason why the future would not hold continued increases in life expectancy, which have averaged about 2.5 years per decade over the past 150 years. Olshansky and colleagues (2009) have contradicted this optimism by suggesting that longevity gains may level off, particularly in the American context, which implies a major break from past trends (see Box 3.1). Regardless of this uncertainty, future developments in terms of mortality and population aging will have massive consequences, from future health-care expenditures, public health initiatives, research priorities, through to basic quality-of-life issues. While demographers have long recognized the importance of changes in the birth rate to individual planning horizons, social structures and policy needs, these large and cumulative shifts in upper-age survival chances also require fundamental socioeconomic and political adaptations.

In many areas of policy, when a social problem such as delinquency is alleviated, there is less need to spend money on it. However, in the area of health and longevity, it appears to be the opposite: The higher the life expectancy and the more successful the prevention of diseases, the higher the need for services and resources to cope with the health problems of survivors.

Although people are living longer, these extra years are not necessarily spent in good health. With longer life come longer periods of poor health and disability, on average. Even though many or most older people are healthy, the fact is that almost one third (31.6 per cent) of people aged 85 and above are living in institutions, and only about one in four report good health (Ramage-Morin et al., 2010). Cranswick and Dosman (2008) expect that with the aging of the population, caregiving for the elderly will become an increasingly difficult problem for Canada's health-care delivery system. While there are clearly average improvements in the health of individuals at any given age, an older population will still result in a greater prevalence of poor health and disability in the population.

Nor do the problems apply only to the elderly: roughly 1 in 10 Canadians aged 15 and over report some disability, with over half of this disabled subpopulation under the age of 65 (Statistics Canada, 2010a). Avoidable disease and premature mortality among younger Canadians continues to be a major burden to the health-care system, as, for example, almost 38 per cent of all deaths in 2011 occurred to persons under the age of 75 (Martel, 2013). Preventable mortality is highest among the most economically marginalized of Canadians, suggesting that greater socioeconomic equality would serve to improve the health and well-being of Canada's population (Mikkonen and Raphael, 2010).

In 1964, the Royal Commission on Health Services recommended that the highest possible health standards for Canadians become a primary objective of national policy. As highlighted by Roy Romanow, who headed the 2002 Royal Commission on the Future of Health Care in Canada, Canada's Health Act can be characterized as "a success." It is very popular with the public; it provides comprehensive care at reasonable cost; and it protects the elderly in particular from the burden of rising health-care costs, from depletion of their financial resources, from the threat of chronic sickness without care, and from death in poverty. Yet, there are pressing problems: the growth of health expenditures, underfunding, quality of services, access, and the mix of services, including curative and preventive measures.

In this chapter, we will review historical changes to patterns of health and disability, the predominant causes of death, and the sociodemographic profile of mortality in Canada. We will argue that health policy could better take into consideration the demographics of health, morbidity, and mortality.

Historical and Expected Change in Life Expectancy

The earliest estimates of life expectancy for Canada as a whole date back to 1831, when it would have been 38.3 years for men and 39.8 for women (Bourbeau and Légaré, 1982: 77). By 1901, Canadians had gained an additional decade of life, with life expectancy at birth up to about 47 for males and 50 for females. These levels were still very low by today's standards, as only a handful of countries currently report a life expectancy of less than 50, and these places are without exception experiencing widespread violence as well as political and economic difficulties. The Democratic Republic of the Congo, for example, after having witnessed some of the most violent fighting since the end of the Second World War, reports a life expectancy of only 50 years; wartorn Afghanistan reports a life expectancy of about 60 years; while Lesotho, one of the world's poorest societies, hit hard by the AIDS pandemic, reports a life expectancy of only 44 years (see Table C.1 in Appendix C).

Canadian life expectancy, estimated for the 2009–2011 period, is 79.3 years for men and 83.6 years for women (Statistics Canada, 2013a). Just a handful of countries have a higher life expectancy than Canada, and most of these nations have only a negligible advantage. Japan, as a world leader, has a life expectancy of almost 80 years for males and a remarkable 86 years for females (OECD, 2010). Greenberg and Normandin (2012) place Canada among the top 10 countries internationally—6 countries have a longer male life expectancy (Japan, Switzerland, Iceland, Sweden, Australia, and Italy) and 8 report a longer female life expectancy (adding Spain and France to the aforementioned list). Recent longevity gains in the United States have lagged behind Canadian gains, with male life expectancy reported for 2010 at 76.2 years and female life expectancy at 81.0 years (National Center for Health Statistics, 2014). While Canadians and Americans had near identical life expectancies a half a century ago, over the last several decades, a gap between the two countries has arisen: up to 2.8 years according to the most up-to-date estimates available (Bourbeau, 2002; National Center for Health Statistics, 2014).

The earlier improvements in life expectancy were largely due to the reduction of infectious diseases like tuberculosis, pneumonia, diphtheria, scarlet fever, typhoid, and diarrhea. These were diseases that struck all ages, though often the very young were particularly vulnerable. In fact, the most important contribution to the improvements in life expectancy was the decline in infant mortality. In 1831, 1 in 6 children did not survive their first year, compared to fewer than 1 in 200 in the 2009–2011 period, when there were 4.86 deaths per 1,000 live births (Statistics Canada, 2013b).

An analysis of why infectious diseases declined in importance brings us to consider standard of living and medical knowledge. As a component of the standard of living, improved nutrition appears to have played an important role (McKeown et al., 1972). Poor nutrition increases the susceptibility to infection, and it also makes it likelier that the infection will be fatal. The medical improvements relevant to infectious diseases have especially involved preventive medicine, including knowledge about the importance of sanitation, improvements in the care and feeding of infants, and the development of effective vaccines.

Infectious diseases were still the most important cause of death one hundred years ago in Canada, as communicable diseases, such as tuberculosis, pneumonia, scarlet fever, and diphtheria were responsible for a substantial proportion of all deaths. Infant mortality was quite high, as a wide assortment of diseases, including those of the digestive system, such as diarrhea and enteritis, took a heavy toll on infant lives (Copp, 1974). In 1921, fully 10.8 per cent of all deaths had been vaguely labelled "deaths of early infancy," with a large proportion the by-product of communicable disease (i.e., deaths now easily preventable with antibiotics and inexpensive health-care interventions). As infant mortality declined dramatically, the likelihood of survival through to middle and old age increased dramatically, as did the importance of degenerative/chronic disease. As of 2011, cancer was reported as being the most common cause of death in Canada (29.9 per cent of all deaths), typically among older Canadians, followed closely by heart disease and stroke (19.7 per cent and 5.5 per cent of all deaths, respectively) (Statistics Canada, 2014b). While in the early 1900s only one third of all deaths occurred above the age of 65, by 2011 this had risen to almost 8 in 10 deaths, or 78.6 per cent (Martel, 2013). As the preventable diseases of infancy, childhood, and young adulthood have declined in importance, the impact of chronic/degenerative disease has logically increased, with morbidity and mortality shifting to older ages.

The improvements over the period 1931 to 2009/2011 have been impressive, bringing life expectancy from 61 to almost 81.5 years. In 1931, a person had about a 90 per cent chance of surviving to his or her first birthday; by 2009/2011, a person had roughly the same chance of surviving past his or her 63rd birthday (Statistics Canada, 2013a). Between 1951 and 2009/11, there was almost a 90 per cent reduction in mortality rates up to the age of 2, but there were also reductions of about 60 per cent between ages 10 and 55 (Bourbeau, 2002; authors' calculations). Over the first decade of the twenty-first century, there was little sign of this progress slowing, with male life expectancy up by 2.4 years since 2001 and female life expectancy up by about 1.6 years (see Table 3.1).

By most indicators, the health of Canadians continues to improve, with a few notable exceptions (Crompton, 2000; Statistics Canada, 2014b). For instance, there has been an improvement in age-standardized rates of heart disease, arthritis, and limitations on activity, although the number of Canadians

Table 3.1 ▣ Canadian Life Expectancy by Sex, 1831–2009/2011

Year	Male		Female		Difference in Years Males—Females
	Years	Average Annual Increase	Years	Average Annual Increase	
1831	38.2	—	39.8	—	−1.56
1841	39.3	0.11	41.2	0.15	−1.94
1851	40.0	0.07	42.1	0.08	−2.11
1861	40.3	0.03	42.6	0.05	−2.29
1871	41.4	0.11	43.7	0.11	−2.27
1881	43.4	0.20	45.9	0.22	−2.50
1891	43.9	0.04	46.5	0.06	−2.66
1901	47.1	0.33	50.1	0.36	−2.97
1911	50.9	0.37	54.2	0.41	−3.28
1921	55.0	0.41	58.4	0.43	−3.41
1931	60.0	0.50	62.1	0.36	−2.06
1941	63.0	0.30	66.3	0.43	−3.27
1951	66.4	0.34	70.9	0.46	−4.50
1961	68.4	0.20	74.3	0.34	−5.82
1971	69.6	0.12	76.6	0.23	−6.99
1981	72.0	0.24	79.2	0.26	−7.13
1991	74.6	0.26	81.0	0.18	−6.35
2001	76.9	0.23	82.0	0.10	−5.10
2009–11	79.38	0.27	83.6	0.18	−4.27

Sources: Bourbeau et al., 1997: 72–81; Martel and Bélanger, 1999: 165; Statistics Canada, 2013a.

with these health difficulties is increasing as Canada's population ages. On the other hand, while the incidence of high blood pressure decreased during the 1980s and '90s, it has most recently increased, with a climbing proportion of Canadians diagnosed with this health difficulty. Similarly, the incidence of diabetes has increased, as associated with a climbing proportion of Canadians reported as overweight or obese.

What has changed less is the differentiation of causes of death over the life course. For younger Canadians (under 35 years), accidents, mainly motor vehicle accidents, falls, suicides, and homicides, continue to be the largest cause of death. Cancer is now the principal killer of people aged 35 to 84, while heart disease is the most common causes of death for those 85 and older (Statistics Canada, 2014d). Up until the 1990s, heart disease was the most common cause of death among Canadians aged 75 and older, although recent advances in the prevention and treatment of high blood pressure and heart disease has managed to shift this to the 85 and older age group. Cancer is now the most common cause of death among Canadians in their latter seventies and early eighties, despite the fact that age-standardized death rates continue to decline. In other words, in the 2000s, we have witnessed greater progress in reducing deaths from heart disease relative to cancer, which has resulted in a shift in the leading cause of death among Canadians in their late seventies and early eighties.

Future Prospects

The prospects for further improvements in life expectancy are difficult to predict. Earlier projections had expected improvements to become slower as further progress becomes more difficult over time. Life expectancy, however, has continued to steadily increase over the last half century, by slightly above two years per decade, after having increased at an even more rapid pace earlier in the twentieth century.

Much of the uncertainty with regard to future life expectancy relates to the prospect for further control of diseases at older ages or for extending the length of life. Until the 1970s, it was observed that improvements in age-specific mortality at older ages were negligible, with most of the gains in life expectancy relating to reduced mortality among the young (e.g., Pollard, 1979; Dufour and Péron, 1979). It is easily recognized that the basic aging of the body makes it inevitably susceptible to one disease or another. More recent improvements in the mortality rates at older ages, however, have brought disagreements regarding the future dynamics. Some of the greatest gains in reducing mortality in recent decades have occurred among older Canadians. For age-specific mortality rates of people in their seventies and eighties, rates were down by 23 per cent and 18 per cent respectively, over the 2000–11 period (author's calculations; Statistics Canada, 2014d).

Past projections of the upper limits of average life expectancy have been underestimates, and the age at which the last members of given cohorts die appears to be increasing. While interventions in basic physiological aging processes as of yet do not explain mortality changes at advanced ages, various medical advancements and treatments are increasingly successful in delaying and preventing disease at older ages. Yet it is still possible that scientific advances will permit the arresting of specific aging processes and that the maximum human lifespan may be extended (Guralnik and Schneider, 1987; Vaupel et al., 2004). In an interview published by the American Association for the Advancement of Science (Vaupel et al., 2004), James Vaupel, a leading authority on human longevity, suggests that past trends are likely to continue well into the future (i.e., past gains of about 2.5 years per decade, as observed over the last 160 years): "maybe a little bit less, maybe a little bit more—but something like that." As Vaupel summarizes, a newborn baby in the developed world today, Europe, Japan, or North America, may very well have a 50/50 chance of surviving

through to his or her 100th birthday. The frontiers of biological research are expanding exponentially, with unclear consequences for human longevity.

Past projections have tended to underestimate the improvements in life expectancy, as, for example, can be seen by reviewing prognostications from Statistics Canada (Beaujot, 2002a). For instance, in the population projections based on the 1991 Census, Statistics Canada had a median assumption on mortality reaching a life expectancy at birth of 84 years for women and 78.5 years for men by 2016, with mortality rates then stabilizing through to 2041. As of 2009, though, male life expectancy had already surpassed this projection for 2016, whereas female life expectancy was only negligibly short of this mark. Alternatively, the United Nations' median variant projects a life expectancy for males of 84 by mid-century and 88 for females (United Nations, 2013a). Regarding their long-term projections (well over 100 years into the future), the UN optimistically forecasts a convergence in life expectancies toward a remarkably high 99.7 for males and 102.7 for females in more developed regions (United Nations, 2004). Within the next several decades, we could legitimately project that life expectancy will rise to 85 years for Canada, putting it among the top countries in the world in terms of its state of population health and socioeconomic well-being.

Explanations of Mortality

The study of mortality needs to start with questions about the cause of death, then you can consider risk factors and treatment. Cause of death may be seen as the proximate factor in mortality, similar to the use of contraceptives in fertility, while risk factors allow us to analyze the more distant causes, and treatment questions play a role in the extent to which illness leads to death.

Over long-term history, changes in causes of death can be described as passing through four stages of epidemiological transition (Olshansky and Ault, 1986; Rogers and Hackenberg, 1987). As we described in Chapter 1, the first three stages in this transition are (1) pestilence, (2) the decline of infectious diseases as the primary cause of death, and (3) their replacement by degenerative diseases, especially

Box 3.1 ▣ Will the Young of Today, on Average, Live Less Healthy and Possibly Even Shorter Lives than Their Parents?

In 2005, the *New England Journal of Medicine* published a highly influential paper questioning the optimism implicit in most official projections on future life expectancy. This paper raised the alarming scenario that in the United States, life expectancy was about to plateau and potentially decline as we moved further into the twenty-first century. The authors, Olshansky and colleagues, made the startling prediction that if recent trends continue, the young of today may very well be the first generation of Americans to actually live shorter lives than their parents. In forecasting this decline in life expectancy, the authors were particularly preoccupied with the health consequences of a growing public health concern in the United States: the climbing incidence of obesity among Americans, and even further, the alarmingly rapid increase in the incidence of childhood obesity.

It is clearly unscientific to forecast the future by merely assuming that gains as witnessed in the past will inevitably continue into the future. As Olshansky and colleagues pointed out, this is like "forecasting the weather on the basis of its history." This serves as a critique of the optimism of Vaupel and other authors, who assumed that past gains in life expectancy would continue well into the future, to the potential heights of 100 years of age in the current century. Such optimism arguably fails to consider the health status of people currently alive and explicitly assumes that the past can predict the future. Yet

Olshansky and colleagues (2005; 1139) suggest that we "look out the window, to see a threatening storm—obesity—that could, if unchecked, have a particularly negative effect on longevity."

While obesity rates have climbed rapidly over the last several decades, smoking rates have simultaneously declined (which at least partially offsets the negative obesity trend). Also, the health-care system had made several gains in terms of the effective medical management and therapeutic treatment of various chronic/degenerative conditions. As a result, most demographers continue to forecast future gains in life expectancy (Soneji and King, 2012), yet there is no disputing the fact that climbing obesity rates will serve to hamper such gains. Furthermore, this public health issue is likely a major factor in explaining why the United States is falling behind many other wealthy nations in the area of reducing mortality. Stateside obesity rates are considerably higher than in Canada, and this is arguably one of several reasons why life expectancy is almost three full years shorter than north of the border (Torrey and Haub, 2004a). As shown in Figure 3.1, 24.1 per cent of adults in Canada were obese—this was below the prevalence of 34.4 per cent in the United States (Shields et al., 2011).

Particularly problematic in both the United States and Canada is the fact that many of the recent significant increases in the incidence of obesity have occurred among children (Benac,

cardiovascular diseases and cancers. In initially proposing this theory in 1971, Abdel Omran limited himself to these first three stages, where in the third stage, mortality declines to low levels and eventually approaches stability. The fourth stage, which Olshansky and Ault (1986) referred to as the "age of delayed degenerative diseases," has subsequently been proposed in light of continued mortality gains, with an ongoing progressive shift toward older ages in the

distribution of deaths among age ranges by degenerative causes (mortality levels have not stabilized). This fourth stage, which now characterizes Canada, involves heart disease and cancer as the main causes of death, but these are occurring at later ages.

It is remarkable how much progress has been made in the age-specific incidence of these causes of death. Heart disease declined first, owing both to improvements in risk factors such as diets and

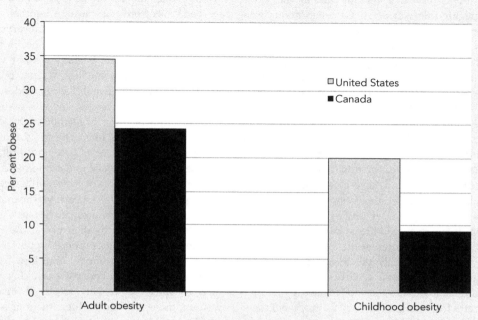

Figure 3.1 ▣ Obesity Rates, Adults and Children in Canada and the United States, 2007–2009

Source: Shields et al., 2011; Roberts et al., 2012.

2010). While childhood obesity is not nearly as high in Canada as in the United States (recent numbers have the child obesity rate at 9 per cent in Canada and at 20 per cent in the States), this is obviously a major health concern in both countries. If left unchecked, the rising prevalence of obesity among children will have long-term consequences as these younger cohorts age, with a heightened lifetime risk of type II diabetes; a decrease in the mean age of diabetes onset; an elevated risk of death from heart disease, cancer, an increased risk of depression and mental illness; among many other health complications. As a priority in promoting population health, public health officials would be wise in Canada in prioritizing this growing problem of inactivity and unhealthy body weight. In aiming to reduce future mortality rates, Canada would be wise to avoid the US situation where fully one third of the population is at a heightened risk of premature death due to obesity.

exercise, and in the medical treatment of heart disease victims. Over the 1979–1995 period, for instance, the age-adjusted death rates due to cardiovascular diseases declined by almost 40 per cent (Nault et al., 1997: 38) while more recently, since 1995, these rates again declined by a comparable per cent (Statistics Canada, 2014c). Once again, medical intervention has had an influence, but risk factors associated with lifestyle are also important. For instance, the age-standardized mortality rate from lung cancer in men has declined with lower rates of smoking (from 78 deaths per 100,000 in 1985 to 50.6 deaths per 100,000 in 2011), but the opposite holds for women (from 23.7 deaths per 100,000 in 1985 to 34.8 deaths in 2011). As lung cancer typically occurs after several decades of smoking, the convergence of death rates by sex relates to shifts in smoking behaviour of Canadian men and women during the 1960s and '70s.

In the 1960s, when smoking rates hit their summit, roughly one half of all Canadian adults were smoking, with over 60 per cent of men smoking and almost 40 per cent of women. Since then, while smoking rates have declined, they have declined in a more pronounced manner among men, to an estimated 22.3 per cent of males and 17.5 per cent of females in 2009—aged 12 and older, who smoke daily or occasionally (Statistics Canada, 2012b). Furthermore, tobacco consumption declined first among men, beginning in the 1960s, whereas among women, the largest decline began in the mid-1980s. As smoking rates converged, so, too, have lung cancer rates, yet with a lag of several decades. With this upturn in the incidence of lung cancer among older Canadian women, it now exceeds breast cancer as the most common cause of cancer death. Back in the 1980s, breast cancer was easily the most common cause (Canadian Cancer Society, 2012). Yet despite the diverging trends, males continue to have higher mortality rates from lung cancer, just as they continue to be slightly more likely to smoke.

Regardless of the phase of the epidemiological transition, it is clear that a variety of factors influence the mortality and health of a population. Though everyone dies from one cause or another, there are various risk factors for each cause, and varying ability of the medical system to handle the health problems that emerge. Clearly, our health is not just a function of the quality of the medical system, but is also affected by environmental factors and individual behaviour in diets, lifestyles, and risk taking. These kinds of behaviours can in turn be analyzed in relation to broader issues like opportunities and social support by social class (Chen and Millar, 1998; Raphael, 2009). The social and economic conditions found in different sectors of society influence lifestyle. The higher mortality due especially to heart disease of lower-class men, for instance, can be partly attributed to the stresses caused by their precarious economic situation, along with lack of social support for healthy living, which can promote unhealthy habits like smoking, poor diet, and excessive drinking. The pressure of work or various kinds of insecurity—surrounding work and/or life situations—can lead people to drink or smoke for relaxation, or to engage in risky behaviour. People of higher socioeconomic status have the advantage of various kinds of

Box 3.2   ▣   Avoidable Mortality in Canada

The Canadian Institute for Health Information (CIHI, 2012a), in collaboration with Statistics Canada, has published several new indicators of mortality, building upon the idea that some deaths are clearly "premature" and/or "potentially avoidable," whereas others will occur at older ages due to senescence and genetic factors. As life expectancy has increased across developed countries, the somewhat arbitrary standard of 75 has been introduced in delineating "premature deaths." In 2011, about 39 per cent of all deaths in Canada were people under the age of 75 (Statistics Canada, 2014d). Yet over the last three decades, Canada has made considerable progress in reducing premature mortality, with age-standardized rates down by 46 per cent.

Of these premature deaths, the CIHI classified some as "avoidable" (72 per cent) whereas others are considered "unavoidable" (28 per cent). The idea that some deaths are avoidable builds upon the idea that much loss of life can be averted or delayed by "preventing disease onset in the first place" (e.g., reducing the incidence of cardiovascular disease by getting Canadians to exercise and stop smoking, or reducing mortality from liver disease by getting Canadians to avoid alcohol abuse). In addition, some deaths are avoidable by averting or delaying death "after a condition has already developed" (e.g., early detection and treatment of high blood pressure to avoid an early death from stroke). Many deaths occur at a relatively young age, yet can be deemed "untimely and unnecessary," and could be potentially eliminated by effective health-care delivery and the promotion of public health initiatives. For potentially avoidable deaths, the study estimates that 72 per cent of premature deaths in Canada are, in fact, avoidable. This theoretically translates into a 4.9-year gain in life expectancy, if under ideal conditions avoidable deaths were eliminated altogether given our current state of medical knowledge. More specifically, life expectancy at birth in Canada would be up to about 86 years of age as opposed to 81 years of age as estimated for 2008.

While this concept of "avoidable" mortality dates back to research first conducted in the 1970s (Rutstein et al., 1976), there is still no universally agreed upon definition of the conditions and associated deaths that can be considered as avoidable. This Canadian research builds upon over three decades of development, with a careful review of previously compiled lists of conditions and associated mortality deemed to be avoidable. In so doing, two specific subcategories of avoidable death have been distinguished: (i) mortality from preventable causes, and (ii) mortality from treatable causes (see Figure 3.2). The first subset includes mortality from diseases with well-established risk factors that could potentially be reduced through successful public health initiatives—for example, by getting Canadians to reduce tobacco use and address issues such as high blood pressure, obesity, physical inactivity, high blood glucose, high cholesterol, poor diet, alcohol abuse, accidents, and occupational risks. The second set of avoidable deaths includes premature mortality potentially averted by early screening, detection, and successful treatment of disease in the Canadian health-care system, with effective and timely interventions.

As of 2008, preventable mortality is estimated to encompass 65 per cent of this avoidable mortality, whereas mortality from treatable causes represents the remaining 35 per cent. Returning to the observation that under ideal conditions, life expectancy rises by an estimated 4.9 years, about 3 years of this can be attributed to preventable mortality with the other 1.9 years attributed to mortality from treatable causes. In other words, much greater potential gain is achieved by disease prevention rather than disease treatment. There are innumerable public health initiatives that, if successful, could in a very cost-effective manner have a pronounced impact on population health and human longevity.

Consider ischemic heart disease as an example. While we have made substantial improvements in treatment (e.g., the development of beta blockers,

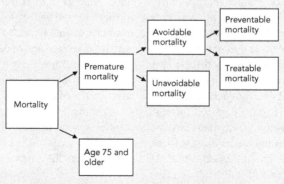

Figure 3.2 ▣ Mortality from Preventable and Treatable Causes

Source: CIHI, 2012a.

Continued

thrombolytic therapy, and cholesterol-lowering medications), there is still substantial potential for further mortality reduction through addressing the many risk factors widespread in the Canadian population. There are several risk factors that could be addressed through basic changes in lifestyle, including tobacco smoking, poor diet, elevated blood cholesterol, high blood pressure, obesity and low physical activity, type II diabetes, along with other less important risk factors. Recent initiatives to reduce trans fats and saturated fats in processed foods can have their impact, as well as efforts to reduce the daily sodium intake of Canadians. Considering that health problems often surface early in the life course, ending the availability of unhealthy foods for purchase in many Canadian school cafeterias could be made a priority in an effort to shift the habits of young Canadians toward a healthier diet.

structural and cultural support for healthy behaviour. Men of higher status in particular may experience less isolation and more social support.

Causes of Death

Since everyone dies of some cause or other, and the causes are fairly well diagnosed and reported, the analysis of causes of death provides useful insight into health questions. As of 2011, cancer was reported to be the most common cause of death in Canada (responsible for about 29.9 per cent of all deaths), followed by heart disease (19.7 per cent), and stroke (as a distant third, responsible for 5.5 per cent of deaths). Completing the top 10 includes chronic lower respiratory diseases (4.6 per cent), accidents (4.4 per cent), diabetes (3.0 per cent), Alzheimer's (2.6 per cent), influenza and pneumonia (2.4 per cent), suicide (1.5 per cent), and kidney disease (1.4 per cent). In terms of relative rank, this list, which accounts for more than 3 out of every 4 deaths, has been unchanged for well over a decade, with the exception of the 9th- and 10th-ranked causes—suicide and kidney disease have shifted place since 2000 (Statistics Canada, 2014e).

The ranking of deaths by cause again highlights a simple fact: that Canada has largely passed through the epidemiological transition. Canadians are no longer likely to die from an infectious disease (here, only influenza and pneumonia fall under this label), while accidental deaths remains the leading cause only among the young. Degenerative diseases and chronic illnesses have become increasingly important as Canadians are much more likely to survive through to old age. And in the modern context, even infectious disease tends to prey on the old; influenza and pneumonia are often described as "opportunistic," as they are of greatest risk to people who are already frail or weakened and not particularly healthy to begin with. In 2011, for example, almost 82 per cent of all persons who died of influenza/ pneumonia were over the age of 75, while over 57 per cent were aged 85 years and older (author's calculations; Statistics Canada, 2014e).

Without exception, the mortality rates associated with all 10 leading causes of death, standardized for age, have declined over the last decade. Some of the most remarkable gains, even among Canadians of advanced age, relates to mortality from heart disease and stroke (see Figure 3.3). The standardized mortality rate from major cardiovascular disease over the 1983–2011 period declined by 65.8 per cent among males and 62.4 per cent among females. While changing lifestyle factors are important and relevant (e.g., the decline in smoking, improvements in diet), various medical interventions, medication, and therapy for persons who develop cardiovascular disease have also been important. Canadians with hypertension and hypercholesterolemia, for example, are much more likely to have such conditions diagnosed with higher proportions receiving appropriate treatment, medication, and preventive care.

The health-care system has also invested substantial resources into the delivery of emergency medical services for heart attack and stroke victims, among other life-threatening events (e.g., increased availability of automated external defibrillators, better-equipped ambulatory services). In appreciating the importance of early intervention with medical emergencies, substantial resources have been directed over the last several decades in providing and expanding access to emergency medical care. Yet as the Canadian Patient Safety Institute has recently pointed out, there has also been a relative paucity of careful empirical research at the national level in Canada that has quantified how successful these initiatives have actually been, or how they might be further improved and enhanced (Bigham et al., 2011).

Many developments have helped reduce case-fatality rates, lengthen survival times, and shorten hospital stays (CIHI, 2012a). In terms of cancer, the gains in reducing mortality have not been as strong, with standardized rates down by 24.9 per cent for males and 10.9 per cent for females (see Figure 3.3). While medical efforts to combat cancer have lead to lower standardized mortality rates for most (yet not all) types of cancer, incidence rates remain high, which implies an ongoing demand for medical intervention and treatment. Since both cardiovascular disease and cancer affect people aged 70 and over the most, any gains in reducing the risk of death from these conditions especially affects the number of survivors at advanced ages.

According to the Canadian Cancer Registry and National Cancer Incidence Reporting System Databases (Statistics Canada, 2010d), the overall number of persons diagnosed with cancer in 2009 was up to about 160,000 new cases—which was a record high and a near doubling in the number of cases reported relative to the early 1980s. With this climb in the overall number of cases, the underlying factors responsible are less obvious. Particularly important in this context is population aging, which in and of itself leads to a climb in the number of new cases, even if the lifetime risk of cancer for the typical Canadian remains much the same or even declines. Canada's population is growing older, due to a variety of factors, including a low fertility rate and the aging of the baby boom generation. In addition, doctors in Canada have improved the diagnosis of cancer, which is clearly a good thing as earlier diagnosis leads to early treatment and reduced mortality risk.

The reality with cancer is that age-standardized incidence rates have gone up slightly over recent decades—the female age-standardized incidence rate

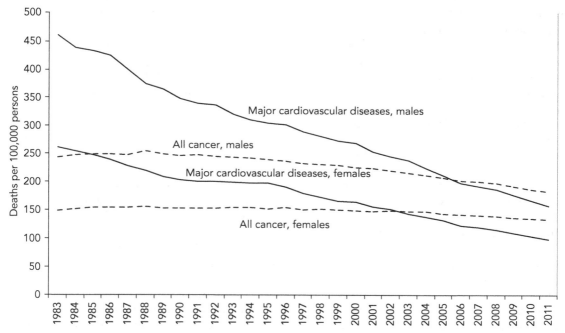

Figure 3.3 ▣ Age-Standardized Mortality Rates, Major Cardiovascular Disease and Cancer, by Sex, Canada 1983–2011

Source: Statistics Canada, 2014e.

rose from 333.1 new cases per 100,000 in 1983 to 364.2 cases for 2009, whereas the male rate rose from 450.5 new cases to 456.1 estimated cases. With these incidence rates, which are at least partially due to a reduced risk of mortality from other causes, forecasts suggest that now probably at least 40 per cent of Canadians will develop some form of cancer during their lifetimes (Canadian Cancer Society, 2012). Of course, not everyone who is diagnosed with cancer will die from the disease. While cancer is a diverse class of diseases, with uncertain etiology, improved treatments are having some effect in reducing the loss of life. To an unknown extent, cancer is linked to many genetic, environmental, and lifestyle factors. Regardless, cancer as the leading cause of premature death represents 27 per cent of the potential years of life lost resulting from all causes of death.

Figure 3.4 portrays the age-standardized mortality rates of the three most serious types of cancer for men and women separately over the 1983–2011 period (lung, colorectal, and prostate cancer among men; lung, breast, and colorectal cancer among women). While mortality from cancer has historically been higher among men than women, this is less so the case today than in the past. Recent gains for men have clearly outpaced those for women. While the mortality rates of most types of cancer have declined, lung cancer among women is an important exception to this pattern, with standardized rates up by 74.9 per cent over the last 25 years. Over this same period, lung cancer among men has continued to decline (–35.5 per cent), such that women now have almost as high a probability of death from lung cancer. This relates to past smoking behaviour and a convergence in the smoking behaviour of men and women in the 1970s and '80s—i.e., smoking rates fell dramatically among men prior to the downturn among women (Trovato, 2007). The mortality rate as associated with breast cancer among women continues to decline (down by 36.5 per cent), as does mortality from colorectal cancer (down by 30.9 per cent). Men have made comparable gains to women on colorectal cancer (down by 27.4 per cent), while the age-standardized mortality rate from prostate cancer among Canadian men is also down substantially, by 33.3 per cent. Improvements in screening procedures, early

diagnosis and treatment all appear to have contributed to reduced mortality (Canadian Cancer Society, 2012).

In combination, these cancers account for about half of all cancer deaths, with a variety of other types responsible for the remainder. For example, pancreatic, non-Hodgkin's lymphoma, leukemia, and stomach and bladder cancer together are responsible for an additional 18 per cent of cancer deaths. While medical efforts to combat these diseases have led to lower standardized mortality rates for most, yet not all, types of cancer, persistent incidence rates, and population aging suggest that health-care costs associated with treating cancer will continue to rise. However with escalating costs, an honest appraisal also acknowledges the substantial gains that have been achieved in terms of extending the lives of Canadians, not to mention lowering morbidity and increasing people's quality of life. There are many other public health initiatives that could be introduced in the future that could potentially have a major impact on longevity. About one quarter of adult Canadians continue to smoke, for example, despite the direct and obvious link with premature death.

Accidents rank 5th as a cause of death (4.4 per cent in 2011), but for people between the ages of 15 and 34, they are clearly the leading cause, accounting for roughly one third of all deaths (Statistics Canada, 2014e). Since the early 1970s, there have been reductions in age-standardized mortality rates due to accidents, especially for teenage boys and men. Traffic accidents are the largest component of accidental deaths (Millar and Last, 1988; Ramage-Morin, 2008). Traffic death rates rose during the first half of the twentieth century, but have declined steadily since then (see Figure 3.5). A number of factors are responsible for this, including technological advances such as anti-lock braking and airbags, the greater use of seat belts, better highway design, lower speed limits, better control of drinking and driving, and improved medical treatment of victims.

A review of the data from various countries makes clear that interventions can reduce traffic-accident mortality (Chesnais, 1985). In Japan, there was a 50 per cent reduction in mortality after the introduction of tough laws regarding drinking and driving, speed

Age-standardized mortality rates, males

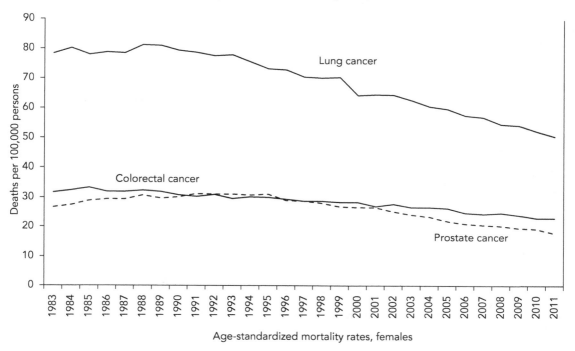

Age-standardized mortality rates, females

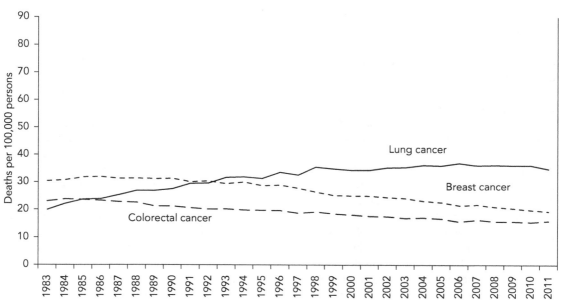

Figure 3.4 ▣ Age-Standardized Mortality Rates for Major Types of Cancers by Sex, Canada, 1983–2011

Source: Statistics Canada, 2014e.

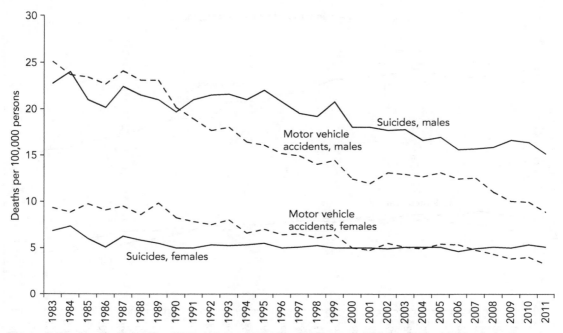

Figure 3.5 ▣ Age-Standardized Death Rates, Accidental (Motor Vehicle) and Suicide, by Sex, Canada, 1983–2011

Source: Statistics Canada, 2014e.

limits, use of seat belts, and control of motorcycles. Chen (2005), in assessing the impact of a photo radar program in British Columbia, suggests that the introduction of this traffic-safety program could "potentially" reduce accidents by as much as 17 per cent. According to Transport Canada (2011), there are over 75 times as many injuries as fatalities from traffic accidents on Canadian roads and highways, with over 170,000 injuries reported annually. The risks, while declining, are not insignificant. As a rough estimate, for every person killed, there are at least five people seriously injured and admitted into our hospitals to receive emergency treatment (Transport Canada, 2011). As a primary cause of death for young adults, and young men in particular, interventions to reduce speed and encourage safer driving are important priorities.

Suicide is another important cause of premature mortality, as for example, among those aged 15–34, it ranks second only to accidental death as a leading cause of death. In 2011, there were 3,728 suicides in Canada, a crude rate of 10.9 per 100,000 persons

(Statistics Canada, 2014e). Attempted suicide is even more common—for every person who actually dies from suicide, there are an estimated 20 attempts to do so (CIHI, 2011). While suicide became more common during the 1960s and '70s, rates have since fallen. The age-standardized rate is down by roughly a fifth among women and a third among men (see Figure 3.5). A complex set of factors is responsible for suicide, although depression is the most commonly linked medical condition—an estimated 60 per cent of all suicide deaths involved people suffering from this form of mental illness (Cavanagh et al., 2003). Men continue to be more likely to commit suicide than women (with the suicide rate over three times as high), although women are more likely to attempt suicide (1.5 times more frequently). Many individual and environmental factors are responsible for these suicide attempts, including physical health; financial hardship; marital and/or family difficulties, and lack of social support; chronic pain or disability; as well as untreated or misdiagnosed mental illness (Beneteau,

1988, Navaneelan, 2012). It is likely that some accidental deaths are in reality suicides, as sometimes it is very difficult for coroners to document accurately the actual circumstances leading to death.

The Sociodemographic Profile of Mortality

Region

In an Institute for Research on Public Policy report covering the 1926–1976 period, titled *Health Status in Canada*, Wilkins (1980) concluded that life expectancy was rising, regional differences in health were diminishing, and social disparities in health persisted. The decline in regional differences was noted by observers at the provincial level, where the difference in life expectancy between the highest and the lowest province declined from 7.3 years in 1921 to only 1.4 years in 1986 (Nagnur, 1986: 31; Nault et al., 1997: 37). Yet, this long-term trend with regard to provincial

differences stabilized and, in fact, has reversed itself slightly over recent years (Manuel and Hockin, 2000; Maynard and Kerr, 2010). The difference in life expectancies across provinces has gone up again slightly, from 1.7 years in the mid-1990s to 2.8 years by 2011. British Columbia continues to have the longest life expectancy across provinces (82.3 years), whereas Newfoundland and Labrador has the shortest (79.5 years). Canada's northern territories continue to be quite disadvantaged in terms of mortality, with all three territories (Northwest Territories, Yukon, and Nunavut) reporting life expectancies noticeably lower than the national average (see Figure 3.6).

Within the territories, living conditions and the state of population health varies—Wilkins and colleagues (2008b) have estimated a life expectancy of only 68 years across the predominantly Inuit territories of Nunavut, Inuvialuit, Nunavik, and Nunatsiavut. Nunavut is particularly disadvantaged, with an estimated life expectancy of only 71.1 years in 2009–2011. Among men, life expectancy in these territories

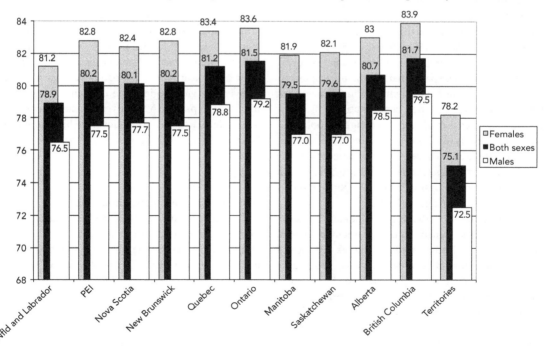

Figure 3.6 ▣ Life Expectancy by Provinces and Territories, and Sex, Canada, 2009–2011

Sources: Martel, 2013; Statistics Canada, 2013a.

was estimated as particularly low, at 68.8 years. In Yukon Territory and the Northwest Territories, life expectancy is somewhat higher, although still well below the national average, at 77.4 and 78.2, respectively. Canada's northern territories are somewhat disadvantaged in terms of unemployment, employment security, income and its distribution, education, housing, health-care services, among other basic social services, all of which are associated with lower states of population health (Sisco and Stonebridge, 2010; Shields and Tremblay, 2002).

It directly follows that mortality is highest in regions of the country that have the greatest unemployment and underemployment, the highest poverty rates, and the least-educated population. Across provinces, some of the differences are relatively pronounced: the unemployment rate in Newfoundland and Labrador at the end of 2007, for example, was almost three times British Columbia's, at 13.2 per cent and 4.2 per cent, respectively (Statistics Canada 2009a). In education, almost one half of BC's population in the 25–64 age group have some form of post-secondary schooling, which compares with only about one third of Newfoundland and Labrador's population (Statistics Canada 2010b). As we've mentioned, living conditions in Canada's northern territories can be particularly difficult—for example, the official unemployment rate in Nunavut has been as high as 16+ per cent (Statistics Canada, 2012c). Statistics Canada reports a high school graduation rate that is much lower than the national average; an estimated 56.6 per cent of teenagers in the Northwest Territories graduated from high school in 2008–2009, and an abysmally low 39.3 per cent did in Nunavut (Statistics Canada, 2010b).

In an effort to provide greater detail by geography, Statistics Canada has documented several health-status indicators across Canada's 139 health regions—administrative areas—that is, geographic regions established by the provinces for local health and social service delivery. While a majority of these health regions suggest limited regional differences, there were some important exceptions to this general rule. Shields and Tremblay (2002) put forth a few generalizations. First, people living in Canada's largest metropolitan areas and urban centres tend to

have the greatest longevity; second, people living in some of the most remote communities of the country tend to be some of the least healthy; and third, without exception, Canada's health regions that rank particularly poorly are in remote areas with prominent First Nations or Inuit presence. While many First Nations peoples in Canada are doing relatively well, others are characterized by major economic hardship that translates into unfavourable health outcomes.

Even within some of Canada's most prosperous cities, there are communities and neighbourhoods that are characterized by difficult living conditions and economic hardship, a fact often obscured when looking at statistical averages. Some of Vancouver's inner city neighbourhoods, for example, are particularly poor, despite the fact that the city itself and the larger metropolitan area are both widely thought of as being prosperous with health indicators that compare quite favourably with the national averages. Vancouver's Downtown Eastside, well known as "Canada's poorest postal code," is a community that struggles with a very high incidence of poverty, homelessness, drug use, sex trade, crime, and violence (Vancouver, Central Area Planning Report, 2007). While Statistics Canada reports a life expectancy of 83 years for the broader Vancouver Health Delivery Service Region, the incidence of avoidable mortality in parts of Vancouver's urban core remains quite high. Regional statistics can hide important heterogeneity within a population.

Age

Mortality in many populations follows a U-curve, with high mortality levels in the first year of life, the lowest rates in childhood, and rising rates with age. Statistically speaking, the safest age in terms of mortality in Canada is typically 10–12 years, with mortality rates that are slightly lower than in infancy (Statistics Canada, 2014d). While mortality rates have fallen across all ages, the declines among the young have been particularly spectacular, with, for example, a declining infant mortality rate from 175 per 1,000 births in 1830 to 85 in 1921 to only 4.9 in 2009–11 (Bourbeau and Légaré, 1982; Dumas, 1990: 29;

Statistics Canada, 2013b). The improved survival rates of low-birth-weight infants have contributed to the more recent decline in infant mortality, although these gains have slowed somewhat over the last several decades. This is at least partly due to an increased incidence of low birth weight, which is related to the fact that we now see more births to women over 35 years of age (Nault et al., 1997).

From past analysis of mortality, the earlier decades of the twentieth century were noted for particular success in lessening premature death, but not in combating death at older ages. Dufour and Peron (1979:52), for example, find in their analysis of mortality in Quebec over the 1931–71 period considerable successes in lessening premature death, but not in combating death at older ages. More specifically, there was a spectacular 80 per cent reduction in the risk of death before age 15 between 1931 and 1971. Yet at ages 60 to 85, the corresponding reduction was only 12 per cent. Major gains were made in increasing life expectancy in Quebec, largely due to reduced mortality among the young. We can now speak of a marked improvement in mortality among older age groups in reducing the risk of mortality as Canadians move into middle and older ages.

A graphical way to demonstrate how mortality and life expectancy has evolved over recent decades is through the use of survival curves (see Figure 3.7). Building upon life tables, these curves demonstrate how a birth cohort might be affected by mortality if the cohort members were to experience over their lifespans the age-specific mortality rates as observed in a given year. Figure 3.7 shows a comparison of the survival curves for Canadians born in 1921 (the lowest curve), 1951, 1981, and 2009–11 (the upper curve). The greatest disparity between the curves is clearly observed in comparing 1921 with 1951, as major gains were made in reducing mortality among infants and the young in the early half of the twentieth century. From a cohort of 100,000 Canadians born in 1921, roughly 85,000 would have survived through to age 5. By 1951, of a cohort of the same size, over 95,000 would have survived the same interval of time. Since 1981, the greatest gains have been in reducing the mortality among older ages. This is demonstrated in Figure 3.7, with modest differences

in the 1981 and 2009–2011 curves prior to middle age, yet with pronounced differences in survival from middle age onward.

We can now speak of a marked improvement in mortality among older age groups; this applied to older women over the postwar period, but also to men since 1971 (Martel and Bélanger, 1999: 165). At age 65, life expectancy increased only marginally from 13.6 years in 1921 to 14.2 years by 1951 (Statistics Canada, 1989, 1995), with more substantial gains observed more recently, up to 20.4 years by 2009–11 (Statistics Canada, 2013a). With death being postponed to later ages, we can speak of the survival curve as becoming more rectangular in shape. In 1921, only 4.7 per cent of people born could expect to survive to the age of 90, compared to 30 per cent in 2009–11 (Canadian Human Mortality Database, 2012; Statistics Canada, 2013a). In 1981, 30.6 per cent of Canadians could expect to reach the age of 85; by 2009–11, this had increased to 40.9 per cent of men and 55.5 per cent of women (Statistics Canada, 2013a). In 1986, Stone and Fletcher noted the increased "positive health attitudes" on the part of seniors, and their increased participation in exercise. Through to the present, seniors are particularly aware of health risks, and they are leading in non-smoking rates.

Longer life expectancy for the population means that growing numbers of elderly people are in poor health. According to Ramage-Morin and colleagues (2010) for instance, among Canadians aged 65 and older, fully one quarter report living with four or more diagnosed chronic conditions (relative to about 1 in 17 among persons aged 45–64). Using numbers from the 2009 Canadian Community Health Survey, the authors found that 52.9 per cent of all seniors reported high blood pressure; 43.4 per cent were living with arthritis; 28.6 per cent were experiencing back problems; 27.9 per cent reported eye problems; and 22.6 per cent had previously suffered a stroke or were living with heart disease (Ramage-Morin et al., 2010). According to the 2005 Canadian Community Health Survey, 44 per cent of people aged 65 or older visited a family doctor at least four times in the previous year, whereas just over a third had consulted a specialist to address more complicated health issues (Nabalamba and Millar, 2007). As Manton (1987)

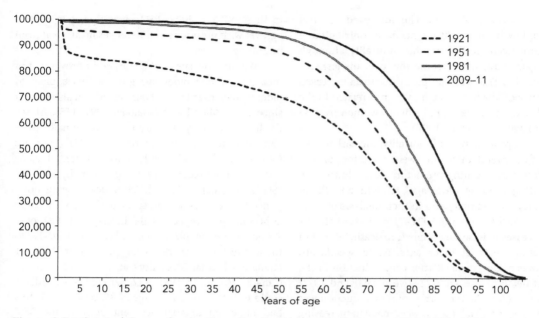

Figure 3.7 ▣ Survival Curves for the Canadian Population, Both Sexes, 1921, 1951, 1981, and 2009–2011

Sources: Canadian Human Mortality Database, Period Life Tables; Statistics Canada, 2013a.

observed, given the strong links between morbidity, disability, and mortality at advanced ages, large increases in lifespan raise questions about the public health costs. It also appears that the same types of interventions are appropriate for younger and older people: improvements in lifestyle and in the treatment of specific diseases. Mortality at advanced ages is dependent on multiple chronic degenerative disease processes that are similar to those that cause mortality at younger ages.

Sex

Differences in mortality by sex also provide insight into health questions. Regarding life expectancy, the difference between the sexes increased from roughly three years in favour of women early in the twentieth century to over seven years in the 1971–81 period. This change as observed in Canada was also witnessed across most western countries, as the average sex gap in life expectancy widened from about two to three years in favour of women to a difference of about four

to seven years (Trovato and Lalu, 2012). At least part of this trend owes to a rapid decline in mortality among young women, and especially to a sharp drop in deaths associated with childbirth. For example, as Dufour and Péron (1979) observed for Quebec—prior to the Quiet Revolution and modernization—young women of child-bearing age were actually at a higher risk of mortality than their partners, a situation that had reversed itself by the 1960s. Female mortality rates among the young declined much more rapidly than male rates; the death rate among Quebec men aged 15–34 in 1931 was only 83 per cent of that for women; by 1971, this situation had more than reversed itself, with the male rate being 236 per cent of the female rate.

More recently, this widening sex differential in life expectancy has not only stabilized, but it has actually reversed itself, from its peak of 7.3 years in 1976 to 4.3 years by 2009–11. Again, this mortality trend was not unique to Canada, as several (yet not all) highly industrialized nations have also witnessed a narrowing of this gap in longevity. But there is still currently no industrialized country in the world with a complete convergence in life expectancy—across wealthy nations, women continue to live longer than men. It appears that biology plays a part in explaining this gender difference, as females have shown over time to be better survivors in the life journey.

In discussing the United States in the 1980s, Keyfitz (1989) estimated that the biological advantages of women would probably account for slightly less than half of the difference. Males are even more likely to die before birth (as miscarriages and stillbirths), and also at very young ages, which means that the differences are not simply a function of lifestyle, environment, and/or gendered behaviour. In Canada from 2000 to 2009, for the first year of life, the male rate of infant mortality has consistently been 115 to 120 per cent of the female rate. After infancy and into early childhood, boys have a slightly higher risk than girls, although this sex difference in mortality risk by gender increases in a pronounced manner as the young move into latter adolescence and early adulthood.

The sex differences are now highest at ages 20–24, where the male probability of death is 2.6 times that of females (Statistics Canada, 2010c), before falling to about 1.5 times as Canadians move into the middle and older ages. In explaining the more recent convergence in mortality, it is especially at ages 45 and over that male mortality rates are now improving in relation to those of women. Men are still at a considerable disadvantage, however. While the overall difference by sex has been reduced to 4.3 years of life expectancy, it took until the 2009–11 period for male life expectancy to reach a level comparable to female life expectancy in the early 1980s: 79.3 years (Bélanger, 2002; 31; Statistics Canada, 2013a).

Beyond biology, others factors need to be considered, as, for example, men have tended to be more disadvantaged by engaging in unhealthy or dangerous activities, especially smoking, drinking, and risk taking. While smoking has become far more equalized by gender over recent decades, it has historically been fundamental in explaining differences in mortality by sex (Gee and Veevers, 1983; Trovato and Lalu, 2012). In the 1980s, for example—when the life-expectancy gender gap was at a maximum—among persons aged 65 and over, where death was

most likely to occur, only 21 per cent of men had "never smoked" relative to fully 67 per cent of women (Statistics Canada, 1987). Underlying the convergence in life expectancy has been a shift in smoking behaviour; by 2011, for example, this difference in smoking behaviour had largely disappeared: 22.3 per cent of men report smoking on a daily basis relative to 17.5 per cent of women (Statistics Canada, 2012b). Among 18- and 19-year-olds who smoke, a useful predictor of future smoking behaviour, this differential is even smaller, at 20 and 19 per cent respectively. As a result, there has been a convergence in a number of cause-specific death rates associated with smoking behaviour, including lung cancer and cardiovascular disease (Nault et al., 1997; Trovato and Lalu, 1996; Statistics Canada, 2012b).

The more reckless attitude of males increases the likelihood of accidental death, although here, too, we have seen a convergence. In the 1980s, Péron and Strohmenger (1985) estimated that the lifetime probability of dying violently was 7.5 per cent for men compared to 4.3 per cent for women. Since this time, the age-standardized death rate in motor vehicle accidents has declined from 25 to about 9 deaths per 100,000 among males and roughly from 10 to 3 deaths per 100,000 among females (Statistics Canada, 2012d). Similarly, the age-standardized rate from suicide has fallen quite precipitously: from roughly 25 to 15 deaths per 100,000 among men, while among women, the rate has remained stable at 5 to 6 deaths per 100,000 (Statistics Canada, 2012d). Men continue to suffer more from dangerous working conditions, a differential that has not changed over time. Among fatalities that were under the purview of workers' compensation boards between 1988 and 2005, the rates fell slightly, whereas the percentages of males have remained relatively stable at about 96 per cent (Marshall, 1996; Sharpe and Hardt, 2006).

While men have the disadvantage of engaging in dangerous or unhealthy activities, women are more likely to admit to discomfort and to solicit assistance. Evidence of this was documented in the Canadian Health Measures Survey (CHMS), where people were asked about high blood pressure and then the actual blood pressure was measured (Wilkins et al., 2010). Among Canadians with hypertension, more than four fifths (83 per cent) were aware of the fact, yet among those who were unaware, a larger proportion was male (20 per cent) than female (14 per cent). Other studies have shown that women are more likely to complain of symptoms and see doctors, even for diseases that are most common among men, as measured by actual mortality. According to Health Canada (2010), about 19 per cent of women aged 20–34 reported that they did not have access to a regular doctor relative to 35 per cent of men at the same age (Health Canada, 2010).

Women are more likely to seek medical attention and to know more about health, and they may acquire the habit of more regular medical visits because of the routines surrounding contraception, pregnancy, and child-bearing. Another example of women living more healthfully is found in the oral health component of the CHMS, which reports that women are more likely to seek preventive dental checkups, practise better dental hygiene, and have better oral health across a wide range of indicators—including tooth decay, untreated decay, and traumatized teeth (Health Canada, 2010). Women are more likely to address their husband's and children's health in a variety of ways. Since they are less likely to receive the same kind of attention from their husbands, women are more likely to turn to doctors for help. For men, traditional gender roles have emphasized the necessity of "toughing it out," and as a result men have a higher tendency to neglect signs of illness, often suppressing or ignoring them longer than women (Gee and Veevers, 1983; Armstrong et al., 2012).

Socioeconomic Status

Across most modernized countries, mortality differences by socioeconomic status are more important than are regional differences (CIHI, 2008; Raphael, 2009). Yet with advanced medicine and medical insurance, one might expect that social differences in mortality would largely disappear. This has clearly not been the case, as several large, nationally representative population-based studies have documented across a variety of nations how social inequality continues to affect health outcomes, mortality, and life expectancy (Muntaner et al., 2001; Johnson and

Blackwell, 2007; Leclerc et al., 2006). In the Canadian context, lower education and income have been shown to be associated with higher mortality and shorter life expectancy (Choinière, 1993; Nault et al., 1997; Ross et al., 2007; Trovato, 2009; Orpana et al., 2010). Certain occupations are also noted for their occupational and environmental hazards (Marmot and Wilkinson, 2005). There is clearly room for major gains in life expectancy and population health, but stakeholders need to act on the social determinants of health, in Canada and elsewhere.

While historically there was a scarcity of individual-level data available on the socioeconomic status of the deceased in Canada, various analyses have attempted to solve this problem by using an assortment of analytical techniques and datasets, including neighbourhood data and administrative records (Wolfson et al., 1993; Chen et al., 1996; Bélanger et al., 2002; Wilkins et al., 2002). A successful effort in this regard has recently been developed by analysts at Statistics Canada, who have managed to link, for the first time, individual mortality information from Vital Statistics with information about people as available from the 1991 and 2001 Canadian Census (Wilkins et al., 2008a). While demographers have long been limited to basic demographic information on mortality in Vital Statistics (age, sex, and the location of the person who died), this successful linkage to the census has expanded what is possible in the analysis of mortality. Data from the 1991 and 2001 Census have now been linked to deaths occurring through to 2006, which has allowed analysts to develop life tables for the Canadian population, and they have done this across a range of census variables.

Such data-linkage analysis provides detail on the socioeconomic gradient: the loftier the socioeconomic status for individuals, the more the risk of mortality declines. Among those who died between the 1991 and 2001 Census, mortality rates were highest among persons with less than a high school education, were unemployed or not in the labour force, were in unskilled jobs, and were in the lowest income brackets (Tjepkema and Wilkins, 2011). When delineating Canadians by income quintile, for example, life expectancy at age 25 was estimated to be shorter, by roughly seven years, when comparing men in the lowest quintile with those in the highest, whereas among women in the lowest quintile, a five-year disadvantage was documented (Wilkins et al., 2008a). Education was similarly shown to be important; men with less than high school were estimated as having a six-year disadvantage relative to the university educated; among women, the difference was roughly four years. This chasm between the most educated and least educated persists in a context of enduring income inequality, despite an often-restated commitment on the part of national and provincial governments toward universal health-care coverage.

Regardless of access to health-care services, higher mortality has been linked to difficult working conditions, poor job security and/or job prospects, and the stresses associated with economic marginalization and social exclusion. That is, people of higher socioeconomic status receive more structural and cultural encouragement for relatively healthy behaviour (Mikkonen and Raphael, 2010). They may be less isolated, have more social ties, and have healthier alternatives available to them as a means of reducing tension. In contrast, the lack of control over external conditions may lead lower-income people to be more fatalistic in the face of risks. Social scientists have long noted that manual workers are more likely than non-manual workers to ignore symptoms and that the latter have earlier recourse to health care. In noting that the disadvantage of blue-collar workers compared to white-collar workers applies more to men, Nathanson and Lopez (1987) suggest that the factors are based largely on lifestyle and environment (i.e., whether a person has social support). Yet they also emphasize that it is not so much a matter of individual decisions but of the social and economic conditions found in different locations in the social structure.

Education is fundamental to mortality risk, largely through various health behaviours that can be considered important intervening variables. Canada has persistent social-class differences in terms of long-term behaviours detrimental to health, including poor diet, smoking, lack of exercise, alcohol and substance use, and risk taking. The pressures associated with difficult work and living conditions and the stress associated with such insecurities lead some people to drink or smoke as a form of relaxation, or to engage in other risky behaviours. In an analysis of health and mortality disparities in Canada, James and colleagues (2007) have suggested that disparities that continue to characterize Canadians, especially regarding causes of death, that are potentially affected by greater public health interventions—for example, lung cancer, cirrhosis of the liver, and accidental death.

There are important differences in level of education as documented in the literature on preventive medical checkups, immunizations and vaccinations, use of seat belts, and sleep habits (Norman, 1986; Nathanson and Lopez, 1987; Crompton, 2000). In some cases, obvious financial obstacles persist—for instance, there are differences in the ability or willingness to pay for preventive dental services, pharmaceuticals, and assorted treatments not necessarily covered by government health care. Differences of socioeconomic status, access, lifestyle, and environment have all been documented elsewhere, across a wide variety of industrialized countries (Guo et al., 1999; Marmot, 2005; Marmot and Wilkinson 2005). The explanation of the class inequality in mortality lies in the complex interaction of two factors: available resources and behavioural patterns, including how effectively the available resources are used, both to prevent illness and to treat illness when it occurs.

Marital Status

Besides the differentials of mortality by age and sex, the differences by marital status are also relevant in understanding the dynamics of mortality (Manzoli et al., 2007). We find in this area that married people (or, for that matter, persons cohabiting) have advantages over others. Data from the 1990s for people aged 30 and over show that, compared to married people, single and widowed women had a three-year disadvantage and divorced women a three-and-a-half-year disadvantage in life expectancy (Nault et al., 1997: 247). Compared to married men, single men had a disadvantage of 7 years, while those divorced were 4.4 years in arrears.

There are again a variety of explanations. Selectivity plays a role. That is, people who enter longer-term relationships may be partly selected on the basis of better health, while persons who separate may be selected for poor health. It is likely, however, that the differences are mostly due to questions of lifestyle. The single and divorced, for instance, are more likely to suffer from cirrhosis of the liver, a disease that is clearly related to lifestyle (Trovato, 1992: 126). Some authors have argued that being alone, without social support, is itself detrimental to health (Hawkley and Cacioppo, 2011). In this regard, both men and women appear to profit from the protective role of marriage (Manzoli et al., 2007). Married people benefit from having someone who can help in times of illness, and they benefit in particular from better diets and lower-risk behaviour (Trovato, 1998).

Cultural Identity and Immigration Status

The highest mortality in Canada when comparing persons defined in terms of ancestry or cultural identity is the Aboriginal population. In drawing a systematic comparison of the mortality experience of various Aboriginal groups, Tjepkema and Wilkins (2011) have estimated a life-expectancy disadvantage at age 25 of roughly 4 to 4.5 years among the Métis, about 5 years among non-status Indians, and over 6 years for the registered Indian population, all relative to the Canadian population overall. Using the Canadian Community Health Survey of 2000–1, Tjepkema (2002) documented how overall health conditions for the registered Indian population have been even more difficult on reserve relative to those who are living elsewhere in Canada—although the off-reserve First Nations population also reports poorer health than the non-Aboriginal population, even after controls for socioeconomic and health-behaviour factors.

The health regions that have a relatively high proportion of Aboriginal residents (19 per cent or higher) have significantly more premature deaths, half of which are attributable to injuries, both intentional and unintentional (Allard et al., 2001). Among First Nations youth and young adults aged 15–39, motor vehicle accidents and suicide are the two most important causes of premature deaths. These causes of death underscore the preventable nature of much of this premature loss of life. A variety of factors are responsible for the relative disadvantage of Aboriginal peoples, in particular their social, economic, and cultural deprivation. Many First Nations people live in residences in remote locations with difficult access to medical services; many also tend to have poor water, sewage, and community services.

Health conditions in Canada's Far North are particularly problematic, a situation that is striking in the predominantly Inuit-inhabited regions of the country. In Nunavut, northern Quebec, and Labrador, mortality is substantially higher than elsewhere in the country (Wilkins et al., 2008b). In 2001, life expectancy in these regions was estimated to be roughly 68, or a 12-year longevity gap relative to Canada's population overall (up from roughly 10 years in 1991). In several regions, mortality was documented as particularly high, in Nunavik (northern Quebec), Nunatsiavut (Labrador), and to a lesser extent in the northern territory of Nunavut and the Inuvialuit region of the Northwest Territories. As the non-Aboriginal population makes up roughly 20 per cent of these regions, it is logical to say that the longevity gap is even greater for the Inuit living in these regions—to the extent that the mortality of non-Aboriginals parallels that of other Canadians. If overall life expectancy is roughly 68 years, and roughly 20 per cent of the population in these regions have mortality rates comparable to the national average, then the majority Inuit population in these regions logically have an even lower life expectancy, estimated at roughly 64 years using basic decomposition methods (Wilkins et al., 2008b).

Other sociocultural differences in mortality have been documented, although they are less pronounced or disturbing. Several studies have documented, for instance, a *healthy immigrant effect*—i.e., the observation that the health of immigrants tends to be better than that of the native-born populations. This phenomenon has been documented across a variety of immigrant-receiving nations in the West (Kennedy et al., 2006; Chen et al., 1996; Trovato and Odynak, 2011; Ng, 2011). There are several factors contributing to this effect, including *selectivity*—the observation that better-educated and healthier people tend to be migrants in the first place, that most recipient countries introduce health screening to exclude those who are unhealthy, and the possibility that migrants live a healthier life prior to immigration. Somewhat consistent with this latter emphasis is the *acculturation thesis*—that the longer immigrants live in Canada, the more closely their lifestyle and behaviours converge with those of other Canadians, such that the healthy immigrant effect tends to decline over time.

According to the 2000–2001 Canadian Community Health Survey, immigrants, especially those who have arrived more recently, have lower mortality risks and lower odds of reporting chronic conditions in general (Pérez, 2002). In estimating life expectancy for 2001, Trovato and Odynak (2011) estimated that in a relative sense, immigrants enjoy an advantage in

survival—possibly up to three or four years on average. In working with Statistics Canada's Census Mortality Follow-up Study, Ng (2011) estimates a non-trivial healthy immigrant effect, with age-standardized mortality rates that were roughly 20 per cent lower among immigrants relative to the native-born. Consistent with the acculturation thesis, this advantage tends to decline with time, as immigrants establish themselves in Canada. Figure 3.8 summarizes this tendency, in comparing age-standardized mortality rates for immigrants, among those who migrated before 1971, in the 1971–80 period, and in the 1981–91 time frame, for men and women separately. In general, the longer an immigrant lives in Canada, that person's mortality advantage lessens—that is, the age-standardized mortality rate is lowest among immigrants living in Canada for the shortest period.

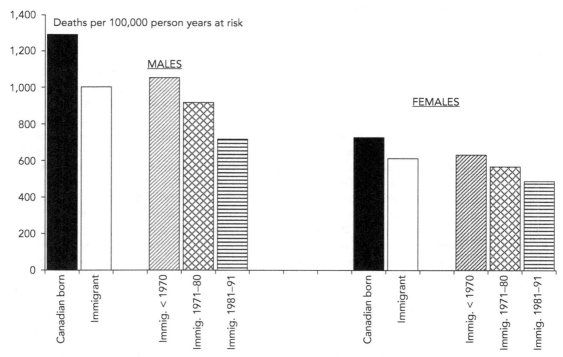

Figure 3.8 ▣ Age-Standardized Mortality Rates for Immigrants, by Sex and Period of Immigration, Compared with Canadian-Born Cohort Members, Persons Aged 25 or Older at Baseline, Canada, 1991–2001

Source: Ng, 2011.

Edward Ng (2011) also demonstrates an additional dimension to this health advantage: the healthy immigrant effect varies somewhat across immigrant communities and various source countries. In drawing comparisons across broad geographic regions, for example, Ng showed that the relative advantage of immigrants was least among those migrating from the United States and most among those arriving from Asia, particularly from South and East Asia. As mortality risk varies by country of origin and period of immigration, there is associated heterogeneity in terms of lifestyle, behaviour, and mortality risk. Ng concludes by emphasizing the need for further research into how this plays out, especially in how socioeconomic determinants might play a role in immigrant adaptation and contribute to or lessen the healthy immigrant effect. With the aforementioned mortality data linkage study that combined vital statistics with the census, it is possible to potentially further distinguish some of the most serious risk factors and how these differ across cultural communities and immigrant groups.

Implications

The sociodemographic profile of mortality indicates that there are significant differences in life expectancy: a 4.3-year difference by gender, 5 years by level of education, 6 years by income levels, a 6-year disadvantage for the registered Indian population, and possibly as much as 15 years among the Inuit. The evidence does not tend to point to hard curative medicine as the factor that would reduce the differences. Equally important are questions of lifestyle—especially smoking, alcohol consumption, and driving habits, and also the effective use of preventive health consultations. Picker (2013) recommends that we pay particular attention to educational programs to promote health and that we study ways to deliver existing services more effectively to the disadvantaged groups. We will return to these questions shortly because they suggest that health policy should take demographic analysis into greater account.

Development of Health Policy

Before 1945, health was largely a private matter, although the government had long been involved in the construction of hospitals and the training of medical students. For general health care, a mosaic of private and public insurance served the public unevenly. For most people in the pre-1945 years, the costs were not particularly high in relation to the standard of living, and various charities helped to defray costs.

In the 1945–77 period, the main elements of state responsibility for health were put into place. The federal government tried to gain more control over this domain at a time when the provinces were in a weak position. The Hospital Insurance Diagnostic Services Act was passed in 1957, and the Medical Care Act in 1966. The purpose of these acts was to increase the supply of health personnel and facilities, and to make the services available to people regardless of their socioeconomic circumstances and geography. As Badgley and Charles (1978) observed, there was certainly the positive outcome of having increased the availability and use of medical services. There were also continuing problems, however: differentials in use of services did not appear to have declined; there were some distortions of services because of what was included (the emphasis was on expensive, highly technical, curative, and individually oriented medicine) and what was excluded (namely, preventive and community approaches), and there were no specific incentives for cost containment.

The period since 1977 has seen attempts to ensure cost containment at the federal level, and more of the responsibility has passed to the provinces. The 1977 Established Programs Financing Act and the 1994 Canadian Health and Social Transfer ensured more predictable federal increases in health and education transfers to the provinces, and they brought reductions in federal transfers in the mid-1990s while also passing more of the control over to the provinces. Some provinces introduced various forms of extra billing in order to cover part of the increased costs. This was stopped in 1985 through the Canada Health Act, with the result that the provinces were largely responsible for the increased costs of health care.

Continuing Policy Issues

Improvement in longevity, in particular through health policy, is very much a success story for Canada. Life expectancy has progressed steadily, and only a handful of countries have better health conditions than Canada. Certain problems remain, however, and are subject to continued discussion.

Costs

The question of health costs is frequently raised. Clearly, personal expenditures on health have long been relatively low. In 1988, when detailed data first became available, out-of-pocket expenditures on health in Canada was roughly $300 per capita, yet this rose to over $800 by 2010 (CIHI, 2013a). As private health insurance expenditures have also increased by a comparable amount (up to almost $700 per capita by 2010), the typical Canadian household is now spending more of its income on basic health-care needs than was true decades back, even after adjustments for inflation.

Over this same period, government health-care expenditures have also risen, at a pace that has clearly outpaced GDP growth. As a percentage of GDP, total health costs (both private and public) increased from 7 per cent in the late 1970s to somewhat above 8 per cent

in the mid-1980s, 10 per cent by 1992, and then up again to an unprecedented 12 per cent in 2010 (see Figure 3.9). Both private and public expenditure have risen such that the private share of total expenditures is now roughly 30 cents on the dollar. Over the past 15 years, this share has remained relatively stable—at 29.9 per cent in 1997, up slightly to 30.3 per cent estimated for 2012—as both public and private expenditures have risen at roughly the same pace (CIHI, 2013a).

There is no doubt those costs are considerable. In 2010, the public sector spent $136.2 billion on health care ($3,990 per capita), whereas total expenditures, including private costs, were 193.1 billion ($5,660 per capita). Relative to the employed population (17 million Canadians), this amounts to about $11,300 per working person (CIHI, 2013a; authors calculations). Since 1986, the total government expenditure for health care in Canada has been higher than the expenditure for education, and it is currently the largest single governmental expenditure.

Evans (1987) compared the health costs in Canada and the United States over the period 1950–85, before and after the introduction of the Medical Care Act. He noted that there was no major jump in costs in Canada following the introduction of this government policy, and that Canadian costs relative to the United States

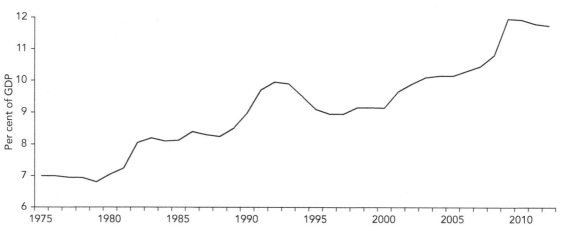

Figure 3.9 ▣ Total Health Expenditures as a Percentage of Gross Domestic Product, Canada, 1975–2012

Source: CIHI, 2013.

actually declined following its introduction. This would imply that public funding of health costs does not necessarily result in higher total costs. As of 2010, the United States was a true outlier among OECD countries in terms of health-care expenditures, amounting to 17.6 per cent of its GDP overall. The second highest in the OECD is the Netherlands, at almost 13 per cent, followed closely by France, Germany, and then Canada, whereas the OECD average is 9.5 per cent (CIHI, 2013a). The higher costs in the United States have not translated into higher life expectancy, as Canada has a nearly three-year life-expectancy advantage at birth (relative to near parity in the 1950s). Other international comparisons confirm that a more socialized approach to health care has a positive impact on life expectancy (Smith et al., 2012).

Fassbender and colleagues (2009) observe that dying is a much more important factor than aging per se in the use of the health system. A dramatic increase in use occurs in the relatively short period before death, with up to 25 per cent of all health costs devoted to caring for patients in their last days of life, typically in high-tech intensive-care hospital beds. People aged 45 and up in Manitoba used an average of 42 hospital bed days in the last year of life, whereas even people aged 85 and up who survived for the next 4 years had less than 7 bed days per year (Roos et al., 1987). Projections of hospital needs might profitably take into account expected deaths as well as the aging of the population. Deaths per 1,000 population, for instance, decreased from 10.1 to 7 over the 1941–83 period, but they have since been increasing and could surpass 11 by 2050 (Statistics Canada, 2013c). That is a doubling in the number of deaths, from about 240,000 in 2012 to roughly 500,000 in about 40 years. This will likely have a significant impact on hospital usage, as roughly 70 per cent of all deaths now occur in hospitals.

While population growth and aging has contributed to this increase in health-care expenditures, several other factors are arguably more important. These include the following: a population that has been vocally supportive of additional government funding; people's attitudes to seeking out care; new medical technology, including new diagnostic and surgical tools; increased spending on physician salaries; the emergence of new drug therapies; and an increase in the volume and costs of drugs sold. Simpson (2012) observes that health-care spending has increased by 7 per cent per year over the 2004–10 period. Canada ranks in the top five OECD countries in health spending, but the outcomes do not measure up. Several suggestions for constraining costs have been made, and many of these have been put into effect. There are several resource-saving measures, such as earlier shifting from acute-care to chronic-care facilities and more use of nurse-practitioners. Health-care costs are related to the availability of hospital beds, the increase in the supply of physicians, and the way in which physicians practise medicine (i.e., their proneness to place patients in hospital). Expensive hospital care is not always the best choice, especially when it is not desired by patients and their families. The option of high standard care can also be provided via community services, both reducing costs and potentially adding to the quality of life for Canadians with chronic disease. Yet, while acknowledging the importance of these reforms, the Ontario Hospital Association (2010), in collaboration with other public health organizations, has highlighted the need for additional measures to contain costs, particularly in the publicly funded drug system, as total expenditures on drugs have risen dramatically, up by an annual rate of over 9 per cent during the 1997–2007 period in Ontario.

It might be argued, however, that rather than have health services reduced, Canadians are willing to pay higher health costs as an important part of their high standard of living. There would appear to be a demand for more health care relative to other goods and services. The Commission on the Future of Health Care in Canada (Romanow, 2002) argues that health is an important value for Canadians, and that health services should be seen by governments as part of the rights of citizenship.

Curative and Preventive Approaches

Another criticism that is made frequently is that the approach to health is overly dependent on the curative model. This critique has been voiced by many people, including several past federal ministers of health. In *A New Perspective on the Health of Canadians*, Marc Lalonde (1974), the Trudeau government's then health minister, argued for less emphasis on diagnosis and treatment and greater emphasis on a holistic approach that should include lifestyle, environment, and the organization of medical care. In the 1980s, health minister Monique Bégin (1987: 225–6) observed that our health-care system is overspecialized and our approach to health is over-medicalized, at the expense of a more holistic approach. She went on to say that there is an "urgent need to reorient the health care system in a fundamental and challenging way. This means greater emphasis on illness prevention and health promotion." Much more recently, Ontario's health minister Deb Matthews (2012), who has a doctorate in demography, stressed the importance of community initiatives into health promotion, in a context of both escalating costs and a greying population.

Our earlier analysis on mortality differentials by sociodemographic characteristics of the population tends to support this conclusion. That is, the differences across social and demographic groups, which are large, appear to be due less to differential treatment by doctors and hospitals than to differential degrees of preventive measures. Many of the gains in life expectancy occurred before the use of high-technology medicine. Nonetheless, medical advances are clearly playing a role, in the improved survival of low-birth-weight infants, for instance, and in the treatment of cancer and coronary heart disease.

The many uncertainties involved in medicine prompt physicians to be particularly careful, to try various alternatives, and to make maximum use of the technology available. When someone dies waiting for an operation or because of inadequate supply of high-technology facilities, the criticism is made that we need more of these resources. Such facilities, however, often cost a great deal without necessarily having much of an effect on the overall longevity of a population. Organ transplants, for instance, are spectacular, but they are also very expensive and their effect on the overall life expectancy in the population has thus far been relatively small. If budgets are diverted to preventive approaches, such as campaigns against drinking and driving, the results may be hard to see in terms of specific lives saved, yet the long-term life-expectancy benefit can potentially be larger for the same amount of expenditure. The financial incentives in the health-care system have been biased in favour of institutional care and curative approaches, and against the development of community approaches and preventive programs. It is hard to combat this, partly because the doctors and hospitals, which have considerable political influence, have vested interests in protecting their budgets.

The evidence would nonetheless suggest that health-budget decision-makers should put more emphasis on preventive approaches: lifestyle changes (e.g., smoking, drinking, exercise), attention to the nutritional value of food, reduction of environmental hazards, the "counselling" role of doctors, and public education on health questions. It can be argued that our high expenditures on health care are excessively aimed at the "doctors plus hospitals" portion of the equation for improved longevity. Barker (1990) argues that a greater emphasis on preventive and community-based services will probably lead to higher-quality care but will not necessarily reduce costs. Mostly, these kinds of new services will complement rather than replace the existing services. A financial savings will occur only if other services are reduced.

Further Ethical Issues: Better Health or Longer Life

With reference to the observation that longer life does not translate directly into better health, either for individuals or for the group, we can ask if it would not be better to orient the health system toward health improvements in old age, rather than being excessively concerned about delaying death (Légaré, 1990; Carriere and Légaré, 2000). The orientation toward prolonging life would put emphasis on cancer and heart disease, because they are fatal, as well as on technologies that lengthen life. The orientation toward health improvements in old age would emphasize diseases that cause chronic disability but not necessarily death: arthritis, osteoporosis, deafness, dementia, diseases that affect eyesight, and fractures.

Légaré argues that we should spend more on research and health care for these non-fatal but debilitating diseases, while being more prepared to accept the inevitable death due to chronic disease when it comes. He therefore advocates a shift in resources from prolonging life to making life better. This would mean trying to make both the mortality curve and the morbidity curve rectangular—that is, attempting to minimize the period of incapacity before death. It may also correspond to ethical preferences of people who want to control the end of life as they now control fertility.

Conclusion

We have noted much change in longevity. The improved health and mortality prospects of children, younger adults, and people of workforce age have significantly reduced the waste of human resources and have increased human capital. But health concerns remain a high priority, partly because health problems and disability affect a significant proportion of the population. Morbidity remains important in the later decades of life, and more people are reaching these stages of life.

As seen from the reductions in the major causes of modern mortality, especially heart disease but also cancer and accidents, the improvements are a function of both risk factors and treatment. Partly through research and its dissemination, we have become more aware of risks, and many are willing to change the way they live to reduce those risks. There is also a push to spend more on the treatment of people subject to poor health. These factors, along with the aging of the population, mean that health policy will remain an important priority.

In reviewing the situation of less-developed countries, the World Health Organization (2010) concludes that low mortality is within the reach of all countries, and that it is a matter of having the political and social will to attain this objective for the benefit of the entire population. One could say the same for the differentials in our own country. There is a need in Canada for further analyses of the dynamics of these differences in population health,

but especially for a political will to work to reduce them.

At the same time, it is important to appreciate that health questions are related to a number of economic and social factors. In a significant way, the extension of life expectancy is a result of the fundamental economic and social changes that produced modern industrial societies. More generally, major demographic transformations followed on the agricultural revolution of times past and on the Industrial Revolution of the nineteenth century.

Since the agricultural revolution entailed a higher level of food production through the deliberate planting of crops and domestication of animals, rather than obtaining food through gathering and hunting, it permitted significant improvements in human welfare and also population growth. Nonetheless, this agricultural revolution brought more deaths from all causes except inadequate nutrition (Muhsam, 1979; Wells, 2010). A more predictable food supply was an important improvement that lowered mortality, but at the same time, denser population settlement increased the spread of infectious diseases, the storage of food permitted rats to spread plagues, and people living near stagnant water resulted in deaths from malaria.

Similarly, the technological and scientific advances of the Industrial Revolution have had significant demographic effects. Until now, the effects on population health have largely been positive through increased food supply, climbing living standards, and more surplus resources that can be used by governments to improve human welfare. Scientific advances and public health initiatives have assisted dramatically in the control of diseases. However, the Industrial Revolution and population growth have had an unprecedented environmental impact, including the increased exploitation of natural resources, disturbance of natural habitats, and reduced global biodiversity.

Dramatic technological and economic change may be having other effects over the longer term, with results we have yet to experience. Industrialization, for example, has and continues to be very energy intensive, which has by and large been driven by the burning of fossil fuels. To the extent that this industrialization increases the CO_2 in the atmosphere, among other greenhouse gases, our climate is being modified, yet to an uncertain extent. While the consequences of increased emissions are highly uncertain, and entail many risks, the ultimate consequences may in fact be higher mortality.

Critical Thinking Questions

1. Use the concepts of the epidemiological transition to discuss the long-term changes in Canadian mortality.
2. Indicate the risk factors and the treatment factors associated with the following causes of death: heart disease, cancer, and accidents.
3. In the light of mortality trends over time, and mortality differentials by various characteristics of the population, what conclusions can be reached with regard to the relative importance of preventive and curative factors in reducing mortality and in reducing mortality differentials?
4. What life expectancy would you envisage for Canada in 2050? Defend your prediction.
5. How should health costs be shared between provincial governments and the federal government, and between individuals, families, and societies?
6. How should public responsibility for health care be defined, and how should we prioritize (1) better health and (2) prolonging life?

Recommended Readings

Bah, Sulaiman M., and Fernando Rajulton. 1991. "Has Canadian mortality entered the fourth stage of the epidemiologic transition?" *Canadian Studies in Population* 18(2): 18–41. This article analyzes Canadian mortality in relation to the epidemiological transition and argues that Canada has entered the fourth phase of this transition.

Bourbeau, Robert. 2002. "Canadian mortality in perspective: A comparison with the United States and other developed countries." *Canadian Studies in Population* 29: 313–69. Besides showing favourable comparisons to the United States, this article points to the differential declines in mortality at various ages over the 1951–1996 period.

Romanow, Roy. 2002. *Building on Values: The Future of Health Care in Canada*. Final report of the Royal Commission on the Future of Health Care in Canada. Ottawa: Canadian Government Publishing. This Royal Commission report, headed by Romanow, argues for giving high priority to health in Canadian social spending.

Statistics Canada. 2015. *Health Reports*. Published by Health Analysis Division, this peer-reviewed journal provides up-to-date Canadian research on issues related to population health and health services.

Wilkins, Russell, Jean-Marie Berthelot, and Edward Ng. 2002. "Trends in mortality by neighbourhood income in urban Canada from 1971 to 1996." *Health Reports* 13 (supplement): 45–71. This analysis of data at the aggregate level shows slight declines in socioeconomic differentials over time.

Related Websites

www.cihi.ca. The Canadian Institute for Health Information (CIHI) is a not-for-profit organization that provides useful health information.

www.statcan.gc.ca/eng/health/index. Statistics Canada regularly updates its health statistics on both the state of population health and Canada's health-care system.

www.bdlc.umontreal.ca/chmd/. The Canadian Human Mortality Database (CHMD) was created to provide detailed Canadian mortality and population data to researchers, students, and others interested in the history of human longevity.

4 Fertility and the Reproduction of Society

The Chapter at a Glance

- There has been a long-term fertility decline from seven births per woman in 1851 to under two births, on average, since 1976.
- The baby boom of the 1946–1966 period was an important departure from the long-term trend.
- From 1976 to 2011, the age patterns of child-bearing changed more substantially than the overall fertility rate, toward older ages for mothers at childbirth.

- Fertility can be analyzed in terms of proximate factors (e.g., fecundity, contraception, marital status), micro-level considerations (especially the economic and cultural value and cost for parents in raising children), and macro-level considerations (especially the interplay of production and reproduction or the structure of paid and unpaid work).
- Policy associated with child benefits, parental leave, and child care can assist parents in achieving their family and work goals.

Introduction

Just as for mortality, there has been a substantial long-term change in fertility, from some seven births per woman in the 1850s to fewer than two births since the mid-1970s. The interpretation of these changes involves a variety of considerations, including basic changes in the socioeconomic structure of society and the changing role of the family in people's lives. As we saw in Chapter 3, the pattern of change for mortality has a certain uniformity, the trend being universally downward, over time and across Canada. With fertility, the changes have not been so uniform, and the postwar baby boom was a major departure from the long-term trend. The analysis of fertility is also more complex: whereas everyone dies just once, usually of an identifiable cause, births are subject to fewer biological constraints.

Public policy discussions about mortality also have a certain simplicity, since the goal is to reduce mortality. For fertility, the issues of concern might include excess births—especially unwanted births—but also low birth rates. Among the countries of the world, governments have paid considerably more attention to reducing births, either in order to reduce population growth or to reduce unwanted births. Since the 1980s, various countries have adopted policies aimed at sustaining births. While the number of children to have, or whether to have children at all, is on one level a deeply personal question, the people around us also have a stake in the matter—be it family, workmates, community, or society. In all societies, families or other groups will try to influence people's decisions about having children in order to promote the well-being of the society.

In this chapter, we first consider the trend in fertility, paying particular attention to age patterns, and then we offer an interpretation in terms of the demographic transition. After looking at fertility differentials and explanations of fertility variation, we will discuss the interplay of production and reproduction, and the family policies that can assist parents in achieving their family and work goals.

The Fertility Trend

The long-term changes in fertility are shown in Figure 4.1. These data are based on the *total fertility rate* for 1871–2011 and the *completed fertility rate* for cohorts of women born in the years 1898 to 1982. The total fertility rate is called a period rate because it takes the rates of child-bearing of women at various ages in a given year and sums them to get a measure of what the average births per woman would be if the rates for this one year represented the lifetime experiences of women. The overall pattern shows a decline from about seven to fewer than two births per woman. The postwar baby boom period of 1946 to 1966 represents an exception to the long-term trend. The total fertility rate tends to exaggerate the baby boom because it was partly a function of an earlier onset of child-bearing and closer spacing of children. The subsequent decline is also exaggerated by this measure because it was partly a function of the delay of child-bearing. The period from the mid-1960s to the early 1970s shows the most rapid change, with the total fertility rate falling below two in 1972. Over a remarkably short period, from 1963 to 1974, the total fertility rate declined by 50 per cent, from 3.61 to 1.84 births per woman (Romaniuc, 1984: 124). It is noteworthy that the 1981–2011 period saw less variability, with a level between 1.5 and 1.7 births per woman.

The rate of 2.1 is traditionally used to mark *replacement fertility*, or the replacement of one generation by the next. Two births are needed to replace the parents, and 0.1 to compensate for the small number of deaths that occur before the next generation reaches reproductive ages. After fertility declines, the inertia of a population's past growth continues for some time. This is known as *population momentum*. In effect, births continue to outnumber deaths because the demographic bulge in the population age structure was at reproductive ages. Even though they are having fewer births than are needed for replacement, this generation is sufficiently numerous to ensure more births than deaths. This momentum will continue for some time. According to projections from Statistics Canada (2010c), with fertility constant at 1.7 births per woman, births would still outnumber deaths at the end of the projection period in the year 2061. However, with a fertility rate of 1.5, deaths would outnumber births as of 2031.

The *cohort completed fertility rate* gives the average number of children ever born to women from given birth cohorts (see Figure 4.1). For the more recent cohorts who have not completed their child-bearing, estimation procedures have been used. Beyond age 30, the age-specific rates that were not observable have been estimated by linear extrapolation of the trend observed over the past 10 years. It can be seen that the cohorts born in the early 1930s had levels as high as 3.4 births on average (during the baby boom), the 1948 cohort was the last to have completed fertility above 2, and the cohorts born in the 1968–82 period are showing constant levels at an average of about 1.75 births per woman.

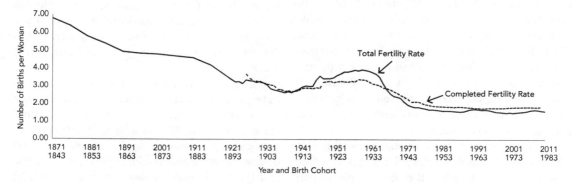

Figure 4.1 ⊡ Total Fertility Rate, 1871–2011, and Completed Fertility Rate for Cohorts Born 1898–1982, Canada

Sources: Romaniuc, 1984, pp. 121–2; Statistics Canada, *Births*, cat. no. 84–210 various years; Beaujot and McQuillan, 1982, p. 54; Milan, 2013a, p. 8.

Table 4.1 ▣ Distribution of Women by Number of Children Ever Born, and Average Children per Woman for Birth Cohorts 1977-81 to 1927-31, Canada

Birth Cohort	1977–81	1972–76	1967–71	1962–66	1957–61	1952–56	1947–51	1942–46	1937–41	1932–36	1927–31
Age in 2011	30–34	35–39	40–44	45–49	50–54	55–59	60–64	65–69	70–74	75–79	80–84
No Children	28.1	19.3	15.7	15.5	18.3	16.2	14.0	10.2	10.7	13.0	10.5
1 Child	22.9	18.1	17.8	17.2	14.6	16.3	16.0	12.7	11.1	12.0	7.4
2 Children	31.5	39.5	43.2	43.1	41.1	43.0	38.1	36.2	26.1	15.9	24.8
3 Children	12.7	16.1	16.3	16.8	18.6	18.0	23.2	24.9	27.4	16.7	10.9
4 Children	3.6	5.2	4.7	5.4	5.5	4.5	6.0	11.7	8.0	16.1	13.3
5+ Children	1.3	1.8	2.3	2.1	1.9	2.0	2.8	4.2	16.8	26.4	33.1
Total	100.0	100.0	100.0	100.0	100.0	100.0	100.0	100.0	100.0	100.0	100.0
Average Number of children per woman	1.46	1.76	1.84	1.87	1.86	1.86	2.01	2.31	2.77	3.12	3.41

Notes: Includes adopted children

Cohorts 1937–41 to 1927–31 were taken from Dumas and Belanger 1997: 41
Source: Special tabulations based on the General Social Survey, 2011.

Besides the averages, it is useful to consider the proportion of women who have various numbers of children. During the baby boom, there was a decline in the proportions of women having one or no children, along with increases in the proportions having three to five children (Needleman, 1986). The subsequent period has seen increased proportions having two children.

As seen in Table 4.1, for cohorts born in the 1927–36 period, the largest category was women having five or more children, representing over 25 per cent of women. For the 1937–41 birth cohort (women who were 70–74 in 2011), the largest category involved three children, with over half of women having three or more children. In the 1942–46 cohort, the largest category is those having two children, representing over 40 per cent of women.

In the 1927–31 cohort, 46 per cent of women had four or more children, and, consequently, three quarters of all children belonged to families of this size (Dumas and Bélanger, 1997: 41). In the 1967–71 cohort, 7 per cent of women had four or more children, representing 17 per cent of children. It seems that the decline in fertility over cohorts has mostly involved lower proportions of women who have three or more children and a greater concentration of

women with two children (Péron et al., 1987). Consequently, three quarters of children belong to families of two or three (about half of children are from families with two children, and a quarter are from families with three children).

For women aged 35–64 in 2011, the proportion with one child was in the range of 15 to 18 per cent, representing about 10 per cent of children. While research suggests that children in one-child families have various advantages, only 5 to 6 per cent of people aged 15–29 said in 1990 that they intended to have one child (Ravanera, 1995: 19).

It is also noteworthy that the proportion of women with no children has not changed as significantly as the average number of children. The proportion of women with no children was as low as 10 per cent during the baby boom era. While this has clearly increased, the rise has not been to the extent that some had predicted (Kneale, 2008). For women aged 35–64, the proportion with no children has been in the range of 15 to 18 per cent. In Quebec, where births by cohort are systematically tabulated, the women having no children increased to some 23 or 24 per cent of women in the 1955–65 birth cohorts, and it has since declined to 17 or 18 per cent for the 1971–79 birth cohorts (Institut de la statistique du Québec, 2013: 49).

There is also a concentration at two children when women in married or common-law unions are asked about the total children that they intend to have (Edmonston et al., 2010). In surveys taken every five years over the 1990–2006 period, the average intended family size, for women aged 15–44, has been in the range of 2.1 to 2.3 children. Total intended children is lowest at ages 40-44, with an average of 1.9 in the 2006 survey. Women and men in their twenties are expecting an average of about 2.5 children. The analysis of intended births shows that some of these births may not materialize, in part because the respondents are assuming that they will be in a stable relationship when the time comes to have children. Other complications associated with planning for children in people's lives, and even the difficulty of conceiving a child, are also difficult to anticipate.

Age Patterns of Child-Bearing

Since the mid-1970s, there has been more change in the age patterns of child-bearing than in the levels of fertility. These age patterns have shifted toward later

child-bearing. The trend in age-specific fertility has mostly been downward at ages under 30, and upward between ages 30 and 39. Before 1969, the 20–24 age group had the highest fertility; now it is the 30–34 age group, followed by 25–29.

The baby boom involved increases in fertility, especially at ages 20–29, with some increases also at ages 30–34 and 15–19. In contrast, fertility at ages 35+ continued its long-term decline during the baby boom period (see Figure 4.2). The subsequent fertility decline has applied to the 15–29 age group since the early 1960s. For older age groups, there has been a turnaround, with fertility increases dating back to the early 1970s at ages 30–34, the late 1970s for the 35–39 age group, and the late 1980s for ages 40–44. At the height of the baby boom, the 20–24 age group had the highest fertility, fertility was higher in the 25–29 age group by 1969, and the highest fertility has been in the 30–34 age group since 2005. Since 2010, fertility at 35–39 years of age has been higher than at 20–24 years.

The average age of mothers, for *all births*, declined over the 1945–1975 period, and it has since increased (see Figure 4.3). From an average age of 26.7 years in

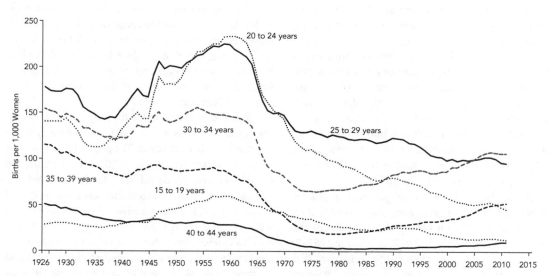

Figure 4.2 ▣ Total Fertility Rate by Age Group, Canada, 1926–2011

Note: Births to mothers for whom the age is unknown were prorated
Source: Milan, 2013a, p.4.

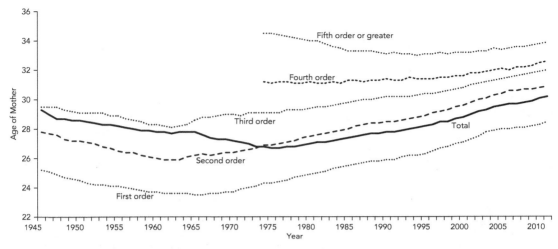

Figure 4.3 ▨ Average Age of Mother by Birth Order, Canada, 1945–2011

Note: Births to mothers for whom the age is unknown were prorated
Source: Milan, 2013a, p. 6.

1975, it reached 30.2 years in 2011. In the mid-1960s, the average age of women at *first birth* was 23.5 years, and it has since increased to 28.5 years. Summarizing the patterns over the past century, Milan (2013a: 6) observes that child-bearing has become increasingly concentrated over a short time span in women's lives, from their late twenties to early thirties.

The patterns can best be described as a postponement of child-bearing and partial recuperation after age 30. As Lesthaeghe and Moors (2000) have observed, there are many reasons for the postponement, but there is less literature on the basis for differential recuperation. Postponement is related to the increased importance of achieved status for both men and women as a basis for forming reproductive relationships. The open questions are (1) Will the tempo shift toward later child-bearing continue? and (2) To what degree will cohorts recuperate after age 30 for fertility forgone in their twenties?

In the Canadian case, successive cohorts after 1945 have had lower fertility up until the ages of 28 or 29, and higher fertility after the age of 30 (see Figure 4.4). For the 1946 cohort, which was the last to have completed fertility above the replacement rate of 2.1, peak fertility occurred at age 24 (Milan, 2013a: 8). This peak fertility was at age 27 for the 1965 cohort,

age 28 for the 1970 cohort, and age 30 for the 1975–1979 cohorts.

As will be seen in Chapter 9, there are similar delays in several other family events, from leaving home, to starting relationships, marrying, and having children. These delays may be interpreted as a longer period of adolescence, or even a "generation on hold" (Côté and Allahar, 1994). But the delays also reflect the needs of both men and women to postpone marital relationships, and especially child-bearing, until they are better able to handle the trade-offs between investing in themselves and investing in reproduction. All species face trade-offs in this regard (Kaplan et al., 1998). A longer period of investment in oneself provides the individual with more resources to then invest in reproduction, but there is the risk that reproduction will not occur. Conversely, early reproduction represents a greater security that reproduction will occur, but also the danger of inadequate investment in oneself to have the resources necessary to bear and raise "quality" children. Women who start having children later are likelier to have more education, or higher occupational status and income.

Part of the trend toward postponement of child-bearing has been a decline in child-bearing

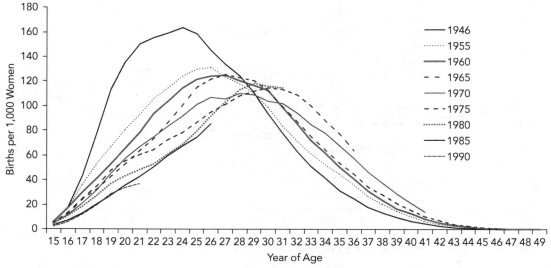

Figure 4.4 ▣ Total Fertility Rate by Age for Selected Cohorts

Source: Milan, 2013a, 7.

among teenagers. In 1974, the 15–19 age group had 35.6 births per 1,000 women, compared to 12.6 in 2011 (see Figure 4.2). This is not because of the post-ponement of first intercourse, which is, in fact, occur-ring at earlier ages on average (Odynak, 1994). Part of the reason for the lower birth rate among teenagers is their higher abortion rate. Canadian teenage fertility rates are about in the middle of comparable countries; rates are lower in Belgium, Finland, Denmark, and Sweden, but they are higher in the United States (Dryburgh, 2000: 11).

Interpreting the Long-Term Trend

In interpreting the long-term trend, demographers often refer to the theory of a demographic transition (see Chapter 1). In the history of the more developed countries, and more recently in the Global South, mortality and fertility have moved from high to low levels over a period of economic and indus-trial transformation, and cultural change (Wilson, 2013; Edmonston, 2014). There is disagreement in the literature about the relative influence of eco-nomic and cultural factors in this transformation. Economic explanations highlight people's adaptation to evolving opportunities, while cultural explanations

concentrate on the social construction of preferences and the normative evaluation of opportunities. In the analysis of fertility decline, economic explanations consider the advantages of smaller families, while cultural explanations consider the "think ability" of control over family size (Coale, 1973). We can also say that economic conditions may make people "ready" to have fewer children, and cultural condi-tions may make them "willing" to do so (Lesthaeghe and Vanderhoeft, 1997).

In the pre-transition stage—say, before 1850 for Canada—fertility tended to be uniformly high, in the order of seven births per woman. The economic explanation focuses on the role of the family in pre-industrial societies. The family was the basic economic unit in society, responsible for not only consumption, but also production and security. From a fairly young age, children were important as labour in family production and sustenance. The cultural explanation suggests that the very idea of planning family size was probably foreign to most people's mentalities (Van de Walle and Knodel, 1980). That is, some forms of contraception were known, especially coitus interruptus and, of course, abstinence, but the spacing of births was not much affected by the number of previous births or by the number of surviving children. Van de Walle and Knodel also suggest that there were considerable unwanted births. For instance, they refer to sayings such as "smallpox is the poor man's friend" (because it eliminated unwanted children) and to the high level of infant mortality that would have partly been due to the neglect of children who were not wanted in the first place (Boswell, 1988). Even if they were ready and willing to have fewer children, however, couples would have needed to find the means to do so. Lesthaeghe refers to these conditions as "ready," "willing" and "able" (Lesthaeghe and Lopez-Gay, 2013). Lapierre-Adamcyk and Lussier (2003) speak of a change from "high" to "desired" fertility.

The transition in fertility can also be interpreted in both economic and cultural terms. With the industrial and economic transformations of society, most economic production became organized outside the family, and the role of the family changed. Children became less valuable in family production, and the cost of children increased since they needed to be in school for a longer period. The movement of economic production out of the household ruptured the close link between economic production and demographic reproduction (e.g., Dickinson and Russell, 1986; Boily, 1987). In addition, social security replaced the family as the basic welfare net in the face of economic hardship, incapacity, and old age. The economic rationale for having children was reduced as family and kin groups became less important as a guarantee of security, and the state took more responsibility for the welfare of individuals. These economic transformations did not occur simultaneously across socioeconomic groups. A detailed study in the Saguenay region of Quebec over the period 1840 to 1971, for instance, shows that the demographic transition started in the 1930s with the class of non-manual and skilled, and it was only by the 1950s that farmers had similar declines (Vézina et al., 2014). This brought a widening of socioeconomic fertility differentials during the transition period.

The cultural explanation suggests that the idea of limiting births within marriage, and the use of contraception, were innovations whose legitimacy spread gradually. That is, besides the adjustments to structural changes and new socioeconomic conditions, with the associated cost–benefit calculations, there

was a decline in patriarchy and shifting patterns of sociability with fewer family-based interactions and more age-related social networks (Dribe and Scalone, 2014; Bras, 2014). These cultural changes can be seen as "innovation–diffusion" of new norms on appropriate behaviour, including fewer gender-based behavioural norms. This spread of the new standards of behaviour has sometimes been impeded by cultural barriers. In his interpretation of the higher fertility in Quebec until the 1950s, for instance, Henripin (1957) speaks of "acceptance of nature" as a "cultural attitude toward life" or an "approach to existence" that contrasts with what he calls a modern "contraceptive control civilization." Minorities, such as First Nations peoples, resisted for some time the "penetration" of different forms of behaviour, including changed modes of fertility. In support of this cultural explanation, Van de Walle and Knodel (1980) note that the fertility decline has begun under a variety of socioeconomic conditions, and that once the decline starts, it appears to be irreversible.

Both economic and cultural factors are crucial to an understanding of fertility trends. In his discussion of a "unifying theory" of global fertility transition, Caldwell (1997) observes that these economic and cultural elements are an integral part of the transition in both Western and Global South countries. The economic elements involve couples making spontaneous adjustments to changed conditions. The cultural elements include ideological debates, like those introduced by Malthus, as well as activist interventions, like those by the birth-control movement or the United Nations conferences on population and development. Once fertility decline starts, it tends to spread rapidly, especially in societies that are linguistically homogeneous, or in which the decline starts later. That is, the "willingness" to control fertility can spread rapidly.

There has been considerable research on the economic and cultural factors affecting the timing of the demographic transition, and its variability over space and time. Taking a 10 per cent decline in fertility as an indicator of the onset of the transition, this would have occurred by 1891 in Ontario and 1901 in Quebec (Beaujot, 2000b: 203–4). There are indications of earlier declines, however. In the industrializing town of Saint-Hyacinthe near Montreal, there were signs of fertility declines in the decades that follow 1850 (Gossage, 1999). In Ontario, the declines became more noteworthy in the 1870s, while certain counties of Quebec showed evidence of a transition by 1891 (Gauvreau and Gossage, 2001; McInnis, 2000a). As in other populations, there were important urban–rural differences in Quebec, especially at the beginning of the demographic transition. Starting in 1881, urbanization rates were lower in Quebec than Ontario (Beaujot, 2000b: 211). The 1901 Census shows an average of 4.3 children in rural agricultural households, compared to 3.3 in the large cities of Quebec (Gauvreau, 2001: 184). It is clear that for the whole of Quebec, the fertility transition was slower to take hold. Comparisons of Ontario and Quebec do not show much difference before 1860 but an increasing difference by 1921, when the total fertility rate was 5.3 in Quebec and 3.2 in Ontario, or 65 per cent higher in Quebec (Beaujot, 2000b: 207). The higher fertility of Quebec lasted a hundred years, from 1860 to 1960, at which point both total fertility rates were 3.8 births per woman. An analysis of newspaper articles shows that cultural factors helped to delay the transition in Quebec; for instance, there was celebration of Quebec's large families, and newspaper articles that appeared during the First World War expressed anxiety about diminished rates of reproduction and less encouragement to have children (Gossage and Gauvreau, 2000; Gauvreau et al., 2007). There was also much anxiety about what methods of birth control were acceptable.

Earlier versions of the demographic-transition theory had expected fertility in the post-transition phase to fluctuate around replacement levels as a function of changing socioeconomic circumstances. The persistent below-replacement fertility has necessitated further theorizing to understand the trends. Since the mid-1960s, there has been extensive family change: not only lower child-bearing, but also a greater propensity to cohabit outside of marriage, lower marriage rates, older ages at first marriage, higher divorce rates, and less specialization of earning and caring activities by gender (Beaujot, 2000a). These

changes are highly interrelated and have occurred widely, first in countries with a European civilization, and then around the world (Roussel, 1989). This pattern of change is now called the *second demographic transition* (Van de Kaa, 1987). Like the earlier transition that brought markedly lower mortality and fertility, these more recent demographic changes have deep economic and cultural roots, and they have profound effects on society.

The timing of the second demographic transition is quite similar in Quebec and Ontario. The beginning of the rise in the mother's age at first birth places this transition in the mid-1960s (Beaujot and Bélanger, 2001). If one takes as an indicator the proportion of births after age 30, Ontario is more advanced in the second transition, but the indicator of number of births in cohabiting unions places Quebec at a more advanced stage. The fertility differences have not been as large, but this time, Quebec showed lower fertility. The largest difference was 21.6 per cent in 1970, but from 1977 to 1980, fertility was slightly higher in Quebec. For the 1991–2005 period, the difference between Quebec and Ontario was less than 2 per cent, but in 2006–11, fertility was 6 to 11 per cent higher in Quebec (Milan, 2013a: 3).

If one takes 1945 as the end of the first transition (McInnis, 2000b) and 1965 as the beginning of the second, the intervening period can be seen as exceptional for being between two transitions. The trends until the mid-1970s suggested to some that fertility patterns were cyclical (Easterlin, 1980). Subsequent trends, however, indicate that there was only one cycle, or that the baby boom is best seen as an exception to the trend (Wright and Maxim, 1987). This exception can be interpreted in both economic and cultural terms. The 1950s were a period of sustained economic growth with much confidence in the future. It was also a time, often dubbed "the golden age of the family," when life was centred on the family unit and there was strong support for an ideal of parents having three or four children, with the mother staying at home to look after the children and the household. People who followed different patterns, including those who did not marry or had no children, were often seen as deviants, and it was considered wrong for women to work outside the home while their children were young (Veevers, 1980; Boyd, 1984).

It should also be noted that in some ways, the baby boom fits into the larger trend. There had been a long-term trend toward more universal marriage, marriage at an earlier age, and less childlessness, which was accentuated during the baby boom (Gee, 1986). Although marriage rates have subsequently declined, the universality of entry into relationships and the ages at which these occur have not changed substantially, especially if one includes all intimate relationships. In addition, the long-term trends, including those of the baby boom period, have involved a greater *compression* of child-bearing and a certain *standardization*, both in terms of age of entry into relationships and the modal category of a two-child family (Gee, 1986).

Proximate Factors

In the following sections, we offer possible explanations for the trends in fertility and the differentials by various characteristics that are described in Box 4.1. Variations in fertility can be considered in relation to three sets of factors: (1) the proximate factors (especially union formation and use of contraceptives), (2) the micro-level determinants (especially the value and cost of children to their parents), and (3) society-level factors (particularly the organization of paid and unpaid work).

Studies of fertility have found it useful to consider the specific proximate factors that are involved in any birth. Except in cases of artificial reproduction, there needs to be the ability to conceive (fecundity), along with sexual intercourse without contraception or abortion. Balakrishnan (1989: 235), for instance, has calculated that under 1984 Canadian health conditions, the "maximum" fecundity would be an average of some 16.4 births per woman. Of these, some 11.5 are eliminated through the use of contraceptives, 0.6 though induced abortions, 1.9 through non-marriage, and 0.8 through lactation, resulting in an actual fertility (excluding births outside of marriage) of 1.6

births per woman. At least in an "accounting" framework, the level of child-bearing is a function of these proximate factors of exposure to the risk of conception and successful parturition. In effect, these factors largely involve union formation and dissolution, along with contraception and abortion. Unions need to be considered both in terms of age at entry and exit, and proportion of people who are in unions.

These immediate factors go beyond the pure mechanics of fertility. Secure and efficient contraception, for instance, can change attitudes and norms toward sex, marriage, and children, as people become accustomed to the idea of sex without marriage and relationships without children (Preston, 1986). Also, as union dissolution becomes more common, women need to be more concerned about their own independence and self-sufficiency (Davis, 1986).

Union Formation and Dissolution

The measurement of fertility has often separated marital from non-marital fertility. Until 1971 in Canada, births outside of marriage were called "illegitimate births." The census question on children ever born has typically been asked only of women who were or had been married. The links between marriage and fertility have since been weakened, to the point that close to two thirds of births in Quebec are occurring outside of marriage (Institut de la Statistique du Québec, 2013: 50). For Canada as a whole, 40 per cent of all births occurred outside of marriage in 2011, compared to 17 per cent in 1981 (Beaujot and Wang, 2010: 415). The births outside of marriage are mostly occurring in common-law unions. For instance, in Quebec, the proportion of births where there is no declared father was stable at about 5 per cent over the 1975–94 period, while births to non-married women increased from 9.8 per cent to 48.5 per cent (Duchesne, 1997: 1).

The proportions of childless couples further document the importance of union status. At ages 35 and over, the percentage of people with no children varies extensively by marital status: 81.9 per cent of people who have never married have no children,

Box 4.1   ▣ Fertility Differentials

The study of fertility differences between subpopulations helps to explain the trends and dynamics of fertility. Differentials can usefully be analyzed by various demographic, socioeconomic, and sociocultural characteristics of respondents. As can be expected, the differentials by marital status are particularly significant (see Table 4.2). At ages 30–44, for instance, both current fertility and total intended fertility are highest for married and formerly married, followed by cohabiting and single.

Table 4.2 ▣ Current Fertility and Total Intended Fertility by Marital Status, Aged 20–44, Canada, 2006

| | Current Fertility | | | | | | | | | |
| | Women | | | | | Men | | | | |
Age group	Married	COH	SDW	Single	Total	Married	COH	SDW	Single	Total
20–4	0.33	0.41	1.23	0.07	0.15	0.55	0.34	*	0.02	0.08
25–9	1.05	0.70	1.39	0.24	0.66	0.83	0.55	0.33	0.04	0.35
30–4	1.61	1.29	1.66	0.63	1.37	1.17	0.99	0.87	0.19	0.86
35–9	1.93	1.39	1.75	0.51	1.64	1.66	1.33	1.51	0.35	1.38
40–4	1.98	1.34	2.00	0.55	1.76	1.96	1.33	1.60	0.29	1.62
n (unweighted)	2336	769	514	1573	5192	1758	638	262	1502	4160
Total	1.69	1.01	1.82	0.25	1.15	1.53	0.95	1.36	0.10	0.89

| | Total Intended Fertility | | | | | | | | | |
| | Women | | | | | Men | | | | |
Age group	Married	COH	SDW	Single	Total	Married	COH	SDW	Single	Total
20–4	2.18	2.32	2.12	2.22	2.23	2.37	2.01	*	2.17	2.17
25–9	2.36	2.05	2.28	1.99	2.14	2.21	1.91	1.47	2.05	2.05
30–4	2.19	1.93	2.08	1.74	2.05	2.10	1.93	2.10	1.57	1.93
35–9	2.10	1.66	1.86	1.22	1.90	2.02	1.62	1.91	1.22	1.82
40–4	2.01	1.36	2.03	0.77	1.81	2.10	1.51	1.74	0.90	1.83
n (unweighted)	2290	758	512	1525	5085	1712	623	259	1419	4013
Total	2.13	1.87	2.01	1.91	2.01	2.09	1.78	1.81	1.88	1.95

Notes: COH for cohabiting, SDW for separated, widowed or divorced.
* no cases for the cell
Data are weighted.

Source: Beaujot and Wang, 2010, p. 427.

compared to 27.5 per cent of people living common-law, 12.2 per cent of formerly married, and 9.1 per cent of married people (based on the 1995 General Social Survey). Fertility thus tends to be reduced by the lower prevalence of marriage, along with the greater prevalence of cohabitation.

The greater prevalence of union dissolutions has less effect on child-bearing, as births tend to be

An analysis of the 2001 Canadian General Social Survey on families shows that different factors affect the likelihood of first, second, and third births (Beaujot and Muhammad, 2006: 33–8). First births were less likely for women who were not in relationships, with more education, working, with few siblings of their own, and not affiliated with a religion. For those who had a first birth, the progression to a second birth is high, and to some extent those who have a first birth simply go on to have a second. In contrast to first births, however, second births were most common for women who had post-secondary education and who endured fewer work interruptions. For those who had two births, the probability of a third child was lower if they already had children of both genders, while it was higher for women who were less integrated in the labour force—as measured by education and work status—more religious, and with more siblings.

In their study of intended child-bearing for women in marital or cohabiting unions, Edmonston and his colleagues (2010) find remarkably little variation in average intended births across various segments of the population, and over the four General Social Surveys on families from 1990 to 2006. On marital status and family considerations, intentions were lower for those cohabiting than those married, for people who had experienced more cohabiting unions or more total unions. Averages were somewhat lower for women who were in the labour force or who had more education, while they were higher for women who were more religious, had more social ties, and a stronger sense of belonging.

Based on the 2001 Canadian General Social Survey, Heintz-Martin and her colleagues (2014) analyzed the probabilities of births in stepfamilies.

That is, families in which at least one child was not the biological or adoptive child of both partners. About half of stepfamily couples had a child within 10 years of the beginning of their union. Births were more likely for women who were younger, married, and not in the labour force. Heintz-Martin and colleagues propose that the birth of a common child justifies a women's maternal role and is a sign of commitment to the union by both partners.

Other studies have analyzed differentials in the timing of childbirth. On the basis of the Canadian Youth in Transition Survey, Hango and Le Bourdais (2009) find that early parenthood is more likely to occur for young adults who exit from full-time schooling and for persons with lower educational aspirations. Conversely, based on data from the Netherlands, Begall (2013) finds that the transition to a first childbirth is delayed for women with high earning potential.

The differentials between foreign-born and native-born Canadians are often studied, especially to see the extent to which immigration is changing the population in subsequent generations. Some first-generation groups, like those from the Middle East, have higher fertility than those who are Canadian-born, but others from China and South Asia tend to have lower fertility. On the whole, foreign-born fertility has been slightly higher than the Canadian-born rate, but there is convergence over time. Adsera and Ferrer (2014), for instance, analyzed the fertility of women who migrated to Canada before reaching age 19. Fertility was found to be high for women who immigrated in their late adolescent years, regardless of county of origin. But findings also show that the younger the children are at the time of immigration, the more likely they are to have the same fertility as the native-born Canadians (Adsera et al., 2012).

compressed into a short part of the life course, and some couples have children in subsequent unions. We can conclude that later entry into unions, more cohabitation, more instability in unions, and more complex family structures are generally reducing fertility compared to that intended at the onset of child-bearing ages (Beaujot and Wang, 2010; Beaujot and Bélanger, 2001).

Contraception

The main proximate factor in fertility is contraception. In *The Bedroom and the State*, McLaren and McLaren (1986) observe that in Canada from 1880 to 1945, birth control and abortion were limited by fairly deliberate state action. The 1984 National Fertility Survey was the first to provide a detailed picture of Canadian contraceptive use (Balakrishnan et al., 1985). Among all women aged 18–49, some 68.4 per cent were using contraception at the time of the survey. Contraceptive use was highest among cohabiting women who had never been married (83.1 per cent), but it was still 50.8 per cent among women who had never been married and who were not cohabiting. Among single women who were using contraceptives, 71.2 per cent were on the pill. Once the desired family size has been attained, there is a high propensity to turn to an irreversible method of contraception, making for fewer unplanned pregnancies and births in marriage. In the 20 years between 1976 and 1995, the rates of contraceptive sterilization almost doubled (Bélanger, 1998: 17). In the 1995 General Social Survey, one of the partners was sterilized for a quarter of couples aged 30–34 and half of couples aged 35–39 (Bélanger and Dumas, 1998: 68–9). While just 14 per cent were sterilized when they had only one child, that rose to 47 per cent when there were two children.

Among people using contraception, sterilization is by far the most common method, followed by the pill at 26 per cent of couples (Bélanger and Dumas, 1998: 79). The continued importance of the pill was partly foreseen from the finding of the 1984 survey that 10 per cent of women had some regrets about having been sterilized, saying that "if they were to make the decision now they would not elect to become sterilized" (Balakrishnan et al., 1993: 226). Among younger couples, male sterilization as a method of contraception has become more common than female sterilization (Boroditsky et al., 1996; Bélanger and Dumas, 1998). This is a significant change since the 1984 survey had found twice as much female as male sterilization (Balakrishnan et al., 1993: 198). Given that the relative use of condoms has also increased and that they are used much more than female barrier methods or the IUD, it would

appear that men are taking more responsibility for contraception.

Abortions increased from 3 per 100 live births in 1970 to 24.5 in 2011 (Balakrishnan, 1987; Wadhera, 1990; Dumas and Bélanger, 1997: 48; CIHI, 2014a). For females aged 19 and under, there are about 90 abortions per 100 live births. Data collection has become more difficult since abortions occur both in hospitals and clinics, and those occurring in other settings are not captured in the statistics. In the 2011 statistics, 70 per cent of abortions involved a fetal gestational age of less than three months, and close to half of females had no previous abortions. In Quebec, the rate per 100 live births was 7.3 in 1976, reaching levels of about 40 per 100 in the 1998–2004 period, and then went down to 30 abortions per 100 live births in 2008–11 (Institut de la statistique du Québec, 2013: 51). It would appear that efficient contraception does not preclude significant numbers of abortions.

The importance of contraception is highlighted by both the Easterlin and Lesthaeghe explanations of the demographic transition. For Easterlin and Crimmins (1985), mortality reduction brings an increased *supply* of children, which may be larger than the *demand* for children. Whether people will act on this imbalance between supply and demand depends on the *cost* of limiting their fertility. The economic and cultural factors noted above are relevant not only to the demand for children, but also for the availability of contraception (Alder, 1992). That is, the demand for children is a function of both the economic value that they represent for parents and the symbolic values that adults place on children. Similarly, contraception depends not only on its availability but also on its cultural acceptability. According to Lesthaeghe and Vanderhoeft (1997), for the transition to occur, people have to be *ready* for a change that represents an advantage for them, *willing* to make a change that is seen to be legitimate, and *able* to make the change through available means of preventing births.

Clearly, this cultural acceptability has changed from the times when Malthus was concerned about the "vice" represented by forms of contraception other than abstinence and coitus interruptus. Now, not only is *responsible parenthood* valued as Malthus had proposed, but also family planning has been deliberately promoted. The 1994 International Conference on Population and Development, for instance, argued for "reproductive health and reproductive rights." That is, there is an increased acceptance of the view that individuals should have the right to decide how many children to have and when, and have access to the facilities that would permit them to exercise these rights.

Fecundity

Fecundity, or the ability to conceive, is another proximate factor in fertility. According to data from various countries, women's fecundity would reach some 93 per cent at age 20, and falls to 70 per cent at age 40, and 40 per cent at age 45 (Nam, 1994: 183). On the basis of a measure of "perceived and inferred infertility" for Canadian women in 1984 who were not using contraceptives and had been in a marriage or common-law relationship for at least 24 months, it is estimated that while 86 per cent of women can become pregnant at ages 30–39, this is reduced to 40 per cent by ages 45–49 (Balakrishnan and Rajulton, 1992: 125). If we define evidence of infertility as being one year of trying to achieve a pregnancy without success, it is estimated that as many as 15 per cent of all couples have some problems in this area (Achilles, 1986). Similarly, analyses from the Canadian Community Health Survey suggest that, of couples who tried to become pregnant at some point in their relationship, 15 per cent reported seeking medical help for conception (Bushnik et al., 2012). Besides tracking ovulation, the most common methods used were assistive reproductive technology and fertility-enhancing drugs.

The Royal Commission on New Reproductive Technologies (1993) has suggested that we "proceed with care" on questions of new reproductive technologies. Given the moral issues and financial costs, this commission proposed that there be various constraints on the use of these technologies. In vitro fertilization, for instance, was recommended only for women with blocked fallopian tubes, representing about half of users. The Royal Commission suggested a ban on couples choosing the sex of their child through artificial insemination or abortion. In spite of these recommendations, there has not been a systematic change in the associated legislation.

These considerations of fecundity, contraception, and unions are not just the proximate factors of fertility—they also shape our identities and our relationships. By removing the link between sex and reproduction, and by permitting relationships without children, effective contraception has had a profound effect on relationships and marriages. Few aspects of family behaviour have changed so fundamentally as the extent and effectiveness of control over marital fertility.

The Value and Cost of Children

In his extensive analysis *Fertility, Class and Gender in Britain, 1860–1940*, Szreter (1995) uses the concept of "perceived, relative childrearing costs" as the underlying thesis to make sense of the trends and differentials. By relative costs, Szreter is referring to the costs relative to the benefits or value of children. He includes not only the economic costs and benefits, but also the social, cultural, and emotional ones. Economic costs are the easiest to identify, however, and economic development brings a rise in the "normatively sanctioned cost of childrearing" (Szreter, 1995: 443). Szreter makes reference to normatively sanctioned costs because many of the costs are a function of norms of proper behaviour.

While it is difficult to measure, the desire (or demand) for children depends on the values and costs associated with them. When asked about the advantages and disadvantages of having children, respondents fairly readily identify the costs. Eventually, they can also identify the benefits, or they may say that the values of children are obvious (see Box 4.2). In reference to women's and men's life strategies, Ni Bhrolchain (1993) makes the important observation that there is no a priori reason for assuming that having children is an end in itself. She observes that having children can serve other purposes, such as improving old-age security or maintaining the stability of a marriage, or it may become a strategy for women to opt out of the labour force. Children can represent various benefits in the life strategies of women and men.

Box 4.2 ▣ Attitudes toward Having Children

In order to understand the cultural context of child-bearing, a qualitative survey of 122 people was taken in the year 2000 in London, Ontario, and the surrounding region (Oxford and Middlesex counties). The purpose of the survey was to obtain people's basic attitudes toward various family questions. So, the survey asked a series of open-ended questions regarding unions, children, and the division of work. Here are some observations from these interviews.

Asked why people have children, many responded that *it is somehow natural, a normal part of life, expected, it simply made sense, was the right thing to do, a stage in life, to have another person to love, to create a family, bringing another life into your world is a gift.* Some saw themselves as creating a family, redeveloping its nucleus over a lineage. Others spoke of somehow leaving someone who is like you in this world, another self, to continue the family and its special characteristics. Many answered in terms of the benefits of having children. These were often stated in terms of the uniqueness of relationships with children when they are young, as they grow older, and even as they are adults. Some respondents added observations on the enjoyment of being with children—*it is fulfilling, there is nothing like the love a child gives, they bring joy, they remind you of the simple things, enjoying childhood again, watching them experience things, seeing them grow and become their own personalities, and moulding them.* Some spoke of the opportunity to be a child again, to play marbles, and make things.

Especially when asked about *advantages* and *disadvantages*, many respondents said that *there are strong time sacrifices, less time for oneself, being tied down.* The disadvantages mostly had to do with time and responsibility, the big workload when they were babies, the longer-term financial expenses, and sometimes the difficulty of raising children. Others spoke of the compromises, a lack of independence—*you "lose your life"; the freedom to do things when you want; the need to be responsible; it is a lifelong process; the difficulty of balancing roles such as mother, wife, and worker.* Life is changed enormously by having children—there is a lack of freedom, increased expenses, frequent fatigue—but most survey respondents did not dwell on the disadvantages, and almost without exception they were very glad to have had children.

When asked about the *best time to have a first child,* most talked about financial stability, having a job, not necessarily two jobs in the couple but sufficient economic security, the income necessary to be able to support children, having things in place before taking on this additional responsibility. Some noted that money was not everything, because if you waited to have enough you might never have a child. When asked if they would have, or would have had, more children if they had twice the income, most said no. Many spoke of the importance of being mature enough to take on the responsibility, to tolerate the disadvantages, and of being both financially and emotionally ready. Many also spoke of the importance of first being in a secure and established relationship, and having financial, emotional, and partnership stability, which mostly included marriage (preferably, a marriage that was at least two years old, or three to five years mature). The respondents were more willing to speak of the ideal age to have kids, which they put at around 25—some said 20 to 25, others late twenties, others still even said early thirties was fine. Many said that before 30 was best, though some said that after 30 was also acceptable, or even in your forties, as long as you have the energy. In speaking of a minimum age, some said that what mattered was to be able to provide for the children. Even if you marry before finishing school, you should certainly finish your education before having children. In speaking of a maximum age, this related to having the necessary energy level, to be able to run around with them and enjoy their energy and their youth. They also spoke of biological questions, of the shifting odds after the early thirties. It would appear that one should be old enough to be emotionally and financially stable, to be able to absorb the various costs, but not too old to have the energy and proper disposition.

Before asking about the ideal number of children to have, the survey inquired about the *conditions under which one should not have children.* A number of respondents started with some extreme conditions, such as genetic deficiencies, or serious emotional problems, mental deficiencies, or not being intellectually able to take care of them. Many also said it was best not to have children if you were not in a stable relationship, that it was not fair to the children if one has kids in a weak relationship, and it was seen as inappropriate to have children in order to secure the relationship with a partner. If someone is in an unstable relationship or is not able to be a good parent, then it's best not to have children. Many said that financial questions should not be a block, as long as one can afford children, and most people should be able to afford children. But others said that you should have enough money or the resources to raise children properly. Maturity was more important than finances. But when asked if it was acceptable not to have children, most said that it was acceptable if one did not want children. Many saw it as selfish not to want to have children, and they should not be so selfish. But if people were selfish, it was best that they not have children. Some thought there was no point in getting married if one did not want to have children. Those who saw it as natural to have children gave more extreme conditions under which one should not have children; those who saw it as a choice largely said that it was acceptable not to have children simply because one did not want children.

The *ideal number of children* was largely indicated in terms of a range, most often two to three; some said two, others two to four, and a few said as many as you want to have. In justifying this ideal, most started by talking about the expenses and costs, the limit on one's time, the desire to give everything that one could to each child. When asked why not have fewer kids, the vast majority expressed disagreement with the idea of having only one child. This was seen as not good for the child, or selfish on the part of parents. An only child was considered to be spoiled or lonely; it was unfair to the child not to have siblings to play with. It was thought that an only child would have poor social skills, not know how to cooperate with peers, not be able to regularly deal with people on a one-on-one basis, and not learn to share—all life skills that one needs. Some said it was acceptable to have only one child if that is all the parents can handle. There seemed to be even more opposition to the idea of having only one child than there was to not having any children. However, the respondents said they did not pressure people to have children if they did not want children. If someone does not want children, it is best that they not have them. While agreeing with not having children, some said it was unfortunate, a shame, they were missing an important life experience.

Having three or four children was seen as a better family atmosphere, but many said it was not realistic. The idea of having five or more was sometimes seen as fine if people could handle it, but most thought it was not realistic, and some even thought it was "crazy," and they could not understand why someone might have that many. A 35-year-old mother of four children under age 5 spoke of being accosted by an elderly woman while grocery shopping who said, "My child . . . have you not heard of birth control?"

Many found two children the easiest to justify—it is financially feasible, reasonably demanding on one's time, the children have someone to make friends with, it is a real family. More than two involves various trade-offs in terms of time and other things that one wants to do, like taking

Continued

holidays. But for some, three was also a good number, a safe number, and a real family—especially since it makes for more interactions among the children. For many, four was difficult, given all the emotional and other things one wants to give to each child; there is simply a limit and not enough time and energy to give each child everything that he or she needs.

When asked if they would have more children with twice the income, or with more government support, they mostly said no. Most wanted some subsidies to help them out, but this would not be a basis for having more or fewer children. Many said that the government should not be involved in this sphere of life—it was an infringement on the privacy of personal lives—or people should be responsible for their own decisions, or that it might even create an incentive not to work so hard.

When asked what a couple should do if there was *disagreement between husband and* *wife* regarding the number of children to have, most found it difficult to answer the question. They said the couple should talk about it, the decision should be made by both partners, perhaps via compromise. Some said that the person who bears the child or who will spend the most time looking after the children should decide, and a few said that the person who is most aware of the family finances should decide. But a good number of respondents said people should only have children that they both want, and thus they should have the smaller number. Many said that they should have talked about this before getting married, implying that having a common ground in terms of understanding how children will fit into their lives should be part of people's establishing of relationships. Couples should have a like-minded logic in this regard—otherwise there would probably be other misunderstandings.

Economic Values and Costs of Children

Children are very costly economically, as they are dependent on their parents and do not contribute to family income. Using data from the 1982 Family Expenditure Survey, Henripin and Lapierre-Adamcyk (1986) as well as Gauthier (1987) have attempted to estimate these costs. This is difficult to do because most of the expenditures for children are not directly identified in the survey. In effect, these authors compared families at the same standard of living (e.g., the proportion of income spent on food and necessities) to see how much extra income it takes with more children to achieve the same standard of living. The two studies place the average annual direct costs of the first child at slightly more than $10,800 per year in 2011 dollars. The costs vary by age of the child, with two children of preschool ages costing a total of $4,300, but two children aged 11 and 13 costing almost $21,600.

Using similar approaches, Gauthier (1991) calculated the direct costs to age 18 of a first child, excluding child care, at $222,000 for a higher-income family and $91,600 for a lower-income family (in 2011 dollars). The average costs for three children would be $337,000. If child care and indirect costs are added, this figure rises to $675,000. Dionne (1989) calculates that three children aged 17, 12, and 10 would reduce the family's standard of living by 33 per cent, compared with a family that has no children.

At the same time, it is useful to consider the direct *marginal* costs in terms of cash outlay. In examining the basic marginal costs necessary for the healthy development of a child, Sarlo (2013) estimates an annual amount of $3,000 to $4,500 per child per year, depending on the community or region and the age of the child. Focusing also on these minimal out-of-pocket costs, Battle (1997) estimates an average figure of $5,400 (in 2011 dollars) per child per year, and argues that the child tax benefit for low-income families should be set at this level in order to cover these direct costs. These are minimal estimates of direct costs, not including other costs that families undertake, such as more expensive housing, let alone child-care and opportunity costs associated with lower involvement in the labour force.

Using US data from 1972 to 2007, Furstenberg and colleagues (2013) found that in the early 1970s, parents were spending more on boys, but by the late 2000s, there was more spending on girls. Prior to the

1990s, parents spent most on children in their teen years, but the spending later was highest when children were under 6 and in their mid-twenties.

Explanations of trends and differentials in fertility need to consider not only the cost of children, but also the levels of income. Enid Charles (1936) long ago pointed to the paradox of economic interpretations of child-bearing. When real incomes have risen, fertility has declined. At the same time, inadequate means is universally given as the most potent motive for limiting the size of a family. Charles stated it very simply: "Hence arises the paradox that people limit their families for one of two reasons, because they are prosperous or because they are not" (p. 189).

In effect, attempts to analyze fertility differences through these economic factors have shown mixed results. Kyriazis (1982), for instance, found that the husband's income had a positive effect on the child-bearing of wives who had no children or one child but a negative effect if the wife already had three or more children. Wright (1988) found that the relationship between income and fertility was U-shaped, with higher fertility at both lower and higher incomes. The point of inflection in the curve, however, was fairly high: only 2.3 per cent of couples were in the upper income range where fertility was positively related to income. Using data from the 1991 Census, Ng and Nault (1996) also observed U-shaped relationships between income and fertility. In this case, women had the highest fertility when their own income was in the middle range, and fertility was lowest when the male partner's income was either below or above average.

It appears, then, that the relationship between income and fertility depends on the measure of income adopted. If it is women's income, fertility is probably highest when they have intermediate income; at higher levels of income, there may be less room for children in busy work lives. For men's income, and also for total family income, the relation to fertility may be positive at higher levels of income, as people are able to afford more children. But this higher income could also be translated into higher quality children, or a desire for forms of consumption that interfere with having children. Low incomes for husbands or families could imply that they cannot afford children. But low income could also mean that having children has more priority than achieving higher income.

In effect, the values and costs of children depend on the relative importance given to various possible life pursuits. A careful economic analysis of the values and costs of children may suggest that one should not have any children (David, 1986). Some of the respondents in the survey described in Box 4.2 specifically said that if you wait until you can afford to have children, you may never have children. It may be that economic rationales are relevant to explaining why people do not have more children, but these rationales do not really explain why people want children in the first place.

Cultural Values and Costs of Children

The non-economic costs and values of children are more difficult to determine. Children are *costly* in the sense that parents have less time and energy for themselves. And children are sometimes emotional or psychological burdens; parents worry about them and have to put up with various inconveniences ranging from a messy place at the dinner table to a dented car fender. Respondents to the survey summarized in Box 4.2 often refer to children as a heavy responsibility.

In a small sample of Australian women who had made transitions to motherhood, Crouch and Manderson (1993: 136) found that motherhood is "laden with responsibilities and, in most cases, socially isolating. . . . Thus many women feel vulnerable, lonely and confused most of the time and all women feel some or all of these things some of the time." Most studies find a drop in marital satisfaction, especially for women, when they and their spouse become parents (e.g., Lupri and Frideres, 1981, Waite and Lillard, 1991). Thompson and Walker (1989: 863) suggest that this drop in marital satisfaction could be due to the increased gender differentiation and specialization that comes with child-rearing. Children may also be a cost in the sense of keeping a parent in a relationship that he or she no longer finds fulfilling.

On the *positive* side, children do offer certain advantages: people's status as adults can be more firmly established when they are parents; having children can provide a sense of achievement and even of continuity beyond death. Survey respondents often refer to the enjoyment of being with children; that it is nice to see them grow and learn things; and that they bring fun, excitement, and laughter into the home. In the Canadian Fertility Survey, 84 per cent said that children "provide an irreplaceable source of affection" and 72 per cent said they "provide an irreplaceable goal in life" (Balakrisnan et al., 1993: 159). Thompson and Walker (1989: 861) summarize by saying that being a mother is a complex and contradictory experience; that it is "frustrating, irritating and overwhelming, but also pleasing and fulfilling."

Children also provide a stable interpersonal relationship, which can be especially fulfilling when other relationships are less stable. Friedman and colleagues (1994) propose that parenthood is a strategy for *reducing uncertainty*, especially for people who do not have stable marriages and careers. In effect, Wu (1995) found that, among cohabiting people, those who have more uncertainty in their lives are more likely to have children. That is, children can provide a certain insurance against unstable relationships. In addition, while marital satisfaction is often lower when there are children in the home, marital stability tends to be higher. Couples with young children are less likely to separate, and marriages with no children are the most prone to end in divorce (Waite and Lillard, 1991). Using data from Sweden, Andersson (1996) confirms that divorce risks are lowest when there are two or more children, especially if these children are young, and highest when there are no children.

Children enhance social integration, not only in terms of family ties but also at the community level. Coleman (1988) calls this *social capital*, because children provide contact with others in the neighbourhood, at school, and in the larger community. This is the *social resource* value of children, since they help establish new relationships among people, along with the support that these relationships can provide.

In an article titled "Why Do Americans Want Children?" Schoen and colleagues (1997) observe that parents of adult children become more likely to provide support when their own children are parents. It was found in the US 1987–8 National Survey of Families and Households that people are more likely to want another child when relationships created by children are seen to be important. Survey respondents also tend to emphasize the increased family ties, along with affection, stimulation, and fun, as intrinsic values of children. In other societies, anthropologists have

long recognized the kinship ties and other relationships that come with children. In some African societies, child placement, or the custom of placing one's child in another family, establishes a special bond between families. Schoen and colleagues (1997: 350) conclude by observing that "childbearing is purposive behaviour that creates and reinforces the most important and most enduring social bonds . . . as the threads from which the tapestry of life is woven."

When people are asked about the things that are important for being generally happy in life, relationships, children, and jobs are among the most salient factors. Among respondents to the Canadian Fertility Survey, 96 per cent chose "having a lasting relationship," 72 per cent chose "having at least one child," and another 72 per cent chose "being able to take a job outside the home" (Balakrishnan et al., 1993: 174).

Child-Bearing and the Structure of Paid and Unpaid Work

The value and cost of children is a micro- or individual-level consideration. In this section, we introduce macro-level considerations, especially in terms of the social organization of paid and unpaid work. That is, the value and cost of children to parents would partly reflect the organization of paid and unpaid work and the family strategies that are adopted to divide this work.

Family strategies can be related to the broader political economy or, in Marxist terms, to the mode of production and the relations of production. In other words, both paid and unpaid work depend on the form of economic production and on the relations of various categories of people to the production process. Marx further thought that different relations of production would involve different dynamics of the population. The relation of women, men, and children to the production process is crucial to an understanding of demographic reproduction in the society. The economy has also evolved in the direction of greater potential to use market mechanisms as substitutes for domestic production. As Li (1996) observes, the family has become ever more dependent on goods and services available in the market. Consequently, the dynamic has involved maximizing earnings through having more wage earners, and economizing on the cost of children by having smaller families.

In analyzing the relation between production and reproduction, Ursel (1986) has argued that labour legislation in Ontario over the 1884–1913 period increasingly limited the use of child and female labour in the production system. The manifest concern was to improve the living conditions of children and women, but the laws also entrenched the distinctions between male and female labour. By putting limitations on the hours women could work, the places they could work, and the kind of work they could do, these laws made it almost impossible for a female factory worker to make a living wage. As women were in an economically dependent position, their livelihood depended on their entering into reproductive relationships. The resulting division of labour, often called the *breadwinner model*, produced a reciprocal state of dependence between the sexes.

Especially since the 1960s, the economy has changed in ways that have produced increased demands for workers in the service sectors of the economy, traditionally dominated by women. The consequent growth in the integration of women into the paid workforce has altered the relations between women and men and has raised the opportunity costs of having children. Women have become less dependent on marriage, and, thus, divorce, cohabitation, and childlessness have become feasible alternatives. Westoff (1986) also argued that the most important force underlying the weakening of marriage has been the growing economic independence of women. Keyfitz (1986) proposed that low fertility is the ultimate natural outcome of gender equality, brought about by the changing roles of women in the economy. Davis (1984) had even questioned the extent to which societies based on an egalitarian gender-role system can survive if people do not reproduce enough to replace themselves. Other views have suggested that, if there is gender equality both at the level of the marital/cohabiting couple and in the broader society, with men absorbing more of the overall costs of children, couples would be more likely to have the number of children that they desire (Matthews and Beaujot, 1997; Matthews, 1999).

McDonald (2000) has theorized that fertility is particularly low when women have attained equal opportunities in education and work, but families have remained traditional, allocating an excessive component of reproductive work to women. Bernhardt (2005) proposes that this low fertility is because only the first half of the gender revolution has been completed; the second half of the gender revolution, in the private sphere, remains incomplete. There is some evidence of higher fertility when men share more of the household burdens (Pinnelli, 2001; Gil Alonso, 2005; Purr et al., 2009). Research from Sweden shows that wives were more likely to have had a second child if their husbands had taken parental leave for a previous birth (Olah, 2003).

Men's participation in housework has been increasing. Reviewing Canadian trends in people's daily activities (based on time-use surveys) over the 1986–2005 period, Marshall (2006) uses the title "Converging Gender Roles." At ages 25–54 in 1986, for instance, men did an average of 43 per cent of the amount of unpaid work that women did, while men in 2005 did 58 per cent of women's average hours per day (Beaujot and Wang, 2010: 424). Among men aged 25–54 who were in a relationship with a child under 5 at home, 57 per cent participated in primary child care in 1986, compared to 73 per cent in 2005. For people with children under 5, the time spent doing child care has increased for both men and women, but especially for men (Gauthier et al., 2004: 661). For those who worked at least three hours on the observation day, the family time with spouse and/or children declined between 1986 and 2005, but the gender differences in this family time are very small (Beaujot and Wang, 2010: 424).

Comparisons across countries suggest that the structure of work is an important determinant of child-bearing. In comparing the pro-natalist policies of France and Japan, Boling (2008) concludes that the difficulties in Japan relate to the labour market, which "extracts high opportunity costs from parents who interrupt their careers to raise children, keeps ideal workers from having much time for their families, assumes and reinforces a traditional gender ideology, and hires few young workers into good jobs." Similarly, McDaniel (2008a) places part of the responsibility for Korea's low fertility on the increased insecurity in the labour market.

A comparison of Germany and France indicates that women without children have higher workforce participation in Germany, but when women have one or more children, it is in France where they have higher participation (Pailhé, 2008). The potential for flexibility of given occupations is another structural factor. Using Canadian data, Ranson (1998), for instance, finds that women in the educational and health sectors had more supports for child-bearing than women in law or business. The earnings of women with children are especially affected by those women having taken more time off from work than women without children (Zhang, 2009).

Comparative analyses also suggest that the relationship between fertility and women's workforce participation is dependent on the specific institutions of given welfare states (Baizan, 2007). The negative effects of women's employment on child-bearing in Italy, Spain, and the United Kingdom, in particular, contrast with the positive effect of having a job in Denmark. Employment status has positive effects in Scandinavian countries, while in other countries, women with low incomes have a higher probability of child-bearing.

These broad structural factors are therefore useful for understanding changes in the family, in gender roles, and in child-bearing. In the fallout from the Industrial Revolution, the family lost much of its function in economic production, and children became economic dependents. Since women were excluded from almost all economic production that moved outside of the household, they also became more dependent on the extra-familial occupations of their husbands. Only more recently did women regain their place in the labour force. Fertility went down first when children lost their economic value to parents, and again when child-bearing became an opportunity cost to employed women. As men and the broader society absorb more of these costs, however, there is less downward pressure on fertility.

Labour-Force Participation, Opportunity Structures, and Child-Bearing

From 1960 to 1985, the total fertility rate declined as fast as women's employment rate increased (see Figure 4.5). Less noticeable is that this inverse relationship between the two time series does not apply for the whole postwar period. During the 1950s, both fertility and women's employment increased. Since 1985, fertility has been relatively stable while women's

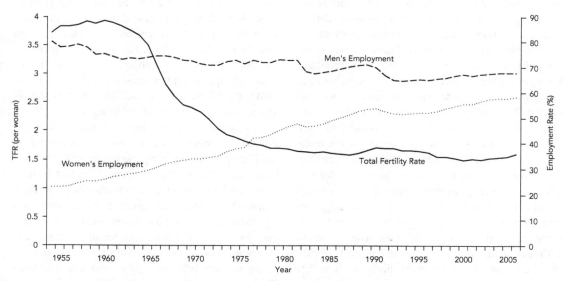

Figure 4.5 ▨ Total Fertility Rate and Employment Rate of Women and Men, Canada, 1953–2006

Source: Beaujot and Wang, 2010, p. 418.

employment rate has continued to rise, other than for the period of the early 1990s.

Across countries, the inverse relationship observed into the 1970s between rates of fertility and women's workforce participation has become positive since the mid-1980s (Morgan, 2003; Coleman, 2005: 438; Never, 2008; Billari, 2008; Thévenon, 2008). The same results are seen when Canadian provinces are used as the units of analysis (see Figure 4.6). In 1976, there was basically no relationship between fertility

rates and women's employment rates, while the linkage became more and more positive until 1996, with positive but weaker relationships in 2001 and 2006. For men, the relationships between fertility and their employment rates have been positive since 1976, but the correlations increased to 1996, with slightly lower but still positive correlations for 2001 and 2006 (Beaujot and Wang, 2010: 420).

The level of child-bearing needs to be placed within the opportunity structures of young people as

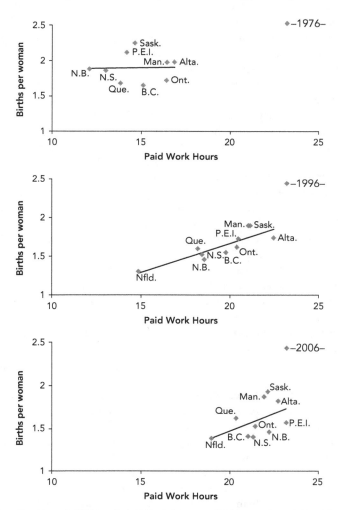

Figure 4.6 ▣ Total Fertility Rate (TFR) by Paid Work Hours of Women Aged 15–44, Provinces of Canada, 1976, 1996, and 2006

Note: Paid Work Hours = Employment Rate × Average Actual Weekly Hours Worked
Source: Beaujot and Wang, 2010, p. 419.

these evolve over time. As Wheeler (2008: 6) indicates, "babies tend to be born where the jobs are." Similarly, Roy and Bernier (2006) propose that employment continues to be the foundation of social and occupational integration, and weak job prospects, like the growth of non-standard work, are not incentives for having children. Bingoly-Liworo and Lapierre-Adamcyk (2006) find that the delay in first births is increasingly due to the longer period of education, as well as the difficulty of obtaining stable employment. First births are related to both stability in employment and the ability to rely on a spouse's employment. In France, two jobs predict the transition to first birth, while employment uncertainty delays the first birth (Testa and Toulemon, 2006; Pailhé and Solaz, 2012). In Sweden, we find that people who are not in the labour force and those in temporary employment are less likely to start a family (Lundstrom and Andersson, 2012). In Italy, the stable employment of both partners predicts higher fertility (Vignoli et al., 2012).

Several commentators have observed that the prospects for young men have deteriorated since the mid-1970s, after the leading edge of the baby boom had entered the labour force (Morissette, 1998; Kapsalis et al., 1999; Beaupré et al., 2006; Clark, 2007). Since the mid-1980s, for workers under 35, especially men, earnings have declined; educational premiums over older counterparts have disappeared; there is lower job quality, less pension coverage, lower unionization rates, increased earnings instability, increased wage gaps between newly hired and those with more experience, and lower likelihood that men under 35 have full-year full-time employment than in the 1970s.

It was thought that the "baby bust," born between 1967 and 1979, would have better prospects, since they were a smaller cohort (Foot, 2000). However, these cohorts have been disadvantaged by following the large baby boom cohort. With a more competitive labour market, they have pursued more education and the two-income model, partly as a means of achieving the desired standard of living. This has brought delays in early-life transitions, including home leaving, union formation, and child-bearing (Beaujot, 2006; Clark, 2007).

Early in this century, men under 35 have made more gains than at ages 35–64 (Morissette, 2008; Chung, 2006). It would appear that recent workforce entry cohorts are sufficiently distant from the baby boom that their opportunity prospects are less affected by the bulge in the age distribution. As mandatory retirement is being set aside, however, and the baby boom cohorts are concerned about the adequacy of their pension funds, the much-anticipated opportunities for younger cohorts have been postponed through the recession of 2007–2008 and subsequent period of high unemployment. Already in 2008, there were employment gains at ages 55+ compared to declines at ages 15–24 (Usalcas, 2009).

Family Policies and Child-Bearing

Gauthier (2008) has theorized that policies would make a difference to child-bearing if they help overcome some of the costs of children, but these costs are not the only element—equally important would be the availability of child care, housing, flexible hours of work, and part-time work. She further proposes that policies reducing gender inequality in households would be important. What may matter the most is not individual policies, but the package of policies, paying attention to the heterogeneity in the population (Gauthier and Philipov, 2008; Thévenon and Gauthier, 2010).

In the following sections, we will consider financial transfers to individuals, parental leave, and child care. In each of these three areas, Quebec has been more proactive than other provinces.

Financial Transfers to Individuals

At the federal level, universal family allowance payments started in 1945 (Blake, 2009). In 1993, the family allowance payments and the tax deductions for dependent children were converted into child tax benefits, allowing for more benefits to low-income families. At first, this change was revenue neutral, but the program has since been augmented by more than the cost of living. The maximum benefits per child were increased by 65 per cent between 1993 and 2012, to reach $3,485. The payments are reduced for incomes above $24,183 and they reach zero at an income of $109,894 for families with one or two children. It is estimated that 9 out of 10 families with children receive some benefit (Battle, 2009). In 2006, a universal child care benefit of $1,200 per child under 6 was added as a further direct payment.

Since 1996, there is also a family supplement to employment insurance for persons with net family income up to $25,921 (in 2012 dollars) for families receiving child tax benefits. This increases the replacement rate of employment insurance to as much as 80 per cent of insurable earnings, compared to the default replacement rate of 55 per cent. In 2006, 7.7 per cent of employment insurance claimants received a family supplement. In 2007, a working income tax benefit was added to tax benefits (Battle, 2009). For single parents and couples, the maximum benefit in 2012 was $1,762, with reductions to zero at incomes above $26,952. Following the lead of the federal government, since about 1998, numerous provinces have added their own versions of working income tax benefits. Quebec, for instance, has a *Prime au travail du Québec*, and there is a child care supplement for working families in Ontario (Laplante et al., 2011; Milligan, 2008).

From 1988 to 1996, Quebec adopted a distinctive family policy through a baby bonus program that followed a French model of larger payments per child if there are more births. For the third and subsequent births, these payments amounted to $1,600 per year for the first five years of the child's life (Rose, 2010).

Parental Leave

Maternity leave was first instituted as part of unemployment insurance in 1971. Mothers with the minimum weeks of insurable earnings could claim up to 15 weeks of benefits. As with other unemployment-insurance benefits, there was a two-week waiting period and the benefits used the same replacement rate as regular unemployment insurance. In 1990, 10 weeks of parental leave were added to the 15 weeks of maternity leave, but if both parents took leaves, they each had to endure a two-week waiting period. In 2001, the parental leave was expanded from 10 weeks to 35 weeks, and there was only one waiting period— even if the parental leave was shared. Now called

employment insurance, the replacement rate is 55 per cent up to a maximum income of $45,900 (that is, a maximum payment of $485 per week or $25,245 per year in 2012).

After several attempts to negotiate an agreement, Quebec began to administer its own parental-leave program in 2006, which also covers the self-employed and does not include a minimum previous weeks of work (Bureau de l'Actuaire en chef, 2008). This Quebec program offers two options: in the basic plan, there are 18 weeks of maternity leave (70 per cent replacement rate) plus 5 weeks of paternity leave (70 per cent replacement rate) and 32 weeks of parental leave (7 weeks at 70 per cent and the rest at 55 per cent); in the alternate plan, there are 15 weeks of maternity leave, 3 weeks of paternal leave, and 25 weeks of parental leave (all at a 75 per cent replacement rate).

By 2006, the take-up rate for mothers was 77 per cent in Quebec compared to 62 per cent in the rest of Canada (Marshall, 2008). For the 20 per cent of mothers who were receiving top-up payments from their employers, the average length of maternal leave was 48 weeks in 2008, compared to 46 weeks for mothers without top-up provisions, and 34 weeks for those with no benefits (Marshall, 2010). For fathers, the take-up rate in 2006 was 56 per cent in Quebec and 11 per cent in the rest of Canada. Quebec fathers took an average of only 7 weeks in 2006, however, while the smaller proportion of fathers in the rest of the country who took parental leave had an average of 17 weeks (Marshall, 2008). For parents who worked before the birth or adoption, 99.2 per cent of new mothers and 76.1 per cent of fathers in Quebec took parental leaves in 2010; outside Quebec, these figures were 90 per cent of mothers and 26 per cent of fathers (Findlay and Kohen, 2012).

Child Care

In 1997, Quebec converted the budget associated with the baby bonus program into a very popular $5-a-day child care program, which has since become $7 a day. Quebec's funding of child care increased much more than in other parts of the country. While in 1995 the total allocated funds in Quebec amounted to 38 per cent of those of Ontario, the Quebec funding was over twice that spent in Ontario in 2007–8 (Childcare Resource and Research Unit, 2009, Table 27). Adjusting for inflation, over this period, the public funding of child care increased 670 per cent in Quebec compared to 140 per cent in the rest of Canada. The higher availability and funding of day-care in Quebec has prompted higher usage in the province. For instance, 72.6 per cent of respondents with children aged 0–4 were using child care in Quebec in 2006, compared to 41.2 per cent in the rest of Canada (Beaujot et al., 2013a: 228).

In *Doing Better for Families*, the OECD (2011) documents that Canada is similar to the average across OECD countries on fertility (total fertility rate of 1.7), on the gender pay gap (20 per cent gap at median earnings), and on child poverty (15 per cent of children under 18 are living in households with less than 50 per cent of the median household income). Female employment in Canada is higher than the average for OECD countries, as is children's reading literacy. Canada is below the OECD average on family benefits spending as a per cent age of GDP, however, and the formal child-care enrolment of children under 3 was 24 per cent in Canada compared to the OECD average of 31 per cent in 2008.

Total Transfers

While Canada's track record is far from that of Nordic countries or France, the movement is in the right direction (Beaujot et al., 2013a). In comparison to other OECD countries, Canadian parental leaves are intermediate, but levels of cash support for families and child-care provisions are low, and transfers are concentrated in low-income families (Gauthier and Philipov, 2008: 8–11; Thévenon, 2008; Thévenon, 2011: 65). Canada has nonetheless made some progress in the variety of structures that need to be in place for prospective parents to feel that they have support from society in overcoming some of the costs and barriers to childbearing: direct transfers, parental leave, child care, and work–life balance features. Within Canada, Quebec has similar levels of direct transfers

associated with child-bearing, but its parental-leave program is more generous, with fewer restrictions and more options, and its funding for child care is higher and more universal.

Family Policies and Fertility Trends

There has long been a debate regarding the effectiveness and appropriateness of policies seeking to influence fertility. It is largely agreed that deliberate pro-natalist policies, designed to "buy children," are not effective—and it's generally considered to be inappropriate for the state to take such actions. At the same time, most authors would agree that there is a range of policies affecting families, gender, and work that have a bearing on fertility (Héran, 2013a). A review of population priorities in the OECD countries, for instance, proposes "appropriate policy responses, responsive legal frameworks, and support, including financial support, facilitating work–life reconciliation . . . [and that] transforming gender norms is vital for the success of family policies" (United Nations, 2013b: 11). It can be argued that the Canadian policies we reviewed in the previous section—enhancing direct transfers to children, parental leaves, and child-care subsidies—have helped Canada to avoid particularly low fertility (Beaujot and Wang, 2010).

Canada is among the low-fertility countries of the world that have seen an increase in child-bearing over the first decade of the twenty-first century. In 2003, there were 21 countries with total fertility rates of 1.3 or lower, but by 2008, there were only 5 such countries (Goldstein et al., 2009). Following on the recession that began in 2008, there have been reductions in fertility, especially in the countries hardest hit economically (Goldstein et al., 2013).

The Canadian upward trend from 2000 to 2008 saw total fertility increase from 1.51 to 1.68, with a subsequent decline to 1.61 (see Table 4.3). In the two largest provinces, Ontario and Quebec, the increase was more pronounced in Quebec. In 2000, the rates were 1.45 in Quebec and 1.49 in Ontario. By 2008, the Ontario rate had increased only to 1.59 while Quebec's rate was 1.74 (Milan, 2013a: 3; Beaujot et al., 2013a: 226). Fertility has also increased in other provinces:

Table 4.3 ▣ Total Fertility Rate, Canada, Provinces and Territories, 1981–2011

Year	NL	PE	NS	NB	QC	ON	MB	SK	AB	BC	YT	NT	NU	Canada
1981	...	1.89	1.62	1.67	1.58	1.58	1.83	2.11	1.86	1.63	2.06	2.88	...	1.65
1986	...	1.80	1.58	1.53	1.38	1.60	1.83	2.02	1.84	1.61	1.96	2.87	...	1.59
1991	1.44	1.86	1.59	1.56	1.65	1.69	1.98	2.05	1.90	1.68	2.17	4.47	...	1.72
1996	1.31	1.74	1.52	1.46	1.61	1.61	1.90	1.91	1.75	1.56	1.70	4.39	...	1.63
2001	1.30	1.55	1.40	1.41	1.50	1.53	1.82	1.90	1.67	1.40	1.57	1.84	3.08	1.54
2002	1.31	1.49	1.38	1.40	1.47	1.48	1.81	1.84	1.69	1.39	1.56	1.89	3.02	1.51
2003	1.33	1.60	1.39	1.43	1.50	1.51	1.82	1.88	1.74	1.42	1.50	2.05	3.09	1.54
2004	1.32	1.58	1.41	1.42	1.50	1.53	1.79	1.86	1.74	1.43	1.63	2.02	2.96	1.55
2005	1.36	1.54	1.40	1.43	1.54	1.54	1.84	1.87	1.74	1.44	1.41	2.07	2.72	1.57
2006	1.41	1.65	1.40	1.48	1.65	1.55	1.89	1.91	1.81	1.47	1.61	2.01	2.82	1.61
2007	1.45	1.63	1.48	1.52	1.68	1.57	1.96	2.03	1.90	1.51	1.58	2.11	2.97	1.66
2008	1.58	1.73	1.54	1.59	1.74	1.59	1.96	2.05	1.92	1.50	1.64	2.08	2.99	1.68
2009	1.59	1.69	1.50	1.59	1.74	1.56	1.98	2.07	1.89	1.50	1.65	2.06	3.26	1.67
2010	1.58	1.62	1.48	1.59	1.71	1.54	1.92	2.03	1.83	1.43	1.60	1.98	3.00	1.63
2011	1.45	1.62	1.47	1.54	1.69	1.52	1.86	1.99	1.81	1.42	1.73	1.97	2.97	1.61

Notes: Births to mothers for whom the age is unknown were prorated. Nunavut is included in the Northwest Territories before 2001. Data by age of mother not available in Newfoundland and Labrador before 1991.

Source: Milan, 2013, p. 6 (Figure 3; Statistics Canada cat. no. 201391-209-X).

Alberta is noteworthy with an increase from 1.66 in 2000 to 1.92 in 2008.

Beaujot and Wang (2010) have suggested that Quebec has followed the Nordic model with supportive family policies, while Alberta has followed the US model where labour-market security tends to prompt higher fertility. Among the factors that are responsible for low fertility, the risks experienced by young people, and women in particular, are especially relevant (McDonald, 2006; see also Bingoly-Liworo and Lapierre-Adamcyk, 2006; Pacaut et al., 2007; Pacaut, 2010). These risks are partly responsible for the delay in family formation. In that context, it is noteworthy that fertility has increased most in Alberta and Quebec—provinces where young families have had the security of either good job opportunities or supportive social policy. Until the recession that began in 2008, the US model of a strong labour market gave young people security that they could find employment even if they took time off to have children. Wheeler (2008) proposes that "children will be born where the jobs are." Trovato (2010) also links the

Alberta trend with the rapid economic growth in the province.

For Quebec, the analysis of trends by generation suggests that the fertility of Quebec women born after 1956 was enhanced by the Quebec policy, starting with the baby bonus program of the 1988–1996 period, and including the subsequent child-care and parental-leave programs (Lapierre-Adamcyk, 2010). Based on a sample of couples with no children with both partners working (from the Canadian Longitudinal Survey of Labour and Income Dynamics) Morency and Laplante (2010) find support for both the economic and policy contexts. For couples who have after-tax incomes in the range of $10,000 to $40,000, the decision to have a first child is affected by the amounts of direct financial assistance available in their province of residence, while higher-income couples are more affected by the generosity of parental leave. In both cases, the security of the woman's employment plays an important role, as do home ownership and the man having access to an employer's pension plan (Laplante et al., 2010, 2011).

Summary

Fertility levels and trends need to be studied in relation to the factors that influence reproduction, starting with the proximate factors (especially union formation and contraception), as well as the economic and cultural values and costs of raising children. At a macro level, the structures of paid and unpaid work, including the associated gender structures, influence both the value and the cost of children, and, consequently, the child-bearing dynamics in society. That is, to understand fertility and its variation, it is important to consider the structure of production and reproduction as a macro-factor at the societal level, and the value and cost of children as micro-factors at the individual level, along with the proximate factors of union formation and contraception.

The first demographic transition changed the value and cost of children since they became dependents rather than producers. Consequently, there is no longer an economic value associated with children, only costs. The costs of children increased further as they became an opportunity cost to employed women. Children have always competed with other demands on the time of adults, but this has been increased systematically with the change in paid work. The economic value and cost of children, however, is clearly an insufficient explanation. In particular, the economic rationale would mean that people should not have children at all (David, 1986).

The non-economic, or cultural, value and costs of children are equally important, and they are also difficult to study. It is clear that most people want children. In a survey in Tunisia, there were two principal answers to a question asking, "Why do people have children?" According to the respondents, children are valued "for support in old age" and because "children are the joy of life" (Beaujot, 1988). In some ways, the Canadian answers are similar. People are not exactly looking for support in old age now that we have extensive pension plans and other benefits for the elderly, but they are looking for "someone who will be there." Especially with marital relationships that have become insecure, there is a desire to have someone in life who represents a close and enduring relationship. Similarly, the joy of children is expressed in a variety of ways, such as the pleasure of seeing children smile, take their first steps, learn new things, develop, and eventually become mature adults with whom one can have a special relationship. In a variety of ways, respondents say that one can experience life more fully with children, including experiencing the unique relationships among children and in the broader family.

Clearly, there are not just values but also non-economic costs. Children are experienced as a heavy responsibility, especially when they are young and completely dependent, but sometimes also when they are older. Children who do not turn out as expected are a source of fundamental frustration and loss. Having a child is a "fateful decision" in the sense that it cannot be reconsidered. A child creates a permanent link to the other parent of the child, and sometimes these are relationships that people would prefer to forget.

That is why, when asked how many children it is best to have, many people, both in Tunisia and in Canada, say something like "not too many and not too few." Not too many because there are significant costs, but not too few to miss out on the experience of children in one's life. It is also seen to be important that spouses agree on these central life questions. For instance, when people were asked, "What if the wife wants more than the husband?" or vice versa, respondents often said to have the smaller number because parents both should want the child.

In the past, higher fertility has depended on the discriminatory treatment of women (Davis, 1984), especially through the separation of economic production and demographic reproduction. The present-day challenge is to devise policies that enhance equality in productive roles while making reproduction possible. It can be argued that the adjustment between production and reproduction has mostly been made to the detriment of the latter (Chesnais, 1987). As we reach for higher standards of living, partly by including most adults of both sexes in the labour force, there is less and less time in our lives for reproduction. Even though reproduction has lost its importance to the economic welfare of individuals, both production and reproduction are obviously important to the long-term welfare of society. At issue is the division of our time between production and reproduction, and the introduction of other changes that will encourage men and women to share in both activities.

As we have seen, the support of the larger society is also important. It would appear that societies are in less danger of particularly low fertility, say 1.3 or lower, if there is state support for families and for gender equality, and if families of various types are accepted (Beaujot and Bélanger, 2001). The societies where fertility is particularly low seem to have a certain rigidity associated with families. In Japan, for example, births outside of marriage are still considered to be illegitimate. Fertility is higher in societies that are more open to cohabitation and to births in cohabiting relationships. A comparison of northern and southern Europe shows that fertility is lower when there are fewer opportunities for part-time work. It would appear that fertility can be sustained in postmodern family settings that include the acceptance of various kinds of families, the de-gendering of child care, and opportunities for both part-time and full-time work.

Policy support is also important. The example of northern Europe suggests that it is not narrow pro-natalist policies that make a difference, but rather having a set of policies that are generally supportive of families, of people's integration into the labour market, and of gender equality (Héran, 2013). Supportive family policy can take various forms, from tax provisions to child benefits and services for families and children. Labour-market integration is important so that people have a sense of security in forming relationships and having children. Assuming that most people want to have jobs and that they also want to have children, this labour-market integration needs various supportive provisions, ranging from parental leaves and child-care facilities, to family-friendly work environments. In terms of gender, we once thought that the only way to boost fertility was to return to a single-breadwinner type of family structure. On the contrary, however, fertility is now particularly low in societies where women have opportunities in education and work but are responsible for most of the child care at home. If they have to choose between opportunities in the workforce and limits in families, many women will find childlessness to be the easiest route to equality.

Critical Thinking Questions

1. Relate the long-term fertility change to the economic and cultural factors underlying the demographic transition.
2. How can the period of the baby boom be interpreted within the context of long-term changes?
3. How does the second demographic transition apply to Canada?
4. Using theoretical and empirical observations, discuss the relation between marital status and child-bearing.
5. What can we conclude from Canadian trends with regard to the relationship between economic change and fertility?
6. What is the relationship between income and fertility? Consider family income, women's income, and men's income separately.
7. How can child-bearing be related to social capital?
8. What generalizations can we make about the relationship between women's workforce participation and fertility? Has it changed over time?
9. Make an assumption about Canada's fertility level in 2030 and defend this assumption.
10. Discuss Canadian policies regarding (1) gender, (2) family, and (3) work in terms of their relevance to fertility levels.

Recommended Readings

Balakrishnan, T.R., Evelyne Lapierre-Adamcyk, and Karol J. Krotki. 1993. *Family and Childbearing in Canada*. Toronto: University of Toronto Press. This is an extensive analysis of the 1984 Canadian Fertility Survey, conducted within the context of changing Canadian families.

Beaujot, Roderic. 2000b. "Les deux transitions démographiques du Québec, 1860–1996." *Cahiers québécois de démographie* 29: 201–30. This article analyzes the demographic transition and the second demographic transition in Quebec, making comparisons to the trends in Ontario.

Charles, Enid. 1948. *The Changing Size of the Family in Canada.* Ottawa: Dominion Bureau of Statistics, Eighth Census of Canada, 1941. This census monograph from 1941 studies especially the differentials in fertility during the demographic transition.

Gauvreau, Danielle, Diane Gervais, and Peter Gossage. 2007. *La fécondité des Québécoises, 1870–1970: d'une exception à l'autre.* Montréal: Les Editions du Boréal. This book uses a variety of data and methods to portray and interpret the exceptionally high fertility in Quebec, which became an exceptionally low fertility.

Hall, David. 2002. "Risk Society and the Second Demographic Transition." *Canadian Studies in Population* 29, no. 2: 173–93. Using the theoretical work of Anthony Giddens and others, Hall argues that the second demographic transition involves a concern about the risks associated with child-bearing.

Henripin, Jacques. 1968. *Tendances et facteurs de la fécondité au Canada.* Ottawa: Dominion Bureau of Statistics. This classic fertility study is based on the 1961 Census and also on earlier vital statistics and census data.

———, and Evelyne Lapierre-Adamcyk. 1974. *La fin de la revanche des berceaux : qu'en pensent les Québécoises?* Montreal: Les Presses de l'Université de Montréal. Based on a 1971 fertility survey, this book shows how quickly fertility patterns changed in Quebec.

———, Paul-Marie Huot, Evelyne Lapierre-Adamcyk, and Nicole Marcil-Gratton. 1981. *Les enfants qu'on n'a plus au Québec.* Montreal: Les Presses de l'Université de Montréal. The subsequent fertility survey in 1976 shows further changes in Quebec fertility, including the adoption of sterilization as a method of contraception.

Milan, Anne. 2013a. "Fertility: Overview, 2009 to 2011." *Report on the Demographic Situation in Canada.* Ottawa: Statistics Canada cat. no. 91-209-X. The section on fertility, from the *Report on the Demographic Situation in Canada*, has up-to-date information on fertility trends and differences.

Romaniuc, Anatole. 1984. *Fertility in Canada: From Baby-boom to Baby-bust.* Ottawa: Statistics Canada cat. no. 91-524. This is a thorough overview of the long-term trends in Canadian fertility, with discussions of causes and implications.

Related Websites

www.statcan.gc.ca/demography. The website of the Demography Division at Statistics Canada carries current information on fertility trends and differences.

www.ippf.org. The International Planned Parenthood Federation links national autonomous family-planning associations in over 180 countries.

www.ppfc.ca. The Planned Parenthood Federation of Canada is an organization dedicated to promoting sexual and reproductive health and rights in Canada and in developing countries.

5 Immigration and the Population of Canada

The Chapter at a Glance

- The history of Canadian immigration can be studied in connection with events happening in Canada and other countries, as well as relations between countries. Globalization has brought a new context to immigration.
- A theoretical understanding of migration needs to consider why people move or do not move, and how they choose their destination when they do move. It is proposed that social factors, including integration in family and community, affect whether people move, and that economic factors are more important in the choice of destination.
- The net balance between immigration and emigration accounted for close to a quarter of population growth in Canada during the twentieth century. From 2001 to 2011, net immigration accounted for about 65 per cent of the country's population growth.
- While immigration contributes considerably to Canadian population growth, it has only a slight influence on the aging of the population. As

demographic change becomes more a function of net migration than of natural increase, there is an increased concentration of population in cities and regions that attract more immigrants.
- The proportion of foreign-born Canadians rose from 15 to 20.6 per cent over the 1951–2011 period.
- Immigration has brought significant ethnic diversity to Canada's population, including, since the mid-1960s, large numbers of arrivals from Asia, Latin America, and Africa.
- Research on the macroeconomic impact of immigration suggests that it has made a small but positive contribution to average income.
- In contrast to earlier cohorts of immigrants, more recent immigrants show more disadvantages in terms of workforce participation and average incomes.
- In sociocultural terms, immigration brings more diversity, growth of visible minorities, and a changed language composition to the disadvantage of French.

Introduction

Immigration is often portrayed as a point of unity across population groups in Canada, with the idea that "we are all immigrants or descendants of immigrants." This immigration is relatively recent for some—who are either immigrants themselves or second generation—whereas for others, this migration dates back to ancestral times. The First Nations population is, of course, an exception to this generalization, with an ancestry on the continent that dates back thousands of years. The original inhabitants of North America

migrated across the Bering Strait from Asia during the Paleolithic era, at least 13,000 to 16,000 years ago (White, 2006).

Among the three demographic processes of mortality, fertility, and migration, the most explicit attempts to influence population trends have occurred in the area of international migration. In effect, discussions of population policy in Canada often limit themselves to questions of immigration. It is not surprising that states pay careful attention to international population movements. The flow of people across international boundaries can affect relations between states, creating either links or conflicts.

Simmons (2010) says that international migration can create a "transnational way of living," as migrants live in a world that has both a "here" and a "there," with many newcomers continuing to live a life in both places. The previous residents of other countries can have specific interests in the political processes of their new countries, and they can attempt to influence the political processes in their countries of origin (Carment and Bercuson, 2008). So it is not surprising that states pay careful attention to questions of international movement of populations, elaborating rules of entry (and sometimes of exit) in order to ensure that the process produces a maximum of benefits. Equally understandable is the deep interest that the public takes in migration questions, for it affects the society in which we live.

Immigration policy is as old as Canada itself; in fact, the original statutes date back to the first two years after 1867 Confederation. Given the fragile beginnings of the country, the federal government was eager for population growth. Particularly pressing was the need to stimulate development in the vast territory of the Canadian West and thus allow for effective sovereignty over these lands. Although the government was committed to encouraging immigration, it was cautious and soon made it clear that not all prospective immigrants would be considered suitable.

Immigration has always been viewed with a certain ambivalence by policy-makers. On the one hand, immigration has been viewed positively, first in nation building, then in promoting economic development, and later in building a multicultural society. On the other hand, the government had concerns about immigrants who used Canada as a passage to the United States, then about immigration undermining the position of labour, and often about the different "stock of people" that prompt a broadening of the very definition of who we were as a society. While government policy over time has attempted to steer a course, sometimes hesitantly, between these conflicting considerations, there has also been a sense that government does not completely control the process. When farmers were sought to settle the West, many

actually became unskilled labourers in Canada's early industries. When specialized skills were sought to fuel the urban industrial expansion of the postwar era, many of the sponsored immigrants were skilled and unskilled labourers (McInnis, 1980). On the refugee side, the control of arrivals has become complex when large numbers make refugee claims from within the country, putting strains on the refugee boards that are seeking to determine which claims are legitimate. Though Canada is geographically removed from the areas of the world that generate refugees, the policies permitting refugees to become permanent immigrants, combined with a humanitarian attitude toward refugees, make Canada an attractive destination for refugees, both political and economic.

The broad policy questions at any one time are (1) What should the level of immigration be? (2) Who should the immigrants be? and (3) How are immigrants to be integrated? Starting with a brief history of immigration trends, policy, and theoretical questions, we will in this chapter consider the demographic, socioeconomic, and sociocultural effects of immigration. We will conclude with discussions of the future of immigration in a globalizing world.

The History of Immigration and Emigration Trends

It is useful to consider why we have immigration at various points of history, and to appreciate this history in relation to Canadian interest, external forces, and political dynamics. Past trends, along with historical phases in these trends, may be described in terms of numbers of immigrants, policy orientation, economic objectives, areas of origin, and areas of destination in Canada. Although the trends in immigration show considerable annual variation, six phases of immigration since 1860 can be considered: 1860–1896, 1897–1913, 1914–1945, 1946–1961, 1962–1988, and 1989 to the present. While these demarcations are somewhat arbitrary, we will pay special attention to government intentions behind immigration, and how this shaped the numbers and characteristics of immigrants, places of origin and destination.

Net Out-Migration, 1860–1896

The first phase, 1860–1896 was a period of net out-migration. As seen in Chapter 2, although large numbers of people immigrated to Canada, even more emigrated. The earlier industrialization of the US economy offered jobs that attracted not only recent immigrants to Canada, but also people born in Canada (Kelley and Trebilcock, 2010). While the estimates remain uncertain, there is agreement that in the years just prior to 1867 Confederation and in the decades to follow, Canada was losing population to its southern neighbour. McInnis (2000a) estimates a total immigration of 892,000 and emigration of 1,891,000, for a net loss of 999,000. While Canada is known as a county of immigration, the four decades from 1861 to 1901 had net out-migration (see also Beaujot and McQuillan, 1982).

The earlier industrialization of the US economy offered employment prospects that attracted both recent immigrants to Canada and persons born in Canada. In addition, dry-farming techniques suitable for the colder climate of Canada's western provinces were not developed until the 1880s. The period surrounding Confederation was a time of depression in international trade, which undermined the markets for Canadian staple products. By 1900, Canada's population was 5,301,000, while that of the United States was 75,994,000, or 14.3 times greater.

The net emigration from Canada was in the context of considerable efforts to enhance immigration. In 1868, one year after Confederation, the Free Grants and Homestead Act sought to increase immigration, especially to the Canadian West. In subsequent years, numerous efforts were made to encourage agriculturalists to immigrate to Canada, including aggressive recruitment in the United Kingdom and Europe. The government entered into various agreements, especially with the railroad companies, for the recruitment, selection, transportation, and establishment of potential agriculturalists. In addition, mining, lumber, and especially railway interests desperately required sturdy labourers willing to accept difficult working conditions and prepared to move to areas where workers were needed. In effect, the period of the mid-1880s to the First World War involved a

deliberate use of immigration as an instrument of industrial development and nation building, including the settlement of the wheat-growing prairies.

In other regards, policy attempted to restrict immigration, and it soon became clear that not all prospective immigrants would be considered suitable. In one of the federal government's earliest pieces of legislation, restrictions were placed on immigrants through the prohibition, among other things, of "the landing of pauper or destitute immigrants in all parts of Canada, until such sums of money as may be found necessary are provided and paid into the hands of one of the Canadian immigration agents" (Beaujot and McQuillan, 1982).

The 1885 Chinese Immigration Act imposed a head tax on prospective Chinese immigrants. At around the same time, the United States, Canada, and Australia all decided that "the Chinese were unassimilable, that they were a positive hindrance to the process of nation-building, and that with few exceptions their immigration should be stopped completely" (Rao et al., 1984: 15). This act was updated several times to restrict the arrival of Chinese workers after the railroads had been built, and was not set aside until 1947.

First Wave of Post-Confederation Immigration, 1897–1913

While the net numbers were negative for the 1891–1901 decade, the turnaround essentially came in 1897, with the numbers of immigrants climbing from 17,000 in 1896 to over 400,000 in 1913. The years 1911–1913 had record numbers that have never since been surpassed (see Figure 5.1). While departures remained important, the gains from 1901 to 1911 more than balanced the net loss of the four previous decades. This followed the improved attractiveness of the Canadian West and the onset of industrialization. Immigrants from the United Kingdom continued to be the largest stream, but there were others, not only from Western and Northern Europe, but also from Southern, Central and Eastern Europe.

The settlement of the Prairie provinces brought a majority whose ethnic origins were neither British

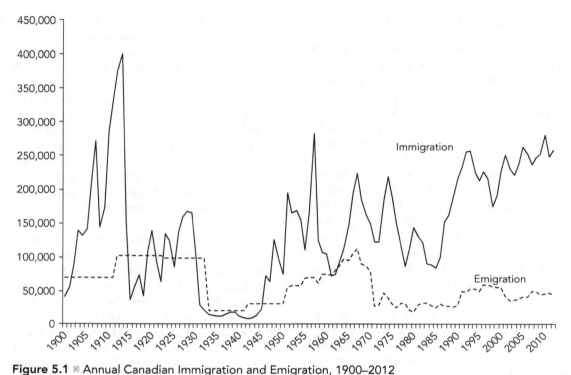

Figure 5.1 ▦ Annual Canadian Immigration and Emigration, 1900–2012

Sources: Beaujot et al., 1989, Dumas, 1990 Figure 1; Statistics Canada, 2013a, CANSIM Tables 051-0009, 051-0004.

nor French. Particular rural areas and towns of the Prairies tended to attract people of a specific origin who established churches and community institutions along ethnic lines. The appointment of Clifford Sifton as minister of the interior in 1896 had brought much energy to the immigration portfolio. Sifton's goal was to promote the arrival of farmers and farm labourers. There were also policies, though, that attempted to restrict immigration. In 1907 and 1908, measures were taken to limit immigration from Japan and India. The Immigration Acts of 1906 and 1910 placed diseased persons as well as those advocating violent political change on the restricted categories. The 1910 Immigration Act allowed the government to introduce regulations on the volume, ethnic origin, and occupational composition of the immigrant flow.

Interlude, 1914–1945

The onset of the First World War brought this period of mass migration to an abrupt end. While

immigration picked up somewhat in the 1920s, the severe economic depression of the 1930s and the Second World War years make the 1914–1945 period somewhat of an "interlude" in immigration. The 1930s saw once again more departures than arrivals. Annual arrivals were under 20,000 from 1933 to 1944. The places of origin were similar to that of the previous period, with the British being by far the largest component, followed by German, Austrian, Scandinavian, and Ukrainian arrivals.

In terms of policy, the 1922 Empire Settlement Act offered assistance in settlement to British subjects. The 1925 railway agreement was especially conducive to the arrival of Central Europeans. There were also exclusions. Amendments to the Immigration Act in 1919 made it possible for non-Canadian strike leaders to be deported, and the prohibited classes were extended to include alcoholics, conspirators, and illiterates (Manpower and Immigration Canada, 1974). These amendments were mostly aimed at excluding persons who had been enemy aliens, but there were also provisions to exclude Doukhobors, Mennonites, and Hutterites on the grounds that their "peculiar customs, habits, modes of life and methods of holding property" made them unlikely "to become readily assimilated" (Simmons, 2010: 56).

While some restrictions were lifted in the 1920s, various categories of immigration were deleted in 1933, and even British subjects were discouraged (Corbett, 1957). The Immigration Act was used in the 1930s to deport persons belonging to the Communist Party of Canada or other persons who had run into trouble with the law, often simply accused of being "public charges" (Avery 1979). The period of the Second World War was also a time of restrictions. Canada did not play a role in admitting refugees fleeing from Nazi Germany. In 1939, the *St Louis*, an ocean liner carrying 907 desperate German Jews, was refused entry into Canada and was forced to return to Europe (Abella and Troper, 1982).

In general, the 1867–1945 period can be seen as involving both the encouragement of immigration and attempts to restrict its flow. Encouragement was strongest in times of economic growth, particularly in 1896–1913 and in the 1920s, while restrictions were strongest in the periods of war and the 1930s. Encouragements tended to focus on British and Northern European immigrants, while non-white arrivals were severely restricted. In the 1920s, there was active opposition to the admission of Ukrainians and others from Eastern Europe on the grounds that this would lead to the balkanization of the country (Simmons, 2010). At the same time, immigrants from Britain were offered inexpensive fares for crossing the Atlantic.

Postwar White Immigration, 1946–1961

The period from 1946 to 1961 can be thought of as a second wave of post-Confederation immigration. While annual arrivals fluctuated considerably, from a low of 64,000 in 1947 to a high of 282,000 in 1957, the total arrivals between 1941 and 1961 amounted to 2.1 million. Although the rate of immigration compared with the total size of the Canadian population was lower than in the 1897–1913 period, and while no single postwar year saw the arrival of as

many people as had come in each of the years from 1911 to 1913, the net migration of 1.25 million persons from 1941–1961 was higher than the comparable figure of 1.12 million net migrants for the 1901–1921 period.

On a year-to-year basis, historical fluctuations in immigration levels followed the path of events both inside and outside the country. There was a spurt right after the war with the arrival of war brides and refugees. After new regulations were in place and the Department of Citizenship and Immigration was established in 1950, immigration was high for the rest of the decade. The high point in 1956–1957 reflects the entry of British subjects escaping the Suez crisis and refugees from the Hungarian revolt. The dip in 1961 coincided with a downturn in the economy.

In policy terms, the end of the Second World War brought considerable uncertainty regarding the appropriate direction for future immigration. In 1944, the Quebec legislative assembly had indicated its opposition to mass immigration. Throughout the country, many argued that priorities should concentrate on the integration of returning soldiers. Others were concerned that Canada might return to the economic situation of the 1930s, for which immigration would be inappropriate. On the other hand, arguments were made that Canada could raise its international stature by helping to rescue persons displaced by the war in Europe (Angus, 1946). In addition, a report to the deputy minister responsible for immigration concluded that a larger population made sense from an economic point of view (Timlin, 1951).

In 1947, then prime-minister Mackenzie King set out the government's policy on immigration in a frequently quoted statement that involved a careful compromise between these divergent concerns. King called for immigration as a support for higher population growth, but cautioned that such immigration should not be in excess of the number that could be advantageously absorbed. While he recognized the obligation to humanity to help those in distress, he clearly indicated that he would not support a massive arrival that would alter the "character of our population." The "character of our population" could mean various things, but it obviously included a desire to continue receiving immigrants mainly from the traditional sources. An important administrative procedure for admissions at this time was the widening of eligibility for sponsored relatives. This was an interesting political solution, since those who had argued for restricted entries could hardly oppose the arrival of relatives. This also assured that immigrants would largely be from the traditional, "preferred" sources—those who already had relatives in Canada. At the same time, gone was the earlier objective of bringing agriculturalists.

This 1947 statement by Mackenzie King is an important point of demarcation, including making reference to the independent (or economic) and family classes of immigrants. Immigration was to serve economic development, build the labour force, strengthen demographic resources, and it was also a humanitarian matter. It is noteworthy that his priority not to change the basic character of our population did not generate any debate in the House of Commons.

The 1953 Immigration Act allowed the government to prohibit the entry of immigrants for a variety of reasons, including nationality, ethnic group, and "peculiar customs, habits, modes of life or methods of holding property." Preference was given to persons of British birth, together with those from France and the United States. Second preference went to persons from Western European countries—if they had the required economic qualifications. Persons from other countries could not enter unless sponsored by a close relative. A small exception involved an arrangement, in force between 1951 and 1962, which allowed for selected arrivals from Asian Commonwealth countries (Hawkins, 1972). Very low limits were set, however: a combined total of 300 people per year from India, Pakistan, and Sri Lanka.

Diversification of Origins, 1962–1988

In his chapter, "Immigration and Nation-Building," Simmons (2010) proposes that the 1867–1960 period can be called "a European nation in the Americas." In the early 1960s, there were rising concerns regarding discrimination on the basis of racial origins. In 1962, the national-origin restrictions to immigration were officially lifted. In 1967, a points system for the

---

Box 5.1 ▪ History of Refugee Arrivals

Refugees have been an important part of immigration to Canada. Starting with the United Empire Loyalists in 1783, various groups of refugees continued to arrive—Quakers, Mennonites, blacks, Doukhobors, Hutterites, Mormons, and Jews in the period before the First World War (Ziegler, 1988). Later, there were displaced persons after the Second World War and refugees from the Hungarian revolution in the mid-1950s and from Czechoslovakia in 1968. In the 1970s, there were the American draft dodgers and deserters, Tibetans, Ugandans of Asian ancestry, Chileans, and Indochinese. In the 1980s, Vietnam, Laos, and Poland comprised a large proportion, whereas during the 1990s, many landings originated from the former Yugoslavia. Into the 2000s, the source countries have become considerably more diversified, with a larger proportion landed from Africa (e.g., Sudan, Ethiopia, Somalia, Congo) as well as Iraq, Iran, Afghanistan, and Colombia.

Migration flows are difficult to estimate for earlier periods, but from 1945 to 1985, the total number of refugees who came to Canada was 564,000, representing about 10 per cent of all arrivals (Nash, 1989: 125–7; Taylor, 1987). Since the 1980s, the Canadian government has carefully documented all refugees arriving in Canada, with an additional 750,000 through to 2010 (Citizenship and Immigration Canada, 2012). Refugees made up 17.7 per cent of arrivals in the 1980s, 14.8 per cent in the 1990s, and the number went down to 11.7 per cent in the first decade of the 2000s. While the total share of immigrant landings varied over the last 30 years, it has generally followed a

selection of independent immigrants was established. This reinforced the non-discriminatory aspects of immigration policy by clearly outlining the education, training, skills and other special qualifications under which immigrants were to be selected. The policy of multiculturalism, promulgated in 1971, underlined an open attitude to the arrival of immigrants from various parts of the world.

There have also been important shifts in the government attitude to immigration. The 1966 White Paper, for instance, was very positive toward immigration: "Without a substantial continuing flow of immigrants, it is doubtful that we could sustain the higher rate of economic growth and the associated cultural development which are essential to the maintenance and development of our national identity" (Taylor, 1987: 3). Just eight years later, the 1974 Green Paper was much more reserved: "When all the arguments are sifted, it would probably be a not unfair assessment of our understanding of the economic consequences of higher against lower population growth rates . . . to conclude that the evidence in favour of higher rates

is uncertain" (Manpower and Immigration Canada, 1974: 6).

Immigration policy was subjected to a thorough review in the period from 1973 to 1975, culminating in the 1976 Immigration Act. The main change introduced by the new Act was the introduction of a target level for immigration, to be set by the minister responsible for immigration. This level is to be determined after consultation with the provinces concerning regional demographic needs and labour market considerations, and after consultation with such other persons, organizations, and institutions as the minister deems appropriate. It is an indication of the importance placed on immigration that the Act requires an annual Statement to Parliament on the federal government's goals with respect to immigration. The 1976 Immigration Act also incorporated the 1951 UN Convention on Refugees. Canada had signed the convention in 1969 and was already obligated to protect people arriving who were found to be refugees, but at the time, few were actually arriving, reaching some 500 per year by 1976.

pattern of decline (from a high of 28 per cent in 1980 to a low of just under 9 per cent in 2010).

Since 1978, the planning of immigration levels has explicitly taken refugees into account. An important change since the mid-1970s has been the numbers of people who have sought refugee status after arriving in Canada. The number rose from some 500 in 1976 to an average of 19,500 over the 1980s and 29,300 in the 1990s (Citizenship and Immigration Canada, 2000). Those who are accepted as refugees are called "refugees landed in Canada." In 2010, this number was down somewhat to 9,041, compared to 7,624 government-assisted refugees (as identified by the United Nations High Commissioner for Refugees), and 4,833 privately sponsored refugees (largely sponsored by humanitarian and church groups), and 3,558 refugee dependants, for a total of 24,696 (Citizenship and Immigration Canada, 2012).

While the international need for asylum is very high, the priority in Canada as of late has been in promoting other types of immigration. In particular, the "economic" class of immigration has increased in importance. In 2010, Canada admitted about 187,000 migrants under the economic class, or roughly two thirds of all immigrants. The corresponding reduction in other classes of immigration has led some to criticize the federal government for an apparent downplaying of its humanitarian tradition of respecting international obligations to the displaced and persecuted (Canadian Council for Refugees, 2013). The UNCHR (2014) estimates that there are more than 10 million refugees who are seeking political asylum in a safe country, with tens of millions of additional persons forcibly displaced from their homes without crossing an international border (referred to as IDPs or "internally displaced persons" by the United Nations).

The 1976 Immigration Act in many regards involved continuity in policy, explicitly affirming the fundamental objectives of Canadian immigration laws, including family reunification, non-discrimination, concerns for refugees, and the promotion of Canada's demographic, economic, and cultural goals. In effect, immigration has been administered through three *classes*. The *independent class* is admitted through the points system, the *family class* gains admission based on a close family connection, and the *refugee class* is administered on the basis of humanitarian concerns.

On an annual basis, the immigrant arrivals increased in the latter half of the 1960s after the establishment of the Department of Manpower and Immigration and the strong economic growth of the period. The peak in 1974 is somewhat artificial since it results from an amnesty program whereby people in the country without landed-immigrant status were admitted even if they did not meet the criteria. The dip in 1983–5 coincided with a downturn in the economy. The increase of the 1986–90 period followed on a deliberate program of "moderate controlled growth" in immigration levels. The total arrivals for the 1961–86 period amount to 3.9 million or an average of 157,000 per year—about 0.7 immigrants per 100 population.

Sustained High Immigration, 1989–Present

There are several bases through which to consider 1989 as the beginning of a new era in immigration. First, the 1988 Canada–United States Trade Agreement (CUSTA) and then the 1992 North American Free Trade Agreement (NAFTA) placed Canada in a new relationship with the United States and Mexico, including a more open and competitive economy. Second, as has been seen since the early 1990s, there is no longer a reduction of immigration when unemployment is high. This was not true of earlier recessions (e.g., the deep recession of the early 1980s), when reduced immigration resulted from difficult economic times. More recently, this has not been the practice of the federal government. With the economic recession of the early 1990s, as well as the economic downturn in 2008–2009, immigration

targets were not reduced. Third, the immigrant arrivals have been sustained at levels that are high compared to all historical periods except 1910–13. Fourth, there is increasing emphasis on the economic class of immigrants, and also on the admission of temporary workers. Since 2004, the number of temporary residents has increased substantially, including foreign workers, foreign students, and refugee claimants, all of whom have access to temporary work permits.

Immigration numbers in the period before the First World War showed the four consecutive years of 1910–13 with levels above 200,000, while all but 2 of the 22 years between 1990 and 2011 saw these levels. The total numbers over the 1986–2011 period amount to 5.9 million, or an average annual arrival of 237,000, representing 0.8 immigrants per 100 population. Immigration policies have sought to attract highly skilled immigrants, but there are also migrant-worker programs bringing increasing numbers of temporary workers for unskilled and short-term skilled jobs. The changes since the mid-1990s have focused on cost recovery in the administration of immigrant arrivals, more refined selection within each class, and a higher proportion of the independent class—while the family and refugee classes have remained relatively stable in terms of total numbers (see Box 5.2).

The adaptations that have been made to the points system in the early part of the twenty-first century have focused less on specific occupational qualifications, with more emphasis on education, skilled trades, work experience, and knowledge of the official languages, in attempts to bring workers who have transferrable skills. With the introduction of the 2001 Immigration and Refugee Protection Act, the federal government encouraged a larger involvement of the provinces in the selection of immigrants and in the arrival of temporary workers, including the introduction of a provincial nominee program.

The last two decades have also been the period during which immigration began to account for a significantly larger proportion of population growth. While in the 1951–91 period, net migration accounted for about a quarter of population growth, it made up about 60 per cent of growth in 1991–2011. At the

Box 5.2 ▣ Planned and Actual Immigration Levels

Given that the period since 1978 has seen deliberate planning of immigration levels, it is worth taking note of the planned levels and their components (see Table 5.1). The middle range of planned levels increased from 100,000 in 1979 to 135,000 in 1981, then declined to 87,500 in 1985, and rose to 170,000 in 1990 and to 250,000 in 1992–1994. From the late 1990s through to the present, targets have remained relatively high, declining slightly to 212,500 in 1998–2001, before rising to 232,500 in 2003–2005, and even higher to 252,500 in 2007–2012.

Table 5.1 ▣ Immigrants, Planned and Actual Numbers, Showing Immigration Classes, 1979–2012

Year	Planned Number	Family	% Total	Economic	% Total	Refugees	% Total	Others	% Total	Total	%
1979	100,000									112,093	
1980	120,000	49,441	34.5	46,431	32.4	40,658	28.3	6,969	4.9	143,499	100
1981	130,000–140,000	50,534	39.2	56,702	44.0	15,062	11.7	6,495	5.0	128,794	100
1982	130,000–135,000	50,187	41.4	51,148	42.2	17,002	14.0	2,994	2.5	121,331	100
1983	105,000–110,000	48,987	54.8	24,186	27.1	14,064	15.7	2,140	2.4	89,377	100
1984	90,000–95,000	44,593	50.3	26,097	29.5	15,556	17.6	2,353	2.7	88,599	100
1985	85,000–90,000	39,355	46.7	26,113	31.0	16,769	19.9	2,102	2.5	84,339	100
1986	105,000–115,000	42,470	42.8	35,837	36.1	19,199	19.3	1,835	1.8	99,341	100
1987	115,000–125,000	53,796	35.4	74,100	48.7	21,466	14.1	2,666	1.8	152,128	100
1988	125,000–135,000	51,397	31.8	80,221	49.7	26,740	16.6	3,172	2.0	161,530	100
1989	150,000–160,000	60,939	31.8	90,141	47.1	36,865	19.2	3,570	1.9	191,515	100
1990	165,000–175,000	74,367	34.4	95,638	44.2	36,101	16.7	10,315	4.8	216,421	100
1991	220,000	85,949	36.9	80,007	34.4	35,880	15.4	30,936	13.3	232,772	100
1992	250,000	96,797	38.0	82,285	32.3	37,024	14.5	38,752	15.2	254,858	100
1993	250,000	110,445	43.0	95,653	37.3	24,895	9.7	25,771	10.0	256,764	100
1994	250,000	93,718	41.8	96,574	43.0	19,750	8.8	14,352	6.4	224,394	100
1995	190,000–215,000	77,228	36.3	100,910	47.4	27,763	13.0	6,970	3.3	212,871	100
1996	195,000–220,000	68,320	30.2	120,282	53.2	28,342	12.5	9,108	4.0	226,052	100
1997	195,000–220,000	59,959	27.8	125,471	58.1	24,134	11.2	6,466	3.0	216,030	100
1998	200,000–225,000	50,886	29.2	94,974	54.5	22,700	13.0	5,612	3.2	174,172	100
1999	200,000–225,000	55,272	29.1	105,463	55.5	24,378	12.8	4,831	2.5	189,944	100
2000	200,000–225,000	60,613	26.6	136,282	59.9	30,091	13.2	469	0.2	227,455	100
2001	200,000–225,000	66,786	26.6	155,716	62.1	27,916	11.1	219	0.1	250,637	100
2002	210,000–235,000	62,287	27.2	137,863	60.2	25,113	11.0	3,785	1.7	229,048	100
2003	220,000–245,000	65,120	29.4	121,046	54.7	25,983	11.7	9,200	4.2	221,349	100
2004	220,000–245,000	62,272	26.4	133,746	56.7	32,686	13.9	7,119	3.0	235,823	100
2005	220,000–245,000	63,373	24.2	156,313	59.6	35,775	13.6	6,781	2.6	262,242	100
2006	225,000–255,000	70,515	28.0	138,249	54.9	32,499	12.9	10,377	4.1	251,640	100
2007	240,000–265,000	66,240	28.0	131,244	55.4	27,954	11.8	11,315	4.8	236,753	100
2008	240,000–265,000	65,581	26.5	149,068	60.3	21,858	8.8	10,738	4.3	247,245	100
2009	240,000–265,000	65,205	25.9	153,492	60.9	22,850	9.1	10,627	4.2	252,174	100
2010	240,000–265,000	60,222	21.5	186,920	66.6	24,697	8.8	8,852	3.2	280,691	100
2011	240,000–265,000	56,445	22.7	156,121	62.8	27,872	11.2	8,310	3.3	248,748	100
2012	240,000–265,000										

Sources: Citizenship and Immigration Canada, 1999, 2000, 2012.

These ups and downs in planned levels have historically been influenced by labour-market conditions and the general state of the Canadian economy. For example, the reduction in planned levels in the 1983–1985 period was due to an economic recession, which was followed by a policy of moderate controlled growth in immigration levels. Yet breaking away from this tendency have been the sustained high targets that have characterized Canada over the last 20 years, even during economic-downturn periods. This was the situation with the recession of the early 1990s, just as it has been true with the most recent economic downturn in late 2008–2009. Immigration targets have remained high despite difficult economic times and a less-than-robust labour market.

Consistent with the federal government's stated goal of creating an immigration system that is more responsive to the Canadian economy and potential workforce needs, the economic class has been prioritized over recent years. For example, the economic class, as a percentage of all immigrants, has risen from a low of only about 30 per cent of all immigrants in the early 1980s to 62.8 per cent in 2011. Conversely, over this same period, both the family class and refugee classes have declined, to 22.7 and 11.2 per cent, respectively.

conclusion of this chapter, we will return to other features that are unique in the current immigration phase. In particular, communication, exchanges, and trade in a globalizing world are all on the upswing, along with more movement of people and, consequently, more diversity. Globalization tends to elicit winners and losers, and the glaring disparities in standards of living around the world are themselves a leading cause of migration. Migration is less permanent and less managed than previously, and more third parties, including traffickers, lawyers, private institutions, and humanitarian organizations, become involved in the migration process.

Most recently, the federal government's 2012 Economic Action Plan prominently featured immigration as a key area of reform, following legislative amendments under Bill C-38, the Jobs, Growth and Long-Term Prosperity Act. These changes reaffirmed Canada's commitment to high immigration targets while prioritizing labour-force shortages and the need for a flexible immigration system that can best meet Canada's economic needs. The explicit assumption underlying this government policy is that immigration "can address labour market shortages and strengthen economic growth" (Kenney, 2012: 2).

Theoretical Understandings of Migration

On both empirical and theoretical grounds, it is harder to make generalizations about migration than about the other demographic processes of mortality and fertility. One empirical generalization seems to be that higher levels of immigration tend to be linked to higher levels of emigration, partially due to the simple fact that a substantial proportion of all emigration is the return migration of immigrants (Beaujot and Rappak, 1989; Michalowski and Tran, 2008). When there is more movement, it will occur in all directions, including onward to other destinations or back to the place of origin. Looking at emigration from Canada, especially to the United States, and immigration to Canada, Zhao and colleagues' study, "Knowledge Workers on the Move" (2000), concludes that people with higher socioeconomic status are generally more prone to migrate because they have more opportunities. As well, young adults and people at other times of life-course transitions are more prone to migrate.

Though it is very difficult to theorize about migration because there are many factors, it is useful to start with what might be called a natural tendency not to move. At the international level, it is noteworthy that about 97 per cent of the world population is living in their country of birth (United Nations, 2006). Staying represents integration with family and friends (Goldscheider, 1971). Questions of integration are consistent with the observation that people who have moved once are more likely to move again and that return migration is a common phenomenon (Aydemir and Robinson, 2006). The importance of social integration is also consistent with chain migration—that is, people who knew each other before they emigrated tend to follow one another to the same destination.

It could be further proposed that life-course and social factors are more important in determining whether or not people move, while economic factors are more important for the choice of destination. People move especially at stages of the life course that involve disruptions, such as leaving home, finishing school, finding a job, starting or ending a relationship, or retiring. Whether or not people move also depends on how comfortable or integrated they are in a given location. Once people are prone to move, their destination is determined by economic factors or, more broadly, by the push and pull factors. When a person is settled, especially in a two-income family with children, a higher salary at a different location will not necessarily induce them to move. But when people are looking for a first job or an early-career advancement, a higher salary may prompt them to move, especially if they see other opportunities at the place of destination.

At the micro level, then, we theorize that social and life-course questions associated with the extent of integration in family and community are more responsible for whether or not people move, and economic questions are more responsible for the choice of destination when people do migrate. At the macro level, there would be movement toward locations that provide greater potential for integration, both economically and socially. Besides these push and pull factors, there are barriers, in the form of lack of information, difficulty of communication, cost of transportation, and distance.

For international migration, the factors to consider include the opportunities for social and economic integration at the place of origin and the destination, along with links and barriers between countries, including policy barriers. Levels of immigration are clearly a result both of things happening in Canada and of other things happening outside the country, along with the links and barriers between countries—both in the short and long term (Simmons, 2010).

In "Migration in Historical Perspective," William McNeill (1984) proposes that we can distinguish four forms of pre-modern migration around the world: radical displacement of one population by another, conquest leading to a symbiosis between two previously diverse groups, infiltration by outsiders with some acceptance on the part of the original population, and importation of populations that have been forcibly uprooted. These migration patterns took place in pre-modern civilizations, where there were small ruling groups, a variety of population groups, and often a division of labour along ethnic lines. McNeill further proposes that the nineteenth-century European ideal of homogeneous populations corresponds neither to the civilizations of the past nor to those that can be envisaged by modern states. Instead, he proposes that civilizations mostly include multi-ethnicity and pluralism.

In *The Age of Migration*, Castles and Miller (2009) argue that international migration is a constant in human history and that population movements accompany demographic growth and technological change, as well as political conflict and warfare. Over the last five centuries, they propose that mass migrations have played a major role in colonialism, industrialization, the emergence of nation-states, and the development of the capitalist world market. They also suggest that international movements have never been as significant as today, linking these high levels of movement to the greater inequality across countries, and to transnational networks and cultural interchange.

In their theoretical synthesis, Massey and colleagues (1994) propose that globalization creates both mobile populations as a result of various economic displacements, and a demand for labour in the largest cities. With communication links, family and other networks, migratory exchanges are perpetuated between places of origin and destinations (Boyd and Nowak, 2011; Fong et al., 2013). Consequently, recent migrants are concentrated in large cities. In Canada, this means Toronto, Montreal, Vancouver, Calgary, and Ottawa-Gatineau (Statistics Canada, 2013e).

In modern times, the differential levels of development over space, and the population pressures associated with the demographic transition, have brought further movement of peoples. As Europe was undergoing its demographic transition, with the associated population growth, there was significant displacement within countries, principally urbanization, but also movement of the "surplus" European population to other continents (Zelinsky, 1971). If we characterize the world as consisting of a North and a South, until about 1950, there was more movement from the North to the South, with Europeans settling not only in North America and Australia, but also in Africa, Asia, and South America. Over the nineteenth century, 54 million people crossed the Atlantic (Coleman, 2009). From the sixteenth century to the early twentieth century, the demographic expansion of Europe changed the face of other continents, sometimes almost replacing the indigenous populations, as in North America.

Since the 1950s, the continents of the South have been undergoing demographic expansion, and the associated population pressures have brought a net movement from South to North. Once again, development is bringing migration, including urbanization and movement beyond national borders. Such movements of people are occurring at a time of greater effective resistance to immigration on the part of the populations in many receiving countries—this in a world that has few "empty spaces." But there is also an interest in taking advantage of these arrivals in terms of productivity and innovation.

Over the twentieth century, the greatest international movements have occurred in two periods of globalization, first in the early part of the century, and then in its later half. In between, through two World Wars and a Great Depression, there was retrenchment.

Migration has always brought a transformation of the ethnic composition of populations. For Canada, the wave of migrations during the early twentieth century brought not only British and French, but also other Western, Northern, then Eastern and Southern Europeans. While these arrivals were almost entirely white, there was visible diversity in language, dress, and customs, including differentials in settlement patterns. In today's globalized world, the movement has come to be dominated by Asians, but it includes peoples from all parts of the South, with diversities that are more visible along ethnic lines. In all of these cases, the movements bring transformations of ethnic composition. Coleman (2006) has aptly characterized the change as another demographic transition, resulting this time from immigration and ethnic composition rather than a change in deaths and births.

In the *sending countries*, the demographic transition, especially the phase of rapid population growth, produces pressure for emigration. Given this out-migration pressure, the medium term will see no shortage of people who want to come to Canada, and these outside pressures are probably increasing (Hatton and Williamson, 2003; United Nations, 2011a). Development itself, which is clearly associated with the demographic transition, brings various displacements as economic change undermines traditional forms of livelihood, especially in rural areas. So, it is understandable why emigration pressure from Europe started in Northern Europe over a century ago, then later came from Eastern Europe and in the postwar period from Southern Europe. As these populations entered the third phase of the demographic transition, along with stable urban economies with high standards of living, the out-migration pressure lessened. World patterns of migration are now dominated by the development, displacement, and out-migration pressure from the Third World.

These theoretical ideas for interpreting international migration suggest that migration can be beneficial to the sending country by reducing the emigration pressure and to the receiving country by helping it build the desired kind of society. At the same time, departures can undermine the availability of skills at places of origin and an excess in arrivals can bring conflicts at the place of destination. The balance between these negatives and positives requires continuous study in the context of changing circumstances. This analysis is complicated by the micro-level situation where migrants themselves largely benefit from increased opportunities, as long as they are making free decisions based on proper knowledge.

Demographic Impact of Immigration

The demographic objectives, as stated in federal legislation, relate to population size, rate of growth, structure, and geographic distribution. We will first address the demographic questions, namely population growth, age structure, and geographic distribution. In subsequent sections, we will discuss the socioeconomic and sociocultural aspects of immigration.

Population Growth

The basic trends in immigration have been reviewed above (see Figure 5.1). We should observe here that the two post-Confederation surges of immigration came when the rate of growth of the native-born labour force had slowed considerably. The 1897–1913 wave made up for the emigration losses of the depressed post-Confederation era, and the 1946–1960 arrivals compensated for the small proportions of young adults in the 1950s that resulted from the decline of fertility in the 1930s. Similarly, the higher numbers from the 1990s to 2012 were occurring during an era when the labour force was growing less rapidly.

The effect of immigration on past population growth in Canada can be examined from three different perspectives: the direct effect of migration on population growth, the effect of children born to immigrants, and the proportion of people in Canada who are foreign born. Annual population estimates provide a summary measure of the *direct effect* of immigration on population growth. This measure includes only arrivals and departures, or the first generation of immigrants. Throughout the twentieth century, the total immigration of some 12.9 million people and emigration of some 6.1 million people produced a net gain of over 6.8 million, representing just over one quarter of population growth (see Table 5.2). The contribution of net international migration to population growth varied considerably over history, reaching a peak in the 1901–11 decade when it accounted for 44.1 per cent, down to a low of –8.1 per cent during the 1930s, when Canada was losing more population through emigration than it was receiving through immigration (see Table 5.2). During the 1950s and '60s, net migration accounted for just under 20 per cent of growth, whereas during the 1970s and '80s, its contribution more than doubled, to about 40 per cent. During the early 1990s, the relative importance of immigration increased even further, up to over half of all growth: on an annual basis since 1994, net migration has made up a larger proportion of total population growth than natural increase (Bélanger, 2002: 10). From 2001 to 2011, over 2.4 million immigrants landed in Canada, whereas roughly 400,000 emigrants left, suggesting that roughly two thirds of all growth can be tied to international migration.

The direct effects of immigration and emigration can also be appreciated from a comparison to the base population. In particular, it is useful to compute the average annual levels per 100 people in the Canadian population (see Figure 5.2). In the period around the beginning of the twentieth century, there was an average of 2.46 annual arrivals per 100 population. The 1950s had levels very close to 1 per 100 of the receiving population. The decades since 1971 have seen annual arrivals in the order of 0.52 to 0.76 per 100 of base population, and departures in the order of 0.11 to 0.18 per 100. From 1971 to 2011, immigration averaged 0.66 per 100 of the base population, and emigration averaged to 0.14 per 100, for a net migration of 0.52 per 100 Canadians.

The second approach to estimating the demographic effect of immigration includes the contribution

Table 5.2 ▣ Immigration, Emigration and the Contribution of Net International Migration to Canada's Population Growth, 1851–2011

	Population (end of period)	Immigration	Average Immigration (per 100 persons)	Emigration[1]	Contribution of Net International Migration to Growth[2] %
1851	2,523,000				
1851–61	3,230,000	352,000	1.22	170,000	25.7
1861–71	3,689,000	260,000	0.75	410,000	−32.7
1871–81	4,325,000	350,000	0.87	404,000	−8.5
1881–91	4,833,000	680,000	1.49	826,000	−28.7
1891–01	5,371,000	250,000	0.49	380,000	−24.2
1901–11	7,207,000	1,550,000	2.46	740,000	44.1
1911–21	8,788,000	1,400,000	1.75	1,089,000	19.7
1921–31	10,376,700	1,200,000	1.25	970,000	14.5
1931–41	11,506,700	149,000	0.14	241,000	−8.1
1941–51	14,009,400	548,000	0.43	379,000	6.8
1951–61	18,238,200	1,531,838	0.95	645,512	21.0
1961–71	21,962,032	1,432,022	0.71	903,868	14.2
1971–81	24,819,915	1,439,808	0.62	297,572	41.6[3]
1981–91	28,037,420	1,383,379	0.52	283,226	42.4
1991–01	31,019,020	2,235,494	0.76	538,916	54.5
2001–11	34,483,975	2,456,333	0.75	422,283	67.5

1 The emigration time series is revised to include the returning emigrant component from 1971 onward and the temporary emigrant component from 1991 through current.

2 Includes the impact of immigration – all the emigration components + from 1971 onwards any change in the number of non-permanent residents in Canada. These estimates do not include any accomodation for the residual term in Statistics Canada's time series.

3 This calculation, from 1971 onwards, includes net change in non-permanent residents (numbers not shown here)

Sources: Beaujot and Rappak, 1989; Statistics Canada, 2003: CANSIM Table 051.004; author's calculations.

of *births to immigrants* on population growth. If we apply birth and death rates observed over the 1951–81 period to the 1951 population, the population would have grown from 14 million in 1951 to 20.4 million in 1981 (Le Bras, 1988: 9). Since the 1981 population was 24.3 million, this implies that 38 per cent of the actual growth was due to immigration and births to these immigrants over those 30 years. Using the "counter-factual" scenario of no international migration from 1951 to 2001, Denton and colleagues (2001) arrive at a 2001 population of 22.2 million, which is 28.5 per cent less than the actual

population of 31.1 million in that year. This implies that 51.5 per cent of the growth from 14.0 million to 31.1 million, over the 1951–2001 period, was due to the direct and indirect effects of international migration.

This indirect effect of immigration is affected by the *relative vital rates* of the foreign-born and Canadian-born populations. Various analyses conclude that the foreign-born Canadians have a slight advantage in health and mortality (e.g., Chen et al., 1996; Trovato, 1998; Ng et al., 2011). This advantage appears to decline over time, pointing to selection

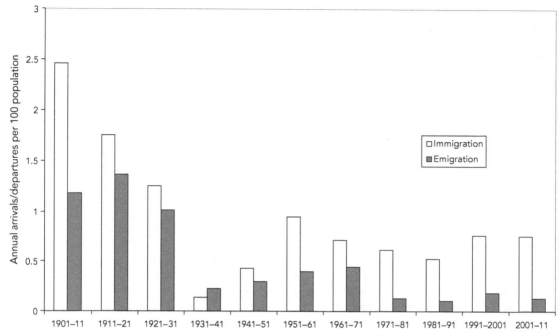

Figure 5.2 ▣ Average Annual Immigration and Emigration, per 100 Mid-Decade Population, Canada, 1901-2011

Sources: Beaujot and Rappak, 1989; Statistics Canada, 2003; Statistics Canada, 2013a, CANSIM Table 051.004; authors' calculations.

factors. In terms of fertility, the Canadian pattern largely shows lower fertility for the foreign born until the 1981 Census and higher fertility since the early 1980s (Bélanger and Gilbert, 2003; Woldemicael and Beaujot, 2012). Using data from the 1991 Census for instance, Ng and Nault (1996) find that foreign-born women who came to Canada between 1986 and 1991 had a higher current fertility than those who immigrated in earlier years. Without the fertility question in the census since 1991, and given the difficulty of using vital statistics to measure fertility of immigrants, Bélanger and Gilbert (2003) and Malenfant and Bélanger (2006) have used the own-children method. For the 2001 Census the total fertility rate of first-generation Canadians is estimated at 1.8, compared to 1.4 for the second generation and 1.5 for the third generation or higher (Bélanger and Gilbert, 2003). Using the 1996 and 2001 Census fertility is

found to be higher for the visible-minority population as a whole, with considerable variation across specific groups (Malenfant and Bélanger, 2006). Data from Quebec over the 1976–95 period indicate strong differences in fertility, with an average of 1.5 births per woman for the Canadian-born women and 2.5 for the foreign-born women (Tossou, 2002: 114).

The third approach to studying the effects of immigration on the population is to consider the *proportion of foreign born* in the census data (e.g., Badets and Chui, 1994; Statistics Canada, 2013c). This figure has increased slowly from 15 per cent in the 1951 Census to about 1 in 5 (20.6 per cent) in the 2011 National Household Survey (Statistics Canada, 2013c). The 1971 Census determined that 33.8 per cent of people were either foreign born or had at least one foreign-born parent (Kalbach and McVey, 1979: 179), whereas Edmonston (1996) calculates, using

Box 5.3   Emigration

The demographic effect of immigration clearly depends on emigration and the proportion of immigrants who stay in Canada. The subsequent departure of immigrants is an important aspect of international migration. Why do some immigrants end up returning to their homeland or migrating again to a third country?

Departures may follow a failure either on the part of the immigrant to adapt or on the part of the receiving society to integrate its newest members from abroad. It could, however, also follow the successful accomplishment of the immigrant's objective and it may have been part of his or her original plan. Conditions may also change, either in the host or sending country. Return migration, for instance, may become more attractive when a person is approaching retirement. Migrants have ties to their places of origin, and modern means of communication and travel make it easier to retain these ties. Partly for this reason, the overall relationship between immigration and emigration is positive. That is, higher levels of immigration are paired with higher levels of emigration.

Especially in a globalizing world, it is an outdated notion to think of immigrants as settlers who never look back after making a fresh start in their chosen country. Emigration is the component of population change that is subject to the most uncertainty (Statistics Canada, 2012g). What is known of emigration is that it tends to be quite selective (as is immigration), as persons who leave Canada tend to be more highly educated than other Canadians and do quite well economically in their new country (Michalowlski and Tran, 2008). The United States appears to be the most important recipient of emigrants, although return migration of emigrants across a wide variety of countries is also important. Dumont and Lemaitre (2005) estimate that roughly 1.1 million people who report Canada as their place of birth are living elsewhere in the OECD, with roughly 4 out of 5 of these emigrants living in the United States. Yet these figures do not include the substantial number of people born outside Canada, immigrating to Canada, and subsequently either returning to their homeland or migrating again to a third country.

In Statistics Canada's population estimates, "emigrants" are people who have taken up long-term residence in another country, especially by declaring that they are not Canadian residents for the purposes of income tax. Some of these emigrants subsequently return to Canada (returning Canadians) and are again difficult to enumerate because they have a right to return without going through immigration procedures. These returning emigrants cannot be called immigrants and therefore are entered separately in the population equation. In addition, a small number of Canadians are living "temporarily abroad" without any intention to permanently emigrate. Any change in this latter number is estimated and is subsequently accounted for in Statistics Canada's system of demographic accounts as "net temporary emigration" (see Appendix A at the end of this text). These difficulties of estimation need to be taken into account when one interprets the emigration levels shown in Table 5.2 and Figure 5.2. From 1951 to 2011, emigration amounted to about 30 per cent of immigration (see Table 5.2).

births and deaths data, that over the 1951–91 period about 35 per cent of the Canadian population was first or second generation, and about half were in the first three generations. The 2011 NHS, which asked the "birthplace of parents," found that 20.6 per cent were foreign born, 17.4 per cent were Canadian born with at least one foreign-born parent—or in other words, 38 per cent of the Canadian population were first or second generation (Statistics Canada, 2013c). The contribution of immigration to Canada's population growth remains high, as almost 4 in 10 Canadians are either immigrants themselves or the children of immigrants (first or second generation), with over half in the first three generations.

Box 5.4 ▣ Temporary Immigrants?

If immigrants are people who move to a new country, then the very concept of the "temporary immigrant" does not make sense. In effect, visitors and others who are in a country for a short time have not been traditionally counted as part of a census population. Yet since the 1991 Census, Canada has counted not only Canadian citizens and landed immigrants, but also *non-permanent residents* (NPRs). Briefly, NPRs can almost be thought of as a type of temporary immigrant, as they are lawfully in Canada, yet only with a temporary residency permit, and are typically expected to leave when their authorization or permit expires.

In Canada, NPRs are regulated by the Immigration and Refugee Protection Act (2001). These people are predominantly persons on temporary work permits, foreign students, and what Citizenship and Immigration Canada broadly refers to as the "humanitarian population" (i.e., refugee claimants and temporary residents who are allowed to remain in Canada on humanitarian grounds). Statistics Canada (2013d) has estimated the number of NPRs living in Canada, which has risen quite noticeably, from roughly 85,000 in the early 1970s up to about 700,000 in 2012 (see Figure 5.3). After a temporary peak of about 400,000 in 1990, the

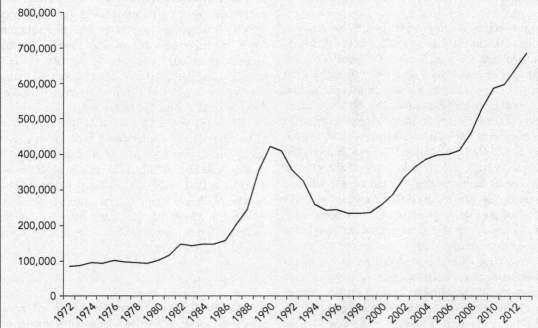

Figure 5.3 ▣ Number of Non-permanent Residents Living in Canada, 1971–2012

Source: Statistics Canada, 2013c, CANSIM Table 051-0020.

Continued

total number dipped to about 250,000 before climbing again quite noticeably over the first decade of the twenty-first century. A large part of this increase has been growth in the number of foreign workers employed by Canadian companies, including many admitted under Canada's Temporary Foreign Worker Program.

In 1996, only about 140,000 people were authorized to work temporarily in Canada, a figure that has more than tripled since, to over 446,000 in 2011 (Citizenship and Immigration Canada, 2012). The underlying government policy that explains this growth is one that "theoretically" is meant to assist employers who face immediate skills and labour shortages. Foreign workers can obtain permits to work in

Canada in order to fill workforce gaps temporarily when Canadian citizens are not available to do the job. In other words, employers are expected to demonstrate the need for temporary workers (i.e., an absence of Canadians able or willing to do the job), whereas workers come to Canada with the understanding that they are expected to leave voluntarily when no longer needed. While this can be considered advantageous to the Canadian economy, it can be particularly challenging for the migrants who have longer-term horizons. As some critics have pointed out, the problem of finding a new job does not disappear, it is merely transferred outside Canada to the home country of the migrant worker (Simmons, 2010; Foster, 2013).

Immigration and Future Population Growth

Population projections provide another useful way in which to assess the demographic effect of immigration. Holding the total fertility rate constant at 1.7 births per woman (which is only slightly higher than the 2011 rate of 1.61 births), projections indicate that an annual immigration of about 200,000 a year will be more than sufficient to avoid population decline over the long term (Beaujot and Matthews, 2000; Dion et al. 2010). With lower natural increase, immigration will play a larger role in future population growth. This can be demonstrated by examining a series of scenarios that accompanied Statistics Canada's 2010 round of population projections, in demonstrating the sensitivity of these projections to alternative assumptions on immigration (see Figure 5.4).

Working with the medium growth scenario (2009 base year), four separate projections were generated, all including a constant fertility rate of 1.7 births per woman and moderate gains in life expectancy (up to 84 years for males and 87.3 for females, by 2036). The migration assumptions involved the following: zero immigration (2009–61), low immigration (at about 6 immigrants per

1,000 Canadians annually), medium immigration (a continuation of current levels at 7.5 immigrants per 1,000) and high immigration (up to 9 per 1,000). Translating these rates into immigration levels, the medium scenario would mean 250,000 immigrants in 2011 and 400,000 in 2061; the low scenario implies levels of 200,000 in 2011 and 250,000 in 2061; and the high scenario implies 300,000 in 2011 and 700,000 in 2061.

These projections demonstrate the importance of immigration to population growth, with population projections by 2061 of 47.6 million, 52.6 million, and 58.2 million, respectively. Over the 30 years from 1981 to 2011, Canada's population grew by about 40 per cent; in comparison, the low, medium, and high scenarios imply growth of 20, 30, and 36 per cent, respectively, in the next 30 years (Statistics Canada, 2010c).

Age Structure

It is often thought that immigration will be a solution to population aging; that is, that young immigrants in the labour force will pay the social security costs of an aging society, especially the costs of health care and pensions. One of the main conclusions of the Review of

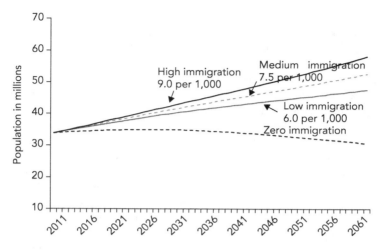

Figure 5.4 ▣ Projected Canadian Population under Different Immigration Scenarios, Medium Growth, 2009–2061

Source: Statistics Canada, 2010c.

Demography and its Implications for Economic and Social Policy (1989), however, was that immigration has a modest effect on the age structure. The greying of the population will continue regardless of the level of immigration. It has also been pointed out that the age structure of foreign-born Canadians is older than that of the Canadian-born population. It has sometimes been concluded from this comparison that immigration ages the population. This comparison, however, does not take into account that children born to immigrants are counted with the Canadian-born population, and so the two age structures cannot be compared fairly.

There are several studies that have demonstrated that variation in immigration levels has a small impact on age structure without ignoring its importance when it comes to the rate of overall population growth (Loh and George, 2007; Guillemette and Robson, 2006). The effect of immigration on the age structure can be appreciated by comparing the median age of immigrants on arrival to that of the Canadian population. The median age of immigrants was relatively stable, averaging 25 years for each year between 1956 and 1976, then increasing to 30 years in 1994–1999 and 31 by 2008 (Beaujot and Rappak, 1989; Citizenship and Immigration, 2012). The median age of the entire Canadian population has changed much more, rising

from 26.3 in 1961 to almost 39.4 in 2008. In effect, the median age of arriving immigrants was one to two years younger than that of the receiving population in 1961, compared to eight to nine years younger by 2008. Both immigrant arrivals and the receiving population have been aging, but arrivals remain younger on average. The overall effect, however, is minimal given that immigrant arrivals represent a small part of the total population.

Other demographic phenomena, including the movement of the baby boom through the age structure, lower fertility, and mortality reductions at older ages, have a larger effect on the age structure than the arrival of immigrants. Other measures confirm that immigration has only a small effect on the age structure. For instance, simulating population change after 1951 as a function only of births and deaths produces a 1981 population with an average age that is only 0.5 years older than the actual average observed in that year. Stated differently, the 1951–1981 immigration reduced the average age of the 1981 population by half a year (Le Bras, 1988: 12). Another example: with no international migration over the 1951–2001 period, the median age in 2001 would have been only 0.8 years older than it actually was (Denton et al., 2001).

Similar results have been obtained with population projections. Consider the four separate projections discussed above, for example (with zero, low, medium, and high immigration). Immigration is important to population growth, yet an inspection of projected age structure demonstrates the relatively modest impact on population aging. Relative to the medium immigration scenario, with a projected median age of 43.6 years in 2036, the high-immigration scenario had a median age roughly one year younger, whereas the low-immigration scenario had a median roughly one year older. With the extreme of zero migration, median age would be only about two years older in 2036.

Geographic Distribution

Immigration, and to a lesser extent the subsequent internal migration of foreign-born Canadians, has an important effect on the geographic distribution of Canada's population. The regional inequalities in demographic growth are becoming accentuated as immigration becomes the principal component of change. Figure 5.5 shows that Ontario and British Columbia are the only two provinces with significantly higher percentages of immigrant populations

(28.5 and 27.6 per cent, respectively) relative to the national average (20.6 per cent). Rather than being a national phenomenon, immigration has tended to add population growth to a limited number of provinces and metropolitan areas.

In terms of absolute numbers, Canada's three largest provinces, Ontario, Quebec, and British Columbia, receive the most of all immigrants. Citizenship and Immigration Canada (2012), for example, reports that from 2002 to 2011, roughly four out of every five immigrants to Canada settled in one of these provinces. Ontario received almost one half (48.3 per cent) of all immigrants, whereas Quebec and British Columbia received 18.5 and 16.1 per cent, respectively. Yet while Ontario and British Columbia receive more than their population share (explaining their respective percentages of foreign-born Canadians), Quebec has always received less. For example, while Quebec received 18.5 per cent of immigrants, its overall share of the national population is about 24 per cent. Over the last half century, it has been Ontario and British Columbia in particular that have consistently

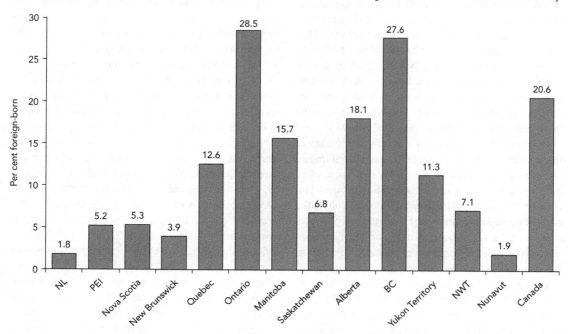

Figure 5.5 ▣ Percentage of the Population that is Foreign-Born, Canada, Provinces and Territories, 2011

Source: NHS, Statistics Canada, 2013b.

received more than their share of immigrants, although there are notable exceptions to this generalization. Alberta received a substantial number in the latter 1970s and early '80s, and the province has been receiving a climbing proportion over the first years of this century (Denton et al., 1997; Milan, 2011a).

Table 5.3 demonstrates the longer-term consequences of such settlement patterns by comparing the distribution of the Canadian- and foreign-born populations across provinces. Overall, immigrants are clearly most concentrated in Ontario and British Columbia and least concentrated in the Atlantic region. In 2011, the Atlantic region made up 8.5 per cent of the Canadian-born population but only 1.4 per cent of the foreign born. Quebec made up slightly more than one quarter of the Canadian-born population (26 per cent) but only 14.4 per cent of the foreign born. In comparison, Ontario had 34.6 per cent of the Canadian-born numbers but over one half of the foreign born (53.3 per cent). British Columbia, with only 11.8 per cent of the Canadian-born population, had the second-largest share of foreign-born Canadians across provinces (17.6 per cent). Among the Canadian born, Ontario's population exceeds Quebec by 33 per cent, whereas its foreign-born

populations is 3.7 times as numerous. Quebec's overall population is more than double that of British Columbia, but BC has a higher number of foreign-born Canadians than Quebec.

Not only has the largest proportion of immigrants settled initially in a few provinces, but the internal migration of foreign-born Canadians has also tended to accentuate these differences. This internal migration of the foreign-born Canadians has tended to be to Ontario and British Columbia. In the first decade of the twenty-first century, Alberta saw a climbing share of immigrants, both in terms of direct settlement as well as internal migration. As of 2011, Alberta was third among provinces in terms of the percentage foreign-born.

Over the 2005–2011 period, there was a modest movement away from the concentrated settlement patterns of the past (Milan, 2011a). The economies of Canada's Prairie provinces (Manitoba, Saskatchewan, and Alberta) all did relatively well in that time frame, whereas southwestern Ontario, for example, experienced economic difficulties. Both internal and international migration tend to be sensitive to economic conditions, and the labour market in Canada's West has outperformed Central Canada, with associated consequences for the

Table 5.3 ⊡ Regional Distribution of Native-Born and Foreign-Born (in percentage), Canada, 1961–2011

Canadian Born	1961	1971	1981	1991	2001	2011
Atlantic	11.9	10.3	10.9	9.9	9.1	8.5
Quebec	31.6	30.7	28.9	27.5	26.6	26.0
Ontario	31.7	33.2	32.2	33.4	34.0	34.6
Prairies	16.7	16.5	17.8	17.7	18.2	18.6
British Columbia	7.8	9.3	10.3	11.1	11.8	11.9
Total	100.0	100.0	100.0	100.0	100.0	100.0
Foreign Born	1961	1971	1981	1991	2001	2011
Atlantic	2.3	2.1	1.9	1.7	1.4	1.4
Quebec	13.6	13.7	13.7	13.6	13.0	14.4
Ontario	47.6	52.0	54.0	54.6	55.7	53.3
Prairies	21.4	16.0	14.0	13.3	11.4	13.2
British Columbia	14.9	15.9	16.2	16.7	18.6	17.6
Total	100.0	100.0	100.0	100.0	100.0	100.0

Sources: Beaujot and Rappak, 1989; 1991 Census; 2001 Census Statistics Canada, 2003; Statistics Canada, 2011, National Household Survey Geography Series.

movement of population (King, 2009). In this context, the Prairie provinces have witnessed a climb in their share of immigrants. Alberta, for example, received over 12.4 per cent of all immigrants to Canada in 2011, its largest share in over a quarter century. Ontario's share fell from 53.6 per cent in 2005 to 40 per cent in 2011 (Citizenship and Immigration Canada, 2012).

Immigrants tend to be drawn to regions that have dynamic economies and culturally diverse populations. This geographic effect is visible at the level of *census metropolitan areas* (CMAs). While postwar immigration has largely been a metropolitan phenomenon, this has been particularly true of metropolitan areas west of Quebec, plus Montreal (see Figure 5.6). East of the Quebec provincial boundary, the highest proportion of immigrants is in Halifax, but this is still under half the national average (Statistics Canada, 2013e). In the percentage of foreign-born Canadians across metropolitan areas, it is especially

Toronto and Vancouver that stand out, with 46 per cent and 40 per cent, respectively. Calgary now ranks third in the country (26.2 per cent), as it has drawn a considerable number of arrivals more recently.

Of Canada's 33 (CMAs), only 8 have a foreign-born population greater than the national average (20.6 per cent), whereas a dozen have percentages below 10 per cent. Some cities in Quebec (e.g., Saguenay, Trois-Rivières, Quebec City) and Atlantic Canada (e.g., St. John's, Saint John, Moncton) have attracted and retained relatively few immigrants, with less than 5 per cent foreign born.

The importance of immigration to population growth is fundamental in this context, as several CMAs in Eastern Canada have consistently lagged behind the rest of the country, whereas Toronto, Vancouver, and Calgary routinely have annual growth rates surpassing 2 per cent (Statistics Canada, 2013e). Some cities, while receiving many immigrants consistently, lose population through

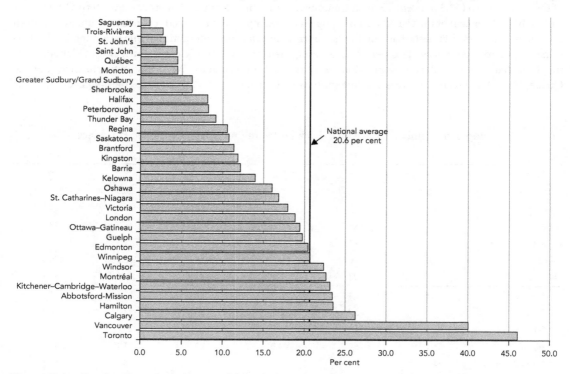

Figure 5.6 Foreign-Born Percentage of Population, Census Metropolitan Areas, 2011

Source: Statistics Canada, 2013k.

out-migration to other parts of Canada. Montreal, for example, which receives a substantial number of immigrants (second only to Toronto), loses considerable population through out-migration to other parts of Canada. Even such cities as Oshawa, Ottawa-Gatineau, Edmonton, and Victoria, while drawing many immigrants, have a slightly lower proportion of foreign-born Canadians than the national average.

The concentration of immigrants in Canada's CMAs is even greater when we consider recent immigrants who arrived between 2006 and 2011. The 2011 NHS estimates that of the 1.2 million immigrants who arrived over this five-year interval, most (92.3 per cent) settled in a census metropolitan area, while slightly more than three in five (62.5 per cent) were in Toronto, Montreal, or Vancouver. In addition, 13.8 per cent of these recent immigrants are in Canada's other large metropolitan areas with populations in excess of a million (Calgary, Edmonton, and Ottawa-Gatineau), with an additional 16 per cent in Canada's 27 remaining CMAs. Consequently, the regions outside Canada's metropolitan areas have attracted fewer than 8 per cent of all immigrants while having 30.8 per cent of Canada's total population.

Immigrants to Quebec are highly concentrated in Montreal. In 2011, 86.8 per cent of Quebec's foreign-born inhabitants were in Montreal. This is similar to the situation in other provinces. For example, 76.6 per cent of British Columbia's foreign-born population lives in Vancouver, 70.2 per cent of Ontario's foreign born live in Toronto, and 84.8 per cent of Alberta's immigrants live in either Calgary or Edmonton. More generally, the metropolitan destination of immigrants is pushing the urbanization trend, a situation that is particularly true for Canada's largest cities. Toronto, Montreal, and Vancouver have all been growing as a result of immigration yet actually losing population as a result of net internal migration. Statistics Canada (2013e) estimates for the 1996–2012 period a net internal migration of about –300,000 for Toronto, close to –200,000 for Montreal, and just over –50,000 for Vancouver. During this same time frame, Toronto is estimated as having received almost 1.4 million immigrants, whereas both Montreal and Vancouver received about half a million each.

Internal migration was documented as negative in 10 of Canada's CMAs, but was more than offset by immigration in all but four of Canada's CMAs (Saint John, Saguenay, Greater Sudbury, and Thunder Bay). Not only is immigration pushing the urbanization trend in Toronto, Montreal, and Vancouver, but it is also more than helping to compensate for any net departure through internal migration for most of Canada's CMAs. In the majority of CMAs, positive internal migration is supplemented with international arrivals, adding to an increased concentration of Canada's population.

Given that immigrants are likely to settle mostly in metropolitan areas and to follow the pathways established by earlier cohorts, immigration will probably continue to accentuate the inequalities in Canada's regional population distribution. While there are efficiencies associated with more concentration of population, this also means that immigration cannot be seen as a means of demographic redistribution toward areas that have smaller populations. In his discussion of the social and political implications of recent immigration trends, Simmons (2010) expresses concern that those provinces that do not have large metropolitan areas will see a decline in their relative population share and the associated political and economic consequences.

Economic Effects of Immigration

Immigration is often justified on economic grounds, and yet the research based on macroeconomic questions tends to be inconclusive. Nadeau (2011) argues that while immigration affects the overall size of the economy (i.e., it tends to increase the size of Canada's GDP), it appears to have a relatively modest effect on per capita measures (e.g., GDP per capita). In other words, while higher immigration implies a larger population and a larger economy, there is a lack of consensus among economists as to the actual impact on per capita measures, unemployment, and standards of living. Dungan and colleagues (2010) suggest that efficiency gains associated with immigration can be found, as immigration can be used to fill gaps in the labour market, potentially increase the productivity of labour, and introduce economies of scale as associated with a larger population. Grubel (2009) contradicts this by suggesting that high immigration tends to result in lower productivity and lower wages, and may have an overall negative fiscal impact on public resources.

McQuillan (2013) proposes that Canadians can benefit from a healthy debate on this topic, since labour-market conditions continue to be difficult, particularly for new entrants to the workforce, with few gains in terms of real wages among Canadian workers over the last 30 years. Green and Green (2004) consider eight possible economic goals often used to justify immigration: filling occupational gaps, expanding human capital, meeting regional needs, generating investment, increasing trade flows, altering the age structure of the population, increasing flexibility, and increasing returns to scale. As might be expected, Canadian immigration policy is not the only tool that can be used to try to meet these economic goals. For example, there are other ways to fill occupational gaps and expand human capital, including investments in post-secondary education and increased commitment on the part of industry to invest in human resources and employee training.

Immigration has an impact on international commerce, as trade, in particular, depends on trust and information, which is easier when someone has emigrated from the country that is being considered as a trading partner. On the other hand, immigration has always had a relatively small impact on age structure, and cannot be viewed as a solution to the problems and challenges of Canada's greying population (Bloom, 2010). While Canada's point system encourages the immigration of young adults, immigrants of all ages do ultimately come to Canada. Bélanger (2013) observes that past immigration may have exacerbated the coming challenges of an aging population. Over the 1989–2011 period, Canada received roughly 1.6 million immigrants who were the same age as the baby boomers (born between 1946 and 1964).

Dungan and colleagues (2010) emphasize the creativity and enhanced productivity associated with immigration, since many immigrants qualify for entrance through the skills-based point system. Similarly, the Provincial Nominee Program has identified specific skills to be in high demand in specific regions and encourages immigration to meet this demand. To the extent that immigrants are highly skilled and actually given the opportunity to use their skills in Canada, then aggregate productivity gains may result with higher GDP per capita over the longer term (Dungan et al., 2010). Immigrants are widely perceived as energetic, productive, and hard-working, and this may cause others to also be more productive. Similarly, arguments are made with regard to the capital resources that immigrants bring—Canada's Immigrant Investor Program is often heralded as an example of successful immigration policy (Ware, Fortin, and Paradis, 2010). While it is relatively limited in size, with only about 2,500 immigrants a year, this program involves about $3 billion in annual investments (or approximately $800,000 per immigrant). The impact of immigration on the industrial structure of regions can be dramatic. Florida (2002) suggests that the ability to attract international talent has long been a defining characteristic of the world's leading and most dynamic cities.

The impact of immigration in terms of tax and dependency effects is often raised in public debate, particularly in the current era of greying populations. Yet since immigration has little impact on age structure, it is clearly not a solution to the forecasted climb in health and social security costs of an aging society. Nadeau (2011) suggests a moderate positive effect, as the net balance of expenditures and taxes may add to government balances modestly—immigrants tend to pay moderately more in taxes than what they receive from government expenditures. Immigrants often come to Canada as young adults, although their age distribution overall is not that different from other Canadians. An upturn in immigration may potentially lower the real per capita costs of health, education, and income security, just as it can help spread out the cost of some public goods (e.g., the Department of National Defence, Parks Canada, and the Supreme Court of Canada). To the extent that immigrants are successful in Canada, one might expect a net contribution from new arrivals in terms of taxes and dependency.

To the extent that immigrants are given the opportunity to use their skills in Canada, aggregate productivity gains can result. Yet while a majority of immigrants are successful in Canada, there is growing concern for those who encounter considerable difficulty integrating into the Canadian labour market. Yssaad (2012) reports that the unemployment rate of very recent immigrants aged 25–54 in 2011 was more than twice the rate for the Canadian born (12.1 per cent versus 5.4 per cent). Gross and Schmitt (2012) highlight the case that high levels of immigration increase labour supply, which in turn increases competition among Canadians and immigrants alike for labour-market opportunities. Although employers and consumers can benefit from a better flow of labour, goods, and services, workers may lose as a result of higher competition—and this would be particularly serious during periods of economic recession. Tal (2012) points to a recent study by the OECD which found that immigration to Canada has been working to reduce productivity gains given the chronic underemployment of many immigrants. According to the OECD, 20 per cent of the increase in the Canadian and US productivity gap over the past decade may be attributed to the economic difficulties faced by more recent cohorts of immigrants (Grady, 2013).

Some suggest that immigration provides economic opportunities for all Canadians by increasing aggregate demand for various services and goods—demand in the housing market, for example (Dungan et al., 2010). While immigrants compete with Canadians for jobs, they also sometimes create opportunities and expand the job opportunities for domestic-born workers. They can start businesses in Canada, and some immigrants are self-employed. The question that is difficult to answer here is the extent to which the economic benefits of immigration, including job creation due to investment and possibly enhanced productivity, offset some of its difficulties.

Throughout most of the twentieth century, immigration policy has had relatively short-term goals, typically with the stated objective of overcoming specific labour shortages during periods of economic upturn, while being flexible enough to curtail immigration during periods of economic downturn. Throughout most of the postwar period, immigration targets have been inversely associated with the unemployment rate—that is, it has been highest

during periods of low unemployment and lowest during periods of high unemployment. Yet since the late 1980s, there has been a fundamental shift in how the federal government views immigration, away from this shorter-term response to labour-market conditions and to a deliberate long-term policy of maintaining population and labour force growth (see Figure 5.7).

Since 1989, then, high immigration has remained a preference for successive governments in Ottawa. The consequence of this has been high immigration, even during the recession of the 1990s and the most recent downturn in 2008 and thereafter. It is symbolic of this shift that the government department responsible for immigration was previously placed with employment (Employment and Immigration) yet more recently designated as a separate department (Citizenship and Immigration Canada). Beach and colleagues (2011) question the wisdom of this shift, and they suggest there might be significant benefits if Canada were to return to its strategy of reducing immigration during times of higher unemployment and increasing targets during better economic times. In a critique of Canada's immigration policy, Stoffman (2002) proposes that the number of immigrants annually admitted into Canada be reduced to about 175,000, observing that Canada is having a hard time absorbing current levels and that the youth unemployment rate remains high.

McQuillan (2013) makes the important point that while Canada may be experiencing certain skill shortages in specific regions and sectors of the economy, it is far from facing a general labour shortage (as many Canadians remain unemployed, some in regions with high unemployment, often with skills that are not in demand). Questioning the perception of there being a widespread skill shortage, Drummond (2014) points out that Statistics Canada's survey of job vacancies shows that there are 6.3 unemployed people for every job vacancy, a statistic that doesn't suggest a shortage of skills but rather an oversupply of workers. A reliance on immigration to fill specific types of jobs can be hindered by the inability of immigrants to gain recognition for their credentials, a lack of relevant Canadian work experience and/or inadequate language skills in one or both of Canada's official

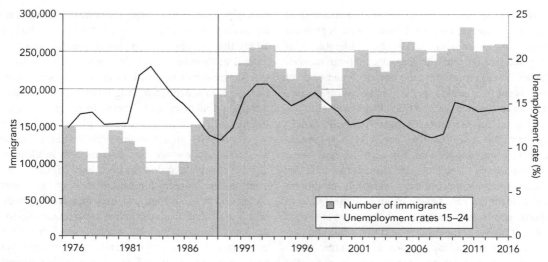

Figure 5.7 ▣ Number of Annual Immigrants and Youth Unemployment Rate, Canada, 1976–2013

Sources: Bélanger, 2013; Statistics Canada, 2013g, *Labour Force Survey*, CANSIM table 28-0086; Citizenship and Immigration Canada, 2012.

languages. In addition, there is also a substantial time lag between the application to immigrate and a person's eventual acceptance and arrival in Canada. Technological change has made certain occupations obsolete very quickly, whereas domestic labour markets and educational institutions can sometimes respond reasonably well to labour shortages. The reality of unemployment and underemployment among immigrants is evidence of the difficulties involved in directing new arrivals to where they are most needed in the labour market, and could be read as evidence that current levels are somewhat high. Yet the reality of underemployment is not unique to immigrants, as a growing proportion of the Canadian labour force appears to now be facing much the same fate, particularly among young adults.

It has been estimated that nearly a quarter of Canadian workers in their early twenties with a university degree are working in jobs that do not require post-secondary credentials (Certified General Accountants Association of Canada, 2012). Unemployment and underemployment is a problem for many new entrants into the Canadian labour force, whether we speak of recent immigrants or young adults who have recently completed their education. With regard to gaps in the labour market and human capital, a reliance on immigration competes to a certain extent with the education system. In particular, the use of skills imported from abroad may keep wages lower, discourage local training, and also discourage the shifts in wage rates that would prompt workers to move to areas that need their skills. Bélanger (2013) projects a rapid rise in the number of Canadians with post-secondary credentials over the next couple of decades without a corresponding climb in the number of jobs requiring these credentials. The result may be a well-educated population with a substantial number of seriously underemployed workers. The degree to which Canada continues to encounter skill shortages in a context of considerable underemployment and high regional unemployment suggests a failure of industry, government, and our colleges and universities to successfully train Canadians with the appropriate skills to meet labour-force requirements.

It is very difficult to project future labour-force shortages, given much uncertainty in forecasting both the supply and demand for workers in specific occupations or industries (Green, 2002). Immigration is important in this context, but there are obviously other strategies possible in terms of meeting future labour-market vacancies. Immigration policy should not leave government to neglect a more effective use of human resources. There are several under-represented groups in the Canadian labour market (including Aboriginal Canadians, visible minorities, and Canadians living in rural regions). McQuillan (2013) highlights the success of Canadian immigration policy while also emphasizing the need for both federal and provincial governments to better promote labour mobility from regions of high unemployment to low unemployment, and the integration of young adults and under-represented groups into meaningful and stable employment.

In the early 1990s, the Economic Council of Canada (1991) concluded that immigration might be better justified on social rather than economic grounds. That is, rather than making a case for immigration in terms of demographic or economic goals, the case should be made in terms of helping to build a diverse and open society. Public opinion has tended to be supportive of immigration targets (IPSOS, 2011). This positive view may be related to these other goals of immigration policy; there are humanitarian goals, such as accommodating refugees and reuniting families; social goals, such as building a multicultural society; and international goals, such as smoothing relations with other countries and establishing ourselves in the international community. This includes building an open, pluralist society, with good international relations in a multicultural world. While it is next to impossible to measure, it may also be that this kind of open society presents economic advantages in a globalizing world.

Socioeconomic Status of Immigrants

We have seen that immigration is often justified on economic grounds. Reitz (2011: 4) summarizes that "the primary purpose of the Canadian immigration program has been to boost the economy." It does not necessarily follow, however, that immigrants will do well economically once they have relocated to

Canada. Discrimination and racism could operate to deny economic benefits to newcomers, as there is evidence to suggest that the human capital of specific immigrant groups has been undervalued (Picot and Hou, 2010). It is therefore important to continuously analyze the economic status of immigrants and to pay attention to disadvantaged groups. The socioeconomic status of immigrants needs to be followed in relation to arrival cohorts and places of origin.

On education, the relative advantage of immigrants was highest in the immediate postwar period, when the Canadian educational system was poorly developed. Even for the 1961–1969 arrivals, the percentage of immigrants with some university education was more than double that of the Canadian population. While this gap narrowed during the 1970s and '80s as Canada's post-secondary system expanded, more recently, it has again widened, suggesting the highly selective nature of Canada's immigration policy (Galarneau and Morissette, 2008). Over the 2001–2006 period, for example, the educational qualifications of recent immigrants rose to almost 6 in 10 men (56 per cent) and roughly half of all women (49 per cent) with at least a bachelor's degree (see Figure 5.8). Not only is this much higher than for the Canadian born (at 19 and 23 per cent, respectively), but it is also higher than for younger cohorts. For those aged 25–34 in 2009, roughly 30 per cent of Canadians report a university degree, or more specifically, 26 per cent of men and 34 per cent of women (Turcotte, 2011).

Even though they are well educated, many immigrants encounter difficulties in finding employment, particularly in their first years after arrival. In 2012, Statistics Canada reported an unemployment rate of 12.1 per cent for immigrants aged 25–54 who arrived during the previous five years, which was more than double that of the Canadian born (5.4 per cent). Similarly for the employment rate, 83.2 per cent of the Canadian born were employed relative to only 66.4 per cent of recent arrivals. The historical pattern has always been that immigrants take some time in successfully establishing themselves in the labour market. Among more established immigrants who have lived in Canada for at least 10 years, for example,

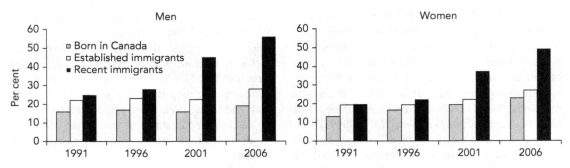

Figure 5.8 ▣ Percentage with a University Degree, Canadian born and Immigrants to Canada, 1991–2006

Source: Galarneau and Morissette, 2008.

these aforementioned rates fall closer to parity with other Canadians (at 6.6 per cent unemployed and 80.3 per cent employed, respectively).

Prior to the 1980s, immigrants actually had a higher employment rate than native-born Canadians (Beaujot, 2002b). The relative ability of immigrants to find employment has since deteriorated, such that by the early 1990s, immigrants had a lower rate. There are differences by immigration cohort, with participation rates higher among cohorts arriving in the 1960s and '70s. While Picot and Sweetman (2012) also document this decline, they find room for optimism with a modest rebounding in employment rates since the late 1990s. The employment prospects of newcomers have historically been sensitive to periods of economic upturn and downturn, as new entrants into the labour force were hit particularly hard during the recession of the early 1990s (Aydemir, 2003).

Finding work is one thing; finding optimal work is another. While almost as many immigrants are employed as native-born Canadians after 5–10 years in the country, higher proportions work in low-quality jobs. The relative labour-market outcomes of immigrants has deteriorated over the last several decades, with recent immigrants overrepresented in low paying, unstable, part-time and/or temporary employment (Green and Worswick, 2004; Galarneau and Morissette, 2008). This translates into incomes that are lower than those earned by native-born Canadians.

To a certain extent, lower wages are expected for immigrants shortly after arrival, as they look for work and frequently settle for a less-than-perfect job. Yet eventually, many immigrants obtain better-paying jobs as they acquire local work experience, improve their language skills, and familiarize themselves with local workforce opportunities (Borjas 1999). This has clearly been the historical pattern, as the earnings of past immigration cohorts consistently saw their wages increase with time spent in Canada. Among immigrant cohorts who migrated to Canada during the 1950s and '60s, not only did their earnings rise with time in Canada, but typically their average earnings converged and even surpassed that of the Canadian born, typically within a decade or two (Richmond and Kalbach, 1980). More recently, there has been a departure from this pattern, as recent immigrants have encountered greater difficulty in establishing themselves in a highly competitive job market.

The comparison of the 1961 and 1971 Census had shown a very encouraging outcome for postwar immigrants (the 1946–60 cohorts). In the majority of age and sex groups, the average income in 1961 was lower than that of the Canadian born, but by 1971, these groups had largely exceeded the averages of their Canadian-born counterparts (Richmond and Kalbach, 1980). Similar transitions occurred over the 1971 to 1991 Census (Beaujot and Rappak, 1989: 139; Beaujot, 1999: 111). In the vast majority of comparisons, earlier immigrant cohorts were above the average of the

Box 5.5 ▣ Who Drives a Taxi in Canada?

The proportion of recent immigrants with post-secondary credentials is much higher than among other Canadians. Despite this fact, many immigrants are underemployed in the labour market, partially due to the low rate of recognition of foreign credentials, usually education and work experience obtained abroad (Green and Worswick, 2004). As a result, many immigrants work in jobs with low educational requirements, such as cashiers, retail sales clerks, office clerks, truckers, and taxi drivers. According to the 2006 Census, 28 per cent of recent immigrant men and 40 per cent of women hold this kind of employment, which compares with roughly 10 and 12 per cent of the Canadian-born population (Galarneau and Morissette, 2008).

In an interesting investigation into the over-qualification of immigrants, Xu (2012) asked the simple question, "Who drives a taxi in Canada?" Of the more than 50,000 taxi drivers, about one half are immigrants. In Toronto and Vancouver especially, more than 80 per cent of all taxi drivers are born in a country other than Canada. While many taxi drivers are overeducated for their occupation, a much larger proportion of immigrant taxi drivers

have credentials greater than required. The National Occupational Classification identifies taxi driving as a C skill level, which usually requires high school and/or specific job-relevant knowledge (e.g., testing on local maps and addresses and the appropriate driver's licence). Yet among immigrant taxi drivers, 53 per cent had at least some post-secondary education compared to 35 per cent of native-born Canadians.

This situation is even worse when we consider recent immigrants (who arrived within five years of the census). Among these immigrant taxi drivers, more than 6 in 10 had post-secondary credentials. Of these cabbies, almost 4 in 10 held a bachelor's or graduate degree (Masters or Ph.D.), a situation that is true of about 1 in 20 native-born taxi drivers. In fact, roughly a third of Canadian-born taxi drivers have less than a high school diploma compared to fewer than 1 in 10 recent immigrants. While underemployment is a problem for all Canadians, it is a very serious issue for recent immigrants. This is for an occupation that has an average annual income of $17,671 when working "full-time, year-round" with very long and irregular working hours (Service Canada, 2013).

Canadian-born population in later censuses. These transitions that did occur were as follows: the 1961–1969 cohort had lower average incomes than the Canadian born in 1971, but exceeded this average in 1981, and women of the 1970–74 cohort had made a similar transition by the time of the 1986 Census. Yet among immigrants who have migrated more recently, the same sort of transitions have not occurred. Regarding the earnings of cohorts arriving in the 1990s and 2000s, it is highly unlikely that they will ever reach parity with other Canadians, in spite of their relative educational advantage.

Recent immigrants often obtain poorly paying employment on arrival, with deeper initial disadvantages for successive cohorts (Frenette and Morissette, 2003). In

turn, this disadvantage is increasingly difficult to overcome even with many years of work experience. Among cohorts arriving in the early 1970s, within five years, immigrant men earned roughly 85 per cent of Canadian-born-males' wage. Among immigrants who arrived in the early 1980s, initial earnings fell to roughly 70 per cent. By the twenty-first century, earnings had fallen even further, to roughly 60 per cent by 2005. This situation of deepening average disadvantage occurred despite the fact that immigrants coming to Canada in the 2000s were increasingly educated, with a climbing proportion having university credentials (Beach et al., 2011).

Picot and Sweetman (2012) demonstrate this disadvantage in the labour market, while taking into consideration relative educational credentials. In their analysis, they used statistical controls in order to compare earnings for persons of similar age, education, and marital status. Figure 5.9 summarizes this analysis, in charting average earnings over time for immigrants who arrived over various periods, beginning with the late 1970s through to the early 2000s. While average earnings consistently rose quite quickly with Canadian experience, recent cohorts are encountering greater difficulties. Immigrants who arrived during the early 1990s, for example, were earning less than 80 per cent of what other Canadians were earning, even after being in Canada for 11 to 15 years. This compares with the earnings disadvantage among immigrants who arrived 15 years earlier (1975–79), who were earning about 92 per cent after living in Canada for the same period of time (11–15 years).

Similar conclusions are reached about low income and unemployment. For the 1980s, Picot and colleagues (2009) show that the likelihood of having a low income was quite similar for immigrants and Canadian-born workers, yet by 1995, the likelihood of low income had gone up to be roughly 40 per cent higher among immigrants than other Canadians. By 2005, the incidence of low income among immigrants had risen to even greater heights, at fully 60 per cent higher than among other Canadians. In terms of newcomers, immigrants who had been in Canada for fewer than five years in 1980 were 1.4 times as likely to experience low income than the Canadian born, whereas by 2000, this had risen to 2.5 times as likely, and by 2005, this had gone up further to 2.7 times as likely. Following male unemployment over the 1982–93 period, McDonald and Worswick (1997) found higher unemployment for the most recent immigrants, but not for those of the 1956–70 arrival cohorts. Especially during periods of recession, like the early 1980s and the early 1990s, unemployment has been significantly higher for those who recently arrived. These same differences also applied to people with university education.

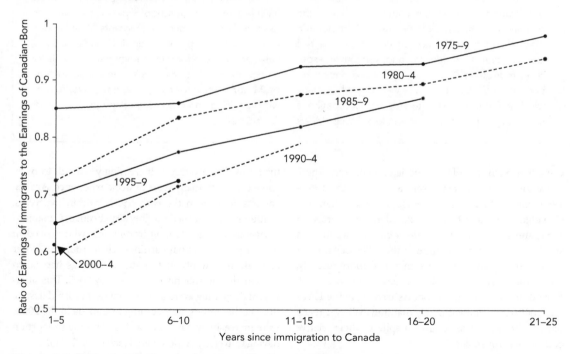

Figure 5.9 ▣ Earnings of Immigrants Compared to Canadian-Born, Full-Time Workers, by Years since Immigration, 1975–2004

Source: Picot and Sweetman, 2012.

There have also been important differences for specific origin groups. The situation has long been more positive for immigrants from Western Europe and the United States, for example. For the majority of recent immigrants, who are mostly visible minorities, serious disadvantages have been encountered. Among immigrants who have lived in Canada for fewer than 10 years, for instance, Picot and colleagues (2007) document a low-income rate of about 20 per cent for those from Western Europe relative to 27.5 per cent of immigrants from the Caribbean and Latin America, 31.7 per cent of South Asians, and 37.3 per cent

among immigrants from Africa. While these statistics apply to immigrants who have been in Canada for fewer than 10 years and all origin groups witness some improvement with the passage of time in Canada, important differences persist. Although immigrants who speak one of Canada's national languages at home have average levels of income that compare much more favourably, controlling for language and education does not fully explain this disadvantage.

Other analyses of past censuses show a trend toward lower rates of employment and earnings for

---

Box 5.6 ▣ Economic Adjustment by Classes of Immigrants

In an analysis of the socioeconomic characteristics of immigrants, it is first important to appreciate the criteria by which they are admitted into Canada. Not all immigrants are admitted under the same criteria, and changes in the distribution of admissions can affect the relative status of different immigration groups. Canadian immigration policy specifies three major classes of immigrants. The *family class* consists of close relatives of permanent residents of Canada. Such immigrants are not assessed under the point system, and their sponsoring relatives agree to provide them with lodging and care for up to 10 years. The *refugee and designated classes* are admitted on the basis of humanitarian considerations. The category of *independent immigrants* consists of people who must meet all the criteria for admission according to the point system. Within this group, *assisted relatives* are people who have relatives in Canada willing to support them for up to 10 years, and who receive points because of this. In addition, the *provincial nominee program* was introduced in 1998 to give provinces a greater say in immigration selection. The basic idea was that the provinces are likely to be more successful in selecting immigrants with the appropriate skills, education, and work experience to meet the immediate economic needs of their region.

Various analyses have highlighted the economic disadvantages of immigrants since the 1990s, in spite of the increase in the relative size of the economic class (Kustec, 2012; Morissette and Picot, 2005). Over the 1990s and early 2000s, the proportion arriving as skilled workers increased while family and refugee classes declined. Among the principal applicants of the economic class, the vast majority have university education and know at least one of the official languages (Ruddick, 2001). Yet while the economic class fares better financially than other migrants (see Figure 5.10), their relative earnings (one year after landing) have declined over this same period, falling below the Canadian average in 1990. While the earnings of economic-class immigrants continues to exceed the family and refugee classes—both initially and over time—the relative earnings advantage of this class has declined the most. In contrast, the newly introduced provincial-nominee program has had some success, with average earnings up steadily since its introduction, reaching parity with the Canadian average in 2008.

Despite their lower earnings, the research that has been done on the family and refugee classes indicates that they have a reasonable level of socioeconomic integration, despite having lower

Continued

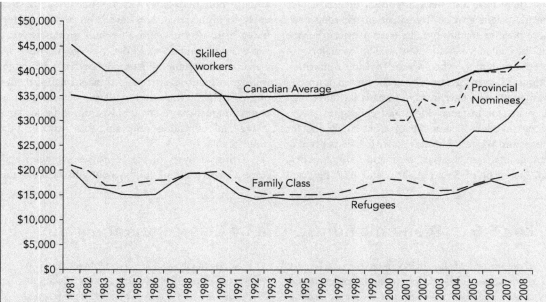

Figure 5.10 ▣ Average Entry Employment Earnings by Immigration Category and Tax year (2008 dollars)

Source: Kustec, 2012.

education, work experience, and language skills on arrival. As they are not selected on job-related criteria, they clearly witness an earnings disadvantage in first establishing themselves economically. The refugee class is the smallest among the three major classes, and since they are not specifically coming for economic reasons but for political asylum, they, too, are consequently less likely to have transferable skills. Yet both the family class and refugee class have demonstrated considerable ability to penetrate the Canadian occupational structure with time. Wanner (2003) finds that there is considerable convergence in the earned income across immigrant categories over time. While all classes struggle

initially upon landing, all seem capable of acquiring the human capital required to adjust to Canada's labour market. After 10 years, nonetheless, the family and refugee classes still have an average earnings disadvantage compared to the independent class. Looking at immigrants with bachelor's degrees or higher among people who had come to Canada between 1980 and 1994, who were aged 20 or older at the time of arrival, and who were aged 25–54 at the time of the 1996 Census, Boyd (2002) finds that men who came from refugee-producing countries had higher unemployment, were more likely to be in low-skilled occupations, and had lower earnings, in spite of their educational credentials.

immigrants compared to the Canadian-born population. Looking at successive cohorts of immigrants, Reitz (2001) finds that the increased education of the Canadian-born population has reduced the relative advantage of immigrants. In addition, the increased

returns to education are stronger for the Canadian-born than for immigrants over time (see also Boyd and Thomas, 2001). In particular, the proportion of immigrants aged 20–64 who are employed has declined, especially among men who have been in

Canada for 0–5 years (Reitz, 2001). In addition, from census to census, the general trend has been downward; that is, the more recent censuses show lower relative incomes for immigrants who have been in Canada for a given length of time. A decomposition analysis reveals that for most comparisons, a significant proportion of the increased disadvantage of more recent cohorts can be attributed to (1) change in the relative immigrant education level, and (2) change in the relative value of immigrant education in the labour market (Reitz, 2001).

Reitz (2001) discusses three possible sources of changes in immigrant relative socioeconomic status: changes in the skills that immigrants bring, changes in the treatment received by immigrants within the labour market, and changes in the structure of the labour market itself. Compared to the 1960s, the skills of newer immigrants have increasingly been defined by academic degrees rather than technical training. Racial discrimination could be the reason for the increased discounting of immigrant skills, but this explanation seems inadequate since white immigrants are also affected, although to a lesser degree. The changed structure of the labour market toward a service economy may undermine the value of educational credentials obtained abroad, and may accentuate the disadvantage of a lack of Canadian experience and Canadian references. In summary, while the average level of education of immigrants has been increasing, so, too, have the credentials of the younger cohorts of internal entrants to the labour force. The cohort differences by labour-force participation and average income clearly show that the strong negative differential at the time of arrival is reduced over time (Badets and Howatson-Leo, 1999). Especially with regard to the average income of immigrants who are not from Europe and the United States, however, the disadvantages of the more recent cohorts are not being reduced as quickly. Contrary to the experience of earlier cohorts, it is unlikely that more recent immigrant cohorts will come to match the average incomes of the Canadian born, in spite of having more average years of education.

Two positive observations can nonetheless be made. First, immigrants who finish their education in Canada receive stronger economic value for this education (Hum and Simpson, 1999; Adamuti-Trache et al., 2013). Second, while immigrants themselves often have economic disadvantages, the children of immigrants (the second generation) have shown very strong levels of economic adaptation (Boyd, 2002; Palameta, 2007). Reitz and colleagues (2011) find that for most immigrant origin groups, the second generation actually do better than other Canadians (third and later generations) of the same age group in terms of educational attainment and occupational achievement. While the first generation struggles, they seem to convey the value of education to their children, which helps ensure employment success. The second-generation members, who have less difficulty with language and Canadian culture because they were raised in Canada, use this education-driven mobility to find meaningful employment, a situation often not available to their parents.

After reviewing studies of immigrant satisfaction, Richmond (1989) concludes that many of the social costs of immigration have been borne by the immigrants themselves: housing problems, language barriers, non-recognition of credentials, experience of racial prejudice and discrimination, obstacles to family reunion, intra-family tension, and frustrated expectations for upward mobility. The receiving society clearly needs to pay closer and continual attention to the opportunity profile of the newest arrivals from abroad. Only if this profile is interpreted positively will immigration itself be seen as a good thing both by immigrants and the receiving society.

Sociocultural Composition of Immigrants

All societies have minorities and need to balance assimilation and the respect for differences. The uniqueness of Canada does not come from the presence of minorities and the dynamics of their integration, but from the fact that immigration plays a predominant role in such questions. These dynamics are somewhat different in Quebec, given the dominant position of the English language on the continent. As a result, there are difficulties both in integrating immigrants into the French majority, and in the

French society redefining itself as a receiving and pluralist society.

Immigration obviously produces a population that is not completely native born. The foreign-born segment made up 15 to 20.6 per cent of the total population of Canada over the 1951–2011 period. Other than Australia at 26.7 per cent, this proportion of foreign-born people is higher than that found in any of the large industrialized countries. In the United States, the figure is 13.0 per cent. The proportions in Australia and Canada are considerably higher than in Europe, where the figure ranges from 13 per cent in Germany, to 11 per cent in France, and 4 to 5 per cent in Finland and Hungary (OECD, 2014). For the world as a whole, the proportion of people who are not living in their country of birth is about 3 per cent. These figures are highest in small oil-rich countries, like the United Arab Emirates at 71 per cent.

The foreign-born members of society can be divided into various categories of place of origin. Figure 5.11 illustrates the changing composition of the immigrant stream over the 1946–2011 period. Until 1970, more than half were from Europe. Since 1979, the Asian component has been the largest. The proportion from Asia, Latin America, and Africa combined increased from 8 per cent in 1961 to 65 per cent in 1980 and has since increased to about 84.3 per cent of total arrivals in 2011.

In effect, there is much diversity in the places of origin of Canada's immigrants. The annual Citizenship and Immigration Statistics lists a total of 175 countries of birth. We often pay special attention to the top 10 sending countries. The nature of these top 10 has changed substantially. In 1960–65, all but one were European, whereas in 2011, all but two were non-European (Citizenship and Immigration Canada, 2012). It is interesting, however, that the top 10 countries account for only about 50 per cent of all immigrants. In 1969, 22 countries each sent more than 1,000 immigrants to Canada, comprising four fifths of all arrivals. In 1988, the equivalent numbers came from 37 countries, and in 2011 there were 47 countries that had each sent more than 1,000, representing 86.2 per

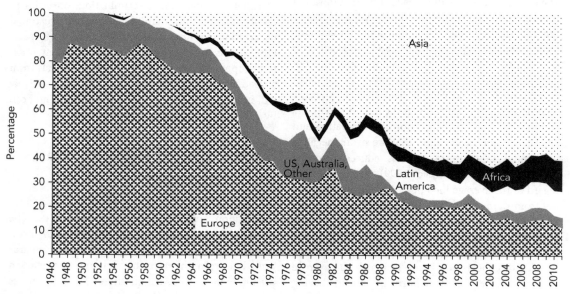

Figure 5.11 ▣ Place of Birth of Canadian Immigrants, 1946–2011

Source: Special tabulations from Employment and Immigration Canada, Immigration Statistics, Citizenship and Immigration Statistics and Facts and Figures from 1946 to 2011.

cent of total arrivals (Citizenship and Immigration Canada, 1999, 2012). This is rather different from European countries, where immigrants are predominantly from one source (e.g., Algerians in France, West Indians in the United Kingdom, Turks in Germany). Since racial criteria were lifted in immigrant selection, the origin of immigrants to Canada has become very diversified. This reduces the formation of ghettos of people from a given place of origin.

Visible Minorities

Since the 1970s, the fastest-growing foreign-born population has consisted of people born outside Europe and the United States. The term *visible minority* has increasingly been used to refer to this population. This term was first coined by the federal government in its employment-equity programs, as the population of people who are neither white nor Aboriginal. In effect, it is the population that originates directly or indirectly from Asia, Latin America, and Africa.

At the 1981 Census, the visible-minority population was estimated at 1,130,000 (4.7 per cent of the total population), of which 85 per cent were of foreign birth (Samuel, 1987). By 2011, Statistics Canada (2013f) documented a major change, with a visible-minority population of 6.26 million people (19.1 per cent). Of the total visible-minority population, roughly 3 in 10 are now born in Canada. On the basis of slightly lower mortality and a continuation of current fertility and immigration trends, it is projected that the visible-minority population will more than double in size to between 11.4 million and 14.4 million (29 to 32 per cent) by 2031 (Malenfant et al., 2010).

These projections of Canada's visible minority and non-Aboriginal population are characteristically based on broad definitions that capture any element of non-Caucasian origin. In particular, all children with at least one visible-minority parent tend to be classified as a visible minority. Thus, the projections are based on strong ethnic retention, yet over the longer term, this retention is not guaranteed, as the very meaning of visible-minority status can change in scope. It can be argued that Canada is becoming a multi-ethnic society where we will especially speak of "pluralism" rather than "visible minorities."

Language Composition

Immigration is fundamental to the demolinguistic evolution of Canada's population. According to the 2011 Census, more than 200 languages coexist in Canada as either a home language or mother tongue. With a history of high immigration, Canada has become very diverse linguistically; the 2011 National Household Survey estimates that 72.8 per cent of immigrants have a mother tongue other than English or French. As a result of the diversification of immigration beyond Europe, Canada's linguistic landscape has evolved. Among immigrants who settled in Canada prior to the 1970s, the most common mother tongues were English, Italian, German, and Dutch. More recently, the most common mother tongues are English, Chinese (including individuals who reported Cantonese and Mandarin), Tagalog, and Spanish (Statistics Canada, 2012f).

Among immigrants who arrived over the 2001–2006 period, only 31.7 per cent were using English and/or French at home in 2006, and more than 9.3 per cent knew neither language (Lachapelle and Lepage, 2010). Yet over time, the majority of immigrants come to associate with one or the other of the official languages—a large proportion of the second generation (born to immigrant parents) live almost entirely in English and/or French. While over 70 per cent of the first generation report a mother tongue other than English and/or French, this declines to 32.5 per cent for the second generation, and even further, to about 1 per cent for the third or later generation (Lachapelle and Lepage, 2010).

The impact of immigration on Canada's official languages is simple: outside of Quebec, immigration contributes to the English language, as the overwhelming majority of immigrants speak English at work and/or at home. Among immigrants outside Quebec, there is even less French than among the Canadian-born population. In Quebec, the opposite occurs, but to a lesser extent. Immigrants are more prone to report using French at work and/or in the home, yet many also report using English. Among immigrants inside Quebec, there is more French than English, but more

English than among the Canadian-born population. In spite of the minority status of English in Quebec, immigrant cohorts have long acquired English, and before 1965, were actually more likely to acquire English than French. For the cohorts arriving since 1980, French has become the more predominant language.

In Quebec, fully 45 per cent of immigrants whose mother tongue was neither English nor French report using French regularly at home, which compares to about 1 per cent outside Quebec. Regarding English, 30 per cent of immigrants in Quebec use it regularly at home, compared to about 65 per cent elsewhere in Canada (Lachapelle and Lepage, 2010). While virtually all immigrants use some English and/or French at work and in the public sphere, English is the more common language, with the important exception of Quebec. While language policy in Quebec has promoted a greater association of immigrants to the French language, this is partly at the expense of departures of English and other linguistic groups. Therefore, it is at the expense of a lower total weight of Quebec in the population of Canada.

The general linguistic trends in Canada involve decreases in the official-language minorities—that is, English in Quebec and French in English Canada. Outside Quebec, immigration contributes to the trend since there is less French among immigrants than in the native-born population. In Quebec, immigration enhances the English minority because there is more English among immigrants than in the native-born population, and a sizable proportion of third-language migrants continue to transfer to the English language. The immigrants to Quebec who are most likely to associate with the French language are those who were selected on the basis of prior knowledge of French, and children who arrive early enough to be schooled in French. For this reason, the Quebec government has been particularly interested in promoting French as the language of instruction for all new immigrants as well as the use of "knowledge of the French language" in its selection of immigrants to the province.

Immigration, therefore, plays an important role in Canada's changing linguistic distribution. Although the distribution by languages changes only slowly, immigration is perhaps the main element producing an increase in the relative size of the English language in comparison to French. Lachapelle (1988) has put it well: "It is hard to envisage scenarios that would both sustain the weight of Quebec in the Canadian total and increase the proportion French in Quebec." The rest of Canada does not have such a problem since more of its international arrivals are English to start with, other immigrants retain their languages less, and almost all transfers favour English.

Sociocultural Implications of Immigration

Reitz (2011) in reviewing survey research over the last 15–20 years suggests that Canadians have consistently been supportive of immigration, relatively unaffected by economic downturns and negative reports on specific immigrant groups. Underlying this situation are two fundamental pillars that support immigration, including the widespread belief that immigration is a plus for the Canadian economy and multiculturalism, which serve to counter concerns about the cultural integration of immigrant communities. Cross-national comparisons of public opinion demonstrate how Canada deviates from the negative attitudes toward immigration that characterizes most industrialized nations. Yet Canada's multiculturalism is not merely government policy, it is also a reality in the day-to-day lives of its citizens, particularly in Canada's largest cities.

The fact that Canada has such a high proportion of foreign-born people is likely partially responsible for these attitudes. As we mentioned earlier, immigrants can influence the political process in both their country of origin and also their country of destination (Carment and Bercuson, 2008). According to the 2011 NHS, 20.6 per cent of Canadians are first-generation immigrants born abroad, and an additional 17.4 per cent are the children of these immigrants (Statistics Canada, 2013f). In other words, almost 4 in 10 Canadians (38 per cent) are either immigrants themselves or the children of immigrants (first and second generation). Politically, government policy has often tended to follow the social climate and, thus, not to deviate excessively from public opinion. All major political parties are wise to the fact that they should not alienate the immigrant vote given their growing demographic weight. All major federal parties are currently pro-immigration, and it is relatively rare that the public and/or media demand in a major way for them to defend their policies (Reitz, 2011).

Clearly, immigration contributes to the change in the sociocultural composition of the Canadian population. However, we would argue that this effect is especially felt at the time of arrival, and that ethnic and linguistic distinctiveness is reduced over time. In effect, the integration of immigrants requires a fine balance between respect for differences and absorption in a common society.

We would also argue that Canada's experiment with a policy of non-discrimination in immigrant selection is relatively successful. Anderson and Frideres (1981: 328) observed several decades back that "it is already very much to the credit of Canada that it has succeeded in incorporating such human diversity into one country." In addition, Canada's commitment to non-discrimination is key to receiving political support in the international community for immigration as well as for other forms of international relationships.

Although immigrants need to be selected without prejudice on questions of race or ethnicity, they also need to know that they are coming to a society where the dominant structures involve English and French, and that they will need to integrate into these structures in order to take effective part in the society. Picot and colleagues (2008), for instance, highlight the importance of language skills and familiarity with Canadian culture to occupational status and earnings. As background to Canada's immigration policy, Employment and Immigration (1989: 13) emphasized, "In the end, Canadians want immigration's economic and demographic benefits and the richness that cultural diversity can bring, but they also want to foster and strengthen Canada's national identity and culture, and to encourage immigrants to embrace certain values which define our identity as a nation."

This also points to the need to avoid situations that would produce immigrant ghettos and instead to ensure that immigrants become integrated into the mainstream of society as quickly as possible. In many regards, this is already the case; for instance, while there is relatively scant research on this topic, Chui and colleagues (1991) provide evidence to suggest that second-generation Canadians are perhaps the most likely to vote and participate in Canadian elections. In general, immigrants have a lower criminality rate than non-immigrants (Giese, 2011).

While integration into the broader society is the greater goal of immigration, it is worth noting that ethnic enclaves can help immigrants to avoid problems of alienation and can give access to various resources that can assist in their integration to the host society. Family and personal networks play an important role in international migration, including the role of being conduits of information and of social and financial assistance (Boyd, 1989; Fong and Hou, 2013). Ultimately, the contribution of immigrants to a host society depends not only on their human capital on arrival, but also on the social context in which they become incorporated. Networks, as well as the social capital of immigrant communities, affect the process of adaptation (Fong et al., 2013).

Conclusion

Canadian immigration can be considered in several broad phases (Simmons, 2010). In the pre-modern period, the arrivals from Europe involved conquest, displacement, and a means of establishing control over land and resources. In the modern period, from the 1850s to the early 1960s, national elites used immigration to help build a modern nation-state by bringing in farmers to settle the land and workers for the industrializing economy. In the following period, which might be called postmodern, immigration is very diverse. This diversity includes the various classes of immigrants, diversity in terms of places of origin, and both *permanent* and *non-permanent* immigrants. It remains a strategy for building an efficient, competitive national economy, but also for finding Canada's place in the world of nations where

European populations are of declining relative importance.

It can be argued that the diversity of this postmodern phase has been accentuated in the twenty-first century. There are mounting outside pressures, including greater numbers of people on the move in the world, and greater numbers of asylum seekers. The changing demographics now include lower internal growth of the population and the workforce. The changing labour markets will see more retirements and worries about shortages in some areas. On the other hand, a substantial proportion of Canadians remain underemployed, and the employment outcomes of recent immigrants have declined. Immigration is important in this context, but there are obviously other strategies possible in terms of meeting future labour-market vacancies. Immigration policy is not a panacea for population aging, nor should it leave government to neglect a more effective use of human resources.

These evolving aspects of immigration can also be related to globalization (Simmons, 2010). There is increased communication and information in a global village, and cultures are becoming more homogenized. Globalization means more trade but also more movement of people, and more diversity, including both winners and losers. There is already free movement of people at the highest levels of skills, but not at lower levels. In the European model of free trade and free movement of people, there were also budgetary transfers to the more disadvantaged regions to achieve greater similarities in socio-economic standards across Europe, and attempts to arrive at common social policy (Alba et al., 1998). These dynamics are different in north–south migration, where the early stages of development bring strong population growth and out-migration pressure, but where standards of living, environmental standards, and social policy are very different (see Golini, 1996). With fewer bases for achieving common standards, immigration brings more diversity.

Globalization also means transnationalism, as many people today develop and retain links with more than one country; there can be dual and multiple citizenships. Movement is temporary rather than permanent. Some people move on to third countries or return to their homeland. Instead of settling in a community, transnationals consider the world to be their community. Issues of sovereignty and social policy are raised as business interests argue for a "level playing field," and transnationals may be more interested in support from their family and networks than from social policy. As economic interests dominate, doubts may be expressed about what values hold us together.

Another aspect of migration in a postmodern and globalizing world is that it is both managed and unmanaged. There is management through selection, but many other people find ways to migrate to places that will provide more opportunities. It has been claimed that trafficking in migrants has become as big a business as the drug trade (see Skeldon, 2000). There are also immigration lawyers, consultants, and volunteer organizations that have an interest in higher numbers of immigration. In these circumstances, debate on migration may become monopolized by special-interest groups.

Clearly, questions of immigration do not involve Canada alone. People from heavily populated countries can come to resent Canada's vast land and resources, arguing that we need to exercise our stewardship over these to the benefit of a humanity that goes beyond our borders. Migration pressures are generated by a world system of economic inequality, political instability, and by development itself, which brings various forms of dislocation. The immigration process is therefore far from being totally under Canada's policy control.

Critical Thinking Questions

1. As minister responsible for immigration, what kind of a statement to Parliament would you make regarding the level and composition of immigration for the short-term future? Why?
2. In what ways has immigration followed the course outlined in the 1947 statement by Mackenzie King?
3. In making population projections for the period up to 2030, what immigration and emigration assumptions would you use? Defend those assumptions.
4. It was suggested that social factors are more important in determining whether people move and economic factors in determining where they move to. Explain and discuss.
5. Immigration is sometimes seen as a demographic necessity and sometimes as an economic necessity, but it is easier to make a case for immigration in sociopolitical terms—that is, as a means of increasing diversity and pluralism in Canada and our contact with a broader world. Discuss.
6. On the basis of theory and evidence, discuss the change in the relative economic well-being of immigrants over cohorts.
7. Immigration reduces the relative size of the French majority in Quebec, and it reduces the relative size of the French minority outside Quebec. What are the prospects of English–French bilingualism when about two-thirds of population change is due to immigration?
8. Discuss ways in which the change of Canada's population is due to immigration.

Recommended Readings

Avery, Don. 1979. *Dangerous Foreigners: European Immigrant Workers and Labour Radicalism in Canada, 1896–1932*. Toronto: McClelland & Stewart. This book considers the various points of view on immigration during the 1896–1932 period.

Castles, Stephen, and Mark Miller. 2009. *The Age of Migration: International Population Movements in the Modern World*. London: Palgrave Macmillan. Immigration is placed in the context of long-term trends at the world level, arguing that the recent period is unique in terms of both the extent and diversity of immigration.

Fong, Eric, ed. 2006. *Inside the Mosaic*. Toronto: University of Toronto Press. This collection by Canadian experts on immigration and its social effects explores how immigration affects social structures and processes, using Toronto as a case study.

McQuillan, Kevin. 2013. "All the workers we need: Debunking Canada's labour shortage fallacy." The School of Public Policy, SPP Research Series (www.policyschool.ucalgary.ca). This paper provides an insightful overview and critique of Canadian immigration policy.

Simmons, Alan. 2010. *Immigration and Canada: Global and Transnational Perspectives*. Toronto: Canadian Scholars' Press. This book puts international migration within the context of globalization, and it pays particular attention to human rights.

Related Websites

http://canada.metropolis.net. This is an international forum for comparative research and public policy development about population migration, cultural diversity, and the challenges of immigrant integration in cities in Canada and around the world.

www.cic.gc.ca/english/about_us/reports.asp. This is the website of Research page, Citizenship and Immigration Canada. This site provides useful information on Canada's immigration policy as well as research on the effect of immigration on Canadian life.

www.iom.int. The International Organization for Migration is a leading international organization working with migrants and governments to provide humane responses to migration challenges.

Growth, Distribution, and Aging

Now that we have studied the components of population change (mortality, fertility, and migration), in the next section of the book, we consider how the population is changing in size, distribution over space, and age composition. These three chapters show how the processes of fertility, mortality, and migration are affecting the state of the population, as seen through size, distribution, and composition by age. With lower fertility and immigration playing a larger part in population change, we see slower population growth, more concentration of that growth in regions that are more attractive to immigrants, and significant population aging.

Chapter 6, on population distribution, puts this distribution in a historical and regional context. The geographical settlement patterns have implied that the populations of the different regions differ considerably: the Atlantic region has the largest proportion of people of British origin; Quebec is of French origin; the Prairie provinces have a concentration of people of European origin, but neither English nor French; and the large urban centres of Toronto, Vancouver, and Montreal have a concentration of visible minorities. In this chapter, we also consider internal migration, including theoretical and empirical questions about the movement of people across areas of the country.

Although population growth has varied over the decades, it has been high in comparison to other countries and will be considerably lower in the future than we have seen in the past. The projections make a case that fertility will remain well below the replacement level, though not as low as in some countries, and that life expectancy will continue to increase. Immigration levels of about 250,000 per year would prevent a decline both in the size of the population and in the size of the labour force. We would argue that there are advantages to avoiding population decline and to having slower rather than more rapid aging.

The aging of the population has been going on for at least a century, but it has become more rapid as a result of low fertility, mortality gains for adults and elderly people, and the aging of the baby boom generation. The change in age structure also shows declining numbers at younger ages and rapid growth at older ages, especially for the oldest people. Long-term projections are particularly important for assessing the number of beneficiaries and contributors to the Canada Pension Plan. We will see that the aging of the population has a number of implications, for pensions, health, and, more broadly, for redistribution in the welfare state.

PART II

6 Population Distribution, Internal Migration, and the Regions

The Chapter at a Glance

- Regional dynamics are a function of geographic and economic questions, compounded by unequal sizes of population and unequal distributions of ethnic groups.
- The regional distribution of population changed extensively during the period of western settlement, and it has since involved a movement to the advantage of Ontario, British Columbia, and Alberta.
- On the basis of the characteristics of migrants, the areas of origin and destination, and the process of migration, it can be suggested that social factors are more important in determining whether people move, and that economic factors determine where they move to. Social

- factors are also important in return migration, while economic factors are important in onward migration.
- Given that net migration has become more important than natural increase in changing population size, there is more growth in regions that contain the largest cities, while regions that do not have large cities are more likely to decline.
- The changing distribution of population puts pressure on constitutional arrangements that treat the provinces equally and on policies that seek to reduce economic inequality among the regions of the country.

Introduction

The 1982 Macdonald Commission, which had the mandate of inquiring into "the long-term economic potential facing the Canadian federation and its respective regions," found the problem of regional disparity to be particularly perplexing:

> For a number of reasons, few of the issues in this Commission's mandate have proved more perplexing than regional development. There is typically, but not always, a fundamental conflict between the goals of regional economic development and those of national efficiency.
>
> Commissioners looked at often-conflicting values and concerns: freedom of movement versus community preservation; uniformity and diversity. . . . In a federal system, migration can weaken

the provincial communities which federalism is designated to protect. (Royal Commission on the Economic Union . . ., 1985, III)

Questions of regionalism and population distribution are as old as Canada itself and are as true today as ever. Starting with a brief review of the factors underlying the regions of Canada, we will focus in this chapter on the geographical distribution of the population, the causes of change in this distribution, and the implications of evolving trends. We will pay particular attention to the influence of internal and international migration on the evolving distribution of population. The interplay of migration and regional disparity can be discussed in relation to the two alternatives of "bringing people to the jobs" or "bringing jobs to the people." As implied in the above quotation, important questions are at stake in this debate; in particular, values of efficiency versus equity, and individual welfare versus community preservation.

Factors Underlying Regional Dynamics: Unity and Diversity

It is no accident that questions of regionalism are studied in a number of the social sciences, especially geography, economics, history, politics, sociology, and demography. From a geographic point of view, the populated areas of Canada consist essentially of a long, thin ribbon along the border with the United States. Even at that, the ribbon is broken twice—once by the Canadian Shield and also by the Rocky Mountains. In a book on Canada in the world, the French historian André Siegfried (1937: 16) noted that, because of the narrowness of this band of habitation, Canada lacks a point of identification and is always tempted to seek a centre of gravity from outside itself. There is much diversity over this land mass, including mountains, plains, islands, and arctic tundra. Canada is second only to Russia in terms of the size of its territory. The size is also evident from the fact that, for example, Victoria is almost as close to Tokyo as it is to St John's.

The specific economic history of Canada, especially the emphasis on the export of resources (staples) and the concentration of industrial development in central Canada, has created further difficulties with regard to national unity. The exploitation of various staples for export has arguably balkanized the nation into several economic areas; the focus of each region has often been on external needs rather than on national aspirations. The economic core of Canada, especially Toronto and Montreal, or, more broadly, the Windsor–Quebec corridor, established itself early as the economic and manufacturing centre of Canada. Atlantic Canada has seen its economy lag behind other parts of the country, as it has had less in-migration and has been less attractive to immigrants (Colgan and Tomblin, 2003). Other regions, especially the Prairies, northern Ontario, and northern Quebec, have long feared that they may decline economically, especially if their respective natural resources (e.g., wheat, wood, fish, minerals, oil) are no longer useful or less valuable (Innis, 1980; Grant and Wolf, 2006). The importance of oil production has especially prompted the population growth of Alberta.

Especially in a North American context, which is the appropriate frame of reference under free trade, parts of Canada are very peripheral. However peripheral the states of Maine or Montana may be within the United States, eastern Quebec, the Atlantic provinces, northern Ontario, and northern British Columbia will always be more peripheral in the Canadian context. Distance affects trade flows as well as the choice of the locations for plants and head offices. In the American context, Central Canada has historically been the region considered best suited to serve continental markets, although other cities, such as Halifax, Winnipeg, Calgary, and Vancouver, have also served as commercial and administrative hubs.

While regional disparities have varied somewhat over the years, Ontario, British Columbia, and Alberta have typically seen average earned incomes that are higher than in the rest of the country. In recent decades, like other parts of North America, the manufacturing sector in Central Canada has faced challenges because of the globalization of economic activity. On the other hand, Saskatchewan and Manitoba, long considered more peripheral parts of the Canadian economy, have joined Alberta in experiencing better economic times, largely due to the vitality of the resource sector and the price of commodities on the world market (Bloskie and Gellatly, 2012). Lower unemployment and climbing incomes in Canada's western provinces have had demographic consequences. The 2011 Census reported that for the first time in Canadian history, the percentage of Canadians living west of Ontario surpassed the number living east of Ontario, at 30.7 relative to 30.6 per cent (Statistics Canada, 2012g).

Beyond purely economic factors, linguistic and cultural differences have contributed to Canada's regionalism. Due to the history of the settlement of Canada, the populations of various regions are quite different. Both Newfoundland and Labrador and Nova Scotia are largely of British origin (or, more specifically, Irish and Scottish), Quebec is largely of French origin, and European ethnic origins other than British or French have predominated in

Saskatchewan and Manitoba. Canada's north has a strong First Nations presence, while the visible-minority component of the Canadian population is concentrated in the largest cities, Toronto, Vancouver, and other southwestern British Columbian munici-palities in particular.

In his introduction to Canadian regional geog-raphy, Bone (2011) suggests that there are four fun-damental "fault lines or tensions" that have contributed to Canada's regionalism including: the French–English dynamic, relations between the First Nations and the rest of Canada, the impact of immi-gration and its unequal distribution across regions, as well as a brand of Federalism that often pits cen-tralist forces in Ontario and surrounding regions against the decentralizing interests of other regions. In other words, we can think of the persistence of regionalism in Canada as due to geography (espe-cially the breaks in the area of settlement imposed by the aforementioned Canadian Shield and the Rocky Mountains); economics (e.g., inequalities of resources and trade links); politics (e.g., inequalities of power, especially between the centre and the periphery); and demography (e.g., unequal size of populations, unequal distribution of linguistic/ethnic groups).

Population Distribution

As we discussed in Chapter 2, before the arrival of European settlers, Canada's First Nations peoples were concentrated in particular regions: on the Pacific Coast and in the St Lawrence Valley, extending into southern Ontario. This is not unlike other distributions that emerged in later periods of Canadian history. For the European settlers, the St Lawrence Valley and Montreal had the advantage of closeness to points of arrival. Population distribution is an important indicator of the relative attractiveness of the various parts of the coun-try and how that has changed with time. It also plays a part in the regional dynamics of the country.

At the time of the 2011 Census, roughly 2 out of 3 Canadians lived within 100 kilometres of the United States border, whereas fewer than 1 in 20 lived over 600 kilometres from the same border. So, for a coun-try with a very low population density overall (at roughly 3.7 persons per square kilometre), Canada's population is highly concentrated in its southern regions. Using another geographic measure, at the time of the 2011 Census almost 7 out of 10 Canadians lived south of the forty-ninth parallel, which marks the southern border of the Prairie provinces, and only 0.3 per cent lived north of the sixtieth parallel, which marks their northern border.

Taking a long historical view, Dumas (1990) observes that in both Canada and the United States, the long-term population movements have been westward and southward. In Canada, *south* means the British Columbia lower-mainland and southern Ontario. If we look at the population distribution by regions that run east and west, around the time of Confederation, Ontario had 42.2 per cent of the population, Quebec 31 per cent, and Atlantic Canada had 19.9 per cent (excluding the British colony of Newfoundland that entered Confederation in 1949). A remaining 2.8 per cent lived west of Ontario (see Table 6.1). Major changes in the distribution of popu-lation have occurred since then, particularly with the massive immigration wave of 1897–1913 (see Chapter 5). While the four western provinces were very sparsely populated in the later nineteenth cen-tury, they constituted over one fourth (27.4 per cent) of Canada's population by 1921.

After this unprecedented immigration wave, Canada's population distribution continued to shift, albeit in a slower and less profound manner. Ontario, Alberta, and British Columbia continued to gain population, as migrants pursued economic opportu-nities in these three provinces. Over the full 1921–81 period, the Atlantic region decreased from 14 to 9 per cent of the total, Quebec shifted from 26.1 to 26.4 per cent, Ontario increased from 32.4 to 35.5 per cent, Manitoba and Saskatchewan decreased from 15.1 to 8.1 per cent, Alberta increased from 6.5 to 9.2 per cent, and British Columbia increased from 5.8 to 11.4 per cent. Another way to characterize these changes is the fact that the population of British Columbia increased by over 400 per cent, Alberta by almost 300 per cent, and Ontario by over 200 per cent; at the other end of the spectrum, Saskatchewan's population increased by less than 30 per cent and Prince Edward Island's by just under 40 per cent. Over this period, some of the rankings of provinces changed. In 1921,

Table 6.1 ▦ Population by Province and Territory, Canada, 1871, 1921, 1981, 2011

Province/ Territory	1871		1921		1981		2011	
	(1,000s)	%	(1,000s)	%	(1,000s)	%	(1,000s)	%
Newfoundland and Labrador[1]	152.5	4.0	263.0	2.9	575.3	2.3	512.9	1.5
Prince Edward Island	94.0	2.4	88.6	1.0	123.6	0.5	145.7	0.4
Nova Scotia	387.8	10.1	523.8	5.8	854.9	3.4	948.5	2.8
New Brunswick	285.6	7.4	387.9	4.3	706.4	2.8	755.3	2.2
Quebec	1,191.5	31.0	2,360.5	26.1	6,547.2	26.4	7,978.0	23.1
Ontario	1,620.9	42.2	2,933.7	32.4	8,812.3	35.5	13,366.3	38.8
Manitoba	25.2	0.7	610.1	6.7	1,035.5	4.2	1,251.7	3.6
Saskatchewan	-	-	757.5	8.4	975.8	3.9	1,057.8	3.1
Alberta	-	-	588.5	6.5	2,291.1	9.2	3,778.1	11.0
British Columbia	36.2	0.9	524.6	5.8	2,826.6	11.4	4,576.6	13.3
Yukon	-	-	4.2	0.0	23.9	0.1	35.4	0.1
Northwest Territories[2]	48.0	1.2	8.1	0.1	47.4	0.2	44.2	0.1
Nunavut[3]	-	-	-	-	-	-	33.6	0.1
Canada	3,841.7	100.0	9,050.5	100	24,819.9	100.0	34,484.0	100.0

Notes:

[1]In this table, the 1871 and 1921 Canadian totals also include Newfoundland and Labrador, prior to the entrance of this former British colony into Confederation in 1949.

[2]In the 1871 enumeration, most of the population of present-day Yukon, Saskatchewan, Alberta, and large parts of northern Manitoba and British Columbia were part of the Northwest Territories.

[3]Prior to the establishment of Nunavut in 1991, its population total was reported in the Northwest Territories.

Sources: Beaujot and McQuillan, 1982; Statistics Canada, 2013i.

Saskatchewan was the third-largest province; by 1981, it was the sixth-largest. Conversely, British Columbia moved from sixth to third rank. Ontario's 1921 population was 24 per cent larger than that of Quebec; by 1981, it was 35 per cent larger.

From 1981 to 2011, there was no change in the relative rankings of provinces by population size, but the total population share east of Ontario has continued to decline, from 35.5 to 30 per cent, while the population west of Ontario has steadily increased, from 28.7 to 30.9 per cent. Both Alberta and British Columbia increased from 20.6 per cent to 24.2 per cent of the total. Quebec's population share has declined, from 26.4 per cent of the total in 1981 down to 23.1 per cent in 2011. The areas of relatively slower

growth are also those of lower population density: the Atlantic provinces to eastern Quebec as well as the central Prairies to northern Ontario. These areas have no cities of over 500,000 people, except Winnipeg.

For the country as a whole, the population increased by 38.9 per cent over those three decades, but all provinces except Ontario, Alberta, and British Columbia had much lower rates of growth (see Figure 6.1). Except for Ontario and Yukon, other provinces and territories are either markedly below or significantly above the national average of growth. Newfoundland and Labrador was the only province to experience population decline over this period, down by over 10.8 per cent over the three decades from 1981 to 2011. In terms of Canada's sparsely

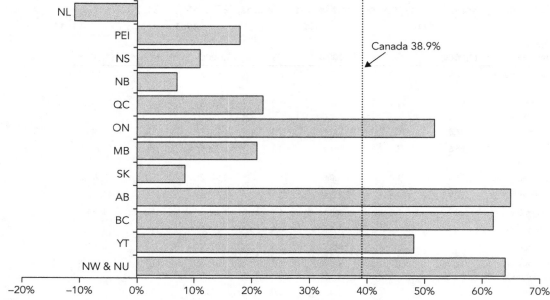

Figure 6.1 ▣ Population Growth, 1981–2011, Canada and the Provinces/Territories

Source: Statistics Canada, 2013a; authors' calculations.

populated North, the territories (Yukon, Northwest Territories, and Nunavut) have all witnessed substantial proportional increase but their populations remain small in relative terms.

Looking at each region separately, we found that the Atlantic provinces have declined in relative population size, commensurate with the waning importance of wood and fish as an economic staple—and the building of the St Lawrence Seaway, which by-passed the eastern provinces as a transportation route, also did not help. The area has received few immigrants and has tended to be an area of net out-migration. As a consequence, the population is relatively homogeneous and has long-established roots in the region.

Quebec has received a considerable number of immigrants, especially to Montreal when it was *the* Canadian destination metropolis. It has not always kept its immigrants, however, especially the non-French arrivals, and it lost some of its own population with the general westward movement in North America.

Ontario has made population gains, both from immigration and, to a lesser extent, internal migration. With the St Lawrence Seaway providing ocean-going transportation, and the proximity to the resources of

the Canadian Shield, Toronto succeeded Montreal as the major Canadian destination metropolis. The 1951 Census of Toronto showed it was 18 per cent smaller than Montreal; by 1976, the two metropolitan areas were equal in size, whereas by 2011, Toronto was 46 per cent larger than Montreal. Overall, 16 of Canada's 33 census metropolitan areas (CMAs) are in Ontario, with 14 located in the Windsor to Ottawa corridor. Immigration since the 1970s has diversified the population ethnically.

The population of the central Prairies (Manitoba and Saskatchewan) has not grown as quickly as Central Canada's because of the decline in importance of their agricultural staple base. Harsh winters and dry conditions limit the agricultural potential of the Prairies and their attractiveness for settlement. The ethnic origins of the population are largely European, but the English and French components are about half of the total only.

Alberta and British Columbia, which may be considered together as the mountain region, have above-average population growth. The oil resources of Alberta have made growth possible as long as external markets are favourable. British Columbia has made continuous population gains as a result of the importance of wood and mineral resources, the moderate climate, and trade links in the Pacific Rim. With new arrivals both from within and beyond the country, about half the population was born outside the province.

The North constitutes a large part of the geography of Canada but a small part of the population. Comprising the Northwest Territories, Yukon, and Nunavut, the North has a relatively young population, with roughly one half (49.7 per cent) reporting First Nations identity (Statistics Canada, 2013h). Although the population of Nunavut grew by 8.3 per cent between 2006 and 2011 and Yukon Territory's population grew by 11.6 per cent, the population of the three territories together amounted to only 107,265 people—across a massive unoccupied land-mass that amounts to almost 40 per cent of Canada's territory (Statistics Canada, 2012g). Its settlements are spread across an enormous wilderness, which leaves for substantial expense and cost in transporting goods and services from the south. Whitehorse, Yukon, the largest settlement, had a population of only 22,815 in 2011, followed by Yellowknife, Northwest Territories (18,830), and Iqaluit, Nunavut (6,595).

Urban and Rural Areas

Another way of analyzing the trends is by distribution of population in urban and rural areas. As late as 1931, over half of Canada's population lived in rural areas and 31.1 per cent were classed as "rural farm". By 2011, this had fallen to fewer than one in five Canadians (18.9 per cent) and only about 2 per cent lived on farms (Statistics Canada, 2012g, 2013j). In 1871, the only city of 100,000 or more people was Montreal, and it accounted for no more than 3 per cent of the Canadian population at the time. By 2011, there were 33 census metropolitan areas of this size, and they contained nearly 7 Canadians in 10 (69.1 per cent). The CMAs of Toronto and Montreal dominate the urban landscape, with populations of 5.9 and 3.9 million respectively, while Vancouver (2.4 million), Calgary (1.4 million), Ottawa–Gatineau (1.3 million), and Edmonton (1.3 million) have all witnessed considerable demographic growth (Statistics Canada, 2012g).

Recent censuses have highlighted four large urban regions that together contain about one half of Canada's population: the extended Golden Horseshoe from Oshawa to Kitchener in southern Ontario (about 8 million people, or 22 per cent of the country's total); Montreal and the adjacent region (a population of 3.9 million, or 11 per cent of the total); British Columbia's lower mainland and southern Vancouver Island (with 2.8 million people, or 8 per cent of the total); and the Calgary–Edmonton corridor (with over 2.5 million people, or about 7 per cent of the total). Compared to the Canadian population overall, which grew by 5.9 per cent from 2006 to 2011, the total population of these metropolitan areas grew by roughly 8 per cent over this same five-year period (Statistics Canada, 2012h; authors' calculations). From 2006 to 2011, Calgary and Edmonton led the country in terms of demographic growth, up by 12.6 and 12.1 per cent, respectively. This is a very rapid rate of growth, leaving for major challenges in terms of providing the necessary urban infrastructure, housing, and municipal services, as both cities have recently Table D2 in the appendix of this book includes Statistics Canada's annual population estimates (2001–2013) for all 33 CMAs listed in Figure 6.2.

Canada's rural population, defined as persons living in areas of less than 1,000 people or with a density of less than 400 persons per square kilometre, has been steadily declining over the last century. Over 80 per cent of the population was rural in 1871, about half in 1931, and 38 per cent in 1951 (Beaujot and McQuillan, 1982). By 2011, this rural population had fallen to fewer than one in five Canadians (18.9 per cent). Most of this population is rural non-farm, often on the distant fringes of the large metropolitan areas where significant proportions commute to major urban centres (Statistics Canada, 2012h). Depending on definitional issues, Munro and colleagues (2011) estimate that perhaps as much as 70 per cent of the rural population live and work in locations that are somewhat integrated into larger urban centres. While the total farm area is relatively stable, the number of farms is declining along with the farm population. The rural farm population declined from 1,420,000 in 1971 to 684,260 in 2006. In 1941, this figure was over 3 million, which was 27 per cent of the total population, whereas it is about 2 per cent of the total today (McSkimmings, 1990; Statistics Canada, 2013j).

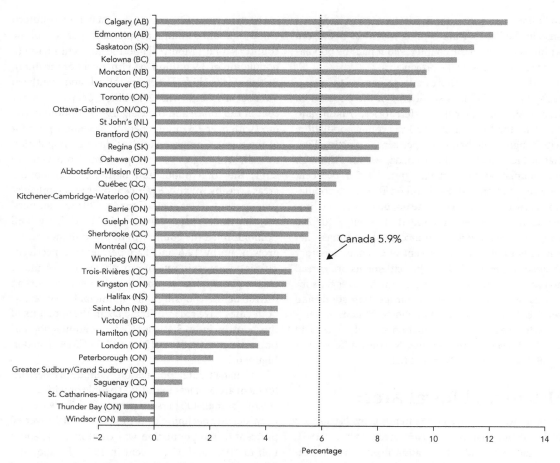

Figure 6.2 ◉ Population Growth (Percentage) for Census Metropolitan Areas, 2006–2011

Source: Statistics Canada, 2012a.

Box 6.1 ◉ Has the 2011 Census Documented a Reversal of Longer-Term Trends?

The 2011 Census documented some interesting shifts in provincial growth rates that go counter to the longer-term trends in Canada. The question is whether these changes are temporary or longer lasting. Newfoundland and Labrador's population growth, for example, was positive for the first time since the 1981–6 period, whereas the population growth of its CMA of St John's ranked ninth in the country (8.8 per cent). All regions of Canada, with the exception of Ontario, Northwest Territories, and Nunavut, witnessed a higher rate of growth in 2006–11 than in 2001–6. Ontario's population growth slowed to its lowest rate of population increase since the 1981–6 period (see Figure 6.3).

While Ontario still had the fourth-highest growth rate among provinces (at 5.7 per cent), it received fewer immigrants than in the previous intercensal period while also losing some population through interprovincial migration. Among Canada's 33 CMAs, 7 of the 8 slowest-growing over the 2006–11 period were located in Ontario, a pattern that departs from past intercensal periods (see

Figure 6.2 above). In the twenty-first century, Ontario's economy has been influenced by structural changes, including some profound difficulties in the manufacturing and auto sector. The global recession that began in 2008 had a particularly pronounced impact on Ontario, whereas other regions, including the western provinces, did not witness a comparable economic downturn.

Saskatchewan's reversal of fortunes is particularly dramatic. As we mentioned, throughout much of the twentieth century, Saskatchewan's growth

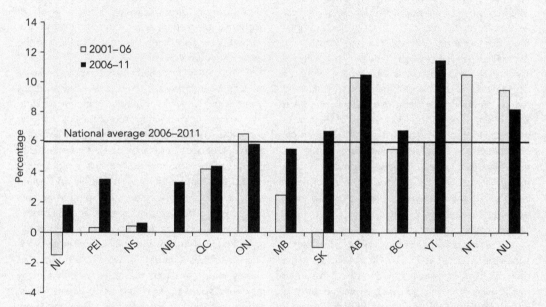

Figure 6.3 ◉ Percentage Population Growth, by Province and Territory, 2001–2006 and 2006–2011

Source: Statistics Canada, 2013c.

was substantially lower than the national average, with a declining population share. After negative growth (–1.1 per cent) for both the 1996–2001 and 2001–6 periods, the province witnessed rapid demographic growth over the 2006–11 period (6.7 per cent), in excess of the national average (5.9 per

cent). This was the third-highest growth rate across provinces, after Alberta (10 per cent) and British Columbia (7 per cent). Saskatchewan's unemployment rate has fallen, with its natural resource and energy sectors generating considerable economic opportunity. The CMA of Saskatoon witnessed high

Continued

growth (11.4 per cent), and Regina also grew at a relatively rapid pace (8 per cent). Over the 2006–11 period, all of Canada's western provinces (Manitoba, Saskatchewan, Alberta, and British Columbia) witnessed an increased influx of immigrants and interprovincial migrants (many from Ontario),

all contributing to a western shift in population. Will the western trend hold? A lot depends on how the Canadian economy fares in the coming years—will the uncertainty in Central Canada's economy abate relative to the resource-based economy of Canada's West?

Box 6.2   A Few Observations on Census Geography

There is some confusion among the general public when it comes to the population of our largest cities. According to the 2011 Census, for example, the Toronto census metropolitan area (CMA) has a population of 5.6 million, whereas the City of Toronto is 2.6 million. The Montreal CMA has a population of 3.8 million, whereas the City of Montreal is 1.6 million. Similarly, the Vancouver CMA is 2.3 million, whereas the Municipality of Vancouver is only slightly greater than 600,000. The simple explanation for these disparities relates to the fact that Statistics Canada releases population data using different types of geography, some of which are purely administrative, as defined by provincial or territorial statute, whereas others have been developed by analysts at Statistics Canada.

The above figures correspond to both census subdivisions (CSDs) as well as CMAs. Most CSDs are municipalities, or areas deemed to be equivalent to municipalities, as defined by a provincial or territorial government. CMAs, on the other hand, are geographic regions developed and defined by Statistics Canada, meant to refer to large metropolitan areas. These involve continuously built-up urban areas that can include several neighbouring municipalities, with a sizable urban core and population of at least 100,000. The Toronto CMA, for example, not only includes the City of Toronto (2.6 million), but also several neighbouring municipalities, including Mississauga (713,443), Brampton (523,911), Markham (301,709) and Vaughan (288,301), among

others. To be included in a CMA, a neighbouring municipality or area must have a high degree of economic integration, as for example, a large proportion of its population commutes to work in the larger CMA's urban core.

The CMA is particularly useful sociologically, as political boundaries are often somewhat arbitrary, whereas the level of social and economic integration across neighbouring municipalities can be very high. The City of Laval, for example, which is actually Quebec's third-largest city, is considered to be part of the Montreal CMA, and it is highly connected to Montreal both economically and culturally. The public transit system, including Montreal's metro system, connects Laval with the larger metropolitan area, as a sizable proportion of its working-age population makes the daily commute to work. The City of Mississauga, just west of Toronto, is so closely integrated with the larger city that many residents would be at a loss as to where Mississauga ends and Toronto begins. CMAs can even cross provincial boundaries, as is the case with the Ottawa–Gatineau CMA on the Quebec–Ontario provincial line. Many who live on the Quebec side cross the Ottawa River on a daily basis to work in Ontario, just as many who live on the Ontario side do the same thing in reverse.

In addition, Statistics Canada provides population figures for *census agglomerations* (CAs), which are urban areas with at least 10,000 population, yet below the 100,000 threshold for CMAs. In the 2011

Census, Statistics Canada reported 114 CAs across Canada, up slightly from 111 in 2006. Roughly 4.3 million people—or 12.9 per cent of Canada's population—live in these mid-sized towns. In other words, slightly less than 7 in 10 Canadians live in Canada's CMAs, just over 1 in 10 live in its CAs, whereas just under 2 in 10 live outside both these CMAs and CAs. The population growth in these different areas have varied, although Canada's largest cities have typically grown most quickly. Over the 2006–2011 period, the greatest population growth was reported for CMAs (7.4 per cent), followed by the smaller CAs (4.2 per cent), while the population outside both the CMAs and CAs remained relatively stable—up by only 1.7 per cent overall (Statistics Canada, 2012i).

Dynamics of Internal Migration

The change in distribution of the population can be the result of natural increase, international migration, or internal migration. In earlier chapters, we have discussed mortality, fertility, and international migration. Before analyzing the demographic components of the changing geographic distribution, it is important to consider certain empirical generalizations and theoretical perspectives on internal migration.

Three generalizations can be made about migration. First, with regard to the characteristics of people who are most likely to migrate, it is often observed that migration is more likely among young adults and among people with above-average education and socioeconomic status (Dion and Coulombe, 2008; Coulombe and Tremblay, 2006). Second, with regard to *areas* of origin and destination, migration is predominantly from smaller to larger places and from places with fewer opportunities to those that offer more options (Cicchino and Newbold, 2007). Hiller (2009) summarizes some of the advantages of resource-rich Alberta over recent decades as a place of destination in attracting people from other parts of Canada. Broadly speaking, this situation can be interpreted in the context of development, which produces areas of higher and lower opportunity. Globalization gives further advantages to certain large cities, and these places become the receiving areas for migrants.

The third generalization relates to the *migration process*, which is disruptive in people's lives; psychologists call it a stressful life event. Implied here is that people mostly would prefer not to move, and when they do move, they will often follow relatives, friends, or acquaintances. This disruption also implies that there will always be a certain number of people who return home (*return migration*) or move again to a third or fourth destination (*onward migration*). Cicchino and Newbold (2007) estimate that *return migration* represents up to 30 per cent of all recorded migration, while *onward migration* is also relatively common. *Primary migrants* who make the initial move from their community of origin also tend to be less socially and economically integrated into their community. This generalization is also true of *return migrants* and *onward migrants*. For this reason, immigrants and other newcomers are more likely to migrate than other Canadians, particularly within the first few years after arrival (Okonny-Myers, 2010). Conversely, those who were born in a region have a much lower propensity to leave than those who were born outside this region. Onward migration rates are also found to be higher than primary migration, and this is especially the case for those who are living farther from their province/territory of birth. That is, those who have experienced migration and who are consequently less integrated in their place of birth are more likely to move again. It is also noteworthy that return migration from British Columbia is lower than for any other province, whereas return migration to this province is higher than elsewhere. In a sense, Canada's westernmost province, British Columbia, can be seen as an absorbing state or terminus for migration. Its growth rate has thus historically been very high relative to other provinces.

There is often an economic motive to migration. Economic questions operate especially as pull factors, and help to explain the choice of the place of destination. Day and Winer (2012) demonstrate how economic incentives are the main forces shaping migration flows, particularly for Canadians of workforce age. Edmonston (2011: 191) emphasizes that "internal migration provides both a mechanism for personal employment improvements as well as a process that maintains a better connection between available workers and job opportunities." Migration is a fundamental demographic process in a dynamic economy, with important consequences for both communities of departure and arrival. In other words, it serves as a central mechanism in the adjustment of labour markets to economic change, with the movement of population away from regions with higher unemployment to those where there is a greater demand for labour.

There are also social factors, however, since people prefer not to move—and a move is often assisted by relatives and friends. This would explain the greater propensity of young adults to move, at a time when they are leaving home and, thus, less integrated into their community (Dion and Coulombe, 2008). Movements also follow changes in marital status and other life-cycle transitions, whereas, conversely, the presence of dependants lowers the propensity to move. Many moves are influenced by wanting to live with or closer to families/friends. It could be concluded that social factors are mostly involved in the decision whether or not to move: people are more prone to move when they are at stages of their life where there is less integration into the community. Once the decision to move has been made, economic factors are paramount in the choice of a destination.

While it is very difficult to theorize about migration because there are so many factors involved, the above research is consistent with an explanation that starts with a natural tendency not to move. Unless there are disruptions, there is a tendency to remain in one's community. Staying represents integration with family and friends. We would further propose that life-course and social factors are more important in determining whether or not people move, while economic factors are more important in the choice of destination. People move especially at stages of their life that involve disruptions, such as leaving home, finishing school, finding a job, starting or terminating a relationship, or retiring. Whether or not people move depends on how comfortable or integrated they are in the place where they live. Once people are prone to move, economic factors, or, more broadly, the push and pull factors, determine the place of destination. When people are settled, especially in the case of a two-income family with children, a higher salary at a different location will not be attractive. But when people are looking for a first job, a higher salary may prompt them to move, especially if they see other opportunities at their potential destination (Bernard et al., 2008). Overall, men have had slightly higher rates of migration than women, and by far the most movement has been among young adults in their twenties (Statistics Canada, 2013k).

This perspective helps to explain various other observations about internal migration. In Quebec, for instance, interprovincial migration rates—both in and out—are noticeably lower than for other provinces (Bélanger and Dumas, 1998; Statistics Canada, 2013k; 2013l). Past research has pointed to the importance of culture and language in this context, as the French-speaking minority in Canada has little choice but to remain in Quebec if it prefers to live and work in its own language (Liaw, 1986; Newbold, 1996). Lachapelle and Lepage (2010) highlight the importance of language, as there is a tendency among French speakers in Canada to migrate toward a francophone environment (i.e., toward Quebec), whereas the opposite is true among English speakers in Quebec (they are much more likely than French speakers to move to another province). While Quebec had a net loss of 11,600 through interprovincial migration over the 2001–6 period, the francophone population actually gained through net migration (+5,000), whereas anglophones and other non-French speakers lost numbers (–16,600). Edmonston (2011) documents a low interprovincial migration rate for Quebec, but highlights how this does not apply to movement within the province. Relative to elsewhere in Canada, Quebec has a very low *interprovincial migration rate* but a very high *intraprovincial migration* (i.e., migration across municipalities and/or regions within the province). It is not that the Québécois are less mobile than other Canadians; it is merely that they are less likely to move across provincial boundaries. While Québécois relocate for economic reasons, both culture and language are important in this context.

The theory stated above on the social and economic factors associated with migration is also consistent with the finding that there has not been substantial change over time in the propensity to migrate. The censuses from 1971 through to 2006 asked about place of residence five years earlier. For the country as a whole, these data show a fairly constant, if not a slightly declining amount of movement. Somewhere between 5 to 6 Canadians out of 10 are living in the same residence as they were 5 years earlier. Some 22 to 26 per cent have changed residence, but within the same municipality, and 12 to 17 per cent changed municipalities within the province. Only 3 to 5 per cent of people are living in a different province than they were 5 years earlier.

Contrary to the common view that there is more and more movement in the modern world, Canadian data shows a gradual decline in internal migration rates between provinces (see Figure 6.4). In 1971, there were 17.9 migrations per 1,000 people between provinces, compared to about 13 in 1990 and 9 by 2011. Similarly, Edmonston (2011) documents a stabilization and slight decline since 1981 in the lifetime migration of Canadians, with roughly 15 per cent of the Canadian born now living in a province other than where they were born. Using the data from the Longitudinal Administrative Database for 1993–2004, Bernard and colleagues (2008) observe that roughly 95 per cent of people were living in the same province in 2004 as they were in 1992. The lowest out-migration was for Quebec, where 97.4 per cent were still in the same province at the end of the period, and the highest was for Newfoundland and Labrador, where 86.5 per cent were living in the same province.

Nonetheless, with a concurrent convergence toward below-replacement fertility (and low natural increase) across provinces, internal migration continues

Figure 6.4 ▣ Interprovincial Migration Rates in Canada, 1971–2011

Source: Statistics Canada, 2013f, authors' calculations.

to be an important component of population change at the provincial, metropolitan, and local levels. Internal migration can potentially change quite quickly, depending on regional economic conditions, producing sizable migratory flows into or out of specific provinces.

Demographic Components of Population Redistribution

The immediate components of change in population distribution involve differences in natural increase (births minus deaths), internal migration, and the extent to which international migrants go to the various regions.

Natural Increase

In the past, changes in population distribution were partly due to differences in natural increase, especially the higher fertility in Quebec from 1881 to 1961. Caldwell and Fournier (1987) point out that this "constituted a demographic investment that alone ensured the survival of French society in geographical Quebec as we know it today, despite political and economic subjugation." Compared to the relative sizes of population, the natural increase of the 1931–61 period represented advantages to the relative sizes of the provinces of Quebec, New Brunswick, Nova Scotia, and Alberta. Quebec had the largest advantage, with a natural increase 25 per cent higher than would be expected from the size of its population (Beaujot and McQuillan, 1982).

In the more recent periods, however, rates of natural increase have become much more uniform across the country. In 2011, for example, all provinces in Canada had below-replacement fertility with the longer-term trend for all provinces of declining natural increase (Statistics Canada, 2013m). While the western provinces of Manitoba, Saskatchewan, and Alberta have slightly higher fertility than elsewhere, the differences in natural increase are not large. As fertility and mortality become relatively homogeneous over space and as natural increase declines, migration becomes the dominant component of differential demographic

growth and of population redistribution over space (Gilbert et al., 2001).

International Migration

The different levels of immigrant arrivals in various parts of the country has a significant effect on population redistribution. We saw in Chapter 5 that Ontario and British Columbia, in particular, have higher proportions of immigrant populations than the national average. The immigration of the postwar period has largely been to the advantage of the populations of Ontario, British Columbia, and increasingly Alberta, while to the disadvantage of the Atlantic provinces, Quebec, Manitoba, and Saskatchewan.

International migration also accentuates the growth of the larger metropolitan areas. Compared to the size of the Canadian-born population, Toronto, Vancouver, and, to some extent, Montreal and census metropolitan areas west of Quebec have received disproportionately large shares of postwar immigrants (Review of Demography, 1989). With lower natural increase, the effect of this international migration on population distribution was particularly evident over recent censuses. As was noted earlier, the provinces that made substantial population gains in the 1990s and 2000s were those that contained Canada's largest urban regions: Ontario's Golden Horseshoe, Greater Montreal, British Columbia's lower mainland and southern Vancouver Island, and the Calgary–Edmonton corridor. These are the regions that are receiving the largest number of immigrants. The growth of Canada's major urban centres is largely due to immigration, while non-metropolitan regions are more strongly influenced by internal migration (Simmons, 2010; Citizenship and Immigration Canada, 2012).

In addition, the subsequent remigration of immigrants tends to accentuate the largest areas of initial destination. Population distribution is thus different from other characteristics that distinguish immigrants. On most characteristics, the impact of immigration in terms of the differences that they represent lessens with time (Beaujot and Raza, 2013). Their fertility and mortality come to resemble those of the Canadian born, as do their economic characteristics. Even the visibility of minorities lessens as styles of dress and speech become more similar with a longer length of residence, certainly into the second and third generations. When it comes to geographic distribution, however, where immigration accentuates the uneven distribution of the population, the subsequent internal migration of immigrants brings a further concentration to the main areas of primary destination.

The provinces that receive disproportionate numbers of immigrants (Ontario, British Columbia, and Alberta), for instance, are the least likely to see them depart for other provinces (Edmonston, 2002). That is, there is no evidence of an increased dispersion of immigrants over time. In following the interprovincial migration of immigrants from 1991 to 2006, Okonny-Myers (2010) documents that it is from the Atlantic region, Saskatchewan, and Manitoba that foreign-born people are most likely to leave, whereas they are least likely to move from British Columbia, Alberta, and Ontario. While all provinces gain and lose immigrants, these latter three provinces were the only provinces to record a net gain in the interprovincial migration of immigrants over this 15-year period. While immigrants are most mobile in the first years after they arrive, after 15 years of residence, their mobility is less than that of the Canadian-born population (Ram and Shin, 1999; Ostrovsky et al., 2008).

Internal Migration

In many regards, the internal migration of native-born Canadians is similar to that of the foreign born. In particular, the departures tend to be from the Atlantic and Prairie provinces, whereas the western provinces of British Columbia and Alberta have seen the greatest gains (Edmonston, 2002; 2011). Migration tends to be from less-populated to more-populated provinces, and to respond to economic conditions like unemployment and wages. While the migration patterns of the Canadian born and foreign born are similar, Quebec is the province where the native-born population is least likely to leave, followed by Ontario (expressed as a rate, but not in absolute numbers).

The annual number of people moving across provincial boundaries has declined slightly over recent decades, averaging 317,300 migrants over the 1971–2012 period (Statistics Canada, 2013l). This compares to an average of about 189,600 immigrants—or, in other words, immigration over this period was equivalent to about 60 per cent of interprovincial migration (Statistics Canada, 2013l). So, while Canada received almost 8 million immigrants over 40 years, a population roughly equivalent to 13 million moved across provincial boundaries. Yet, while there is considerable movement of population overall, to a certain extent this movement balances itself out in terms of population distribution, as specific provinces have not only gained considerable population, but also lost population though out-migration.

As a result, the net movement (in-migration minus out-migration) is considerably smaller than the total movement. In 2010–11, for example, Nova Scotia saw 29,147 people moving across its border (14,553 in-migrants and 14,594 out-migrants) to make a net loss of only –41 people through interprovincial migration. Similarly for Alberta, the gross movement was 119,507 (63,975 in-migrants and 55,532 out-migrants) for a net gain of +8,443. Table 6.2 shows only these net changes for all provinces and territories without providing the detail in terms of flows into and out of specific provinces. These annual estimates for the extended 1971–2012 period are made by the Demography Division of Statistics Canada, using administrative indicators of change in residence, especially from taxation records.

Looking at the net flows on a year-by-year basis shows patterns that are consistent over time. We can see that the flows are mostly showing losses for the Atlantic region, Quebec, Manitoba, and Saskatchewan, with the most pronounced gains being for Alberta and British Columbia. Only four provinces witness a net gain over four decades (Prince Edward Island, Ontario, Alberta, and British Columbia), although only Alberta and BC witness substantial gains (with net inflows of over half a million each). The advantage that Ontario observes with regard to international immigration clearly does not exist for interprovincial migration, as this province gained

Table 6.2   Net Migration for Canadian Provinces and Territories, 1 July–30 June 1971–2012

Year	NL	PEI	NS	NB	QC	ON	MB	SK	AB	BC	YT	NWT	NU	Total Migrants
1971/2	864	349	-586	384	-21,637	14,462	-8,880	-18,995	4,190	28,088	686	1,075	–	395,432
1972/3	-777	782	4,851	2,102	-19,754	940	-5,489	-16,524	5,498	27,193	458	720	–	396,138
1973/4	-2,719	821	1,014	2,269	-12,581	-9,802	-1,656	-10,472	2,911	31,505	-504	-786	–	437,549
1974/5	543	1,334	2,422	6,037	-10,361	-28,194	-6,119	697	23,155	9,615	339	532	–	411,709
1975/6	132	456	3,639	5,907	-13,354	-18,932	-4,982	5,296	26,579	-5,035	115	179	–	375,351
1976/7	-4,149	154	-799	-82	-26,366	-6,402	-3,531	3,182	34,710	5,016	-400	-1,333	–	357,389
1977/8	-4,311	700	-416	-1,348	-46,429	8,510	-4,674	-1,719	32,543	17,576	261	-693	–	364,421
1978/9	-3,374	-74	-357	-1,171	-30,884	-4,325	-10,746	-2,878	33,426	22,005	-643	-979	–	358,805
1979/80	-3,597	-358	-2,732	-2,761	-29,976	-22,362	-13,864	-4,493	41,435	40,164	-464	-992	–	371,388
1980/1	-3,552	-1,251	-2,836	-4,989	-22,841	-33,247	-9,403	-3,808	44,250	37,864	313	-500	–	382,932
1981/2	-5,693	-856	-1,936	-2,842	-25,790	-5,665	-2,625	-323	36,562	8,705	81	382	–	357,919
1982/3	1,829	636	3,791	3,554	-24,678	23,585	2,544	3,580	-11,650	-1,489	-1,653	-49	–	305,486
1983/4	-2,026	797	3,804	1,792	-17,417	36,400	339	2,133	-31,986	6,636	-435	-37	–	279,372
1984/5	-3,445	250	2,557	-678	-8,020	33,885	-595	-1,425	-20,771	-1,969	-223	434	–	270,565
1985/6	-5,716	-76	-1,321	-1,891	-5,349	33,562	-2,297	-6,939	-3,831	-4,501	-545	-1,096	–	287,260
1986/7	-4,423	-205	-941	-2,026	-3,729	42,601	-2,759	-4,957	-29,998	7,426	575	-1,564	–	302,602
1987/8	-3,504	295	-1,788	-1,957	-7,693	35,215	-5,875	-12,107	-23,223	21,479	349	-1,191	–	322,375
1988/9	-1,655	381	537	-598	-7,618	9,739	-9,313	-17,071	-1,528	27,821	-180	-515	–	327,700
1989/90	-2,889	-253	-162	169	-8,642	-5,961	-10,361	-19,442	5,593	41,394	90	-293	–	356,807
1990/1	-930	-325	595	923	-11,325	-11,627	-7,540	-12,176	8,983	34,053	243	-117	–	316,567
1991/2	-1,669	-237	306	-253	-12,552	-11,045	-7,641	-8,481	2,983	38,004	645	-26	-34	316,659
1992/3	-3,078	654	96	-1,402	-8,420	-14,189	-5,544	-6,348	-1,181	40,099	-265	-330	-92	303,294
1993/4	-4,952	622	-1,887	-671	-8,758	-9,420	-4,614	-5,431	-1,630	37,871	-1,094	-19	-17	289,391
1994/5	-6,974	349	-2,741	-813	-8,947	-2,841	-3,220	-3,652	-556	29,291	269	78	-243	285,464
1995/6	-7,436	638	-1,245	-369	-12,626	-2,822	-3,566	-2,161	7,656	22,025	564	-554	-104	291,764
1996/7	-8,134	136	-1,648	-1,263	-17,436	1,977	-5,873	-2,794	26,282	9,880	-54	-696	-377	292,873
1997/8	-9,490	-416	-2,569	-3,192	-16,958	9,231	-5,276	-1,940	43,089	-10,029	-1,024	-1,316	-110	309,234
1998/9	-5,695	193	201	-1,244	-13,065	16,706	-2,113	-4,333	25,191	-14,484	-747	-555	-55	276,930
1999/2000	-4,263	104	-270	-1,183	-12,146	22,369	-3,456	-7,947	22,674	-14,610	-691	-651	70	285,817
2000/1	-4,493	165	-2,077	-1,530	-9,442	18,623	-4,323	-8,410	20,457	-8,286	-572	-160	48	269,220
2001/2	-3,352	62	-898	-1,218	-4,350	5,354	-4,344	-8,820	26,235	-8,556	-221	84	24	290,490
2002/3	-1,683	165	510	-843	-1,829	637	-2,875	-5,141	11,903	-1,037	149	242	-198	274,899
2003/4	-2,027	144	-772	-760	-822	-6,935	-2,565	-4,521	10,606	7,865	27	-105	-135	261,380
2004/5	-3,710	-139	-3,041	-2,074	-4,963	-11,172	-7,227	-9,515	34,423	8,214	53	-668	-181	285,544
2005/6	-4,342	-639	-3,024	-3,487	-9,411	-17,501	-7,881	-7,083	45,795	8,800	-73	-954	-200	285,868
2006/7	-4,067	-849	-4,126	-2,632	-12,865	-20,047	-5,500	1,549	33,809	15,005	101	-221	-157	305,062
2007/8	-528	-291	-1,794	-908	-11,682	-14,750	-3,703	4,171	15,317	14,643	235	-420	-290	301,237
2008/9	1,877	-536	-751	-237	-7,419	-15,601	-3,111	2,983	13,184	9,995	228	-577	-35	277,846
2009/10	1,558	60	612	571	-3,258	-4,662	-2,412	2,153	-3,271	8,728	325	-351	-53	259,234
2010/11	30	-210	-41	-158	-4,763	-4,007	-3,517	545	8,443	3,421	363	-179	73	257,085
2011/12	-1,556	-1,252	-3,008	-2,182	-3,886	-8,091	-4,675	2,846	28,170	-4,648	265	-1,491	-492	311,921
TOTAL	-122,599	2,280	-18,831	-23,054	-540,042	24,196	-201,262	-190,771	546,427	545,737	-3,054	-15,692	-2,558	13,008,979

Source: Statistics Canada, 2013, CANSIM Table 051-0012;

only +24,000 persons over the full 1971–2012 period. While immigrants to Canada continue to move to Ontario (and to the Greater Toronto Area in particular), the province has not been growing through interprovincial migration. In fact, Ontario has witnessed nine straight years of net negative interprovincial migration over the last decade.

All but Alberta, British Columbia, Yukon, and Prince Edward Island witness more years of net out-migration than net in-migration over this period. In Quebec, the net losses were greatest in the 1976–83 period, where they were above 20,000 per year with a high of 46,429 in 1977–8. Since 2003, Quebec's net losses have actually been less than Ontario's, with average annual losses of –6,560 and –11,420, respectively. Manitoba and Saskatchewan have had net losses, with the exception of some small gains in the 1982–84 period, and most recently for Saskatchewan, with six consecutive years of positive net migration. For Canada's North, while the numbers are smaller, the overall pattern shows net departures for Northwest Territories and Nunavut. Alberta is the province to record gains over more years than any other, while British Columbia recorded gains across most years except for a period of economic downturn in the late 1990s and early 2000s. Atlantic Canada continued to lose population due to the common practice of migrating to Central Canada and farther west in search of employment. People have generally tended to move to provinces that were nearby, large, or farther west.

An important observation surfaces when one looks at total flows: Ontario can still be considered the "hub of the migration system" since the overall numbers coming into and out of Ontario are very large, involving about one half of all interprovincial moves nationally (Bélanger, 1999; Statistics Canada 2013k; authors' calculations). Over the 1971–2011 period, Ontario actually received more than 3 million in-migrants from other provinces (primarily from Atlantic Canada and Quebec) while losing almost an identical number through out-migration (including both return migration as well as primary

and onward migration to Canada's western provinces). Based on Demography Division's time series, with a total movement of over 6.3 million people, Ontario's net gain over four decades was a mere +24,000 persons (3.171 million in-migrants; 3.145 million out-migrants). The substantial demographic growth that Ontario has experienced over recent decades is the result of international migration and natural increase, and not due to movements into and out of the province from elsewhere in Canada.

In sum, only 4 out of 10 provinces in Canada have made net gains in terms of migration, in considering the combined impact of internal and international migration: British Columbia, Alberta, Ontario, and, to a lesser extent, Quebec. While Quebec has consistently lost population through migration to other provinces, this has been offset by the fact that it continues to be one of the preferred destinations for international migrants. Ontario, while gaining only marginally overall through interprovincial migration continues to attract a sizable share of all international migrants. Both British Columbia and Alberta have gained through both internal and international migration, although BC in particular has received a disproportionate share of international migrants. The fact that all other provinces have either lost population or have been negligibly affected by this migration is striking, as Canada is a country of immigration that in 2011 had 6.5 million non-native-born people. Among the provinces that have gained the most, people born in another province or abroad constitute a very large share of overall population, at over half of BC's population and over 4 in 10 Albertans.

Political Implications of Differential Growth

It is useful to anticipate the future of differential growth and distribution in various elements of Canadian society. Regional population growth has been highly uneven, and there is little reason to believe that this will not continue well into the future.

Migration, both international and internal, has been important in this context, particularly as natural increase across Canada's regions has become more homogeneous. Canada's reliance upon immigration in maintaining demographic growth has had a large impact on metropolitan Canada, whereas other parts of Canada without large cities have seen their relative demographic weight decline. Similarly, the relative demographic weight of Ontario, British Columbia, and Alberta has increased relative to the rest of Canada, as these three provinces have all received a disproportionate share of migrants, whether we refer to internal or international migration.

For some of Canada's largest cities, the pace of growth has been particularly dramatic, as, for example, the CMAs of Toronto, Calgary, and Edmonton have all seen their populations more than double in fewer than four decades. At current rates of growth, both Edmonton and Calgary could well observe a further doubling of their population over the next half century (Alberta Treasury Board and Finance, 2012), while the Greater Toronto Area is projected to increase by as much as 38 per cent over the next 20 years (Ontario Ministry of Finance, 2010). On the other hand, the relative demographic weight of other regions, outside Canada's CMAs, has declined in terms of absolute numbers and/or population share. For example, of the roughly 2,000 municipalities across Canada with at least 1,000 population in 2011, about one third had zero or negative population growth over the previous intercensal period (Statistics Canada, 2012h; authors' calculations). For the remaining 3,000 villages with populations of fewer than 1,000, roughly two thirds experienced zero growth or population decline. So, across much of Canada's geography, regions face the prospect of demographic decline, the out-migration of the young, aging populations, natural decrease, and fewer immigrants.

In an analysis of migration and population distribution, Boyd (2005) refers to a "growing demographic divide" between Canada's rapidly growing metropolitan centres and the remainder of the country. Matthews (2006) elaborates upon the many challenges faced by not only rapidly growing cities and regions, but also those that are experiencing slow growth, zero growth, or even negative growth. For governments at all levels (municipal, provincial, and federal), the problems of planning are particularly difficult when the pace of demographic growth is either particularly high, or particularly slow or negative. For mid-sized cities and small towns outside Ontario, British Columbia, and Alberta, the problem is not only one of very slow growth, but also of declining influence, both politically and economically. Alasia and Rothwell (2003) document for rural and small-town Canada a declining share of aggregate income, particularly in the most peripheral areas of the country.

For Atlantic Canada, about 70 per cent of all municipalities witnessed a decline over 2006–11, many of which were already very small. Over the same five-year period, more than half of rural municipalities in Manitoba and Saskatchewan lost population, while almost one third lost an equivalent of 10 per cent or more (Statistics Canada, 2012g). Similar population losses were witnessed across many communities in Canada's North, with the exception of a few areas important to the resource sector. As an exception, the urban centre of Fort McMurray, 420 kilometres northeast of Edmonton, witnessed a population boom of over 28 per cent growth between the 2006 and 2011 Census. Migrants have flocked to northern Alberta, primarily because it is near the Athabasca oil sands, one of Alberta's most important hubs of oil production. In the resource industries of Northern Canada, there is the growing phenomenon of workers who commute long distances, a practice that can strain the communities and supply centres near a mine or other resource site (Radke, 2006). The result is that workers in resource industries like mining and logging live in a limited number of centres, often with highly transient populations, while much of the sparsely populated North remains unaffected by such economic activity.

The patterns of differential growth in cities, towns, and rural areas are further compounded in an aging population. Two phenomena are at work here:

older people are less prone to move, resulting in an "aging in place" (Dandy and Bollman, 2008); on the other hand, older persons who do move are likely to go in fairly large numbers to the same places, thereby having a significant effect on housing markets and the need for services (Turcotte and Schellenberg, 2007). The age composition of given places is a function of the age profile of those who move as well as of those who stay. It is for this reason that many small towns and rural areas have higher proportions of elderly people, who do not necessarily find the services they need there. Dandy and Bollman (2008) note that small towns and villages more distantly removed from larger metropolitan areas tend to be the oldest (or "greyest" in age), due to lack of jobs and educational opportunities for the young. The resultant out-migration from these locations leaves a population that is predominantly old and retired. This implies a number of needs: health care, public housing, subsidized transportation, formal and informal care facilities, and recreational facilities (Hodge, 2008).

While Canada's population is becoming increasingly concentrated into a limited number of municipalities, none of these municipalities, whether large or small, exercise real fiscal or legislative autonomy. Even though cities and towns are largely responsible for many local services (e.g., water, sewage treatment, garbage collection, roads, public transit, snow removal, policing, fire services) the degree of autonomy in planning and paying for these services varies by province and municipality (Stevenson and Gilbert, 2005). The boundaries of municipalities tend to be under provincial rather than municipal control, and cities have none of the constitutional guarantees that have been conferred on provincial boundaries and jurisdictions. Yet the demographic reality is that 28 CMAs now have a larger population than the province of Prince Edward Island, and 6 of the largest (Toronto, Montreal, Vancouver, Calgary, Edmonton, and Ottawa–Gatineau) have more citizens than any of the Atlantic provinces. In this context, municipal governments continue to be limited in their powers,

and are often caught under the unilateral control of the provinces. As a lobby group for municipal government in Canada, the Federation of Canadian Municipalities (2013) has criticized the federal government for failing to develop policies on cities and not fostering cooperation across different levels of government. Conflict over jurisdiction has left a vacuum: little is being done to promote more balanced urban growth, redistribute urban growth to smaller municipalities, or to improve the quality of the environment in large urban centres.

There are clearly political implications of this growth, just as there are economic implications of Canada's regional disparity. The evolving patterns of population distribution will put further strain on constitutional and political arrangements that need to properly represent the regions at the federal level. Kerr and Mellon (2010), for example, highlight the manner in which the current representational order in Ottawa's House of Commons arguably penalizes regions of the country that are growing most rapidly—the average federal electoral district in Atlantic Canada, Saskatchewan, or Manitoba represents a population that is much smaller than the average one in Ontario, British Columbia, or Alberta. In addition, Senate seats have been established on the basis of four "equal" regions: the Atlantic provinces, Quebec, Ontario, and the West. The Supreme Court traditionally has three judges from each of Quebec and Ontario, one from the Atlantic provinces, and two from west of Ontario. Given that the largest province is 90 times larger than the smallest, it can become difficult for provinces to be treated equally.

The federal government nonetheless attempts to appoint cabinet ministers from each province, regardless of population size. Just as Quebec has sought new arrangements with the feds that would recognize it as being a distinct society, the West has sought to have more power in the federal government—an unsurprising fallout from the growth in its population. As several cities have now become larger than many of the smaller provinces, there are further problems of representation in metropolitan Canada, including an under-representation of new

Canadians in the political process (Choudhry and Pal, 2007). Quebec's declining share of the national population has its political implications—in 1867, for example, the province held 35.9 per cent of the country's ridings, but this percentage was down to only 24.3 by 2011. In 2015, when the latest representation formula is introduced, Quebec will hold 23.1 per cent of the ridings (Mellon and Kerr, 2012). The 2011 federal election was unique in Canadian history, as a majority government was elected in Ottawa with virtually no support from within the province of Quebec (the governing party won only four seats there), a situation that was at least partially due to the province's declining share of overall population.

Thirty years ago, the Royal Commission on the Economic Union and Development Prospects for Canada (1985) concluded that there needed to be a better way of including the regions in the workings of federal policy-making institutions. Some representation from each region in the governing party could be ensured through a form of proportionate representation based on popular vote in each region. Another alternative would be a stronger Senate with a focus on representing regional interests.

Population Distribution and Regional Economic Inequality

The trends in population distribution have long been associated with economic inequality across the country. In 2011, the median earned income for individuals in Canada's richest province (Alberta) was 67 per cent higher than the poorest (Prince Edward Island), and the median total income was 34.3 per cent higher (Statistics Canada, 2013n). Despite such differences, the general trend over the last half century has been a lessening in these regional differences. For example, the average income per capita in Quebec has hovered at about 90 per cent of Ontario's over recent years, up from roughly 60 per cent in the 1950s (Capeluck, 2014;

Beaujot and McQuillan, 1982). The largest differences across provinces are in unemployment, whereas the differences in average earned income per employed person are not as large. Across provinces, the 2013 unemployment rate ranged from 11.5 per cent in PEI to 4 per cent in Saskatchewan. For people involved in the labour market, provincial labour-force participation rates varied from 61.2 per cent in Newfoundland and Labrador through to 73 per cent in Alberta (Statistics Canada, 2013i).

These ongoing economic disparities continue to be among the most serious of economic problems faced by Canadians. Canada has a long history of national policies meant to address these inequalities at the regional level. In the 1960s, for example, the federal government established the Department of Regional Expansion with the intent purpose of targeting and promoting development in some of the most depressed economic regions. More recently, this department was dismantled and replaced by four regionally based agencies (Western Economic Diversification Canada, the Atlantic Canada Opportunities Agency, the Economic Development Agency of Canada for the Regions of Quebec, and the Federal Economic Development Initiative for Northern Ontario), all with the intent of introducing developmental policies to the benefit of Canada's regions. In an analysis conducted over 25 years ago on Canada's regionalism, Polèse (1987) draws the somewhat obvious conclusion that still seems to largely hold true today: "There are definite limits to the capacity of public policy to alter long-run patterns." At the same time, as Polèse continues, this is not to suggest that regional policy is of no consequence.

In effect, a variety of policies have been promoted, including investments in infrastructure, investment in education and training, rural stabilization policies, industrial assistance, mega projects, resource and sectoral development, as well as compensatory or transfer policies. The general idea behind these developmental initiatives is that the federal government can potentially assist the provinces in efforts to improve regional productivity and the efficiency in their labour markets. The implicit assumption is that the national government is obligated to treat each region as a separate community, supporting its economy to ensure its longer-term viability. Many people are attached to their communities, would prefer to stay where they are, and view the out-migration of young adults as potentially a serious problem for the future vitality of their home regions. Dupuis and colleagues (2000), for example, find a strong association between educational credentials and the propensity to out-migrate, such that the more depressed regions in Canada have always lost their most dynamic and educated people of working age. Nolan (2007) argues for the preservation of a way of life in the outports of Newfoundland, where traditions and quality of life cannot be measured in economic terms.

In disadvantaged regions with higher unemployment and difficult labour-market conditions, the federal government has supplemented developmental initiatives with compensatory policies meant to directly assist individuals and families. For example, in regions with higher regional unemployment or with a sizable proportion of its workforce in seasonal employment (e.g., the fisheries), the federal government has modified its employment insurance program accordingly, making it easier to qualify, and in so doing, allowing for benefits over a more extended period. Canada has a broader system of transfer payments, to both individuals and governments, meant to equalize somewhat any differences in the economic conditions across its regions. (For a useful overview, see Finance Canada, 2012.) As stated in the Constitution Act of 1982, "Parliament and the Government of Canada are committed to the principle of making equalization payments to ensure that provincial governments have sufficient revenues to provide reasonably comparable levels of public services and reasonably comparable levels of taxation." In the 2011–12 fiscal year, six provinces in Canada received roughly $16.1 billion in equalization payments from the

remaining wealthier provinces, as determined by the population count of each province and the relative ability of provincial governments to raise revenues to provide public services for its residents (Finance Canada, 2012).

The internal migration decisions of individuals clearly have consequences for the communities involved, regardless of government policies and efforts to curtail out-migration. As an alternative to these developmental and compensatory policies of the federal government, the inter-regional market-adjustment approach has also had its impact on public debates relating to regional development. The underlying logic of this argument is associated with a seminal academic paper, published several decades ago, that argues for the free movement of factors of production (capital, labour, and goods), expecting this to equalize wages across regions (Courchene, 1981). That is, as wages decline in disadvantaged regions, the unemployed would move out and industries seeking cheap labour would move in, bringing an eventual increase in wages. The "logic" of this argument is somewhat contradictory to the developmental and compensatory approach outlined above. For instance, the inter-regional market-adjustment approach might argue against transfer payments. Courchene (1981) argues that transfer payments protect the lagging regions from the discipline of the market and, in so doing, lock them into a dependent state that he calls "transfer dependency." This makes the disparities worse, and the economy less efficient.

The views on these alternatives depend in part on whether we seek to maximize individual welfare or the welfare of communities. If we take the point of view, as Courchene (1981) does, that it is not the welfare of geographic communities that counts, but rather the welfare of individuals, then it would follow that we would want to maximize the national economic efficiency by eliminating barriers to trade and mobility. If the individual is not achieving well-being where he or she is living, the important thing is to be able to find opportunities elsewhere, and these opportunities will be maximized if the overall economic efficiency is maximized. In the alternative approach, developmental initiatives and transfers are promoted in order to maximize the viability of all communities, regardless of location.

There is arguably a basic conflict between attaining overall economic efficiency and achieving regional development. Inasmuch as questions of equity and preservation of community remain important values, we need to resign ourselves to some economic inefficiency. The conflicting points of view can be thought of as two geographic grids, one representing the distribution of resources and economic opportunity, and the other representing the distribution of population. Two strategies are possible for making the two grids more symmetric: bring the people to the jobs, or the jobs to the people. While there are difficulties involved in taking somewhat conflicting approaches simultaneously, this may be unavoidable.

Even the Canadian Charter of Rights and Freedoms recognizes this contradiction in the section on migration. It speaks of the right of citizens and permanent residents "to move and take up residence in any province; and to pursue the gaining of a livelihood in any province." It goes on to set certain limits to this broad stipulation, however, saying that this does "not preclude any law, program or activity that has as its objective the amelioration in a province of conditions of individuals in that province who are socially or economically disadvantaged if the rate of employment in that province is below the rate of employment in Canada." In effect, provinces that have higher-than-average unemployment can give preference to the employment of residents of the province— the right of individuals to move needs to be balanced with the impact that the movement has on the communities to which they move.

There will be continuous debate on the relative importance of individual and community welfare, along with the specific mechanisms to achieve these objectives. Where people are situated geographically will also influence their willingness to entertain one or the other alternative. Sensitive national-unity issues are at stake in this debate. The inter-regional market-adjustment approach implies that, on average, individual welfare will improve if we build on the strong economic areas, submit every region to the discipline of the market, minimize the inefficiency that results when we support the lagging regions, and encourage people to move out of these areas. After all, it is best for them if they move, and everyone should be equally at home anywhere in the country. On the other hand, those who promote the political and economic interests of Canada's regions would support developmental and compensatory policies, ensuring the economic and demographic viability of all provinces and regions. There are historical, cultural, and political arguments for treating each region as a separate community, ensuring its sustainability so that it stays within the fold, and remembering that most people typically prefer to stay where they are.

In terms of migration, then, the inter-regional market-adjustment approach prefers to move people to the jobs, whereas the developmental and compensatory approach prefers to move the jobs to the people. The tax system, for example, supports migration by allowing tax deductions for the cost of moving. There are many policies related to human resources and employment on both sides of this ledger, some that promote local communities and others that promote the mobility of labour. As natural increase becomes a less-important source of growth, and, consequently, as we can no longer think of relative growth but of some regions declining while others grow, the debate between these policy alternatives is not likely to lose its intensity. There are likely to be continued calls for approaches that would bring more development to the disadvantaged regions and for policies that would benefit the country as a whole. At stake are the very visions of the country, either as various communities that need to be sustained, or as a whole where economic efficiency should be maximized.

Critical Thinking Questions

1. In what ways are the trends in regional dynamics a source of unity rather than diversity?
2. Describe and interpret the relative growth of the regions of the country.
3. How does globalization affect the demographics of urban and rural areas, and what are the implications for the age structure of those areas?
4. What generalizations can be made about the characteristics of migrants, places of origin, destination, and the migration process?
5. Use theoretical interpretations of migration to discuss the relative importance of primary, return, and onward migration.
6. Analyze the following demographic components of population redistribution: natural increase, international migration, and internal migration. Show how the conclusions may differ depending on the areas under consideration.
7. What constitutional arrangements are under stress in the evolving distribution of population?
8. Contrast the inter-regional market-adjustment approach with other developmental policies for reducing economic inequality across regions.

Recommended Readings

Bone, R.M. 2011. *The Regional Geography of Canada*, Fifth Edition. Don Mills, ON: Oxford University Press. This book serves as an introduction to the basic physical, historical, cultural, social, and economic features of Canada's regional geography, taking into account their relevance within a global context.

Day, K., and S.L. Winer. 2012. *Interregional Migration and Public Policy in Canada*. Montreal and Kingston: McGill-Queen's University Press. This text critically reviews four decades of empirical research on the relationship between internal migration and regional variation in the generosity of Canada's many transfer and equalization programs.

Dion, Patrice, and Simon Coulombe. 2008. "Portrait of the mobility of Canadians in 2006: Trajectories and characteristics of migrants." *Report on the Demographic Situation in Canada, 2005 and 2006*. Statistics Canada cat. no. 91-209-X, pp. 78–98. This issue of the annual report has an extensive analysis of internal migration.

Okonny-Myers, Ima. 2010. *The Interprovincial Mobility of Immigrants in Canada*. Research and Evaluation, Citizenship and Immigration Canada, June. This document highlights some of the key analytical findings from the study of the interprovincial mobility of immigrants and their retention, based on data extracted from the Longitudinal Immigration Database.

Statistics Canada. 2014. *Annual Demographic Estimates: Canada, Provinces and Territories*, cat. no. 91-215-X. This annual publication presents estimates of the total population, done by age and sex, for Canada, the provinces, and the territories. It also presents estimates of the components of population change: births, deaths, immigration, emigration, returning emigration, net temporary emigration, net non-permanent residents, and inter-provincial migration.

Related Websites

www12.statcan.gc.ca/census-recensement/2011/as-sa/index-eng.cfm. Contains a wealth of information from the 2011 Census about thousands of municipalities in Canada.

www.prl.ualberta.ca. Maintained by the Population Research Laboratory, a centre for social science research established in 1966 at the University of Alberta in Edmonton. It conducts research in social policy, health, population, education, and public opinion.

http://data.gc.ca. This federal government site, introduced in 2013, contains datasets compiled by over 20 departments and agencies. The datasets cover a broad range of topics, including housing, immigration, the environment, health issues, and crime statistics. The site also has datasets that allow for mapping data across Canada's geography.

7 Changing Growth Patterns and Their Implications

The Chapter at a Glance

- Over the last 100 years, Canada's population has multiplied sixfold, a higher growth rate than that of the world population.
- Whereas the fifty year period 1961–2011 has seen the Canadian population grow by almost 90 per cent, Statistics Canada's medium-term projection suggests a slowing of growth to about 46 per cent over the next 50 years.
- The medium population projections are based on the fertility assumption of 1.67 births per woman, life expectancy reaching an average of about 88.5 years in 50 years, and an annual immigration rate of 7.5 immigrants per 1,000 (gradually rising from about 260,000 immigrants in 2013 to almost 400,000 by 2062–63).

- The population of labour-force age, which grew extensively with the entry of the baby boom into the workforce, is expected to slow considerably over the 2011–31 period.
- Immigration of some 225,000 per year would prevent population decline, and also labour-force decline, in the foreseeable future but would not stop the relative growth of the number of people older than labour-force ages.
- Issues of slower growth and aging raise questions about both attempting to sustain growth and adapting to changed demographic conditions.
- From an environmental perspective, questions are raised about sustainable development rather than growth.

Introduction

There are alternative points of view about the effects of population growth. Some people take the view that population growth reduces the average well-being because the resources have to be shared by more people. If we put in the numerator the total resources and in the denominator the number of people, then the lower the denominator the higher the average well-being. A larger population, however, can also produce more resources of some (though not all) types. Therefore, the simple division of resources by population gives an inaccurate view of the impact of population change. The resources under consideration could be natural resources, or the overall goods and services, or jobs. Although population growth can mean the division of goods, jobs, or other resources among more people, it can also mean the production of more of these goods, jobs, or other resources.

Ehrlich (1968), in his book *The Population Bomb*, argued that population growth would undermine human welfare on the planet. However, his work exaggerated the effects of population growth on pollution and the depletion of resources, as per capita consumption has more effect than total population. Alternatively, Julian Simon (1981) saw population growth as the "ultimate resource," which would benefit our standard of living through economies of scale and more frequent inventions. He failed to appreciate that technology and the quality of the labour force are more important than the size of the population itself. The effects of population growth are complex; they involve interplay of environmental questions, consumption patterns, and technology. We might agree that the environment sets limits. In particular, the economy needs to exist within the limits of the environment, including the inputs of natural resources and the outputs that affect the environment (Cohen, 2010; Smil, 2013). Although we can make a case that population growth has contributed to Canada's past development, the same need not apply to the future.

Having analyzed mortality, fertility, and migration in previous chapters, we can follow the overall picture of changes to the population. In this chapter, we will consider the growth patterns in Canada's past and the prospects for the future. There will be a specific focus on growth of the labour-force population. We will end the chapter with a discussion of concerns about population growth and related policy questions.

Past Population Growth

Canada's population grew from 5.4 million in 1901 to 34.5 million in 2011, or a more than sixfold increase

(see Table 7.1). Although we pay much attention to the rapid growth of the world population, it is noteworthy that over the same period, the global population actually increased at a slower rate than Canada's: globally the numbers went up by about fourfold, from 1.6 billion to roughly 7 billion.

Population growth has also varied considerably over Canadian history. There have been three periods when growth was close to 3 per cent a year: 1851–61, 1901–11, and 1951–61. These are high rates of growth indeed, surpassing the more recent figures for many Global South countries. By way of comparison, it is estimated that population growth for the total of developing countries peaked in 1965–70 at 2.5 per cent a year (United Nations, 2001: 12). This was also the peak period of world population growth, at 2.04 per cent a year.

There have also been three periods of Canadian population growth has been closer to 1 per cent per year: 1881–1901, 1931–41, and 1981–2011. With a

Table 7.1 ▣ Population Growth, Showing Net Migration Component, Canada 1851–2011

	Population at End of Period	Population Growth Rate%	Contribution of Net International Migration to Growth% [1]
1851	2,523,000		
1851–61	3,230,000	2.5	25.7
1861–71	3,689,000	1.3	−32.7
1871–81	4,325,000	1.6	−8.5
1881–91	4,833,000	1.1	−28.7
1891–01	5,371,000	1.1	−24.2
1901–11	7,207,000	2.9	44.1
1911–21	8,788,000	2.0	19.7
1921–31	10,376,700	1.7	14.5
1931–41	11,506,700	1.0	−8.1
1941–51	14,009,400	2.0	6.8
1951–61	18,238,200	2.6	21.0
1961–71	21,962,032	1.9	14.2
1971–81	24,819,915	1.2	41.6
1981–91	28,037,420	1.2	42.4
1991–01	31,019,020	1.0	54.5
2001–11	34,483,975	1.1	67.5

[1]From 1971 onward, net change in NPRs is included in the time series, as are all of Statistics Canada's migratory components. These estimates do not accommodate for the residual term in Statistics Canada's time series, which potentially modifies this column.
Sources: Keyfitz, 1950; McInnis, 2000; Statistics Canada, 2012m.

growth rate that averaged 1.1 per cent in the most recent decade (2001–11), it remains higher than the average elsewhere—for example, the annual growth rate for Europe as a whole was only 0.2 per cent over this same decade, or less than one fifth of Canada's rate. Figure 7.1 shows further comparisons between Canada and other relevant countries from 1950 to 2010 using data compiled from the United Nations Population Division (United Nations, 2013a). For this period, Canada's population growth has been slightly slower than that of the world as a whole, much lower than its North American neighbour, Mexico, as well as lower than most less developed countries (LDCs). On the other hand, Canada's growth was higher than that of the United States, France, the United Kingdom, or, more generally, all of Europe, and other more developed countries (MDCs).

The higher growth in Canada as compared to most other developed countries is due both to immigration and to the after-effect of the baby boom. Even though they were having fewer than two children each, the large number of couples at child-bearing ages ensured that there were considerably more births

than deaths in the population. In terms of population growth, Canada was living off the baby boom into the end of the twentieth century.

Patterns by Historical Decade

As we saw in Chapter 2, the fact that the population of New France had not exceeded 70,000 by 1760 (after 150 years of colonization) had significant political consequences. Given the international tensions of the Seven Years' War (1756–63), it is not surprising that the French population lost military and political control over the territory. By contrast, the population of the area now known as Canada grew rapidly in the first century of British rule. Heavy immigration and high fertility brought the total to 3,200,000 in 1861. The average rate of growth of the population of non-Aboriginal origin was 3.7 per cent per year between 1760 and 1861. This rapid growth helped Canada to become a separate political entity among the nations of the world.

Between 1861 and 1901, Canada's annual growth rate declined to an average of 1.3 per cent. This period included the long depression during which the

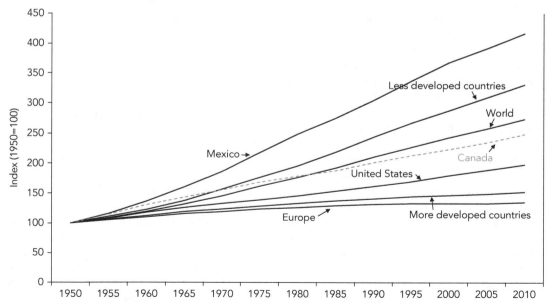

Figure 7.1 ▣ Change in Population Size, Various Countries and Regions, 1950–2010

Source: United Nations, 2013a.

demand fell for Canadian grain and raw materials. Although the flow of immigrants continued, about half of them moved on to the fast-industrializing New England states south of the border. In addition, some 1.5 to 1.8 million native-born Canadians emigrated to the United States during this period (Lavoie, 1972: 39; McInnis, 2000a: 422). This is a very large figure when one considers that the population of Canada was only 3.2 million in 1861 and 5.4 million in 1901. Emigration to the United States had serious consequences for Canada—in effect, it helped to establish a pattern of dependence on the neighbour to the south. Given the lack of employment possibilities in the country, Canada was exporting a surplus population as well as raw materials and was thus promoting industrialization in the United States. Another important consequence of the emigration stemmed from the fact that most of the Canadians who moved south (to the New England states) were French speaking. If the movement had been west rather than south, the two languages would have been distributed more evenly throughout the country.

In discussing Canada's population in the twentieth century, the historical demographer McInnis (2000b) begins with the "era of mass immigration, 1901–31" and ends with "immigration to Canada since 1945," treating the 1931–45 period as an "interlude." In effect, the beginning of the previous century witnessed a turnaround in growth patterns, due to immigration, that brought population growth to 2.9 per cent per annum from 1901 to 1911. The transcontinental railway had been completed, and earlier-maturing varieties of wheat, culminating in the introduction of the famous Marquis strain in 1903, pushed the farm frontier northward (Cartwright, 1941: 4). This coincided with the upturn in world economic conditions and the decrease in the availability of virgin land in the United States. This population growth in Canada around the turn of the century extended the area of settlement by populations of European origin and in effect permitted the Canadian state to maintain political control over the vast western and northern reaches of the continent.

After 1901–11, population growth declined during each successive decade owing to decreases both in fertility and in net immigration; it reached a low of 1

per cent a year during the 1931–41 period. Barber (1978, 1979) has speculated that the lower rate of population growth may have contributed to the economic difficulties of the period. Clearly, there are a series of factors—economic, environmental, political, and even psychological—underlying the Depression, but the demographic factors should not be ignored. The decrease in population growth started before the Depression, and it may have weakened the incentive for long-range business investment. The Depression also certainly affected population growth: the 1931–41 decade saw the only net emigration of the century and the total fertility rate fell to 2.6 children per woman in 1937, a level which was not to be seen again until 1967.

Population growth regained momentum during the war years, reaching a high of 2.6 per cent annually in the 1951–61 period. These were the peak years of the baby boom as well as an era of high immigration. The 1950s and '60s were unique in Canada as a long period of almost uninterrupted economic growth. Though there have been fluctuations from year to year, the general trend since the height of the baby boom has been downward, although the last two decades have seen a stabilization of sorts, with a growth rate close to 1 per cent per year. The principal source of slowing growth relative to the 1950s has been a decline in the number of births. Over the 1961–86 period, immigration also declined in relation to the size of the population.

The Future of Canada's Population

Some of the first attempts to project Canada's population were disastrous. Using data to 1931, Hurd (1939) projected that the population of Canada would reach 15.4 million in 1971. At the end of the war, demographers at what was then known as the Dominion Bureau of Statistics projected even lower figures. They forecast that the 1971 population would be between 13.8 and 14.6 million (Charles et al., 1946). The DBS further estimated that it would reach a maximum of 15 million in 1990. We now know that by 1951, the population had already reached 14 million and by 1971, it was 21.6 million. These projections essentially failed to foresee the baby boom, and they also assumed that international migration would continue to be negligible, as it had been during the Depression and the war.

Since the 1971 Census Statistics Canada has made population projections after each census. Partly because the underlying demographics have been more stable, these projections have been much closer to the mark. For instance, the projections released in 1974 gave a range that easily included the actual figure for 2001 (Statistics Canada, 1974). The closest was Projection B, which yielded a 2001 population of 30.7 million (only 1.4 per cent off the mark). Especially in the context of the changes in population definition, wherein non-permanent residents are now considered part of the population, and the adjustments that are now made for under-enumeration, these are quite accurate results. The band of projections for 2001 was 28.4 to 34.6 million. There were compensating errors, however, in that fertility was overestimated and immigration underestimated. Consequently, in Projection B, the population over 65 was expected to be 3,314,800 in 2001, whereas the actual figure was 3,917,900, representing a shortfall of 15 per cent. The under-projection of the population aged 65+ was mostly because of conservative assumptions on improvements in life expectancy.

Some subsidiary projections have also been far from the mark, such as those for post-secondary school enrolments. The projections made in the mid-1970s were 31 per cent off the mark for total full-time post-secondary enrolment by the mid-1980s (Zsigmond et al., 1978). It was not the demographics that were wrong, but participation rates were expected to be stable, as they had been in the late 1970s, especially for men. Though reasonable at the time, this turned out to be an inaccurate assumption since post-secondary participation rates rose after a period of being flat.

Projections tell us as much about the present as about the future. We see, for instance, that it took some time for demographers to conclude that fertility would stay below replacement levels (see Table 7.2). Though we had not seen fertility above replacement since 1972, the high assumption after the 1986 Census was still using a total fertility rate of 2.1 births per woman. We have seen a tendency to consider that there is something magical about replacement fertility, but patterns in a number of countries show that the trends pay no attention whatsoever to the figure of 2.1. As indicated, the assumptions for life expectancy have had to be raised over time, especially as we have seen reductions in adult mortality. For immigration, the assumptions pay considerable attention to the numbers at the time of the projections.

One of the values of these population projections is that they are based on a cohort-component method. That is, the population by age and sex is advanced year by year, with assumptions about fertility,

Table 7.2 ▣ Assumptions Underlying Statistics Canada Projections, 1971–2011

	Total Fertility Rate			Immigration			Life Expectancy M/F		
	L	M	H	L	M	H	L	M	H
1971 Census	1.80	2.20	2.60	120,000	–	160,000	–	70.2/78.3	–
1976 Census	1.70	–	2.10	125,000	150,000	175,000	–	70.2/78.3	–
1981 Census	1.40	1.66	2.20	100,000	–	150,000	–	74.9/81.6	–
1986 Census	1.20	1.67	2.10	140,000	–	200,000	–	77.2/84.0	–
1991 Census	1.50	1.70	1.90	150,000	250,000	330,000	77.0/83.0	78.5/84.0	81.0/86.0
1996 Census	1.30	1.48	1.80	180,000	225,000	270,000	78.5/83.0	80.0/84.0	81.5/85.0
2001 Census	1.30	1.50	1.70	204,000	280,000	360,000	81.1/85.3	81.9/86.0	82.6/86.6
2006 Census	1.50	1.70	1.90	245,000	335,000	435,000	82.3/86.0	84.0/87.3	85.4/88.4
2011 Census[1]	1.53	1.67	1.88	202,000	343,000	462,000	83.8/86.0	85.1/87.3	87.0/89.5

[1]Projections are for the reference period 30 years following the census.

Sources: Statistics Canada, 1979, 1985, 1990; 1994; 2001; 2005; 2014a.

mortality, and migration. Before considering in more detail the results from the projections released after the 2011 Census it is worth indicating alternative assumptions and their justification through current theory and evidence. The sections that follow will review the materials presented in Chapters 3, 4, and 5 with a view to formulating projection assumptions.

Fertility

In the projections based on the 2011 Census Statistics Canada has used fertility assumptions of 1.53, 1.67, and 1.88 births per woman. These assumptions on fertility are slightly higher than the projections based on the 1996 and 2001 Census. The assumptions used for the projections based on 2006 and 2011 Census are reasonable, given that the 2011 fertility rate was 1.61 children per woman, down slightly from 1.69 a few years earlier. The low assumption of 1.5 would return Canada's fertility to its lowest level ever observed (roughly a decade earlier), yet still slightly higher than what has been labelled the *low-low fertility* countries of Southern and Eastern Europe. Theorizing about particularly low fertility, McDonald (2002) proposes that these latter countries, which also include Japan and Hong Kong, have witnessed particularly low fertility (1.3 births and even lower) due to constraints, as represented especially by opportunity costs that children represent for women and young adults. Fertility might increase in these countries if these opportunity costs could decrease with institutional arrangements like greater paid leave, part-time work with good benefits, and subsidized child care.

The broader theoretical interpretation of fertility needs to be based on the demographic transition. The first transition involved a change in the economic value and cost of children and a new appreciation of the advantages of controlling one's reproductive destiny. The second transition involved various family changes, especially a greater looseness in entering and leaving relationships, along with later ages at entry into relationships, later age at child-bearing and lower fertility.

As we saw in Chapter 4, further theoretical reflections on the dynamics of fertility in modern societies needs to consider the proximate factors, along with the value and cost of children, and the interplay of production and reproduction. The main proximate factors are union formation and contraception. Unions occur later, with a somewhat lower proportion of people living in a union, and there is a greater willingness to have children in cohabiting unions. Contraception is quite reliable, especially for people in a stable relationship, and abortion is available for unwanted pregnancies.

Research suggests that most people want children and that fertility intentions are typically higher than fertility outcomes (Beaujot and Bélanger, 2001; Edmonston et al., 2010). Children are valued as a source of enjoyment in life, including the special relationships that children represent, and as long-term links with other people. The costs are mostly in time and energy, given that people have other interests and responsibilities. Given the changed family models, the interplay of production and reproduction is felt not only by families but also by individual women and men. There are situations where this interplay makes it very difficult to have children, especially if most of the opportunity costs are borne by women (Ranson, 1998). Yet there are other situations where the division of paid and unpaid work makes possible a better sharing of the costs of children (Beaujot and Ravanera, 2009; Ravanera et al., 2009). These questions of supportive marital relationships and flexibility at work are probably the factors most responsible for the extent to which delayed births are recuperated after age thirty. Child-bearing has been fairly stable since the mid-1970s, while women's workforce participation has continued to rise. Although some of this stability was due to women's double burdens, there are also improvements in the sharing of the work on the part of men and the larger society (Marshall, 2011).

At least with the proper policies, it can be proposed that Canada is not likely to be among the countries to experience low-low fertility, and a cohort projection of 1.5 to 1.9 is an easier assumption to defend (Beaujot and Bélanger, 2001). Societies are in less danger of particularly low fertility if there is state support for families and for gender equality, and if families of various types are accepted. It would appear that fertility can be sustained in post-modern family conditions, which include the acceptance of births in cohabiting relationships, the de-gendering of child care, and the flexibility of opportunities for both part-time and full-time work. Though Canada does not have all of these features, we may be moving in the right direction to avoid particularly low fertility.

Although it is very difficult to foresee the future, even into the medium term, available theory and empirical evidence suggest that Canadian fertility will remain within the range of 1.5 and 1.9 births per woman. If one assumption is to be chosen, we would prefer the cohort level of 1.7, which was used in projections following the censuses of 1981, 1986, 1991, 2006, and 2011. As we saw in Chapter 4, the lowest cohort level that has been experienced is 1.75, for women born in 1968. More recently, completed fertility is up slightly, as, for example, Milan (2013a) estimates a completed fertility rate of at least 1.8 for women born in the late 1970s. Myrskyla and colleagues (2013) forecast a similar levelling off and slight upturn in cohort fertility across a range of Western countries, including Canada.

Mortality

Taking an average of men and women, the most recent Statistics Canada projections use life expectancies in the range of 85 to 88.2 years by 2042–43, up from a life expectancy at birth of 81.5 at the beginning of the projection period (Statistics Canada, 2014f). As seen in Table 7.2, life expectancy has been revised upwards from one projection to the next. Just as it was hard to think that fertility could remain permanently at below-replacement levels, the tendency has been to expect that there are real limits in terms of future gains in life expectancy, and that further reductions in mortality will be much more difficult to achieve. One reason for this is that there has been the tendency to pay particular attention to things that are getting worse, rather than vice versa, things as getting better over time. There is now considerable concern, for instance, both in Canada and

the United States, with the climbing incidence of obesity among North Americans and its potential impact on future longevity (Olshansky et al., 2005). Yet over this same period, we have managed to reduce quite dramatically the number of deaths from heart disease, at least partially due to medical advances in the treatment of high blood pressure and its associated risks.

In 1971, Omran argued that the improvements in life expectancy were likely reaching some limit, and in effect the improvements had been declining from census to census (Omran, 1971); yet the changes since have been larger than anticipated. Life expectancy in 1971, for example, was roughly 73 in Canada, whereas over the four decades or so that have passed since, it went up by roughly 8 years. It was also expected that the divergence between women and men would continue to grow (Gee and Veevers, 1983). On the contrary, the divergence has declined from over 7 years in 1971 to 4.27 years in 2009–11, not because women are dying sooner, as some pessimists had thought, but because men have made significant gains (Trovato, 2007; Bohnert et al., 2014).

It was largely unforeseen in the early 1970s that adult mortality would be significantly reduced. In effect, much of the previous gains had been due to reductions in infant and childhood mortality, along with fewer deaths of women in childbirth, and by the early 1970s, there was little room for further improvements in these forms of mortality. But we subsequently saw improvements in cardiovascular mortality, then in accidental deaths, and now, to a lesser extent, in cancer mortality (Dumas and Bélanger, 1997; Milan, 2011b). That is, all three of the modern causes of death are in decline. We can usefully speak of a fourth phase of the epidemiological transition toward delayed degenerative diseases and hubristic causes (Olshansky and Ault, 1986; Bah and Rajulton, 1991). *Delayed degenerative* means that cardiovascular and cancer deaths are occurring at older ages. *Hubristic* mostly means an overconfidence that produces reckless behaviours in the face of risks—for example, continuation of smoking, alcohol abuse, and the consumption of fast foods and/or other unhealthy foods.

The proximate factors or causes of death, requires a fuller analysis in relation to risk factors and treatment. It is probably safe to say that, for many major causes of death, these are improving significantly, and there is room for further improvement. In terms of risk factors, with the exception of certain subpopulations, there is increased concern about health in areas ranging from diets and exercise to harmful habits like smoking tobacco (Ramage-Morin et al., 2010). For accidental deaths, safety measures are being enhanced in the home, at work, and on the roads, and there has been a greater recognition of certain dangers, such as drinking and driving (Ramage-Morin, 2008). In the case of cancer, where the declines have been slight, improvements in environmental quality may be an important means of reducing risks, but this may be particularly difficult in a world where standards of living depend on high use of manufactured energy and other environmentally unfriendly forms of consumption.

To be sure, treatment factors are particularly hard to predict because they involve scientific and technological advances. While many complain about the underfunding of the health system, there are several reasons for optimism. First, the high quality of the personnel in the health-care system would suggest that technological advances are likely. Second, the public tends to be very favourable to further public spending for health. Third, there is a growing willingness to seek help from the health-care system; the interactions with the system are increasing more than population growth or aging would predict.

While it is easy with 20–20 hindsight to say that we were too conservative in the past in anticipating changes, we may also be too conservative in our predictions of further changes. For instance, while Statistics Canada's medium projection based on the 2011 Census projects an average gain of roughly 1.5 years per decade over the next 30 years, Oeppen and Vaupel (2002) propose that life expectancy could continue to rise by more than 2 years per decade, as it has in the past 150 years. Until the revisions for the year 2000, the United Nations used a projection model in which the highest possible life expectancy was 85; this has now been revised to show 92.5 years.

For the 10 countries with the highest life expectancy in the 2012 revision, the UN projects gains that are comparable to Statistics Canada's (with decennial gains in the range of 1.47–1.65 years), yet the highest life expectancy is projected for Hong Kong at roughly 88.5 by 2040. As health conditions in Canada are among the top countries in the world, it could be argued that Statistics Canada's most optimistic assumption on life expectancy is also reasonable, projecting a 2.2 year per decade increase (88.2 years by 2042–43).

Immigration

Immigration assumptions have also varied considerably in the projections summarized in Table 7.2. The projections following the 1981 Census for instance, used a range from 100,000 to 150,000, whereas those following the 2001 Census used 204,000 to 360,000. In these latter figures, we see immigration levels of roughly 1 per cent of Canada's population, an attractive number to use in policy statements, but with little obvious demographic justification. The most recent projections are even higher, with a wider range on immigration projections, from 202,000 to 462,000 immigrants annually by 2042–43.

Empirically, the main generalization seems to be that if immigration is going up, it will eventually come down, and if it is going down, it will eventually come back up. Given this variability, it would seem best to use longer-term averages rather than short-term fluctuations if projections are to be based on past trends. Figure 7.2 demonstrates how Canada's immigration rates have varied widely, while also summarizing the rates that correspond to its three immigration assumptions. Given past variability, the medium assumption is closest to the rates as observed over the two decades prior to the projection, the low-growth assumption is closer to rates as observed during the late 1970s and early '80s and the high growth is closer to the high levels witnessed in both the early 1970s and the early '90s. More specifically, the medium assumption sets the immigration rate at 7.5 immigrants per 1,000, the low assumption assumes a decline to 5 immigrants per 1,000 and the high

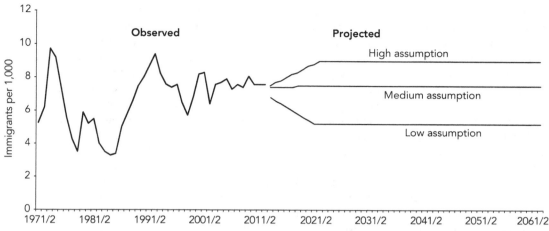

Figure 7.2 ▣ Canadian Immigration Rates Observed (1971/72–2012/13) and Projected (2013/14–2062/3) According to Three Assumptions

Source: Statistics Canada, 2014.

growth assumes an increase, up to 9 immigrants per 1,000. With all three assumptions, the rate is held constant from 2022–23 onward. Regardless of scenario, the by-product is sustained immigration for all assumptions, as tied closely to the corresponding immigration rates and corresponding rates of population growth.

Theoretically, mortality has a certain simplicity in the sense that everyone dies, and only once, of a given cause, and there are also certain biological constraints on fertility, but migration is considerably more complex. For international migration, there are push and pull factors, along with various barriers between places of origin and potential destinations. These barriers, represented especially by policy, are probably the main way in which to understand shifting trends (Beaujot and Matthews, 2000). At the very least, we need to appreciate that levels of immigration are a function of things happening both in Canada and outside the country, along with the links between countries (Simmons, 2010).

Given the pressure for out-migration resulting from the demographic transition, the medium term will show no shortage of people who want to come to Canada, and these outside pressures are probably increasing (Castles and Miller, 2009). In other words,

there is no upper limit in the number of immigrants that would potentially migrate to Canada, if provided the opportunity, from a global population of over 7 billion. Yet, of course, the factors that must be analyzed are from within Canada, especially economic and demographic, but perhaps social and political factors should be given even greater prominence. Politically, immigration policy has tended to follow the social climate, and thus not to deviate excessively from public opinion.

Currently, Canadians appear to support the notion that Canada benefits from immigration, yet there is in fact relatively little public or political debate on this issue. There are certainly a number of people who are seeking to make a case for high immigration, including many first- and second-generation Canadians who hope to sponsor relatives and others from their home country. While Statistics Canada's medium- and high-growth targets are higher than current levels, so, too, will be Canada's total population size, as these levels are determined by rates and directly tied to the country's population size. In providing a rationale for these higher assumptions, Statistics Canada (2014f) points out that higher immigration targets might also be perceived as important in a context of rapid aging and slowing natural increase. The low assumption, which allows immigration levels to fall slightly (to below 200,000 annual immigrants by 2022), presents a hypothetical situation whereby the push and pull factors that attract immigrants to Canada lessen somewhat into the future (Bohnert and Dion, 2014).

As we saw in Chapter 5, unemployment no longer seems to be a particularly useful predictor of immigration. Canada has maintained relatively high immigration targets throughout the recession of the early 1990s as well as during the most recent economic downturn in 2008 and onwards. Historically, though, the social and political tendency was that Canada was less open to immigration when economic conditions were more difficult, with a public mood that we should look after ourselves first when economic times get tough. If this interpretation is correct, to the effect that receptivity to immigration is mostly a function of social and political climate, then predictions of changes in trends are particularly difficult to make. When the social mood is more favourable, there is the tendency to see immigration positively, especially for its contribution to the cultural richness of Canada and the contact it provides with a broader pluralistic world. Nonetheless, these social and political climates are subject to change and difficult to predict over the long term.

Projection Results

Among the various possible combinations of these assumptions, Statistics Canada (2014f) has chosen the following to represent alternatives in population growth nationally:

- Projection 1: Low Growth—with low fertility, low life expectancy, and low immigration
- Projection 2: Medium Growth—with medium fertility, medium life expectancy, and medium immigration
- Projection 3: High Growth—with high fertility, high life expectancy, and high immigration

The discussion of the assumptions would suggest that each of these is a legitimate projection, on the basis of available theory and evidence. Nonetheless, we would argue that Projection 1 uses too low a level of fertility, while Projection 3 uses too high a level of immigration. Although it might be argued that Projection 2 also has too high immigration, it uses a somewhat conservative projection on life expectancy—it is likely closest to the current trends, is most consistent with the UN projections, and thus easiest to defend. As seen in Table 7.2, the assumptions in Projection 2 are a fertility of 1.67, an immigration of 7.5 immigrants per 1,000 (i.e., levels rising from about 260,000 in 2012–13 to about 343,000 by 2042–43), and a life expectancy climbing to 86.2 years by 2042–43 (or 85.1 years for males and 87.3 years for females).

Figure 7.3 shows these three projections to 2063 working with the 2011 Census and the 2013 post-censal population estimate as its base year. All three scenarios show population growth for the full projection period. In the low series, the population grows from 35.2 million in 2013 to 39.6 million in 2043, and then projects very slow growth to about 40 million by 2063. In the medium series, the population grows to 44.9 million in 2043, and even further to 50.5 million by 2063. In the high series, the growth remains substantial throughout the projection period, from 35.2 million up to 63.5 million by 2063. In contrast to the sometimes-widespread impression among the general public that Canada is on the edge of population decline, all scenarios project growth for the next 50 years. This, of course, does not guarantee the fact, as none of the scenarios had particularly low fertility (the low-low fertility that has characterized some countries in Europe), nor do any involve particularly low immigration—a circumstance that is certainly possible given the history of immigration to Canada (all scenarios, including the low growth, project an average of more than 200,000 immigrants annually for the full projection period).

In the 50 years from 1961 to 2011, the population of Canada increased by 89 per cent. Only the high-growth scenario shows a similar comparable growth, up 80.5 per cent for the 2011–61 period. In contrast, the low- and medium-growth scenarios see, perhaps more realistically, increases of 16.3 per

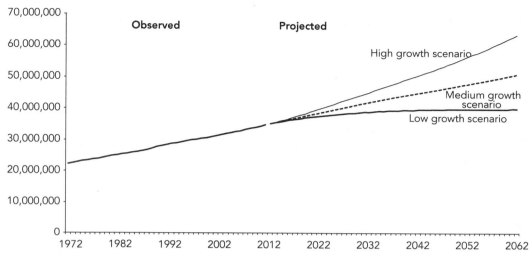

Figure 7.3 ▦ Population of Canada, Observed (1972–2013) and Projected (2014–63), according to Statistics Canada's Low-Growth, Medium-Growth, and High-Growth Scenarios

Source: Statistics Canada, 2014a.

cent and 46.4 per cent, respectively. If we look at the medium-growth projection, we see that population growth is expected to gradually slow, from 1.06 per cent over the 2006–11 period to 0.81 per cent after 2026 and 0.65 per cent after 2056, all in a context of below-replacement fertility and population aging (see Table 7.3). While the medium-growth scenario sees a slowing of population growth, only the low-growth scenario suggests a future with close to zero growth, down to 0.36 per cent for the 2026–31 period and as low as 0.03 per cent by mid-century. On the other hand, the high-growth projection suggests an immediate upturn in growth (up to 1.33 per cent by 2021–6), with growth rates remaining at 1.1 per cent or higher for the full projection period.

All three scenarios project population growth for the full projection period, despite the fact that all three also assume below-replacement fertility. A particularly important factor in this context is the projected immigration, which is expected to climb in importance in underlying demographic growth over the next several decades. In addition, both the medium- and high-growth scenarios also

project, somewhat counterintuitively, positive natural increase (births minus deaths) for the entire projection period. Figure 7.4 charts births and deaths over almost a century of demographic change, first working with Statistics Canada's historical time series (1971–2013) as well as with the medium-growth projection (2014–63). While below-replacement fertility has characterized child-bearing in Canada since the early 1970s, natural increase has remained positive and is expected to continue to do so well into the future. While the gap between births and deaths narrows considerably, this is not due to a projected decline in the number of births but instead to a significant upturn in the number of deaths, as associated with population aging.

When fertility falls below replacement, the natural increase of a population can remain positive due to what demographers refer to as the *population momentum* inherently built into a population's age structure. Even in closed populations (not influenced by migration), when total fertility declines, there is typically a lag period before the rate of natural increase also declines. Canada's fertility rate fell

Table 7.3 ◎ Average Annual Rate of Canadian Population Growth, 1986–2013, and Projected, 2014–2061

1986–91		1.43	
1991–96		1.09	
1996–01		0.93	
2001–06		0.98	
2006–11		1.06	

Projections	Low	Medium	High
2011–16	0.94	1.07	1.16
2016–21	0.64	0.95	1.27
2021–26	0.47	0.89	1.33
2026–31	0.36	0.81	1.24
2031–36	0.25	0.73	1.16
2036–41	0.16	0.66	1.11
2041–46	0.10	0.63	1.10
2046–51	0.05	0.61	1.11
2051–56	0.03	0.62	1.14
2056–61	0.04	0.65	1.18

Sources: Statistics Canada, 2014m; authors' calculations using mid-year population estimates, 1986–2013, and projections, 2014–2061.

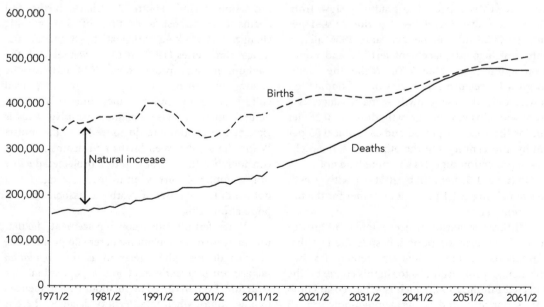

Figure 7.4 ◎ Births and Deaths, 1971–2013; Projected 2014–2063, Canada

Source: Statistics Canada, 2014n, CANSIM 053-0001.

below replacement in the early 1970s and declined to a low of 1.5 births per woman in 2000 before rebounding somewhat since. Yet the number of births has continued to outnumber deaths, leaving a positive rate of natural increase throughout this period. This population momentum is ultimately explained in terms of age structure, as Canada was relatively youthful in the early 1970s due to the baby boom of previous decades (1946–64). The analogy is often drawn of a moving train, which continues to move even after the engineer slams on its brakes; similarly, a relatively youthful population would not stop growing even if it were to immediately witness a precipitous drop in fertility.

Population momentum can occur because of the relative sizes of different age cohorts, or, in other words, the relative size of older cohorts that are at a much greater risk of mortality in comparison to the size of younger cohorts that are either currently bearing children or are soon to enter into the reproductive years. The relative size of these different age groups then affects in an immediate manner both the absolute number of births and deaths. The women already born build momentum into the population, even if on average they have below-replacement fertility. In the Canadian context, natural increase will likely remain positive for many more decades, yet will also likely decline in importance as the particularly large cohorts born during the baby boom move into their most senior years. Those born during the height of the baby boom in 1959, for example, will not reach their seventieth birthday until 2029 and their eightieth until 2039. In terms of future mortality, even with climbing longevity, demographers forecast a substantial climb in the absolute number of deaths as the largest of the baby boom cohorts move into the highest mortality years.

For both the medium- and high-growth projections, natural increase remains positive, whereas even with the low-growth projection (with a fertility of 1.53), an additional 17 years of positive natural increase is projected, through to 2029–30. Also relevant in this context is the projected number of immigrants received by Canada, as a large proportion of migrants are of child-bearing age (i.e., strong immigration has a positive effect on the number of births).

This is illustrated in a simulation that accompanied Statistics Canada's 2006 round of projections—a simulation that projected Canada's population into the future, yet with zero net migration. This provides insight as to how Canada's population would evolve without international migration, if, hypothetically, it were to act like a "closed population." Using rates of fertility and mortality very similar to the medium scenario, a closed population would grow exclusively through natural increase to reach a maximum by 2025, before declining to 30.6 million by 2061 (Statistics Canada, 2010c). Comparing this result to the actual medium projection shows that an immigration rate of 7.5 immigrants per 1,000 adds 9.4 million people to the population over 26 years and about 22 million over 50 years. This unlikely assumption of zero immigration nonetheless indicates that immigration levels will play a large role in Canada's future population growth.

While the medium growth scenario projects continued positive natural increase, natural increase declines, from about 130,000 a year at the beginning of the projection period down to about 26,000 toward the end (see Table 7.4). Over this same period, net international migration increases in importance, from roughly 200,000 a year in 2010–11 to over 300,000 by 2060–61. Yet despite the declining share of growth explained by natural increase, it is important to appreciate that this situation still includes population renewal through births, but the increase in deaths is expected to outpace the increase in births. In the medium projection, for instance, the number of births exceeds the number of immigrants throughout the projection period. When natural increase is expected to be responsible for most of the growth by the end of the projection period, there are still 504,600 births in 2060–1 compared to 388,500 immigrants. In effect, rather than speaking of the net change brought about by births minus deaths and immigrants minus emigrants, it is equally important to compare births and immigrants in population renewal. Although natural increase declines in importance, making net migration responsible for 92 per cent of all growth by 2060–1, the births continue to outnumber immigrants by about 30 per cent (see Table 7.4).

Table 7.4 ▣ Population and Components of Population Growth (in thousands), Canada, 2010–2061

Period	Population at Beginning of Period	Births	Deaths	Natural Increase	Immigrants	Emigrants	Net International
2010–11	34,005.3	377.0	245.0	**132.0**	259.1	56.7	**205.5**
2015–16	35,872.6	397.5	266.6	**130.9**	267.4	63.7	**225.5**
2020–21	37,646.5	418.0	288.0	**130.0**	283.8	66.4	**217.4**
2025–26	39,385.8	421.9	311.3	**110.6**	298.9	68.2	**230.7**
2030–31	41,052.8	417.8	341.1	**76.7**	312.7	69.6	**243.1**
2035–36	42,605.3	422.5	378.9	**43.6**	325.7	71.3	**254.4**
2040–41	44,067.1	440.1	418.9	**21.2**	338.1	73.4	**264.7**
2045–46	45,485.9	461.0	452.8	**8.2**	350.2	76.2	**274.0**
2050–51	46,903.4	479.9	475.7	**4.2**	362.4	79.1	**283.3**
2055–56	48,370.9	494.3	482.6	**11.7**	375.0	81.7	**293.3**
2060–61	49,946.8	504.6	478.2	**26.4**	388.5	84.2	**304.3**

Source: Statistics Canada, 2014n; authors' calculations.

Given these different patterns of growth and decline, it is also useful to compare Canada to some other countries. Figure 7.5 compares both the medium- and low-growth projections from Statistics Canada with the medium-growth UN projections for the same set of countries shown earlier (see Figure 7.1). Unless demographic trends shift in both the United States and Mexico, the medium projection suggests that Canada's share of the North American total could easily increase over the next several decades, whereas the low-growth scenario suggests that Canada's share could actually decline slightly. There is considerable uncertainty as to Canada's relative demographic weight in the broader North American context in upcoming decades. Yet both projections still show growth that is substantially higher than in Europe or across most other more developed countries. The population decline elsewhere is at least partially explained in terms of lower fertility, but also in terms of lower levels of immigration. Few countries have been as open to immigration as Canada.

Population at Labour-Force Ages

The labour force is defined as "people who are either employed or actively seeking work (unemployed)." In "One Hundred Years of Labour Force," Crompton and Vickers (2000) show that the labour force grew from under 2 million in 1901 to almost 16 million by 2000. The periods of most rapid growth were those of particularly high immigration, especially the decades of 1901–11 and 1951–61. In addition, the labour force grew as a result of the increased female participation in the workplace that characterized the second half of the twentieth century. Among women aged 25 and older, for example, the labour-force participation rate was only about 20 per cent in 1955, yet increased quite rapidly to over 40 per cent by the early 1970s and over 60 per cent by the early 2000s.

The trends in the labour force and in the whole population have been different in terms of both growth and aging. While the growth of the full Canadian population slowed, for example, from about 2.6 per cent annually in the 1950s to roughly 1.2 per cent in the 1970s, the growth in the Canadian labour force accelerated, with a peak growth of some 4 per cent a year from 1971 to 1976 (Martel et al., 2011). The labour force grew rapidly into the 1970s and '80s as the largest of the baby boom cohorts born during the 1950s and early '60s completed their education and moved into the workplace. Regarding aging, though the whole population had been aging

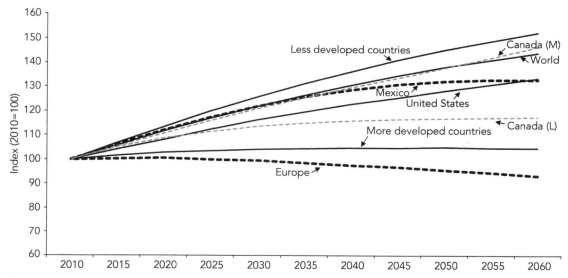

Figure 7.5 ▣ Projected Populations, Various Countries and Regions, 2010–2060

Sources: United Nations, 2013a. Population Division of the Department of Economic and Social Affairs of the United Nations Secretariat, *World Population Prospects: The 2012 Revision, Medium Projection*; Statistics Canada, 2014a: medium and low projections.

for more than a century, the average age of the labour force did not rise until the mid-1980s, when the entire baby boom was of labour-force age.

More recently, the patterns for the population and the labour force have become more similar, although growth in the labour force has continued to outpace growth of Canada's overall population. For example, the labour force grew at about 1.8 per cent per year from 1980 to 1985, down slightly to average 1.5 per cent from 2000 to 2012 (Statistics Canada, 2013o). In maintaining this growth, the workforce participation rate has continued to climb, reaching an all-time high of roughly 68 per cent of Canadians aged 15 years and older in 2008 (Statistics Canada, 2013o).

More broadly, the impact of demographic change on the labour force can be examined by considering the population at labour-force ages, defined here as persons aged 18–64, regardless of whether or not they are employed or seeking a job. By considering this age group, we can derive hints as to future labour-force growth. Working with Statistics Canada's projections, we can concentrate on this subpopulation, while recognizing that these age boundaries are somewhat arbitrary, as, for example, many older Canadians

retire well before or well after the conventionally defined retirement age of 65, just as an increasing proportion of young adults are delaying employment and continuing full-time studies well into their twenties.

Figure 7.6 summarizes Statistics Canada's projections for this population at labour-force ages. For two of the three scenarios, the 15 years from 2013 to 2028 shows little or no growth, whereas the high-growth scenario shows a slowing rate of growth. In the low-growth projection, this population is projected to increase slightly through to 2018 before declining—down by 1.4 per cent over the 2013–28 period. The medium-growth population is projected to increase by only 3.5 per cent between 2013 and 2028, prior to witnessing a more pronounced growth in the decades to follow. Even in the high projection, total growth in this subpopulation is projected to be only 7.5 per cent from 2013 to 2028. This compares with a growth of fully 18.8 per cent over the previous 15-year period, from 1998 to 2013. Thus, all scenarios provide evidence to suggest that the growth rate in the labour force will likely slow, even with the relatively high immigration levels that underlie Statistics Canada's medium- and high-growth projections.

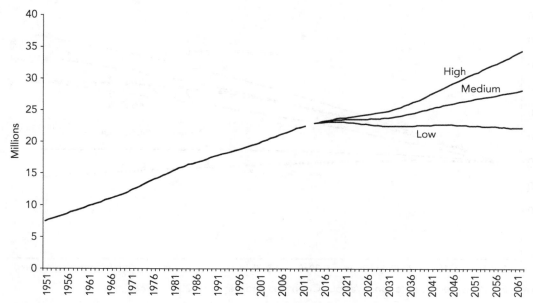

Figure 7.6 ▣ Growth of the Population Aged 18–64, 1951–2012 (estimated) and 2013–2016 (projected), Canada

Sources: Statistics Canada, 2013b; Statistics Canada, 2014a.

A fundamental factor in explaining this slow-down is the unique shape of Canada's current age structure; just as the entrance of the baby boom generation into the labour force had a pronounced impact on its rate of growth, so, too, will its eventual exit. A particularly useful comparison in this context can be made between the populations at ages 15–24 and 55–64, which are typical ages for entering and leaving the labour force. When the age and sex profile from the 2011 Census was released, much publicity was given to the fact that the oldest people of the baby boom generation were about to reach their 65th birthday in the census year. With this, the census showed that for the first time, there was roughly the same number of people in the 55–64 age group as the 15–24 age group. Large cohorts of boomers will reach their 65th birthday over the next 15 years, and for the first time, these boomer cohorts will be considerably larger than the youngest cohorts who follow them into the labour force. Figure 7.7 demonstrates this fact, by providing the ratio of the population aged 15–24 years to those aged 55–64 years, for the extended period of 1971–2061.

This ratio was down substantially from the period of peak labour-force growth in the early 1970s, when almost 2.5 persons were newly entering the workforce to roughly every 1 person exiting it (i.e., precisely when the largest baby boom cohorts were first entering the labour market). While this ratio was near parity in 2011, in forecasting future labour force growth, this ratio is expected to decline further, to about 0.8 for all three of Statistics Canada's projections by 2021. For the next 20 years, then, there will likely be fewer people about to enter the labour force than exiting it through retirement. Even with high immigration and climbing participation rates, which can affect the size of all age groups in the labour market, it is quite likely that growth in the Canadian labour force will slow quite noticeably, with uncertain economic consequences.

Replacement Migration

Given the changes expected in the population, it is useful to study the extent to which immigration could counter some of these trends. A United Nations (2000) study has called this a question of "replacement migration." That

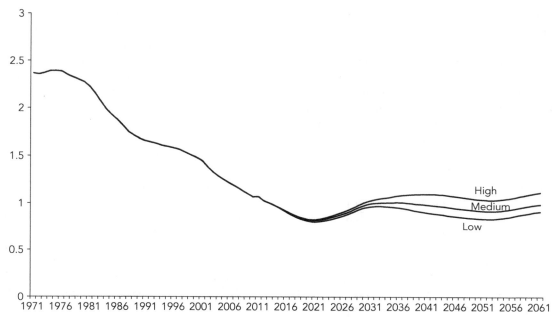

Figure 7.7 ▣ Ratio of Population Aged 15–24 Years to Population Aged 55–64 Years, 1971–2012 (estimated) and 2013–2061 (projected), Canada

Sources: Statistics Canada, 2013i; Statistics Canada, 2014a.

is, how could migration bring forms of replacement that would keep the population more similar to what it has been in the past?

One of the definitions of replacement migration is the number of immigrants necessary to prevent long-term population decline as a result of below-replacement fertility. Ryder (1997) uses the concept of replacement migration to mean the level of migration that would achieve the same ultimate population size as we would achieve if fertility were at replacement levels. Using the fertility and mortality rates of the early 1990s, Ryder places the replacement migration figure at about 215,000. Other studies have used this idea, suggesting that immigration somewhat above 200,000 would prevent population decline at recent levels of fertility and mortality (see Beaujot and Matthews, 2000).

Besides having enough migration to prevent the population from declining, a second meaning of replacement migration would be to use migration to maintain the size of the labour force. If the objective is

to prevent the labour force from declining, it is useful to realize that there are other factors that can be manipulated. McDonald and Kippen (2001) have outlined scenarios where, besides immigration, other factors are considered—in particular, the participation rate in the labour force (including ages at entry and departure, and women's participation) and the level of fertility. In Canada, along with United States, New Zealand, Australia, and Singapore, decreases in labour supply can be avoided through a continuation of the present rates of fertility, immigration, and labour-force participation. These results are similar to those obtained by Denton and colleagues, where immigration of 200,000 per year shows the labour force declining slowly between 2026 and 2036; in 2036, nevertheless, it is still 16 per cent larger than in 1996 (Denton et al., 1997: 38–9). Compared to the other 16 countries studied by McDonald and Kippen (2001), Canada and Australia have "moderate fertility, high immigration, and low labour force participation." With zero net immigration, the current fertility and labour-force participation rates would bring declines in labour supply after about 2015. With current immigration, their results show the labour force rising only slowly but not declining. Increased labour-force participation rates, moving men's rates at ages 35+ toward their rates in 1970, and moving women's rates at ages 25+ toward Swedish rates, would lead to large increases in labour supply (at least a 20 per cent increase from 2000 to 2030). A return to fertility of 1.8 would bring growth of the labour force after 2025, compared to holding fertility and migration constant.

Thus, there are various means to prevent the labour force from declining, including having a continued annual immigration of some 225,000 per year (see Box 7.1). The third scenario of replacement migration used by the United Nations (2000) seeks to maintain the relative size of the population aged 15–64 to that aged 65 and over. As recognized by the authors of the report, this scenario leads to absurd results, requiring astronomically high immigration targets (Coleman, 2000). This would be an extreme meaning of replacement migration, with migrants eventually replacing the original population (Lachapelle, 2001). As shown by various projections, including those by Denton and colleagues (1997), there is no demographic solution to aging. The aging of the population cannot be prevented by replacement migration, and this is demonstrated in Figure 7.7, which compares the ratio of people at ages 15–24 to those aged 55–64 (ages for typical labour force entry and exit). This ratio was at about 1 at the time of the 2011 Census but all scenarios show a ratio of about 0.8 by 2021, when the largest of the baby boom cohorts will be on the cusp of retirement. This ratio is 0.80 in the low projection from Statistics Canada, with annual immigration of roughly 220,000 over the 2013–2021 period, 0.82 in the medium projection, with annual immigration of about 270,000, and 0.83 in the high projection, which assumes an average immigration of almost 300,000 over this same period.

Box 7.1 ▣ Immigration and Labour-Force Growth

The public discourse on immigration often misrepresents the underlying demographic dynamics associated with labour-force growth. In a 2009 speech by Canada's federal minister responsible for citizenship, immigration and multiculturalism, for example, it was observed that "with the demographic changes that will soon start to take hold, within a few years, 100 per cent of Canada's labour market growth will be attributable to immigration" (Kenney, 2009). Similarly, the 2002 Annual Immigration Plan (Citizenship and Immigration Canada, 2001: 2) observed that "70 per cent of labour force growth was due to immigration." Such figures are derived by merely dividing the number of workforce participants who arrived over a specific period by the change in the size of the workforce over the same period. That shows what percentage of the change in the size of the labour force is due to immigration. When the

workforce is growing slowly, as is now the case, this figure is not very meaningful. If, for instance, the labour force grew from 10,000,000 to 10,000,001 but 1 member of the workforce was an immigrant, then 100 per cent of the labour-force growth would be due to the arrival of that single person. It is more useful to look at the relative size of the internal and external sources of entry into the labour force.

The number of people turning, say, 20 in 2012 was roughly 480,000, for example, while immigration was about 260,000. Of course, neither group would be completely in the labour force. If we estimate that 90 per cent of those who reach labour-force age will be in the workplace at some point, and that about 75 per cent of immigrants are aged 15–64 and would immediately enter the labour force, then we would have 627,000 additions to the labour force, of which 68.9 per cent would be due to internal recruitment and only 31.1 per cent due to immigration.

That is, while immigration is an important source of recruitment to the labour force, its importance has been exaggerated. On the basis of projections using zero immigration, for instance, Baxter is quoted as saying, "If we didn't have immigration, we'd stop regenerating our labour force in about four years" (Hutchinson, 2002: 32). This implies that there is little regeneration by all the people leaving Canadian schools to enter the labour force. It is absurd to say that our labour force will not be renewed unless we have immigration!

Immigration is clearly an important source of recruitment, but there are other options. Moreover, depending excessively on immigration can also make us lazy about encouraging other sources of recruitment from within; it is not productive if we fail to make the necessary investment in education and training and neglect domestic population groups that have low labour-force participation. In 2012, for instance, the average hours worked per week was 38.9 for employed men and 32.9 for employed women. If women's average hours were increased to that of men, it would be the equivalent of a 7.9 per cent increase in the size of the labour force (Statistics Canada, 2013o; authors' calculations). Similarly, at ages 25 and over, the employment rate was 68.3 per cent for men and 58.4 per cent for women. Reducing that difference would be equivalent to a 6.9 per cent increase in size of the labour force (Statistics Canada, 2013p; authors' calculations).

Concerns about Population Growth and Decline

There are both individual and collective interests in demographic phenomena. In particular, the number of children to have and where to live are immensely personal questions. At the same time, fertility and immigration are the fundamental mechanisms through which populations, countries, or societies are regenerated in the face of departures through death and emigration. These demographic processes not only determine the number of people, but they also change the character of the population and, thus, of the society. The characteristics of the population are changed in terms of age and sex structure, socio-economic composition, cultural makeup, and regional distribution.

Given the importance of demographic events at both the micro and macro levels, it is natural that there is considerable attention to ensuring that these operate in the best interests of both individuals and societies. Summarizing the situation in the mid-1980s, Marr (1987) concluded that the orientation had been relatively simple: "Canada had a small population relative to her needs and so that population should be enlarged." Focusing especially on the population of Quebec, Henripin (1954) expressed a similar point of view, to the effect that rapid growth had been beneficial and that a "contraceptive society" might mean a society where individuals were self-absorbed and unwilling to create life. More recently, Saunders (2012) made the case that Canada remains a victim of underpopulation: "We do not have enough people, given our dispersed geography, to form the cultural, educational and political institutions, the consumer markets, the technological, administrative and political talent pool, the infrastructure-building tax base, the creative and artistic mass necessary to have a leading role in the world."

On the other hand, others have long argued for slower growth. Back in the 1970s, for example, a publication by the Conservation Council of Ontario and the Family Planning Federation of Canada (1973: 54) clearly came out in favour of a policy to reduce growth: "Canada is already overpopulated . . . . [There is an] urgent need to . . . reduce . . . the absolute size of the human population of this country. . . . Even today, Canada has more people than it can support comfortably on a sustainable basis." Marsden (1972: 142) argued that there was a need for a comprehensive policy: "a policy concerning numbers, distribution and what we intend to do about them is essential." She was clearly in favour of slower growth: "We have not shown that continued growth is economically, politically, ecologically or socially desirable or necessary for the continued harmonious development of Canada" (Marsden, 1972: 133). More recently, the well-known Canadian science-and-nature broadcaster and environmentalist David Suzuki, in an interview published in the Paris weekly *L'Express* (2013), criticized Canada's fixation on economic and demographic growth, implying that current trends are environmentally unsustainable.

Until the 1980s, there had not been much Canadian demographic research that was aimed at policy concerns (Beaujot, 1985). The Royal Commission on the Economic Union (Macdonald Commission, 1985, II: 668) found that population was an area of Canadian policy which was "little debated, under-researched, and extremely important." In the 1986–92 period, the federal government established the Review of Demography and its Implications for Economic and Social Policy. The resulting report, entitled *Charting Canada's Future*, which was released in 1989, tended to take a neutral stance (Review of Demography, 1989). There was much discussion among academics and the public at large, but no clear directions were established by the time the review was shut down (Wargon, 2002: 209–14). The report suggested that there was no crisis, much of the change had been inevitable, and policy intervention was not advocated.

Issues Concerning Population and Policy

The neutral stance of the Review of Demography is similar to the concerns expressed by Keyfitz (1982) in *Population Change and Social Policy*, where he argued that the issues are very complex: "Whether we should be concerned about the low birth rate, about immigration, about age distribution in relation to social security, each involves a host of conflicting questions." Similarly, Ryder (1985) warns that by and large governments can have but little influence on the

onrush of social change. If there is concern about population dynamics, a crucial question is to know whether to try to influence these dynamics or to adapt to the changing population. McDaniel (2009: 50) argues that "policy challenges are determined not only by demographic structures and challenges per se but by the flow and interaction of multiple shifting processes, demographic, economic and social, national and global, in contexts of other policy priorities."

Hohn (1987) has observed that there is the potential for considerable conflict between the aims of various policies. Pro-natalist approaches are those that would encourage more births. However, she also notes that both immigration and pro-natalist strategies tend to conflict with the goals of other important and powerful social and economic policies. While Hohn favours policies that have explicit demographic aims, she points out that these can often be in conflict with other policies. For instance, many of the factors historically reducing fertility were rooted in the very emergence and expansion of the welfare state: the expansion of education reduced the extent to which parents could profit from the labour of young children, social security for health and old age reduced the dependence of elderly on their own children, and the emancipation of women provided opportunities outside the family and beyond the traditional role of mother. More broadly, low fertility and high life expectancy were the result of an enhanced quality of life. These blessings of the welfare state can be enjoyed even without children, from the individual point of view. But from the vantage point of society as a whole, children are, of course, needed. Consequently, parts of the conflict are between the goal of maximizing individual welfare in the short term and maximizing social welfare in the long term. Children in many respects offer present sacrifice for future gain. While social security allows the individual to avoid this dilemma, it cannot be avoided at the level of the society.

Chesnais (1996) speaks of the conflict as one between production and reproduction. Production and wealth are maximized, both at the individual and collective level, by maximizing the time spent in the labour force. But reproduction also takes time. There needs to be, then, an adjustment between production and reproduction, and that adjustment has increasingly been to the detriment of the latter. Equal opportunity in the labour force has come with a growing scarcity of children. This poses issues with regard to gender models that would allow for both emancipation and reproduction.

Environmental considerations bring another set of concerns that are related to population. Many have argued that the problem is found less with population growth than with the level of consumption, but both population growth and standards of living contribute to environmental damage. In its policy statement on population, for example, the Sierra Club of Canada (2013) has acknowledged that while human numbers are a cause of a worsening environment, it is overly simplistic to ignore a web of interrelated factors associated with resource consumption, technology, and the potential for ecologically sustainable production. Yet if one considers it very important to sustain the environment, possibly also wanting to maximize the cohabitation of the human species with the other species of the planet, then one is very likely to conclude that the population is already too large or that population growth is too high. If one feels strongly that "small is beautiful," then again a smaller population makes sense. In Chapter 12, we will return to these issues by addressing the role of population in environmental deterioration.

Issues of Low Fertility and Related Policy

In order to justify a policy, it is necessary to make the case that there is a problem, that the problem can be remedied, and that the proposed remedy will cost less than the problem itself (Demeny, 2011). In the case of low fertility, there is the additional complexity that the consequences are long term. The economic consequences of low fertility are probably mixed. Bloom (2010) argues that the "main economic effects" depend upon time frame; that is, while initially there is a "demographic dividend" associated with fewer child dependents, over the longer term, the consequences are uncertain in terms of the labour force, technological change, investments, and consumption.

Eventually, the "distribution effects" may be more negative; that is, as the old-age share of the population rises, there may be more inequality. Population aging makes higher demands on social security and health care, among other public expenditures, to such an extent that the welfare of other age groups, including children and younger adults, may suffer.

If we consider these questions at the family level, children are no longer needed as a means of old-age security. In the short term, families and adults may well be better off with few or no children. Minimizing the number of children reduces the number of dependents and gives adults more opportunity to join the labour force. In the longer term and at the level of the society, however, there is no escaping the need for younger generations to take care of the aged. In effect, there may be a conflict between promoting the welfare of the increasingly numerous older population and maintaining a standard of living of the young working-age population in order to provide a secure basis for child-bearing.

In his article "Demographic Recruitment in Europe," Lesthaeghe (1989) concludes that there may be advantages to low fertility, but only in the short term. Low fertility, he argues, is a high-risk path: "At the present state of knowledge about the social and economic effects of future aging, it seems unwise to trivialize the demographic issues." He especially argues against moving resources from the young to the old, because investment in the new generation is of paramount importance.

While there are difficulties in deciding to what extent low fertility is a problem, it is equally difficult to decide whether the problem (if it is a problem) can be remedied. The assessment of the impact of fertility policy is a very difficult question. The mechanisms that theoretically link policies with demographic outcomes are complex, involving imperfect and incomplete information, with often mixed outcomes (Gauthier, 2007). The most convincing case for the utility of pro-natalist policies involves East Germany, France, Sweden, and Norway. Comparing East Germany to West Germany, Buttner and Lutz (1989) note that the fertility trends were very similar from 1957 to 1972, but after East Germany introduced a series of measures in 1976, including high family allowances and housing benefits for families with children, its total fertility rate was higher by 0.4 to 0.5 more births per woman. Similarly, France once had one of the lowest fertility rates in the world, but in the last quarter of the twentieth century, it had higher fertility than the rest of the European Economic Community. France also has one of the most developed and ambitious family policies among Western European countries (Laroque and Salanie, 2004). In Sweden, the policies are more recent, but fertility has been raised in a country that has high female labour-force participation, in particular by promoting the idea, and associated policy, that adults should be seen as workers who would mostly want to have children (Bjorkland, 2006; Hoem and Hoem, 1996). Taking advantage of strong economic growth, Norway has promoted child-bearing through policies that are supportive of gender equality and the welfare of the family and that are not biased toward any particular kind of family (Ronsen, 2001).

Finally, part of the justification for a policy must be that its costs will be lower than the problem being addressed—in this case, low fertility. This is again a very difficult question, partly because the costs of low fertility are in the future while the costs of policies must be broached today. It was once thought that promoting higher fertility involved the unacceptable cost of limiting women's opportunities. Contemporary theorizing on low fertility, however, suggests that the main issue is that of addressing opportunity costs, through institutional arrangements like paid leave, part-time work with good benefits, and subsidized child care (McDonald, 2002). The right policies could also promote a more equal sharing between men and women of the costs of children (Beaujot, 2002a). The cost of such policies, which would support families and promote greater gender equality in families, could be justified on a variety of grounds.

Immigration versus Pro-natalist Policy

At least in the short term, immigration policies are probably less expensive than pro-natalist policies, and are therefore an easier way to increase the population. Nonetheless, Bouvier (2001) observes that immigration policies are not easy, especially when the

immigrants are very different from the native born. As the potential for receiving immigrants from other European populations decreases, more developed countries have increasingly faced issues associated with admitting and integrating "more distant foreigners." While the immigrant solution to below-replacement fertility may be not as serious in Canada as elsewhere, Ceobanu and Koropeckyj-Cox (2012: 261) have documented that across several more developed nations there is "considerable public resistance to population policies that encourage large scale immigration."

There are a variety of opinions on the issue of immigration as a means of compensating for low fertility. Statements on the policy implications of low fertility, based especially on the European experience, have tended *not* to identify immigration as a viable solution. With this in mind, perhaps it is best to think of a combination of policies to sustain fertility and to admit and integrate migrants. Lutz and colleagues (2003) argue that immigration policies that favour higher immigration might be considered more politically feasible if they were combined with efforts to also raise fertility among other potential reforms.

Ceobanu and Koropeckyj-Cox (2012) document that across Europe anti-immigrant sentiments are highest in the least prosperous of economies, and among the poorly educated and economically marginalized. Noting the very high levels of immigration needed to counter population aging, Coleman (2008) concludes that high immigration might be judged as inappropriate in this context. Bijak and colleagues (2007) suggest that immigration is typically a less popular and effective policy in countering population aging than efforts to increase the fertility rate. Bouvier (2001) emphasizes that populations that are not replacing themselves may especially resist an increase in the proportion of foreigners, particularly among European publics that have a history of anti-immigrant sentiment. While noting that immigrants enrich a society materially and culturally, the noted Quebec demographer Jacques Henripin (1989: 119) has argued that using immigration to compensate for a fertility deficit is giving an essential role to what should be a supportive role. In other words, the arrival of immigrants cannot be in excess of what the society can absorb, and that the original society would disappear if immigrants became substitutes for births.

These difficulties of an immigration solution may not be as serious in Canada. Many of the above statements are based on political rather than social or economic considerations. In the Canadian context, all of the country's major political parties (the Conservatives, Liberals, New Democrats, Bloc Québécois, and Greens) have pro-immigration platforms, while Canadian government statements have emphasized the economic, social, cultural, and humanitarian benefits of immigration. Reitz (2011) documents how Canadian public opinion support for immigration has been highly stable over time, largely unaffected by economic downturn and/or negative media reports on specific immigrant groups. Canada may be quite distinctive, among more developed countries, both in being willing to accept variety in its population and also in making policies and taking measures that facilitate the arrival and integration of diverse groups. It may be possible in Canada, then, to promote both immigration and fertility as means of sustaining the size of the population.

Population Policy: Can We Endogenize the Demographics?

It is not popular to talk about population policy. Even the Cairo Conference on Population and Development tended to avoid setting demographic goals at the macro level or promoting population policy, preferring instead to promote services that would allow individuals to control their reproductive destiny. In effect, population control has too often been used as a top-down approach that abuses individual rights. It is essential that ethical questions be brought forward and that only acceptable means of changing the population processes be adopted. In terms of child-bearing, as the Cairo conference indicates, people should have the means to make free and responsible decisions on the number and timing of their children. Policy that would infringe on this human right must be condemned, along with deliberate incentives that would constrain behaviour (United Nations, 1994, 2011b).

People should not be forced to have unwanted children, and they must be permitted to have the children they do want. However, we would add that it is legitimate for the society to call for certain behaviour that would enhance collective well-being, in child-bearing as in other domains. The size and composition of a society is obviously of interest to all its members, and there is a legitimate reason for people to influence one another on the question of having children.

What might we suggest as a population policy for Canada, in the sense of a vision of the preferred demographic future and a discussion of the means to move in that direction? This might start with two elements: (1) the advantages of some population growth or at least avoiding decline, and (2) slower rather than more rapid aging. Substantial demographic growth can be economically useful, or at least it has been in the past, but avoiding decline is probably more important from an economic point of view (United Nations, 2000). Decline would mean that various investments, such as housing stock, would lose their value. Population decline would also include particularly significant aging. On the other hand, environmental arguments point to the disadvantages of high growth. While population growth could encourage renewal in the form of more environmentally friendly consumption and technology, there is no avoiding the direct multiplier of population size on environmental impact, given our standard of living, which is based on high use of energy and other forms of damaging consumption (Daly, 2007). In the context of uncertainties associated with environmental questions, the wise course of action would be to seek to minimize the impact (LeGrand, 1998).

In terms of specific components, fertility is key to both growth and aging. There is clearly limited potential for increasing fertility—some would say there is none. Gauthier's (2007) review of the empirical evidence on the impact of public policies (direct and indirect cash transfers to families with children, means-tested child-welfare benefits, maternity- and parental-leave benefits, as well as child-care facilities) on people's fertility desires, the timing of fertility, and completed family size suggests that their effects are relatively modest overall. The example of Northern

Europe suggests that it is not narrow pro-natalist policies that make a difference, but instead having a set of policies that are generally supportive of families, of people's integration into the labour market, and of gender equality (Héran, 2013b). This set of policy conditions may not bring fertility above replacement, but it could allow more people to have the children that they originally intended. In effect, reflections on countries that have particularly low fertility, such as in Southern and Eastern Europe, suggest that these very low levels occur when women have opportunities in education and the labour force but the family remains traditional (McDonald, 1997). If women have to bear the burden of the domestic work, especially once there are children in the family, they are very likely to turn to the paid-work sphere, where opportunities are more equal. Fertility in a modern society may be sustained by policies that support families, regardless of the type of family, reduce the dependent position of women in families, and prompt a better sharing of paid work and child care between men and women (Beaujot, 2000a). That is, we should seek to remove the barriers to child-bearing by ensuring that fathers and the broader society share more in the cost of children.

Policies on mortality are easier since longer and healthier lives are a widely shared value. As indicated earlier, in an era of delayed degenerative and hubristic mortality, the key to longer life expectancy lies in the risk factors and treatment. This key points to the importance of continued public education on risk factors, along with advances in treatment. It also points to the various other bases for disadvantage that discourage individuals from taking control of their lives. Other risk factors are environmental, where more research is needed, but there is considerable evidence of the impact of environmental quality on human health. In fact, more is known about the effect of environment on population than about the effect of population on environment. But here again, the greater danger is the lack of political will to adopt policies based on the research.

That leaves international migration, where the policy basis is best established. While the immediate demographics of immigration are reasonably well established, the influence that these should have on immigration levels is far less clear. There are the short-term benefits to employers and the labour market, along with the short-term costs of integration, but the long-term benefits of a larger population depend on the relative weight given to economic and environmental considerations. While immigration targets work quite well, there is need for more discussion on the basis for setting these targets. The costs and benefits of immigration to the receiving society need fuller analysis, especially the differential costs and benefits to the varied interests and parts of the society. For instance, it has been concluded in Sweden that by avoiding the cheap solution of temporary workers, Swedish society was prompted to make more space for women in the labour force, including policies that would allow workers to have children (Hoem and Hoem, 1996). While immigration is largely appreciated for bringing diversity, richness, pluralism, and contact with a broader world, population renewal that is excessively based on migration rather than fertility means much change and possibly less potential for integrating new members into a common society. We need to evolve a society that will have good adaptive capacity—by being both diverse and cohesive.

These specifics are subject to discussion, but the broader problem is the lack of an institutional basis for policy that would seek to directly influence the demographics, or to endogenize population. Looking at the Australian case, McNicoll (1995) finds that there are various impediments to population policy in liberal democracies.

Besides the lack of a political basis for long-term planning, the emphasis on individual welfare, and the lack of attention to scale, there is also a tendency for "government to see its constituency only in terms of organized groups and its role that of arbitrating competing claims (McNicoll, 1995:18)." In the Canadian case, Pal (2013) has analyzed how various "civil society" groups, often set up by the state, are also attempting to benefit through the political system and may control agendas based on their specific interests. It would appear that these interests have less to do with the population as a whole than with specific issues, such as families, feminism, the environment, health, business, multiculturalism, or refugees. That is, the potential participants in a discussion of population policy are absorbed in distinct political domains and are consequently more interested in separate than common interests. Some of them would even be opposed to any discussion of population policy (Hodgson and Watkins, 1997; Hodgson, 2009).

Conclusion

The history of Canadian population growth has shown much variety, including periods of more rapid and slower growth. Although population growth has slowed since 1961, the workforce continued to grow rapidly with the entry of the baby boom and women into the job marketplace. The projections suggest that both the population and the labour force will grow more slowly in the future. This brings discussions of means of avoiding population decline, including through fertility and immigration.

There is much room for further research. We need to understand more about the trends in the components of population change in order to have a more secure basis for the assumptions on which we base our projections. There is need for further analyses of the implications of both the actual and the potential demographic change. There is also need for further thinking on the policy side of the evolving demographics. We are encouraged here by the basic democratic orientation of demography, which counts everyone equally in the total population. While there is room for those who think of the interests of specific groups, like the elderly, children, women, visible minorities, families, or immigrants, there are also advantages to looking at the welfare of the whole population and counting everyone equally.

Critical Thinking Questions

1. Interpret the variation in growth rates over specific past decades, and suggest what they may mean for the future.
2. Why have demographic projections been more accurate since 1971?
3. Suggest one central reasonable assumption for each of fertility, mortality, and immigration in the medium term. Defend these assumptions both theoretically and on the basis of past trends.
4. What are the means through which the labour force could be increased in a slow-growing and aging population?
5. Describe different interpretations of replacement migration, and state the applicability to the Canadian case.
6. What is the potential for policy that would sustain child-bearing?
7. Compare immigration and pro-natalist approaches to achieving population growth.
8. What issues would you consider important when discussing population policy.

Recommended Readings

Gauthier, Anne. 2007. "The impact of family policies on fertility in industrialized countries: A review of the literature." *Population Research and Policy Review* 26: 323–46. Gauthier reviews the theoretical arguments and empirical evidence linking public policies with fertility across more developed nations.

George, M.V., Shirley Loh, and Ravi Verma. 1997. "Impact of varying the component assumptions of projected total population and age structure in Canada." *Canadian Studies in Population* 24: 67–86. Based on the population projections published after the 1991 Census this study shows how the results are sensitive to the various assumptions.

Germain, Marie-France, Claude Grenier, and Gilles Montigny. 2001. "Demographic profiles of Canada, the United States and Mexico, 1950–2050." In the Federation of Canadian Demographers' *Demographic Futures in the Context of Globalization: Public Policy Issues*, pp. 35–63. This paper compares the fertility, mortality, and immigration assumptions in recent projections for Canada, the United States, and Mexico.

Statistics Canada. 2014a. *Population Projections for Canada, Provinces and Territories*. Ottawa: Statistics Canada cat. no. 91–520. StatsCan's publication provides the results of several population-projection scenarios by age group and sex up to 2063 for Canada, the provinces, and territories. Using the 2011 Census and 2013 population estimates as the starting point, these projections are based on assumptions relating to components of fertility, mortality, immigration, emigration, and interprovincial migration.

United Nations. 2013a. *World Population Prospects: The 2012 Revision*. New York: United Nations. This report is available online from the Population Division of the United Nations and provides results from the UN's most recent set of projections, globally and for specific countries and regions.

Related Websites

www.canpopsoc.ca. The website of the Canadian Population Society, an organization that promotes population studies in the Canadian research community. Graduate students at Canadian universities are welcome to join this society.

http://socserv2.mcmaster.ca/qsep. This is the site of the McMaster University QSEP Research Institute. There are several papers a year, and they often make projections about population and the labour force.

https://fcdweb.wordpress.com/. The website of the Federation of Canadian Demographers, an organization created through the joint initiative of the Association des Démographes du Québec and the Canadian Population Society. The objectives of the federation are to promote research and the scientific study of demography throughout Canada.

www.demographesqc.org. The website of the Association des Démographes du Québec.

www.facebook.com/actioncanadaSHR. The Facebook page of Action Canada for Sexual Health and Rights, a Canadian non-governmental organization that was formed after the 1994 Cairo–United Nations Conference on Population and Development. The Facebook page publicizes and discusses issues of population and development.

8 Population Aging

The Chapter at a Glance

- Canada's population has been aging for a long time, but it accelerated in the 1970s owing both to lower fertility and lower mortality at adult ages. It is also accelerating in the 2010s as the baby boom moves into older ages and with greater survival of the oldest old.
- The causes of an aging population are analyzed in terms of fertility, mortality, and immigration.
- The aging of the population began because of a decline in the number of children—that is, aging because there were fewer people at the bottom of the age pyramid. Now the baby boom generation is moving to older ages (aging at the middle of the pyramid), and more people are surviving to older ages (aging at the top of the pyramid).
- The demographic ramifications of aging include fewer births, more deaths, and less movement of population.

- From 1981 to 2011, significant proportions of the population were at labour-force ages, and so there has been relatively low dependency.
- Aging has various economic consequences, including an aging workforce that may be less adaptable.
- Aging enhances the role of government in a welfare state, and it can undermine the status of children compared to the elderly.
- Aging has significant consequences for the relative numbers of contributors and beneficiaries to pension plans.
- In an older population, there are more people at an age when health problems are more likely to occur; this entails difficult decisions regarding the allocation of increasingly expensive health technology.

Introduction

One of the essential features of the changing population of Canada, caused primarily by the long-term changes in birth and death rates, is the transformation of the age distribution. Although population aging has been going on for many decades, the 2011 Census release on age and sex composition made headlines across the country. And, in fact, demographic projections are particularly useful for predicting specifics about population aging. For the viability of the Canada Pension Plan, it is important to be able to anticipate at least 50 years ahead the relative size of the populations of labour-force age compared to retirement age—that is, the contributors and beneficiaries of the plan. For Canada's health-care system, population aging is relevant to its longer-term sustainability, as larger cohorts move into ages that make much higher demands. Shifts in the age structure have important implications for Canada's economy, including consequences in terms of consumption and investments, and to issues relating to the labour-force size, productivity, and flexibility.

The importance of understanding the changing age structure is evidenced by the fact that the book *Boom, Bust & Echo* by the demographer/economist David Foot (2000) made the national bestseller list in Canada for many months. Foot wrote eloquently and convincingly about the importance of population aging and demographics for understanding both individual-level questions, like one's relative life chances, and macro questions, like social and economic trends. More recently, Gomez and Foot (2013) have discussed how we are at the beginning of what is certain to be several decades of transformative economic changes. More specifically, we face a decline in the ratio of Canadians of working age relative to those of retirement age, and a slowing in labour-force growth. This suggests that society faces potential trouble ahead, if we fail to adapt from a twentieth-century model of economic growth, driven by rapid population expansion and a youthful population, to a twenty-first-century reality of slowing growth and greying of the population.

In this chapter, after describing and explaining the past and future trends in aging, we will analyze the ramifications for the economy and society. The policy issues associated with aging include questions associated with the labour force, pensions, and health care.

Trends in Aging

The age profile of a population can mostly be described by the use of a population pyramid, the median age, and the proportion over age 65. In a stable demographic setting, age distributions will take one of two forms. With high fertility, the distribution looks like a pyramid with a wide base and an even slope. Under stable low fertility and low mortality, the distribution looks more like a vase with a rounded top. Until about 1961, Canada's age profile looked like a pyramid, and by 2036, it will have more the appearance of a vase (see Figure 8.1).

By juxtaposing the 1991 and 2011 pyramids, Figure 8.2 shows the dynamism underlying the age structure. By 2011, the youngest of the baby boom bulge (born in 1964) were in their late forties, whereas the oldest (born in 1946) were reaching their 65th birthday. The more stable total births since 1990 are visible in the more even base, with less variation in the relative size of the youngest of cohorts. This age structure looks somewhat like a Chinese vase, narrower at the top and bottom.

The shape of Canada's population pyramid will gradually evolve to even more top-heavy distribution (again, refer to the 2036 pyramid as shown in Figure 8.1). By 2036, the baby boom will be aged 72–90 and will be less visible because many of the very oldest will have died. Unless there are unexpected fluctuations in fertility or mortality, Canada's age pyramid will eventually by mid-century have a more even shape, with few surviving baby boomers at the very top of the age structure. The base will remain more or less narrow, depending essentially on future levels of fertility.

The age structure can also be described in terms of the median age and the percentage over 65 (see Tables 8.1 and 8.2). The median age has risen from 17.2 in 1851 and 26.2 in 1971, to 39.9 years in 2011, with a medium projection of 43.7 years by 2036. The percentage over 65 increased from only 2.7 per cent in 1851 to 7.6 per cent by 1961, up further to 14.4 per cent in 2011. These numbers show that aging has historically been a gradual and long-term phenomenon, yet the arrival of the baby boom involved a temporary departure from this longer-term trend. While average age increased from 1851 to 1951 (from only 17.2 to 27.7 years), it then declined slightly, down to 26.2 years by 1971, prior to returning to its upward trajectory. Since the end of the baby boom, the population has continued on its course of aging, yet the speed of this aging has increased even further. Over the 1961–81 period, for example, the percentage of people over 65 increased by roughly two percentage points, whereas from 1991 to 2011, this segment increased by about three percentage points.

The oldest age groups are now growing most quickly; the 2011 Census demonstrated that the age group for 80 and over had grown by 47 per cent in only 10 years, more than 4 times the rate of the entire population (Statistics Canada, 2012j). Over the long term, the fastest growth will likely occur in the population aged 80 and above. Even in the medium scenario, this population more than doubles from 1.38 million in 2011 to 3.3 million in 2036, while the whole population increases by about 25 per cent (Statistics Canada, 2014f). Keefe and colleagues (2005) refer to an "acceleration in the growth in the number of the elderly," a trend that is expected to continue for at least the next 30 years as a result of the aging of the baby boomers and increased life expectancy. By 2061, this same medium-growth scenario projects that Canada's population aged 80 and over could be as high as 4.82 million, up by a factor of 3.5 from 2011.

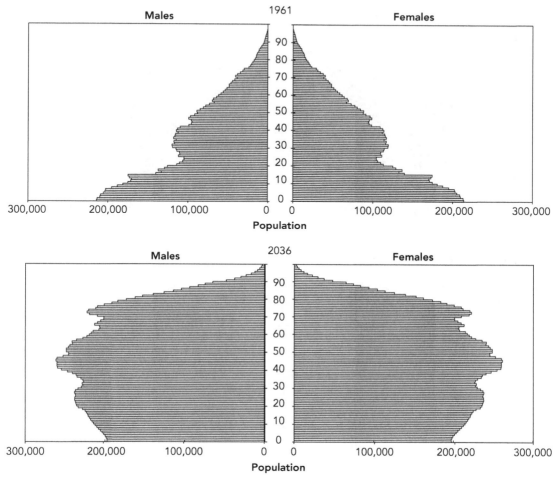

Figure 8.1 ◉ Population by Age and Sex, Canada, 1961 and 2036

Sources: 1961 Census five-year age groups (Basavarajappa and Bali Ram, 1983); single-year estimates by the authors; Statistics Canada, 2014a, medium projection.

At the other end of the age profile, the number of children under the age of 15 declined slightly by 2.5 per cent from 2001 to 2011, while the total population increased by 11.2 per cent. As seen in Figure 8.2, age groups under 15 have remained relatively stable in absolute size between 1991 and 2011, whereas the number of older teenagers and young adults is up modestly; the number of persons aged 15–24 rose by 8.9 per cent over this same period. It is especially important to follow the aging of the baby boom cohort, which corresponded to just over 1 in 4 Canadians (26 per cent), or about 9

million out of a population of 34.5 million in 2011. Landon Jones (1980) famously coined the expression "the pig in the python" to refer to the aging of the baby boom, as these very large birth cohorts move through the age distribution, becoming dominant at older and older ages. The 2011 pyramid shows that the baby boom bulge is currently middle-aged, and is about to begin exiting the labour force in a major way. For this reason, many demographers and economists are anticipating potential difficulties in meeting the demand for labour over the next 20 years or so (Gomez and Foot, 2013).

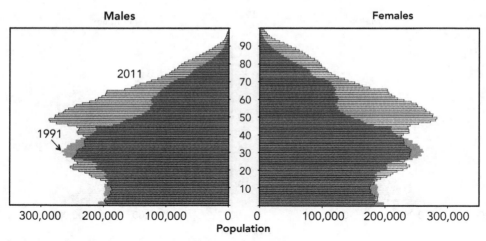

Figure 8.2 ▣ Population by Age and Sex, Canada, 1991 and 2011

Source: Statistics Canada, 2013i, population estimates, CANSIM Table 051-0001.

Table 8.1 ▣ Median Age of Canada's Population, Observed (1851–2011) and Projected (2016–2061), According to Three Growth Scenarios

Year	Median Age		
	Low	Medium	High
1851		17.2	
1861		18.2	
1871		18.8	
1881		20.1	
1891		21.4	
1901		22.7	
1911		23.8	
1921		24.0	
1931		24.8	
1941		27.1	
1951		27.7	
1961		26.3	
1971		26.2	
1976		27.7	
1981		29.5	
1986		31.4	
1991		33.3	
1996		35.1	
2001		37.2	
2006		38.9	
2011		39.9	
2016	40.8	40.7	40.6
2021	41.8	41.4	41.0
2026	43.0	42.2	41.4
2031	44.1	42.9	41.9
2036	45.0	43.7	42.4
2041	45.8	44.2	42.6
2046	46.0	44.1	42.2
2051	45.9	43.9	41.9
2056	46.1	44.0	41.6
2061	46.4	44.1	41.6

Sources: Statistics Canada, 2013i, 2014a.

Table 8.2 ▣ Percentage of Canadians 0–14 Years and 65+ Years, Observed (1851–2011) and Projected (2016–2061), According to Three Growth Scenarios

Year	Children (0–14 years)			Seniors (65 years +)		
	Low	Medium	High	Low	Medium	High
1851		44.9			2.7	
1861		42.5			3.0	
1871		41.6			3.7	
1881		38.7			4.1	
1891		36.3			4.6	
1901		34.3			5.3	
1911		32.9			4.7	
1921		34.4			4.8	
1931		31.6			5.6	
1941		27.8			6.7	
1951		30.3			7.8	
1961		34.0			7.6	
1971		29.3			8.0	
1976		25.4			8.6	
1981		22.3			9.6	
1986		21.0			10.5	
1991		20.7			11.6	
1996		20.2			12.1	
2001		18.9			12.6	
2006		17.3			13.3	
2011		16.4			14.4	
2016	16.1	16.1	16.2	16.6	16.5	16.5
2021	16.0	16.3	16.8	18.9	18.7	18.5
2026	15.5	16.3	17.3	21.7	21.1	20.7
2031	14.9	16.0	17.6	24.0	23.1	22.4
2036	14.3	15.6	17.3	25.1	23.9	23.1
2041	14.0	15.3	16.8	25.7	24.2	23.3
2046	14.0	15.2	16.8	26.2	24.5	23.4
2051	14.1	15.4	17.0	26.7	24.8	23.5
2056	14.1	15.5	17.3	27.1	25.1	23.6
2061	14.0	15.5	17.5	27.7	25.5	23.8

Sources: Statistics Canada, 2013i, CANSIM Table 051-0001; Statistics Canada, 2014a.

The changes foreseen in the population aged 65 and over will represent an increasing proportion of the total; the largest increases are from 2011 to 2031, when the baby boom moves into these ages. Similarly, the population under 15 years of age will represent a slightly smaller proportion of the total, except in the high-fertility scenario, where their proportion is up slightly, albeit relatively stable. According to the medium projection, Canada should have by 2016 slightly more persons aged 65 and over than under 15 years (16.5 per cent and 16.1 per cent, respectively). In fact, all projections show more elderly people than children by this date. By 2036, the medium projection suggests that there could be greater than 50 per cent more people aged 65 and over than under 15.

While the trends are systematic for the youngest and the oldest, other parts of the age distribution do not change as systematically. As we have seen in Chapter 7, the population aged 18–64, which is relevant especially for the labour force, is expected to show slowing rates of growth over the next 15–20 years, or possibly even show a slight decline in total numbers. In the low-growth projection, this population is projected to decrease by 1.4 per cent between 2013 and 2028. In the medium projection, this population is projected to increase by only 3.5 per cent by 2028, whereas in the high projection, total growth in this subpopulation is projected to be only 7.5 per cent by 2028. This compares with a growth of 18.8 per cent over the previous 15-year period, from 1998 to 2013. In other words, by 2036 in all scenarios, the population aged 18–64 will

make up a smaller proportion of the total than it did in 2011.

Population aging has for many decades been at a more advanced stage in Europe, where Chesnais (1989) spoke of an "inversion of the age pyramid." By 2010, the percentage over 65 was already at 20.3 per cent in Italy, 20.8 per cent in Germany, and 23 per cent in Japan (see Table 8.3). A major reason for this is that many of these more developed countries have had low fertility for many decades, without the baby boom that especially characterized North America and Australia. The percentage over 65 is slightly lower for Canada (14.4 per cent) than the average for the more developed countries (16.1 per cent), and according to Statistics Canada's projections (2014f), this percentage is not expected to reach 20 per cent until sometime after 2023.

In many ways, the current age structure in countries like Germany and Japan will be Canada's future. According to the medium projection, for example, Canada's portion of people aged 65+ is not

Table 8.3 ▦ Selected Age-Distribution Indices, Canada and Selected Countries, 2010 or 2011

	Median Age	0–19 %	20–64 %	65+ %	80+ %
Canada (2011)	39.9	22.7	62.8	14.4	4.0
Other countries (2010)					
United States	37.1	26.9	60.0	13.1	3.6
Germany	44.3	18.6	60.6	20.8	5.1
France	40.0	24.4	58.8	16.8	5.4
United Kingdom	39.8	23.8	59.6	16.6	4.7
Italy	43.3	18.9	60.8	20.3	5.9
Japan	44.9	18.0	59.0	23.0	6.3
Russia	38.0	21.1	65.8	13.1	2.9
Australia	36.8	25.7	60.9	13.5	3.7
Mexico	25.9	39.7	54.3	6.0	1.2
World (2010)	28.5	35.4	56.9	7.7	1.6
More Developed Countries	39.9	22.5	61.4	16.1	4.3
Less Developed Countries	26.4	38.2	55.9	5.8	1.0
Least Developed Countries	19.3	51.6	45.0	3.5	0.5

Sources: Statistics Canada, 2013i, CANSIM Table 051-0001, United Nations Population Division of the Department of Economic and Social Affairs, 2012 Revision, 2013a.

forecast to reach 23 per cent, as is currently observed in Japan, until 2031. Nonetheless, the Canadian change is now as rapid as that observed elsewhere, and it will be more rapid while the larger baby boom generations move into retirement ages. Whereas just over 1 in 10 people were over 65 in 1986, some 25 years later, in 2011, roughly 1 in 7 Canadians were over 65, while in an additional 25 years, almost a quarter of the population will be at these ages (23.9 per cent in 2036 according to the medium projection). Along with a median age of some 43.7 years, and with about 8 per cent of the population aged 80 and over, this will make for a different demographic profile and a very different type of society.

Box 8.1 ⬚ The Cohort as a Useful Concept in the Study of Social Change

Cohort analysis is fundamental to the science of demography, and, more broadly, an essential method in the social sciences (Ryder, 1959). The word *cohort* can be defined as "a group of persons who experience the same significant event in a particular time period, and who can thus be identified as a group in subsequent analysis" (Wilson, 1985). This significant event can be almost any baseline-defining event (birth, marriage, employment), yet most commonly, cohorts are defined in terms of year(s) of birth. All persons born between 1946 and 1964, for example, are widely referred to as the baby boom cohort by demographers and the general public alike. While this is a very broad birth cohort, mixing the experiences of persons born in the latter 1940s through to those born in the early 1960s, the relative size of this cohort is important in understanding the dynamics of population change in Canada.

The juxtapositioning of various population pyramids effectively demonstrates the movement of specific cohorts through their life course (review Figures 8.1 and 8.2). For example, the birth cohort in its infancy in the 1961 pyramid is aged 30 in 1991, middle-aged in 2011 (aged 50 years), and elderly in the projected 2036 pyramid (aged 75 years). People belonging to the same birth cohort move into their formal schooling over roughly the same period, complete their education and establish themselves in the labour force over roughly the same time, raise their families and enter into middle age over roughly the same years, and eventually retire and grow old together. The utility of cohort analysis is that the experience of one birth cohort might be somewhat distinct from that of another one. The experience of the baby boomers who came of age during the 1960s and '70s, for example, is quite different from the much smaller cohorts born in the 1990s. This latter group comprises people who are just now beginning to establish themselves in the labour force. By following specific birth cohorts over successive years, demographers can build up a picture of how the collective history of specific cohorts may have differed from that of other cohorts, at least partially determined by their year of birth.

Demographic analyses that focus on the collective history of specific birth cohorts provide useful insight, as the life chances and opportunities have been shown to vary across distinct cohorts (Ryder, 1959; Foot, 2001). The general idea is that some people fare better than others, merely as a result of chance, being at the right place at the right time and belonging to the right cohort. The demographer Richard Easterlin (1980) has made the specific argument that persons born to smaller cohorts may witness certain advantages because they face less competition in terms of workforce participation. This was arguably the reality for cohorts born during the 1930s and '40s

Continued

in North America, as they were relatively small cohorts that came of age when Canadian society was expanding rapidly, both economically and demographically. Similarly, Foot (2001), with the help of his colleague Daniel Stoffman, has argued in this context that these shifts in fertility and the subsequent sizes of birth cohorts are of fundamental importance in shaping the relative life chances of various cohorts through to the present.

The concept of *cohort* has also been used interchangeably with the term *generation* in the popular media. Media outlets have often referred to the life chances of distinct cohorts, loosely defined, including those that followed the baby boom, the so-called "baby bust generation" (1965–79), Generation X (1966–80), Generation Y (1980–2004), Millennials (1982–2000), among others. Unfortunately, these labels have been loosely applied by some social commentators, with considerable oversimplification and sometimes misleading generalizations. The problem in the non-scientific literature is that many stereotypes have been used to characterize different generations, even though there is considerable diversity within each cohort.

While demography is obviously relevant in shaping the life course of Canadians, Foot and Stoffman have been criticized for overstating the importance of cohort size. With this in mind, it is useful to remember that current age structure can always be described in terms of past fertility, or, more specifically, the sizes of specific birth cohorts as we move back further and further in time. A substantial upturn in fertility has long-term consequences for the age structure and social fabric of any society, just as does a significant downturn. Yet in using and extending some of the cohorts adapted by Foot and Stoffman (2001), Table 8.4 demonstrates the simple reality of Canada's age structure—that is, excluding the baby boom cohort, there has been much less variation in the size of birth cohorts born over the last half century. As seen in Table 8.4, the annual births during the baby boom outnumbered those of the previous cohort by over 50 per cent (averaging 425,000 annually relative to the 280,000 births that characterized the Second World War era). This upturn in fertility was unprecedented, with much less variation in cohort size both before and after the baby boom. While Canadian society continues to make all sorts of adjustments in accommodating aging boomers, there are certainly far fewer adjustments necessary in accommodating the variation in size of the cohorts that precede and follow the baby boom.

Table 8.4 Relative Cohort Sizes, Canada, 2011

Cohort	Year of Birth	Age in 2011	Average Number of Annual Births
Pre-WWI	Before 1914	98+	201,000
WWI	1914–19	92–97	244,000
1920s	1920–29	82–91	249,000
Depression	1930–39	72–81	236,000
WWII	1940–45	66–71	280,000
Baby Boom	1946–1964	47–65	425,000
Baby Bust	1965–1979	32–46	366,000
Children of the Boomers	1980–1995	16–31	382,000
Children of the Baby Bust	1996–2005	6–15	340,000
Recent	2006–2011	0–5	373,000

Source: Statistics Canada, 2013v, CANSIM Table 053-0001.

What is certain is that specific cohorts have faced greater competition in establishing themselves in the labour force, as directly tied to both the general state of the economy when they came of age and their relative cohort size (Garloff et al., 2013). Canadians born at the tail end of the baby boom (early 1960s), for example, encountered stiff competition for entry-level jobs in the early 1980s when they were first attempting to find full-time work, which happened to overlap with a period of economic recession and high youth unemployment. Yet while demography is relevant, it is certainly not destiny. There are many factors influencing the life chances of various cohorts beyond the year in which cohort members were born or the relative size of their birth cohort, including the demand for labour, the general state of the economy, globalization, the level of immigration, the skill set and education that each cohort obtains, the cultural context, among many other factors.

Causes of Aging

The causes of the aging—or, as some call it, "greying"—of a population, as with any demographic change, inevitably involve fertility, mortality, and migration. A population that did not have any births, deaths, or migrants would age systematically by one year at a time. That is one easy thing about studying age—everyone ages at the same rate. From this perspective, Preston and colleagues (1989) speak of a *"natural tendency to age."*

The impact of vital events and migration will depend on the age at which they occur. Since all births take place at the same age, which is at the bottom of the population distribution, they obviously counteract population aging. An upturn in births leads to a more youthful population, whereas a reduction makes for more aging because there are fewer entries at the bottom of the age structure. The effect of deaths will depend on where most of them occur. Since they are usually spread out over many ages, deaths tend to have less effect than births. A reduction in deaths that especially benefits the young can actually reduce the average age, while one that benefits the old will increase the aging. In terms of migration, there is also a tendency for migrants to be of all ages, and subsequently, the impact of migration tends to be even more moderate and spread out in terms of the age structure (see Box 8.2).

With this in mind, one could consider three stages of population aging. In the first stage, which is only of historical interest (nineteenth century and earlier), aging of the population was slow because fertility reduction was largely compensated for by mortality reductions at young ages. Concurrent with a gradual reduction in fertility was a gradual decline in infant mortality, such that a greater proportion of all births survived infancy, leaving for a larger proportion of the population at younger ages. In the second stage, which lasted until about 1971, the population was aging mostly as a function of the decline in fertility. The mortality decline that also took place during this period especially benefited the young, and, therefore, had a slight tendency to counteract the impact of reduced fertility. In the third stage, after about 1971, population aging has been due to both low fertility and falling mortality rates. Recently, most of the gains in reducing mortality have occurred for the older population. Now that there is less room for mortality decline at younger ages, reduced mortality at older ages serves to increase the relative weight of the top of the pyramid.

Aging at the Bottom, Top, and Middle

In the 1970s, it was widely thought that the principal influence on age structure was fertility. This made sense since fertility had fallen precipitously after the baby boom, such that the observed impact on the bottom of Canada's age pyramid was obvious and with immediate consequences. We can usefully call this *aging at the bottom*—that is, a decline in the relative size of the young population.

It should have been understood, however, that fertility was not the only factor, given that both the number and proportion of older Canadians was also increasing. In addition, at older ages there was a clear imbalance in the sex ratio (for example, 7.2 per cent of the male population was 65 and older in 1971, relative to about 9 per cent of the female population). Since the births of males and females follow an identical trend (i.e., move up or down with the overall birth rate), it must have been that the mortality advantages of women were showing up in these different age structures. There has been a tendency to underestimate the ways in which the improved mortality conditions at adult and older ages are producing *aging at the top*— that is, in the number of survivors at older ages.

There is now much awareness of aging, with considerable attention focused on the aging baby boom. This might be called *aging at the middle*. It is easy to recognize the large baby boom moving up the age structure, as it moves from middle age into its senior years (recall Landon Jones's pig in the python metaphor). This aging process is accelerating due to a continuation of low fertility combined with a further decline in mortality, particularly at the oldest ages. As Canada's epidemiological transition has moved into its fourth stage (the *age of delayed degenerative diseases*), there has been a progressive shift toward older ages in the distribution of deaths by degenerative causes.

In effect, earlier research tended not to anticipate the extent to which mortality could decline at older ages. Yet, as we discussed in Chapter 3, life expectancy at birth climbed by roughly three years per decade during the first half of the twentieth century, and it continued to climb by roughly two years per decade through to 2010. Life expectancy at birth, for example, went up by roughly 10 years between 1961 and 2011 (from about 71 years in 1961 to over 81 years in 2011). The latest revisions to the projections prepared for the Canada Pension Plan anticipate further gains, and the projections are particularly optimistic in terms of reducing mortality among the elderly. The Office of the Chief Actuary of Canada (2011) forecasts a life expectancy at age 65 of 23.6, or a total of 88.6 years by 2050. That is, if someone were to spend the whole 45 years between 20 and 64 in the labour force, there would be another 23.6 years of retirement, or about 1.9 years in the labour force per year of retirement. While there is a clear understanding that low fertility brings aging, as does the movement of the baby boom through the age structure, we may not be sufficiently appreciating how potential mortality reductions at adult and older ages may be particularly important in influencing population aging into the future. The twenty-first century will see very significant changes in the number of years people spend in retirement compared to those spent in the labour force.

Box 8.2 ▣ Is Increased Immigration a Solution to Population Aging?

In Canada, immigration is often considered a way of sustaining the labour force in the face of population aging and low fertility. In 2012, for example *The Globe and Mail*'s editorial board, in a substantive series about immigration reform, recommended that Canada dramatically increase its annual intake of immigrants to a level roughly equivalent to 1 per cent of Canada's total population. The *Globe*'s editorial board argued that Canada needs to radically boost immigration numbers in a context of rapid population aging and slowing labour force growth (Friesen, 2012). The thrust of their argument was that markedly increased immigration, although not a panacea, would be immediately necessary to help stave off the worst of Canada's challenges in terms of population aging and labour-force decline.

To provide a sense as to the magnitude of such a reform, a 1 per cent annual immigration target would imply an immediate intake of roughly

350,000 immigrants a year, up from an average of about 240,000 that has characterized Canada since the turn of the century. While public opinion polls suggest that Canadians are quite supportive of immigration, it is far from certain as to whether an immediate 40 per cent increase in immigration targets would be widely accepted as reasonable. Yet assuming that such targets be accepted, what sort of impact would this have on Canada's age structure? To what extent might this slow the pace of population aging? As demonstrated here, relative to the status quo, immigration levels of this magnitude are not likely to have much of an impact on age structure, although, of course, they would have a sizable impact on the extent to which Canada's population and labour force grows as we go deeper into the twenty-first century.

Historically, variation in immigration has had a relatively modest impact on Canada's age structure (George et al., 1990; Matthews, 1988; Denton et al., 1997). Similarly, into the future, immigration of the order of 1 per cent is also not likely to have much of an impact, either over the short or long term. Unlike shifts in fertility that exclusively affect numbers at the bottom of the age distribution, and unlike mortality gains that are now almost exclusively affecting numbers toward the top, shifts in overall immigration levels tend to influence numbers across all ages, and if anything, in the middle of the distribution. As Statistics Canada documents (2013q), while the majority of immigrants who come to Canada are between the ages of 25 and 44 years, their median age on arrival is about 8 years lower than Canada's overall median. While there is an overrepresentation of working-age adults among international migrants, newcomers of all ages tend to settle in Canada, including both their children and parents (as potentially sponsored under the family class). In addition, the fertility of immigrants after arrival in Canada has tended to converge with that of other Canadians, such that high immigration has not had much of an impact on the overall fertility rate.

While the current publication has relied upon Statistics Canada's population projections (2014a), the Canadian Socioeconomic Database (CANSIM) available from Statistics Canada also provided a less publicized projection, identical to the medium-growth scenario of Statistics Canada's 2010 projection (2010c), yet with the notable exception of its immigration component. More specifically, rather than extrapolating on the immigration rates as observed over the 1991–2009 period (true of the medium scenario), this projection assumed a 1 per cent immigration target, or, in other words, levels that are consistent with the recommendations of the *Globe*'s editorialists. For comparative purposes, while the medium-growth scenario assumes levels rising from about 240,000 in 2009 to about 335,000 by 2036, the 1 per cent scenario works with immigration levels that start at 40 per cent higher (350,000 immigrants), reaching about 475,000 immigrants by 2036. In total, by comparing the medium and 1 per cent scenarios, this allows us to isolate the impact on age structure of an additional 3.1 million immigrants over the 2010–36 period, and 7.8 million immigrants over the full 2010–61 projection period.

The results from these projections are summarized in Table 8.5. Briefly, for comparative purposes, this summary also includes the results from a third projection—i.e., again identical to the medium-growth scenario, but this time with a revision on the fertility component. While the 2010 medium-growth scenario assumed a TFR of 1.7 births per woman over the projection period, this third projection considers the potential impact of replacement-level fertility (a TFR of 2.1 births per woman). While this is quite a jump in fertility, it is not completely outside the realm of possibility if a society were to be particularly supportive of family life and pro-natalist in the encouragement of fertility. Furthermore, in terms of the projected growth in total population over the projection period, an increase of this order in fertility is comparable (slightly less) to the aforementioned

Continued

increase in immigration to a 1 per cent annual target.

What is striking in Table 8.5 is the negligible difference across the two immigration scenarios in terms of median age—by 2036, the median ages are 43 years and 43.6 years. In other words, an additional 3.1 million immigrants manages to reduce median age in Canada by only 0.6 of a year over a 25-year period. Furthermore, over the full 50 years, a total of 7.8 million immigrants will reduce this median by less than 2 years (42.2 years and 44 years, respectively). While additional immigrants obviously bring about greater population growth (including the eventual births to these immigrants), the relative impact on age structure is surprisingly small. In terms of the replacement-level-fertility scenario, while its impact on overall growth is slightly less, the difference in median age is greater (or 2.2 years after 25 years and about 4 years after 50 years).

For the population aged 65 and older, the 14.1 per cent estimated for 2010 is projected to increase to anywhere between 22.3 and 23.7 by 2036, regardless of scenario. In other words, these alternate projections highlight the wisdom of preparing for a top-heavy age pyramid regardless of future immigration and fertility. By increasing immigration to levels unseen except for short periods in Canada's history, these projections demonstrate that there is still no obvious demographic solution to the basic reality that Canada's population will continue to age over the next several decades.

Table 8.5 also summarizes the projected proportion aged 15–64, often considered useful as a proxy of the population of labour-force age. Relative to 2010, with 69.4 per cent of the population aged 15–64, the medium-growth scenario projects a decline to 60.6 per cent by 2036, the 1 per cent immigration target projects 61.5 per cent, and the replacement fertility projects 59.5 per cent. The policy-related consequences of these projections should be clear enough. While the size of the labour force will likely increase into the future, the proportion of Canada's population of labour-force age will continue to decline. There is obviously no demographic fix to this basic population trend.

Table 8.5 ▣ Population Age Indices Observed (2010) and Projected (2036 and 2061), Canada

	Median Age	% under 15	% 65+ years	% 15–64 years	Population Size (millions)
Population Estimate 2010	39.7	16.5	14.1	69.4	33.7
Projections 2036					
Medium-Growth Scenario	43.6	15.7	23.7	60.6	43.8
– revised on immigration (1% target)	43.0	16.1	22.4	61.5	47.5
– revised on fertility (replacement fertility)	41.4	18.2	22.3	59.5	46.6
Projections 2061					
Medium-Growth Scenario	44.0	15.7	25.5	58.9	52.6
– revised on immigration (1% target)	42.2	16.0	23.9	60.1	62.7
– revised on fertility (replacement fertility)	40.0	19.1	22.1	58.8	61.3

Note: The three projections have identical assumptions to Statistics Canada's medium-growth scenario unless specified otherwise.

Source: Statistics Canada, 2014a.

In summary, fertility reduction makes for population aging at the bottom, while mortality reduction now contributes to population aging at the top (Krotki, 1990; Keyfitz, 1990). Thus, the particularly rapid aging that we are experiencing is due to low fertility, lower mortality at older ages, and the movement of the baby boom through the age structure. The consequences of aging may be different at the bottom, middle, and top, and most assessments of aging have not paid attention to this differential impact. Aging at the bottom means fewer young dependents, also liberating adults to be in the labour force. This form of aging clearly has no negative short-term effect on the number of people who are entering labour-force ages. Aging at the top can result in older dependents, especially as the frail elderly increase in relative size, while aging in the middle can first result in a rapidly growing labour force, and then a labour force that is more experienced but possibly less adaptable. From 2011 to 2031, the impact of this movement of the baby boom will see large numbers of departures from the labour force. The first members of the baby boom cohort reached their 65th birthday in 2011, whereas the last of the boomers will do the same in 2029.

Demographic Ramifications of Aging

Before considering the economic and social implications of aging, it is worth paying attention to the demographic impact. Although the extent of aging is determined by fertility and mortality rates, the reverse is also true—population aging, in and of itself, also influences in a direct manner these vital rates. As Chesnais (1989) observed, just as youthful populations tend to grow rapidly, the potential for slower growth and even demographic decline can be inscribed in the age distribution of older populations. There are self-reinforcing mechanisms at work: aging is due to low fertility, but an older population also produces fewer births and more deaths.

At the beginning of below-replacement fertility in the early 1970s, there were still almost twice as many births as deaths, and the crude death rate (deaths per 1,000 population) continued to decline well into the 1980s. This was related to the momentum for population growth as tied to Canada's age distribution at the time, with a relatively youthful population and very large cohorts of reproductive age. A youthful population can continue to grow even though its fertility falls to well below replacement, as long as there continue to be fewer deaths than births. Yet just as there is a momentum to population growth in youthful populations, there is also a momentum to population decline (i.e., older populations may experience slow growth or even negative natural increase for an extended period, even with a return to above-replacement fertility). In other words, if fertility were to move to above-replacement levels, the smaller numbers at reproductive ages could still imply fewer births than might be expected.

Relevant in the Canadian context is the country's relatively high immigration, which has helped to sustain both natural increase and population growth through to the present. Unlike many other countries that have had low fertility but remained largely closed to immigration, Canada is not expected to witness negative natural increase or population decline anytime soon. Nonetheless, demographic growth is expected to slow, as population aging has the self-reinforcing mechanism of having a downward pressure on birth rates and an upward pressure on death rates. In a somewhat counterintuitive sense, we can anticipate both substantial gains in terms of life expectancy while simultaneously a substantial rise in the number of deaths. Canada's life expectancy is expected to rise such that the risk of premature death declines, while simultaneously, the total number of deaths increases due to population aging and an increase in the number of persons at a high risk. In the aforementioned projections, all of Statistics Canada's (2014f) scenarios point to a near doubling in the number of deaths over the next several decades, from roughly 260,000 in 2013–14 to about 470,000 by 2062–63.

Besides exercising a downward pressure on birth rates and an upward pressure on death rates, the aging of the population has affected the sex ratio at higher ages. As was observed in Chapter 3, the female advantage in life expectancy increased from some two years in 1931 to seven years in 1971. This resulted in higher numbers of surviving women, especially at older ages. While the female life-expectancy advantage is now closer to 4.5 years, the 2011 Census showed women outnumbering men by almost 25 per cent at ages 65 and over. At particularly advanced ages, there was a very strong imbalance by sex. At ages 90 and over, there were only 39 men per 100 women in 2011 (Statistics Canada, 2013r). This differential in survival means a greater likelihood that elderly women will be widowed and living alone. Given that the mortality differentials have declined since 1971, the gender imbalance in the proportions of aged people by sex has since declined slightly.

Population Aging and Its Geographic Distribution

The aforementioned generalizations at the national level can potentially obscure the fact that the pace and extent of population aging can vary somewhat across different provinces and regions (see Table 8.6). As an extreme example, the territories in the Far North have particularly young populations, much younger than documented elsewhere. The predominantly Aboriginal populations of Nunavut and the Northwest Territories

have a long history of well-above-replacement fertility and higher mortality. As a result, they have much lower median ages, of only 24.8 and 31.8 years, respectively, relative to the national average of 39.9 years (Statistics Canada, 2013i).

Parts of Canada that have witnessed higher-than-average fertility (e.g., the Prairie provinces) tend to be younger than elsewhere, whereas provinces that have long had lower fertility tend to somewhat older (e.g., Atlantic Canada, Quebec, British Columbia). Yet at the subnational level, both internal and international migration can also be of some importance. This is particularly true when the absolute number of migrants is large relative to the size of the population at origin and/or destination. Quebec's age structure, for example, is less influenced by migration, with relatively low rates of interprovincial migration and less than its share of immigrants. Alberta's age structure, on the other hand, has been influenced by interprovincial migration in light of the economic opportunities related to the resource sector of its economy. The Atlantic provinces, among other regions with

Table 8.6 ▣ Median Age and Selected Age Groups, Provinces and Territories, Canada 2011

		Percentage		
	Median Age	65+	0–15	15–64
Newfoundland and Labrador	43.8	15.8	14.8	69.4
Prince Edward Island	42.2	15.8	16.1	68.1
Nova Scotia	43.1	16.5	14.7	68.8
New Brunswick	43.0	16.2	15.1	68.7
Quebec	41.4	15.7	15.6	68.7
Ontario	39.6	14.2	16.5	69.3
Manitoba	37.6	13.9	18.8	67.3
Saskatchewan	37.3	14.6	19.0	66.4
Alberta	36.0	10.8	18.4	70.8
British Columbia	41.1	15.3	15.0	69.7
Yukon	39.2	8.8	17.2	74.0
Northwest Territories	31.8	5.6	21.2	73.2
Nunavut	24.8	3.2	31.4	65.4
Canada	**39.9**	**14.4**	**16.4**	**69.2**

Source: Post-censal Estimate, July 1st, 2011; Statistics Canada, 2013.

higher-than-average unemployment, have some-what older population structures due to the out-migration of young adults while also receiving less than their share of immigrants.

As we have mentioned, population aging in and of itself has self-reinforcing mechanisms: for example, aging is due to low fertility, yet an older population also produces fewer births. Similarly, an older population also tends to produce fewer migrants. Older people are less likely to move, particularly as their ties with local neighbourhoods increase and family and community life becomes more established. So, three phenomena are at work here: the lower migration propensities of older people produces "*aging in place*"; the greater like-lihood of younger people to move from the more depressed regions leaves more older people behind; and the differential choice of destination also accentuates the proportion of older people in specific locations.

All of this has influenced Newfoundland and Labrador, which by 2011, had the highest median age in the country (43.8 years), with 15.8 per cent of its population over the age of 65 (see Table 8.6). Newfoundland and Labrador has a relatively low pro-portion of its population in their twenties and thir-ties, the result of a net outflow of young adults to other parts of Canada. Likewise, other parts of the Atlantic region are also older, with all four of Canada's oldest provinces situated here. In terms of median age, both Nova Scotia and New Brunswick are quite close to Newfoundland and Labrador (43.1 and 43 years, respectively), followed closely by Prince Edward Island (42.2 years). With a net outflow of young adults to other parts of the country, the pres-ence of fewer young adults strongly implies fewer births and fewer children, which correspondingly entails proportionally more seniors. This is even more pronounced in some of the most economically depressed regions. The census division of Cape Breton in Nova Scotia has almost 20 per cent of its population over the age of 65, whereas Queen's coun-try in rural New Brunswick has almost 25 per cent. Both regions have consistently lost population to elsewhere in the Atlantic region or to other provinces, given higher-than-average unemployment and fewer economic and/or educational opportunities.

For Ontario, Canada's largest province, its age distribution most closely mirrors the national distri-bution, whereas both Quebec and British Columbia are slightly older than the country as a whole. Across provinces, Alberta had the lowest median age (36.0 years) with only about 11 per cent over the age of 65, whereas the two other Prairie provinces, Saskatchewan and Manitoba, are also relatively young (with medi-ans of 37.3 and 37.6 years, respectively). Alberta has gained population both through net inflows of young adults from other provinces and also through the receipt of more immigrants and having higher fertil-ity. Young adults from Atlantic Canada have been heading west for several decades, while the continu-ing decline in Canada's manufacturing sector has led to more migrants coming from Central Canada.

With the exception of Canada's northern territo-ries, all three Prairie provinces have higher fertility than elsewhere, and as a result, have higher proportions aged 0–14 years. For the working-age population (15–64), Saskatchewan has the lowest percentage across provinces (66.4 per cent) whereas neighbouring Alberta has the highest (70.8 per cent). At least part of this relates to the history of migration in the Prairies, as young adults from rural Saskatchewan have tended to migrate to Alberta for educational opportunities and employment. In addition, Saskatchewan has consistently had the highest fertility across provinces, at or close to replacement level, and subsequently has had the highest proportion of children under the age of 15.

Briefly, as is the case with the provinces, urban and non-urban areas also show some variation in terms of age distribution. Like certain provinces, Canada's largest cities have tended to not only draw most of Canada's immigrants but also attract migrants from rural areas and smaller centres. As a result, census metropolitan areas (CMAs) tend to be younger than elsewhere, with 13.4 per cent of their populations aged 65 and older relative to almost 17 per cent in non-CMAs (Statistics Canada, 2013t; note: authors' calculations using population esti-mates rather than the census). The median age is also noticeably younger, at 38.8 years relative to 42.9 years outside CMAs. Figure 8.3 portrays the

All Census Metropolitan Areas (median age = 38.8 years)

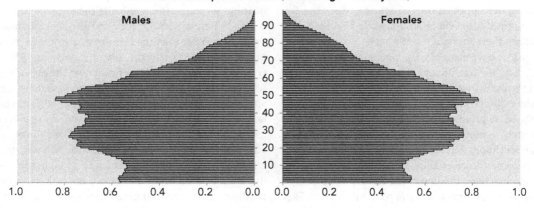

Outside Census Metropolitan Areas (median age = 42.9 years)

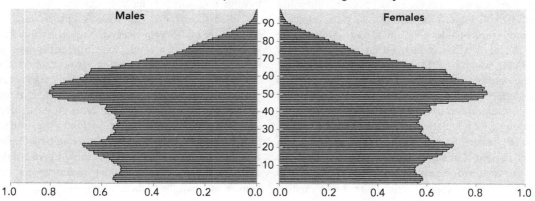

Figure 8.3 ▣ Population Pyramids (in percentage) for CMA and non-CMA Populations, Canada, 2011

Sources: Statistics Canada, CANSIM Table 051-0046, Estimates of Population by Age and sex, 1 July, 2011; authors' calculations.

population pyramids of Canada's population living in CMAs for 2011 relative to the population living outside these cities. Clearly, the proportion of elderly people is considerably higher outside the CMAs, as, in fact, the most top-heavy age structures tend to be in towns and cities with populations below 10,000. In addition, the outflow of young adults from smaller centres is obvious in comparing the two pyramids, with only 23.1 per cent of the non-CMAs aged 20–39 relative to almost 30 per cent of the CMAs. This distribution does not always coincide with the distribution of services, especially for health; on the contrary, the largest cities have the most services.

To further complicate matters, across CMAs, there remains considerable variation. The percentage of people 65 and older, for example, ranges from a low of only 9.8 per cent in Calgary through to a high of about 19.5 per cent in Peterborough (see Figure 8.4). In 2011, all major metropolitan areas located west of Ontario had younger-than-average populations, with the exception of the retirement communities of Victoria and Kelowna in British Columbia (Statistics Canada, 2012j). While a majority of CMAs do not depart dramatically from the national picture (within a year or two in terms of median age), some are substantially younger (e.g., consider the three western cities of Edmonton, Calgary, and Saskatoon, with median ages

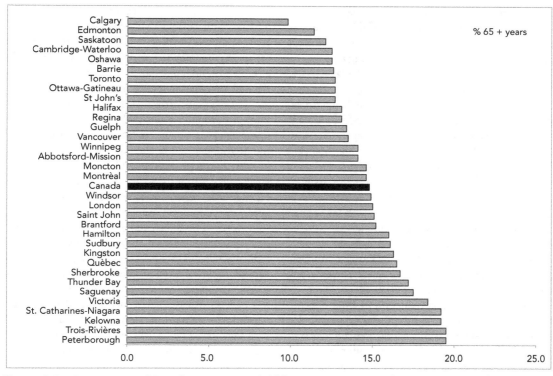

Figure 8.4 ▣ Percentage of People 65 years and Older, Census Metropolitan Areas, Canada, 2011

Source: Statistics Canada, 2012a.

of 36.1, 35.9, and 34.9 years, respectively), whereas others are much older (including the Central Canadian cities of St Catharines–Niagara, Peterborough, and Trois-Rivieres, with medians of 43.4, 44.1, and 45.1 years, respectively).

In general, CMAs with the most economic opportunity have tended to have the youngest age structures, whereas those that have witnessed economic decline tend to be older. An exception to this generalization applies to cities with a particularly attractive climate for retirement purposes, which would apply to Victoria and Kelowna, with median ages of 43.1 and 43.5 years, respectively. Even older in age are a few smaller centres that have been particularly successful in selling themselves as retirement communities—for example, both Elliot Lake, Ontario, and Parksville, British Columbia, have more than a third of their population over the age of 65 (Statistics Canada, 2012j).

Aging and Dependency

The aging of the population has a number of demographic ramifications, including fewer births, more deaths, lower population growth, an accentuation of the imbalance between the numbers of women and men at older ages, and a regional imbalance in the proportion of elderly people. An additional demographic observation is related to what has been called "*dependency*", or the ratio of people in age groups that are not usually in the labour force (0–14 and 65+) to those who are.

Over the last half century, there has been a substantial increase in the number of people over 65 per 100 people aged 15 to 64 (sometimes referred to as "*old-age*" or "*aged dependency*"). In 1961, there were 13 people of retirement age per 100 people of workforce age, compared to 20.3 in 2011 and a projected 39.5 in 2036 (Statistics Canada, 2014f). This means that in 1961, there was one retirement-age person for every eight people of labour-force age, whereas in 2036, there may be more than one retirement-age person for every three people of working age.

While the number of older dependants has risen, the number of younger dependants has declined (aged 0–14, or sometimes referred to as "*child dependency*"). For every 100 people of labour-force age, the decline has been from 58 persons under the age of 15 in 1961 to 23.8 persons by 2011. While Statistics Canada's projections suggest that this level is not likely to decline much further, this is not impossible if the birth rate were to fall much below existing levels. There are currently several countries with lower child dependency than Canada—for example, this ratio has fallen to below 21 in both Italy and Japan, to about 20 in Germany, and as low as 19 in the Eastern European countries of Latvia, the Czech Republic, Slovenia, and the Ukraine (United Nations, 2012).

Taken together, this reduction in child dependency and upturn in old-age dependency actually left for a relatively stable level of overall dependency over the 1981–2011 period. With fewer children and the baby boom generation still largely in the labour force, the proportion of dependants in the population has been at historically low levels. Yet in terms of population aging, we are on the cusp of considerable change: while child dependency is not likely to fall much further, we are about to witness major growth in the proportion of Canada's population at older ages. As we mentioned, the first of the boomer cohorts reached retirement age as of 2011, with up to 8 million baby boomers set to reach this milestone by 2026.

A high dependency ratio can be a challenge for any society, to the extent that government expenditures rise in order to support or service the youngest and/or oldest age groups in that population. For example, a high level of child dependency implies a greater proportion of government expenditure to be spent on child care, education, and labour-force training. A high level of old-age dependency implies a greater proportion spent on health care and pensions. With this in mind, it is noted that government expenditures associated with old-age dependency tend to be high, given the costs of the health-care

system and public pensions. This can become problematic to the extent that dependency costs rise to levels potentially judged as burdensome by the remaining population (i.e., those who are economically active and contribute to government revenue through taxes on their earnings).

Yet an exclusive reliance on age group in the definition of dependency has its limitations: for example, many older Canadians continue to work well beyond the traditional retirement age of 65, remain very healthy, and are not particularly reliant upon the government for income or other forms of support. Furthermore, many who are aged 15–64 are not necessarily employed, may have health problems or some form of disability, and even employed people in this age range often depend on public resources. Similarly, persons classified as dependent often provide various supports through family and other networks. In effect, most people are dependent on others in a variety of ways. Worries about increasing (demographic) dependency should thus be taken with caution as it's clear that not everyone over the age of 65 is dependent, just as many of working age are not employed.

In the early 1990s, the now-defunct Economic Council of Canada (1991) produced a useful summary of how Canada's age distribution and dependency are important in determining government expenditures. In so doing, they produced a useful summary of how various government transfers and services to both individuals and families tend to vary, on average, across various age and sex groups. Figure 8.5 updates this research with 2010 data, in providing estimates of per capita expenditures spent by government on health, education, and social security, delineated by sex and five-year age groups. For social security, these estimates include not only Canada's system of public pensions, but also disability payments, employment insurance, social welfare, child tax benefits, and other sources of income support provided to Canadians of various ages.

Clearly, the costs of pensions and health care are much higher than those of education, per person using the services. Though there are dependency costs at all ages (e.g., employment-insurance benefits are disproportionately paid out to younger adults), there are markedly higher public expenditures for children and older Canadians, and, in particular, older persons at ages 70 and over. For public expenditures, the per capita costs of the population aged 65 and over are of the order of 2 to 3 times that of the population under 15. As a result, the shift in the nature of dependency, from child to old age has contributed to rising government costs, just as population aging will do so into the future. As a by-product of population aging alone, even if per capita costs remain much the same, we can anticipate a major increase in the budgetary pressures faced by governments.

Figure 8.5 includes only estimated public expenditures and excludes private costs incurred by individuals and families. These costs are not minor, as, for example, roughly 30 per cent of all health care in Canada is paid out of pocket by individuals or are covered by private health-care plans (CIHI, 2014a, 2014b). Similarly, while the government pays the lion's share of the costs associated with primary and

secondary education, parents are largely responsible for early child care (with the notable exception of Quebec), while there are substantial costs incurred by young adults and their parents in support of post-secondary education through tuition and fees. Wolfson (1990) made the useful observation that while public costs are higher for the aged, private costs tend to be higher for the young, and consequently the total of public and private costs may be about equal for the young and the elderly. Aging, therefore, involves a shift in the burden from parents and young adults to the public sector, or a growth in the public sector. More of the burden will be financed through governments rather than by families. In addition, Wolfson observes that lower costs to individuals mean more ability to pay taxes. The expenses are nonetheless different: costs for the young are a form of investment in the future labour force, while costs for the elderly relate more directly to consumption.

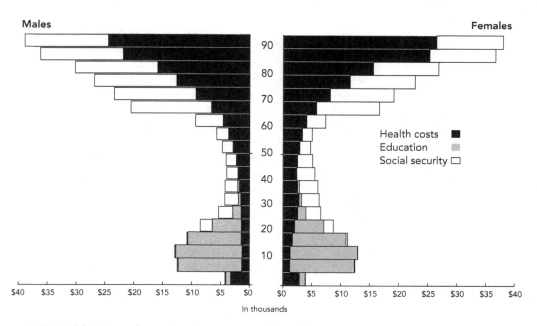

Figure 8.5 ▣ Public Expenditures Per Capita on Health, Education and Social Security, by Sex and Age Group, Canada, 2010

Sources: Based on the Economic Council of Canada, 1991—updated with estimates by authors using data from Canadian Institutes of Health Information, 2013a; Statistics Canada, 2013z; Office of the Chief Actuary of Canada, 2012.

The Economic Impact of Aging

It is clear that the early stages of aging produce net economic benefits (Bloom et al., 2003). There are more survivors at younger ages and eventually a higher proportion of the population is in the labour-force age range. In Canada, the labour force itself was getting younger from 1966 to 1986, in spite of the aging of the population. The median age of the core working-age population (20–64 years) was 39.2 in 1966 and 36.5 in 1981, but this trend has since reversed, with the median surpassing 40 in the 1990s and reaching 42.9 in 2011 (Statistics Canada 2013r). A somewhat older population also has more savings because there are fewer family expenses for the young. In the short term, lower fertility means fewer government expenditures directed toward child tax benefits and education, along with an increase in tax revenues because there are more two-income families. Women's labour-force participation advances because there is less need for their services to smaller families.

It is less clear if these advantages persist to later stages of aging. Subsequent stages include a higher proportion of the population beyond labour-force age, a higher ratio of pensioners to workers, and possibly more rigidity in the labour force. A higher proportion of pensioners would mean a tendency to convert investments into consumption, which could possibly undermine economic growth. There are also higher public expenditures, which would give governments less manoeuvrability to support the economy. It would appear that the things that may be more problematic are particularly difficult to measure: the lower flexibility, innovativeness, and productivity of an aging labour force (Beach, 2008). As we noted earlier, an older labour force would probably be less geographically and occupationally mobile and therefore would be less able to adapt to economic change (Mercenier et al., 2005). Legoff (1989) observed that while productivity might not necessarily decrease with age, at least until age 65, age does act as a restraint on mobility, because of seniority, family responsibilities, home ownership, and company pensions.

As one ages, there are clearly fewer economic returns to a change in career and/or location. Moreover, while older people may not be less productive, seniority practices may pay them more for a given level of productivity. The question then becomes whether there is too large a gap between the productivity and earnings profiles by age, which requires either an increase in productivity through retraining or a reduction in earnings at older ages. Handa (1986) argued that as workers age, they acquire skills relevant to the job but sometimes relevant only to the firm in which they work. Consequently, an older labour force could introduce more rigidity and a lower rate of acquisition of new skills or of upgrading of skills. A study by the Skills Research Initiative (2008) at Human Resources and Social Development Canada concludes that the rate of skill growth in Canada may slow somewhat, which in turn could exercise a downward pressure on economic growth and living standards.

While technological change and an increased investment in skills and human capital throughout the life course could serve to mitigate the impact of population aging, a structural rigidity as associated with aging may contribute to some obsolescence of the workforce and its misallocation with regard to sector. Tabah (1988) long ago observed that rich countries have a "universal concern" about the structural rigidity that aging creates and aggravates in the production apparatus. This may be compensated for by a more experienced labour force, along with the potential to invest more in those that remain employed, which could benefit productivity. In turn, whether Canadians continue to work through to older ages and whether employers take advantage of their experience could well become a particularly important issue as Canada's population continues to age. This could be of some importance as a potential means of reducing economic dependency ratios, meeting labour shortages, improving public finances, and promoting economic growth.

While many Canadians continue to work well into their sixties, there is currently considerable room for greater workforce participation among older Canadians. Table 8.7 portrays the participation rates

Table 8.7 ▣ Rates of Labour Force Activity, by Selected Age Groups and Sex 1976–2011, Canada

	Ages 55+			Ages 55–59		
	Both	Males	Females	Both	Males	Females
1976	31.4	47.2	17.7	60.4	84.2	38.2
1981	29.8	44.3	17.6	59.7	82.1	38.9
1986	27.3	39.8	16.8	59.8	78.3	41.8
1991	25.3	35.6	16.7	61.0	75.9	46.2
1996	23.8	32.2	16.6	59.8	71.6	48.4
2001	26.0	33.6	19.4	62.6	72.2	53.3
2006	32.1	39.1	26.0	69.1	76.1	62.2
2011	36.4	42.5	30.9	73.0	77.5	68.7
	Ages 60–64			Ages 65–69		
	Both	Males	Females	Both	Males	Females
1976	44.7	66.5	24.4	15.6	24.5	7.8
1981	43.2	63.7	25.0	13.0	19.9	7.1
1986	38.5	55.3	23.6	11.6	17.5	6.8
1991	35.5	47.6	24.1	11.6	17.3	6.8
1996	33.1	43.5	23.2	11.6	16.5	7.1
2001	36.7	46.5	27.3	11.8	16.1	7.8
2006	45.0	53.3	37.0	17.8	23.3	12.7
2011	51.1	58.0	44.5	23.9	29.9	18.2

Source: Statistics Canada, 2013p, table 282-0002.

of older Canadians, aged 55 and up, for the 1976–2011 extended period. What is clear is that the most recent trend has been upward, with a greater proportion of people working and a delay in the average age at retirement. In 2011, 73.0 per cent of Canadians aged 55–9 were involved in the labour force, up from 59.8 per cent in 1996. Among persons aged 60–4, roughly one half were employed in 2011 (51.5 per cent), up from about one third in 1996 (33.1 per cent). Even among Canadians aged 65–9, almost one in four (23.9 per cent) report some involvement with the labour force. Carrière and Galarneau (2011) point out that the average age at retirement has been climbing as of late; in 2008, for example, they forecast that a 50-year-old could expect to work an additional 16 years, or roughly 3.5 years longer than workers of the same age

15 years earlier. This shift since 1996 toward delayed retirement was found to be true of both older men and women.

Despite these changes, there remain more than one in four Canadians aged 55–9 with no involvement in the labour force (27 per cent) and roughly one in two aged 60–5 without any involvement (48.9 per cent). With this in mind, the question of whether an older person chooses to retire or leave a job as a result of involuntary unemployment becomes an important issue. The climbing proportions of working people may be partially a function of improved health and less physically demanding work, yet as health and working conditions have improved, there has been considerable room for more involvement in paid employment.

Box 8.3 ⊞ Factors Affecting Age at Retirement

The analysis of why older workers leave the labour force is far from straightforward, and even on a descriptive level, there are major obstacles to accurately documenting the pattern (Pyper and Giles, 2002; Rowe and Nguyen, 2003). Probably the largest obstacle is methodological—empirically distinguishing retirement from other forms of early labour-force exit. For example, the Canadian Labour Force Survey directly asks respondents why they left their previous job, with reasons broadly classified as either voluntarily (retirement, personal or family responsibilities, dissatisfied with job, and other reasons) or involuntary (laid off or illness/disability). The problem with relying on this definition is that, in many cases, the act of withdrawing from the labour force may, in fact, involve a combination of several of these factors. In addition, there are also questions relating to validity in measurement, as not everyone is necessarily going to be entirely forthcoming regarding the real reasons for leaving a previous job.

A proportion of all older Canadians leave the labour market on a voluntary basis, while for others, this is not a matter of choice. Many Canadians decide to retire early in light of accumulated wealth and savings, while others leave paid employment as a result of health problems, disability, or perhaps difficulties in maintaining a job or finding a new one if they are unemployed (McDonald and Donahue, 2000).

Some older workers lose their last job through layoffs and/or some other form of forced exit from the labour market, never to re-establish themselves in the workforce. Other people retire from a job and begin to draw their pensions and yet, for whatever reason, continue to work on a part-time basis. Still others retire early, only to decide to return to the labour market after a period out of the marketplace. Merely asking respondents via a cross-sectional survey whether they "retired" over the previous 12 months does not capture the wide range of experience that characterizes this transitional period.

Many cases of permanent withdrawal from the labour force will never be classified as retirements. As people approach retirement age, many enter an extended transitional stage, characterized by periods of employment (full-time and/or part-time) interspersed with periods of unemployment and non-employment (McDonald et al., 2000). Increasingly, researchers are coming to appreciate that retirement might be better thought of as a process rather than a well-defined event that occurs at a specific point in time and that it is consequently not easy to operationalize in empirical research (Habtu, 2002). Retirement is not easily defined, which presents difficulties in trying to explain recent trends, let alone providing a forecast of future trends.

As Osberg (1988) has pointed out, a reliance on self-definition can potentially provide misleading information, particularly in light of the stigma that often accompanies being laid off or unemployed. While this stigma persists, there is an increasing acceptance of early retirement among Canadians, even among those who could potentially continue to work for many years. In a situation where older workers lose a job, Osberg has suggested that a certain proportion may misreport the reason for exiting the labour force and identify themselves as retired rather than involuntarily unemployed. In this manner, an analysis of the labour-force participation of older workers may miss a form of hidden unemployment that in the survey data resembles retirement. Schellenberg (2004) has observed that older workers seem to be overrepresented among discouraged workers (i.e., those who have abandoned their job search) and also tend to be unemployed for longer periods of time. If an older worker loses his or her job, without the skills for easy re-entry into the labour market, might this same worker report that she/he has retired to preserve self-esteem? According to the 2002 General

Social Survey, a significant proportion of all recent retirees would have continued to work if their health permitted and/or if suitable employment was available (Schellenberg and Silver, 2004).

Beyond labour-market events, many careers have ended through illness or disability. Yet, with improvements in population health, the risk of morbidity and serious disability has declined in quite a pronounced manner for older workers over recent decades. The likelihood of heart disease has declined, as have high blood pressure, arthritis, among other chronic conditions that place limitations on activity (Chen and Millar, 2000; Hogan and Lise, 2003). Among Canadians reaching their 65th birthday, only about 15 per cent report a disability affecting the ability to work that could clearly justify the end of a working career (Michaud et al., 1996). The climbing participation rates of older Canadians over recent years may be partially a function of better health and less physically demanding work, because both health and working conditions have improved. Life expectancy at birth has been steadily increasing in Canada—up to 83 years for women and 79 years for men (Statistics Canada, 2013t). In a similar manner, "disability-free life expectancy" has risen—i.e., the number of years on average one could expect to live in good health and without serious disability (Public Health Agency of Canada, 2013). Recent improvements in the state of population health serve to highlight the arbitrary character of the marker typically associated with the beginning of old age or normal retirement (i.e., the age of 65). In light of better living conditions, lifestyle, and quality of health care, the average 65-year-old (or even 70-year-old) is not as old today as 30 years ago. As Denton and Spencer (2002) have argued, this marker for old age should be moved upward, to the extent that we succeed in retarding what is inevitable—the aging process).

Thus, the retirement decision is the result of a truly complex set of interacting factors that include changing labour-market opportunities, health, pension benefits, technology, and attitudes to work and leisure. There appear to be many powerful incentives and reasons for an early workforce exit. Among working Canadians, almost one third report that they are not sure about the timing of their retirement, a fact that suggests considerable potential for increasing participation rates among older workers if proper incentives and working conditions are introduced (Schellenberg, 2004). While retirement seems to express a clear intention to withdraw voluntarily from the labour market, most of the other reasons listed in the Labour Force Survey suggest an involuntary exit from paid work. In this context, barriers or disincentives to re-employment for older workers may be an important issue in the future. There may be considerable interest among older workers to continue with paid employment if they are provided proper incentives and real opportunities for re-entry.

In an explanation of why participation rates have recently climbed for both Canadian men and women, Beach (2008) highlights improved health levels, climbing female workforce participation, and shifting pension entitlements. Improved health may have shifted the time frame of older Canadians as they face the prospect of a much longer retirement period. An increased involvement of women in the labour force seems to be contributing to delayed retirement, as many have had shorter careers and so choose to work longer in order to build up benefits and pension entitlements. In addition, there has been a substantial climb in the number of older dual-earner households, which might delay retirement as couples attempt to coordinate their retirement plans. And, finally, Beach suggests that change in both public and private pension plans may be at least partially shifting retirement income risks onto workers. With this in mind, delayed retirement might be a way of coping with increased risk. In addition, mandatory retirement is now largely a thing of the past in Canada, as most jurisdictions have done away with it completely (Ibbott, Kerr and Beaujot, 2006).

The Role of Government and the Welfare State

While there is some uncertainty about the effect of aging on the economy, one of the least ambiguous consequences of aging is the increase in the role of government in transferring resources from the working age population to the elderly. Various studies have observed that government transfers to individuals tend to rise as a consequence of population aging (Sanz and Velázquez, 2007; Visco, 2000). Stone (2006) concludes that across countries, major financing pressures have surfaced in connection with income support and health-care systems, with the associated redistribution from the working-age population to older people. Although Denton and Spencer (2000, 2010) do not expect particularly large increases in government expenditures overall, they do foresee substantial changes in the composition of this expenditure, changes that will entail major economic and political adjustments. This pressure to redistribute for the benefit of the elderly has arguably limited government options, especially in view of such goals as reducing government deficits and reducing taxes.

In a larger context, Myles and Pierson (2001) have outlined the importance of population aging in shaping the welfare state, as its expansion has occurred primarily around the provision of support for the elderly. As argued, the conjunction of population aging and the postwar political economy across Europe and North America provided the historical setting for the creation of a welfare state. It is for the elderly and the retirement principle that the welfare state is most complete, for it substitutes a social wage for a market wage. The overall costs are considerable, as the largest component of federal social spending is now on the elderly; for example, Statistics Canada (2012j) reports that old-age security (OAS) and the guaranteed income supplement (GIS) now comprise roughly 40 per cent of all federal transfers to people.

Relative Positions of Young and Elderly

An overly simplistic argument for addressing the fiscal challenges of an aging society is to merely transfer resources from the young to the elderly. Funds previously allocated to families for raising children (e.g., child benefits or support for child care) might merely be transferred to providing pensions and health care. However, there are many unmet needs for the young that an aging society would ignore at its peril. The greater willingness to favour the aged can undermine transfers in favour of the younger dependants, and for that matter can undermine the standard of living of younger workers (who must pay the social security costs), inducing them to have fewer children. In effect, transfers from workers to the elderly can be thought of as transfers away from children. Consequently, transfer payments favouring children and young families continue to be important, if only as an investment in the future labour force.

Cheal (1999) observed that among the major client groups for social policy, the elderly have been the most successful and children much less so in mobilizing support. For instance, after taxes and transfers, the proportion of elderly people with low-income status declined from roughly 20 per cent in 1980 to about 10 per cent in the early 1990s, before falling even further to about 5 per cent in 2011 (see Figure 8.6). Since 1989, these rates have been systematically lower for people aged 65 and over than for children up to the age of 17. The fact that many older Canadians exit the workforce well before the traditional retirement age of 65 implies that many have the "luxury" not to work, with accumulated wealth and property. As older Canadians have low income rates that are almost half of that for other Canadians, OAS in combination with the guaranteed income supplement (GIS) has been enough to keep the majority of older Canadians out of poverty.

In his presidential address to the Population Association of America several decades back, Preston (1984) contradicted the common wisdom of his time that the elderly were America's neediest dependants, and provided evidence to suggest that the aging of American society would likely further promote some improvement in the economic and political position of the elderly. There appears to be a fairly natural tendency for an aging society to favour the elderly. Not only are there greater numbers of elderly people

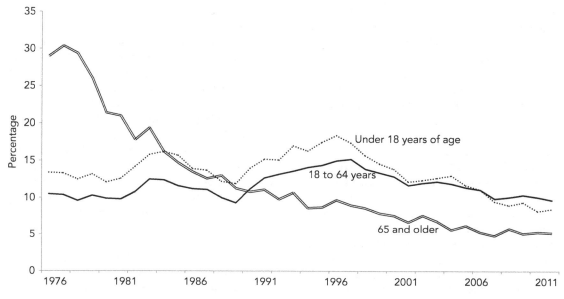

Figure 8.6 ◙ Percentage in Low Income, by Age Group, 1976–2011, Canada

Source: Statistics Canada, 2013e, CANSIM 202-0802, Persons in Low Income Families, LICOs 1992 Base, After-Tax.

looking after their own interests, but the age groups following them want to ensure that there are adequate structures for their own retirement. On a variety of levels, it appears that "young dependants" receive less public support than "old dependants," a generalization that is true of both Canada and the United States (Newacheck and Benjamin, 2004; Pati et al., 2004). In general, the very young in society have less political power since they do not vote. Households with children under 18, and consequently with a direct self-interest in youth, have become a minority.

Nonetheless, Canada has most recently had some success in reducing the incidence of low income among children, albeit low income rates still remain more pervasive in this age bracket than for many other age groups. Particularly relevant in this context has been the introduction of the National Child Benefit Supplement in the late 1990s, a progressive reform that has helped to push a proportion of the working poor with children above Statistics Canada's low-income threshold (Paterson et al., 2004). Since 1996, the low income rate for Canadians under the age of 18 has declined from 18.4 per cent down to 8.4 per cent (Statistics Canada, 2013u).

Retirement and Pensions

While aging affects a number of social programs, pensions are particularly affected because benefits and contributions are closely linked to age. Given the provisions of access based on age, but also the provisions for spousal allowances, widows' allowances, and disability allowances, along with the contributions based on employment and income, several demographic factors are involved in the evolution of pension programs. The demographic factors of age, sex, marital status, fertility, and immigration affect both the number and types of beneficiaries and the number and types of contributors (Siegel, 2002).

Particularly relevant is the relative number of contributors and beneficiaries. As Keyfitz (1988) has observed, when the population and economy are growing rapidly, no one need be much worried about equity between the generations. As long as the people in the labour force are more numerous and richer than their parents were, they will have little difficulty in supporting their elders, even at standards of living higher than they had when they were working. When demographic and economic growth start to slow, however, the transfer of resources can become more onerous. Large retired cohorts followed by small working ones may be at a particular disadvantage.

In effect, these considerations bring into question some of the underlying assumptions that were made when our public pension plans were being instituted. The late twentieth century was a time of considerable demographic and economic growth in Canada with a relatively young population. As Béland and Myles (2012) have summarized, this was also a period whereby the modern Canadian retirement income system came to be crystallized across three fundamental tiers—the first tier and cornerstone of which was OAS and the GIS; the second major tier includes the Canadian Pension Plan (CPP) and Quebec Pension Plan (QPP), two non-universal, contributory, earnings-related programs; and the third tier, private, tax-subsidized, employer-sponsored registered retirement plans (RRPs) and individual retirement savings accounts such as registered retirement savings plans (RRSPs). Of the above, only the OAS and GIS are exclusively public "*pay-as-you-go*" programs (i.e., pensions that are financed by current revenues of the federal government, with benefits paid directly from current workers' contributions and taxes), whereas the others are at least partially self-financed through current and future investments. Given the relatively small numbers of elderly people back in the 1960s and '70s, it was possible to establish programs without particularly high start-up costs, anticipating that economic growth would keep up to future costs.

With considerable confidence that the future would be able to fund an expanding welfare state, the OAS and GIS programs were introduced to reduce hardship among older Canadians. Socially, there was a desire to expand social security, especially to benefit the elderly, who were at the time a significant pocket of poverty (Myles, 2000). In this regard, both the OAS and GIS continue to be particularly important means of income support for low-income Canadians—that is, the OAS is a flat-rate pension for all persons aged 65 and over, whereas the GIS is an income-tested supplement directed to exclusively lower-income seniors in

particular need. While the OAS is universal, after meeting residency requirements, it is clawed back when income exceeds set thresholds (as of 2013, this threshold for an individual was set at $70,954, with benefits clawed back at 15 cents for every dollar for persons with incomes above this amount). On the other hand, the GIS is a "means-tested" program—it is provided only to Canadians with little or no other income. For example, the combined maximum of OAS/GIS was $15,546 for singles and $25,063 for couples in 2013 (i.e., for older Canadians with absolutely no employment income or CPP/QPP or any other private or public pensions). With roughly half of this amount the GIS, this is enough to bring many elderly Canadians to above or close to the aforementioned low income cut-offs.

While the OAS was first introduced through the Old Age Security Act in 1951 (albeit in a less generous form), the CPP/QPP started in 1966. Unlike the OAS, the CPP/QPP were never set up to be pay-as-you-go schemes. These plans were introduced as mandatory social insurance plans, in which employees and employers contribute toward a longer-term retirement pension, which would be properly invested, and subsequently drawn upon by future pensioners. In other words, the CPP/QPP are earnings-related schemes financed by mandatory payroll taxes (i.e., only employed persons and their employers pay into these plans) whereas future entitlements depend ultimately upon how much a worker contributes and for how long. In this context, the GIS was initially introduced as a stopgap measure to assist low-income seniors until the Canadian Pension Plan became fully operational. Yet since many Canadians have an on-again off-again history of involvement with the labour market, it soon became obvious that many would not be paying sufficiently into CPP/QPP to avoid hardship in retirement. For this reason, the GIS became a full-fledged part of Canada's retirement income system during the 1970s, in providing income support to those older Canadians who benefit little from other earnings-related pension schemes.

The third tier of Canada's retirement system includes the private retirement plans (RRPs and

RRSPs)—plans subsidized through the tax system to encourage Canadians and their employers to put aside income and revenue available now for future retirement. Such registered retirement plans typically allow contributions and savings for the future to be deductible from current taxable income (reducing the amount of income tax paid now to a later date when the income is actually needed in retirement). As Gougeon (2009) has documented, private pension plans continue to be an important source of retirement income, such that all private pension plans (self-sponsored or employer-sponsored) comprise roughly a third of the average retirement income (or 32 per cent in 2006). Yet the obvious problem is that not all Canadians can take advantage of these programs; for example, Morissette and Ostrovsky (2007) report that only about one quarter of all Canadians aged 15 to 65 have some form of registered pension plan through their place of employment. In addition, Pyper (2008) reports that only about 6 out of 10 Canadian families take advantage of individual RRSPs, and again middle- and upper-income Canadians are far more likely to do so than lower-income people. Investments in such plans vary quite strongly by family income, as lower-income Canadians have a harder time putting aside resources for future benefit. Pyper (2008) reports that nearly 90 per cent of families with after-tax annual incomes of $85,000 or more owned RRSPs, while among families with lower income (less than $36,500), this percentage drops to only 35 per cent. While upper-income Canadians gain little or nothing through either the OAS or GIS, lower-income Canadians tend to gain relatively little through either RPPs or RRSPs.

The evolution of these programs have been heavily influenced by the shifting demographics of Canada's population. For example, in its earlier years (in the 1960s and early '70s), the CPP/QPP took in more funds than it distributed because only past contributors could be recipients and Canada's population at the time was relatively young. Consequently, there was an irresistible urge to use these extra funds to meet other needs in the welfare state, by adding widowhood and disability provisions and granting full benefits to those retiring in 1976 after just 10 years of contributing. That is, the system was very profitable when it was first instituted. All workers made contributions, but only people who had made contributions could receive benefits, the level of which depended on the number of years of contributions. As more people became eligible to receive benefits, there was a tendency to run out of reserves, a problem that could be solved either by increasing the contributions or reducing the benefits. The reserves came under pressure owing both to the aging of the population and to the aging, or maturing, of the system itself. As of 1985, the Canada Pension Plan fund would have started to pay out more than it was receiving. Instead of returning the money that they had borrowed from the Canada Pension Plan, which would have increased other taxes, the provinces easily agreed to allow an increase in the level of contributions. From 3.6 per cent of income, the rate rose to 4.6 per cent by 1991. The program underwent another significant review in 1996, and the contributions were increased further, to reach a stable state of 9.9 per cent of income by 2003. The advantage enjoyed in the profitable earlier period can be seen from the fact that the contributions almost needed to triple in order to maintain the same benefits. It should also be observed that the changes have involved increasing the contributions rather than reducing the benefits. In some countries like Sweden and Italy, benefits have instead been reduced (Blanchet, 2002).

Population projections have long been relevant to planning the future of the Canada Pension Plan, although past projections by the chief actuary of Canada have tended to understate the extent to which Canada's population was expected to age (see Table 8.8). Reviews are undertaken every three years, including revisiting the projection assumptions and the anticipated population dynamics (Office of the Chief Actuary of Canada, 2010). By legislation, the CPP must be renegotiated every five years in order to review potential increases in expenditures and to adjust contributions and benefits in line with these projections. When the CPP was established, it was expected that contributions would have to represent 5.5 per cent of income by

Table 8.8 ■ Ratio of Population Aged 20–64 to those Aged 65+, 1950–2075, Canada

Historical data

1951	6.97		
1976	6.49		
2001	4.77		
Projected for	**2000**	**2050**	**2075**
Initial CPP Report (1964)	6.22	5.61	
CPP Report 6 (1977)	5.62	3.47	
CPP Report 12 (1988)	4.83	2.48	2.32
CPP Report 18 (2000)	4.90	2.36	2.23
Observed in 2000	**4.79**		
CPP Report 25 (2010)		2.20	2.10
Statistics Canada Projections, 2013 base		**2026**	**2051**
Low		2.90	2.22
Medium		2.97	2.42
High		3.00	2.53
Projected with alternate immigration levels Statistics Canada, 2009 base;		**2026**	**2051**
Zero Immigration		2.37	1.65
Medium Immigration		2.73	2.20
1% target Immigration		2.74	2.40

Sources: Statistics Canada, 2010c, 2014a. Office of the Chief Actuary, 2001; 2010.

2030. Underlying this projection was the expectation that the ratio of persons aged 20–64 to 65+ years would be roughly 5.6 to 1 by 2050. But according to forecasts made in 2010, the contributions will need to be at least 9 per cent of income and possibly as high as 10.4 per cent of income, not surprising in light of the revised projections that underlie the latter review (Office of the Chief Actuary of Canada, 2010). Part of this difference is due to enriched benefits, including disability benefits that had not been anticipated when the program was started, yet in addition, this rate has risen due to changed demographics, especially more aging than had been initially foreseen back in the 1960s.

The relative size of age groups that are contributors and beneficiaries is particularly relevant to the CPP/QPP. In 1976, there were 6.49 persons aged 20–64 for every person aged 65 and over (see Table 8.8). By 2000, this ratio had fallen to 4.79, somewhat lower than was forecast in previous projections by the chief actuary (e.g., the 1964, 1977, and 1988 reviews forecast ratios of 6.22, 5.62, and 4.83, respectively). By 2051, Statistics Canada's (2014a) projections expect this ratio to fall further, to anywhere between 2.22 to 2.53. These are amazing numbers: what was once a ratio of over 6 workforce-aged people ages to every 1 retirement-aged person could fall to a ratio of under 3 to 1 by 2026 and perhaps as low as 2 to 1 by mid-century. The life expectancy assumed here would imply that even those who spent the whole 45 years between 20 and 64 in the labour force would have spent only about 2 years in the labour force for at least 1 additional year of retirement (Beaujot, 2002a).

Given the increased weight of government expenditures on pension plans, it is understandable that there have been attempts to reform these programs. In 1996, for instance, the finance minister proposed that the OAS be converted into a super-GIS. This would have maintained the benefits for poor elderly while reducing the benefits of elderly with other sources of income. There was considerable opposition, including the view that the reform was part of a conservative agenda to use population aging as an excuse to downsize the welfare state (Gee and Gutman, 2000). One could nonetheless argue that the situation has changed considerably since the 1960s when these programs were being established, and that reforms are justifiable now that significant numbers of the elderly have their own sources of income. In discussing alternative possibilities for changes in pension plans, it is important to note that these are ultimately distributional policies. In discussing policy change, Deaton (1989: 342) had the foresight to predict that reforming the pension system would ultimately be "a potentially volatile political issue because it involves the structurally determined interests of all major groups and institutions in a capitalist political economy: workers, unions, finance and industrial sectors, the state, and the increasing proportions of the elderly." Since the redistribution is largely from people in the labour force to retired people, a sense of the appropriate level of transfer is, of course, needed.

Any change to Canada's pension system would be advisably introduced slowly with enough advance warning, corresponding to the long-term nature of retirement plans. With this in mind, the 2012 federal budget introduced a controversial reform, which increased the age of eligibility for both the OAS and GIS, from 65 to 67 years. In recognizing the importance of advance warning, the finance minister indicated that this reform would not take effect until 2023—and with this, it would be phased in over a six-year period (2023–9). The government highlighted the fact that Canadians are living much longer than was true in the past, typically in better health, and that the labour force would benefit by a greater involvement of older Canadians (Flaherty, 2012).

As Scoffield (2012) has pointed out, it is possible that the need for reform was increasingly being appreciated by the general public, in light of the growing concern about population aging and whether the federal government's policies would be sufficient in addressing the large number of retirements as forecast. Yet the federal leader of the opposition was quick to go on the record that he would reverse this decision if elected, largely as a matter of equity, since low-income Canadians are most dependent on the OAS and GIS. By raising the age of eligibility, these Canadians especially would be forced to continue working past the traditional retirement age of 65 (Mulcair, 2012). In addition, hinting at the difficulties involved in reforming our public pensions, the polling firm Ipsos Reid estimated in the months leading up to this reform that a clear majority of Canadians (roughly 75 per cent) continued to be opposed to raising the age of entitlement from 65 to 67 (Kennedy, 2012).

Aging and Health

Compared to pensions, health costs are more spread out over the life cycle and consequently are less affected by aging. Nonetheless, costs are higher in the older ages and, consequently, aging increases health costs. In addition, health is very much funded through pay as you go. The working population largely pays for improvements in health services that extend life; then it also pays for the health and pension costs of the persons who live longer. While improved health and longevity are clearly important for individuals and societies, longer lives can also mean longer periods of ill health, and, consequently, higher medical costs.

Canada's health-care system has grown much more rapidly than other areas of government spending, such that total health costs are now the single most important expenditure by Canada's provinces, with education a distant second. Overall, Canadians spent over $207 billion for health services in 2012 (both private and public), which works out to roughly $5,900 per capita, or $9,500 per person aged 20–64. In constant dollars, overall expenditures on health have more than doubled since the early 1990s, whereas Canada's population has grown by only about one quarter over this same period (CIHI, 2014b, 2014a). Yet the analysis that has been made of the components of increase in health costs show that aging has thus far played a relatively minor role compared to other causes (Evans et al., 2001; Constant et al., 2011). Climbing health-care costs have been fundamentally a function of a series of other factors, including technological progress, alternative sources of care, extent of public funding, tolerance for pain, supply of services, salaries in health care, as well as the climbing costs of pharmaceuticals. Evans and his colleagues (2001), for instance, find that the increased costs of pharmaceuticals for people 65 and over in British Columbia were mostly due to higher expenditures per person under treatment for particular illnesses.

The CIHI (2014b) has estimated that for the 1998–2008 period, public expenditures on health care increased by an annual rate of 7.4 per cent, but that less than one quarter of the increase was the by-product of demographic factors. More specifically, population growth in and of itself was responsible for roughly a 1 per cent annual increase, with population aging being responsible for another 0.8 per cent annual increase. In a direct sense, it is easy to see the impact of population growth: when a population grows by roughly 1 per cent a year, you would expect at the least that overall expenditures would also increase by roughly 1 per cent. Yet isolating the impact of aging is not as immediately obvious. This estimate is possible through a simple simulation: in observing population aging over the 1998–2008 period, how much would overall costs increase if there had been a constant level of service and cost per capita by age and sex group? In other words, while age-specific costs remain the same, overall expenditures increase as a climbing proportion of the population moves into older age groups where the per capita costs are higher. As to the future, while further population growth and considerable population aging is certain, the difficulty is that it is far from certain as to how non-demographic factors might contribute to escalating costs.

There have been many past attempts to project the impact of demography, by assuming a constant level of service and cost per age group (Denton et al.,

1997; Fellegi, 1988). In general, this research has tended to conclude that population aging, in and of itself, is not likely to overly burden the ability of Canadian society to pay for its health-care needs, although it certainly will not help, as aging clearly contributes to overall costs. While demography is important, we should not overstate or exaggerate its impact. We should also appreciate the difficulty of attributing increased costs to a changing age structure. These calculations start with the assumption of constant age-specific health costs. This underlying assumption of "constant" age-specific health costs in a growing economy is not particularly realistic, as, for example, it involves the difficult assumption that the economy grows but the real wages of health-care workers do not. In this context, the CIHI (2011) has recently estimated that physician salaries as well as hospital staff and nurses have all seen gains at a much faster rate than compensation in other non-health sectors of the economy. As another contributing factor, prescription-drug expenditures grew at an annual rate of 10.1 per cent per year over the 1998–2007 period. With many other contributing factors, expenditures continue to climb, as health care as a percentage of GDP has continued to steadily increase from 7 per cent in 1975 to 11.9 per cent in 2009 (CIHI, 2014b).

It is estimated that the average lifetime health costs for the typical Canadian in terms of publicly funded health care has surpassed $220,000 (Corscadden et al., 2013). Health spending is increasing more rapidly than the rate of economic growth, igniting some concern about the longer-term sustainability of Canada's publicly funded health-care system. There is also concern about the possibility that health-care costs might crowd out expenditures on other government-funded services and programs. Brown (2012) has argued, for example, that beyond a certain threshold, increased expenditures on health care may in fact lead to some worsening in health outcomes, to the extent that resources become less available to support other health-enhancing activities. Well documented is the importance of income security and education as predictors of individual and population health. Over the long term, from the standpoint of population health, it may actually be counterproductive to redirect funds that are useful in other social- and economic-policy spheres: education, employment insurance, social security, pensions, welfare, child support, and so on.

A basic insight from the public health literature is that upper-income, better-educated Canadians are in much better health than others, not only because wealth implies adequate food, shelter, and other necessities, but also because more fundamentally, better-educated people have more knowledge, choices, and control over health-related decisions in their lives. Consistent with this insight, Corscadden and colleagues (2013) have estimated that average lifetime health costs also vary considerably across income groups, such that, on average, the public costs of the richest 20 per cent of Canadians are fully 15 per cent less than those of the lowest 20 per cent. This was found to be the case even though wealthier Canadians can expect to live much longer—in fact, the highest-quintile group was documented to have a life expectancy fully five

years longer than the lowest-quintile group. Interestingly, from a life-course perspective, across all age groups from young adulthood through to the 80–84 range, expenditures were shown to be less for higher-income groups than for lower-income ones (see Figure 8.7).

Regardless of population aging, resources devoted toward education, income security and improving the living and health conditions of all Canadians can serve to potentially reduce overall health-care costs over the longer term. For example, consider that Canada's largest cohorts who are set to move into the 50–9 year old age group—i.e., into ages where health-care costs start to climb quite noticeably. Figure 8.7 demonstrates that for this age group the public health-care costs of the lowest income quintile are more than double that of the highest quintile. In addition, the richest quintiles have average health-care costs negligibly greater than the lowest quintile group, even 15 years younger, aged 40–45. Population aging is but one factor among many in determining both current and projected health-care costs.

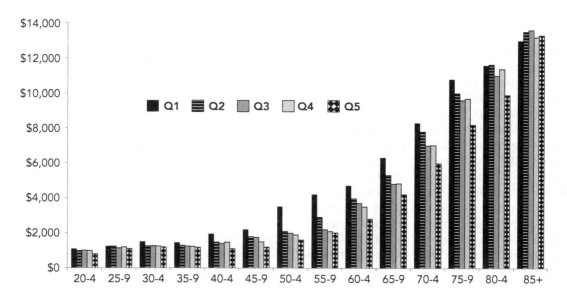

Figure 8.7 ▣ Per Capita Public Sector Health-Care Costs, by Income Groups and Age, Canada

Source: Corscadden et al., 2013.

Conclusion

As we consider the various policy questions associated with aging, it is important to remember that the older population is very heterogeneous. Some need extensive services and support while others are quite independent and in fact pay more in taxes than they receive in government transfers. Most of the elderly live on their own and the majority report that they have fair to excellent health (Connidis and Willson, 2007). The elderly make important contributions to unpaid work, and it should be noted that disabled people are often productive (Galarneau and Radulescu, 2009). Also, families do not abandon their elderly relatives, and a large part of the needs of the dependent elderly are provided for by spouses and children (Connidis, 2010). As aging continues, however, the proportions of older people with working-age children will decline. If life expectancy increases dramatically, with fewer people dying of chronic diseases but larger proportions of frail and disabled elderly, then the needs of the aged will clearly surpass the support possibilities of their immediate families (Carrière et al., 2008). The weakening of family ties, as a result of divorce and the geographic mobility of Canadian society, may also result in a greater need for formal services.

The economic ramifications of aging are difficult to disentangle. In the decades that followed the baby bust of the late 1960s, population aging was initially accompanied by an increase in the proportion of the total population of labour-force age, as lower fertility initially implied significantly fewer child dependants. These smaller cohorts moved through the school system in the 1970s and '80s and into the labour market in the 1980s and '90s. This likely contributed to reduced unemployment overall, as a smaller proportion of the population was at ages whereby unemployment is typically at its highest (ages 18–24). Initially, dependency burdens declined with smaller numbers of child dependants, yet eventually, they were to stabilize due to a compensating climb in the number of older persons. Nonetheless, this dependency burden is set to change quite noticeably during the second and third decades of our current century, as some of the largest baby boom cohorts are set to move into retirement. Costs should increase, as the expenditures associated with old-age dependency are quite different from those associated with child dependency, with pensions and health care substantially more expensive than education or other transfers directed toward the young. Until now, the increase in health and pension costs has been due less to aging and more to higher benefits and the maturation of pension plans. In the future, however, aging will play a larger role, as there will be larger numbers of frail elderly needing health care, and pension costs are closely linked to age (OECD, 2001a).

In addition, population aging in the Canadian context may imply problems in terms of labour productivity and the rate of skill growth, due to the reduced mobility of older workers and a tendency for employers not to invest in the training of older workers, particularly among those who are approaching retirement (Schellenberg, 2004; Mercenier et al., 2005). To some extent, automatic adjustments will take place, yet changes may be slow in light of societal norms relating to work and retirement. Yet one major adjustment that could reduce the dependency burden would be to extend the working life and to spread education out over the life course in order to compensate for fewer people entering the labour force. The relatively recent upturn in workforce participation rates among older workers may very well signal change in this direction, which could be considered the logical outcome of improved health and less physically demanding work. The meaning of age could also change, moving the marker of old age upward as health and longevity improve (Denton and Spencer, 2002). Correspondingly, the increased labour-force participation of women may lead to gains for older Canadians in retirement, as an increased number spend a much larger part of their adult life in the labour force and will subsequently qualify for pensions and be less disadvantaged in retirement (Ménard, 2009).

More generally, population aging is clearly a function of improved socioeconomic conditions, including higher income, education, and improved population health. Aging and income per capita are linked around the world. Putting aging in its socio-economic context, McDaniel (2008b) sees it as an indirect and unintended consequence, in an affluent and industrialized society, of successful planned parenthood. She therefore observes that aging, along with zero growth, stem from good fortune and affluence. Yet in this connection, it should be remembered that out of positive causes can sometimes come unintended negative consequences. While aging is associated with economic success and control over fertility, in terms of public policy and its associated costs, it can also be considered as somewhat of a mixed blessing.

Tabah (1988) summarizes what he calls a "universal concern in rich countries" about two things: (1) structural rigidity that aging creates and exacerbates in the economic production process, and (2) future financial viability of health-care and retirement systems. He suggests that two actions are needed: launching a lasting recovery of the birth rates, and making appropriate changes in retirement

arrangements. This raises the question of who is going to pay for the adjustments that are needed. If workers pay the main costs, then it could well be at the expense of investments in children. Already, the compensation for family costs is not keeping up with pension increases, and young couples have difficulty finding room for children in their lives. Possibly, the costs of aging could be divided somewhat differently between younger and older workers, along with the retired population. Older people who are not particularly disadvantaged could pay more through lower retirement benefits and by postponing their departure from the labour force. It may be that more of the pension costs could be paid especially by the older workers, who have fewer family responsibilities and whose own retirement is closer at hand. If young families paid less of the social expenditure costs of aging, they could be more involved in supporting the younger generation, which is the most secure of long-term investments.

Critical Thinking Questions

1. Explain the various stages of population aging and their different causes and consequences.
2. Explain the demographic effects of aging.
3. Analyze the changing levels of dependency in Canada, taking account of the trends for both people 65 and over and those under 20.
4. Criticize the concept of dependency and explain how it can be used appropriately.
5. How could Canadian public pension plans be reformed to maximize intergenerational equity?
6. What other factors besides aging influence health costs? Assess their relative importance.

Recommended Readings

Chappell Neena L., and Marcus J. Hollander. 2013. *Aging in Canada*. Don Mills, ON: Oxford University Press. This excellent overview considers many of the social and economic consequences of population aging in Canada, providing an eye-opening look at how the needs of older adults are currently met and how we can improve upon this in the future.

Chappell, Neena, Lynn McDonald and Michael Stones, 2008. *Aging in Contemporary Canada*, Second Edition. Don Mills, ON: Pearson Canada. This edition explicitly considers the relevance of Canada's multicultural character in outlining the changing realities of population aging.

Connidis, Ingrid Arnet. 2010. *Family Ties and Aging*. Thousand Oaks, CA: Pine Forge Press/Sage. On the basis of both theory and evidence, this book finds that family ties remain important in societies with low fertility and significant population aging.

McDaniel, Susan, and Zachary Zimmer, eds. 2013. *Global Ageing in the Twenty-First Century: Challenges, Opportunities and Implications.* London, UK: Ashgate. This book brings together an excellent selection of international research on the implications and possibilities of global aging,

Settersten, Richard A., and Jacqueline L. Angel, eds. 2011. *Handbook of Sociology of Aging.* New York: Springer. This comprehensive resource contains 45 chapters on the most pressing topics related to aging today, including the many consequences of this demographic trend for individuals, families, institutions, and societies.

Related Websites

www.statcan.gc.ca/ads-annonces/91-520-x/pyra-eng.htm. This link shows animated population pyramids illustrating the changing age structure of Canada's population from 1971 to 2056.

www.census.gov/population/international/data. Shows a series of dynamic population pyramids for different countries, created by the International Programs Center at the US Census Bureau.

www.cagacg.ca. The website of the Canadian Association on Gerontology. This organization encourages studies in gerontology and disseminates information among the many professions and disciplines whose mandate includes the elderly.

Consequences of Population Change

Having studied the processes of population change (fertility, mortality, and migration) and resulting changes in the size, distribution, and age structure of the population, in this part, we move on to consider some of the consequences of these sorts of changes. This includes changes that have occurred in Canada's population composition. It has been transformed over recent decades in terms of family and household units, as well as in its sociocultural and socioeconomic characteristics. We include a separate chapter on the demography of Canada's first peoples, the Aboriginal population, as well as a separate chapter on the consequences of population growth for Canada's environment.

The second demographic transition has brought greater flexibility in the entry and exit from relationships, and consequently more flexibility and diversity in families. Over the life course, we observe a delay in leaving home, a greater propensity to cohabit, along with more separation and divorce. Common-law families and single-parent families have become a larger proportion of all families. There is also a growth of single-person households. This complicates the family-life trajectories of both adults and children. It also means that there is more growth in the number of households than in the size of the population.

In addition to greater diversity in family and living arrangements, Canada's population can also be characterized by greater diversity in its linguistic and ethnic composition. Canada is becoming increasingly multilingual and multi-ethnic, a fact that is largely due to the growing ratio of immigration to overall population growth. As natural increase continues to decline, this trend is projected to continue, and that will bring a number of changes and require various adaptations. In this connection, Canada has established itself as a socioeconomic success story. Canadians enjoy a relatively high standard of living, just as the country's citizens are among the most educated. This is not to deny the persistence of some problems: for example, many new Canadians (and visible minorities) encounter considerable obstacles in establishing themselves economically in Canada; not all Canadians share equally in income and opportunity; and there is some evidence of increased inequality over recent years.

It is among the Aboriginal peoples where we encounter probably the most disadvantaged of Canada's citizens. The demographic situation of Aboriginal Canadians demonstrates a few important points not always obvious from the larger picture in

PART III

Canada. More specifically, there are plenty of exceptions to national trends; for example, Aboriginal Canadians continue to experience relatively high fertility and mortality, a high rate of natural increase, and a relatively young age structure. In the broader context of this book, our chapter on Aboriginal demography can be taken as a sort of case study, focusing in greater detail on the demographic dynamics of a specific subpopulation within Canada, while demonstrating the various associated difficulties of definition and methodology.

Our final chapter considers the consequences of population change for the environment. This includes a brief overview of the neo-Malthusian position on the impact of population growth and consumption, as well as opposing economistic arguments. In drawing from the natural sciences, economics, and other related social sciences, we consider arguments relating to the primary human driving forces of environmental change, including population growth, technological change, and consumption patterns. Although Canada is a relatively sparsely populated country, its ecological footprint (and affluence) is high and a substantial part of its prosperity comes from international trade. Yet due to globalization, the demand for resources and the associated impact on the environment in Canada is strongly linked with demographic, economic, and political developments far away.

9 Families and Households

The Chapter at a Glance

- The demography of families and households considers living arrangements of persons at various stages of the life course. Union formation and dissolution affects the life circumstances of adults and children.
- Families have become increasingly diverse. There are fewer traditional families with two married parents and children, more cohabiting couples, lone-parent families, stepfamilies, and same-sex couples.
- Demographers have interpreted the family changes since the 1960s as a second demographic transition, with greater flexibility in the entry and exit from unions, along with later home leaving, later union formation, and later child-bearing.

- Family change can be related to both structural transformation (how the family relates to institutions of society) and cultural transformations (the meaning given to the family) in society.
- Family change can also be related to the gender revolution, especially with regard to the changing associations between gender and earning, and between gender and caring.
- The diversity across families represents more options for individuals, but also more risks and inequality across individuals and families.
- It is increasingly complex for policy to support individuals and families that are diverse in their family life course and in their self-sufficiency.

Introduction

Although much demographic research is based on the individual as the unit of analysis, families and households are particularly relevant units for activities ranging from living arrangements and the purchase of major household goods to reproduction and the socialization of children. There is much interplay between family and demographic questions: what is happening to families affects the population, and population change affects families.

Family behaviour influences demographics in a variety of ways. Fertility, for instance, is lowered by later marriage, more divorce, and more cohabitation. The geographic mobility of at least one adult, and often the person's children, is affected by the entry and exit from relationships. Morbidity and mortality are also affected by changing family patterns: for instance, married people benefit from the social support received from spouses.

Population change also affects family patterns. Low mortality and fertility and the resulting aging of the population imply a restructuring of the individual life course and family life cycle. The changes in mortality and fertility have reduced the proportion of an average person's life spent as the parent of a dependent child. Lower fertility means fewer siblings and cousins. Gee (1990) shows that people are spending less of their lives as parents of dependent children and more as adult children of possibly dependent parents, and the number of children available to older parents has decreased.

Particularly since the mid-1960s, the number of households has grown faster than the population.

This is a result of several factors, including a higher proportion of adults (or fewer children) in the population and a larger number of one-person households. Over the 2001–11 period, for instance, the population increased by 10.7 per cent, while the number of private households increased by 15.2 per cent.

After discussing family change and family diversity, and analyzing the trends in relationships over the life course, we will examine the changing composition of families and households, along with the associated inequality. The increased diversity raises a number of policy issues associated with the welfare of individuals and families across the various family arrangements.

Families and Their Diversity

Just as demography pays particular attention to births and deaths, the demography of families pays particular attention to the means by which people form family relationships and leave them. We have seen changes in the way people form such relationships, including a delay in marrying, a prevalence of cohabitation as a means of forming relationships, along with fewer and later births of children. Regarding the termination of relationships, voluntary departures have come to play a larger role, in addition to death. The entries and exits are also more fluid. For instance, separations and divorces are not necessarily "terminations." Especially if there are children from the relationship, it might be said that separation and divorce bring the relationship to a different phase, rather than to its termination. From the point of view of children, both parents usually remain relevant to family life, even if the parents are not in the same household. Consequently, marital instability can bring both an expansion of a person's family network and greater uncertainty regarding family relationships.

These changing means of entering and leaving family life create more diversity among families. Thus, there are families with or without children, marriage and common-law unions, children who live with one or two parents, along with both heterosexual and same-sex unions. Depending on the biological and social bonds between parents and children, this diversity includes step-relationships and blended families. So, from the point of view of children, there may be two parents, one parent, or several parents. The diversity across families can also be defined in terms of the division of paid and unpaid work between the spouses or partners, including breadwinner and dual-earner models.

As we think of families becoming more diverse, it is also important to observe that, in certain regards, there is less variability in present-day families than at earlier times. In particular, the decline of the premature death of parents means that few children are orphaned and exposed to the resulting uncertainty. As far as living arrangements are concerned, there are more people living alone, but there are fewer multiple-family households, and fewer households that include people beyond the immediate family, such as a grandparent, another relative, a boarder, an apprentice, or servant. The changing means of entering relationships and people's longer lifespan mean that there is considerable diversity across families in the earlier or later parts of the life course. At mid-life, however— say, between ages 30 and 55—there are strong commonalities of experience. Most adults are living in relationships, raising children, and working (Beaujot, 1995).

With all this focus on diversity, it can become difficult to see what families have in common and, consequently, what *family* really means. Box 9.1 proposes that families can be defined in terms of sharing of resources and caring for each other. Of course, this pooling of earning and caring may be imperfect. Our definitions must not blind us to the exploitation, abuse, or violence that occurs in families. In effect, earning and caring are variables that can be more or less present, and more or less pooled, in a family. Coltrane (1998) further proposes that families are defined not only in terms of shared activities, but also shared knowledge and practices. Families have unique histories, experiences, and rituals. These experiences and histories, especially as recalled in family stories, recreate a sense of belonging and uniqueness.

Box 9.1 ▣ Defining Family

The difficulty of defining the word *family* is obvious from the fact that even some textbooks on families do not include a definition (e.g., Broderick, 1979: 394–6). In their extensive discussion, entitled "Conceptualizing a Family," Fox and Luxton (1991: 35) observe that the legal definition of family is based on rights and obligations for certain legally described people, principally parents and children, and husbands and wives. Without giving a strict sociological definition, they go on to propose that the family can be thought of "as the relationships that bring people together daily to share resources for the sake of caring for children and each other." Glossop (1994) suggests a similar concept in terms of "relationships of affection and obligation."

In effect, families can be defined in terms of a sharing of resources and caring for each other, or in terms of a pooling of earning and caring. For the purpose of an operational definition that would be usable in the field, families have sometimes been simply defined as "the people eating out of the same pot." This is an interesting concept because "the same pot" represents the crucial life-maintaining resources that have been both obtained and prepared (through paid and unpaid work), and eating together is clearly a means of looking after each other or caring for each other. This pooling of earning and caring is more likely to occur when people are living in the same household. The idea of "coming together daily" can also be interpreted as living in the same dwelling. With this in mind, let's look at the definitions used by Statistics Canada for data-gathering purposes:

census family a married or cohabiting couple, with or without never-married children, or a lone parent with at least one never-married child, living in the same dwelling.

economic family a group of two or more persons who live in the same dwelling and are related to each other by blood, marriage, common-law or adoption.

Though the concept of economic family is broader, it retains the limitation of being based on dwelling units. However, data gathering needs to start with something easily identifiable in the field.

Some of the conceptual difficulties can be avoided by not trying to define the family unit, and focusing only on family relationships. It is then possible to speak of relationships between partners, who may be married, cohabiting, or formerly married, along with relationships between parents and children, who may or may not be living together, and relationships with other relatives.

This focus on relationships allows us to observe that given sets of people have various associations that are sometimes coordinated and sometimes uncoordinated. On the one hand, individuals are constantly being pulled apart by the various activities in life, but we can also look at what brings people together as a family. Smith (1997) describes this as "coordinating the uncoordinated," which "produces an ordinary family day."

Family Change and the Demographic Transition

Paying particular attention to child-bearing, demographers have largely theorized family change in terms of two demographic transitions: a long-term change (from about 1870 to 1950), which brought smaller families; and another change (from about 1960 to the present) that especially involved increased flexibility in marital relationships (Lesthaeghe, 1995, 2010; Beaujot, 2000a: 85–96; Beaujot and Ravanera, 2008).

As we have seen in Chapter 4, the first demo-graphic transition involved a change in the economic costs and benefits of children, along with a cultural environment that made it more appropriate to control family size. The second transition is marked by a greater flexibility in the beginning and ending of rela-tionships, as manifest especially through cohabitation and divorce. Cohabitation first changed premarital relationships, but it also changed post-marital rela-tionships, and, in effect, cohabitation changed mar-riage itself, introducing less rigid understandings of unions. There are also various types of cohabiting relationships, from those that are best seen as dating or loose relationships, to others that are a prelude to marriage or an alternative to marriage. Although the majority of marriages remain intact until death, the substantial increase in separations means that mar-riage is no longer defined as lasting forever.

Table 9.1 presents various indicators of the sec-ond demographic transition in the Canadian case. The annual divorces per 100,000 married couples increased from 180 in 1961 and 600 in 1971 to over 1,100 in the 1981–2011 period. Common-law couples amounted to 6.4 per cent of all couples in 1981, compared to 19.9 per cent in 2011. Similarly, births to non-married women increased from 9 per cent of births in 1971 to 39.8 per cent in 2011. Lone-parent families as a pro-portion of all families with children increased from 11.4 per cent in 1961 to 27.1 per cent in 2011.

Besides the greater flexibility in entry and exit from relationships, the second demographic transi-tion has seen a delay in family formation. There has been an increase in the period of education, and, thus, a later completion of education and later entry into full-time employment, in part due to insecurities in the labour market (Beaujot, 2004, 2006). The fam-ily transitions associated with home leaving and union formation have involved not only a delay, but also more fluidity through less-well-defined transi-tions, and variability from case to case.

The delay in life-course transitions can be seen in the increase of the age at first marriage, from a mean

Table 9.1 ▣ Summary Statistics on Family Change in Canada, 1941–2011

	1941	1951	1961	1971	1976	1981	1986	1991	1996	2001	2006	2011
Divorces per 100,000 married couples	- -	180	180	600	990	1129	1220	1110	1130	1100	1140	1086
Common-law couples as a per cent of all couples	- -	- -	- -	- -	0.7	6.4	8.2	11.2	13.7	16.4	18.6	19.9
Lone-parent families as a per cent of all families with children	9.8	9.8	11.4	13.2	14.0	16.6	18.8	20.0	22.3	24.7	25.8	27.1
Births to non-married women as a per cent of all births	4.0	3.8	4.5	9.0	- -	16.7	18.8	28.6	36.9	38.2	37.7	39.8
Mean age at first marriage												
Brides	24.9	23.4	22.6	22.6	22.9	23.7	24.7	25.8	26.7	27.7	28.9	29.1
Grooms	28.1	26.3	25.3	25.0	25.3	25.9	27.0	27.8	28.6	29.7	30.9	31.1
Births to women aged 30+ as a per cent of all births	35.6	36.2	34.1	21.6	19.6	23.6	29.2	36.0	43.7	46.9	48.9	52.1
Mean age at first birth	25.2	24.3	23.6	23.9	24.4	25.0	25.6	25.9	26.5	27.3	28.0	28.5
Total fertility rate (average births per women)	2.8	3.5	3.8	2.1	1.8	1.7	1.6	1.7	1.6	1.5	1.6	1.6

Notes:
1. 1941–1971 births to non-married women are designated as illegitimate births.
2. Divorces per 100,000 and mean age at first marriage: data for 2008 shown as 2011.

Sources: Beaujot and Wang, 2010: 415; *The Daily*, 19 September 2012; 2011 data from (1.) Census of population, 2011, 98-312-xcb2011006; (2.) Statistics Canada, CANSIM, Tables 102-4505, 102-4503, 102-4506, 051-0042, 101-6501, Milan, 2013b: 10; "Mean age at first marriage": Human Resources and Skills Development Canada. Indicator of well-being in Canada (www4.hrsdc.gc.ca/.3ndic.1t.4r@-eng.jsp?iid=78); "Mean age at first birth": Statistics Canada, Health Statistics Division, Vital Statistics and Demography Division, demographic estimates.

of 23 years for brides and 25 for grooms in 1961–71 to mean ages of 29 and 31 years, respectively, in 2008. Similarly, the age at women's first birth increased from a mean of 23.6 years in 1961 to 28.5 in 2011. The decline in cohort fertility at younger ages has been partly compensated for by increases at ages of 30 and above.

Comparisons across Western countries have shown considerable similarity in the timing of the second transition. Lesthaeghe (1995) proposes that it is useful to consider three stages in this second transition. The first stage, from about 1960 to 1970, involved the end of the baby boom, the end of the trend toward younger ages at marriage, and the beginning of the rise in divorces. In Canada, the law permitting divorces on grounds other than adultery dates only from 1968. The second stage, from 1970 to 1985, saw the growth of common-law unions and, eventually, of children in such unions. The third stage, since 1985, includes a levelling off of the divorce rate, an increase in post-marital cohabitation (and, consequently, a decline in remarriage), and a plateau in fertility due in part to higher proportions of births after the age of 30. These changes in births, marriage, cohabitation, and divorce have brought fewer children, but also a higher proportion of children who are not living with both biological parents (see Table 9.1).

These data also confirm the uniqueness of the 1950s as a period between the two transitions. Not only was this the peak of the baby boom, but it was also a period of a marriage rush, in that people married at a young age and high proportions of people married at least once in their lives. It has been described as a "golden age of the family," in which many families corresponded to the new ideal of domesticity, especially in the suburbs; consequently, there was less variability (Skolnick, 1987: 6–16).

Subsequent research has made it clear that not all was ideal in this golden age. Isolated housewives in particular experienced the "problem with no name" (Friedan, 1963: 15). The idealism of the time served as blinders that obscured some difficult realities of family life, including violence and abuse. Given a general denial that such things could ever occur in families, there was little recourse for the victims of violence. There was also a lack of autonomy, especially for women, to pursue routes other than the accepted path

(Veevers, 1980). Childless couples were considered selfish, single adults were seen as deviants, working mothers were thought to be harming their children, and single women who became pregnant were pressured either to marry right away or to give up the child for adoption in order to preserve the integrity of the family.

Structural and Cultural Interpretations of Family Change

The broader explanations of the demographic transitions include structural and economic questions (macro-level structural changes and micro-level economic calculus) and cultural questions (attitudes and value orientations).

In the long term, the structural explanation relates changes in the family to changes in society, especially in terms of economic structures. We can speak of structural differentiation and deinstitutionalization, through which families have become less central to the organization of society and to the lives of individuals (Harris, 1983). This reduced role allows for more flexibility in family arrangements and fewer constraints on family behaviour. Note that in some other areas of life, there are more constraints on behaviour: for instance, with regard to smoking in public places, throwing out garbage, or sexually offensive behaviour in the workplace. So, not all areas of life have seen the diminished constraints on individual behaviour that we have seen in the family.

In regard to the more recent transformations, the structural explanation pays attention to the shift to a service economy, which increased the demand for women in paid work, especially jobs that might be seen as extensions of women's unpaid work, such as clerical work, teaching, and nursing (Chafetz and Hagan, 1996). Until the 1960s, the division of labour encouraged a state of reciprocal dependence between the sexes. The new work patterns put pressure on women to postpone marriage as they extended their period of education and invested in their work lives. For both young women and young men, marriage became less important as a means of structuring their relationships and understandings, and, consequently, cohabitation became an alternative. As women became less dependent on marriage, divorce and cohabitation became more feasible for both sexes.

The gender revolution, then, is a central part of this structural explanation, as it has involved changing power relationships between men and women. Since both men and women need to position themselves toward the labour market, Oppenheimer (1988) speaks of a "career entry theory of marriage timing." In order to make the most profitable match, prospective partners need to know how each will be positioned for income earning. Two incomes have become important to maintaining stable middle-class standing (Coltrane, 1998). Consequently, the completion of education and higher income prospects have come to be positively related to women's marriage probability, as has always been the case for men (Sweeney, 2002; Ravanera and Rajulton, 2007). By comparing the propensity to marry by level of education in 25 European countries, Kalmijn (2013) further finds that in countries where gender roles are traditional, more-educated women are less likely to be married, but in countries that are more gender-egalitarian, more-educated women are likelier to be married.

The cultural explanations focus on what is happening within families and on the understanding that people have regarding family questions. Burgess and colleagues (1963) spoke of a movement from institution to companionship, or Farber (1964) from orderly replacement of generations to permanent availability, or Scanzoni and Scanzoni (1976) from instrumental to expressive relationships. As is well recognized, relationships based on companionship are less stable than those based on division of labour. Relationships are not maintained as institutions, but as a projet de couple (Roussel, 1979), or as a "pure relationship" defined by the couple themselves (Giddens, 1991). In *La fin de la famille moderne*, Dagenais (2000) also describes the postmodern family as high in individual and humanistic values. That is, the cultural explanation links family changes to secularization and the growing importance of individual autonomy. This includes a weakening of the norms against divorce, premarital sex, cohabitation, voluntary

childlessness, and same-sex relationships. Value change has promoted individual rights along with less regulation of the private lives of individuals by the larger community. There is a heightened sense that both women and men should make their own choices in terms of relationships and child-bearing. Diversity is valued, in living arrangements and in family forms.

Lesthaeghe (1995) has proposed that it is possible to identify two somewhat separable cultural transformations related to family, intimate behaviour, and children. The second of these transformations coincides with the second demographic transition over the period since the early 1960s, whereas the first transformation took place in the nineteenth century, at different times in different cultural groups. He notes that several authors have proposed these themes. For instance, in *The Making of the Modern Family*, Shorter (1975) identifies two sexual revolutions. In the first, young people began choosing their marriage partners themselves, and the result was the removal of the barriers to marriage that had previously been placed by parents and society. This first revolution, however, was based on the idea of "one true love" that was expected to last a lifetime. The second sexual revolution accentuated the sexual aspects of the choice of a mate and introduced experimentation with eroticism along with the possibility of sex without love. Eventually, sexual gratification was seen as indispensable for unions.

There were also two contraceptive revolutions. The first involved the use of inefficient methods, including abstinence and non-coital sex. This first contraceptive revolution occurred quietly, among individual couples who sought to stop having children after they had the number of children they wanted. The second contraceptive revolution involved highly effective methods, principally the pill and sterilization. This was far from a quiet revolution in the privacy of married couples' bedrooms—on the contrary, it liberated premarital sexual activities from the fear of pregnancy and allowed people to enter relationships earlier. Efficient contraception also permitted the postponement of births and strong control over the timing of children. For couples, perhaps nothing has changed as much since the early 1960s as the degree of control over child-bearing. For the non-married, there was a significant reduction in the risks of sexual expression. For both groups, the links between sexuality, marital life, and reproduction were broken.

Ariès (1980) also speaks of two transitions in the relative priority given to children and adults. The first transition centred on children, on what he called the child-king, and motherhood even emerged as a full-time vocation (Shorter, 1975; Stone, 1977). The second transition involved a move to adult-centred preoccupations with self-fulfillment and the quality of the dyadic relation between partners. Children are largely viewed as a means through which adults could receive affective gratification and blossom as individuals (Romaniuc, 1984: 64). Of course, some have concluded that children can also interfere with this affective individualism. Though children remain important for most people, they are no longer so important as to be impediments to parental divorce and subsequent self-fulfillment in other relationships.

Lesthaeghe (1995) further identifies two transitions in individual autonomy and political control. The period until 1950 involved enhanced institutional control, first by the church through the reform movements and then by the state through an extension of its power over individual lives. More recently, there has been a resistance to external institutional authority: for example, the student movements of the 1960s, the second wave of feminism in the 1970s, and the decline of deference of the 1980s. In regard to the latter, Nevitte (1996: 280) finds increases between 1980 and 1990 in the value placed on egalitarianism both between husband and wife and between parents and children. For women in particular, asymmetric gender roles were being questioned as limitations on both achievement and self-fulfillment.

Relationships over the Life Course

We can speak of family change in terms of greater looseness in the entry and exit from relationships, and, thus, the importance of separation and cohabitation as indicators of this change. We can also speak of a shift in the average timing of family events. After

a trend toward younger ages at first marriage, first birth, last birth, and home leaving of children over cohorts born in 1916–20 to 1941–45, the subsequent trend has been toward these transitions occurring at later ages (Ravanera and Rajulton, 1996; Ravanera et al., 1998a, 1998b). Compared to 27 countries from around the world, union formation is on average earlier in Canada, at 25 years for women and 27 for men, than in France, Greece, Spain, and the United States (Bernard et al., 2014). The age of women at the birth of their first child is also younger in Canada, an average of 28 years, compared to average ages in Greece, Australia, Spain, and France. On the other hand, the average age at completion of education and entry into the labour force, at 22 and 23 years, respectively, is older in Canada than in most other countries.

The delays in these life-course events may be interpreted as a longer period of adolescence—Côté and Allahar (1994) have referred to this development as a "generation on hold." But the delays are also due to the needs of both men and women to put off forming relationships and, especially, having children until they are better able to handle the trade-offs between investing in themselves and investing in reproduction. That is, there are trade-offs in the timing of the various life-course transitions, with advantages to both early and late patterns. Having children early ensures that there *will* be children, and early departures from the parental home ensure that the maturing child has somehow become independent. Those who have children later, however, are able to invest longer in themselves before investing in the next generation. Similarly, when children do not leave home until they are older, they are likely to receive more transfers from their parents and to eventually be more self-sufficient.

Home Leaving

After having declined decade by decade, the average age at home leaving started to rise in the late 1970s. In addition, some adult-aged children have become boomerang kids, returning home after having been away for a period of time, something that was very rare in the past. For instance, the proportions living in the parental home at ages 20–24 increased from 41.5 per cent in 1981 to 59.3 per cent in 2011 (Statistics Canada, 2012b). At ages 25–34, the increase over this period was from 8.2 per cent to 18.1 per cent. Compared to other countries, the Canadian levels are intermediate, with some 4 per cent of people aged 25–34 in Norway and Sweden living with parents, and 45 per cent in Portugal and Italy (Imgur, 2014).

There are clearly economic reasons for the delays in home leaving, such as the difficulties that young people are having in establishing themselves in the labour market, and the need to pursue more education in order to be competitive. Also, with more people living in cities, there is a greater likelihood of finding post-secondary education near home.

However, there are also cultural factors, which have probably made the parental home more pleasant for older children as the generation gap has declined. Parents have developed more flexible and tolerant attitudes toward their adolescent children. In the United States in the 1960s, for instance, the typical first sexual experience occurred in a car, whereas in the 1980s, it was more likely to occur in the parental home, admittedly when the parents were away. Bibby and Posterski (1985: 82) find a surprising amount of similarity between the basic attitudes of Canadian teenagers and parents on a range of factors, from the acceptability of sex before marriage for people who are in love, to attitudes on abortion and the rights of gays and lesbians.

While there may be some problems of lack of independence, Boyd and Norris (1995) observe that later home leaving presents various advantages in terms of parental investment in children. It is significant, then, that the average age at home leaving is highest in intact families.

Cohabitation

Though some common-law unions have always existed between people who were not allowed to marry, the modern phenomenon of cohabitation started with university students, especially in Scandinavia and the United States in the 1960s. The practice then spread to professional classes in the 1970s and subsequently to much of the population.

Initially, cohabitation was often a short pre-honeymoon period. It then became a longer period that most often led to marriage, but sometimes resulted in separation. It has now become the normal form of entry into unions for people who are single, but especially for the previously married. According to the 2001 Canadian General Social Survey, 62 per cent of people aged 20–9 who had been in a relationship had cohabited as their first form of union (Statistics Canada, 2002: 4). At the time of the 2011 Census 19.9 per cent of all couples were cohabiting, compared to 6.4 per cent in 1981 (Statistics Canada, 1997: 3; Statistics Canada, 2012a).

To a certain extent, less formal relationships are simply being substituted for marriage. Yet, in some respects, cohabitation is not a true replacement for formal marriages. By comparing various characteristics of cohabiting people with those who are single and those who are married, Rindfuss and VandenHeuvel (1990) found that the cohabiting were more similar to the single than to the married. Cohabitation can be viewed as an alternative to being single, as a prelude to marriage, or as an alternative to marriage. At the level of societies, Kiernan (2001) proposes that there are four stages. At a first stage, cohabitation is essentially seen as a prelude to marriage; later it is seen as a probationary period to test the relationship prior to marital commitment; then as a socially acceptable ongoing relationship; and finally as a substitute or alternative to marriage.

The prevalence of cohabitation is much stronger in Quebec, where 37.8 per cent of couples were cohabiting in 2011, compared to 14.5 per cent in the rest of Canada (see also Le Bourdais and Lapierre-Adamcyk, 2004). With its legal tradition under civil law, as contrasted to common law in the rest of the country, Quebec has had a long tradition of two alternate forms of marriage in terms of the extent to which goods are held in common (Beaujot et al., 2013a: 222–4). With the advent of cohabitation, other provinces have made common-law unions largely equivalent to marriage if the union has lasted some three years, or if a child has been born in a stable union. In Quebec, the *union libre* or *union de fait* is treated differently than marriage, in terms of the separation of goods and the responsibilities of partners toward each other after the relationship has ended. This difference between marriage and cohabitation was supported by a February 2013 decision of the Supreme Court of Canada (SCC). The SCC ruled that the differential treatment of cohabitation in comparison to marriage did not constitute discrimination, in the case of the Quebec civil code. In effect, the SCC ruled on the side of permitting alternative choices in a free and democratic society.

Economic factors play a role in these alternate forms of unions. Bélanger and Turcotte (1999) propose that greater financial autonomy may allow employed women greater freedom to choose their conjugal arrangement. That is, cohabitation may express an exchange between two people who are economically independent. Across countries, the time allocations to paid and unpaid work are more similar between men and women who are cohabiting than it is in couples who are married (Bianchi et al., 2014). Being less based on dependency, cohabiting unions are considerably less stable than marriages. Using data from the 2002–7 Survey of Labour and Income Dynamics, Bohnert (2011: 83) finds that compared to an odds ratio of dissolution of 1 for first marriages, the odds are 4.5 for never-married cohabitations outside Quebec and 3.3 in Quebec.

In addition, cultural factors are central to an understanding of the growing prevalence of cohabitation, and these factors have also influenced marriage itself, including its greater instability. The study of change in France suggests to Leridon and Villeneuve-Gokalp (1994) that there is a denunciation of the hypocrisy of bourgeois marriage, a growth of hedonism, and attempts at personal growth without the constraints of marriage. For many, such trends affect not only those who cohabit, but also marriage itself. Leridon and Villeneuve-Gokalp also relate these trends to the greater security of contraception and to the rising status of women. That is, women who have access to status in other ways than through marriage can more easily enter "pure relationships." Clearly, the devaluation of the institution of marriage has not involved a comparable devaluation of *la vie à deux*. Another indicator of cultural factors is the higher propensity to cohabit among those who had not attended any religious services in the past year (Dumas and Bélanger, 1997).

It is interesting that the 1981 Census did not even ask about cohabitation for fear of raising sensitive issues, whereas in 2008, Statistics Canada decided to no longer collect and publish the vital statistics of marriage because these capture a decreasing proportion of union formations. There is also little use in publishing data on births to non-married women since these data give the false impression that the births are occurring outside relationships. In Quebec, it has been found that the number of cases of "no declared father" on the birth registration has been about 5 per cent of total births from 1976 to 1998, declining to about 2.7 per cent in the 2006–12 period (Institut de la statistique du Québec, 2013: 50). For Canada as a whole, the 2011 Census indicates that 45.1 per cent of common-law couples included children living at home, compared to 54.1 per cent of married couples.

Consequently, Leridon and Villeneuve-Gokalp (1994) see the spread of cohabitation as a radical change for families. Cohabitation is displacing marriage as a form of first union, and it is lasting longer. While cohabitation could be interpreted as simply an alternative form of entry into unions, it has also transformed premarital, marital, and post-marital relationships. It signals flexibility in unions, which has significant consequences for children.

Marriage

At the beginning of the twentieth century, marriage took place at a relatively late age (often in the mid- to late twenties), and significant proportions of people did not marry (Gee, 1986). Over the next six or seven decades, except for a slight reversal in the 1930s, marriages were occurring earlier and earlier in people's lives and higher proportions were getting married at some point. Then, suddenly, these trends reversed. In 1971, the mean age at first marriage was 22.6 for brides and 25 for grooms, but by 2008, it had risen to ages even higher than at the turn of the previous century, with mean ages of 29.1 for women and 31.1 for men. In 1965, 30.8 per cent of first-time brides were under 20 years of age, compared to 3.5 per cent in 2000.

Not only is marriage occurring *later in life*, but it is also happening with less frequency. The use of life-table techniques to combine the 1971 age-specific marriage rates implied that over 90 per cent of adults could be expected to marry at some point in their lives, compared to under 75 per cent in 1991 (Adams and Nagnur, 1988; Nault and Bélanger, 1996). The changes at entry into first marriage are partly a result of more cohabitation. But especially under age 55, the combined proportion of those who were married or cohabiting has declined appreciably between the 1981 and 2011 Census (see Table 9.2).

Table 9.2 ▣ Marital Status of Population by Sex and Five-Year Age Group, Canada, 1981 and 2011 (in percentages)

	Marital Status									
	Never Married		All Unions				Separated/ Divorced		Widowed	
			Cohabiting		Total					
	M	F	M	F	M	F	M	F	M	F
1981										
15–19	98.8	93.7	0.7	2.8	1.1	6.1	0.0	0.2	0.0	0.0
20–4	72.8	51.9	7.2	9.4	26.1	45.4	1.1	2.6	0.0	0.1
25–9	32.6	20.2	8.3	7.3	63.1	72.8	4.2	6.7	0.1	0.3
30–4	15.7	10.7	6.2	4.8	77.9	79.5	6.3	9.2	0.1	0.6
35–9	9.7	7.3	4.9	3.7	81.9	81.4	8.2	10.1	0.2	1.1
40–4	8.2	6.2	3.6	2.8	82.8	81.6	8.6	10.1	0.4	2.2
45–9	7.6	5.8	2.8	2.1	83.4	80.8	8.2	9.3	0.8	4.1
50–4	7.9	6.0	2.0	1.6	83.1	78.2	7.4	8.3	1.6	7.6
55–9	7.9	6.3	1.6	1.2	82.9	73.7	6.6	7.0	2.6	13.0
60–4	7.6	7.1	1.4	0.9	82.5	66.0	5.6	5.7	4.2	21.1
65+	8.5	9.5	1.2	0.9	74.0	39.5	4.2	3.2	13.3	47.8
2011										
15–19	99.3	97.6	0.6	2.1	0.7	2.4	0.0	0.0	0.0	0.0
20–4	87.2	78.7	8.9	13.4	12.3	20.6	0.3	0.6	0.1	0.1
25–9	59.9	47.5	20.2	21.7	38.4	49.7	1.6	2.7	0.1	0.1
30–4	36.7	26.3	20.7	19.6	59.2	67.2	4.0	6.3	0.1	0.2
35–9	23.5	17.6	17.2	15.4	69.4	72.2	6.9	9.8	0.1	0.4
40–4	19.5	14.0	14.9	13.6	70.4	72.1	9.8	13.0	0.3	0.8
45–9	17.4	12.0	13.7	13.2	70.1	71.7	12.0	14.9	0.5	1.4
50–4	14.2	10.1	12.3	11.3	71.6	71.3	13.4	15.9	0.8	2.7
55–9	10.6	8.2	10.4	8.7	74.3	70.4	13.6	16.6	1.5	4.8
60–4	7.6	6.5	8.5	6.2	77.0	68.0	13.0	16.6	2.4	8.8
65+	5.0	5.4	4.8	2.3	74.8	45.9	9.1	10.4	11.1	38.3

Note:
Married and Cohabiting includes persons who were previously Never Married, Separated/Divorced, or Widowed.

Source: Statistics Canada, CANSIM Table 051-0010, estimates of population, by marital status, age group, and sex for 1 July, Canada, provinces and territories, annual (persons).

Over time, there has been an increased similarity in the average age at first marriage of men and women, with a difference of two years, having declined from a difference of about three years in the 1960s and four years in the early part of the twentieth century. Although a two-year gap is small, it can have considerable implications. A younger person is likely to be less experienced, while an older person would on average be more established and earn a higher income.

Goldscheider and Waite (1986) have analyzed the propensity to marry in light of the relative costs and benefits of marriage for the sexes. They find that in the United States before 1980, long-term employment increased the likelihood of marriage for men but not for women. It would seem that women were more likely to use a higher personal income to "buy out of marriage," and that greater options outside marriage were reducing their relative preferences for marriage. In terms of benefits, women tend to gain financially from marriage while men gain more in non-economic benefits, including a longer life expectancy and better health, both mental and physical (Goldscheider and Waite, 1986). These authors propose that, leaving out finances, "his" marriage is more desirable than "hers" in many ways. Having gained other options for financial support, women would be less prone to marry. For men, the greater "access to wife-like social and sexual services outside marriage . . . [reduces] their incentive to make longer-term commitments of financing and support" (p. 93). On the other hand, Goldscheider and Waite (1986) expected these differential effects by sex to weaken with the transformation that is occurring in the role of marriage in males' and females' transitions to adulthood.

In effect, among American cohorts marrying in the 1980s, Sweeney (1997) found that economic prospects had become positively related to marriage for both men and women, suggesting, as Goldscheider and Waite (1986) had expected, that men and women have come to resemble one another in terms of the relationship between economic prospects and marriage propensity.

That is, socioeconomic characteristics have always been important in men's marriageability, but this now also applies to women. For instance, Ravanera and Rajulton (2007) find on the basis of Canadian data for 1993–8 that the higher level of education attained is the main factor in the postponement of marriage, and that having greater economic assets increases the risk of marrying.

In a study of marriage trends in the United States over the 1973–2007 period, Sironi and Furstenberg (2012) document that it has become more difficult for young people to establish economic independence, and that union formation increasingly depends on the capacity to combine men's and women's wages.

These patterns of selectivity by socioeconomic status imply that persons who make transitions early can be relatively disadvantaged. Focusing on women born between 1922 and 1980, in the 2001 Canadian General Social Survey, Ravanera and Rajulton (2007) find women with high social status are more likely to have delayed their entry into motherhood, having first completed post-secondary education. In contrast, women with low social status are more likely to become mothers at a younger age, often without first completing post-secondary education or having a period of regular full-time work. These authors also find that the 10 per cent who do get married at a young age are more likely to have fathers with less education (Ravanera and Rajulton, 2007). Within any particular cohort, later marriage is also associated with higher socioeconomic status (Ravanera et al., 1998b).

Selectivity in Union Formation and Assortative Mating

While common culture, ethnicity or religion, were once dominant characteristics in union formation, education has come to play a much more important role. Potential mates socialize in given educational settings, and people with similar educational assets are more likely to strike a bargain.

Since 1970, there has been an increase in educational *homogamy*—that is, a greater likelihood of spouses having a similar level of education (see Pew

Research Center, 2010, and Kalmijn, 2013). Among men with a university degree, in 2006, 67 per cent were married to women with a university degree, compared to 38 per cent in 1981 (Martin and Hou, 2010: 71). Hou and Myles (2008) further document that the increase in educational homogamy has more to do with changing patterns of mate selection than with the growing similarity in the educational attainments of young men and women. Using data from the 2001 Census Hamplova and Le Bourdais (2008) find similar patterns in Quebec and the rest of Canada, including higher educational homogamy for married than for cohabiting couples.

In effect, the increased homogamy by education implies greater differentiation across couples. As another example, the average employment earnings of married mothers in 1980 were highest when husbands had intermediate earnings, but by 1990 and 2000, the higher the earnings category of the men, the higher the average employment income of their partners (Myles, 2010: 69). Similarly, Gaudet and her colleagues (2011) find that the proportion of women working within two years of a first birth is highest for women whose husband's income is highest.

Considering the association between spouses' earnings on the basis of the US Current Population Survey for 1967 to 2005, Schwartz (2010) finds that there are two factors at stake: over time, there has come to be an increased similarity in the earnings of husbands and wives in dual-earner couples, and second, there has been a decline in the negative association between husbands' earnings and the odds that wives work. This growing economic similarity of spouses has resulted in increased inequality across married couples.

Separation and Divorce

Separation and divorce have increased significantly since the 1960s, but it is also important to appreciate that the most common situation is for people to be married only once. For instance, at ages 30–54 in 1990, some 10 per cent of people had never married, another 10 per cent had formerly been married, 67 per cent were married or cohabiting with no previous marriage, and 12 per cent were married or cohabiting after a previous marriage (Beaujot, 1995: 42). For people aged 20–64 who were living with children in 2011, 79.7 per cent were in intact families, 9.7 per cent were lone parents, and 10.7 per cent were in stepfamilies (Vézina, 2012: 9).

On the basis of duration-specific divorce rates, it was found that 30 per cent of marriages occurring in 1969 had ended in divorce within 25 years, compared to 35.7 per cent for the 1983 marriage cohort (Milan, 2013b: 14). Canadian divorce rates are higher than in Japan, France, and Germany; roughly the same as in Sweden and the United Kingdom; and considerably lower than in the United States. Canadian data show an increase in the proportion of the population aged 15+ who are separated or divorced, from 5.1 per cent in 1981 to 11.5 per cent in 2011—however, the trends have shown considerable stability since 2001 (Milan, 2013b: 3).

In analyzing "what holds marriage together," Trost (1986) proposes that most of the bonds have declined. The legal bonds have been redefined to permit divorce by mutual consent. Two-income families mean less economic interdependency. Fewer children means weaker bonds through parenthood (see Box 9.2 on divorce trends).

Given the prevalence of cohabitation, along with its longer duration, sometimes as a substitute for marriage, it is useful to look at the separation of unions of all types. The separations, in effect, vary considerably according to the type of union. Relative to first marriages, which are assigned an odds ratio of 1, the odds of dissolution of second marriages are 1.7; while outside Quebec, the odds of post-marital cohabitations dissolving are 1.5; and never-married cohabitations have an odds ratio of 4.5 (see Table 9.3).

For both married and common-law unions, Bohnert (2011) finds that unemployment and other difficult employment situations, such as holding multiple jobs, are associated with a higher likelihood of dissolution, while home ownership has the opposite effect. In a meta-analysis of the educational gradient in marital disruptions across a number of European

Table 9.3 ▧ Relative Odds of a Union Dissolving (Odds Ratios), All Union Types, Quebec and the Rest of Canada, 2002–2007

Type of Union	Odds Ratio
First Marriage (reference category)	1.000
Second Marriage	1.722*
Common Law Never Married – Outside Quebec	4.482***
Common Law Post-Marital – Outside Quebec	1.512
Common Law Never Married – Quebec	3.260***
Common Law Post-Marital – Quebec	3.527**

N=8397

*=p<.05, **=p<.01, ***=p<.001

Sources: Bohnert, 2011, p. 83.

countries, Matysiak and her colleagues (2014) find that there has been a weakening of the positive educational gradient over time, and even a reversal of this gradient in some countries, with a higher likelihood of divorce for those with less education. As divorce has become more accessible, there is less selectivity, where people with more education can more afford to divorce, and there has been a move toward more divorce for those with less education. On the basis of data from Sweden for 1970–99, Kennedy and Thomson (2010) find that educational differentials in family instability were small in the 1970s, but have since increased due to the rising union disruption among less-educated parents. Consequently, children in more advantaged families experience less lone parenthood and family instability. In effect, the trends indicate that Sweden has joined the patterns in other countries, showing socioeconomic differentials in family stability.

Remarriage, Repartnering, and Stepfamilies

Given the growing prevalence of separations in society, there has been more repartnering. For marriages taking place in 2004, at ages 25–9, 21.7 per cent of the men and 34.1 per cent of the women were previously married, and this rises to some 90 per cent for the marriages that occur at ages 45–9. In addition, a

significant amount of repartnering occurs through cohabitation rather than marriage (Statistics Canada, 2012l). Among separated or divorced persons in 2011, 25.3 per cent were cohabiting. At ages 40–4, among all people whose marital status was separated, divorced, or widowed, 30.4 per cent of men and 25.1 per cent of women were living common-law. Within five years of separation, 37 per cent of women and 51 per cent of men have repartnered (through marriage or cohabitation), and these figures rise to about 70 per cent of women and 80 per cent of men after 20 years (Wu and Schimmele, 2009: 173).

This repartnering has increased the number of stepfamilies where at least one child is the biological or adopted child of only one of the spouses or partners. Among couple families with children, the General Social Survey estimates that 10.1 per cent were stepfamilies in 1995, and 11.8 per cent in 2011 (Vézina, 2012: 9). Stepfamilies were also enumerated in the 2011 Census where 12.6 per cent of couple families with children were stepfamilies (Statistics Canada, 2012l: 11). Among stepfamilies, 41.3 per cent were complex in the sense that not all children had the same biological or adoptive parents.

In her study titled *Being a Parent in a Stepfamily: A Profile*, Vézina (2012) finds that stepfamilies are much more likely to involve cohabitation rather than marriage. For intact families with children, 14 per cent were cohabiting, compared to 48 per cent in stepfamilies. It also found that 43 per cent of stepfamilies have a child in common (Vézina, 2012: 10). In the further analysis of parents in stepfamilies, Vézina (2012) finds that stepfamilies are more likely to have both parents in paid employment, and to be both working full-time, compared to intact families with children. However, stepfamilies are more likely to be financially stressed, with 18 per cent being "unable to meet a financial obligation at least once in the previous year," compared to 11 per cent for intact families and 31 per cent for lone parents. The complex nature of financial obligations, within and beyond the immediate family, contributes to this greater financial stress in stepfamilies and in lone-parent families.

Box 9.2   ▣   Divorce Trends: Instrumental, Expressive, and Commitment Factors

The understanding of divorce trends can be placed in the context of instrumental and expressive factors in marriage and the changing nature of the marriage commitment. Since there has been a decrease in the instrumental functions fulfilled by families, families have less holding them together. This is particularly true in the economic domain, where members of families are now less economically interdependent. For women in particular, employment outside the home makes it easier to leave an unhappy marriage. Bohnert (2011) finds that first marriages with a traditional division of labour were less likely to experience separation, while those where the female spouse earned more than the male spouse had a higher likelihood of separation. Stated differently, the greater independence of women makes the divorce alternative more viable.

The consideration of instrumental questions also helps us to understand several other things about the incidence of divorce. Divorces are less likely when there are young, dependent children because the family is more economically interdependent at that time. Indeed, both childless couples and those in the empty-nest stage have higher risks of divorce (Rowe, 1989; Hoem, 1995).

Divorce rates are also higher at lower levels of socioeconomic status. A lower income means that the instrumental exchanges in the marriage are less rewarding and consequently the prospect of divorce is not so disagreeable. In Sweden, the relationship between education and the propensity to divorce has changed (Hoem, 1995). In cohorts born before 1940, those with more education were more likely to divorce, possibly because of more liberal attitudes toward divorce. In subsequent cohorts, however, those with more education are less likely to divorce, possibly because of the more rewarding nature of their instrumental exchanges.

The greater importance placed on the *expressive* dimension in relationships is also important in

understanding the divorce trend. That is, marriage is now seen much more as an arrangement for the mutual gratification of participants. Spouses expect more from families in terms of intimacy and interpersonal affect. In addition, individual well-being and self-fulfillment are seen as significant values. Families are expected to serve individual needs rather than individuals serving family needs. Divorce today, then, may be more prevalent because it offers a natural solution to marriages that do not serve the mutual gratification of the persons involved. In particular, 88 to 95 per cent of respondents think that divorce is justified if there is "lack of love and respect from the partner," "unfaithful behaviour," or "abusive behaviour" (Frederick and Hamel, 1998: 8). According to the 1995 General Social Survey, the most common grounds for divorce are abusive behaviour, infidelity, lack of love and respect, and excessive drinking by a partner, all factors at the expressive level. For Hareven (1983), high rates of divorce are proof that people care about marriage and about the quality of their relationships. On the other hand, Ambert and Baker (1988) find that significant numbers regret their decision to divorce. In a third of separations, there were no serious grounds for divorce. Some divorces happen because of circumstances that have little to do with the marriage, such as problems at work, mid-life crises, or continuing emotional problems. Other divorces are due to "taking a risk" with an affair that ultimately does not lead to a permanent relationship.

One of the most consistent findings in divorce research is that the probability of divorce is higher for those getting married at an early age. For women aged 35 to 49 in 1984, the probability of marital dissolution among those who married at 19 years of age or younger was almost twice as great (26 per cent versus 14 per cent) as among those who married at the age of 25 or older

(Balakrishnan and Grindstaff, 1988; Desrosiers and Le Bourdais, 1991). The same applies to the risk of dissolution of common-law unions, which is higher for those entering unions at young ages or if there was a conception before the union (Turcotte and Bélanger, 1997). There are several reasons for the higher divorce rates among those marrying young. Some of these reasons are related to instrumental questions. The lower income common in youth means that the instrumental exchanges may be less rewarding. Regarding the expressive dimension, one can hypothesize that as these young married people mature, they find their spouses to have been poor choices and they do not receive the expected gratification. It may even be that for people who marry young, emotional gratification is particularly important. Early marriage may have been a way of escaping an unrewarding situation in their families of origin. If the expressive dimension is especially important to them, they will hesitate less to separate when this dimension is not satisfactory.

The higher incidence of divorce for second marriages can also be seen in this light. Compared to an odds ratio of 1 for first marriages, the dissolution rate of second marriages is 1.72 (Bohnert et al.

2014b: 2–3). People who have already been divorced are more likely to consider the purpose of marriage to be mutual gratification and to leave a marriage that is not rewarding.

Obviously, divorce would be less common if everyone frowned on it and if the legal restrictions were more severe. But there has been a significant change in the attitudes toward marriage dissolution in Western societies. Over time, the social stigma attached to divorce lessened considerably, and it is now accepted that it occurs frequently among "normal" people. There has also been considerable change in the definition of acceptable grounds for dissolving a marriage. Until 1968, adultery was the only legally acceptable reason for divorce in Canada. The 1968 Divorce Act extended the grounds to include both fault-related grounds and marriage breakdown. Fault-related grounds include adultery and other sexual offences, prolonged alcohol or drug addiction, as well as physical and mental cruelty. To obtain a divorce on these grounds, there must be an injured party who brings the other spouse to trial, and a determination of guilt. By 1986, a divorce could be obtained on the ground of marriage breakdown after the spouses have lived apart for one year, for whatever reason.

Box 9.3 ▣ Children in Families

The demography of families is often presented from the point of view of adults. But the changed patterns of entry and exit from relationships have had important consequences on the family living arrangements of children. In 1961, 6.4 per cent of children aged 24 and under living in census families were with a lone parent, compared to 21.5 per cent in 2011 (Bohnert et al., 2014: 2–3).

For children aged 0–14 in 2011, 69.6 per cent were in intact families, and another 3.7 per cent

were the child of both parents in a stepfamily (see Table 9.4). In addition, 15.7 per cent were with a lone mother and 3.4 per cent with a lone father. Using the ratio of 83.5 per cent of children in stepfamilies being with their biological or adoptive mother and stepfather (Beaujot, 2000a: 271), it can be estimated that 5.3 per cent of all children are with their biological mother and a stepfather, and 1 per cent are with their biological father and a stepmother. From the data in Table 9.4, it can be

Continued

estimated that 73.3 per cent of children under age 15 are with both biological or adoptive parents, 21 per cent are with their biological or adoptive mother but not their father, 4.4 per cent are with their biological or adoptive father but not their mother, and 1.3 per cent are with neither parent. Altogether, 94.3 per cent of children aged 0–14 are with their biological or adoptive mother and 77.7 per cent are with their biological or adoptive father.

Table 9.4 Number and Distribution (in percentage) of Canadian Population Aged 0–14 by Detailed Census Family Status, 2011

	Number	% Distribution
Total population aged 0–14	5,587,165	100.0
Total children in a census family	5,540,225	99.2
Child in lone-parent family	1,065,910	19.1
Child in female lone-parent family	876,750	15.7
Child in male lone-parent family	189,160	3.4
Child in couple family	4,444,315	79.5
Child in intact family	3,886,970	69.6
Child in stepfamily	557,345	10.0
Child of one parent in a simple stepfamily	186,680	3.3
Child of one parent in a complex stepfamily	164,640	2.9
Child of both parents in a complex stepfamily	206,020	3.7
Grandchild in skip-generation family	30,010	0.5
Total population not in a census family	46,940	0.8
Foster children	29,595	0.5
Others not in a census family	17,345	0.3

Source: Based on a special tabulation received 12 September 2014 from Anne Milan, Demography Division, Statistics Canada.

Considering family patterns over generations, Kiernan (2002) has proposed the concept of "the long arm of demography." Early home leaving and taking on parenthood at a young age, for instance, can involve lower investments in children from parents and the broader society, along with less-stable relationships, making for vulnerability to lone parenthood and "fragile families" in the next generation. Based on the 1990 Canadian General Social Survey, Le Bourdais and Marcil-Gratton (1998) found that young people who had experienced their parents' separation were more likely to enter cohabiting relationships early, less likely to have a direct marriage, more likely to give birth before age 20, and more likely to experience union dissolution. Using data from 14 countries, Bernardi and Radl (2014) found that children of separated parents had on average a 7 per cent lower probability of achieving a university degree, compared to children from intact families. Based on Canadian longitudinal data, Bignami-Van Assche and Adjiwanou (2009) find that girls who experienced their parents' separation as children were more likely to also experience earlier sexual activity in comparison to children from intact families. On the basis of data from the United States, Hofferth and Goldscheider (2010) find that women who have grown up with a lone parent, and men who have experienced family instability, are more likely to make early transitions to parenthood, and this is more likely to occur through cohabitation or fathers who are not resident with the mother and child.

In a study of multi-partner fertility of Norwegian men born between 1955 and 1984, Lappegard and her colleagues (2009) found that men's education and income are positively related to the likelihood of having a first birth, and also to the probability of a second birth with the same partner, while men with lower education are more likely to have a subsequent birth with a new partner. That is, men with lower status are less likely to retain a stable partnership. The consequences are significant in terms of the differentials among children. The children of men with higher status benefit both from this status and from the higher union stability of these higher-status men, while children of men with lower status are more likely to be from different mothers, with the associated difficulties in providing and caring for children located in different families.

The family lives of children have also been affected by trends in the timing and number of children. For instance, the proportion of children aged 24 and under living in families with three or more children has declined from 42.2 per cent in 1961 to 18.5 per cent in 2011, while the per cent in one-child families increased from 28.6 to 38.6 per cent (Bohnert et al., 2014: 4). In the early 1960s, 25 per cent of all births were first births, compared with 43 per cent in 2011 (Marcil-Gratton, 1988; Statistics Canada, 2013v). Consequently, greater proportions of children have "inexperienced" parents. With fewer brothers and sisters, they also have fewer older siblings. Half of the generation born in the early 1960s, for instance, had two older brothers or sisters, compared with one fifth of those born 20 years later (Marcil-Gratton, 1988). In the earlier generation, 1 child in 5 had a brother or sister 10 or more years older, compared with 1 in 20 for the later generation. That is, fewer births—and their concentration over a shorter time in the lives of adults—implies more potential parental resources per child, but it also means that children have less opportunity to interact with and learn from siblings.

On average, children have benefited from trends in later parenting and in more dual-earner families, along with parents having on average more education and fewer children (Kerr and Beaujot, 2003). It is probably the increased prevalence of lone parenthood that has affected children the most. For children under 18, the proportion with low-income status has declined both in lone-parent and two-parent families, but the higher prevalence of children living with a lone parent has made for very limited gains overall (Beaujot et al., 2011). For instance, Crossley and Curtis (2006) find very little change in child poverty between 1986 and 2000, partly because the decrease in the poverty rates of children living in lone-parent families was offset by an increase in the proportion of children in this group. Burton and his colleagues (2014) find that children from lone-parent families, children with young parents, and children whose parents have low levels of education are at most risk of being "stuck" at the bottom of the income distribution.

In summarizing how children are faring in the second demographic transition, McLanahan (2004) uses the concept of "diverging destinies." Regarding parents in the United States who are not married, for instance, Tach and her colleagues (2010) find that the father's involvement declines sharply after the end of the relationship, or the mother's transition to a new romantic relationship. Even in Quebec, where the majority of children are now born in cohabiting relationships, these relationships are less stable, and there is less father involvement after the relationship ends, in comparison to children born to married parents (Le Bourdais and Lapierre-Adamcyk, 2004). Father involvement is important to children, promoting physical activity, risk taking, and independence (Doucet, 2009; Beaupré et al., 2010).

Not Living in Union and Living Alone

In 1981, 20.2 per cent of women at ages 30–4 were neither married nor cohabiting, compared to 32 per cent in 2011. For men, the proportion at ages 30–4 who are neither married nor cohabiting has increased from 21 per cent to 38.1 per cent. Except at ages over 60 for women and over 70 for men, the proportion not in couples was higher in 2011 than in 1981 (Milan, 2013b: 5).

In 1961, 9.3 per cent of households consisted of one person, compared to 27.6 per cent in 2011 (Milan and Bohnert, 2012: 5). The 2011 Census enumerated more one-person households than couple households with children. Of the whole population aged 15 and over living in private households, 13.5 per cent were living alone in 2011. By age group, the figures are around 10 per cent at ages 25–44, going up to 15 per cent at ages 55–9, and 40 per cent at ages 80 and over (Statistics Canada, 2012l: 12). Union forming at older ages is contributing to this trend, as is the greater likelihood of separation.

Living alone is particularly widespread among older women, including 35 per cent of those over 65 living in private households. While many elderly people are living alone, most remain in touch with their families, especially through children and siblings (Stone, 1988; Péron and Légaré, 1988; Strain, 1990; Connidis, 1989).

Composition of Family and Household Units: Diversity

The diversity of life-course patterns results in a diverse composition of Canadian families and households. The data presented in Table 9.5 are based on census definitions. The census defines a household as one or more people living in a separate dwelling, which in turn is defined as a living space that can be reached either from outside or from a common hallway without having to pass through another dwelling. As we have seen, the census family is defined as a husband and wife with or without children who have never married, or one parent with at least one never-married child, living in the same residence. In 2011, 68.3 per cent of all households consisted of families, and 81.7 per cent of Canadians lived in families (20.5 per cent of 15+ and 0.8 per cent of 0–14 were not living in families). The average number of people per family declined from 3.9 in 1961 to 2.9 in 2011 (Milan and Bohnert, 2012: 4).

Over the 1981–2011 period, the number of one-person households increased by 118.5 per cent, while lone-parent families increased by 114 per cent (see Table 9.5). In contrast, the number of couple families with children at home increased by only 14.2 per cent. In effect, the largest increases are what might be called non-traditional family forms. Common-law families made up 16.7 per cent of the families in the 2011 Census and lone-parent families another 16.3 per cent (Statistics Canada, 2012l: 3). Thus, one third of families were either lone-parent or common-law ones. For families with children, 27.2 per cent are lone-parent and 12.6 per cent are step-parent families, with the remaining 60.2 per cent being intact.

The 2011 Census was the first to enumerate step-families, which represented 12.6 per cent of couples with children (Statistics Canada, 2012a: 3). Same-sex couples were first enumerated in the 2001 Census where they represented 0.5 per cent of couples. By 2011, same-sex unions represented 0.8 per cent of couples, with one third married and two thirds common-law (Statistics Canada, 2012a: 7).

In the review of change in families and households for the 1971–91 period, Péron and his colleagues (1999) emphasize that households with two or more people have maintained their "family" character, and they largely involve only members of the immediate nuclear or census family. In addition, people in non-family households are mostly elderly persons who have previously lived in families and young people who are between families. Though we often make note of increasing diversity, at the level of households, there is considerable simplicity: non-family households largely consist of only one person, while family households largely include only one family and no additional people. Consequently, in 2011 more than 9 out of 10 households consisted of either one family or one person.

Table 9.5 ▦ Family and Household Types (in thousands), Canada, 1981 and 2011

	1981	2011	% Change 1981–2011
Total households (private)	8,281.5	13,320.6	60.8
Family households	6,231.5	9,104.0	46.1
Non family households	2,050.0	4,216.7	105.7
One-person households	1,681.1	3,673.3	118.5
Other non-family housholds	368.9	543.3	47.3
Total Families	6,325.3	9,389.7	48.4
Couple families	5,611.5	7,861.9	40.1
Couple families with children at home	3,599.1	4,109.3	14.2
Couple families without children at home	2,011.4	3,752.6	86.6
Total married-couple families	5,257.3	6,294.0	19.7
Married with children	3,478.9	3,402.7	-2.2
Married without children	1,777.4	2,891.2	62.7
Total common law families	354.2	1,567.9	342.7
Common-law with children	120.2	706.6	487.8
Common-law without children	234.0	861.4	268.1
Lone parent families	713.8	1,527.8	114.0
Male-led	124.4	327.6	163.3
Female-led	589.4	1,200.3	103.6

Sources: Statistics Canada, 1981 Census of Population, cat. no. 92–325; Statistics Canada, 2011 Census of Population, cat. nos. 98-312-XCB2011020 and 98-313-XCB2011022.

The growth of lone-parent families has drawn the most attention. Among families with children, 11.4 per cent were lone parent in 1961 but 27.2 per cent were such by 2011. In 1961, the majority of lone parents were widowed (61.5 per cent), while in 2011, the largest category was people who were divorced or separated (50.8 per cent), and 17.7 were widowed (Milan and Bohnert, 2012: 4). On the other hand, the proportion of men in lone-parent families has been stable, up slightly to 21.4 per cent of one-parent families in 2011 (Statistics Canada, 2012l: 5).

Family and Household Units: Inequality

The trends toward more diversity have been celebrated as representing more options and pluralism in family forms, beyond the type of heterosexual couples with children in a traditional division of labour. At the same time, these trends represent more inequality across families and individuals. With the increase in women's economic contributions to families, there are important contrasts between two-earner couples, compared to breadwinner and lone-parent families. As we have seen, selectivity into union formation and dissolution, along with assortative mating, are further drivers of inequality.

Particularly important has been the growth of two-earner families. In 1981, among families with earned income, 37.2 per cent had the husband as the only earner, 3.1 per cent with the wife as only earner, and 59.7 per cent with both earning (Beaujot et al., 2013b). By 2001, these figures were 19.8 per cent for the husband only, 7.2 per cent for the wife only, and 73.1 per cent for both earning.

For couple families with children, the proportion with two or more persons working full-time increased from 21.5 per cent in 1980 to 38.4 per cent in 2005

(Statistics Canada, 2008a: 27). This has increased the differences in comparison to lone-parent families, where the median earnings represented 49.9 per cent of those of couple families with children in 1980, compared to 44.3 per cent in 2005 (Statistics Canada, 2008a: 28, 35). In 2005, the median earnings of female lone-parent families made up 63.8 per cent of the income of male lone parents, compared to 52.6 per cent in 1980.

The variations in low-income status are particularly noteworthy (see Table 9.6). Among two-parent families with children, the gap has widened between one-earner and two-earner families. The gap has declined between lone-parent families and two-parent families with children, but the differences remain large, especially for female lone parents. The most significant gains have occurred for elderly families, who had a low-income rate of 9.6 per cent in 1981 compared to 2.4 per cent in 2011.

The overall trend shows improvements both for people in economic families and unattached individuals in the 1996–2011 period. The exceptions to this trend are for unattached non-elderly male non-earners (rising to 80.7 per cent low-income status in 2011), elderly female non-earners (to 18.8 per cent), as well as male lone parents (to 12.4 per cent) and elderly couples (to 1.9 per cent low-income status).

In 2011, the most disadvantaged categories were female lone-parent families (21.2 per cent with low income) and unattached individuals (27.7 per cent). In contrast, the low-income rates were below 3 per cent for couples with two earners and for elderly couples. Among one-earner couples, there are much higher rates of low income when children are present.

For children under age 6, the low-income rate has declined only marginally, from 20.0 per cent in 1980 to 19.3 per cent in 2005 (Statistics Canada, 2008a: 46). There have been improvements for children both in intact and lone-parent families, but the higher proportion of children in lone-parent families has played against overall improvements for children.

The low-income rates in lone-parent families have improved considerably, from 49.3 per cent in 1996 to 19.7 per cent in 2011 (see Table 9.6). The disadvantages of lone-parent families remain significant, at almost four times the rate for two-parent families with children. Older female lone parents made significant income gains from 1980 to 2000, especially as they were having fewer and older children, they were getting better educated, and they were working longer hours (Myles et al., 2007; see also Richards, 2010). At the same time, the income gains for married women parents are even stronger, especially through increases in hours worked.

The income situation of younger lone parents did not improve from 1980 to 2000. Lone parenthood is a significant risk factor for women who marry early. For instance, among women under 25, the proportion with children is highest for the formerly married, in contrast to women who are currently married, cohabiting, or single (Ravanera and Beaujot, 2010).

Conclusion

The greater variability and fluidity in family transitions and family patterns have brought much diversity across families and in the family experiences of individual children, women, and men. This has been celebrated as less rigidity and more pluralism in family forms, but it has also brought other forms of inequality in the earning and caring ability of families. It is worth noting that among families with children, 27.2 per cent are lone-parent and 12.6 per cent are step-parent families.

These patterns pose major challenges, as some families need much more support than others, and one cannot prevent competent parents from giving advantages to their own children. The questions to be considered refer to individuals, families, and society, seeking to promote individual self-sufficiency, family support for dependants, and community/societal support for individuals and families (Esping-Andersen, 1990). Policy considerations also need to face the associated tensions: societal support can undermine the self-sufficiency of individuals, and promoting family support of dependants can undermine the self-sufficiency of the individual who provides this support.

Table 9.6 ▣ Percentage with Low-Income Status by Economic Family Type and for Unattached Individuals, Canada, 1981–2011

Economic Family Type	1981	1986	1991	1996	2001	2006	2011
Persons in all family units	11.6	12.1	13.2	15.2	11.2	10.3	8.8
Persons in economic families, two persons or more	8.8	9.3	10.0	12.0	8.1	7.1	5.5
Persons in elderly families	9.6	4.9	3.1	3.0	2.9	2.9	2.4
Persons in elderly married couples	8.3	4.5	3.2	1.7	1.6	1.2	1.9
Persons in other elderly families	11.2	5.4	3.0	5.5	6.2	6.9	3.9
Persons in non-elderly families	8.8	9.8	10.8	13.0	8.6	7.6	5.9
Persons in married couples	5.0	5.9	7.7	8.4	6.4	5.5	4.1
Persons in married couples, no earners	41.3	30.6	35.3	33.3	30.8	28.5	23.3
Persons in married couples, one earner	7.3	8.7	10.7	9.7	9.2	6.9	7.1
Persons in married couples, two earners	1.5	2.0	2.8	3.2	2.2	2.7	1.2
Persons in two-parent families with children	7.5	8.5	8.7	10.7	7.3	6.8	5.1
Persons in two-parent families with children, no earners	82.8	79.7	78.3	78.4	76.6	82.4	75.7
Persons in two-parent families with children, one earner	14.5	17.6	18.8	22.0	20.9	19.9	14.0
Persons in two-parent families with children, two earners	3.9	4.4	4.9	5.4	3.4	4.0	2.1
Persons in two-parent families with children, three or more earners	2.5	1.8	2.9	2.7	1.0	1.3	1.1
Persons in married couples with other relatives	2.6	3.0	2.8	4.6	4.4	2.1	2.0
Persons in lone-parent families	39.3	44.0	46.1	49.3	30.4	24.5	19.7
Persons in male lone-parent families	12.2	16.3	18.7	24.5	11.4	6.5	12.4
Persons in female lone-parent families	44.2	48.7	49.8	52.9	34.2	28.3	21.2
Persons in female lone-parent families, no earners	92.7	87.3	82.6	88.4	88.6	80.4	76.2
Persons in female lone-parent families, one earner	36.0	39.2	36.6	35.9	25.7	21.7	15.7
Persons in female lone-parent families, two or more earners	13.2	21.0	23.6	21.5	7.3	11.2	4.9
Persons in other non-elderly families	11.8	11.6	12.7	13.3	7.4	9.0	7.9
Unattached individuals	35.5	33.6	35.4	36.1	30.8	29.4	27.7
Elderly males	39.0	26.2	23.8	17.7	16.8	14.0	12.2
Elderly males, non-earner	43.3	28.8	26.0	19.4	19.3	16.9	15.3
Elderly males, earner	15.5	8.0	2.1	5.1	2.0	3.0	3.4
Elderly females	53.5	37.2	30.9	28.1	18.6	15.8	16.1
Elderly females, non-earner	56.4	38.4	31.7	28.9	19.6	16.9	18.8
Elderly females, earner	22.5	14.0	5.6	8.8	5.0	6.2	1.5
Non-elderly males	24.8	30.4	34.8	37.7	30.3	31.8	29.9
Non-elderly males, non-earner	80.9	81.8	77.0	81.0	82.6	78.0	80.7
Non-elderly males, earner	18.2	23.6	24.9	26.4	20.3	23.8	18.5
Non-elderly females	35.6	36.7	41.5	44.2	42.2	37.3	36.0
Non-elderly females, non-earner	81.7	72.0	73.2	74.8	78.5	72.5	71.1
Non-elderly females, earner	25.5	28.3	31.8	32.9	30.1	28.2	24.9

Note: Calculated after taxes and transfers.

Source: Statistics Canada, CANSIM Table 202-0804.

What directions should social policy take, given the context of diverse and less stable families? In addressing these policy questions, we would first make three assumptions: First, reproduction necessitates the support of others across generations, in the community, and at the societal level. Second, in regard to individuals, families, and society, policy should promote the self-sufficiency of individuals, the family support of dependants, and community support of families and individuals who are not able to be self-sufficient. Third, policy should promote a model of gender equity in the division of earning and caring. As a report for the United Nations Economic Commission for Europe proposes, "Transforming gender norms is vital to the success of family policies" (United Nations, 2013b: 11). In particular, the two-income model should be promoted at the expense of the breadwinner model.

In the past, family policy followed the breadwinner model with a focus on men's family wage and associated pension and health benefits, along with widowhood and orphanhood provisions in the case of the premature death of a breadwinner. That is, the focus of family policy was the loss of a breadwinner and supporting the elderly who were beyond working ages. The challenge of current policy is to accommodate children who receive less parental investment and young parents who have difficulty coping with both the earning and caring functions. Policy also needs to address the disadvantages faced by couples where neither has secure employment, and the difficulties of unattached persons at older labour-force ages who have limited employment potential. While there has clearly been a decline in the proportion of the population with low-income

status, this has especially benefited the elderly, and there are new forms of inequality across individuals and families. As we move toward entrenching a two-income model, we should discuss putting aside widowhood benefits, tax deductions for dependent spouses, and pension splitting. These provisions are based on a breadwinner model and they tend to promote dependency.

Across family types, it is especially lone parents who are disadvantaged. The widowhood and orphanhood provisions are clearly inadequate when the death of the breadwinner is infrequently the avenue of lone parenthood. The policies promoting the employment of the lone parent have been important, as are the child tax benefits and child-care subsidies tailored to families with lower income. There is also an "equivalent to spouse tax credit" that counts the first child of a lone-parent family as equivalent to a dependent spouse, for tax purposes. We would propose that tax deductions for dependent spouses should be abolished and replaced with a tax deduction for the first dependent child, for all families. That would leave room for an alternative like what has been used in Norway, such as doubling the child tax benefit for the first child of a lone-parent family.

We should promote a more egalitarian type of family that includes greater common ground between women and men in family activities. Just as policy has promoted the degendering of earning, we would argue for approaches that increase equal opportunity through the degendering of child care (Beaujot, 2002b). There is need for more discussion of provisions that would further modernize the family in the direction of co-providing and co-parenting.

Critical Thinking Questions

1. How should family be defined?
2. What are the similarities and differences between the first and second demographic transition?
3. In explaining what caused the changes in the family, would you give greater priority to structural or cultural elements? In your answer, be specific with regard to given family changes—for instance, on average age at entry into union, proportion cohabiting, or proportion separating.
4. How would you explain the changes in the typical ages when home leaving occurs?
5. Is cohabitation an alternative to marriage?
6. What factors predict a greater likelihood of (a) marriage and (b) separation?
7. How should we interpret the rise in the proportion of people living alone?
8. Among families with children, in what ways are there economic advantages and disadvantages in stepfamilies as compared to intact families?
9. How has the change in the composition of family units brought more diversity among families? In what way is there less diversity?

Recommended Readings

Beaujot, Roderic. 2000a. *Earning and Caring in Canadian Families*. Peterborough, ON: Broadview Press. This book on family and work considers how families earn a living and care for each other.

Bohnert, Nora, Anne Milan, and Heather Lathe. 2014. "Enduring diversity: Living arrangements of children in Canada over 100 years of the Census." *Demographic Documents*. Ottawa: Statistics Canada cat. no. 91F0015M – No. 11. This article covers major changes in the lives and living arrangements of children, ranging from their life chances and contributions to family income to their living arrangements.

Gauthier, Anne Hélène. 1996. *The State and the Family*. Oxford: Clarendon. Based on data from several countries, this book analyzes the various ways in which policy seeks to influence family behaviour and support families.

Milan, Anne. 2013b. Marital Status: Overview, 2011. *Report on the Demographic Situation in Canada*. Ottawa: Statistics Canada cat. No. 91-209-X. This section of the *Report on the Demographic Situation in Canada* outlines the change in legal marital status and in unions (marriage and cohabitation).

Péron, Yves, Hélène Desrosiers, Heather Juby, Evelyne Lapierrre-Adamcyk, Céline Le Bourdais, Nicole Marcil-Gratton, and Jael Mongeau. 1999. *Canadian Families at the Approach of the Year 2000*. Ottawa: Statistics Canada cat. no. 96-321, no. 4. This 1991 Census monograph takes advantage of both census and survey data to give a picture of families as units and of the family trajectories of women, men, and children.

Sager, Eric W., and Peter Baskerville, eds. 2007. *Household Counts: Canadian Households and Families in 1901*. Toronto: University of Toronto Press. Based especially on the 1901 Census this edited collection includes chapters on demographic and geographic questions, as well as the social history and cultural context of families.

Statistics Canada. 2012l. *Portrait of Families and Living Arrangements in Canada. Families, Households and Marital Status, 2011 Census of Population*. Ottawa: Statistics Canada cat. no. 98-312-X2011001. This profile, based on the 2011 Census considers the types and changes in families.

—. 2012k. *Living Arrangements of Young Adults Aged 20 to 29*. Ottawa: Statistics Canada cat. no. 98-312-X-2011003. This report observes that there is a decline in the proportion of young adults living as couples, a stable proportion living in the parental home, but an increase of those living in other arrangements, like non-family households.

Vézina, Mireille. 2012. *General Social Survey: Overview of Families in Canada—Being a Parent in a Stepfamily: A Profile*. Ottawa: Statistics Canada cat. no. 89-650-X—No. 002. Based on the General Social Survey, this publication documents the increased numbers of stepfamilies and the socio-economic characteristics of their parents, in comparison to intact and lone-parent families.

Related Websites

www.statcan.gc.ca/pub/91-209-x/91-209-x2014001-eng.htm. The Statistics Canada website of the Report on the Demographic Situation in Canada contains several items related to families, including analyses of change in marital status, fertility, families, and households.

www.vifamily.ca. The website of the Vanier Institute of the Family, a national charitable organization dedicated to promoting the well-being of Canadian families.

www.familiesandwork.org. The Families and Work Institute (FWI) is a non-profit research centre that publishes data to inform decision-making on the changing workplace, family, and community.

10 Sociocultural and Socioeconomic Composition

The Chapter at a Glance

- The demolinguistic balance in Canada has been continuously modified by both natural increase and immigration.
- Canada's linguistic duality reflects a territorial duality; that is, the use of each official language has largely maintained itself where it is in the majority yet decreased where it is in the minority.
- A growing proportion of Canadians have neither English nor French as a mother tongue, as Canada is becoming increasingly multilingual.
- A sizable proportion of new immigrants to Canada are visible minorities, many of whom experience difficulties in first establishing themselves economically in Canada.
- Canada's educational system was dramatically modified by both the postwar baby boom and

  the subsequent baby bust of more recent years.
- By international standards, Canada fares well in education: both the percentage of people who complete high school and of those who pursue post-secondary education are high.
- With a period of sustained economic growth and job creation throughout the late 1990s and into the 2000s, Canadians made up for the ground they lost during the recession of the early 1990s.
- Average income and the incidence of low income vary considerably among Canadian households, depending upon living arrangements, type of family, and the number of wage earners.

Introduction

Demography has been defined as the study of population—its size, distribution, and composition, as well as the factors that make for population change, including mortality, fertility, and migration. We have studied changes in population size (in Chapter 7) and geographical distribution (in Chapter 6). The composition of the population can be studied according to various characteristics, including age (see Chapter 8), labour-force status (see Chapters 7 and 8), and family structure (see Chapter 9). We will focus here on sociocultural composition (i.e., language, ethnicity, and visible minorities) and socioeconomic composition (i.e., education and income groups). In Chapter 11, we will consider the specific case of the Aboriginal

population. Policy issues raised in the discussion of such questions bring into consideration the very definition of Canadian society and how it adapts to the changing aspirations of its constituent groups.

Language

The French constitute a distinct minority in Canada and a numerical majority in the province of Quebec. In distinguishing Canadians according to whether they are English or French, the emphasis is usually placed on language rather than ethnic origin. We will consequently focus on Canada's two national languages, their relative magnitude, and the dynamics of change. In addition, by 2011, about 11 per cent of the population spoke languages other than English or French at

home (Statistics Canada, 2012f). The largest components of this subpopulation are immigrants. Issues relating to language groups other than English and French
are treated in the next section on ethnicity.

Recent censuses have included three language
questions. Mother tongue is the language first spoken
and still understood. Home language is the language
used most often in the home. A question about the
respondent's knowledge of the official languages asks
if the person knows English or French or both well
enough to carry on a conversation. The comparisons
of mother tongue and home language provide a
measure of language retention or transfer.

Demographic Trends

In 1760, the French population of what is now Canada
amounted to at least 80 per cent of the non-Aboriginal population (Lachapelle and Henripin, 1982:
10–11). It is estimated that by around 1805, the
English population was in the majority. By 1850, the
French portion of the total had fallen to 30 per cent, a
level that would remain almost constant for the next
100 years. There has been a noticeable change, however, since the latter half of the twentieth century. The
percentage of Canadians who say that French is their
mother tongue declined from about 29 per cent in
1951 to 21.6 per cent by 2011 (Harrison and Marmen,
1994; Statistics Canada, 2012f).

From 1850 to 1950, fairly stable proportions were
maintained, with approximately 60 per cent English
and 30 per cent French in Canada. These proportions
resulted mainly from the underlying demographics:
the higher French fertility compensated for immigration that largely supported the English group. The
underlying dynamic was broken in the 1960s when all
factors played against the relative size of the French
group. In particular, the French lost their fertility
advantage while the English maintained their immigration advantage, and language transfer favoured
English over French, especially outside Quebec. As a
result, only 20.9 per cent of Canada's population spoke
mostly French at home by 2011, 67.4 per cent spoke
mostly English in the home, 0.5 spoke English and
French equally, and 11.1 per cent spoke neither English
nor French as a home language (see Table 10.1).

Assessing the relative importance of the various
factors, Lachapelle (2009) concludes that international
immigration plays the largest role in the relative decline
of the French group in Canada. Over recent decades,
fertility and mortality differences have been small.
Linguistic transfers from French to English are not very
common: the net transmission of French from mother
to child is fairly constant at about 95 per cent. In contrast, international migration clearly reinforces the
English group, since immigrants continue to shift
toward the English language. This tendency is seen in
recent statistics on home language and mother tongue,
which provide some indication as to language retention
or transfer. The fact that a larger proportion of Canadians
speak English in the home (at 67.4 per cent) rather than
as a mother tongue (at 58.2 per cent) is consistent with
the above observation on language shifts among immigrants (see Table 10.1). The fact that a slightly smaller
proportion of Canadians speak French in the home (at
20.9 per cent) than as a mother tongue (at 21.6 per cent)
suggests modest language transfers toward English, a
tendency particularly true outside Quebec.

A major fact in explaining this decline in the relative weight of the French language in Canada is the
geographic distribution of new immigrants as a disproportionate share continue to settle in English Canada.
For example, over the 1971–2011 period, about
7.6 million people immigrated to Canada, but only
about 1.3 million (17.1 per cent) settled in Quebec
(Statistics Canada, 2012m; Citizenship and
Immigration Canada, 2012). Since Quebec constitutes
about 24 per cent of Canada's population, it can be seen
that this province receives less than its share of immigrants. The vast majority of immigrants to other
regions of Canada learn English (as the language of
work and daily interaction) and many of their children
already have English as a mother tongue. In light of this
settlement pattern and the importance of immigration
to Canada's overall population growth, it is quite likely
that these trends will continue into the future.

Although the above generalizations apply to
both mother tongue and home language, for various
reasons, the situation is somewhat different with
regard to the third language question available from
the census; that is, knowledge of the official languages.
In 1951, about 32 per cent of Canadians said they
could converse in French (Grenier and Lachapelle,

Table 10.1 ▣ Distributions by Mother Tongue, Knowledge of Official Languages, and Home Language, Canada, 2011

	Canada	Quebec	Rest of Canada
Mother Tongue			
English	58.2	8.0	73.7
French	21.6	78.8	3.9
Both English and French	0.5	1.0	0.4
Other	19.7	12.2	22.1
Total	100.0	100.0	100.0
Knowledge of Official Languages			
English	68.1	4.7	87.7
French	12.6	51.8	0.5
Both English and French	17.5	42.6	9.7
Other	1.8	1.0	2.1
Total	100.0	100.0	100.0
Home Language			
English	67.4	10.4	85.0
French	20.9	81.2	2.3
Both English and French	0.5	1.3	0.3
Other	11.1	7.1	12.3
Total	100.0	100.0	100.0

Notes: "English" includes English only, and English and non-official language; "French" includes French only, and French and non-official language; "Both English and French" includes English and French as well as English and French and non-official language.

Source: Statistics Canada, 2012f.

1988), and this figure has remained relatively stable, down only slightly to 30.1 per cent in 2011 (i.e. 12.6 per cent reported knowledge of French in 2011 and an additional 17.5 per cent reported knowledge of both French and English). As to knowledge of English, the corresponding figures are 79.3 per cent in 1951 and 85.6 per cent in 2011 (i.e. 68.1 per cent reported knowledge of English and an additional 17.5 per cent reported French/English bilingualism). The explanation for this relative stability with regard to French and this upturn with English is related to the increased knowledge of either English or French as a second language in Canada. In 2011, 17.5 per cent of Canada's population said they could converse in both of Canada's official languages. This figure had increased substantially, from only 12.3 per cent in 1951 (Harrison and Marmen, 1994).

Official Language Minorities

French-language minorities outside Quebec and New Brunswick have undergone considerable erosion. Language transfer has played a major role in the decline of French outside Quebec and New Brunswick. As long as they could maintain a certain isolation, often in rural areas or in extractive industries, and maintain communities around religious affiliation, there was considerable persistence of these minorities. However, with the broader scale of social interaction and the reduced role of religion in defining communities, the French minorities have been undermined (Beaujot and McQuillan, 1982).

By 2011, only about 2.3 per cent of Canadians living outside Quebec reported French as their home language. As this percentage is at a historic low and has continued to decline over recent decades, some observers have little hope for the French-speaking communities outside Quebec and Acadia (Thériault, 1989; Beaujot, 1998). The rural isolation, based on a parish identity, is no longer available. The groups no longer have the necessary compact relationships that would ensure their long-term existence as language communities. Intermarriage has also played a significant role, because in most cases English is adopted as the home language (Castonguay, 1979; 2002). In fact, outside Quebec, about one third of people whose mother tongue is French do not cite it as the language used most often at home. Beyond New Brunswick and Ontario, this figure rises to well over 50 per cent.

Just as the French minority outside Quebec has declined, so, too, has the English minority in Quebec. The English-mother-tongue group in the province has been declining as a proportion of the total population for more than a century. In 1844, they made up one fourth of the population, whereas recent censuses have shown them to be down to about 8 per cent (Caldwell, 1988; see Table 10.1). Since 1971, the English mother-tongue group has declined in absolute numbers and has increasingly become concentrated in Montreal. While historically, the English group benefited considerably from language transfers (particularly from new immigrants), this is true to a lesser extent today than in the past. In addition, the English population continues to suffer substantial departures to other provinces. For example, over the 25 years before the 1991 Census approximately 450,000 people of English mother tongue left Quebec, out of a population that was only about 626,000 in 1991 (Harrison and Marmen, 1994). Non-French speakers are significantly more likely to leave Quebec than are other residents.

Given these trends, it has been pointed out that Canada's linguistic duality is increasingly coming to reflect a territorial duality (Beaujot, 1998). The official languages are maintaining themselves where they are in the majority (particularly in the case of home language) and are decreasing where they are in the minority. The French majority has managed to maintain its relative weight in Quebec—at over 80 per cent for the last several decades. As far as mother tongue is concerned, over 85 per cent of all French Canadians lived in Quebec in 2011; most of the rest were in either Acadia or eastern Ontario. In contrast, almost 97 per cent of Canadians with English mother tongue lived in other provinces, where they accounted for about 75 per cent of the population.

The Multilingual Aspect of Canada's Population

The 2011 Census documented over 200 distinct languages in Canada. While the majority of Canadians obviously speak English, French, or both, an increasing proportion have a language other than English or French as their mother tongue or home language. For example, this number has risen dramatically, from about 2.8 million with an "other" mother tongue in 1971 to just over 6.6 million in 2011 (Harrison, 2000; Statistics Canada, 2012f). This was an increase of about 136 per cent, or from about 13 per cent of Canada's population in 1971 to 19.7 per cent in 2011. A smaller percentage of people report a language other than English or French as their home language—at about 11.1 per cent in 2011.

With the important exception of Aboriginal languages (which are discussed in Chapter 12), Canada's linguistic and cultural diversity is a by-product of its historic openness to immigration. In recent years, the increase in Canada's linguistic and cultural diversity has been at least partly due to the fact that immigration has been responsible for a larger and larger share of population growth. The combination of high immigration and the decline in Canada's rate of natural increase (births minus deaths) have contributed to the increased importance of "*immigrant languages*" (i.e., languages other than English, French, or an Aboriginal tongue).

Since fluency in English or French is part of the selection criterion for immigrants to Canada, a significant proportion already arrive with some knowledge of one of Canada's official languages. For example, despite the importance of immigration, Statistics Canada (2012f) reports that over 98 per cent of Canada's population is able to conduct a conversation in either English or French. As language skills are also fundamental to socioeconomic success, many immigrants attempt to shift to either English or French sometime after they are settled here. In general, the degree of language retention is much lower among new Canadians than it is among either English or French speakers; the proportion speaking an immigrant language drops noticeably from the first to second generation. As successive waves of immigrants eventually take on the language of the majority, there have been some important shifts in the distribution of linguistic groups over time.

In drawing comparisons over many decades, Harrison (2000) has documented how the most prominent immigrant languages, as identified in past censuses, have changed, beginning with the 1941 Census (the first census to adopt the modern definition of mother tongue). In updating these data to 2011, Table 10.2 demonstrates that Chinese is now the most common immigrant language, with over 1.1 million speakers. Punjabi is the second-most common language, a by-product of recent immigration from South Asia, whereas Spanish has risen to third, as a by-product of immigration from Latin America during the 1990s and 2000s. Just as significant numbers of Chinese, South Asian, and Latin American immigrants have settled in Canada, so, too, did large numbers of Italians and Germans during the 1950s and '60s. As a result, the most common immigrant language in 1981 was Italian, followed closely by German (each with over a half million speakers). More recently, as the source countries of immigration have shifted, the number of Italian and German speakers has steadily declined. The numbers speaking an immigrant language declines from the first to second and later generations, as time in Canada and intermarriage have their impact on the degree of language retention.

As immigrants to Canada are increasingly Asian in origin, the linguistic balance of Canada's immigrant languages has shifted. Among the top 10 heritage languages in 2011, European languages have been replaced by various non-European languages, a trend that is expected to continue well into the twenty-first century. While 9 out of the 10 most common languages in 1941 were European, this had slipped to 5 out of 10 in 2011. For example, Ukrainian is much less common today than in the past, several generations removed from the substantial Eastern European migration of the early twentieth century. The top 10 now include such non-European languages as Punjabi, Tagalog, Arabic, and Urdu—not

surprising, in light of recent trends in immigration and the various source countries of migrants (Citizenship and Immigration Canada, 2012).

The increase in Canada's linguistic diversity over recent years has been especially pronounced in the cities. Since Canada's largest cities receive a disproportionate share of immigrants, this geographic concentration has led to some highly heterogeneous populations, particularly in some neighbourhoods of Toronto, Vancouver, and Montreal. In 2011, 44.7 per cent of the census metropolitan area of Toronto had a mother tongue other than English or French (as a single response or in combination with English and/or French). Similarly, in the same census, 42.6 per cent of Vancouver's population reported a mother tongue other than English or French. In Quebec, a high proportion of immigrants settle in the metropolitan area of Montreal, with the result being that about 23.9 per cent report a mother tongue other than French or English. Since the overwhelming majority of Quebec's English population also lives in Montreal, this city has become more and more ethnically and linguistically heterogeneous. Although recent immigrants to Quebec are more likely to associate with French than was previously the case, the English population continues to gain more immigrants than its relative share in the overall population (Termote et al., 2011).

Ethnicity

Ethnicity, another significant sociocultural dimension on which to study the composition of the Canadian population, refers to membership in a group with a specific origin. At the time of Confederation, 90 per cent of the non-Aboriginal population of Canada consisted of two groups, British and French. Since then, the English and French languages have continued to dominate—but ethnically, Canada gradually became a more diverse multicultural society during the twentieth century. The explicit recognition of this fact by the federal government is often traced to the 1968 Royal Commission on Bilingualism and Biculturalism, where it was specifically emphasized that "biculturalism" was an incomplete reflection of Canadian

Table 10.2   Ranking of Top Ten Immigrant Language Groups, Canada, 1941–2011 (in thousands)

	1941	1961	1981	2001[1]	2011
Top 10 in 1941					
German	322	564	516	438	430
Ukrainian	313	361	285	148	120
Yiddish	130	82	31	19	16
Polish	129	162	127	208	201
Italian	80	340	531	469	438
Norwegian	60	40	19	9	6
Russian	52	43	31	95	170
Swedish	50	33	17	9	8
Finnish	37	45	33	22	18
Chinese[2]	34	49	224	854	1,113
Top 10 in 2011					
Chinese	34	49	224	854	1,113
Punjabi	n.a.[3]	n.a.	54	271	460
Spanish	1	7	70	246	439
Italian	80	340	531	469	438
German	322	564	516	438	430
Tagolog	n.a.	n.a.	8	174	384
Arabic	n.a.	n.a.	69	200	374
Portuguese	n.a.	n.a.	165	214	226
Polish	129	162	127	208	201
Urdu	n.a.	n.a.	12	81	194

Notes:

[1] Prior to 2001, data include only single responses. Data for 2001 and 2011 include both single and multiple responses.

[2] Historically, Statistics Canada did not distinguish between the different Chinese languages. Yet since 2006, the language classification has distinguished Mandarin, Cantonese, Hakka, Taiwanese, Chaochow, Fukien, Shanghainese and "Chinese not otherwise specified." In general, these languages tend to be quite different from each other; for example , Mandarin and Cantonese are as different from one another as French and Spanish. While specialists frequently refer to these languages as "dialects" of Chinese, they are in reality distinct languages (Gordon, 2005). Yet in order to maintain continuity with past censuses, information about the entirety of the Chinese language family is included here as "Chinese."

[3] n.a.—data not gathered in earlier censuses.

Sources: Harrison, 2000; Statistics Canada, 2012f.

reality. A more explicit recognition came in the 1971 Multiculturalism Act.

The concept of ethnicity involves a variety of meanings, and of late it has become particularly difficult to document among Canadians. As defined historically, the ethnicity item on the Canadian Census was meant to document the origins of one's ancestors on first arriving on this continent, because Canadians identified themselves as coming from a wide variety of other countries. For some, this ancestry is an important aspect of their identity, but for others, it is irrelevant. It is generally recognized that the concept of ethnicity has lost some importance, since a significant proportion of Canadians are many generations removed from the culture and language of their ancestors (Krotki, 1990; Satzewich and Liodakis, 2013).

As Canada's cultural heterogeneity has increased, so, too, has the proportion of Canadians with multiple origins. Thus, the measurement of ethnicity has had to capture a changing social reality among Canadians who do not necessarily have a strong sense of identity with their ancestry or cultural origins. Until 1971, ancestry data were collected exclusively along the male line (patrilineally), whereas more recent censuses have permitted or even encouraged multiple replies to questions about ethnicity. The 1986 Census was the first to explicitly encourage multiple responses to the ethnic origin question, encouraging people to list a variety of ethnic origins, following both paternal and maternal lines of descent. As a result, some 28 per cent of respondents indicated more than one ethnic origin, more accurately reflecting the heterogeneity of Canada's population. By 2011, this percentage had risen to 57.9 per cent, as multiculturalism had become increasingly important, even at the individual level where people identify with a variety of cultures (Statistics Canada, 2013w). On the other hand, this has also been interpreted to suggest that the concept of ethnicity is becoming less meaningful, as Canadians report an assortment of origins without necessarily any strong sense of identity with any of them.

Under these circumstances, there has been considerable pressure to modify the census question on ancestry (Boyd and Norris, 2001). As mentioned above, the ethnicity question on the census has historically asked Canadians, with the exception of those with Aboriginal origins, to report on their ancestors upon arrival in North America. Yet in the 1991 Census nearly 4 per cent of the population gave themselves a purely "indigenous" label, in reporting themselves as "Canadian" (ignoring explicit instructions not to do so). As suggested by Boyd (1999), the reporting of "Canadian" as a write-in response in the 1991 Census suggested that "Canadian" should be included as a possible response. In 1996, after some debate, "Canadian" was included as a potential response on the ethnicity item of the census. As a result, fully 31 per cent reported that they were Canadian, with the result being that this category has come to represent the largest ethnic group in Canada, exceeding even the two charter groups with British and French origins.

As suggested by Kalbach and Kalbach (1999), much of the discussion surrounding the ethnic-origin question in the Canadian Census conflates what are essentially two distinct yet interrelated concepts, namely, ethnic ancestry and ethnic identity. The "Canadian" response is not a measure of one's ethnic roots, but rather a measure of how an individual identifies him- or herself regarding the specific group to which he or she feels some sort of allegiance. As a result, it has become increasingly difficult to obtain any insight into the ethnic ancestry of Canada's population, since people from an assortment of backgrounds may call themselves "Canadian." There is nothing to keep a first-generation Canadian from identifying with the Canadian label, just as an uncertain proportion of tenth-generation Canadians might use the same label. Self-identification as Canadian occurs for a wide variety of reasons, including nationalist sentiment, or objecting to the very idea of ethnic origins.

According to the 2011 National Household Survey (NHS), there were more than 200 different ethnic and cultural categories, and as a consequence, no single ethnic or cultural group is truly dominant. The ethnic origin that was most commonly reported continues to be "Canadian," at just over 10.5 million, either reported alone or with other origins. This response was followed by English, reported by about 6.5 million; French, by about 5 million; Scottish, by 4.7 million; Irish, by 4.7 million; and German, by 3.2 million. Additional ethnic origins that surpassed the 1 million mark included Italian, Chinese, First Nations (North American Indian), Ukrainian, East Indian, Dutch, and Polish.

Data from earlier censuses have demonstrated how ethnicity varies from region to region, as, for example, both Ontario and British Columbia have the highest proportion of "non-European" in ancestry, reflecting the tendency of recent immigrants to select these two provinces for settlement. On the other hand, in all provinces east of Ontario, a relatively high proportion report either British origin (true throughout Atlantic Canada) or French origin (true of both Quebec and, to a lesser extent, New Brunswick). In the Northwest Territories, Yukon, and Nunavut, people of Aboriginal descent make up a large share of the population, as is true of Canada's North in general. In the Prairies, populations also report a diversity of origins, including both substantial Aboriginal and British populations, yet also people with ancestors from many other parts of Europe, including South, Central, and Eastern Europe. As an example, roughly one in five residents of Manitoba, Saskatchewan, and Alberta report German ancestry (20.7 per cent), and one in five report either Ukrainian (11.4 per cent) or Scandinavian (9 per cent). These provinces were strongly influenced by the mass immigration that characterized the early 1900s, peaking in 1913 with over 400,000 immigrants. The Prairie provinces have considerable diversity in terms of ancestry, yet this is not as obvious to the casual observer, as much of this diversity comes from various parts of Europe several generations ago.

Generation Status in Canada

As of 2011, 22 per cent of Canada's population were first generation (born elsewhere and currently in Canada), 17.4 per cent of Canadians were second generation (i.e., the children of at least one immigrant parent), and just over 60 per cent were third generation or later. This statistic on the first generation is slightly higher than Statistics Canada's estimate of the foreign-born population (at 20.6 per cent), as the latter excludes non-permanent residents (i.e., people who have been granted the right only to live temporarily in Canada, with a work or study permit, or who are currently refugee claimants). As we discussed in Chapter 5, the number of non-permanent residents in Canada has risen sharply over recent years, up from about 100,000 in the early 1980s to over 750,000 in 2013 (Citizenship and Immigration Canada, 2014). In terms of country of origin, Canada has experienced a well-documented shift away from what was largely a European-based immigration, a situation that is true of both non-permanent residents and permanent immigrants. As of 2011, only about one third of the first generation in Canada reported origins in Europe, whereas over one half reported origins in Asia and more than 1 in 10 reported origins in

either Latin America or Africa (Statistics Canada, 2013w).

The combination of high immigration targets and the shift in the source countries of immigration has contributed to what Malenfant and colleagues (2010) refer to as "the ethno-cultural diversification of Canadian society." Correspondingly, provinces and regions that receive the largest share of immigrants have the highest percentage that are either first or second generation, and by extension, the highest percentage of non-European ancestry. For example, both Ontario and British Columbia have for some time received a disproportionate share of immigrants; as of 2011, over one half of Ontario and British Columbia's population reported that they were first or second generation, at 52.9 and 52.4 per cent, respectively (see Figure 10.1). For Canada overall, this percentage declined to 39.3 per cent, while it was 34.9 per cent in the Prairies, 22.5 per cent in Quebec, and only 10.4 per cent in Atlantic Canada.

In terms of ethnicity and ancestry, Atlantic Canada is the least diversified, whereas Ontario and British Columbia are the most. This has been particularly true for metropolitan Canada, as more than 90 per cent of all newcomers settle in one of Canada's 33 census metropolitan areas (CMAs). At one extreme, consider the CMA of Toronto whereby over 7 in 10 are either immigrants or the children of immigrants (48 per cent are born in another country and 25 per cent are second generation) or the CMA of Vancouver (42.7 per cent are born in another country and 25.2 per cent are second generation). At the opposite extreme, the CMA of St John's, Newfoundland and Labrador, has only 3.9 per cent first generation and an additional 3.5 per cent second generation. Atlantic Canada in general has long faced obstacles in attracting newcomers, as overall the region has 4.9 per cent first generation and 5.6 per cent second generation. Newfoundland and Labrador, Prince Edward Island, and Nova Scotia have populations that are ethnically homogeneous by Canadian standards (largely of English, Irish, and Scottish origin), whereas the British presence in New Brunswick is accompanied by a healthy Acadian presence. This greater homogeneity is also true of much of rural Canada in general,

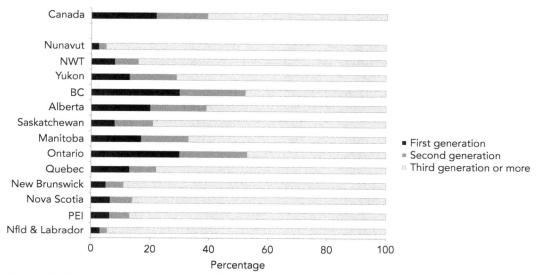

Figure 10.1 ▣ Generation Status, Canada, Provinces, and Territories, 2011

Source: Statistics Canada 2013q.

particularly in the eastern and central parts of Canada.

Visible Minority Status

Beginning with the 1981 Census the classification *"visible minority"* was established, using the questions on ethnic origin, birthplace, religion, and mother tongue. In effect, this identified people who were non-white, non-Caucasian, and non-Aboriginal. A total of about 4.7 per cent of the 1981 population was classified as visible minority, about 85 per cent of these being of foreign birth (Samuel, 1987). In Toronto and Vancouver, visible minorities made up about one seventh of the total population.

By 2011, the national percentage who were visible minority had quadrupled, to 19.1 per cent of Canada's total population (Statistics Canada, 2013w). This esti-mate is based on a question in the NHS which asks whether the respondent is a member of one of the popu-lation groups defined as a visible minority under the provisions of the Employment Equity Act. Under this definition, the regulations to the Act specify the follow-ing groups as visible minorities: Chinese, South Asians,

Blacks, Arabs and West Asians, Filipinos, Southeast Asians, Latin Americans, Japanese, Koreans, and Pacific Islanders. In the CMAs of Toronto and Vancouver, the percentage of visible minorities was up considerably by 2011, to 47 per cent and 45.2 per cent of their respective populations. Specific municipalities within these larger census metropolitan areas are more than one half visible minority, such as the cities of Markham (72.3 per cent) and Brampton (66.4 per cent) in the Greater Toronto Area or the cities of Richmond (70.4 per cent) and Burnaby (59.6 per cent) in the Greater Vancouver Area.

About 6.3 million people identified themselves as members of a visible minority in 2011 (see Table 10.3 for a breakdown by group). About 3 out of every 10 people who identified themselves as a visible minority were born in Canada (27.1 per cent second generation and 3.5 per cent third generation or more), while the rest were first generation (69.3 per cent). In keeping with immigrant settlement patterns, more than 95 per cent of members of visible minorities lived in census metropolitan areas in 2011, as compared to 69.3 per cent of the total population. Moreover, 7 out of 10 vis-ible minorities lived in one of Canada's three largest metropolitan areas: Toronto, Vancouver, and Montreal.

Table 10.3 ▣ Visible-Minority Groups, by Generation Status, Canada, 2011

	First generation	%	Second generation	%	Third + generation	%	Total	%
Total Population[1]	7,217,300	22.0	5,702,725	17.4	19,932,300	60.7	32,852,325	100
Total Visible Minority	4,342,695	69.3	1,700,190	27.1	221,860	3.5	6,264,745	100
South Asian	1,086,060	69.3	457,150	29.2	24,200	1.5	1,567,410	100
Chinese	970,430	73.3	317,010	23.9	37,310	2.8	1,324,750	100
Black	537,060	56.8	324,050	34.3	84,555	8.9	945,665	100
Filipino	476,465	76.9	133,810	21.6	9,035	1.5	619,310	100
Latin American	300,990	78.9	77,260	20.3	3,030	0.8	381,280	100
Arab	279,710	73.5	97,900	25.7	3,015	0.8	380,625	100
Southeast Asian	204,965	65.7	94,655	30.3	12,450	4.0	312,070	100
West Asian	171,240	82.8	35,120	17.0	480	0.2	206,840	100
Korean	134,385	83.4	25,185	15.6	1,560	1.0	161,130	100
Japanese	32,220	36.9	26,835	30.8	28,210	32.3	87,265	100
Visible minority, n.i.e.[2]	63,690	59.8	36,560	34.3	6,220	5.8	106,470	100
Multiple visible minorities	85,480	49.7	74,655	43.4	11,795	6.9	171,930	100
Not a Visible Minority[3]	2,874,595	10.8	4,002,535	15.1	19,710,440	74.1	26,587,570	100

Notes:

[1] Excludes NHS data for one or more incompletely enumerated Indian reserves.

[2] The abbreviation "n.i.e." means "not included elsewhere."

[3] Includes respondents not considered to be visible minority and those who reported Aboriginal identity.

Source: National Household Survey, Statistics Canada, 2013q.

The visible minority population in Canada has grown very rapidly as a result of immigration. Of all arrivals in Canada since the early 1990s, the 2011 NHS shows that over 3 out of every 4 are in the visible-minority category. Among immigrants arriving in the 2006–11 period, 78 per cent fall into this category. In stark contrast, for Canadians who reported that they immigrated prior to 1971, the NHS shows that about 1 in 8 is a visible minority (Statistics Canada, 2013w). The proportion of the visible-minority population that is Canadian born clearly varies widely from group to group, and this is in large measure a reflection of historical immigration patterns. For example, about 63 per cent of the Japanese were born in Canada, owing to their relatively early immigration to this country. This is followed by 43 per cent of blacks and 34.3 per cent of Southeast Asians.

West Asians (e.g., Iranians and Afghanis) and South Koreans are the most likely to be immigrants, as only about 16–17 per cent were born in Canada (see Table 10.3). Overall, about 3 in 10 of the 2011 visible-minority population were native-born Canadians (30.6 per cent), compared to about 9 out of 10 people (89.2 per cent) who reported that they were not a visible minority.

While people of non-European origin may be quite "visible" in the first few years after their arrival, or in the first generation, they become less so as their styles of dressing, speaking, and living come to resemble those of the majority population. Once ethnicity becomes unimportant in marriage, as a concept it takes on a rather different meaning (Krotki and Odynak, 1988)—visible minority will most certainly evolve in the Canadian culture of the twenty-first century. Owing to slightly lower mortality and slightly higher fertility than the national average, and with a continuation of immigration trends, it is projected that the visible-minority population will increase to between 11.4 and 14.4 million persons by 2031, or between 29 and 32 per cent of Canada's population (Malenfant et al., 2010). These projections are based on broad definitions, such that most children born of mixed parentage (including Caucasian and visible minorities) are classified as visible minority. Thus, the projections are based on strong ethnic retention, whereas the very meaning of visible minority status can change considerably over a 20-year period. What is clear is that Canada is a multi-ethnic society characterized by pluralism rather than homogeneity. Members of diverse ethnic, racial, and religious groups, including those currently defined as visible minorities, will continue to contribute to the development of a distinctly Canadian culture.

Socioeconomic Profiles and Their Determinants

There is considerable research on the socioeconomic profile of ethnic and visible-minority status groups. Past census data have consistently documented that visible minorities in Canada have on average more education but they earn less than other Canadians (Samuel, 1987; Richmond, 1988; Abada et al., 2009; Pendakur and Pendakur, 2011). Part of this difference in earnings can be attributed to their recent arrival, for immigrants usually experience some difficulty settling in Canada in their first few years.

Overall, a relatively large proportion of the visible-minority population has a university degree. In 2011, among people aged 25–64, 38 per cent had a university degree, compared with about 23 per cent of their non–visible-minority counterparts (Statistics Canada, 2013x). Similarly, 8.3 per cent have attended, though not completed, a university program, which compares to 4.1 per cent among other Canadians. Among recent immigrants, Hou and Picot (2013) document that about 50 per cent of first-generation people go to university relative to 31 per cent of second-generation Canadians, and about 25 per cent

of the third or higher generation. Yet in spite of their remarkable accomplishments in education, visible minorities continue to be disadvantaged in terms of income and occupation (Hou and Balakrishnan, 1996; Pendakur and Pendakur, 2011; Abada and Lin, 2014).

It has long been documented that minority groups immigrating since the 1970s have had higher educational attainment but lower incomes than the national average, even after controlling for age, year of immigration, education, and knowledge of the official languages (Li, 1996; Palameta, 2004). The 2011 NHS found that the average annual income from all sources for the visible-minority population (15 years of age and over) was about $30,600, almost $10,000 less than for the rest of the population, which had an average income of $40,400 that year (Statistics Canada, 2013x). Unemployment was also higher for the visible-minority population: 9.9 per cent, as opposed to about 7 per cent of all Canadians in 2011 (Statistics Canada, 2013x). In view of their educational attainment, the achievements of visible minorities in the labour market are somewhat lower than might be expected.

Among the visible-minority population, important differences exist between groups—from the relatively high average income of Japanese Canadians (at about $40,000 in 2011) through to the much lower incomes among other subpopulations (e.g., Latin Americans report an average of $28,000, whereas blacks and Arabs report about $29,000). Similarly, 14 per cent of Arabs (aged 15–64) were unemployed in 2011, as were almost 13 per cent of blacks and West Indians, compared with just 6 per cent of Filipinos and Japanese (Statistics Canada, 2013x). A relevant factor in this context is the proportion of each group that has recently settled in Canada. While not all visible minorities are recent immigrants (e.g., many black citizens have roots in Canada that go back several generations), a large majority are newly or recently arrived (7 of 10 were born in another country). As highlighted in Table 10.3, this ranges from a low of 36.9 per cent among the Japanese to a high of 83.4 per cent among Koreans.

Canadians who are visible minorities are about twice as likely as other Canadians to be classified as low income on the basis of Statistics Canada's low-income cut-offs. The 2006 Census reported that 22 per cent of the visible-minority population are classified as low income relative to about 11.4 per cent for Canada's population overall (National Council of Welfare, 2012). This likelihood of low income varies considerably among different visible-minority groups: so, for example, about 40 per cent of all Korean Canadians report low income, as do 35 per cent of Arab/West Asians and 26 per cent of black Canadians (Statistics Canada, 2013x). In addition, visible minorities and recent immigrants account for a higher share of the population living in Canada's poorest neighbourhoods. Statistics Canada has estimated that across low-income neighbourhoods in Canada's metropolitan areas—that is, neighbourhoods where at least 30 per cent of all households are classified as income-poor—about 4 in 10 people are visible minorities (Statistics Canada, 2013x).

These differences cannot be explained easily. One explanation is that lower wages and higher unemployment can be attributed to racial discrimination (Pendakur and Pendakur, 2011); alternatively, some may be due to other factors, such as the age profile of a given group, its language skills, its work experience, or other factors relating to occupation and the labour market. Any attempt at explanation is complicated by the simple fact that not all visible minorities in Canada have the same ethnic origin, education, work experience, length of residence in Canada, or degree of assimilation into the Canadian labour stream. As suggested by Hum and Simpson (1998), it may not be so much that visible minorities face disadvantages, but more specifically, that recent immigrants who are visible minorities tend to encounter major obstacles. It is primarily among visible minorities born abroad that the wage disadvantages are particularly severe, suggesting major obstacles for first-generation Canadians. The relative success of Japanese Canadians, most of whom have had family in Canada for generations, is generally supportive of this idea.

While immigrants to Canada experience substantial economic disadvantages, the second generation have shown higher levels of economic adaptation. Aydemir and colleagues (2005) document that for the second generation, those of European parents have been doing relatively well, and often outperform other Canadians. On the other hand, other groups continue to encounter difficulties; for example, the second generation from the Caribbean and West Africa earn, on average, lower wages and encounter higher unemployment, despite having above-average education. Pendakur and Pendakur (2011) document a persistent earnings gap for Canadian-born visible minorities, after introducing relevant controls, notably among South Asians and blacks, particularly in Canada's two largest cities, Montreal and Toronto. On the other hand, with the exception of black Canadians, Hum and Simpson (1998) conclude that the wage disadvantage for most visible-minority groups born in Canada is now relatively small, and that for many groups, the disadvantage is no longer significant after introducing appropriate controls. In focusing on the second generation in Ontario, Abada and Lin (2014) find more disadvantages among visible-minority men than among women, yet they document considerable variation across groups in terms of their relative success in intergenerational educational and labour-market mobility.

For the first generation in Canada (born abroad), analyses of recent census data has shown a trend toward lower rates of employment and earnings, compared to the Canadian-born population (as we discussed in Chapter 5). This has occurred even though the relative number of economic-class immigrants has risen, a class of immigrant that has relatively high levels of education. Reitz (2001) discusses three possible sources of changes responsible for this trend in the socioeconomic status of immigrants: changes in the skills that immigrants bring, changes in the treatment received by immigrants within the labour market, and changes in the structure of the labour market itself. Compared with the 1960s, the skills of immigrants have increasingly been defined by academic degrees rather than technical training. Racial discrimination could be the reason for the increased discounting of immigrant skills, but this explanation seems incomplete since white immigrants are also affected, although to a lesser degree. The changed structure of the labour market toward a service economy may undermine the value of educational credentials obtained abroad and may accentuate the disadvantages of a lack of Canadian experience and Canadian references. In addition, while the average level of education of immigrants has been increasing, this increase has not been as strong as that of the younger Canadian cohorts entering to the labour market.

The concept visible minority has encountered some criticism as of late, given that it lumps all visible minorities together, regardless of the fact that overall they vary considerably in terms of ethnic origin, education, work experience, length of time in Canada, and degree of assimilation into the Canadian labour stream (Woolley, 2013). As Justice Rosalie Abella (1984:46) wrote several decades ago in her work with the Royal Commission on Equality in Employment, "To combine all non-whites together as visible minorities for the purpose of devising systems to improve their equitable participation, without making distinctions to assist those groups in particular need, may deflect attention from where the problems are greatest." As Hum and Simpson (1998) argue, such exercises can be incomplete and misleading, as not all visible minorities seem to be facing the same sort of labour-force discrimination. Hou and Coloumbe (2010) highlight how in terms of earnings, education attainment and occupation, Canadian-born Chinese and South Asians are very different from blacks, and in several dimensions seem to be doing even better than whites. More specifically, these authors document large gaps in average earnings between blacks, particularly black men, and whites, even when focusing on the Canadian born.

Standard assimilation theory, as associated with the Chicago School of Sociology, considered the integration of successive generations of Europeans who settled in the United States in the early 1900s (Park and Burgess, 1925). The general argument here was that each successive generation would show upward social mobility in terms of both education and occupation, as the second generation was more integrated than the first, just as the third was more integrated than the second. Part of this process involved the education of immigrant children in the North American school system, which allowed for the achievement of

fluency in the majority language, less ethnic distinctiveness, increased out-marriage, and reduced residential segregation. While this appears to have characterized both the United States and Canada for much of the twentieth century, there are exceptions to this rule, just as there is evidence to suggest that this understanding of immigrant assimilation has less applicability in the twenty-first century. By way of contrast, an alternate theoretical framework has developed: segmented assimilation theory, in light of evidence that not all minority communities in the United States are integrating to the same extent. Segmented assimilation posits that there are different paths of assimilation, as conditioned by (i) the economic resources available to newcomers, (ii) economic class, and (iii) discrimination (Portes and Zhou, 1993).

As North America has considerable economic inequality, some groups have been more successful than others in joining the middle class; others remain segregated and overrepresented among the ranks of racialized, impoverished groups at the bottom of the income scale. Portes and Zhou (1993) delineate three possible paths of assimilation. The first is consistent with classical assimilation theory (i.e., increased acculturation and economic integration into the US middle class). The second is acculturation and assimilation into an urban underclass, leading to poverty and downward mobility. The third is the possibility for both selective acculturation and economic integration, which combines both success in the labour market with considerable continuity in terms of an immigrant community's culture, language, and values. As Fong (2006) points out in his collaborative study *Inside the Mosaic*, it is essentially an empirical issue as to what extent segmented assimilation applies to the Canadian context.

Reitz and colleagues (2011) conclude "regarding the expectations based on segmented assimilation theory, there is some but fairly weak confirmation." Boyd (2002, 2009) concludes that there are important differences in the historical and contemporary race relations between the United States and Canada that has allowed the latter to avoid some of the worst of the problems encountered by the former. Relative to the United States, Canada is characterized by a lower level of economic inequality and does not have the same history of ethnic and racial segregation (Balakrishnan and Gyimah, 2003; Corak, 2010). In addition, in terms of official ideology, the Canadian emphasis on multiculturalism can be contrasted with the melting pot idea in the United States. Yet segmented assimilation theory emphasizes that there is more than one way of "becoming American," and that Americanization is not necessarily beneficial (Bankston and Zhou, 2003). In a similar manner, over 30 years ago, the Special Parliamentary Committee on Visible Minorities in Canadian Society specifically defined integration as meaning participation while retaining as much cultural heritage as desired without being denied equality of opportunity.

We still find considerable agreement on certain fronts. For instance, there is widespread consensus on the importance of equal opportunity and on attacking the barriers that prohibit equal participation, especially in employment and in the economy. Since Canada is becoming a more culturally diverse country, laws, policies, and programs have been needed in a variety of areas, ranging from settlement services for immigrants to human rights codes prohibiting discrimination. The 1961 Bill of Rights, the 1977 Human Rights Act, and the 1982 Canadian Charter of Rights and Freedoms prohibit discrimination. By international standards, the emphasis on multiculturalism and economic integration seems to have achieved considerable success. The gains of second-generation Canadians, particularly in terms of education, are impressive in a country with high immigration (Boyd, 2009).

As Halli and colleagues (1990) pointed out over 25 years ago, the reality in Canada is that "the French, the Aboriginals of the northlands, recent visible minorities, bilingual and multicultural policies . . . have made Canada into a plural mosaic." Yet since this point in time, Canada has become even more diverse, as the proportion of foreign-born and non-European people has risen. Canada's Aboriginal population has witnessed considerable demographic growth and Quebec has managed to maintain its cultural and linguistic vitality. To the extent that Canadian society is able to manage this diversity as we move further into the twenty-first century, this diversity gives Canada

advantages in the evolving international arena. In a context of increased economic and cultural globalization, a more diverse Canada might have many advantages, including sustained economic and cultural exchanges with various countries, and the associated cultural richness.

Education: Trends and Directions

In the immediate postwar period, Canada's educational system was poorly developed. In 1951, the total number of post-secondary students numbered about 95,000 (Vanderkamp, 1988). There followed a period of considerable reform in education, especially increased funding that eventually brought Canada into line with other industrial countries. By 2011–12, the number of full-time post-secondary student enrolments had risen to 1,466,148, with an additional 530,052 part-time students (Statistics Canada, 2013y). While the Canadian population is about 2.5 times larger than at the beginning of this period, the total number of post-secondary students has increased by more than twentyfold.

Expenditures for education rose especially in the 1960s. In 1971, education accounted for 22 per cent of all government expenditures, compared to only 14 per cent in 1961 (Pike, 1988: 266). Yet with the growth of other programs, especially for health and pensions, and a decline in the relative numbers of persons of school age, expenditures on education compared to other expenses subsequently declined to about 13 per cent of total government expenditures by the 1990s, with this proportion remaining relatively stable (OECD, 2013). Since the mid-1980s, total government expenditures for health have been higher than for education—a situation that is likely to continue.

A large part of this shift in public expenditures away from education and toward health care can be understood as a response to changes in Canada's age structure. The sizable baby boom cohorts are well beyond the years usually devoted to education and are firmly established in the labour force. Yet despite this fact, Canada does continue to spend quite a bit on education, as, for example in 2010, Canada ranked

10th among 33 OECD countries in terms of total expenditures (public and private) as a percentage of GDP (OECD, 2013). While Canadian expenditures per student on elementary and high schools are quite close to the OECD average, Canada ranks second only to the United States in terms of total expenditures (private and public) on what the OECD labels as "tertiary" education (college and university in the Canadian context).

An increasing proportion of overall expenditures on education are now coming from private sources, especially for Canadian colleges and universities. While Canadians continue to place priority on education, resulting in a highly skilled and well educated population, the OECD reports that about 24 per cent of total funding in Canada for education comes from private sources relative to the OECD average of about 16 per cent. At the tertiary level, the difference is even greater as 43 per cent of Canadian funding comes from private sources compared with the OECD average of 32 per cent (OECD, 2013).

Primary and Secondary Levels

From the early 1950s onward, the postwar baby boom produced a dramatic increase in enrolment in elementary and secondary schools. This enrolment peaked in 1970, at fully 5.9 million, with total enrolment up by 134 per cent over the 1950–70 period. In accommodating this massive enrolment increase, government expenditures on education increased by over 700 per cent, even after one accounts for inflation (Clark, 2000). In efforts to address this substantial climb in enrolment, schools could not be built fast enough.

After the 1970 peak, total enrolment in elementary and secondary schools subsequently dropped, reaching a low of only 4.9 million in 1985. As the baby boomers moved on to colleges and universities, the much smaller cohorts that followed them moved through their elementary and high school years. Yet in spite of the drop of about 1 million in overall enrolment, the total costs of elementary and secondary education continued to increase over the 1970–85 period (Wilkinson, 1986: 537). The number of teachers was much the same at the beginning and end of

the 1970–85 period, but they had some five years more teaching experience on average. The increased costs were largely a function of lower student–teacher ratios and better-educated and more experienced teachers.

Although total enrolments at the primary and secondary level have yet to return to their 1970 peak, the numbers have rebounded somewhat since this 1985 low. By 2005, the total number of primary and secondary students had risen to about 5.4 million (Statistics Canada, 2013z). Just as the Canadian population grew at a moderate pace throughout the 1990s, the total number of children in Canadian schools also increased. During the 1990–2005 period, the number of enrolments in elementary and secondary schools increased at an annual rate of about 0.6 per cent—while Canada's population grew by about 1.1 per cent annually (Statistics Canada, 2013aa). More recently, there has been a stabilization and slight decline in the total number enrolled, down to about 5.3 million students in 2011 (Statistics Canada, 2013z). This situation is largely due to the decline in the number of births that characterized the 1990s, which fell from about 405,486 births in 1990 to a low of only 327,882 births in 2000 (Statistics Canada, 2013ab).

Since this point in time, there has again been an upturn in births, up to 385,179 births by 2013. As a result, we can anticipate a modest growth in the number of students enrolled in Canada's elementary and secondary schools over the shorter term. Expenditures on primary and secondary education have continued to climb, up to $61.9 billion by 2010, a doubling in expenditures over 1990 figures, not adjusted for inflation (Statistics Canada, 2013z). Yet over the same period, Canada's gross domestic product rose by 140 per cent, indicating a slight decline in the proportion of GDP devoted to the young (OECD, 2014b). Since primary and secondary education is mostly under provincial jurisdiction, government expenditures have varied widely across provinces.

Canada continues to fare well in educational outcomes, both in terms of the percentage of Canadians who complete high school and those who pursue post-secondary education. As the Canadian public has come to appreciate that high school graduation is the minimum requirement for most types of employment, the high school dropout rate in Canada has declined at a steady and uninterrupted pace (de Broucker, 2005). As an indicator of the relative efficiency of Canada's secondary school system, Statistics Canada (2014h) has estimated that the percentage of high school students who graduate "on time" (as a percentage of the 18-year-old population, and 17-year-old population in Quebec) is about 74 per cent, which compares well with other countries. In addition, among those who do not graduate at age 17 or 18, over one half eventually do obtain their high school degree. Canada's education system readily allows for the opportunity of a second chance—that is, many young adults who drop out of school early or struggle with their education eventually do obtain certification through adult education (Raymond, 2008). Correspondingly, among 25- to 34-year-olds, the percentage who have successfully completed at least a high school education has risen to an all-time high of 92 per cent (Statistics Canada, 2014i).

Post-Secondary Education

Post-secondary enrolment, which was at a very low level 50 years ago, rose even faster. In universities, the average annual rate of growth for full-time students over the 1951–1985 period was 5.5 per cent at the undergraduate level and 8.9 per cent at the graduate level (Vanderkamp, 1988: 5). This extremely rapid growth through to the 1980s was not unique to Canada, and was at least partially due to shifts in the age structure of the Canadian population. As relatively large cohorts (the baby boomers) moved through young adulthood, the demand for spaces in Canadian universities and colleges increased. At the same time, there was a substantial increase in participation rates of young Canadians in post-secondary education.

Full-time university enrolment grew by 35 per cent during the 1980s, peaking in 1994, and then levelling off somewhat throughout the remainder of the 1990s. For example, Statistics Canada (2001) reported 580,400 full-time enrolments in 1998–1999, up only negligibly from 574,300 in 1993–1994. This flattening in the growth curve of new

enrolments was attributed to several factors, including a stabilization of the size of the young adult population. In community colleges, full-time enrolments were up moderately over this same five-year period, from about 380,000 to 403,500 (growing at an annual rate of about 1 per cent).

More recently, the upward trajectory of total enrolment has continued to rise, to a record of 938,718 full-time university students and an additional 325,032 part-time students in 2011–12 (Statistics Canada, 2013ac). This is due to two factors. First, from the year 2000 through to 2011, the size of the population most likely to attend university (i.e., people aged 18–24 years) increased, at an annual rate of roughly 1.1 per cent (Statistics Canada, 2013ab). Second, participation rates have also increased, as the total number of students attending university grew at an even faster pace, at an average rate of 3.6 per cent. The percentage completing university has risen, from 25 per cent of 25 to 34 year olds in 2001 up to 31 per cent by 2013. Similarly, in terms of the number attending CEGEP and community college, total enrolment increased at an annual rate of 2.7 per cent, climbing from 545,277 in 2000 to 732,450 by 2011.

Overall, the proportion of young adults in post-secondary education is high by international standards (see Figure 10.3). Among 25 to 34 year olds, almost 6 out of 10 Canadians have a community college diploma or a university degree—which puts Canada in third place across OECD countries, behind only Korea and Japan (again, see Figure 10.3). Yet in taking a closer look at this statistic, we see that Canada's high ranking in tertiary education is largely due to the high proportion attaining a college education rather than a particularly high level of university attendance. While in 2001, Canada's relative rank in university education was third (behind only Norway and the United States), it is now in the middle of the pack among OECD countries; for example, 31 per cent of 25 to 34 year olds in Canada report at least a bachelor's degree relative to the OECD average of about 30 per cent (OECD, 2013).

A relevant issue here is the extent to which university enrolment could be even higher in Canada if

Box 10.1 ▣ The Continuing Importance of a University Education

The Canadian economy and occupational structure have witnessed important changes over recent decades, moving into what many refer to as the "post-industrial economic order" (Myles and Picot, 1993; Krahn et al., 2011). This involves a shift from an economic system based primarily on manufacturing to one based on the production of knowledge goods and personal services. Education has been described as fundamental in the adaptation to these changes, for the skill requirements of the typical job have increased over recent years. For both men and women, higher levels of education are generally associated with a wide assortment of benefits, not the least being a much lower likelihood of unemployment.

Both Canadian men and women with a post-secondary education have long benefited from lower unemployment—that applies particularly to university graduates. Whereas the two economic recessions of the early 1980s and the early 1990s were associated with double-digit unemployment, people with a university education fared relatively well throughout both periods. Over the 40-year period from 1975 to 2014, the unemployment rate for university graduates has never once surpassed the 6 per cent mark, even during periods of relatively severe economic downturn (Statistics Canada, 2014i). Typically, community college graduates have fallen somewhere in between university and high school graduates, hinting at the benefits of university education as opposed to the more technical and career-oriented programs.

There are also important differences in earnings, as, for example, Frenette (2014) documents a substantial wage premium associated with the university degree that typically begins early in one's working life and tends to grow larger with more years on the job (see Figure 10.2). In working with longitudinal data over a period

of two decades (1990–2010) and following a specific cohort (aged 35 in 1990), Frenette estimated an overall earnings premium of the university degree over the high school certificate of about $728,000 for men and $442,000 for women. For the community college certificate, this premium was not quite as large, at $248,000 for men and $180,000 for women. Frenette also identified other advantages for the well educated, including greater job security, better benefits, and more years of coverage in employer-sponsored pension plans. Yet while these advantages were experienced by this cohort that was well established in the labour market back in the 1990s, it is uncertain as to what extent more recent cohorts will benefit from a comparable education. As Frenette (2014) points out, "The results of this study applied to one particular cohort . . . . Long-term outcomes for more recent cohorts are not yet available, and may or may not be similar . . ."

Morissette and Frenette (2014) document among younger workers (aged 20–34 in 2012) that those with a university degree earn on average about $1.42 for every $1.00 earned by those with a high school certificate. As for the non-economic returns to schooling, a higher level of education is also strongly correlated with a longer and healthier life, owing to the likelihood of less physically demanding occupations and lifestyle (Tjepkema and Wilkins, 2011). Higher education is associated with greater levels of community involvement, both in volunteer activities and politics (Vézina and Crompton, 2012). Beyond the benefits of a highly qualified labour force and greater labour productivity, there are various benefits to an investment in public education, both for the individual and for society in general. Better-educated parents are also far more likely to pass on such benefits to the next generation (Sticht, 2010).

Continued

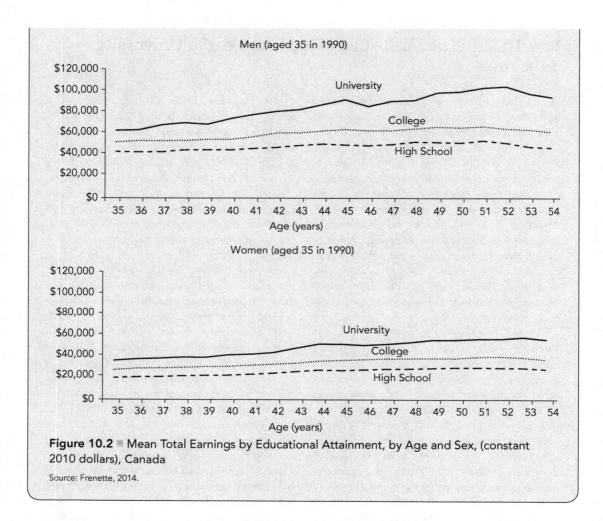

Figure 10.2 Mean Total Earnings by Educational Attainment, by Age and Sex, (constant 2010 dollars), Canada

Source: Frenette, 2014.

the economic obstacles to paying for a university degree were reduced. As we have mentioned, at the tertiary level, over 40 per cent of Canadian funding comes from private sources compared with the OECD average of about 30 per cent (OECD, 2013). In terms of costs, average tuition in Canadian universities more than doubled over the 1990–2010 period, after making adjustments for inflation (Luong, 2010). Post-secondary education has experienced a shift in the nature of its funding, with students paying proportionally more and governments paying proportionally less. As a result, the level of student indebtedness has increased in a context of stiff competition for employment on

graduation (Schwartz and Finnie, 2002). Yet despite these rising costs, participation rates have continued to rise, as a university education is widely understood as being fundamental to obtaining meaningful and better-paid employment (Keeley, 2007). While expenditures on post-secondary education are relatively high, so, too, would appear the benefits of that investment (see Box 10.1).

The Distribution of Income in Canada

Three distinctive types of events shape economic well-being: (1) economic events that influence the

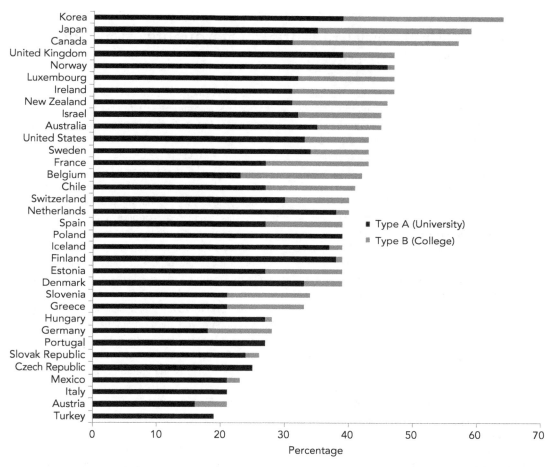

Figure 10.3 ▣ Percentage of People Aged 25–34 Who Have Attained Tertiary Education, OECD 2013

Source: OECD, 2013.

availability of jobs and the wages available in the Canadian labour market; (2) political events that influence the types of transfer payments that Canadians might receive from government; and (3) demographic events that influence the types of families and living arrangements in which Canadians share and pool income (Picot et al., 1998). Of the three types of events, the first two receive considerable attention, particularly in public debates on economic and social policy, whereas the third type—demographic events—tends to be neglected (Lichter, 2006). Yet in an overview of how income is distributed in Canada and how this has changed over recent years, it is crucial that we consider three sets of factors simultaneously.

When income trends are being assessed, the choice of time period is always somewhat arbitrary. Over the last several decades, there have been some noticeable ups and downs in the North American business cycle, which have at times made it difficult to maintain a perspective on long-term trends. Since 1980, for example, Canadians have experienced three economic recessions, one in the early 1980s, another in the early 1990s, and most recently, in 2008–9. This latter recession, brought on by the collapse of the dot-com bubble and the financial crisis in the United States, hurt the Canadian economy, but in terms of unemployment, it was not nearly as severe as the earlier two recessions. For example, while the monthly

Box 10.2 ▣ University Credentials, Overqualification, and the Canadian Labour Force

Despite this growing pool of university graduates, there is the reality that many new entrants into the labour force encounter major difficulties in finding work in jobs that correspond to their expectations and education. As a result, some young adults are *overqualified* after graduation—that is, they work in occupations that require a lower level of education than the university degree (Herbert-Copley, 2013). The question surfaces: has this issue of overqualification become worse in recent years? Has the growing supply of university graduates outpaced the corresponding growth in the number of skilled positions in the Canadian labour market? To the extent that there is a *skills mismatch* in the labour market, we find a corresponding problem for the Canadian economy, as the overqualification issue tends to lead to lower earnings and productivity over the longer term. An absence of an appropriate entry-level job can also prevent a young adult from acquiring the experience necessary in order to find a better job in the future.

The overqualification of university graduates can be measured in various ways, including the use of subjective measures in post-graduation surveys that merely ask respondents if their jobs matched their education. As a preferred alternative, Uppal and LaRochelle-Côté (2014) worked with a particularly objective measure: a unique skills-based classification system of occupations, as originally developed by Employment and Social Development Canada. In this research, occupations were classified in terms of whether the job typically required (i) a university degree, (ii) a college certificate (with or without an apprenticeship), or (iii) a high school degree or less. In working with the 1991 and 2001 Census as well as the 2011 National Household Survey, it was then possible for the authors to match specific types of jobs to educational

credentials. Furthermore, with the 2011 NHS, it was also possible to examine separately the percentage of graduates (aged 25–34) who were overqualified by the specific field of study followed in university.

Uppal and LaRochelle-Côté's findings were mixed (2014). The good news was that while the number of young graduates with university credentials has gone up, so, too, has the proportion of jobs that require a university degree. Similarly, as the proportion of young adults who merely complete high school has declined, so, too, has the proportion of all jobs that require at most a high school certificate. Yet the bad news is that while the problem of overqualification has not worsened, it has not improved, and there are major difficulties in finding the appropriate work for a substantial proportion of young university graduates. In 2011, almost one in five of university-educated men and women (aged 25–34) were in jobs that required a high school degree or less (17.7 and 18.3 per cent, respectively), whereas another one in five (22.8 and 20.9 per cent) were working in occupations requiring only a college education (again, remaining relatively stable over this period). In terms of field of study, this situation was even worse for students who graduated from such programs as the visual arts, humanities, and social sciences (see Table 10.4).

Many university graduates eventually do find jobs consistent with their education, although a degree alone is clearly not a guarantee to a well-paid professional occupation. While the figures in Table 10.4 apply to all people aged 25–34, the authors found that with the passage of years, and with more years of work experience, individuals were typically more likely to find the appropriate job. In both 1991 and 2011, for example, people aged 30–4 had lower rates of overqualification than did those aged

Table 10.4 ▣ Percentage Distribution of University-Educated Canadian Workers (aged 25–34) across Occupations, Classified by Skill Level and Field of Study, Canada, 2011

	Percentage in occupations usually requring:					
	High school or less		**College**		**University**	
	men	women	men	women	men	women
All university educated workers (aged 25-34 years)	17.7	18.3	22.8	20.9	59.5	60.8
Visual and performing arts and communications	22.2	28.2	41.3	37.9	36.5	33.9
Humanities	32.5	32.7	28.3	27.2	39.2	40.1
Social and behavioral sciences and law	24.7	23.8	28.5	27.6	46.8	48.6
Agriculture, natural resources and conservation	21.1	20.3	31.6	28.2	47.3	51.5
Business, management and public administration	21.7	21.6	24.8	23.6	53.5	54.8
Physical and life sciences and technologies	16.8	21.3	25.4	29.7	57.8	49.0
Health and related fields	13.4	8.8	18.1	11.9	68.5	79.3
Mathematics, computer and information sciences	9.3	20.8	19.0	17.8	71.7	61.4
Architecture, engineering and related technologies	9.1	11.9	16.9	19.0	74.0	69.1
Education	9.2	8.7	7.7	9.4	83.1	81.9
Other	34.0	26.5	51.0	46.4	15.0	27.1

Notes: These tabulations exclude persons employed in managerial occupations, which includes roughly 1 in 10 workers aged 25–34. Uppal and LaRochelle-Côté excluded these workers in their tabulations given that the management category is very difficult to classify. Managers tend to have various educational requirements depending on the exact nature of the position; i.e., they tend not to be easily associated with a particular level of schooling. Some managers need little more than high school whereas others require higher education. A substantial proportion of these jobs were filled by persons with less than a university degree.

Source: National Household Survey, 2011; Uppal and LaRochelle-Côté, 2014.

25–9. Other risk factors associated with overqualification include obtaining a degree prior to immigration to Canada (as foreign credentials are often not recognized in the Canadian labour market), living outside a metropolitan area (non-metropolitan areas appear to have fewer opportunities for well-educated Canadians), and completion of education at the undergrad level (people with a master's degree or a Ph.D. are almost half as likely to be overqualified). It is difficult to quantify the importance of family background, ability, motivation, and potential employment connections, all of which have been shown to be important to success in the labour market, regardless of area of study (Coates and Morrison, 2013). Correspondingly, these factors also vary greatly among university students (e.g., some are far more engaged with their studies than others), both within and across academic disciplines.

unemployment rate rose to over 14 per cent in the spring of 1983 and about 12.5 per cent in early 1993, the most recent recession saw unemployment peaking at just over 9 per cent in the summer of 2009, up from the 35-year low of 5.3 per cent in October 2007. More recently, economic conditions have again improved somewhat, with an unemployment rate close to 7 per cent in 2013–14 (Statistics Canada, 2014i).

In 1982–1983, the North American economy witnessed climbing unemployment, high inflation, and declining real earnings. After a period of economic recovery through to the late 1980s, a second recession took hold in 1991 and 1993, again introducing considerable downward pressure on incomes. The early 1990s were turbulent years for many Canadians, with unemployment at persistently high levels at a time of government constraint and large deficits (Picot et al., 1998). Budgetary constraints halted employment growth in the public sector, and unemployment insurance and income-assistance programs became more restrictive (Morissette, 1998). Yet after this period of economic difficulty, labour-market conditions in North America improved noticeably, such that from the late 1990s, unemployment rates declined and moderate gains were made across the income distribution. With a period of sustained economic growth and job creation to 2007, Canadians had more than made up the ground they lost during the earlier recessions. The fallout from the economic crisis of 2008–9 brought

about slow employment growth into 2014. Nonetheless, the data on income and unemployment for the first decade of the twenty-first century document a smaller proportion of Canadians reliant upon government transfers (Statistics Canada, 2012c).

These trends are illustrated in Figure 10.4, which shows income for Canadian families over the 1980–2011 period, after adjustments for inflation (in 2011 dollars). Three different indicators of economic well-being are presented: (i) mean family income, (ii) median family income, and (iii) median family income after tax. Particularly useful in this context is "median income"—that point on the income distribution at which 50 per cent of all income units fall below and 50 per cent fall above. This conceptualization of typical income is not influenced by extreme values and is distinct from the more commonly relied-upon measure of mean income that is merely the arithmetic average. Furthermore, "median income after tax" allows us to identify trends in take-home pay, after all transfers have been received minus all reported provincial and federal income tax paid.

While all of our indicators suggest some improvement in economic well-being, the extent to which this is true varies by indicator selected. The decision to rely upon the *median* as opposed to the *mean* is no small matter when it comes to documenting income trends. If a relatively small proportion of a population becomes particularly wealthy, this can have a substantial impact on the mean, whereas the median would remain largely

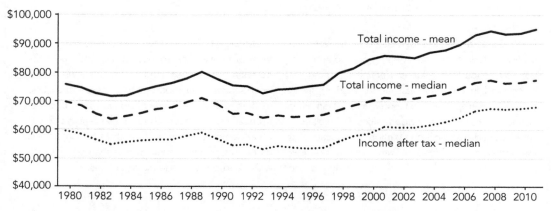

Figure 10.4 Mean and Median Family Income, Total Income and Income after Tax (2011 dollars), Canada, 1980–2011

Source: Statistics Canada, 2014c.

unchanged. If we use mean income, we are left with the impression that the gains of this period have been quite high—up by about 25 per cent over the 1980–2011 period. If we use the median, which is not disproportionately affected by gains at the top of the income distribution, the gains are more modest—up by 10.7 per cent. The climbing disparity between mean income and median income in this case is consistent with the idea that the greatest gains have been made by those at the top of the income distribution. Furthermore, median income after tax rose by about 14 per cent over this 30-year period, consistent with the impression that families have made some moderate gains. Not reported in Figure 10.4 is the corresponding amount for unattached

persons (people not part of an economic family), who report in 2011 a median income of about $28,000 dollars—up moderately by about 9 per cent from 1980.

While moderate gains have been made in terms of purchasing power, the 1980–2011 period also witnessed a substantial climb in the proportion of families that involved two rather than only one wage earner. As we saw in Chapter 9, many families appear to be committing more time to the labour market while increasing their overall purchasing power moderately.

Table 10.5 illustrates the importance of family type and living arrangements to the economic well-being of Canadians, for median income is

Table 10.5 ▣ Median Income in Constant (2011) Dollars for Selected Family-Unit Types, Canada, 1981–2011

	1981	1986	1991	1996	2001	2006	2011
Economic families, two persons or more	$68,300	$67,300	$65,700	$64,700	$71,400	$74,400	$77,300
Non-elderly families[a]	$71,700	$71,500	$70,000	$69,000	$76,500	$79,600	$84,400
Married couples	$69,900	$65,800	$65,100	$65,200	$71,600	$75,800	$78,500
One earner	$52,500	$54,800	$50,700	$53,900	$57,900	$60,900	$61,000
Two earners	$79,000	$75,200	$77,500	$77,500	$81,300	$85,600	$88,500
Two-parent families with children	$74,400	$75,400	$75,400	$76,100	$84,300	$88,600	$97,800
One earner	$59,000	$58,300	$56,300	$54,200	$54,200	$55,100	$63,000
Two earners	$76,100	$77,900	$77,600	$80,000	$86,000	$89,200	$100,000
Three or more earners	$98,400	$98,000	$95,500	$98,400	$109,400	$113,900	$118,500
Lone-parent families	$32,900	$29,800	$27,000	$26,600	$36,000	$41,100	$43,000
Male lone-parent families	$57,700	$53,500	$46,700	$44,800	$50,800	$60,100	$57,300
Female lone-parent families	$29,100	$27,000	$25,400	$25,000	$33,000	$36,500	$41,000
No earners	$15,700	$17,000	$18,500	$18,500	$17,600	$20,100	$19,300
One earner	$32,900	$32,000	$30,400	$32,600	$35,600	$35,700	$41,000
Elderly families[b]	$36,400	$40,400	$43,200	$43,300	$46,400	$50,900	$51,700
Unattached individuals	$25,700	$24,200	$23,000	$22,200	$25,900	$27,300	$28,000
Elderly males	$17,700	$19,900	$21,200	$22,100	$24,300	$25,400	$29,800
Elderly females	$15,700	$18,000	$19,200	$19,900	$21,900	$23,000	$23,500
Non-elderly males	$38,000	$31,900	$30,400	$27,200	$31,900	$32,700	$32,800
Non-elderly females	$28,000	$27,400	$23,800	$22,000	$23,600	$25,900	$25,100

[a] Families in which the major income earner is less than 65 years old.
[b] Families in which the major income earner is 65 years or older.

Source: Income Statistics Division, table 202-0411, Statistics Canada, 2014j.

Box 10.3 ▣ Rising Income Inequality in Canada

The Conference Board of Canada (2013) has argued that income inequality is problematic to the extent that a society fails to fully benefit from the skills and potential of all its citizens. The economic marginalization of a substantial number of citizens, in either an absolute or relative sense, can undermine social cohesion and potentially lead to increased social tensions. While income inequality is not as high in Canada as in the United States or in Britain, there is evidence that indicates it has been rising over recent decades. This rise in income inequality has been attributed to various factors, including globalization, technological developments that displace labour, declining unionization rates, and tax reductions (Krugman, 2009; Yalnizyan, 2010).

Research on income inequality has documented a number of similarities between Canada and the United States. In particular, Murphy and colleagues (2007) highlight the rise in the concentration of income in both countries at the very top of the income distribution. Veall (2012) estimates that in terms of market income (excluding capital gains), the top 10 per cent of income earners in Canada saw their share of total income rise from about 34 per cent in 1986 to over 40 per cent by 2009. Similarly, if we focus on the top 1 per cent of all income earners, we will find that this concentration in income share has risen from about 8 per cent in 1986 to over 12 per cent by 2009.

This rise in income inequality is well documented, with no small help from the "Gini coefficient"—a summary indicator that measures the relative degree of income inequality in a society across people and families (see Figure 10.5). This coefficient ranges from a low of 0 (minimum inequality where each person receives an exact equal share of national income) to a high of 1 (maximum inequality, were one person receives a 100 per cent share). Although the interpretation is not straightforward, comparisons of its value over time or between populations can allow for some clear conclusions: the higher its value, the higher the inequality, and vice versa. Across OECD countries, for example, Canada's Gini coefficient is lower than in

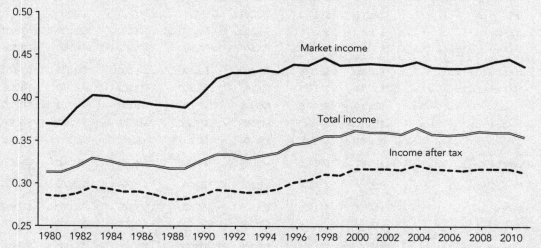

Figure 10.5 ▣ Gini Coefficient for Market Income, Total Income, and Income after Tax, Canada, 1980–2011

Source: Statistics Canada, 2014d.

the United States or Britain but slightly higher than the OECD average and higher than a slight majority of OECD countries. Income inequality, after taxes and transfers, has been shown to be significantly higher in North America in general than is true of much of northern and continental Europe.

In focusing on Canada, we see that Figure 10.5 portrays this coefficient over the 1980–2011 period, separately for (i) market income (earnings from employment, self-employment, investment income and private retirement income), (ii) income after transfers (market income plus all government transfers, including employment insurance, old age security, welfare payments, etc.), and (iii) income after transfers and taxes (total income minus provincial/federal taxes paid). As would be expected, income inequality in 2011 is highest for "market income" (.436), lower for "total income" (.355), demonstrating the impact of government transfers, and lower still for "income after tax" (.313) demonstrating the impact of progressive taxation. Regardless, though, the Gini coefficient has gone up across income types, including, most importantly, an increase in inequality for "income after tax"—in the take-home income of Canadians (from .286 in 1980 to .313 in 2011). While not presented here, similar conclusions have been drawn in connection with the evolution of wealth inequality, wealth meaning all financial resources available

to a family when it defines its net worth, including real estate, personal property, and investments (Yan, 2001; Morissette et al., 2002).

This increase in income inequality has been attributed to various factors, including the aforementioned polarization in market earnings. During the early 1990s in particular, the Canadian workforce became more polarized by the unequal distribution of earnings and hours among workers of different ages and skill levels. Additionally of interest from the point of view of demography are changes in family composition (Picot et al., 1998; Beaujot and Ravanera, 2009). Because of divorce and separation, a growing proportion of all families are headed by single parents—up from about 9 per cent in 1971 to 16.3 per cent in 2011 (Statistics Canada, 2012l). Similarly, the number of people who are living alone has increased, from about 20 per cent of all households in 1981 to 27.6 per cent in 2011. There has been a simultaneous rise in the proportion of husband-and-wife families with at least two wage earners, an option obviously not available to lone parents or people living alone. To the extent that couples (with or without children) are able to improve on their market earnings through increased labour-force participation, we can anticipate further gains in terms of their relative economic advantage into the future.

shown to vary dramatically across family-unit types. Income data are provided by family type (including unattached persons) and number of earners, for selected years from 1981 through to 2011. Female lone-parent families are clearly in a disadvantageous position, particularly among those who report no earner in the family. The median income of female lone-parent families (without an earner) was only $19,300 in 2011, actually down slightly from $20,100 in 2006. Among female lone-parent families with one earner, economic circumstances improve significantly—median income was up from $35,700 in 2006 to $41,000. The obvious implication is that the likelihood of

experiencing severe economic hardship is very high for lone-parent families without some form of workforce involvement. Government transfers are insufficient in meeting the needs of these families, with obvious consequences for children.

Regarding two-earner families, the relative advantages of pooling resources through labour-force involvement become strikingly obvious. For example, dual-earner families (with children) reported a median income of about $100,000 in 2011. This is more than double that of female lone-parent families with one earner and about five times the median of female lone-parent families with no workforce involvement. In addition, it is noted that unattached individuals reported a median income of $28,000 in 2011. A significant proportion of unattached individuals are young adults who have yet to fully establish themselves in the labour market; many others are elderly men or women, often widowed and living alone. Neither lone-parent families nor unattached individuals can benefit from the pooling of resources available to married couples.

Low Income in Canada

In the spring of 2000, Statistics Canada introduced a new indicator of low income, its "low income rate as based on after-tax income" (Statistics Canada, 2000). This was a break from past practice that had calculated low income rates with "before tax income." As a result of this basic change in definition, Statistics Canada's low-income rate was significantly lower than what was reported previously. For example, when working with the "low income rate—after tax," Statistics Canada reported that about 12.5 per cent of Canadians experienced low income in 2000, which compared to the 16.4 per cent classified as low income with the previous definition (Statistics Canada, 2014e). Similarly, the low-income rate among children fell from being almost one in five (18.2 per cent) to just over one in seven (13.9 per cent). Despite there being absolutely no change in the real economic circumstances as faced by the young, a substantially lesser "low-income rate" was circulated among the Canadian public, with relatively little attention paid to the subtle definitional issues involved.

While Statistics Canada has long emphasized that its low-income cut-offs should not be read as poverty lines (Fellegi, 1997), these have come to be widely considered as Canada's unofficial poverty rates. While this shift in rate appeared to be arbitrary, Statistics Canada justified this change by emphasizing that both income taxes and transfers are essentially two methods of income redistribution. The before-tax rates only partly reflect the redistributive impact of Canada's tax and transfer system, by including the effect of transfers but not the effect of income taxes. Consequently, depending

upon which indicator is used, the public could be left with the impression that poverty was less of a problem than it was before the definition was changed.

Suggestive of further complications, Statistics Canada has introduced two additional measures of low income, including a strictly relative measure, set at 50 per cent of median income, adjusted for family size, and a "market-based measure," which, in consultation with Employment and Social Development Canada, identified low-income thresholds dependent on a predefined set of essential goods and services (for further details on the methodological issues involved, see Statistics Canada, 2013g; 2013ad). While these measures lead to results that differ somewhat from one another, they typically give a consistent picture of low income, particularly when examining low income at a specific point in time, demonstrating how it tends to vary by living arrangements, family type and number of earners.

Using the aforementioned after-tax indicator, among unattached Canadians who are living alone, 27.7 per cent were reported as experiencing low income in 2011, which contrasts with only 5.5 per cent of all persons living in families. At one extreme, only 2.1 per cent of persons in two-parent, two-earner families experience low income, while at the opposite extreme, fully 76.2 per cent of persons in female lone-parent, no-earner families are classified as income-poor. While overall, 19.7 per cent of people in lone-parent families are classified as income-poor, a lack of labour-force involvement is a particularly strong predictor of economic hardship. For people living in families with one earner, about 15.7 per cent in female single-parent families are classified in this manner, as are 14 per cent of people in two-parent families with children.

With the availability of longitudinal data, which follows the same families over time, researchers have gained some insight into the extent to which low income can be considered a temporary or permanent phenomenon (Picot et al., 1998). Throughout the 1990–2009 period, for example, Murphy and colleagues (2012) have estimated that over one third of the individuals who started a spell of low income in any given year were no longer income-poor one year later. Corak and colleagues (2002) have estimated that among those who report low income in a given year, only about one in five could be expected to again report low income five years later, and a significant number of these were not income-poor for the full period. In effect, the dynamics of poverty are such that many lower-income persons live precariously close to what Statistics Canada would classify as low income, with an ongoing flux of people entering and exiting income poverty over time.

Of particular concern for public policy are those factors that lead to long-term poverty—that is, who is most likely to remain in poverty or close to poverty for an extended period. Murphy and colleagues (2012) provide evidence to suggest that Canadians with a low level of education are more likely to experience long-term poverty, as are those living alone or in a lone-parent family and people with Aboriginal and visible-minority status, as well as recent immigrants. A sizable proportion of people who have some form of physical disability are also likely to experience extended spells of low income (Crawford, 2013).

Conclusion

Canada is a very heterogeneous country, both in terms of language and culture. As natural increase continues to decline as a component of population growth, the importance of immigration to Canada's demographic development will further contribute to this heterogeneity. At the same time, because of Canada's socioeconomic characteristics, it is reasonable to describe this country as a success story. By any international measure, Canadians enjoy a high standard of living, as reflected in income statistics at the turn of the twenty-first century. Furthermore, not only is Canada among the most heterogeneous countries in the world, but its citizens are also among the most educated.

This is not to deny the persistence of some problems: many new Canadians (and visible minorities) experience considerable difficulty in establishing themselves in Canada. Not all Canadians share equally in its income and opportunity, and there is evidence of increased inequality over recent years. While many Canadians take pride in Canada's heterogeneity, there are obviously both benefits and costs to this situation. In effect, the greater ethnic diversity in Canada's population brings a number of changes and requires various adaptations. Since Canada is becoming a more socially diverse country, laws, policies, and programs have been needed in a variety of areas, ranging from settlement services for immigrants to human-rights codes prohibiting discrimination. If we rely on immigration to maintain Canada's population growth in the years ahead, these policy issues will become even more pressing.

Ironically, it is in turning to our next chapter on Canada's Aboriginal peoples that we encounter probably the most disadvantaged of Canada's citizens. Just as Canada's newest citizens have encountered serious obstacles to economic integration, so, too, have the country's First Nations people, the descendants of the original populations. The demographic situation and history of Canada's Aboriginal peoples are quite distinct from that of other Canadians, and for this reason, they require a separate chapter here.

Critical Thinking Questions

1. According to most projections, Canada's population is expected to become more heterogeneous in the future, both culturally and linguistically. Why do you think this is the case, and what consequences of these trends do you foresee?

2. Many new immigrants experience difficulties in their first years settling in Canada, with higher unemployment than average and lower income than average. Why do you think this is the case, and what might be done to remedy this situation?

3. Describe how Canada's education system has been modified by changes in this country's age structure over recent decades. Do you feel that the education system has done a good job in preparing young Canadians for life after graduation?
4. Various demographic trends have had an impact on the living arrangements of Canadians over recent years. Describe some of these trends and discuss their implications for income patterns and the incidence of income poverty.
5. Statistics Canada revised the manner in which it collects information on ethnicity in the 1996 Census. More specifically, it began to actively encourage "Canadian" as a possible answer. Do you think this was a good idea? Why or why not?

Recommended Readings

Fong, Eric, ed. 2003. *Inside the Vertical Mosaic.* Toronto: University of Toronto Press. This book is a collection of studies by Canadian experts on immigration and its social impact. The basic theme of the book, which uses Toronto as a case study, is to explore how immigration affects social structures and processes.

Malenfant, Éric Caron, André Lebel, and Laurent Martel. 2010. *Projections of the Diversity of the Canadian Population, 2006 to 2031.* Statistics Canada cat. no. 91-551-X. Using a micro-simulation model named Demosim, these comprehensive projections prepared by a team of analysts at Statistics Canada emphasize characteristics such as place of birth, generation status, visible-minority group, religious denomination, and mother tongue.

Satzewich, Vic, and Nikolaos Liodakis. 2013. *Race and Ethnicity in Canada: A Critical Introduction.* Don Mills, ON: Oxford University Press. This is a thorough look at sociological research and thinking on ethnicity in Canada.

Termote, Marc, Frédéric Payeur, and Normand Thibault. 2011. *Portrait démolinguistique. Perspectives démolinguistiques du Québec et de la région de Montréal (2006–2056).* Gouvernement du Québec. This instructive work carefully charts the influence of four main phenomena on the evolution of linguistic groups in Quebec, including natural increase, international migrations, interprovincial migrations, and language mobility.

Zawilski, Valerie, ed. 2009. *Inequality in Canada: A Reader on the Intersections of Gender, Race, and Class.* Don Mills, ON: Oxford University Press. This edited collection reflects research on various spheres in which people experience inequality: family, education, health, justice, labour, and global inequality.

Related Websites

www.pch.gc.ca. The official website of Heritage Canada, the federal department responsible for promoting Canadian culture, including the Canadian Multiculturalism Act and the Official Languages Act.

www.umanitoba.ca/publications/ces. The website of the Canadian Ethnic Studies Association, which is an interdisciplinary organization devoted to the study of ethnicity, multiculturalism, immigration, intergroup relations, and the cultural life of ethnic groups in Canada. This site includes links to other Canadian and international websites that deal either directly or indirectly with ethnicity and immigration.

www.ccsd.ca. The site of the Canadian Council on Social Development, a non-profit social policy and research organization focusing on issues such as poverty, social inclusion, disability, cultural diversity, child well-being, and employment.

www.cmec.ca. This is the website of the Council of Ministers of Education Canada, the national voice for education in Canada. Since education in Canada is primarily a provincial/territorial jurisdiction, this organization centralizes much of the research currently being undertaken on education.

11 The Demography of the Aboriginal Population of Canada

The Chapter at a Glance

- In the 2011 National Household Survey (NHS), 5.5 per cent of Canada's population reported that they had Aboriginal ancestry (1,836,035 people). This is not an insignificant number; in fact, it surpasses in size all but 4 of Canada's 13 provinces and territories.

- According to the 1982 Constitution Act of Canada, there are three major groups of Aboriginal peoples in Canada: North American Indians, Métis, and Inuit.

- The North American Indian population can be further subdivided into two groups: those with legal Indian status (status Indians) and those without (non-status Indians).

- In the demographic evolution of Aboriginal peoples in Canada, the late nineteenth century

can be thought of as initiating a period of demographic stabilization and recovery.

- While Canadian society overall is among the world leaders in the health of the population as a whole, the situation is not true for much of the Aboriginal population.

- There are important differences in the fertility and mortality of Canada's Aboriginal populations, not only varying by Aboriginal group but also by place of residence (e.g., on or off reserve, urban or rural).

- Because of Aboriginal peoples' higher rate of fertility, the population is younger than the rest of Canada. This is particularly true among the Inuit, and to a lesser extent, status Indians.

Introduction

As we saw in previous chapters, Canada has witnessed some remarkable demographic developments over time. International comparisons suggest that Canada ranks among the healthiest countries in the world, with an estimated life expectancy at birth for 2010–2011 of about 81.5 years (Martel, 2013). As far as the birth rate is concerned, Canada entered the twenty-first century with its total fertility rate falling to a historic low—at about 1.5 children per woman in 2005—prior to rebounding somewhat more recently, up to 1.6 in 2011 (Statistics Canada, 2013ae).

Related to these changes have been continuing improvements in Canada's social and economic development. As an indicator of this progress, the United Nations Development Programme (UNDP) has consistently placed Canada near the top of its

annual ranking of countries according to its Human Development Index. Meant to capture differences in life expectancy, per capita gross domestic product, and level of education, this ranking has often been loudly touted by successive federal governments, usually with gushing government officials suggesting that Canada is "one of the best countries in the world to live in." While Canada's relative rank has slipped somewhat most recently (at least partially due to "greater" progress being made in other countries), it has remained very high on this index, or, more specifically, it was 6th out of 185 countries listed in 2011 (UNDP, 2012).

As demonstrated through an innovative application of this index to the First Nations peoples of Canada, Aboriginal Canadians have clearly not shared equally in this affluence. In considering persons designated as *status Indian* by the federal government and in focusing exclusively on those who live on reserves, Cooke and Beavon (2007) rank the First Nations as 48th, only slightly above countries like Uruguay and Mexico. While living conditions are known to be better off reserve than on reserve, Cooke and Beavon rightfully highlight the frustration of the First Nations' political leaders. Ovide Mercredi, a former Grand Chief of the Assembly of First Nations, has condemned the wide circulation of the UNDP ranking, emphasizing that Canada is certainly not among the best countries in the world to live for its First Nations (Mercredi, 1997). While Cooke and Guimond (2009) report modest progress since the 1980s in reducing the gap between Aboriginal and non-Aboriginal Canadians on this index, unemployment remains very high, housing conditions are often substandard, and health care and educational services are often inadequate.

Given the importance of First Nations people to Canada's history and identity, we have devoted this chapter to Aboriginal demography. In light of the confusion and inadequate information that characterizes public discussions of Aboriginal peoples, this chapter necessarily begins with the many definitional issues. For example, what is meant by the term *status Indian* as opposed to *non-status Indian*? What demographic data are available in the study of Canada's Aboriginal population, and how can the Aboriginal population be described in these data? The discussion of definitions is followed by an overview of what is currently known of population size, fertility, and mortality, as well as some of the implications of recent trends for population structure and composition. This will all be related to evidence on the evolving social and economic conditions of Aboriginal Canadians, as well to the broader context of Canada's demographic development.

Defining the Aboriginal Population: Difficulties Due to Changing Identities

Most demographic research focuses on countries or on populations as defined in terms of political boundaries and place of residence. Consequently, the definition of who is to be included in the target population of any analysis is usually straightforward, since it can rely on rules relating to citizenship or usual place of residence. Yet in the study of Aboriginal peoples, it is much more complicated to define exactly who is to be included. Aboriginal peoples are spread throughout Canada, across provincial and territorial boundaries, and live in both rural and urban regions of the country. There are no clear residency rules that can be used in identifying this population, nor is there a clear and objective legal status that can be used in identifying *all* Aboriginal people.

At one point in Canada's history, the Aboriginal population could be defined easily on the basis of ancestry and way of life. In spite of the great variety among Aboriginal languages, customs, and material culture, there were recognizable common elements of culture and biology. Today, however, the situation has become far more complicated—owing to several centuries of cultural exchange, assimilation, intermarriage, and births of mixed ancestry. Though it may have been obvious to the seventeenth- or eighteenth-century observer who was Cree or Mi'kmaq, as opposed to British or French, it is now often far from obvious.

For one thing, there is the question of how we classify persons of mixed ancestry. This issue is not of minor consequence, since the majority of Canadians who currently identify themselves as having Aboriginal ancestry do so as part of a reported mixed ancestry. Of the 1,836,035 people who reported Aboriginal ancestry in the 2011 National Household Survey (or about 5.5 per cent of Canada's population), almost two thirds (1,207,575) also reported other, non-Aboriginal origins (Statistics Canada, 2013af). Similarly, some people of Aboriginal ancestry report no specific affiliation or identification with a given Aboriginal ancestry or culture (Siggner et al., 2001). Is it enough to rely upon the reported ancestry in the identification of this population, and if not, what are some of the other criteria that have been proposed?

In the next few sections of this chapter, we will specifically address some of these issues. We will broadly sketch how the census and, more recently, the National Household Survey have historically defined the Aboriginal population, namely, by asking people their "ancestry or cultural origins," their legal status under the Indian Act, and whether they identify themselves as Aboriginal. Briefly, the data available in studying the demography of Aboriginal peoples is far from straightforward; it essentially reflects definitions developed by government officials and researchers. The use of these definitions led demographers to document a rapidly growing Aboriginal population over the last few decades of the twentieth century. Yet depending upon how the Aboriginal population is delineated, very different conclusions might be drawn about the dynamics of this growth and the corresponding demographic characteristics.

The Canadian Census as a Source of Demographic Data

The Canadian Census has historically been the most comprehensive source of demographic data on Aboriginal peoples in Canada. Historically, the census has calculated the number of Aboriginal people in Canada by asking respondents about their ancestry (as obtained through the "ethnic or cultural origin" question). In the 2006 Census for example, respondents were asked "to which ethnic or cultural group(s)" they belonged while encouraging respondents to report as many origins that they deemed appropriate. Whereas some respondents have answered that question with very specific responses (such as Objiway, Mohawk, or Cree), others have simply identified themselves as North American Indian, Métis, or Inuit.

Although the census is perhaps the most comprehensive source of demographic data on Aboriginal peoples, there are several difficulties associated with this information. One of these problems relates to the fundamental issue of data comparability over time. For example, while the definition of *Aboriginal* has relied on the ethnic or cultural origin question in the census, there have been frequent changes in the wording involved, along with important changes in methodology and in the way in which people answer these questions. Until the 1971 Census the ethnic origin was to follow the male line of descent only. Before 1986, multiple responses to the ethnic-origin question were either disallowed or at least discouraged—a situation that was completely reversed from 1986 onwards. In addition, the long-form census was replaced in 2011 by the National Household Survey (NHS), a voluntary

survey, unlike the mandatory census. This produced an uncertain level of bias in the 2011 NHS, as its final response rate was 68.6 per cent, considerably lower than the response rate of the 2006 long-form census, at 93.5 per cent (Statistics Canada, 2012n).

The encouragement of multiple origins has led to more people reporting Aboriginal ancestry, compared to the situation when multiple or matrilineal origins were neglected. As demonstrated in Figure 11.1, the number of people reporting Aboriginal ancestry has increased dramatically over recent years—from only 496,500 in 1981 up to 1,678,235 in the 2006 Census and up further to 1,836,035 in the 2011 NHS (Statistics Canada, 2013af). In just 30 years, the size of this ancestry-based population has skyrocketed by over 250 per cent. Underlying this change was an increase in the number of people who reported Aboriginal ancestry as part of a multiple response, increasing from 79,085 in 1981 to 997,715 in 2006, and up further to 1,207,575 in 2011. As Canada's population overall was growing at only about 1 per cent a year over this same period (with about half of this growth due to international migration), the growth of the Aboriginal population was obviously far beyond pure demographics.

It would nevertheless be quite wrong to suggest that all such growth was merely the result of the change in census methodology. There have also been important shifts in the propensity of Canadians to report Aboriginal ancestry, independent of any other change. After documenting a similar situation in the United States among American Indians, Passel (1997) refers to a whole series of social changes that may very well have influenced the propensity on the part of Americans to report American Indian heritage. Of particular importance was a new-found political awareness and self-confidence, which has contributed to a raising of North American Indian consciousness.

It has been argued that in societies such as Canada and the United States, most racial and ethnic identities are in a state of flux; that is, it is extremely difficult to establish fixed identities and stable boundaries in the delineation of ethnicity or cultural origins (Eschbach, 1995; Hout and Goldstein, 1994). Among many Canadians of mixed ancestry, for example, respondents to the census often change their declared ethnic

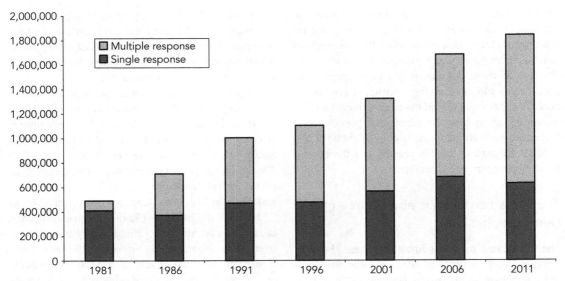

Figure 11.1 ▣ Census Counts of Aboriginal Populations, based on Ancestry, Canada, 1981–2011

Source: Statistics Canada, Census of Canada, 1981–2006; National Household Survey, 2011.

affiliation from one census to the next, in a manner that is often very difficult to predict. Consequently, the size of ethnic groups appears to change, independently of natural increase or migration (Goldmann, 1998; Guimond, 2003). To the extent that subjectivity and choice enter into how populations report on their ancestry, one would expect reduced comparability of demographic data over time. With recent shifts in declared ethnic affiliation, Canadians appear to be far more likely to report their Aboriginal ancestry today than was the case historically.

In similar research on the population growth of indigenous peoples in Latin America, Chackiel and Peyser (1993) refer to a fundamental "demographic paradox," not easily explained by simple demographic accounting formulae. Even though many indigenous populations in both Central and South America have for many decades experienced high rates of natural increase, for a variety of reasons, the available data on these populations indicate that they can barely sustain their numbers from one census to the next. This research points to the constant loss of cultural identity, particularly the tendency to assimilate toward the dominant cultures and languages of these societies. In

reference to this research, Romaniuc (2000), who draws a few parallels to Canada, speculates about the extent to which the same thing may have happened in Canada in the past. In the absence of direct empirical research, Romaniuc suggests that until fairly recently, losses of population as a result of shifts in cultural affiliation and assimilation have outweighed gains. Consequently, we would suggest that the Canadian census likely understated the actual size of Canada's Aboriginal population as defined by ancestry, a situation that has only recently corrected itself, to an uncertain extent.

Aboriginal Populations

According to Section 25(2) of the Canadian Constitution, there are three major groups of Aboriginal peoples in Canada: "the Indian, Inuit and the Métis." While some might suggest that such a classification obscures a virtual "kaleidoscope of cultures and traditions" (Frideres, 1998), this classification has had wide circulation among social scientists and has certainly had a strong influence on the character of most demographic research. While the constitution recognizes these three broadly defined Aboriginal groups, the corresponding populations are not carefully defined. As a result, many researchers have merely relied upon information collected through the census on ancestry or cultural origins in classifying people into one of the above categories.

A further subdivision into two additional groups is provided in the Indian Act (first passed in 1867): North American Indians (First Nations peoples) who hold legal Indian status (status Indians) and those who do not (non-status Indians). By virtue of the Indian Act, status Indians have certain specified entitlements, including the right to elect representatives to negotiate with the federal government over land-claim settlements and many other rights under treaties concluded with the Crown. Although the Indian Act has undergone many revisions and iterations since the nineteenth century (Savard and Proulx, 1982), it does provide for a specific but partial definition of Aboriginal peoples by setting the legal criteria for associated identification. As suggested by Romaniuc (2000: 123), the status population can almost be thought of as de jure members (or citizens, if you like) of Canada's First Nations.

According to the 2011 NHS, which also asked Canadians whether they are "registered under the Indian Act," only about one third (34.7 per cent) of the Aboriginal "ancestry" population are in fact status Indians (637,660 people out of 1,836,035). In reality, this percentage is probably higher, as past census-based estimates have understated the true size of this population, owing to difficulties in data collection (see Box 11.1). This observation also very likely holds true with the 2011 NHS.

Beyond the status Indian population, there are many other Canadians with Aboriginal ancestry, often with similar social and cultural traits, yet without the same rights as formally recognized by the federal government in a legal sense (non-status). For a wide variety of reasons, most Canadians with Aboriginal ancestry are not on the register as maintained by Aboriginal Affairs and Northern Development Canada (AANDC), as, for example, the 2011 NHS reports 1,198,375 persons with Aboriginal ancestry who are not registered under the Indian Act (Statistics Canada, 2013af, 2013ag).

Some merely have ancestors who either refused or were not allowed to establish treaties or agreements with the Crown. Others, throughout the nineteenth and twentieth centuries, experienced "enfranchisement"—that is, they lost their status, sometimes by choice, but more often because of restrictions relating to out-marriage, as spelled out in the Indian Act. In addition, much of the rapid growth of the Aboriginal population that has been recorded in recent censuses has occurred among the non-status and Métis populations, while the number of people reporting as status has been more stable and predictable from one census to the next.

The original inhabitants of Canada's arctic regions, the Inuit, are the least numerous of the three major groups. The question on ancestry in the 2011 NHS revealed about 72,615 people of Inuit ancestry. That figure is based on both single and multiple replies regarding ancestry (Statistics Canada, 2013af). In Canada, the word *Eskimo* has gradually been replaced by *Inuit*, the Inuktitut word used by the Inuit to refer to themselves. Largely situated in Nunavut, Yukon Territory, and the Northwest Territories, as well as in northern Quebec and Labrador, the Inuit share more of an affinity with other arctic groups in neighbouring countries than with other Aboriginal groups in Canada. With a very different history and culture, the Inuit of Canada's arctic regions are quite distinct from the neighbouring Athabascan and Algonquian peoples to the south, and they have much more in common with many of the original inhabitants of Alaska and Greenland, not to mention the Chukotka of the northern regions of Russia.

The third Aboriginal group is the Métis; in the 2011 NHS, about 447,655 people reported Métis ancestry, either in single or multiple responses (Statistics Canada, 2013af). The word *Métis* has two different meanings: it has been used to denote any person of mixed Indian and European ancestry (*Métis* just means "mixed" in French), but perhaps more commonly, it is used to denote a hybrid culture that developed primarily in Western Canada from the marriages of Cree, Ojibwa, and Salteaux women to French and Scottish fur traders. In areas that were remote from European influence, a hybrid culture grew up under the influence

Box 11.1 ▣ How Many Status Indians Are There?

According to the National Household Survey (NHS) that was conducted at the same time as the 2011 Census the size of the status population in Canada is 637,660 persons, up modestly from the 2006 Census tally of 623,780 people (Statistics Canada, 2009b, 2013ag). This figure was much lower than expected, as it implies a total population growth of only 2.2 per cent over a five-year period. While Canada's overall population grew by 5.9 per cent over this same interval, the growth as documented for the status population suggests error, as this relatively young population was expected to at least maintain its population share. For example, the status population grew by more than 10 per cent between the 2001 and 2006 Census. In addition, the 2011 NHS figure is noticeably lower than the official tally compiled by Aboriginal Affairs and Northern Development Canada, which documents a 2011 population of 868,206 people (AANDC, 2013). The true population likely falls somewhere between the NHS and AANDC figures, and is probably closer to the latter figure.

Whereas Aboriginal Affairs and Northern Development Canada is the federal department responsible for meeting the federal government's constitutional, treaty, political, and legal responsibilities to First Nations peoples, Statistics Canada is this country's official statistical agency. Although neither organization would appear to have any vested interest in misreporting the true size of this status population, neither has ever fully explained the reason for such a large discrepancy. Whereas Statistics Canada's figure is based on the 2011 NHS, Aboriginal Affairs relies upon a population register, commonly referred to as the Indian Register. The NHS collects information by directly contacting and asking Canadians whether or not they are registered under the Indian Act; AANDC's Indian Register is, in essence, a list of all persons who have at one point or another been registered as having status and who continue to be classified as such according to

especially of the fur trade, the Catholic Church, and the Hudson's Bay Company. Whereas most people in the western provinces who describe themselves as Métis in the census do so in reference to these origins, an unknown number continue to use other meanings. Consequently, there are Aboriginal persons reporting Métis ancestry in all provinces of the country, including areas that are far removed from the traditional Métis homeland in the Prairie provinces.

Beyond their recognition in the Canadian Constitution, the Supreme Court of Canada confirmed in 2003 that the Métis are a "rights-bearing people," setting out in principal a definition for the purpose of claiming Aboriginal rights under the Constitution Act. Since 1983, the Métis National Council has represented the Métis Nation in negotiations with federal authorities, and currently maintains a register of citizenship. More specifically, it is now possible to be registered as Métis, in much the same way that First Nations are registered as Indians in the Indian Registry. As defined by the Métis National Council, "Métis means a person who self-identifies as Métis, is distinct from other Aboriginal peoples, is of historic Métis Nation Ancestry and who is accepted by the Métis nation" (Teillet, 2010).

Aboriginal Identity

To further complicate matters, Statistics Canada has evolved an additional definition of the Aboriginal population, which is a definition based on identity rather than ancestry. As mentioned above, the use of ancestry to define the Aboriginal population results in a total population count in 2011 of 1,836,035 (or about 5.5 per cent of Canada's population).

Alternatively, the identity-based definition produces a smaller total of 1,400,685 people in 2011—that is, roughly 4.3 per cent of Canada's population

the Indian Act. The NHS is attached to the Canadian Census and was conducted for the first time in 2011; the Indian Register is updated continually, documenting all new persons to be added to the register (predominantly through births) and all persons to be removed (predominantly through deaths).

Various factors are responsible for the discrepancy, including the fact that the 2011Census/NHS was not permitted or was interrupted on 36 different First Nations before it could be completed. For largely political reasons, these communities refused access to Statistics Canada, arguing that the Government of Canada did not have the right to collect information on their territories. In addition, the more general problem of census undercount and/or survey non-response has reduced the accuracy of figures coming out of past censuses (e.g., both individuals and households have been missed by enumerators despite the best of efforts on the part of Statistics Canada to count the full population). As suggested by the Strategic Research Directorate at AANDC, the voluntary nature of the NHS is also likely to be particularly problematic for the Aboriginal population, as it has historically been a segment of the Canadian population with a relatively high non-response rate in survey research (Penney, 2013). So, the 2011 NHS estimate, due to its voluntary nature, is likely to be less accurate than figures coming out of previous mandatory censuses. To an uncertain extent, this shift in methodology is likely responsible for the widening discrepancy between Statistics Canada's figures and those of the register maintained by AANDC.

The NHS is also not capable of documenting status Indians who are living abroad on Census Day (yet these persons are included in the Indian Register), nor are status persons who live in institutions or collectives included in the NHS count (as, for example, those who are living in long-term-care facilities, hospitals, or federal/provincial correctional facilities). In combination, a correction for all these factors would bring the NHS count of the status population closer to the AANDC figure. There may also be inaccuracies in the AANDC register—in particular, the late registration of deaths (and possibly births) that could lead to inaccurate population figures.

(Statistics Canada, 2013ag). This latter, more restrictive, definition has subsequently been used by Statistics Canada in most of its 2011 NHS releases (whereas information on the size and characteristics of the ancestry-based population was given less attention).

Efforts to establish time-series data on Aboriginal populations will always be hindered by the "fluid or situational character" of such concepts as ancestry, cultural origins and identity (Boxhill, 1984; Lieberson and Waters, 1993). Some people of Aboriginal ancestry may deny their origins; others may have a passionate commitment to these origins; still others may be indifferent or simply unaware. It was in direct response to some of these difficulties that Statistics Canada introduced, for the first time in 1996, a new question on Aboriginal identity (beyond the ethnic origin or ancestry question) with the ultimate goal of more narrowly focusing on Canada's First Nations. This new question, which was again used in 2001 and 2006, specifically asked Canadians whether or not they "consider themselves as being Aboriginal, that is, North American Indian, Métis or Inuit" (Statistics Canada, 2008b). Whereas one might argue that a count based on ancestry is more objective, the question on identity is arguably more meaningful, determining whether or not individuals feel an allegiance or association with Aboriginal culture. Unsurprisingly, the numbers are somewhat smaller, as about 76 per cent of persons reporting Aboriginal ancestry state that they "consider themselves" to be Aboriginal.

If we use this narrower definition of the Aboriginal population, about 62.2 per cent of people with First Nations ancestry (North American Indian) say that they "identify" themselves as First Nations peoples (or 851,560 people out of

1,369,115), whereas among the Inuit, 81.9 per cent of those with ancestry identify themselves as Inuit (or 59,445 people out of 72,615). Among the Métis, curiously the identity estimate was slightly greater than the ancestry count in the 2011 NHS, at 451,795 persons identified relative to 447,655 persons who report Métis ancestry (Statistics Canada, 2013ag). The "fluidity" of this reporting over time is striking. Nonetheless, Statistics Canada documents major growth for all major Aboriginal identity populations over time (see Table 11.1). Since 1996, when this information was first collected in the census, the Aboriginal identity population has grown by roughly 75 per cent overall, an increase that could not possibly be the result of only demographic factors. Particularly striking in this context is the phenomenal growth in the numbers of people identifying as Métis, more than doubling (+121.3 per cent) in only 15 years since 1996. Closer to expectations, the Inuit population grew by 47.8 per

cent over 15 years, which implies a very high rate of demographic increase, equivalent to a rate of slightly greater than 2.5 per cent annually.

As Statistics Canada has subsequently used this "identity population" in most of its data releases from all censuses since 1996, as well as in the 2011 NHS, the implication is that this more accurately captures the essence of what one might define as a core Aboriginal population. Systematic comparisons have demonstrated that people who report a particular ancestry yet do not identify with it tend to be much more like the general Canadian population than is the case with those who do identify with that ancestry. For example, Canadians of Aboriginal ancestry who do not report this identity are far less likely to speak an Aboriginal language, live in a rural or more remote region of the country, be registered, or live in a First Nations community (Norris, 2000; Frideres and Gadacz, 2012). Furthermore, whereas virtually all of the status respondents identify with their ancestry,

Table 11.1 ▣ Size and Percentage Increase in the Population with Aboriginal Identity, Canada 1996–2011

	1996	2011	% change
Total Population	28,528,125	33,476,688	17.3
Aboriginal Identity Population	799,005	1,400,685	75.3
First Nations Peoples (North American Indian)	529,040	851,560	61.0
Métis	204,115	451,795	121.3
Inuit	40,220	59,445	47.8
Multiple and Other Aboriginal Responses	25,640	37,885	47.8
Non-Aboriginal Population	27,729,120	32,076,003	15.7

Sources: Statistics Canada, 1996 Census Statistics Canada, 2011 National Household Survey.

Box 11.2 ▣ On Language

Over 60 distinct Aboriginal languages were reported in the 2011 Census. And yet, only three of those 60 languages have been described as belonging to large enough populations to be considered truly secure (Norris, 2011). According to the 2011 Census 213,490 people report an Aboriginal

mother tongue, yet over two thirds of them spoke Cree, Inuktitut, or Ojibwa (see Table 11.2).

Of most commonly reported mother tongues, the 10 largest comprise 89.1 per cent of all people with an Aboriginal mother tongue, whereas about 50 languages comprise the remaining 10.9 per cent.

Of those with an Aboriginal mother tongue, 83,475 speak Cree, 34,110 speak Inuktitut, and 19,275 speak Ojibwa. Of all the Aboriginal languages reported, all but 8 have fewer than 5,000 people, whereas more than 40 languages have fewer than 500 speakers. On the basis of such statistics, UNESCO has suggested that Canada's Aboriginal languages are among the most endangered in the world (Moseley, 2010). A significant number of languages have either already disappeared or are close to doing so, with at least a dozen on the brink of extinction.

Whereas Table 11.2 defines linguistic groups on the basis of *mother tongue* (or the first language learned in the home), it is also possible to distinguish populations on the basis of *home language* (the language most frequently spoken or regularly spoken in the home). In working with this information, sociologists often compare the number of persons reporting each in order get some sense as to the vitality or continuity of language use (Harrison,

1997). In this regard, Table 11.2 includes what demographers refer to as the *"index of continuity,"* which compares the number of people who speak a language at home to the number who report this same language as their mother tongue. The lower the score on this index, the greater the decline or erosion, because it means that a larger percentage are no longer speaking the language that they first learned in infancy.

In exploring some of the factors responsible for either a high level of linguistic continuity (e.g., among speakers of Inuktitut) or considerable language loss/decline (e.g., among many of the smaller linguistic groups not listed in Table 11.2), a wide assortment of factors have been identified (Ponting, 1997). On perhaps the most fundamental level, outside Aboriginal settlements and reserves, there have long been obstacles to obtaining employment or a formal education without a strong command of either English or French. Whether intentionally or unintentionally, this has often led to

Table 11.2 ▦ The Ten Most Commonly Reported Aboriginal Mother Tongues in Canada, 2011

Language	Mother Tongue 2011	Index of Continuity[1]
1 Cree languages	83,475	82
2 Inuktitut	34,110	95
3 Ojibwa	19,275	71
4 Dene	11,860	89
5 Innu/Montagnais	10,985	95
6 Oji-Cree	10,180	90
7 Mi'kmaq	8,030	80
8 Atikamekw	5,915	97
9 Blackfoot	3,250	64
10 Stoney	3,155	85
Other Aboriginal languages[2]	23,255	59
Total	213,490	82

Notes:
[1] Percentage of those with an Aboriginal mother tongue that report it as a home language (i.e., used regularly or most often at home).
[2] More than 50 additional languages account for roughly 11 per cent of all persons reporting an Aboriginal mother tongue. Among the most common languages not listed here include the Ticho (2080 persons), Slavey (1595), Carrier (1525), Dakota (1160), Gitsan (925), Shuswap (675), Nisga'a (615), Halkomelem (570), Mohawk (545), Kwakiut (495), and Nootka (320). Particularly endangered are the Tlingit, Kutenai, and Haida languages, with fewer than 130, 100, and 75 speakers, respectively.

Sources: Statistics Canada, 2012n; authors' calculations.

Continued

the neglect of Aboriginal languages. Other contributing factors include the simple fact that some indigenous languages were explicitly prohibited, a practice that was common in many residential schools throughout the first half of the twentieth century.

Consequently, groups that live in remote communities or in settlements with concentrated populations of indigenous speakers appear to find it easier to retain their language. In the 2011 Census for example, Statistics Canada (2012n) document that the index of continuity was over 96.8 for people who lived in communities with at least 70 per cent

Aboriginal mother tongue. This is clearly the case among the Inuit of the Far North: the continuity index shows that 9.5 out of 10 people whose mother tongue was Inuktitut continue to speak it as a home language. Similarly, Aboriginal people who live on a First Nations reserve are far more likely to retain their language, whereas the levels of language loss are greatest for non-status Indians living off reserve. Among people living in communities with fewer than 30 per cent speaking an Aboriginal mother tongue, the index of continuity drops to about 60, with even lower levels in Canada's larger urban centres.

this is far less likely to be the case among persons who are non-status.

The growth of this population remains dramatic, suggesting problems in terms of temporal reliability regardless of whether we are working with the identity-based or ancestry-based figures. If, in fact, the census documents significant change in the socioeconomic characteristics for either population, it remains difficult to discern how much of the change is due to real change in these characteristics of Aboriginal Canadians and how much is merely due to a different population reporting itself as Aboriginal identity or ancestry. This is a major problem in trying to document change over time in the socioeconomic characteristics of Canada's First Nations, let alone the demographic change associated with trends in fertility, mortality, and migration.

The Dynamics of Population Change: From Stabilization to Rapid Growth

In the demographic evolution of Aboriginal peoples in Canada, the late 1800s can be thought of as pivotal. After close to 300 years of population decline, the late nineteenth century is often noted as the beginning of a period of demographic stabilization and recovery. Although mortality remained very high, the most

serious of epidemics were eventually to subside, and the total number of Aboriginal deaths gradually began to be lower than total births. Toward the late 1800s, the limited evidence available suggests that a negative rate of natural increase was gradually replaced by moderate growth. As a result, the Aboriginal population has been estimated to have grown from its nadir of about 100,000 during the late nineteenth century to 166,000 by 1951 (Goldmann and Siggner, 1995).

Nevertheless, both mortality and fertility continued to remain high; the former, as documented among status Indians in the early 1900s, appears to have been comparable to that of the European population 100 years earlier (Romaniuc, 2000). Similarly, fertility appears to have been quite high, with little evidence of anything other than natural fertility (i.e., there is no evidence of any voluntary control over reproduction). While the Aboriginal population was eventually to experience major reductions in both fertility and mortality, the timing and pace of these changes departed significantly from that of other Canadians (Young, 1994; Trovato, 2000, 2001).

Canadian mortality overall has dropped quite noticeably, but the epidemiological transition of Aboriginal peoples has lagged far behind. Although deaths ultimately declined first (in a manner that is consistent with the demographic transition of most populations), fertility decline still did not immediately follow suit. Contrary to expectations, fertility appears to have risen somewhat during the postwar period (Romaniuc, 1981). Further details on this transition are provided in the sections to follow, demonstrating how the demographic history of Canada's Aboriginal population cannot easily be described in terms of classical demographic transition theory. In other words, the demographic history of Canada's Aboriginal population is quite distinct and demonstrates the heterogeneity of experience that has characterized Canada's demographic history.

Mortality

In an overview of mortality patterns among Aboriginal peoples in both Canada and the United States, Trovato (2001) points to common problems that have emerged. While there have clearly been long-term gains in both life expectancy and infant mortality, Aboriginal North Americans continue to experience mortality conditions that are worse than that of the whole population. Whereas Canadian society on the whole is among the world leaders in the health of its population, current features of Aboriginal mortality and morbidity clearly indicate epidemiological patterns that are at odds with the Canadian norm.

The information that is currently available on mortality is less than complete and can provide only a partial picture, unfortunately. Part of the reason is that Canada's system of vital statistics, which should document all births and deaths in this country (including cause of death), has never collected information on ancestry or cultural origins. Historically, the best source of information available on the mortality of Aboriginal peoples was the Indian Register, the population register maintained by AANDC (2013). This register, which includes information exclusively on the status population, has been continuously updated in documenting births and deaths as far back as the nineteenth century. In addition, there is the lesser-known population register on the Inuit of northern Quebec, which has documented births and deaths since the 1940s (Robitaille and Choinière, 1985). For Aboriginal peoples, without access to a population register, there have been more

recent efforts made at both indirect estimation (Norris et al., 1995) and data linkage that connects the information collected on deaths, as documented in vital statistics, with ancestry and identity information, as recorded in the Canadian Census (Wilkins et al., 2008a; Peters, 2013; Tjepkema et al., 2009).

Canada has witnessed some dramatic overall reductions in mortality, with average life expectancy at the end of the twentieth century about 30 years longer than at the century's beginning. This is a result of some important changes in the pattern of disease dominance. More specifically, male and female life expectancies at birth in 1901 were only about 47 and 50 years, respectively (Statistics Canada, 1999). In comparison, mortality was particularly high among the Aboriginal population—based on data from the Indian Register, Romaniuc (1981) has estimated a life expectancy at birth in 1900 for First Nations of only 33 years, more than 15 years lower than the Canadian average at the time (see Table 11.3).

For the Inuit, the earliest direct evidence available, which was collected in the 1940s, indicated a life expectancy at birth of only about 35 years (Robitaille and Choinière, 1985). Again, even by the standards of the day, this suggests a very high level of mortality. Canadian life expectancy in the 1940s was almost 30 years longer (66 years for females and 63 years for males). Among First Nations people, the situation was not much better, with only modest gains throughout the first several decades of the century. By 1941, the status Indian population had an estimated life expectancy of just 38 years.

The epidemiological transition was delayed among both First Nations peoples and the Inuit; important changes were not to occur until the postwar period. By 2001, First Nations peoples (status) in Canada continued to have life expectancy noticeably shorter than average, at 73 years (70.4 years for males and about 75.5 years for females). For the Inuit, Tjepkema and colleagues (2009) estimate a 2006 life expectancy of slightly less than 70 (67.6 years for males and 72.8 for females). For the Métis, they estimate a mortality experience that falls somewhere between that of the non-Aboriginal population and other Aboriginal groups (about 73 for males and

Table 11.3 ▣ Estimated Life Expectancy at Birth for First Nations (Status), Inuit, and Total Canadian Populations, Selected Periods and Years, Canada, 1900–2006

Year or Period	First Nations (status) Both Sexes		Inuit				Total Canada
			Northern Quebec	Northwest Territories	Inuit Nunangat		
1900	33					1901	47.0M / 50.0F
						1921	58.8M / 60.6F
1940	38	1941–51	35	29		1941	63.0M / 66.3F
		1951–61	39	37			
1960	56	1961–71	59	51		1961	68.4M / 74.2F
1960–4	59.7M / 63.5F						
1965–8	60.5M / 65.6F					1966	68.7M / 75.2F
1976	59.8M / 66.3F	1971–81	62			1976	70.2M / 77.5F
1981	62.4M / 68.9F					1981	71.9M / 79.0F
1982–5	64.0M / 72.8F					1984–6	73.0M / 79.8F
1991	66.9M / 74.0F	1991	58M / 69F		63.5M / 71.1F		
1995	68.0M / 75.7F				64.7M / 71.6F		
2001	70.4M / 75.5F	2001			65.0M / 70.0F	2001	77.1M / 82.2F
2006		2006			67.7M / 72.8F	2006	78.2M / 82.3F

Sources: INAC, 2005; Wilkins et al., 2008b; Romaniuc, 1981; Medical Services Branch, Health and Welfare Canada, 1976; Nault et al. 1993; Loh et al., 1998; Robitaille and Choinière, 1985; Norris, 2000; Statistics Canada, 2008b; Peters, 2013.

76 for females).[1] All relative to the total Canadian population, the longevity disadvantage of the Métis can be estimated to be about 5 years; for the First Nations, about 6–7 years; and for the Inuit, about 10 years. Stated differently, the longevity estimated for the Métis in 2001 was roughly comparable to the longevity of other Canadians in the late 1970s; for the First Nations, their longevity was comparable to that of other Canadians in the early 1970s; and for the Inuit, mortality risks in 2006 were comparable to what other Canadians faced in the 1950s.

Among the changes that occurred over the postwar period, the reductions in infant mortality have been particularly striking. As late as the 1940s, the infant mortality rate among First Nations was as high as 200 deaths per 1,000 live births (Romaniuc, 2000), a rate that was to drop dramatically to about 40 deaths per 1,000 by the 1970s and further to roughly 12 deaths per 1,000 by the 1990s (Loh et al., 1998).

Among the Inuit, similar reductions have been documented, from at least 200 deaths per 1,000 births down to about 28 deaths per 1,000 by the early 1990s (Frideres, 1998). Again, this decline lagged behind that among other Canadians; for example, the infant mortality rate for Canada overall has fallen to only about 5 deaths per 1,000 (Statistics Canada, 2008c). According to Health Canada (2003), among First Nations, this rate has edged closer to the rate observed nationally, at about 6.5 deaths per 1,000 births. The Inuit rate in 2001 was about 15 deaths per 1,000, or roughly three times that as observed among other Canadians (Department of Health and Social Services, Nunavut, 2004).

Causes of Death

The epidemiological transition has involved important shifts in the pattern of disease dominance, particularly a decline in mortality associated with infectious disease.

---

[1] These estimates of life expectancy (at birth) for the Métis are the authors', as roughly based on Tjepkema and colleagues (2009). While they estimated Métis life expectancy at age 25, it is possible to use indirect estimation procedures to roughly convert these estimates to life expectancy at birth (using available model life tables).

Currently, the big killers in Canada are no longer parasitic or infectious disease, but degenerative disease—in particular, cancer, heart disease, and cardiovascular disease. To a large extent, this shift in the pattern of disease dominance in Canada has been the result of success in reducing the risk of premature death. This has involved the gradual introduction of various public health measures, an improved standard of living, and the intervention of modern medicine and antibiotics.

Yet while this is true for the Canadian population overall, this is less the case for the Aboriginal population where the mortality profile continues to be somewhat distinct. From birth to old age, mortality rates are consistently higher for Aboriginal Canadians across most causes of death, and there are some particularly striking differences. Persistent differentials can be found among children and infants. For infants, part of the difference is due to post-neonatal mortality (beyond 28 days), which is suggestive of differences in lifestyle and socioeconomic conditions (INAC, 1999). As has become well established through epidemiological research, infant mortality is sensitive to variations in socioeconomic conditions and lifestyle, not to mention access to health-care resources. The health of Aboriginal Canadians has long been compromised by what Trovato (2001) calls the "geographic, socioeconomic and even social psychological marginalization of many Aboriginal communities."

The 1991–2001 Canadian Census Mortality Follow-up Study (which linked information from vital statistics with the census) has recently provided comprehensive information on the mortality experience of Canada's Aboriginal population, including information on cause of death (Tjepkema et al., 2009). Working with a 15 per cent sample of the national population (aged 25 and older), this study followed the mortality experience of a very large representative sample of Canadian adults over the 10-year 1991–2001 period (Wilkins et al., 2008a). This study included a representative sample of people who self-identified as Aboriginal in the census and/or reported that they held status under the Indian Act. This research confirms that First Nations peoples have a shorter life expectancy than other Canadians, whereas the Métis are also

disadvantaged, yet to a lesser extent. The study found that Aboriginal people, and status Indians in particular, continue to be more likely to die prematurely, true across a wide range of causes (see Figure 11.2). This is true whether it be the result of a heart attack or stroke, or due to some external cause—for example, a motor vehicle mishap or some other unintentional injury, such as a hunting accident or a drowning.

Since the age structure of the Aboriginal population is relatively young, it is useful to first standardize death rates prior to comparing populations; that is, to explicitly adjust for differences in age structure across populations before comparing the risk. For example, as First Nations have a much higher proportion of their population at younger ages, one would expect that they would proportionately have a higher number of deaths due to accidents. Similarly, one would expect that they would have a smaller proportion of deaths due to diseases that are typically associated with old age, such as cancer or heart disease. This is merely due to age structure, or the proportion of a population at risk to a specific type of death (i.e., younger people in general tend to be at a much greater risk of injuries and accidental death, whereas older persons are at a much greater risk of death due to degenerative causes).

After standardizing for difference in age structure, Figure 11.2 lists the six leading causes of death for the Aboriginal population, with systematic comparisons across population groups. In so doing, it demonstrates a simple fact: for both men and women, death rates as associated with the First Nations (status) are typically higher than among non-Aboriginal Canadians—with the exception of the age-standardized cancer rate among Aboriginal men. Whereas First Nations appear to be particularly disadvantaged, the Métis also experience higher rates, yet to a lesser extent, typically falling somewhere between First Nations and the non-Aboriginal population in this regard (Tjepkema et al., 2009).

Particularly striking in this context is the importance of "external causes"; Statistics Canada includes here all deaths caused by motor vehicle accidents, suicide, falls, drowning, among other external causes.

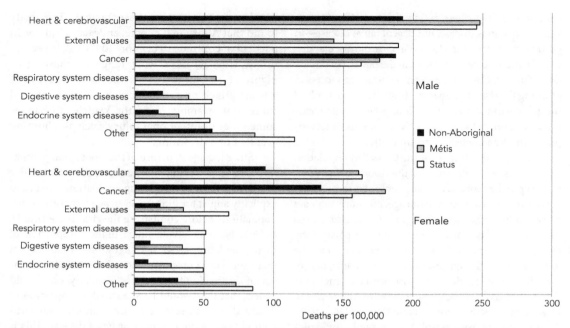

Figure 11.2 ▣ Age-Standardized Mortality Rates (Deaths per 100,000 person years) by Leading Causes of Death, for First Nations (Status), Métis, and Non-Aboriginal Populations, Aged 25 or Older at Baseline, Canada, 1991–2001[1]

Notes:

[1] See the full report by Tjepkema et al., 2009, for 95 per cent confidence intervals as associated with these sample-based estimates.

Source: Tjepkema et al., 2009.

For First Nations (status) men, deaths due to external causes are second only to deaths from heart and cerebrovascular disease, whereas among Métis men, external events are the third-most prevalent cause of death behind heart/cerebrovascular disease and cancer. The standardized rates on external causes for both First Nations men and women are roughly three times that of the non-Aboriginal population, whereas for the Métis, the standardized rates are roughly twice as high. Similarly, the disadvantage in terms of heart and cardiovascular disease is particularly pronounced, for both First Nations and Métis. Here, the age-standardized rates are reported to be about 25 per cent higher for men and about 50 per cent higher for women, all relative to the non-Aboriginal population.

With regard to the additional causes of death shown in Figure 11.2 (respiratory system, digestive system, and endocrine system diseases), without exception, the status group remains the most disadvantaged

(true of both men and women), while the Métis also consistently report higher age-standardized rates. The remaining category in Figure 11.2, "other" causes, serves as a residual category, including all other major types of deaths listed in vital statistics, including deaths that result from musculoskeletal system disease, genitourinary system disease, mental disorders, nervous system diseases, infectious diseases, and ill-defined conditions. Consistently across all of these major categories, without exception, the Aboriginal population experienced a higher age-standardized rate, with the status population typically experiencing the highest rates.

Survey research into the living conditions and health status of Aboriginal peoples has further demonstrated the difficulties that Aboriginal people experience compared to other Canadians. According to evidence from the First Nations and Inuit Regional Health Survey, Aboriginal Canadians are significantly more likely to report a range of chronic health conditions. Diabetes is especially problematic, in that it tends to be predominantly of the non-insulin-dependent type, with a relatively young age at onset and several complications, such as kidney disease and related endocrine and digestive diseases. As shown in Figure 11.2, the age-standardized rate of death due to both endocrine system disease and digestive system diseases is more than twice as high among the Métis and more than three times as high among First Nations (status) peoples relative to other Canadians. As suggested by Romaniuc (2000: 119), these relatively new illnesses among Canada's Aboriginal population (i.e., illnesses that were relatively rare in pre-contact populations) are due to factors that are at least partly "poor men's afflictions" that can be attributable to an underprivileged status. Economic marginalization has widely been linked to poor diet, obesity, inactivity, and smoking, all associated with higher levels of morbidity and mortality (Cooke et al., 2013). In addition, higher mortality is certainly linked, to an unclear extent, with inadequate housing conditions, water supply, and public sanitation, among other logistical difficulties (Romaniuc, 2000; INAC, 1999). As an example, Health Canada (2009) advised in October 2009 that there were 119 First Nations communities across Canada under a drinking-water advisory.

The higher age-standardized rates of death from heart disease and cardiovascular disease (stroke) are clearly linked to these disadvantages, as smoking, inactivity, and obesity are all strongly associated with education and socioeconomic status. While major killers of the past have now been virtually eliminated (e.g., smallpox, typhoid, scarlet fever), other types of diseases and risks associated with poverty continue to maintain a grip on Aboriginal peoples (e.g., heart disease, stroke, diabetes, lung cancer). The much higher rate of accidental death, a major issue relating to public safety, is a particularly serious problem in terms of years of life lost through its impact on younger adults. As estimated by Tjepkema and colleagues (2009), almost two thirds of the difference in terms of excess mortality between Aboriginal men and the general population can be traced to heart disease, circulatory-system diseases, and external causes

(accidents), whereas for women, differences across a wider range of factors are responsible, including cancer and endocrine system diseases (e.g., diabetes). It is important to note that the mortality contexts of First Nations people share many similarities with other Canadians who experience serious socioeconomic disadvantage (Tjepkema et al., 2009); in other words, much of the public health and mortality disparity can be explained by negative socioeconomic factors. To the extent that Aboriginal Canadians make gains in education, income, and occupation, one can anticipate continued improvements in population health and reduced mortality.

Fertility

The evidence available on the child-bearing behaviour of Aboriginal peoples early into the twentieth century suggests that fertility was high—although nowhere close to the theoretical maximum that could occur if a population had absolutely no constraints on fertility. As was the case in most pre-modern societies, a number of factors explain a fertility level below the theoretical maximum. For example, involuntary infecundity was likely much more common than in present-day populations, owing to untreated disease as well as the nutritional constraints imposed by often difficult ecological conditions. In addition, overall fertility levels were reduced by the practice of prolonged breastfeeding, often for as long as two years. While prolonged breastfeeding widened the spacing of births, it contributed to effective reproduction by maximizing the chances of infant survival.

As with the epidemiological transition, there is relatively little evidence to suggest that fertility levels changed extensively for Aboriginal peoples until the postwar period of the twentieth century. Estimates of crude birth rates (the number of births expressed per 1,000 persons) for First Nations peoples from 1900 to the 1940s suggest that the birth rate was about 40 births per 1,000 population (Norris, 2000). Among the Inuit, the crude birth rate was about 30 to 35 births per 1,000 in 1941, somewhat lower than one might expect for a pre-transitional population (Robitaille and Choinière,

1985). With this level of fertility, combined with high mortality, there was moderate growth. Among First Nations, the crude birth rate fell to about 22 births per 1,000 by the 1990s (Frideres, 1998), at a time when the overall rate was about 11 births per 1,000 (Statistics Canada, 2009b).

Whereas mortality declined in quite a pronounced and steady manner from the postwar period onward, fertility did not. The evidence currently available indicates that rather than dropping in the 1950s and '60s (as did mortality), Aboriginal fertility actually increased somewhat over this period. For example, the crude birth rate among First Nations climbed to about 50 births per 1,000 during the 1950s and '60s, and fertility among the Inuit climbed to even greater heights. Although highly accurate data are not available, there is some evidence to suggest that fertility may have peaked at extremely high levels, approaching the phenomenal rate of almost 60 births per 1,000. In explaining these levels, Romaniuc (1981, 2000) has argued that Aboriginal peoples experienced "a rise in natural fertility" owing to rapid social change and modernization. Again, this is contrary to what one might expect in light of classical transition theory, since modernization is expected to introduce a period of fertility decline, following closely on the heels of mortality decline.

During the 1950s and '60s, an increasing proportion of Canadians obtained comprehensive health care, which, in conjunction with the introduction of various social-assistance programs, had a major impact on both the quality of life and general state of population health. In contrast to the situation historically, where medical intervention was often very limited, the risks of premature death for both mother and child were reduced. For Aboriginal peoples, the very high rate of both neonatal and maternal mortality fell dramatically over this period. In addition, the likelihood of stillbirths, spontaneous abortions, and pregnancy accidents were also reduced. In view of these changes, one would expect a slight upturn in fertility. In providing a fuller explanation, Romaniuc (2000) also emphasizes a reduction in the likelihood of involuntary infecundity (owing to an improved diet and less disease) as well as changes in breastfeeding practices. During the 1950s and '60s, health-care professionals actively discouraged protracted breastfeeding among Aboriginal and non-Aboriginal women alike, which removed an important fertility-depressing factor in the absence of birth control. In addition, at least partly because of the geographic and social isolation of many First Nations communities, it is likely that many people did not have easy access to efficient means of birth control.

Although the birth rate went up in the 1950s, this situation was relatively short-lived, and more recently, fertility among Aboriginal peoples has dropped in quite a pronounced manner (see Figure 11.3). From the early 1960s onward, the fertility of Aboriginal Canadians has been on a downward trajectory. While the available time series on First Nations and the Inuit indicate that fertility has not fallen to levels as low as the below-replacement fertility of Canadians overall, by 2005, fertility rates had declined to 2.6 and 2.7 births per woman respectively, as measured by the total fertility rate. In many ways, such as in terms of the timing and level of child-bearing, the gap in fertility outcomes between Aboriginal and other Canadians has lessened. While rates have stabilized somewhat over recent years, it is possible that Aboriginal fertility could continue its downward trajectory into the future.

Demographic Differences by Aboriginal Group

As we previously indicated, Canada's Aboriginal population can be divided into four major groups: (1) First Nations peoples (status), (2) First Nations people (non-status), (3) Métis, and (4) Inuit. In light of their distinct histories, it is not surprising that there are some important differences across these subpopulations. Whereas all four groups have witnessed both mortality and fertility decline, the evidence suggests that this is true to a lesser extent among the Inuit and the status populations.

Since the non-status and Métis populations have the highest level of intermarriage with other Canadians, it is not surprising that their demographic behaviour also more closely resembles that of the

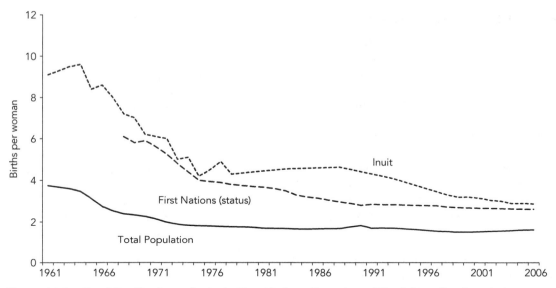

Figure 11.3 ▣ Total Fertility Rates for Inuit, First Nations (Status), and Total Canadian Populations, Canada, 1961–2005

Sources: Statistics Canada, 2008a; Nault et al., 1993; Norris et al., 1995; Loh et al., 1998; Robitaille and Choinière, 1985; Norris, 2000; Ram, 2004; Clathworthy, 2009; Malenfant and Morency, 2011.

larger population. Census data have shown that along a whole range of socioeconomic variables—e.g., education, labour-force participation, language(s) used, place of residence—the non-status population and the Métis have much more in common with other Canadians than do either status First Nations or Inuit peoples. More specifically, a majority of the Inuit continue to live in remote northern regions and a significant proportion of status First Nations peoples continue to live on reserves and in some of Canada's more remote settlements. In contrast, both the non-status population and the Métis are more likely to be living in urban areas or in non-Aboriginal communities and do not experience the same level of geographic and social segregation.

Past estimates of mortality and fertility have consistently ranked the Inuit as having the highest fertility and mortality. In turn, they are followed by the status population, who have higher fertility and mortality than either the Métis or non-status persons (Norris et al., 1995). According to a series of indirect estimates of fertility for 2001, the total fertility rate

was about 3.21 children per woman for the Inuit, 2.68 for status First Nations people, and 2.15 for the Métis (Ram, 2004). A similar ranking is suggested in the limited information available on the state of population health, where the Inuit and the status population are much more likely to be suffering from an illness, disability, or chronic disease.

The census data also indicate that fertility is lower among the Inuit who live in southern Canada than among those in the Far North (Robitaille and Choinière, 1985). Similarly, the mortality and fertility of First Nations people living on reserves is higher than among those living elsewhere (Loh et al., 1998). As a result, important differences can be found in the demographic dynamics of the Aboriginal populations, not only varying by Aboriginal group but also by place of residence. Among Inuit and First Nations peoples who have migrated from their home communities and more remote settlements into Canada's larger cities and towns, the demographic behaviour and experience more closely resemble that of the non-status and Métis populations.

Population Structure

In keeping with the differences in fertility, the age structure of Canada's Aboriginal population continues to be much younger than that of other Canadians. This implies a distinctive set of challenges and priorities. Age and sex influence the working of society in important ways, and Canadian society overall has witnessed important changes over recent decades; for example, its population pyramid is no longer triangular, but instead is becoming increasingly top heavy in shape. This is in contrast to the structure of the Aboriginal population, which has a large proportion of children and young adults (see Figure 11.4).

According to Statistics Canada's Population Estimates program, the median age in Canada in 2011 was 40 years; that is, 12.3 years older than that of the collective Aboriginal-identity populations, which was only 27.7 years (Statistics Canada, 2013ag, 2013ah). Median age is the age at which half the population is older and half is younger. Furthermore, the median age of both First Nations and Inuit peoples is even younger—about 26 among First Nations and only about 23 among Inuit (Statistics Canada, 2013ag). Among the Métis, the population is not quite as young (31), but still almost a decade younger than for Canada overall. It is not an exaggeration to suggest

that this situation has a fundamental impact on the social fabric of First Nations communities. A very young age structure (and a very high proportion of children) has important implications for many societal institutions, while potentially representing a major force for social change into the future.

Populations can also be classified as young or old, depending on the proportion of people at different ages. For example, while only 16.3 per cent of Canadians are under the age of 15, among the Aboriginal-identity populations, about 28 per cent is under 15. There are further differences among the various Aboriginal groups: the Inuit, for example, have 33.9 per cent of the population under the age of 15. At the other end of the age distribution, it is noteworthy that while about 1 in 7 Canadians (14.4 per cent) were 65 or older in 2011, about 1 in 17 (5.9 per cent) of Aboriginal Canadians were in this age group; among the Inuit, the figure was almost 1 in 25, or 4.1 per cent (Statistics Canada, 2013ag).

As we have mentioned in previous chapters, public-policy debates about the impact of age structure and population aging often cover the need to redirect public resources away from the young toward the old. The large major differences in population structure are an excellent example of how issues of broader public concern in Canada are often completely out of line with the needs of Canada's

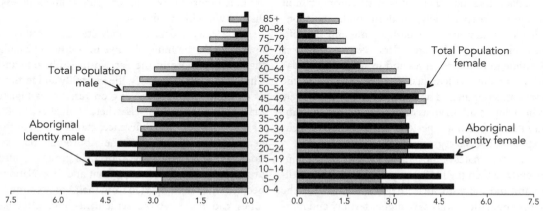

Figure 11.4 ▦ Percentage Distribution by Age Group and Sex of Total and Aboriginal-Identity Populations, Canada, 2011

Sources: Statistics Canada, National Household Survey, 2011; Statistics Canada, 2013c, 2013d.

Aboriginal peoples. The age structure of Aboriginal Canadians suggests a whole different set of priorities, from meeting the educational requirements of the young to assisting young adults and families as they attempt to establish themselves in the labour market or seek affordable housing. What is clear is that the role of the welfare state and government is very different in a young population than in a rapidly aging population. An acknowledgement of the underlying demographic situation of Aboriginal Canadians can assist in the development of informed policy.

Legislative Change as an Unconventional Growth Factor

With a history of higher-than-average fertility, the Aboriginal population is growing rapidly. As we pointed out above, this rapid growth is due to a wide range of factors, and not exclusively to high natural increase. For example, since populations are defined according to their cultural origins, the fact that people have become much more willing to report having Aboriginal ancestry is of fundamental importance in explaining past trends. Yet in defining Aboriginal persons according to legal status (status versus non-status), it is also necessary to consider an unconventional growth factor: namely, legislative reform.

The federal government has introduced revisions to the Indian Act, which has at times had an appreciable influence on the size and rate of growth of the First Nations population. A legislative change of some importance in this regard was made in 1985, when the Act was amended to restore Indian status to people (and their children) who had lost their status under certain provisions of previous legislation (Bill C-31). The amending of the Act has had a dramatic impact: 117,000 people were reinstated as "status" from 1985 through to 2007 (INAC, 2009). Since the total status population in the Indian register is about 868,206 persons, according to 2011 figures, this legislative change is fundamental in explaining the rate of growth and composition of this population.

Making up a significant portion of these reinstatements were First Nations women (non-status) and/or their offspring. Before 1985, a woman who married a person not registered under the Indian Act lost her registered status, whereas a man who did so not only retained his status, but he also conferred eligibility on his wife. Similarly, only the children of registered men would acquire Indian status. The reason for amending the Act was to eliminate the discriminatory status-inheritance rules prescribed in the Indian Act. A whole new series of status-inheritance rules were subsequently introduced, such that descent was no longer simply defined on a patrilineal basis. Most recently, the Indian Act has again been amended (Bill C-3), allowing for the potential reinstatement of not only the children but also the grandchildren of women who had previously lost status (AANDC, 2013). This legislation resulted from a court challenge in the British Columbia Court of Appeal (McIvor v. Canada), which subsequently came to force in 2011. The federal government has estimated that somewhere between 20,000 and 40,000 additional persons may become newly entitled to registration under this provision (INAC, 2009).

Although legislative reform has increased substantially the total size of the status population, the number of reinstatements declined in the 1990s, once most of those who could qualify had been reinstated. In this regard, it is useful to think through some of the long-term implications of Bill C-31, some of which are far from obvious. According to recent projections, for example, it is quite possible that this legislative change will actually reduce the total number of persons who qualify in the long term to be registered under the Indian Act, compared to what the situation would have been without this legislation (Clathworthy, 2003).

In examining this point further, we should consider how Bill C-31 has reformed the status-inheritance rules. Additional amendments to the Indian Act (specifically Section 6 of Bill C-31) contained descent rules that specified two separate ways in which one could acquire status under the revised Indian Act: under either section 6(1) or section 6(2). Children born to parents who were both currently status Indians acquired entitlement under Section 6(1). Children with just one parent registered under section 6(1) and a non-registered parent acquired entitlement under section

6(2). But people with one non-registered parent and one parent registered under section 6(2) became, from 1985 onward, not entitled to Indian status. Therefore, to the extent that status Indians produce children with non-status people, we can expect an increase in the number of children registered under section 6(2) as well as an increase in the proportion not eligible for Indian status at all in the long term.

According to research on the effects of out-marriage, by as early as 2010, perhaps a quarter of all births to status Indians living off reserve were no longer eligible for Indian status (INAC, 2000). With each subsequent generation, the proportion of all children who acquire entitlement under section 6(2) as opposed to section 6(1) is projected to increase. This implies that a growing proportion of births will also be liable not to qualify at all. Without further changes to the Indian Act, it is possible that over several generations, the majority of births will eventually not be eligible. That is what will happen if there is little change in the propensity of First Nations peoples to have children with unregistered people. Intrinsic to this legislation are inheritance rules that can lead to a substantial reduction in the size of the status population.

Conclusion

We began this chapter by observing that Aboriginal Canadians have not shared equally in the affluence of Canadian society. Unemployment remains very high, housing is often substandard, and health care and education are often inadequate. We charted here the demography of Aboriginal Canadians in terms of population size, fertility, and mortality, as well as some of the implications of recent trends. As there are several broader profiles available on the socioeconomic conditions of Aboriginal peoples (e.g., Ponting, 1997; Frideres and Gadacz, 2012), we intentionally narrowed our scope by sketching what is known of the demography of Canada's Aboriginal population.

In the broader context of our book, this chapter can be taken as a case study, focusing in greater detail on the demographic dynamics of a specific segment of Canada's population. In so doing, it demonstrates a few important points that are not always obvious when one scrutinizes the larger picture. One such point is the fact that the demographic behaviour and experience of Canadians is not always the same for all segments of the population. Whereas the overall demographic situation in Canada is such that fertility and mortality have fallen to unprecedented low levels (with the rate of natural increase steadily declining), Aboriginal peoples continue to have relatively high fertility and mortality (and a high rate of natural increase). Consequently, the age structure of Aboriginal peoples is also dramatically different from that of other Canadians, with important implications for both the internal dynamics of Aboriginal communities as well and the broader realm of public policy.

In addition, we have pointed out the enormous definitional challenges that demographers often face in conducting demographic research. The conventional practice by most users of census or demographic data is to accept the census definitions and categories and then to make sense of whatever data or time series are available. Nonetheless, it should be appreciated that most classifications used in the census and the federal statistical system are in fact socially constructed composites that have arisen from a variety of historical and contemporary influences. Definitions of Aboriginal have been incorporated into the legal infrastructure of Canadian society and have largely been imposed on Aboriginal peoples.

As indicated by Frideres and Gadacz (2012), the existence of the Indian Act implies a power relationship of sorts, in that the federal government has long been involved in defining exactly who might be considered a North American Indian in a legal sense. This has significant economic and political consequences, for some Aboriginal people consider themselves well represented by this definition whereas others do not. Consequently, the demographic future of the Aboriginal peoples holds much uncertainty, depending not only on demographic trends but also on various unconventional growth factors (such as legislative reform, intermarriage, and the degree to which cultural continuity is maintained from one generation to the next). Various socioeconomic, cultural, and political unknowns will have a direct impact upon how people self-identify in the future, perhaps even a larger impact than strictly demographic factors. This observation is certainly of concern to many Aboriginal elders, teachers, and political leaders, who have an interest in maintaining symbols of culture and group identity.

In presenting a very general overview of recent trends, we find reasons for both optimism and pessimism. Yet, if one takes a long-term view of the demographic development of Aboriginal peoples, the last half century might be best labelled as a period of demographic recovery.

Critical Thinking Questions

1. Discuss some of the definitional difficulties of conducting demographic research on Canada's Aboriginal population.
2. In policy debates, certain issues of broader public concern are often completely out of line with the needs of Aboriginal people in Canada. Provide a few examples of this and discuss how this is related to the underlying demographic dynamics of Aboriginal communities.
3. How has the demographic transition of the Aboriginal population been different from that of Canada's overall population?
4. Legislative reform has been identified as an unconventional growth factor in the demographic growth of the status Indian population in Canada. How is this the case?
5. Describe how the epidemiological patterns of Aboriginal peoples differ from those of other Canadians.
6. Canada's federal government has long been involved in defining who exactly is to be considered a North American Indian in a legal sense (i.e., who qualifies as a status Indian). What do you think of this situation?

Recommended Readings

Frideres, James, and Rene Gadacz. 2012. *Aboriginal Peoples in Canada*, Ninth Edition. Don Mills, ON: Pearson Canada. The ninth revised edition of Frideres and Gadacz's comprehensive overview of the socioeconomic conditions and political challenges facing Aboriginal peoples in Canada.

Long, David, and Olive Patricia Dickason, eds. 2011. *Visions of the Heart: Canadian Aboriginal Issues*. Don Mills, ON: Oxford University Press. This excellent edited collection provides in-depth research on issues facing Aboriginal peoples in Canada. The book provides an overview of the relationship between Aboriginal peoples and other Canadians throughout the country's history up to the present.

Romaniuc, Anatole. 2000. "Aboriginal population of Canada: Growth dynamics under conditions of encounter of civilizations." *The Canadian Journal of Native Studies* 20: 95–137. Romaniuc provides a very useful summary of past research and evidence on the demography of the Aboriginal population, including much of his own research, which carefully charts the demographic history of registered Indians throughout much of the twentieth century.

Trovato, Frank, and Anatole Romaniuc, eds. 2014. *Aboriginal Populations: Social Demographic and Epidemiological Perspectives*. Edmonton, AB: University of Alberta Press. This edited collection provides a valuable overview of Aboriginal demography, with a primary yet not exclusive emphasis on Canadian research.

White, J.P., J. Peters, P. Dinsdale, and D. Beavon, eds. 2010. *Aboriginal Policy Research, vol. 1–9*. Toronto: Thompson Educational Publishing. This collection includes 10 volumes of research by social scientists on Aboriginal peoples in Canada, including discussions of Aboriginal demography and the policy implications of recent trends.

Related Websites

www.aadnc-aandc.gc.ca. This site is maintained by Aboriginal Affairs and Northern Development Canada (AANDC). This federal department has primary, but not exclusive, responsibility for meeting the Canadian government's constitutional, treaty, political, and legal responsibilities to First Nations, Inuit, and northerners.

www.afn.ca. The website for the Assembly of First Nations, a political organization that represents registered Indians in Canada.

www.itk.ca. The website of Canada's national Inuit organization, the Inuit Tapiriit Kanatami.

www.metisnation.ca. The Métis National Council site, which has defined itself as the national representative of the Métis Nation in Canada, following the recognition of the Métis as a distinct people in the Constitution Act, 1982.

12 Population and the Environment

The Chapter at a Glance

- The global population surpassed 7 billion in late 2011, and signs of environmental stress and overconsumption of the world's resources are becoming increasingly manifest.
- While the global population growth rate has slowed since its peak in the 1960s, most projections suggest considerable population growth to come for several decades, up to perhaps 9 billion by mid-century. The accommodation of this demographic growth while promoting a sustainable use of the natural resources and minimizing environmental impact will be a major challenge to the global economy.
- The population of Canada comprises one half of 1 per cent of the global population. The country is 37th in population size, but it is the 10th-largest country in terms of total CO_2 emissions.
- Despite considerable debate as to the impact of population growth and its sustainability over the long term, there is no serious scientific opposition to the basic idea that "human numbers matter". The theoretical views range from the problems of growth in a limited world, to considering that the size of the population as "the ultimate resource."
- A particularly difficult issue is how to assign responsibility for the variety of environmental externalities—that is, the real overhead costs incurred in the production process that are borne not by particular producers or consumers, but by third parties, the larger community, or the environment.
- In a context of globalization and the increased internationalization of trade, what happens in other countries will matter to Canada, both demographically and economically. As a major exporter of natural resources and energy, Canada's economy and environment will be strongly affected by developments elsewhere.

Introduction

In October 2011, the United Nations marked, with considerable media fanfare, what was considered an important demographic milestone: the global population was estimated as reaching and surpassing the 7 billion mark. In the news conference that accompanied this event, the UN Population Fund executive director Babatunde Osotimehin noted that in many ways this can be considered a "good news" story (UNFPA, 2011). The unprecedented global population growth that has characterized the last century has largely been propelled by lower mortality, with people living longer and more children surviving. Yet as Osotimehin also emphasized, not everyone has benefited from this achievement, in a world marked by harsh inequalities, mounting evidence of environmental decline, and grave economic setbacks.

Of particular concern has been the pace of this population growth, as, for example, the global population reached the 6 billion mark only 13 years earlier in 1998 and 5 billion roughly 12 years prior to that in 1986. While the global population growth rate has slowed since its peak in the 1960s, most projections suggest considerable population growth for several more decades, up to perhaps 9 billion by mid-century.

There remains considerable concern about how this growth will place greater strains on the global environment and on socioeconomic and political stability (Smil, 2012). As observed by Bongaarts (2011), the simple fact that the world had managed to add 5 billion people since the 1920s and about 4 billion since 1960 without a complete breakdown of our natural environment is a tribute to human adaptability and creativity. Yet, as he also points out, signs of environmental stress from demographic growth and the consumption of the world's resources are becoming increasingly manifest.

Canada's population in 2014 of over 35.5 million is roughly equivalent to half of 1 per cent of this global total of over 7 billion people. With one of the lowest population densities in the world at only about 3.7 persons per square kilometre, some might suggest that Canada is arguably underpopulated by world standards, or, at the least, that Canada does not face an overpopulation problem (Saunders, 2012). In many ways, Canada has clear advantages, as there are few countries in the world as favoured, with a geographic land mass that is second in size only to Russia, and with abundance in terms of forests, arable land, mineral and energy resources, not to mention an estimated 20 per cent of the world's renewable freshwater. At least partially due to its population size, geography, and standard of living, Canada has consistently ranked among the more environmentally healthy countries in the world (Prescott-Allan, 2001; Yale Center for Environmental Law and Policy, 2005). Yet in a sense, Canadians may have a somewhat false sense of security. In reference to the concern across the wealthier nations like Canada with issues such as slowing population growth and population aging, the Canadian public intellectual Thomas Homer-Dixon (2006) has written, admittedly in a provocative manner, that in terms of future global population growth, "this is the world's real demographic crisis—one we are unprepared to meet because, when we consider the subject of population at all, we usually dwell rather myopically on falling birth rates within the developed world. The forgotten population bomb, in the meantime, has detonated, and the shock wave is about to hit our shores."

Despite considerable debate as to the impact of population growth and its sustainability over the longer term, there is no serious scientific opposition to the basic idea that "human numbers matter," albeit how they matter is a difficult issue to address. Clearly, concerns about rapid population growth are not new. Contemporary worries can draw a direct line of descent back to the eighteenth century, in Malthus's "An Essay on the Principle of Population as It Affects the Future Improvement of Society" (1798). It is worth noting that in the latter eighteenth century, when Britain's population was only about 10 million (relative to almost 65 million in 2012), Malthus concluded that the power of population growth was "indefinitely greater than the power in the earth to produce subsistence for man" (1798: Chapter 1). In his impoverished homeland at this time, Malthus was incapable of forecasting the enormous impact that both the industrial and scientific revolutions would have on living standards, nutrition, and state of population health. Yet through to the present, there continue to be many equally pessimistic neo-Malthusian thinkers who argue that overpopulation on a global scale is set to increase resource depletion to such a degree that it is not sustainable and that ecological collapse is almost inevitable, if not right around the corner (Ehrlich and Ehrlich, 2004; Hengeveld, 2012). On the other hand, there are others who counter with greater optimism, in suggesting that such an emphasis on overpopulation is perhaps somewhat misplaced, if not prone to exaggeration (Simon, 1999).

While considering in this chapter the relationship between population and the environment, we will provide a brief overview of some of these arguments, including the neo-Malthusian position, as well as opposing economistic arguments. Since it is not possible to consider Canada's situation in isolation from other countries, this chapter begins with the bigger picture—that is, a very brief overview of the history of population growth on a global scale as well as growth patterns that will likely characterize the world well into the twenty-first century. In drawing from the natural sciences, economics, and other related social sciences, we will consider arguments relating to the primary human driving forces of environmental change, including population growth, technological change, and consumption patterns. As we will discuss, the demand for resources and the associated impact on the environment in Canada is strongly linked with globalized demographic, economic, and political developments in all four corners of our planet. In other words, what happens elsewhere—for example, in such demographically giant places like China, India, and the United States—will have enormous implications not only for Canada, but also, more generally, for the global economy and environment.

A Short History of Global Population Growth

Physical anthropologists have documented that our genus has been around for fewer than 2.5 million years, whereas Homo sapiens became first identifiable in the fossil record in Africa only about 200,000 years ago (Lewin, 2005). Throughout most of our history, the impact of human numbers was relatively small and localized, as small bands of hunter-gatherers survived by eating a wide assortment of edible wild plants, insects, and seafood, while also hunting animals and sometimes tracking game over relatively large territories (Wells, 2010). At the time of the Neolithic (agricultural) revolution, which first occurred roughly 10,000 to 11,000 years ago, the global population has been estimated to be only about 6 million persons (Livi-Bacci, 2012). Yet due to the adaptability of early humans and their tendency to follow migrations in the tracking of game, this population of only a few million was very widely dispersed geographically, across Africa, Europe, much of Asia, Australia, and the Americas. For example, as we mentioned in Chapter 5, the original inhabitants of North America migrated across the Bering Strait from Asia during the Paleolithic era, at least 13,000 to 16,000 years ago (White, 2006).

The natural sciences, including biology, geology, atmospheric science, and physical geography, have all contributed to our understanding of environmental change, both prior to and after the emergence of Homo sapiens. From this collaborative work we have come to understand how all biological systems have a degree of equilibrium in terms of how they adapt to their environment, and we also know that all systems are continuously changing and reconfiguring themselves over thousands, if not millions, of years. From a standpoint of evolution, which includes a biospheric time scale of billions of years, the human species is fairly new relative to many other plant, insect, and animal species. Yet originally, due to the small numbers involved and the subsistence technologies available (e.g., a reliance on muscle power, arrows, spears, baskets), the environmental impact of human beings was typically small and localized. Yet from this, the human species gradually evolved to dominate other species, to such an extent that we are now predominant in terms of our effect on the planet's ecological systems.

Particularly important to this transition was the emergence of agriculture, which occurred independently in several distinct locations, including the Fertile Crescent in southwest Asia roughly 11,000 years ago, the Yangtze and Yellow River basins in China roughly 9,000 years ago, the New Guinea Highlands about 8,000 to 9,000 years ago, and in central Mexico and the Andean regions of South America roughly 4,000 to 5,000 years ago (Livi-Bacci, 2012). This basic change in the nature of subsistence and the technologies employed in producing food had an important demographic impact: horticulture and the domestication of animals allowed for a larger and more certain food supply, which in turn permitted larger settlements and greater population growth. Yet by contemporary standards, mortality remained very high and population growth remained relatively low (high mortality continued to largely offset high fertility). Sedentary life did not always improve living conditions, as the higher density associated with agriculture and the domestication of animals created problems with sanitation, poor nutritional variety, and the increased risk of communicable diseases.

Gradually, over thousands of years, populations increased and the environmental impact of human settlement expanded, such that by the beginning of the common era (2,000 years ago), global population was estimated to have increased to roughly 200 million. Over this period, mortality remained relatively high, yet populations slowly increased, as a sedentary, agricultural way of life became more widespread. It would take roughly another 1,200 years before the global population would again double (up to roughly the 400 million mark by 1200 CE) and another 400 years for global population to reach roughly 600 million by the year 1600 (see Figure 12.1). The environmental impact of this growth became more obvious as human settlements came to use resources much more intensively across large territories. For example, as wood remained a primary source of fuel and since land was needed for the growing of crops, large regions of human settlement across Europe, Northern Africa, and Asia witnessed major deforestation. Similarly, grasslands were often seriously overgrazed by pastoralists, whereas many agricultural societies seriously degraded the productivity of their soils through overuse and inappropriate irrigation practice (Harper and Fletcher, 2010).

While early contact with Europe led to a serious depopulating of the Americas, the pace of global population growth maintained itself through the seventeenth and eighteenth centuries, prior to accelerating and picking up some steam in the late eighteenth century. As with the emergence of agriculture, the Industrial Revolution of the nineteenth century produced a qualitatively and quantitatively different type of society, which in turn produced a whole series of cultural, scientific, and economic innovations. Industrialization, fuelled by the burning of coal, stoked the power of society to produce economic surpluses, with a much more extensive exploitation of physical and biotic resources, while simultaneously

having a dramatic impact on the environment. The good-news story in this context was that mortality was declining across Europe, with improved nutrition and public health. Yet natural systems were also increasingly being altered and degraded, as growth in human numbers was having an unprecedented impact on the earth's biodiversity and the environs around human settlements, for both natural and built-up environments (Pimm et al., 1995).

While the precise timing of the demographic transition is known to have varied considerably with respect to both date of onset and duration across different countries, the later eighteenth century is generally identified as a period whereby this transition first moved forward in Europe and North America with important mortality improvements. Public services such as urban sewerage, water systems, and garbage disposal, not to mention the eventual introduction of antibiotics and other medical advances, were to dramatically reduce infant mortality and improve the state of population health. Mortality rates fell well before birth rates, with important consequences for population growth during the demographic transition. While for tens of thousands of years, the population of the world grew very slowly, with periods of decline at least in specific regions, the world has seen the global population mushroom over the last 200 years from about 1 billion at the beginning of the Industrial Revolution to over 7 billion early in the twenty-first century.

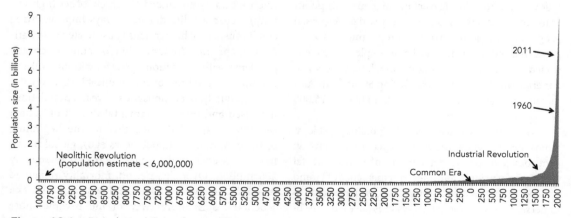

Figure 12.1 ▣ Population Growth over History

Sources: Livi-Bacci, 2012; United Nations Population Division, 2013.

Current Global Population Growth

In 2012, the Population Reference Bureau (PRB) estimated a global rate of population growth of about 1.2 per cent annually. This is near identical to the average rate of increase, as documented for Canada over the last several years, at roughly 1.1 per cent. Yet while much of Canada's growth is due to international migration, all of such reported global growth is obviously due to natural increase (more births than deaths). While for Canada this implies a natural increase in 2012 of only about 130,000 persons (with an additional 267,000 due to international migration), the estimated global population increase is staggering: in 2012 alone, the world experienced an estimated 140.5 million births and 56.3 million deaths, leaving for a natural increase of 84.3 million persons. This is equivalent to adding a population roughly the size of Germany to the global population in one year.

Another way to foreground the magnitude of this growth is to consider the fact that on a *daily basis* in 2012, the PRB estimated that there were roughly 385,000 births (about 4 births per second) and 154,100 deaths (roughly 2 deaths per second), for a total daily increase of 230,900 persons (PRB, 2014). In other words, on a typical day, a population nearly equivalent to the city of Regina, Saskatchewan, is added to the global population (CMA 2012 estimate: 226,300 persons). In less than a month (26 days), a population roughly equivalent to the Toronto CMA is added (2012 estimate: 5,941,500 persons), whereas in just over 5 months, a population roughly equivalent to Canada's 35.5 million is added. Within five to six years, the global population will increase by a number on par with all of North America (the United States, Canada, and Mexico combined), which had a 2012 population of about 465 million. This global population continues to grow at a rapid pace, as many countries are still in the second stage of the demographic transition (i.e., death rates have fallen more rapidly than birth rates, with the resultant natural increase).

Most obviously the current rate of global population growth cannot continue as is, nor is this expected. The UN (2011a) approximates that 64 out of the world's 195 countries have below-replacement fertility, with a disproportionate share situated in Europe, yet also China and many of its neighbours, including Japan, South Korea, Macau, and Hong Kong. The global fertility rate has dropped by almost one half over recent decades, from an average of about 4.5 births per woman in the early 1970s to about 2.5 in 2011. As declining fertility has characterized all major world regions, most demographers expect further fertility decline over the next half century. This in turn is expected to lead to a substantial slowing of population growth. Table 12.1 summarizes the UN projections across major world regions for 2050 and 2100, as well as figures on past population and its distribution for 1950, 1980, and 2011 (United Nations, 2011c). While North America (Canada and the United States in this context) are projected to maintain about 5 per cent of the global population, Europe's share is expected to decline further. While 21.6 per cent of the world's population lived in Europe in 1950, this has declined to only 10.6 per cent in 2011, and is projected to fall further to about 7.7 per cent by mid-century. In contrast, Africa had only 9.1 per cent of the global population in 1950, currently has about 15 per cent, and is projected to have a 23.6 per cent share by mid-century.

There is considerable uncertainty with regard to future growth, given the difficulties involved in forecasting the future path of fertility. The UN's median variant projects a global population of 9.3 billion by 2050, relative to 8.1 billion for its low variant and 10.6 billion for its high variant. The low variant assumes a global fertility rate declining to 1.71 children per woman by 2050, which is roughly one half of a child below the medium variant (at 2.17 births by 2050), and almost a full child below the high variant (at 2.64 children by 2050). A comparison of the three projections allows us to appreciate the importance of future fertility decline: a half child less implies a global population that is more than a billion less than the median variant by 2050, whereas a half child more implies a population of about a billion greater than the median variant. If we consider the medium-growth variant as the most realistic, the world's population is still expected to add an additional 2.3 billion over the 2010–50 period (i.e., an increase that is not inconsequential, as it is close to the current population totals for China and India combined). Even with the low variant, with a fertility rate that falls well below replacement, the world's population is expected to grow by an additional billion over the

Table 12.1 ▣ Population Size and Distribution of the World and Major Areas, 1950, 1980, 2011, 2050, and 2100

Major area	Population (millions)			Population in 2050 (millions)				Population in 2100 (millions)			
	1950	1980	2011	Low	Medium	High	Constant	Low	Medium	High	Constant
World	2,532	4,453	6,974	8,113	9,306	10,614	10,943	6,177	10,125	15,805	26,844
More developed regions	811	1,081	1,240	1,158	1,312	1,478	1,252	830	1,335	2,037	1,090
Less developed regions	1,721	3,372	5,734	6,955	7,994	9,136	9,691	5,347	8,790	13,768	25,754
Least developed countries	196	394	851	1,517	1,726	1,952	2,434	1,772	2,691	3,954	12,430
Other less developed countries	1,525	2,978	4,883	5,437	6,268	7,184	7,257	3,576	6,100	9,813	13,325
Africa	230	483	1,046	1,932	2,192	2,470	2,997	2,378	3,574	5,198	14,959
Asia	1,403	2,638	4,207	4,458	5,142	5,898	5,908	2,624	4,596	7,522	9,530
Europe	547	693	739	632	719	814	672	405	675	1,056	482
Latin America and the Caribbean	167	362	597	646	751	869	863	385	688	1,154	1,252
Northern America	172	254	348	396	447	501	444	342	526	777	512
Oceania	13	23	37	49	55	62	60	42	66	98	110

Percentage Distribution:				Population in 2050 (%)				Population in 2100 (%)			
	1950	1980	2011	Low	Medium	High	Constant	Low	Medium	High	Constant
More developed regions	32.0	24.3	17.8	14.3	14.1	13.9	11.4	13.4	13.2	12.9	4.1
Less developed regions	68.0	75.7	82.2	85.7	85.9	86.1	88.6	86.6	86.8	87.1	95.9
Least developed countries	7.7	8.8	12.2	18.7	18.5	18.4	22.2	28.7	26.6	25.0	46.3
Other less developed countries	60.2	66.9	70.0	67.0	67.4	67.7	66.3	57.9	60.2	62.1	49.6
Africa	9.1	10.8	15.0	23.8	23.6	23.3	27.4	38.5	35.3	32.9	55.7
Asia	55.4	59.2	60.3	54.9	55.3	55.6	54.0	42.5	45.4	47.6	35.5
Europe	21.6	15.6	10.6	7.8	7.7	7.7	6.1	6.6	6.7	6.7	1.8
Latin America and the Caribbean	6.6	8.1	8.6	8.0	8.1	8.2	7.9	6.2	6.8	7.3	4.7
Northern America	6.8	5.7	5.0	4.9	4.8	4.7	4.1	5.5	5.2	4.9	1.9
Oceania	0.5	0.5	0.5	0.6	0.6	0.6	0.5	0.7	0.7	0.6	0.4

Sources: Population Division of the Department of Economic and Social Affairs of the United Nations Secretariat, 2011; United Nations, 2011d.

next half century, which demonstrates the population momentum inherent in the world's current age structure.

The Malthusian Argument

The political economist Thomas Malthus (1766–1834) was the first to develop a systematic theory of population change and its relation to economic conditions. In publishing his "Essay on the Principle of Population" (1798), Malthus produced what is one of the most influential works ever to be written on the consequences of population growth. His central concern was that population had a tendency to grow faster than food supply. Subsequent writers have called this a *Malthusian trap* (see Figure 12.2). The consequence would be a deficit in the food supply, widespread poverty, and misery—or what Malthus coined the *positive checks* of high mortality: food shortages, famine, disease, and conflict. Particularly in his early writings, Malthus did not hold out much hope of finding a solution to the problem. If, for some reason, the food supply increased more than the population did, people would probably marry earlier and have more children, so there would eventually be even more people living in poverty. He feared that if the conditions of the poor were somehow improved, there would be even more population growth and, thus, a larger problem in the longer term.

Subsequent developments in agriculture and trade have produced much more increase in food supply than Malthus had foreseen. However, the concern that Malthus had with questions of food supply, has been replaced with a concern about the damage to the environment from the by-products of our affluent society: polluted air and water, the concentration of carbon dioxide and other greenhouse gases in the atmosphere, increased threats to the planet's biodiversity, and increasing worries relating to the potential for climate change. In effect, the concerns are less with the number of people who can be fed over the shorter term, and more with consequences for health and mortality of a changing environment over the longer term.

The IPAT Equation

In the early 1970s, Ehrlich and Holdren (1971) formulated what has come to be known as "the IPAT equation." It was proposed as a starting point for investigating the impact of human populations on the environment. A proper understanding of any country's environmental record would have to begin with current population size and pace of population growth.

These interrelationships have been summarized in the form of the IPAT equation, or *impact equation*:

$$\text{Impact (I)} = \text{Population (P)} \times \text{Affluence (A)} \times \text{Technology (T)}$$

Impact (*I*) refers to the amount of a particular kind of environmental degradation (e.g., the amount of sewage that is produced or the amount of smog that is released into the atmosphere). *Population* (*P*) is merely the size of a population, whether we speak of a specific city, region, or country. *Affluence* (*A*) refers to the per capita level of affluence, whereas *Technology* (*T*) entails the extent to which the technology used to produce this affluence is environmentally friendly or

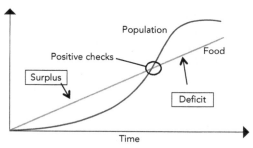

Figure 12.2 ▣ The Malthusian Trap

damaging. The basic idea of the equation is that the impact is a function of the multiplication of population size times per capita income times the technological efficiency of production vis-à-vis environmental by-products.

As an example, the utility of the IPAT equation can be demonstrated by comparing the environmental record of Canada with the United States. Let us consider the greenhouse gas (GHG) emissions produced by the two countries. Very briefly, it is recognized that the US population is roughly nine times that of Canada's—at 320 million relative to about 35 million in 2012 (United States Bureau of the Census, 2013). In keeping with US and Canadian population proportions, the expectation is that the United States should have roughly nine times the environmental impact (*I*), to the extent that we are comparing countries with a comparable standard of living (*A*), economic infrastructures, and patterns of energy use (*T*). And consistent with expectations, the United Nations Framework Convention on Climate Change (UNFCCC, 2009) has estimated that the United States produces roughly 9.5 times the amount of GHGs that Canada emits—at 6,702 million metric tons CO_2 equivalent relative to 702 million metric tons CO_2 in Canada. While the United States is frequently criticized as the world's second-largest producer of GHGs (responsible for about 20 per cent of global emissions), on a per capita basis, Canada has almost the same level of environmental impact (responsible for about 2 per cent of emissions).

While this application reminds us as to the primary importance of population size in explaining environmental impacts (the United States has approximately nine times the population whereas it also has roughly nine times the environmental impact), if we were to draw further comparisons with other leading producers of GHGs, the relative importance of the other components in IPAT become more obvious (see Table 12.2). For example, while China produces more GHGs than any other country, followed by the United States and India (a distant third), if we shift our emphasis to per capita emissions, a very different picture emerges. More specifically, while Canada produces 16.1 metric tons of CO_2

emissions per person annually, China only produces 6 tons per capita. The world's second-largest producer, the United States, emits more than does Canada (16.9 tons per capita), whereas the world's third-largest emitter, India, produces significantly less than any other of the large GHG producers, at only 1.5 tons per capita.

Dietz and Rosa (1997) have emphasized that it is not so much *P* alone that matters, but the *P* × *A*, or the multiplier of population and per capita consumption. More generally, it must be noted that the IPAT equation is but a simplistic expression of the role of population, affluence, and technology in terms of environmental impact. For instance, it is not only per capita affluence that counts, but whether this affluence is achieved in ways that are more or less environmentally friendly (e.g., comparing types of consumption that use more or less energy). A key question is the technology and the associated impact per unit of affluence. Note that there are also indirect effects here, with more affluence probably also helping an economy to generate more environmentally friendly technology. A larger population may also be more efficient in developing technologies that have less impact. While it is important to appreciate these indirect effects that may work in the opposite direction (less impact associated with higher affluence and larger population), we are probably safe to say that the direct effects are stronger than the indirect effects, with more population and affluence having more detrimental impact.

The technology component can be considered fundamental in this context, in recognizing that some societies are more successful than others in *decoupling* or *breaking of the link* between "environmental bads" and "economic goods." For example, while population increase and economic growth can both be considered driving factors behind the increased production of GHG emissions, several European countries have managed both to grow demographically (albeit less than Canada) and economically, with some success, while moving away from this reliance upon fossil fuels. For example, as demonstrated by Kerr and Mellon (2012), Sweden, a country that is similar to Canada in terms of its economy and level of affluence, produced in 2009 less than one third of

Table 12.2 ▨ Total Emissions of CO$_2$ by Country (Top 20), 2012

Country	Total CO$_2$ emissions in kilotons[1]	% of global emissions	Per capita (metric tons/person)
1 China	8,106,430	25.09	6.0
2 United States	5,270,422	16.31	16.9
3 India	1,830,938	5.67	1.5
4 Russia	1,781,720	5.51	12.4
5 Japan	1,259,058	3.90	9.9
6 Germany	788,321	2.44	9.5
7 Korea, South	657,093	2.03	13.6
8 Iran	603,586	1.87	8.1
9 Saudi Arabia	582,670	1.80	21.4
10 Canada	550,829	1.70	16.1
11 Brazil	500,228	1.55	2.6
12 United Kingdom	498,877	1.54	8.0
13 South Africa	473,165	1.46	9.2
14 Indonesia	456,210	1.41	1.9
15 Mexico	453,833	1.40	3.8
16 Australia	420,633	1.30	18.8
17 Italy	385,813	1.19	6.4
18 France	364,538	1.13	5.8
19 Spain	312,442	0.97	6.8
20 Taiwan	307,147	0.95	13.2

Note: [1]On a global scale, CO$_2$ emissions are responsible for roughly 75 per cent of all GHG emissions.
Source: United Nations, 2013a; EIA, 2013.

Box 12.1 ▨ Taking a Closer Look at Canada's Record on GHG Emissions

Following the guidelines set out by the United Nations Framework Convention on Climate Change (1992), Canada on an annual basis carefully documents a national inventory of human-induced greenhouse gas (GHG) emissions from various sources (industry, transportation, fuel combustion, and agriculture) as well as removals from sinks (most of Canada's land mass is covered by forest, with only the southernmost portions used for agriculture and other land uses). An upward trend in GHGs characterized Canada between 1990 and 2007, with an estimated increase of fully 21 per cent over that time frame. This is higher than in most other developed countries—for example, it is almost twice the increase estimated for the OECD overall, at about 12–13 per cent, and dramatically higher than estimates for the OECD Europe, up by only 2–3 per cent (Kerr and Mellon, 2012). Underlying this Canadian upward trend in GHGs is a phenomenal growth in CO$_2$ emissions associated with the consumption of fossil fuels, which continues to be by far the single most

Continued

important type of GHG, in Canada as elsewhere. By 2013, there were only a select few countries in the world that produce higher emissions on a per capita basis than Canada, with many of these being the relatively small yet extremely rich oil-producing states of the Middle East (Qatar, Kuwait, the United Arab Emirates, Saudi Arabia, Bahrain). As with the United States, Canada's carbon footprint is large and, for a variety of reasons, there has been a relative lack of progress over recent decades in reducing the size of this footprint.

Canada has clearly failed to respect some of its most important international commitments, including the Kyoto Protocol, which committed the country to achieving total GHG emissions at 6 per cent below 1990 levels by 2012. While the federal government has since withdrawn Canada from Kyoto, the government has more recently signed on to the non-binding Copenhagen Accord, which commits Canada to reduce its GHG emissions by 17 per cent below 2005 levels by 2020. While emissions declined somewhat over the 2007–9 period (partially due to the economic recession of 2008–9), it started to climb again, through to 2013. While emissions remain lower than their peak in 2007, overall emissions must still fall by about 15 per cent over the next 7 years in order to reach the Copenhagen 2020 target, which is still almost 10 per cent higher than the abandoned Kyoto target (see Figure 12.3). And while emissions have grown significantly in the North American context, many countries in Europe have managed to not only meet their Kyoto targets (with emissions below 1990 levels) but also to bypass such targets. On the other hand, emissions in the rest of the world have increased sharply—especially in China and in other countries with emerging, sizable economies (Jos et al., 2012).

While there are many different gases that also contribute to the greenhouse effect (including methane, nitrous oxide, ozone, halocarbons, perfluorocarbons, and other halogenated compounds), CO_2 emissions are by far the most important, responsible for about 80 per cent of all GHGs (Environment Canada, 2011a). In terms of documenting why GHG emissions have risen over recent decades, a primary driver has been a consistent increase in CO_2 emissions from the burning of fossil fuels. Kerr and Mellon (2012) have applied the IPAT framework in an effort to better understand Canada's record on CO_2 emissions, relative to other more developed countries (i.e., across many of the more developed economies of the OECD).

While Canada witnessed sustained population growth over recent decades (putting it at a distinct disadvantage in meeting its international commitments relative to the slower-growing populations of OECD Europe), it also has witnessed sustained gains in terms of economic growth, as measured by GDP per capita, and, perhaps most importantly, a continued increase in its demand for energy—fossil fuels in particular. While there has been some progress in reducing the energy intensity of economic activities over recent years (i.e., in generating technologies that require less energy input in obtaining the same output), Canada has actually lagged behind most other more developed countries on this front and remains one of the most energy-intensive economies in the world—second highest in the OECD (Kerr and Mellon, 2012). While there are many factors responsible for this, Canada's particularly energy-intensive industrial structure is certainly relevant, as is the importance of its trade relations with the United States, and the importance of the primary and resource sectors of its economy relative to most developed nations.

There is little disputing the fact that North Americans use a great deal of energy, as they tend to purchase less-fuel-efficient vehicles and drive them more, live in larger homes and heat them more, and work in buildings that use substantially more energy than do Europeans (Environment Canada, 2006). In terms of

Canada's particularly heavy energy use, at least part of this situation relates to the simple fact that its climate is among the coldest in the OECD, requiring far more heating days than most other countries, a situation shared by only a few of the northern Scandinavian countries. In addition, Canada has a particularly large land mass, combined with low overall population density, which serves to increase the demand for energy in the transportation of both people and goods. The distances travelled in moving both freight and people tend to far surpass those observed in most smaller-sized European countries (MKJA, 2005). In turn, the transportation sector—both personal and freight—is responsible for a large proportion of Canada's energy use, which was reported at roughly 29 per cent of total secondary energy use in 2007 (Natural Resources Canada, 2010).

Other economic and political factors are relevant to explaining Canada's high energy use, including the globalization of trade and the implementation of the North American Free Trade Agreement (NAFTA). Canada has become

increasingly a part of the continental energy market, with high levels of foreign ownership and constrained governmental policy flexibility. On a deeper level, in both Canada and the United States, energy use remains very high in an energy-policy context of relatively low taxes (in contrast to OECD Europe) and low energy prices. For example, the International Energy Association (IEA, 2014) produces summary statistics on the cost of energy, allowing for systematic comparisons across the OECD. In drawing international comparisons, the price of gasoline has been lower in Canada than in any other OECD country (with the exception of the United States and Mexico) for well over a decade. Similarly, Canadian electricity prices have consistently been second lowest, behind only Norway, while the price of natural gas for Canadian households and industry has consistently been second lowest, behind just Finland. In the North American context, lower taxes on energy (relative to elsewhere in the OECD) are responsible for relatively low prices for both consumers and industry, which have arguably undercut some of the potential for

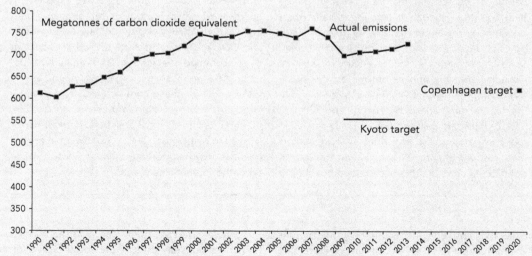

Figure 12.3 ▣ Greenhouse Gas Emissions in Canada, 1990–2013

Source: Environment Canada, 2014.

Continued

conservation, with fewer incentives to increase efficiencies. In reviewing IEA data, countries with higher prices tend to consume less, an observation often voiced by environmentalists in advocating carbon taxes in order to reduce environmental impact.

In this context, governments and industry have actively encouraged growth in the Canadian energy sector, with investments producing an expanding supply of fossil fuels, for both domestic consumption and export. Of particular importance in Canada, for example, have been ongoing efforts to expand access to major reserves of bitumen in the Alberta oil sands, with total production already reaching a height of 47 per cent of Canadian petroleum production in 2007 (Government of Alberta, 2008). Oil sands extraction is more environmentally damaging than conventional crude oil, with much higher energy demands and significant water requirements in moving from the well to the pump. Fossil fuels are used in extracting and upgrading bitumen reserves into synthetic crude, with about one barrel of oil equivalent of energy required to produce roughly five to six barrels of oil for the market (National Energy Board, 2006). Canada's willingness to satisfy burgeoning North American energy demands (as now the largest exporter of crude oil to the United States) has only added to the energy intensity of Canadian industry and compromised the country's ability to meet its climate-change commitments. As summarized by Harper and Fletcher (2010), there are few regulatory limits on fossil-fuel consumption and emissions in those sectors most responsible for GHGs, including transportation (25 per cent), fossil-fuel development (19 per cent), electricity generation (17 per cent), and industrial activities (15 per cent).

Under NAFTA, Canada applies open-market principles and is obliged to trade its major energy resources without excessive regulation. The country is also noted for having a particularly energy-intensive industrial structure relative to most OECD countries. For many energy-intensive commodities, Canada produces far more than its population consumes, with a large proportion of production being oriented toward export. Canada currently produces over 10 per cent of the world supply of its aluminum, 5 per cent of its copper, 9 per cent of its gypsum, 12 per cent of its nickel, 15 per cent of its wood pulp, 23 per cent of its newsprint, and nearly 30 per cent of the world's supply of potash fertilizers—all for a country that has less than 0.5 per cent of the global population (Environment Canada, 2006). As all of these industries are particularly energy intensive, production of these commodities contributes significantly to Canada's overall record of energy intensity. With a substantial proportion of these commodities produced for export, Canada differs in a major way from most OECD countries as a net exporter of energy and natural resources rather than a net importer. The heavy energy demands and resultant CO_2 emissions associated with producing these commodities for export continue to be associated with Canada, regardless of the eventual market for these commodities. This plays a large part in why Canada's record is so poor in meeting its international emissions commitments relative to many other OECD countries that are, in contrast, major importers of energy, not to mention other primary resources.

Canada's CO_2 emissions per capita (4.48 metric tons per capita relative to 15.46 metric tons). Figure 12.4 demonstrates this contrast by juxtaposing GDP per capita across OECD countries for 2009, with a ranking of countries according to CO_2 emissions on a per capita basis.

While GDP/Population (the *A* in the IPAT equation) does not fully capture the social dimension of environmental impact, it is typically considered a critical determinant of environmental degradation—high rates of consumption tend to be associated with a large ecological footprint and rapid rates of resource use and

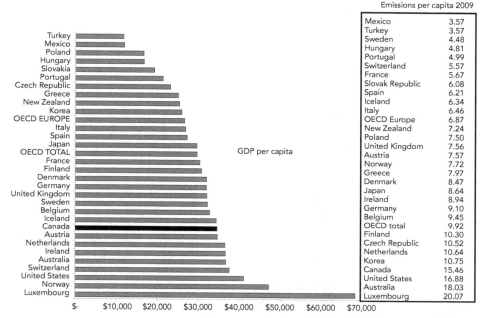

Emissions per capita 2009	
Mexico	3.57
Turkey	3.57
Sweden	4.48
Hungary	4.81
Portugal	4.99
Switzerland	5.57
France	5.67
Slovak Republic	6.08
Spain	6.21
Iceland	6.34
Italy	6.46
OECD Europe	6.87
New Zealand	7.24
Poland	7.50
United Kingdom	7.56
Austria	7.57
Norway	7.72
Greece	7.97
Denmark	8.47
Japan	8.64
Ireland	8.94
Germany	9.10
Belgium	9.45
OECD total	9.92
Finland	10.30
Czech Republic	10.52
Netherlands	10.64
Korea	10.75
Canada	15.46
United States	16.88
Australia	18.03
Luxembourg	20.07

Figure 12.4 ▣ GDP Per Capita and CO_2 Per Capita (Metric tonnes) for OECD Countries, 2009

Source: OECD, 2010; IEA, 2014; Kerr and Mellon, 2012.

waste production (Rees 1992). Yet while Canada is by global standards a relatively affluent country, other societies of comparable affluence have succeeded in reducing their environmental impact (I). It is clearly necessary, then, to move beyond population (P) and affluence (A) in the explanation of Canada's outlier status on CO_2 emissions. While the EIA (US Energy Information Administration, 2013) ranks Canada 10th overall among countries in terms of total GHG emissions (behind much larger countries, demographically speaking, including China, the United States, Russia, Germany, Japan, and India), we note that for total population, Canada currently ranks 37th among nations (United Nations, 2013c). In other words, there are 27 other countries with a larger population than Canada, yet they produce fewer emissions with a lesser environmental impact in terms of GHGs.

Human Ecology

Human ecology, that is, the study of how humans interact with their environment, is a broad perspective that embraces the subject of the causes and

consequences of population processes. The study of ecology is essentially the study of categories of organisms, or populations, in their environment—of how those populations gain their sustenance from the environment and, in so doing, how they introduce certain changes to that environment. The term *population*, then, can be used for species other than humans. This reminds us of the similarity of humans to other species, each of which needs to find its sustenance and niche in the environment.

In considering human ecology, however, we must take into account two major factors that do not apply to other species. In gaining their sustenance from the environment, human populations employ organization and technology. The ways in which humans organize themselves, and the technologies they develop, are central to understanding how they adapt to and influence the environment.

The dynamic interplay of these four basic considerations (population, organization, environment, and technology—POET for short) presents an overarching picture of population dynamics (see Figure 12.5). Each factor influences the others. For instance, more

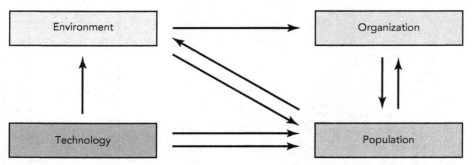

Figure 12.5 ▣ Human Ecology

rapid population growth has historically tended to follow the introduction of new forms of organization or new developments in technology. Thus, the urban revolution involved a new way of organizing human settlements that permitted considerable growth in population. Similarly, the Industrial Revolution involved major changes in technology that fostered population growth; particularly important in this regard were developments that allowed resources to be extracted more efficiently from the environment.

Changes in the environment, such as climate change, can also produce opportunities or hazards for population. Some observers have argued that population pressure on the environment together with technological developments can bring about environmental changes (as, for example, has the intensive use of fossil fuels) and, thus, changes in the potential for sustenance. Conversely, difficulties imposed by the environment can induce a population to find new forms of organization and technology that will enable it to survive and prosper—a process commonly known as adaptation.

The human ecology perspective highlights the fact that both benefits and problems can result from large numbers of people. Population growth can be seen as reducing average well-being because resources have to be shared with more people. In this view, larger numbers simply mean more competition for scarce resources. With higher numbers come various forms of crowding, which place people at a relative disadvantage in the competition for resources. In another sense, however, larger numbers could mean greater strength, in that there are more people to solve the problems. With more scientists, for instance, better and more efficient technologies might be developed to compensate for scarcities in natural resources. Crowding can also reinforce positive factors—larger cities, for example, offer more amenities of various kinds. In effect, this alternative assessment contrasts with the Malthusian view that, with more people, there are more problems. In a more open-ended manner, the impact of population is an empirical issue, potentially producing both opportunities, and hazards.

Box 12.2 ▣ How Large Is Our Ecological Footprint?

In 1996, the Canadian population ecologist William Rees first published the book *Our Ecological Footprint: Reducing Human Impact on the Earth*, co-authored with his then Ph.D. student, Mathis Wackernagel. Their book introduced the concept of an *ecological footprint*, a widely used measure of environmental impact that has had a large impact on the field of environmental studies. Currently, the ecological-footprint concept is frequently used by environmental scientists to more systematically monitor ecological resource use and the demand that human societies place on the earth's systems. Perhaps due to what Rees (2013) refers to as the term's "metaphorical power," it has also had wide circulation in the general public, as many environmentalists, educators, and public commentators have used the ecological-footprint concept to discuss the human impact on the environment.

Briefly, the ecological footprint can be understood as a measure of the demand that human activity puts on the biosphere. As more recently defined by Ewing and colleagues (2010: 8), the ecological footprint more precisely "measures the amount of biologically productive land and water area required to produce all the resources an individual, population, or activity consumes, and to absorb the waste they generate, given prevailing technology and resource management practices." Ecological-footprint analysis (EFA) has been applied on a variety of levels (globally, nationally), but also with a more localized focus on the regional resource issues of specific provinces (Wilson, 2001; Stechbart and Wilson, 2010) and Canadian cities (Wilson and Anielski, 2005). As affluence and wealth are characteristically associated with a larger footprint, the average Canadian has a larger footprint than is the case for people of most other countries. In a similar manner, the average high-income Canadian typically has a much larger ecological footprint than somebody with a low income, just as more prosperous regions typically have a larger footprint than regions with comparable populations that are more economically depressed.

Rees's former student Wackernagel has been credited for continuing to refine this methodology, while establishing the Global Footprint Network, an international group of environmental scientists with the intent purpose of widening the application of this concept and improving its scientific rigor (Wackernagel et al., 2005). The ecological footprint is usually expressed in terms of what are called *global hectares*—hectares with

world-average biological productivity. The calculations obtained for specific countries and regions are now much more detailed, with a more refined accounting of differences in the biological productivity of specific lands. More specifically, the biological productivity of croplands in one country might be quite different from that in another, just as the productivity of lands in different regions of the same country can vary considerably. In the Canadian context, for example, compare the biological productivity of the rich fertile soils of southern Saskatchewan with those of eastern Ontario, or, for that matter, the much less fertile lands associated with the boreal forests of the more northern reaches of the country.

These estimates also consider differences in the demand for ecological services in terms of six major land-use types (cropland, grazing land, forest land, carbon sequestration, fishing ground, and built-up lands used for a variety of human purposes). These land-use types in turn vary considerably in terms of the resources they provide for human consumption and/or in their absorptive capacity for waste. The consumption of energy and biomass (food, fibre), the use of building material, mining of metals, exploitation of water resources, and many other demands are all converted into this same normalized metric: biologically productive land, as expressed in global hectares.

On the basis of such research, the per capita Canadian's ecological footprint has been estimated to be very large (7.01 global hectares in 2007) relative to a global average of only 2.7 hectares (Ewing et al., 2010). Table 12.3 demonstrates the enormous variation across societies in terms of their respective demand on ecological resources, by summarizing the 20 countries with the largest ecological footprint (Canada ranks 7th) and the 20 countries with the smallest. As an indicator of resources used per capita, the range of footprints is large, from an extreme high of 10.68 in the oil-rich state of United Arab Emirates to an

Continued

Table 12.3 ▣ Ecological Footprint of Countries, Top 20 and Bottom 20 on International Rankings

Top 20 Countries	Footprint (per capita)	Bottom 20 Countries	Footprint (per capita)
1 UAE	10.68	1 Timor-Leste	0.44
2 Qatar	10.51	2 Bangladesh	0.62
3 Denmark	8.26	3 Afghanistan	0.62
4 Belgium	8.00	4 Haiti	0.68
5 USA	8.00	5 Malawi	0.73
6 Estonia	7.88	6 DR Congo	0.75
7 **Canada**	**7.01**	7 Pakistan	0.77
8 Australia	6.84	8 Mozambique	0.77
9 Kuwait	6.32	9 Eritrea	0.89
10 Ireland	6.29	10 Burundi	0.90
11 Netherlands	6.19	11 Zambia	0.91
12 Finland	6.16	12 India	0.91
13 Sweden	5.88	13 Yemin	0.94
14 Czech Republic	5.73	14 Guinea Bissau	0.96
15 Macedonia	5.66	15 Congo	0.96
16 Latvia	5.64	16 Togo	0.97
17 Norway	5.56	17 Tajikistan	1.00
18 Mongolia	5.53	18 Angola	1.00
19 Spain	5.42	19 Ivory Coast	1.01
20 Greece	5.39	20 Rwanda	1.02
Global Average	**2.70**		

Source: Ewing et al., 2010.

extreme low of only 0.44 hectares in the newly sovereign yet greatly impoverished Southeast Asian country of Timor-Leste.

Ecological-footprint analysis (EFA) serves to highlight a fundamental question in discussions of population growth and environmental impact: What is the relevance of the vastly unequal distributions in terms of wealth and the per capita resources consumed? Ewing and colleagues (2010), for example, have estimated that the average per capita footprint for the world's 36 richest countries (6.09 global hectares) is more than 5 times the average for the world's 46 poorest nations (1.18 hectares). As Dietz and Rosa (1997) have observed, it is not the P alone that matters, in definitions of carrying capacity and population growth, but the PA in IPAT, or the per capita impact multiplied by the population.

While the average Canadian is estimated as using roughly 7.01 global hectares, there is also obviously considerable variation across individuals when it comes to environmental impact (visit www.footprintnetwork.org—described in more detail at the end of this chapter—to calculate your own ecological footprint). Let us consider, for example, someone who vacations in Florida every winter, owns 2 cars, has a 5,000-square-foot home, regularly dines in upscale restaurants, eats a lot of red meat, is an avid shopper, and, in fact, manages to spend most if not all of a very high income on personal consumption and recreation. Compare this person with someone who has a particularly low income, who might walk or rely on public transit, rarely or never travels, lives in a small apartment, sometimes relies upon food banks, and has little disposable income beyond what is available for the most basic of necessities. As is true in making comparisons across countries, the ecological footprint, and subsequent environmental impact, of the former is several times larger than the latter.

In addition, a person's ecological footprint is not only determined by individual consumption patterns but is also influenced by environmental and societal factors. More specifically, an individual's ecological footprint is also partially shaped by (1) a region's energy supply (does your electricity come from coal generation, natural gas, nuclear, or some other renewable source of energy, such as wind, solar, or geothermal?); (2) its transportation infrastructure (is public transit available, and, if so, is it well developed?); (3) local environmental conditions (is the local climate particularly cold or hot?); (4) the state of the locally built environment (have planners managed to promote smart growth that reduces traffic congestion among various other inefficiencies?); (5) the manner in which industry uses technology and energy in producing goods (does industry manage to minimize waste and energy consumption and use technologies that minimize environmental impact?); and (6) the state and nature of many public services that government provides (are these services provided with minimal environmental cost?). With this in mind, Wackernagel and Rees (1996) have pointed out the importance not only of individual change, but also of the necessity for political change to improve how societies use, distribute, and manage resources.

Population Growth as a Stimulus for Innovation

In direct contrast to the neo-Malthusian position, there are others who argue that population growth in and of itself should not be considered a problem and that if anything, under the right conditions, the increased numbers can act as a driver of innovation, technological progress, and current-day economic growth and climbing standards of living (Boserup, 1981; Simon 1996). The general idea is that when a specific resource becomes scarce—due to population increase or some other factor—societies respond through inventiveness and innovation. The solution to scarcity is that human populations either search out alternatives to the resources that become scarce or find new ways of making more from less. Human populations are considered to be empowered by ingenuity, technological progress, and the ability to organize and reorganize in ways that allow for more successful adaptation (Cohen, 1995).

Relevant in this context is the intellectual contribution of the Danish economist Ester Boserup (1965, 1981), noted for comprehensive research on the interrelationship between population growth and agricultural development, both in terms of historical populations as well as more contemporary populations in Africa. In her book *The Conditions of Agricultural Growth: The Economics of Agrarian Change under Population Pressure* (1965), Boserup challenged the dominant Malthusian paradigm of her time, providing evidence on how growth in food production has continued to outpace population growth, primarily due to what she referred to as the "induced intensification" of agriculture. If there are real limits in terms of the "extensification of agriculture" (or the extension of agricultural production to new lands), then populations tend to respond through an "intensification of agriculture"—by making "production more intense"—getting more out of the land that is currently available. For Boserup, population growth has been a fundamental driver powerful enough to make traditional communities change their agricultural methods, not only forcing people to bring more land under cultivation, but also to grow new types of crops, use new fertilizers and/or irrigation methods, to drain swamp lands, to attempt new intercropping efforts, all in order to make more from less, to increase productivity in a context of real fixed limits.

As Boserup (1999) later wrote, "My conclusions were the opposite of the general opinion at the time, when it was believed that the carrying capacity of the globe was nearly exhausted and that the ongoing demographic transition in developing countries would result in soaring food prices and mass starvation." From this point of view, the aforementioned concept of carrying capacity looks to be far more ambiguous and difficult to define. Returning to its definition, carrying capacity makes reference to the number of people supported given available physical resources of a specific environment, and the "manner in which populations make use of these resources." Borrowing from human ecology, particularly important in this context is not only the size of the population or the limits of the physical environment, but more comprehensively, it is the way in which specific societies organize themselves (and distribute resources) and make use of technologies that allow for successful adaptation.

As we apply this thinking to questions of environmental impact, a key issue to consider is our ability to organize ourselves and develop technologies that lessen environmental impact. This has proven more difficult than the case of food production.

Population as the Ultimate Resource

In the late 1970s, Paul Ehrlich was widely considered as one of the most important voices behind the so-called population crisis, with his writings deemed to be a cornerstone of the thinking of many environmentalists at the time. Similarly, the 1970s futuristic think tank the Club of Rome published an influential, and controversial, monograph *The Limits to Growth*, which also argued that observed demographic and economic trends were not sustainable, particularly in

the long term (Meadows et al., 1972). On the basis of several simulations and longer-term forecasts, with observed time series on population growth, resource consumption, food production, as well as known reserves of natural resources and energy, the central thesis of this work was that humanity was already in an "overshoot" mode—beyond the planet's carrying capacity. As a result, the worrisome forecast was made that some type of economic and "ecological crash" (or, at the very least, a substantial degrading of the global environment and a serious decline in overall living standards) would occur on a global scale, likely in the mid- or late twenty-first century.

At least partially in response to this argument, the economist Julian Simon wrote an equally controversial book *The Ultimate Resource* (1981), whereby he set out the diametrically opposite view: that current trends in terms of population and economic growth are not only unproblematic, but, in fact, something that could and should be encouraged. More fundamentally, Simon argued with great optimism, there are essentially no limits to population growth and that this notion of a finite carrying capacity is without empirical merit. For Simon, there are no limits for the simple reason that people and their economies can adapt well to scarcity, as they have in the past and will continue to do so in the future. In other words, the "ultimate resource" for Simon is humanity's ingenuity, resourcefulness, and creativity. A large population not only means there are more "mouths to feed," but ultimately, more "skilled, spirited and hopeful people who will exert their will and imaginations for their own benefit, and so, inevitably, for the benefit of us all" (1981). In defence of this position, Simon again pointed to the considerable progress that we have witnessed, regardless of population growth, as many resources, including food, have become more plentiful. Regarding population health, more people are living better, healthier, and longer than ever before.

Fundamental to Simon's mindset was his training in economics, or even more profoundly, the prominence he placed on the marketplace in driving economic and technological change. Neo-classical economics has been characterized by a concentrated focus on the circular movement of investment, production, distribution, and consumption, arguably in a manner that is somewhat of an abstraction from the physical reality of both local ecosystems and broader environment limits. While the neo-Malthusian emphasis has been on the "limits to growth," Simon's argument has focused on how markets generate adjustments to scarcity, and as a result, have the capacity to redefine where these limits might actually be. While Boserup (1965) had initially pointed to the importance of population growth as a fundamental driver of social change and technological innovation, Simon elaborated upon how this innovation can operate in a modern economy, or, more specifically, in the free-market capitalist economy of the late twentieth century.

Essential to Simon's argument is what economists have labelled the market response model, defined by Robbins and colleagues (2014) as "a model that predicts economic responses to scarcity of a resource, whereas an increase in price results in either a decreased demand for the specific resource and/or an increased supply." At the heart of this line of thinking is the importance of price as determined in the market place, as a mechanism that provides both potential incentives and/or disincentives for economic adaptation and technological innovation. The price of a specific resource or commodity (e.g., wood, copper, corn, electronics, steel) is determined by the marketplace in light of its supply and corresponding demand. Given the reality of fixed environmental limits (there is only so much wood available to be cut, or land available to be farmed), when a good becomes over-exploited, scarcity results, which in turn has an impact on supply, and subsequently on its price.

In the market response model, it is the price that serves as a major incentive (or disincentive) for economies to change and adapt. If the price goes up (with climbing scarcity), the response of producers is to (1) try to find new sources of this resource under consideration; (2) develop new technologies that allow for the extraction or production of the same resource that had previously been deemed uneconomical or technologically unfeasible; and/or (3) find useful substitutes for the resource under consideration. As elaborated by Simon, population growth often leads to scarcity, which in turn increases price, then

correspondingly provides a major impetus to either expand the potential supply of the resource under consideration or to innovate by finding substitutes for what has become expensive. In many ways, Simon was merely restating the widely held view that "necessity is often the mother of invention." In Simon's view, the by-product of such invention and creativity was a continued increase in the supply of economically useful goods, as modified by technological innovation, which in turn leads to economic growth and climbing living standards.

Returning to the central thesis of the neo-Malthusian position, fundamental are real environmental limits, given available technology and known reserves of natural resources and energy. On the other hand, the market response model shifts the emphasis toward economic and technological innovation, which in turn holds the potential for modifying how we define these same environmental limits. In many ways, the T in the IPAT equation gains prominence in this context, in light of the potential for technological innovation as a response to scarcity. Simon provides several different examples of the workings of the market response model, from how Western societies have met their energy needs over time (using wood, coal, oil/gas, hydro/nuclear, among other alternatives) to the demand for food (which intensified with the Green Revolution). Similarly, he demonstrates the innovation and substitution that have characterized our use of various minerals and metals over time, as widely used by industry in the production of consumer goods, including copper, nickel, tin, tungsten, among others.

Whereas the limits to growth thesis emphasizes known reserves in a physical world with obvious real limits, the market response model suggests that the logical reaction to scarcity is adaptation, innovation, and substitution (e.g., responding to an increase in the price of copper by replacing expensive copper pipes with less expensive polymer plastic pipes). In looking to the future, the energy available for human use is considered unlimited (despite discussions of peak oil or limits on known reserves), as climbing prices breed innovation, allowing us to develop alternatives, including renewable energy (solar, wind, and geothermal). In following the logic of the market response model, if the price of fossil fuel increases (due to climbing scarcity), then the price of renewable energy becomes more competitive, such that the energy transition away from carbon-based fuels would likely accelerate, as producers seek economic opportunities by meeting the high demand for energy, regardless of source.

Finding a Middle Ground

In a critique of mainstream economic thinking on growth and the environment, Harper and Fletcher (2010) point to a few issues that are not easily resolved in a free-market, capitalist economy, including

(i)   How can values ("prices") be assigned to goods that are held in common (the "commons") that are used by many and owned by none, such as the atmosphere, rivers, oceans and public space?

(ii) How can economic analysis incorporate and assign responsibility for the variety of environmental externalities; that is, the real overhead costs incurred in the production process that are borne not by particular producers or consumers, but by third parties, the larger community, or the environment? (Harper and Fletcher, 2010: 59)

For the remainder of the chapter, we shall elaborate on these issues, while making reference to some specific Canadian environmental issues and problems. In a sense, these issues demonstrate some of the most fundamental challenges that Canada currently faces in terms of resolving its economic and environmental problems, all in a context of sustained demographic growth.

The Tragedy of the Commons

A fundamental idea underlying neo-classical economics is the general notion that individual actors who set out to maximize their own gain, in a free-market context, can also serve to benefit society, even if in so doing there is no specific intent to do so. Tracing this general idea back to the eighteenth

century, Adam Smith's *The Wealth of Nations* (1776) popularized the widely held view that the self-regulating behaviour of the marketplace (or its so-called "*invisible hand*") allows for the simultaneous pursuit of private interest and collective well-being. In 1968, population geneticist Garrett Hardin published a short but widely cited article in the journal *Science*, wherein he used the metaphor of "the tragedy of the commons" to demonstrate that under certain circumstances, decisions reached individually by many, who are each pursuing their own private interests, can collectively lead to ruin. In so doing, he addressed a fundamental question (and problem) that modern economies often face: *What of resources that are essentially held in common, or, more specifically, used by many yet owned by none (e.g., the atmosphere, rivers, oceans, and public space)?*

Hardin's metaphor begins with a type of British land tenure, "the commons," that existed prior to the enclosure movements of the eighteenth and nineteenth centuries, whereby herders often shared a common parcel of land, on which they were each entitled to allow their herds of sheep and cattle to graze. Originally, the pasture was open to all, and this situation generally worked well under low population density (with fewer animals grazing). Each herdsman, being a rational being, would seek to make the most of the situation and consider the utility of adding one more animal to his herd. The benefit to the herder was obvious, as he immediately gained all the proceeds from an additional animal's eventual sale. Yet the costs were less obvious: the additional animal contributed to overgrazing, which in turn was shared by all herders in the community (Hardin, 1968). These costs were typically not immediate, but were potentially felt in the long term, after many years of overgrazing and improper land use. The overgrazing of livestock has repeatedly proven to be one of the major causes of land desertification and erosion throughout history and in many different parts of the world. With climbing population densities and increased pastoralism, the earliest examples of this go back thousands of years. In current times, for example, large regions in the Middle East and North Africa are unsuitable for agriculture due to centuries of desertification (Moseley and Jerme, 2010).

The general idea is that the utility of adding an additional animal gained by the individual herdsman (all the proceeds obtained from its eventual sale) clearly outweigh the costs (the herder's small share of the diminished usefulness or productivity of the land, which is borne by the entire community). As Hardin (1968) summarized,

> The rational herdsman concludes that the only sensible course for him to pursue is to add another animal to his herd, and another, and another ... but this is the conclusion reached by each and every rational herdsman sharing a commons. Therein is the tragedy. Each man is locked into a system that compels him to increase his herd without limit—in a world that is limited. Ruin is the destination toward which all men rush, each pursuing his own best interest in a society that believes in the freedom of the commons. Freedom in a commons brings ruin to all.

One can find many examples of "the tragedy of the commons" in the literature, from the mismanagement of rangeland by pastoralists to the biodiversity loss that has occurred via the overhunting or overforaging of public lands (Snyman and Smit, 2007; Sullivan and Swingland, 2006). Others have pointed to the mismanagement of our forests through the large-scale clearance of public lands, through to the

misuse of groundwater resources and the mismanagement of irrigation communities (Ostrom, 1990; Berkes, 2002). In Canada, a major example of this mismanagement of the commons was the overfishing of the Grand Banks by both national and international fishers that eventually led to the collapse of the Atlantic cod fisheries in the early 1990s (Hutchings and Reynolds, 2004). Many decades earlier, the cod of the Grand Banks, just east of Newfoundland, was considered one of the world's greatest fish stocks, with both Canadian fishers and trawling fleets from around the world harvesting unprecedented amounts of fish. But by the early 1990s, after decades of unsustainable fishing practices by both Canadian and international fleets (including the Soviet Union, Spain, France, Portugal, as well as smaller numbers from Asia, the Caribbean, and elsewhere), the northern cod stocks suddenly collapsed.

As estimated by the Dalhousie marine biologist Ransom Myers (2003), the average annual East Coast cod catch gradually climbed from around 100,000 tons in 1850 to about 300,000 tons by the 1950s, in sustaining a vibrant fishery off the coast of Newfoundland and Labrador. Figure 12.6 demonstrates the substantial increase in the annual catch that characterized the 1960s and '70s, peaking at over 800,000 tons in 1968. Thousands of independent fishers, some small yet others quite large, in competitively harvesting the North Atlantic cod, contributed to its eventual collapse,

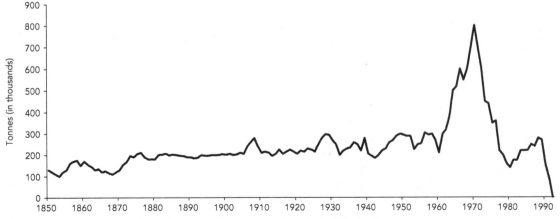

Figure 12.6 ▣ Catches of Northern Cod, Estimates for 1850–1993

Source: FOA, 2002.

estimated to have fallen from a spawning biomass of over 1.6 million tons in 1962 to somewhere between 72,000 and 110,000 by 1992 (Myers, 2003).

While an increased number of trawlers was important in explaining this decline, an additional factor responsible was the development of large factory freezer trawlers that allowed for the harvesting of massive amounts of cod. The large trawlers made it easy to fish much larger areas at deeper depths, and to pursue schools of fish for a longer time. In addition, many of the big trawlers used sonar, which would allow for the precise targeting of the fish that remained. From an ecological point of view, one of the most damaging technologies was the development of draggers, which involved enormous nets being dragged along the ocean floor, harvesting whatever was in their way, including undersize cod and many other species upon which the health of the entire ecosystem depended. As we mentioned, the T technology component in the IPAT equation can operate in various ways, to either increase or lessen environmental impacts—in this context, the development of new fishing technologies had a devastating effect.

Efforts to regulate the harvesting of cod faced considerable opposition from the many interested stakeholders in the fisheries, including both national and international fishing interests. When Canada eventually managed to push for the ratification of a UN convention that extended Canada's authority over fishing rights to a 320-kilometre offshore limit, the heavy fishing continued, but with Canadian trawlers taking the place of international ones. While the 320-kilometre offshore limit covered most of the Grand Banks, it did not cover all of it, and quite predictably, the trawlers from other countries continued to fish in some of the richest areas just outside this limit. Consecutive Canadian governments, while criticizing the overfishing of other countries, largely downplayed the concerns of scientists who were recommending the introduction of low quotas for Canadian trawlers. A major consequence of this inaction was the eventual collapse of the fishery in 1992, as a mere fraction of the cod remained compared to a few decades earlier. When the federal government first introduced its moratorium, the legislation was meant to last for only three years, yet after a couple of

decades, the moratorium remains in place, with only a small recovery in selected areas (MacDonald, 2012).

While the emphasis in this chapter is on the impact of demographic change on economic growth and the environment, the collapse in the cod fishery demonstrates in quite a dramatic manner the opposite sort of situation: how environmental change, or in this case, the loss of a resource, can have a major impact on the population. Outside the province's largest city of St John's, Newfoundland and Labrador has since experienced considerable depopulation, through both low fertility (it has consistently had among the lowest fertility rates in the country since the early 1990s) and major out-migration (largely to other provinces). Overall, Newfoundland and Labrador is the only province to be smaller in 2013 than it was in 1992, declining by about 12 per cent from 1992 to 2007, before rebounding somewhat more recently, up by about 5 per cent over the 2007–13 period. According to the 2011 Census all regions outside St John's and the neighbouring Avalon Peninsula region experienced population loss from 2006 to 2011. The province's fertility rate has been between 1.2 and 1.45 births for virtually every year since the difficulties in the fisheries began, which is considered indicative of the extent to which young adults have been struggling to establish themselves economically and in family life (Higgins, 2008; Hamilton and Otterstad, 1998).

Economic Analysis and Environmental Externalities

In economics, an externality is an indirect effect of consumption or production, which has an impact on others who are not directly involved in the original economic exchange (Laffont, 2008). In environmental science, an *"environmental externality"* is an uncompensated environmental effect that can have an impact upon the wider community and/or environment, yet is not accounted for through the market or through the assignment of prices for specific goods, services, or commodities (Goodwin and Institute, 2011). An externality can be either a benefit (positive externality) or a cost (negative externality), and as a result, might serve to either understate or overstate the full costs associated with an economic activity. As an example, consider the economic decision to either conserve a large tract of property that in its current state is an undeveloped forest, or to use this land for a variety of economic purposes. The decision to preserve it might result in a substantial positive externality by preserving a water recharge source for an aquifer that is shared by a neighbouring community. On the other hand, the decision to develop it (e.g., clear-cutting the woodland, selling the wood to the highest bidder, and using the land for a residential development, or perhaps a large industrial farm) results in considerable economic activity and potential economic gain to those directly involved. Yet this development decision also holds the potential for substantial negative externalities for others. As a result of this decision, there is also the externality of losing the aquifer (a cost that is borne by the neighbouring community), and the risk of environmental toxins or wastewater being released into the local environment as a result of residential development and/or agricultural practices. There is always the potential for seepage from underground storage and septic tanks, sewage, and wastewater drainage, not to mention accumulated nitrates, pesticides, and herbicides that can result from both urban development and/or agricultural practices.

To an uncertain extent, our rivers and groundwater are affected by a variety of pollutants that are released into the environment, sometimes unintentionally, but also at times with the full knowledge of the perpetrators, as a result of a cost–benefit decision by industry, government, and/or individuals. For this reason, such pollutants might best be thought of as important negative externalities that could result from these decisions. Consider the present state of municipal wastewater management in Canada, for example, as there are currently over 3,500 wastewater facilities nationwide, many of which are in desperate need of repair and upgrading (Federation of Canadian Municipalities, 2012). Although many Canadian municipalities have managed to upgrade the quality of wastewater treatment over recent decades, there remains over 150 billion litres of untreated/undertreated wastewater (sewage) that is released into our waterways on an annual basis (Environment Canada,

2013b). While sewage is collected into city sewer systems from Canadian homes, industries, and businesses, the quality of municipal water-management practices varies widely across the country—ranging from non-existent management in some communities through to state-of-the-art oversight in others. In addition, many municipal wastewater systems in Canada continue to combine sewage with stormwater (from rain and melting snow) into the same wastewater-management system, which in turn both increases the costs associated with wastewater treatment and risks overflow during periods of spring runoff and flooding.

The externalities of not investing in proper wastewater management can be substantial, as, for example, neighbouring communities might have to bear greater costs in locating suitable drinking water and/or they might witness a general degrading in the health of a local river system or neighbouring lake, which in turn reduces the quality of life for all concerned. There are several externalities not easily quantifiable in releasing untreated or undertreated sewage into the environment, from the effect it might have on local wildlife, fisheries, wetlands, aesthetics, and recreation through to other quality-of-life issues, including odours and poor air quality. A wide variety of pathogenic micro-organisms are found in undertreated wastewater, including bacteria, viruses, protozoans, among other parasites, many of which can have a devastating impact on a local ecosystem. There are municipalities on both of Canada's coasts that merely release sewage directly into the ocean, with uncertain environmental impacts (e.g., roughly 50 per cent of Newfoundland and Labrador's population live in such municipalities). On the other hand, there are other municipalities that have reduced dramatically such externalities by investing in wastewater-treatment facilities that meet the gold standard in terms of sewage treatment (what is referred to as tertiary treatment). In this regard, Alberta's record on municipal wastewater treatment is far superior to other Canadian provinces, with, for example, both Calgary and Edmonton having tertiary-treatment wastewater systems. This in turn has the positive benefit of helping to preserve the health of Alberta's Hudson Bay watershed, which includes both Edmonton's North Saskatchewan River and Calgary's Bow River.

Tertiary treatment is credited for removing up to 98 per cent of all the impurities from sewage, producing an effluent that is almost of drinking-water quality (Environment Canada, 2013b). While the technology of tertiary treatment can be quite expensive, involving considerable initial expense and ongoing technological expertise, the obvious benefit to this investment is far fewer negative externalities for the local environment. While municipal sewage is one of the largest sources of pollution of surface water in Canada, provinces and municipalities vary widely in terms of level of treatment. Keep in mind that the higher the level of treatment (primary, secondary, tertiary), the cleaner the effluent and the smaller the negative impact on the environment. In primary treatment, wastewater is merely placed in large tanks, whereby screening, sedimentation by gravity, and mechanical processes are used to remove suspended solids from the water prior to allowing the wastewater to be released back into our waterways. Secondary wastewater treatment involves some combination of both physical and biological treatment processes, through which some 95 per cent of conventional pollutants are removed prior to releasing the treated water back into our waterways. The preferred tertiary

treatment uses a variety of physical, chemical, and biological processes (e.g., carbon filters, reverse osmosis) that move beyond secondary treatment to remove not only grit, debris, biological wastes, and disease causing bacteria, but also many nutrients that are not completely removed by secondary treatment (e.g., most nitrogen and phosphorous). As well, tertiary treatment removes heavy metals, dissolved solids, and hundreds of chemicals found in wastewater as a by-product of many household products regularly used by Canadians—including pharmaceuticals, cosmetics, shampoos, and various types of cleaning products (Environment Canada, 2013b).

Figure 12.7 provides a breakdown, by province, in terms of population serviced by these alternative water-management technologies. Environment Canada estimates that as of 2009, only about 15 per cent of Canada's population was living in municipalities with tertiary water-treatment facilities, whereas 3 per cent were living in municipalities with absolutely no treatment at all (again, these communities tend to be concentrated in some specific regions: in Newfoundland and Labrador, Canada's North, and in other more remote coastal communities). In addition, about 13 per cent of Canada's population rely on

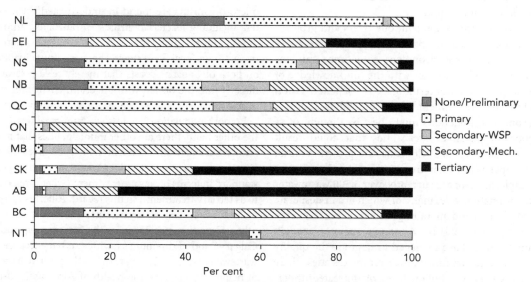

Figure 12.7 ▣ Wastewater Management Level, by Province/Territory, 2009

Source: Environment Canada, 2011b.

private residential septic systems (primarily in rural Canada), 16 per cent have waste-management systems that are classified as primary, whereas 53 per cent live in municipalities with what is classified as secondary treatment of wastewater. By province, with the exception of Alberta, and to a lesser extent Saskatchewan (with 77.9 per cent and 58.2 per cent of their populations with tertiary treatment, respectively), all other provinces in Canada have relatively low tertiary treatment of wastewater (Prince Edward Island has 23.6 per cent), whereas fewer than 1 in 10 Canadians living in Ontario, Quebec, and British Columbia live in municipalities with such a service (at 8 per cent, 8.4 per cent, and 7.4 per cent, respectively). With regard to the province of Quebec, roughly half of all the sewage involves primary treatment or even less, primarily due to Montreal's relatively poor performance in treating its wastewater before releasing it directly into the St Lawrence River system (Emond, 2009). Very briefly, in making some international comparisons, there are many countries that far outperform Canada on the wastewater-management front. For example, according to the European Environment Agency (2012), over 90 per cent of the wastewater-treatment systems in Germany and the Netherlands are tertiary, or more than 7 persons in 10 in both Northern and Central Europe are generally connected to tertiary treatment plants, and nearly half of the populations of Southern and Eastern Europe receive tertiary treatment.

While the various levels of government debate jurisdiction, and, in particular, who is to pay for the costs of upgrading systems, municipalities currently own and provide for the bulk of the funding, responsible for the operation of about 70 per cent of wastewater infrastructure in Canada (CCME, 2009). The bulk of the funding for collection systems, wastewater facilities and combined sewers is directly provided by municipalities and recovered by revenues generated primarily through municipal taxes and service charges. The Canadian Council of Ministers of the Environment (CCME, 2009) have estimated that the costs involved in upgrading municipal facilities to levels that approach or reach the tertiary level to be substantial (in the billions of dollars), a cost that would largely be borne by the municipalities, with the potential for supplemental funding by federal,

provincial, and territorial governments, to the extent that reducing this source of pollutants could be prioritized. Yet the cost (or negative externalities) of inaction have been estimated to be substantially greater than the expected upgrading costs. For example, Environment Canada (2013b) estimates, without providing detail, that the positive externalities that could be gained via a decision to clean up our current sewage-treatment plants could lead to a "potential benefit-to-cost ratio of over 3:1 for the country as a whole." In other words, untreated and undertreated wastewater continues to wreak havoc on the ecosystems of many of our rivers, lakes, and coastal zones, with a real social, economic, and environmental costs.

Returning to Hardin's work, the tragedy of the commons is relevant in this context, yet with a slightly different twist. Rather than overexploiting the commons, the problem here is that we are putting our waste-ridden effluent back into the commons. Nonetheless, the calculations are much the same: the utility of economic decisions involving the commons ignore the most basic of externalities—that is, the gradual degradation of our rivers, lakes, groundwater, and other bodies of water. More broadly, other observers have pointed to similar types of problems, as, for example, the idea that our atmosphere be thought of as a "global commons," or, in other words, as a sort of waste-disposal site, free of charge, for CO_2 emissions and other GHGs. Very briefly, this is one of the rationales behind the idea of introducing a carbon tax on fossil fuels, in addressing the problem of emitters of greenhouse gases who do not pay the full costs of their actions (e.g., the negative externalities of burning coal or oil as opposed to cleaner sources of energy). By increasing the price of fossil fuel, one could put a price on the amount of carbon that is released into the atmosphere, which in turn could serve as a major incentive for consumers and producers alike to seek out alternatives in meeting their energy needs. If there are difficulties in the political decisions associated with allocating the costs of waste management across the municipalities, provinces, and the feds, these negotiations are that much more complex at the international level. Beyond the issue of externalities is the further problem that these costs are both differentially experienced and long range.

Box 12.3   ▣   Is Canada's Climate Warming?

The buildup of GHGs in the atmosphere is an international problem, regardless of which country is the source of the emissions. While the largest current emitter of GHGs is China (producing almost one quarter of today's global total of CO_2 emissions), Canada is responsible for a disproportionate share (roughly 2 per cent of the global total for a country with about 0.5 per cent of the global population). Our atmosphere has been treated as a global commons, a waste disposal site for CO_2 emissions and other GHGs. Yet regardless of who is responsible, the concentration of these gases in the atmosphere is a common problem faced by all of humanity and will continue to be a problem in the future to the extent that fossil fuels continue to be a primary source of energy.

The International Panel on Climate Change (IPCC, 2013) has estimated that on a global scale, atmospheric CO_2 concentration increased by only 20 PPM over the 8,000 years prior to industrialization (+7.1 per cent), yet since the beginning of the Industrial Revolution, it has increased dramatically from about 280 ppm in 1750 to over 400 PPM by 2013 (+42.9 per cent). In extrapolating these trends, the IPCC estimates that this concentration could easily move well beyond 500 PPM by mid-century and perhaps double before stabilizing sometime later this century. With this, we have witnessed an increase in global temperatures (average combined land and ocean surface temperature) of roughly 0.85°C since 1880 (IPCC, 2013) with an uncertain amount of warming forecast for the future. While this might not seem like a large amount, from the point of view of a climate scientist, the rate of warming has been quite rapid. In capturing these trends, the IPCC reports that each of the last three decades has been successively warmer than any preceding decade since 1850, and that levels of atmospheric CO_2 have reached heights that have not occurred for over 800,000 years.

As summarized in the IPCC's Fifth Assessment Report, the evidence for anthropogenic climate change is now unequivocal—that is, the warming of the climate is due to human activities, and, in particular, due to this increased concentration of CO_2 among other GHGs (IPCC, 2013). After an exhaustive review of over 9,200 scientific publications, the IPCC has provided additional forecasts: that global temperature could climb through to the late twenty-first century, from anywhere between a low of 0.3°C (if immediate and dramatic action takes place in curtailing the burning of fossil fuels) to a high of 4.8°C (if relatively little is done and emissions continue to climb). While the low forecast might be considered unlikely as CO_2 emissions continue to climb rapidly, an increase of 4.8°C might be also considered improbable (although not impossible), as it is built on the assumption that emission levels continue to rise in almost an unabated manner over the next half century. In addition, the IPCC also projects a rise in sea levels, of anywhere between 26 and 82 centimetres over the current century, as well as more frequent extreme weather events. And as pointed out by scientists at Environment Canada, climate change has not and will not be experienced uniformly across different world regions; more specifically, climate change and warming tends to be most amplified at northern latitudes and in arctic regions, and for this reason, Canada will be more influenced than most countries (Fyfe et al., 2013; Flato and Morotzke, 2013).

For the northern hemisphere overall, the IPCC estimates that the 1983–2013 period was likely the warmest 30-year period in over a millennium, with temperature anomalies most dramatic during the winter months. Canada has already observed substantial warming over recent decades, as documented in data compiled by Environment Canada (see Figure 12.8). With the mandate of collecting and compiling weather and meteorological information for the country as a whole, this federal department has been releasing quarterly data for over 65 years, which summarizes information collected at weather stations across the country. For example, in estimating the trend line, Environment Canada (2013a) documents a warming in temperatures, averaged across the country, of about 3°C for the winter months and about 1°C for summer months, over the 1948–2011 period.

These national averages obscure a simple reality: the extent of warming has not been uniform across geographic regions of Canada. Some of the most substantial changes, for example, have occurred in Canada's Far North (e.g., in the Arctic and Subarctic). From the point of view of population distribution, these are precisely areas of the country that tend to be the most sparsely

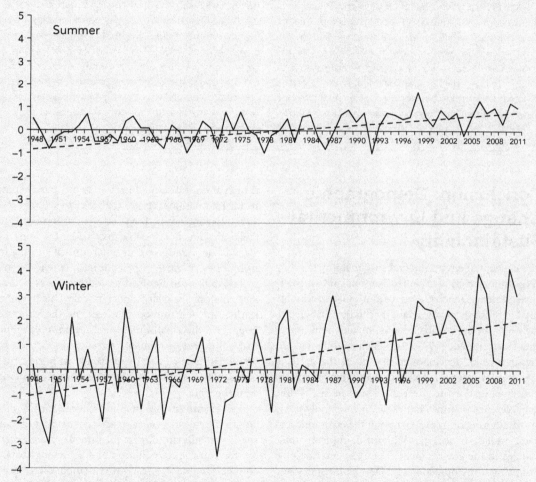

Figure 12.8 ◉ National Temperature Departures[1] and Long-Term Trends, Summer and Winter Months, Canada 1948–2011

Notes: [1]Departures from longer term average, 1961–1990.
Source: Environment Canada, 2012.

Continued

populated. As was seen in Chapter 6, almost 7 in 10 Canadians lived south of the 49th parallel, which marks the southern border of the Prairie provinces, and only 0.3 per cent lived north of the 60th parallel, which marks their northern border. With considerable variability across regions, Canada's most densely populated regions have witnessed much less warming in temperatures (e.g., in the Great Lakes area of Ontario; the St Lawrence lowlands of Ontario, Quebec, and the Atlantic provinces), while there are weather stations in some of the more remote northern regions that have witnessed a warming trend of more than 5°C.

It has been in Canada's Far North that the greatest warming has occurred, as the arctic sea ice and northern spring snow cover have continued to decline. While glaciers continue to shrink almost worldwide, of particular concern to climate scientists has been the warming of the polar regions of the world's climate system as well as the uncertainty associated with the warming of the world's oceans. Both the massive Greenland and Antarctic ice sheets have been losing mass for several decades, as has the northern ice cover in Canada. According to summaries by Natural Resources Canada researchers, with the warming of ocean currents, the Arctic Ocean could easily become virtually ice-free in summer before the middle of the century (Lemmen et al., 2008). If the worst of the IPCC's forecasts come to fruition, the northernmost reaches of Canada could see an increase of 10°C before the end of the century, which surely has uncertain and worrisome implications for both the global climatic system and Canada's leaders.

Conclusion: Demographic Change and Environmental Sustainability

The concept of environmental sustainability has long been endorsed by the United Nations and its many development agencies. One of the most commonly cited definitions of sustainability can be attributed to early work by the World Commission on Environment and Development (1987:43), which highlighted the importance of "development that meets the needs of the present without compromising the ability of future generations to meet their own needs." While this reference is somewhat vague, it essentially refers to maintaining or improving upon the economic and social welfare of societies without doing irreparable damage to the environment. The 1994 International Conference on Population and Development devoted a chapter of its final report to environmental questions and developed a Program of Action that would result in population growth "at levels below the United Nations medium projection."

Although Canada is a relatively sparsely populated country, its ecological footprint (and affluence) is high and a substantial part of its prosperity comes from international trade (Engelman, 2007; Rees 2007). In considering the issue of environmental sustainability, it is not possible to consider the impact of Canada's population on its environment in isolation from other countries. The concept of environmental sustainability can be used to address issues that are local, national, and also global in scale. Due to globalization, the demand for resources and the associated impact on the environment are related to economic and political developments far away, as Canada has developed major trade relationships with the United States, Mexico, China and the European Community, among others.

In examining the situation internationally, difficulties often surface as many developing nations spend virtually nothing on the infrastructure necessary for controlling pollution and achieving sustainable development. Clearly, the demographic trends in Canada can be seen as inconsequential relative to the impact of some of the world's demographic giants, such as China and India. If these larger nations do not pursue a path of sustainable development, this will have major ramifications for Canada, regardless of what happens with domestic policy. For example, China is now the world's largest importer of pulp, while Canada is the largest exporter—and the second-largest supplier to China after the United States (Roy, 2005). Similarly, Canada is currently the single biggest foreign supplier of energy to the world's largest economy, the United States, providing 21.5 per cent of US oil imports and 87 per cent of natural gas imports stateside (IEA, 2014). While this is a major driving force behind Canada's dynamic energy sector and the planned exploitation of tar sands in Alberta, it is also a major contributor to greenhouse gases.

Canadian demographers have published, and continue to publish, relatively little on the topic of the environment, which suggests that they are not in a very well-situated position to advise on environmental policy. In the context of relatively low fertility and mortality, much demographic research has focused on why Canadians are not having children, and has examined some of the immediate consequences of low fertility, including population aging and a declining rate of natural increase. Similarly, there is considerable interest among demographers in the topic of immigration—given its ongoing importance to the demographic evolution of Canada. Other factors are also responsible for this lack of interest on population and the environment, including the fact that there has been very little dialogue or exchange between demographers and environmental scientists. Demography is more influenced by related social sciences (sociology, economics, and human geography) than the natural or environmental sciences. This leaves major challenges for social scientists who have relatively little expertise in constructing indicators of environmental quality—necessary in studying the trade-offs and interrelationships between people and environmental well-being.

In a frequently cited paper on public policy and social science, Demeny (1986) argued that three conditions need to be met to justify a population policy. First, there needs to be a population problem, or a situation where individual decisions do not add to the recognized collective welfare. Second, there needs to be a sense that the population problem can be remedied, and at a cost lower than the cost of the problem itself. Third, there needs to be a sense that the

problem will not solve itself automatically. In discussions of population policy and the environment, issues could be raised at all of these levels: What is the problem? Can it be remedied at a cost lower than the cost of the problem itself? Clearly, these are core issues for a society—they relate to questions of how many people are to be added to the society, by what means, and at whose cost and benefit. It should not be surprising that these questions can generate considerable discussion and disagreement. Demeny perceives them as relating to the very "constitution of the society."

The classic neo-Malthusian argument is that overpopulation is the problem, and that rapid population growth is intimately connected with most aspects of the current human predicament, including a rapid depletion of non-renewable resources and a general deterioration of the environment (Ehrlich and Ehrlich, 1990; Hardin, 1968). While the term "*overpopulation*" has been used, with some debate, in discussions of the global situation, the word is rarely encountered in discussions of Canada's demographic situation (for an exception, see Cassils and Weld, 2001). In considering Canada in isolation from the rest of the world, there is a widespread view—likely shared by most demographers—that Canada is more correctly thought of as being underpopulated than overpopulated. In this context, any discussion of Canada's environmental problems typically shifts to a focus on consumption patterns, international trade relations, and/or the corresponding technologies we use in maintaining our standard of living. The implicit assumption for many demographers appears to be that Canada's population is *not* growing too rapidly, and—if anything—faces problems over the longer term of slowing growth, population aging, and potential decline.

Among policy analysts, there is actually little consensus as to what, if any, population problems characterize Canada, with perhaps a few notable exceptions, including the fact that Canada's population is rapidly aging and that the geographic distribution of people is becoming increasingly uneven (see Policy Research Initiative, 2007, "Population at 2017," for a review). Selected parts of Canada are facing some major policy challenges in terms of rapid population growth, while others have been witnessing population decline and out-migration. Yet the general orientation of the federal government has been that overall, Canada needs more people in order to maintain its economy and labour force (Citizenship and Immigration Canada, 2008). Governmental policy has been committed to high immigration levels to offset low fertility, especially since the late 1980s.

As argued by Rees (2008), there are several values that underpin Canadian society, with its emphasis on material wealth and economic growth through competitive market mechanisms. More specifically, one can detect a prevailing cultural belief that there are potential costs to our economy associated with slower demographic growth, which might outweigh benefits associated with moving toward population stability. Also, for many Canadians, there is a commitment to maintaining population growth through immigration and taking pride in the relative successes of multiculturalism and immigration. Recent reforms in the Immigration and Refugee Protection Act are specifically concerned with facilitating further economic growth by addressing shortages in the Canadian labour market (Citizenship and Immigration Canada, 2008). The fact that the United Nations (2014) has forecast climbing numbers of environment-related migrants, including tens of millions of environmental refugees by the end of this decade, has not yet made it into debates among public officials in Canada. Again, population policy returns us to core issues for our society, as they relate to questions of how many people are to be added to the society, by what means, and at whose cost and benefit.

To again place Canada's demographic situation into an international context, it has a population roughly the size of Tokyo (the world's largest metropolitan area) spread across a massive territory of 922 million hectares (second only to Russia's 1.69 billion). Because of Canadian geography, most social scientists think of the concept of overpopulation here as being largely irrelevant. Yet in taking the long-term perspective, both domestically and internationally, demographers recognize the power of exponential growth and acknowledge that populations cannot grow indefinitely. Yet without a more explicit focus on the relationship between our population and the environment,

demographers are not particularly well situated in answering a fundamental question which has, to date, remained unanswered in developing a population policy: What would be a sustainable level of population for Canada, considering not only issues relating to quality of life and economic well-being, but also the carrying capacity of the Canadian environment, the need for biodiversity, and the preservation of wilderness areas? In returning to the science, there are major challenges in efforts to answer this question, as demographers have relatively little expertise in constructing and working with indicators of environmental quality.

Examining the extent to which given populations or societies are environmentally sustainable is far from straightforward, as societies can differ dramatically in terms of their level of industrialization and economic development, just as they differ in population size and having available natural resources. Just as population is an important multiplier in examining the impact of human societies on the environment, it is obviously not the sole or perhaps even the most important multiplier. Societies differ in terms of the use and availability of technology, their success in reducing waste, in introducing recycling, reducing pollution, and maintaining reasonable water and air quality (Prescott-Allan, 2001). Some societies have had greater success in developing sustainable natural-resource-management strategies (including, for example, large-scale efforts at reforestation, the establishment of territories under protected status, and the safeguarding of biodiversity). Some societies have the human capital and political institutions that potentially allow for accountability and democratic response to environmental problems, while others are corrupt and non-democratic. Canada's abundance of resources has clearly contributed to its high standard of living, but so have Canada's democratic political institutions, highly educated workforce, and innovative economy. Growth in the size of the population, and of the economy, has permitted Canada to be part of the G8 group of advanced industrial nations.

The question is, on what to optimize? The world has been fixated on growth, but international conferences have concluded that we must turn from growth to sustainability as a primary objective.

Globally, there is little disagreement that slower population growth is best, reaching a maximum size as soon as possible. Of course, greater efficiency in sustainably using the environment is a top priority, as are higher per capita standards of living, especially in poorer countries. Size of the total economy and of the total population also matter. While Canada's present and future population growth are globally miniscule, Canadian levels of consumption imply a greater average impact than implied in its population share. Canada has other unique aspects, such as cold climates and long distances that absorb energy, and an economic dependence on the export of natural resources (Simpson et al., 2007). We need to do our part toward maintaining the natural capital for future generations. As natural population increase moves toward zero, Canada has the advantage of maintaining population growth through immigration—without involving growth of the total population at the world level. In this context, one might think that Canadian population questions play a minor role in environmental stress. However, international agreements are made in terms of the total population of the country, not just its natural-increase component. In effect, as world population trends seek to achieve stability and sustainable development, so should Canada's.

Critical Thinking Questions

1. Why is Canada's ecological footprint so high, ranking seventh internationally? Discuss what might be done about this issue, both on the level of environmental policy and at the individual/household level.
2. How can "*values*"(prices) be assigned to goods that are held in common (the "*commons*") that are used by many and owned by none, such as the atmosphere, rivers, oceans, and public space?
3. How can economic analysis incorporate and assign responsibility for the variety of environmental externalities—that is, the real overhead costs incurred in the production process that are borne not by particular producers or consumers, but by third parties, the larger community, or the environment?
4. What insights can we draw from Ehrlich's IPAT equation in understanding Canada's record on greenhouse gas emissions?

Recommended Readings

Cohen, Joel. 1995. *How Many People Can the Earth Support?* New York: W.W. Norton. This is a compelling book on the global population problem, providing a cautious analysis of some of the more fundamental implications of current and projected population growth in the twenty-first century.

Harper, Charles, and Thomas Fletcher. 2011. *Environment and Society: Human Perspectives on Environmental Issues.* Don Mills, ON: Pearson Education Canada. *Environment and Society* is a comprehensive Canadian text that considers how population; human behaviour; culture; and social, political, and economic systems affect the environment.

Population and Environment. New York: Springer Publishers. This excellent academic journal focuses on the social demographic aspects of environmental issues.

Simpson, Jeffrey, Mark Jaccard, and Nic Rivers. 2007. *Hot Air: Meeting Canada's Climate Change Challenge.* Toronto: McClelland & Stewart. This award-winning book considers why past environmental policy in Canada has failed to meet its international commitments in terms of reducing carbon and other greenhouse gas emissions.

Related Websites

http://epi.yale.edu. Sponsored by the Yale Center for Environmental Law and Policy, Columbia University, and the World Economic Forum, this site provides a detailed ranking of countries (including Canada) on high-priority environmental issues. Included here is a ranking of countries in two broad policy areas: protection of human health from environmental harm and protection of ecosystems.

www.footprintnetwork.org. This is the website of the Global Footprint Network, an international think tank set up to promote the use of ecological-footprint accounting tools. The site has a footprint calculator, which allows you to estimate your own ecological footprint. You can find out how much land area it takes to support your lifestyle.

www.ipcc.ch. You will find here the International Panel on Climate Change (IPCC), the international body established by the United Nations for the assessment of climate change. On this site, you can find the Fifth Assessment Report, published in 2013–2014, which provides a clear and up-to-date view of the current state of scientific knowledge relevant to climate change.

www.ec.gc.ca. This is the website of Environment Canada, the federal government department with the mandate to not only preserve and enhance the quality of Canada's natural environment, but also to monitor and coordinate environmental policies and programs.

13 Conclusions

While births, deaths, and changes of residence are very personal events, taken together, they delimit the life of societies over history. Fertility and immigration are the fundamental mechanisms through which populations, countries, or societies are regenerated in the face of departures through death and emigration. These regeneration processes not only determine the number of people, but they also change the character of the population and, thus, of the society. The characteristics of the population are changed in terms of age and sex structure, socioeconomic composition, cultural makeup, and regional distribution. Given the importance of the evolution of demographic events to societies, it is natural that considerable importance is attached to understanding the changes and their implications, as well as to ensuring that these operate in the social interest.

The Canadian demographic story is exciting. It begins with the diversity of pre-contact Aboriginal populations and continues through the dominance of populations of French and then British origin to the new diversity brought by immigration from all parts of the world. We have also changed from a young and rapidly growing country to a slower-growing and aging population that is largely urban. There have been strong declines in mortality and fertility, increases in urbanization, much family change, and a more educated society. As we have seen, little is known for certain about the demography of the original inhabitants of the land. Given the available means of subsistence, Aboriginal peoples had probably inhabited the land as much as was possible, given climate conditions and the technology that had been developed. There were probably periods of growth, at least when particular Aboriginal groups controlled the resources in their region, and when the climate was favourable to food supply—and other times when

famine and disease brought declines in some Aboriginal groups.

Two things are quite clear. First, population density was not the same everywhere. It was highest on the Pacific Coast, owing to the favourable climate and the availability of fish and other food. There was also a concentration of population in the St Lawrence Valley, extending into what is now southwestern Ontario. Settled farmers in these regions had developed crops like corn and squash, which have since been important for sustaining populations in other parts of the world. In other areas, especially on the prairies and in northern regions, Aboriginal populations were more nomadic, often following seasonal patterns.

The second thing that is quite clear is that the contact with European populations brought disaster for Canada's original inhabitants. In all likelihood, the population of the large and varied Euro-Asian land mass had profited not only from various technological innovations, but also from exposure to various forms of bacteria and viruses, to which they subsequently built up some resistance. Consequently, the European populations brought diseases to which the Aboriginal populations lacked resistance. The effects of disease were compounded with warfare, as the new arrivals sought to exploit the resources and pushed the original inhabitants to more remote and less desirable regions.

It is probably not too much of an exaggeration to speak of almost three centuries of demographic decline in the Aboriginal population. Given the difficulty of estimation and enumeration, the censuses preceding 1911 may have underestimated the population. Nonetheless, it is likely that somewhere around the beginning of the twentieth century, the mortality of the Aboriginal population had declined sufficiently to finally ensure population growth. The demographic transition of the Aboriginal population is not well mapped, but it would appear that fertility increased, at least in some groups, before starting its decline in the later 1950s. An increase in fertility is not unknown in demographic transitions, for fecundity benefits from better health, more sustained availability of food, and lower lactation, before deliberate means of controlling births are adopted. More recently, the fertility of the status-Indian population has declined—in 1968, for instance, there were about 6 births per woman, compared to 2.6 in 2005. Though mortality has continued to improve, life expectancy is still six or seven years shorter than the Canadian average. In other words, the mortality level of the Aboriginal population in the 2000s is comparable to the Canadian average in the 1970s. Given this later transition, the age structure of the Aboriginal population is much younger, with a concentration at ages for entry into the labour force. The Aboriginal population has always been difficult to study, but there is the further complication that since the 1981 Census more people identify with their Aboriginal ancestry, and, thus, there is much more growth than would be expected by the difference between births and deaths in a population that is essentially closed to migration.

In contrast to the First Nations population, much is known about the original French population of what is now Quebec. That we have this knowledge is due to the detailed record keeping of the Catholic Church, the diligence of civil authorities who conducted the first modern census in 1666, and the demographic reconstruction that researchers have since undertaken. It was not hard, in 1666, to take a census of a population that numbered only 3,215. During the whole history of New France, immigration is estimated at not having been much more than 10,000.

It is the growth of this French population that makes its story particularly noteworthy. The mortality advantages that resulted from the selectivity of migration, the relatively favourable hygienic conditions, and especially the delay in the fertility transition brought a long period of remarkable growth. There has been some immigration beyond the original 10,000 people who crossed the Atlantic, but the French arrivals have always been limited. Yet the population of French origin in North America may now be close to 10,000,000, a number that represents a thousandfold increase in four centuries. Without this demographic vitality, the French population would not have been able to maintain its distinct status in this part of the North American continent. The burgeoning of the French population is also an example of the growth potential of human populations. If there had been an Aboriginal population of 300,000 people in the current area of Canada in 1600, and if they had grown as rapidly, they would now number 300,000,000, or as much as the whole population of North America. Though the European settlers created the myth that the original inhabitants were a "dying breed" to justify taking away resources, from a demographic point of view, there was no need of immigration to populate this land.

Population Processes

For the whole population of Canada, the reduction in mortality has been crucial. A century and a half ago, life expectancy was only 38 to 40 years; by 2010, it was about 81. Until about 1971, the decline in mortality benefited the young especially, and women more than men. Since then, there have also been reductions in the mortality levels of older people and the sex differential has begun to decline. In earlier times, reductions in mortality did not have a substantial influence on the aging of the population, because the improvements benefited mainly the young or were spread out over all ages. Now that the improvements occur at older ages, the extension of life expectancy contributes to population aging.

There are also good prospects for a further decline in mortality, since we see declines in all three of the major modern causes of death: heart disease, cancer, and accidents. These reductions can be attributed to both risk factors and treatment factors. Partly with the benefit of research, there is much awareness of the various causes of poor health, and we have a medical system that is among the best in the world, along with considerable willingness to invest further in health care. There are only a few countries, representing 3.4 per cent of the world population, that have higher life expectancy than Canada.

The fertility story is equally spectacular. In some groups, the transition started as early as 1870, or not much later than in the earliest groups to undergo the beginning of fertility transition in Europe; in some groups, however, the transition was much later. Then there was a baby boom that is essentially unmatched among the countries of the world. More recently, the birth rate has fallen to much lower levels, bottoming out at about 1.5 births per woman at the turn of the twenty-first century, before climbing slightly more recently, at 1.61 births per woman in 2011.

By now, about 12 per cent of the world population lives in countries that have lower fertility than Canada. Besides the later transition of the Aboriginal population, the delayed transition of the French population is also noteworthy. In the 100 years from 1860 to 1960, Quebec had much higher fertility than Ontario, whereas for the last four decades of the twentieth century, it had lower fertility than the national average. Though there are various reasons for Quebec's delayed transition, the influence of religion is not to be ignored, from the call for a *revanche du berceau* to the ability of the Catholic Church to control health care, education, and welfare into the 1960s. When the 1867 Constitution Act gave health, education, and welfare to the provinces, this played into the hands of the Church, which controlled these areas in Quebec. It was not until the Quiet Revolution of the 1950s and especially the 1960s that the state came to control these key areas of life and social policy. Whereas the first demographic transition was delayed in Quebec, the opposite holds for the second transition, where more than half of first births now occur in cohabiting relationships.

For the country as a whole, the fertility changes over the past half century have been equally substantial. If we take a total fertility rate of 2 as representing equal numbers in the generation of parents and children, the rate for 1965 implied that that generation of children was 48 per cent larger than the generation of parents, whereas under the conditions of the year 2011, there were 23 per cent fewer children than parents. It is sometimes difficult to appreciate the significance of the fertility trends because the total fertility rate has been below the replacement level of 2.1 births per woman since 1972, but according to Statistics

Canada's projections, births are still likely to outnumber deaths well into the twenty-first century. The natural increase that we are experiencing is a function of the growth potential accumulated in the age structure during the past period of demographic expansion. Yet if present trends continue, this potential will eventually begin to exhaust itself, with a slowing rate of natural increase. It may be that people handle the greater individual risks associated with globalization through higher investments in human capital and delayed child-bearing (MacDonald, 2002). According to this theory, low fertility does not occur because of the lack of desire to have children, but due to constraints, especially the opportunity costs people must face.

Compared to most other countries, immigration has made a large contribution to Canada's population growth. Besides the period of settlement by Europeans and displacement of the First Nations people, net immigration accounted for a quarter of population growth over the twentieth century. This figure is obtained by counting only the direct effects of immigration and emigration. If one adds the births to immigrants and their descendants, we see that this combination of the direct and indirect effects of immigration was responsible for about 60 per cent of the population growth from 1951 to 2011.

The broader understanding of international migration needs to take into account what is happening outside Canada, inside the country, and in relations between countries. These factors played to the disadvantage of immigration to Canada in the 1861–96 period, when the country experienced a long era of net emigration to the earlier industrializing New England states. The first wave of post-Confederation immigration, especially from 1895 to 1914, brought 2.9 million arrivals during an initial phase of globalization. These relations between countries were largely interrupted by two world wars and the Great Depression of the 1930s. The second wave of immigration, in the postwar era, brought 5.9 million arrivals from 1946 to 1989 as Canada became more open to the other countries of the world—first welcoming immigrants from Europe and then admitting new arrivals without regard to their ethnic background or race. The period since 1990 can be seen as a new phase of immigration, occurring in another period of major globalization. Since the late 1990s, population growth has consistently been driven mostly by immigration, with about two thirds of current population growth the result of migratory increase. Immigration to Canada is clearly also affected by the population growth that is occurring as a number of developing countries go through their demographic transition. Just as Canada received immigrants from Europe when that continent was going through its demographic transition, this now applies to Asia, Latin America, and Africa. In the longer term, the demographic transition should reduce the pressure for out-migration, as it did in Europe, but that will take at least another 50 years.

What is happening within Canada is also important for understanding immigration. Compared to most other countries, Canada has been very open to immigrants, especially when economic conditions are good, and more so if the prospective immigrants appear to have a good economic future in Canada. Some argue that the current demographic conditions require even higher immigration, but economic growth in a globalizing world can take place as a result of trade rather than population growth. An annual immigration of some 225,000 would enable Canada to avoid population decline, and, more important, avoid a decline in the labour force. While immigration has benefits, we clearly cannot depend on immigration to "solve" our demographic or economic problems. Rather than being made in economic or demographic terms, the case for immigration should be made especially in sociopolitical terms—that is, in view of the kind of multicultural, pluralist, and open society we wish to build. This diversity also benefits adaptability in a globalized world. In this regard, Canada is well placed with policies that promote the selection and integration of immigrants. At the same time, there are limits, as witnessed by the poorer economic performance of immigrants who have arrived since the 1990s. It may be that further diversity will not provide the same benefits, and that as far as the labour force is concerned, immigration cannot be seen as a solution to low fertility.

Population States

These patterns of mortality, fertility, and international migration have clearly brought much demographic growth in Canada. Over the twentieth century, when the world population grew at record rates, Canada's population growth was significantly higher than the world average, bringing almost a sixfold growth of the population. Even from 1961 to 2011, Canada saw more rapid growth than in other comparable places, such as the United States, United Kingdom, or Europe as a whole.

The main components of Canada's shifting demographic situation are lower fertility, lower growth, and population aging. These are setting parameters that are in many regards different from those that have operated in the past. Over the 50 years following 1961, Canada's population more than doubled, growing from 14 million to roughly 35 million. Projections made in the 1940s did not foresee this growth, having expected that the population would stabilize at some 15 million. These projections did not anticipate the baby boom or postwar immigration. It could be argued that the demographic situation as it actually evolved ensured more domestic control over resources, increased the status of the country among the nations of the world, and contributed to economic growth and social development.

According to current medium projections from Statistics Canada, the population in 2061 could be 46.4 per cent larger than it was in 2011, and that over this period, immigration will be the primary source of growth. According to the medium scenario, the average age of the population would increase from 39.9 years to 44.1, and the proportion aged 65 and over would grow from about 1 person in 8 to 1 in 4. These are different situations than those we have known in the past, making it difficult to anticipate their effects on society.

Besides slower growth and aging, Canada's population distribution is also shifting. The 2011 Census reported that for the first time in Canadian history, the percentage of Canadians living west of Ontario surpassed the number living east of the province, at 30.7 relative to 30.6 per cent. As regional disparities have always been relevant in explaining patterns of settlement and migration, British Columbia and Alberta have continued to witness rapid demographic growth, while recently, like in other parts of North America, the manufacturing sector in Central Canada has faced challenges, largely because of the globalization of economic activity. On the other hand, Saskatchewan and Manitoba, long considered more peripheral parts of the Canadian economy, have joined Alberta in experiencing better economic times, chiefly due to the vitality of the resource sector and the price of commodities on the world market. Lower unemployment and climbing incomes in Canada's western provinces have had demographic consequences.

Canada has also tended to have the greatest growth in places that have had the largest cities, with Toronto, Montreal, and Vancouver continuing to receive many immigrants. These regional patterns may also be related to globalization, which brings both surplus populations to regions of the world that are less developed and jobs to the world's largest cities.

Implications

While the theory of the demographic transition is the best framework within which to interpret Canada's demographic evolution, the ideas of Malthus and Marx reviewed in Chapter 1 are not irrelevant. Recall that Malthus argued that the population would increase depending on the amount of food available. It is said in Ecclesiastes (5:11), "As goods increase, so do those who consume them." This is the corollary of the basic Malthusian idea that the population is limited by the available resources. In Canada, we could say that resources have been abundant, and so, too, has been population growth. If one considers the effects of human activity on the environment, however, we may be facing limits of a different kind. Discussions concerning the means of achieving the Copenhagen targets in greenhouse gas emissions, for instance, need to take into account not only the level of consumption per person, but also the number of consumers.

Marx saw the population as labourers rather than as consumers, and he would say that we should pay particular attention to human resources. In effect, there have been considerable consequences for human capital of the changed demographics. This is clearest for mortality and morbidity, where the reduction of deaths, first among young people and later in the adult population, reduced the wastage of human resources. While morbidity remains important even in young and healthy populations, as observed, for instance, by the levels of sickness at times of university examinations, it is clear that morbidity was higher in earlier times, making for more days of serious sickness and loss of work time. The human-capital consequence of the reduction of fertility includes the potential for women to be more involved in the paid labour force. It is clear that, especially over the 1960–75 period, there was a direct relation between the lower level of child-bearing and the greater involvement of women in the labour force.

It goes without saying that immigration has increased the amount of human capital. That applies especially to the period of western settlement in Canada, where the first wave of post-Confederation arrivals also provided the labour needed for Canada's early industrialization. It also applies to the postwar period, when immigration compensated for the poorly developed education system and lack of skills in the Canadian population.

Migration more generally can be seen as an improvement in human capital, because it permits a better match between the need for labour and the availability of human resources at given locations. Of course, migration also brings losses at the places of origin, and people living in the places that are losing populations would generally prefer the movement of "jobs toward people" rather than "people toward jobs."

We have seen, then, a tremendous growth in human capital, as further accentuated by the improvements in education. The number of people pursuing post-secondary education, for instance, multiplied fourteenfold between 1951 and 1999. Since 2000, the number of enrolments has continued to go up; for example, the number of full-time university students increased by about one half from 2000 to 2010. Similarly, over the last half century, the labour force has continued to grow, especially with the movement of women into the workforce, and the movement of the baby boom into labour-force ages. Prior to the recession of 2008–9, Canada's employment rate, defined as those who are employed as a percentage of the population aged 15 and over, was at an all-time high, at 63.5 per cent, and then dipped down to about 62 per cent in 2013.

This employment rate is higher than in past decades; for example, it was at about 57 per cent in the 1970s, 59 per cent in the 1980s, and 60 per cent in the 1990s. At the turn of the twenty-first century, it was thought that the reductions in the employment rate would result from more early retirements and more people going to school. It has become clear that older workers are deciding to work longer and some people who were not even looking for work have now joined, or more likely rejoined, the labour force.

In spite of this past record of an increase in human resources, there is reason to believe that the future may not be as positive with regard to the demographics of human capital. First, the movement of the baby boom and women into the labour force were one-time events. Although the labour force grew at rates close to 3 per cent a year in the 1966–81 period, the rate was down to 1.5 per cent a year from 2001 to 2012, and it expected to show only modest growth over the next 15 years. Besides, other elements of demographic change may not bring such increases in human capital (Livi-Bacci, 2000). On the mortality side, the improvements in the fourth phase of the epidemiological transition are now more likely to occur for people who are beyond labour-force age. Lower fertility has no direct consequences for the labour force in the short term, and the effect on the age structure is at first attenuated through population momentum. Eventually, lower fertility results in slower growth of the labour force, as there are fewer young people at ages for entry in the workforce. As the baby boom moved into reproductive ages, the lower fertility was muted in terms of its translation into fewer births. Over the 1981–2011 period, however, the number of children has been lower than in earlier decades, and in absolute numbers, there were fewer people under 30 in 2011 than in 1981—this in spite of the fact that the whole population grew by 38.4 per cent. Regardless of the projection chosen,

after 2016, there will be more people at workforce-exit ages (55–64) than at workforce-entry ages (15–24). While this ratio was near parity in 2011, in forecasting future labour-force growth, the ratio is expected to decline further, to about 0.8 for all three of Statistics Canada's projections by 2021. For the next 20 years, then, there will likely be fewer people about to enter the labour force than exiting it through retirement.

These changes can also be interpreted through the phenomenon of aging at the bottom, aging in the middle, and aging at the top. When population aging started, it was mostly due to aging at the bottom—that is, fewer births, which did not immediately have a direct affect on the labour force, and it had the indirect effect of liberating women for more entry into the labour force. From the 1960s to the '80s, the aging at the middle involved the positive element of the movement of the baby boom into labour-force ages. It is, thus, understandable that in her 1986 book *Population Aging*, McDaniel (1986) had a largely positive interpretation. The aging at the middle, however, will eventually mean that the baby boom will move into phases of life where they are less productive. At the time of the 2011 Census the oldest of the baby boomers reached the milestone age of 65, while this cohort (aged 47 to 65) made up about a third of the labour force. Besides, we now have the phenomenon of aging at the top, which implies a greater number of people who are at ages beyond those usually found in the active labour force.

It may also be that there will be less human capital gain from immigration than has been the case in the past. First, the Canadian labour force is well educated, and there are fewer relative gains from importing skilled labour. Second, the education and credentials obtained abroad may be less valuable in a service economy. In fact, people who completed their education before coming to Canada have often done poorly in the labour market since the 1980s, whereas second-generation Canadians have done well, as have those who successfully obtained further education or completed their education in Canada.

For internal migration, the older population, and the fact that most people now live in larger places, means that there is likely to be less human capital gain through movement of people across regions. Contrary to the common view that there is more and more movement in the modern world, Canadian data shows a gradual decline in internal migration rates between provinces. In 1972, there were 17.9 migrations per 1,000 people between provinces, compared to about 13 in 1990 and 9 in 2011. There may also be some disadvantages to large urban concentrations, including the loss of time, and, thus, of human capital, caused by long commuting times.

Following on these lines of thinking about human capital, there are several possible implications. In an older and slower-growing population, the contributions of all elements to human capital must be maximized. This, of course, applies to women's contribution to the paid labour force, which cannot be endangered, and must be further enhanced. On the mortality side, it means that reductions in morbidity and disability are even more important than prolonging life. It can be argued, for instance, that an undue amount of financial resources are allocated to the last days and months of life and that more resources should be allocated to improving the quality of life rather than the length of life.

While the human-resource implications of migration are significant, we must not exaggerate the potential to solve human resource deficiencies through immigration. Even the annual report to Parliament on immigration (Citizenship and Immigration Canada, 2014) continues to make the misleading statement that immigration has become the primary source of our country's "net labour force growth." While this observation is technically correct, it is very misleading, as this inference is obtained by merely taking as the denominator the amount of growth in the labour force over time, and as the numerator the number of immigrants received. The resulting ratio can be misleading if the size of the labour force is fairly stable. For instance, if the labour force increased from 10,000,000 to 10,000,001 persons, but one immigrant had joined the labour force, then 100 per cent of the labour force growth would be due to immigration. It is better to compare the internal and external sources of labour-force entry, and to appreciate that most of it is due to the internal source of people leaving the Canadian educational system and entering the workplace. Kustec (2012) has estimated, for example, that in 2010, roughly 80 per cent of all new labour-force entrants were people leaving school and roughly 20 per cent were immigrants. Anyone who has some association with Canadian education would know that there is a large internal source of new entries into the workforce.

In effect, these human-capital questions call attention to all three of the demographic processes. Immigration has clear implications for human resources, including the advantages of diversity and openness to the world. There is need for continued attention to ways of reducing health risks and disability, especially for people of labour-force age. Population renewal through births needs to be supported by reducing some of the opportunity costs of having children. Besides these purely demographic elements, there is also a need to maximize the employment rates, by investing in the human resources of disadvantaged groups and encouraging participation at older ages. It is well understood, for instance, that raising the male age-specific labour-force participation rates back to 1970 levels, and bringing women's rates much closer to parity with men could increase the total size of the labour force substantially.

John Maynard Keynes, the father of modern economics, frequently said that big historical events are often caused by slow demographic processes (United Nations, 1989: 1–2). Today, he would surely pay attention to the rift that separates the rapidly growing and young Global South populations from the aging and slow-growing or declining populations of the world's more developed countries. In the long term, these different demographic dynamics will surely bring changes in the relations among nations. The changes within Canada are no less striking, especially in comparison to the recent past. While demographic changes are slow, continued attention is required to understand their impact and to meet the challenges of adaptation.

There are many reasons for students, researchers, and the public to pay continued attention to Canada's changing population. A greater focus on the demographics will ensure that discussions are based on the actual facts and the underlying population processes. Besides, these facts and processes have important implications for our well-being, both individually and collectively.

Appendix A: The Life Table

The life table is among the most versatile of the demographer's analytical tools. The structure of the life table varies from the simple conventional life table (described below) to more complex multiple-decrement and multistate life tables (these are clearly beyond the scope of the current text; for further detail, see Rogers, 1980; Ledent and Rees, 1986). Best known as a statistical device for summarizing the mortality experience of a population, life tables have been used in a wide variety of applications and not just in the study of mortality. The simple conventional life table can be used to analyze mortality or any other non-renewable process. By *non-renewable process*, we mean any demographic process in which the constituent events cannot be repeated—for example, mortality is clearly not repeatable, just as the birth of a first child is not repeatable, nor is the establishment of a first union.

The most commonly cited statistic from the life table is life expectancy at birth, although it is possible to use a life table to calculate life expectancy at any age. The tables (see Tables A.1 and A.2) referred to here are from the 2009–11 Canadian life table. This is the complete life table (by single years of age) constructed by Statistics Canada from vital statistics on deaths (by age and sex) and population estimates based on the census (for methodological details, see Martel et al., 2013). Although not presented here, Statistics Canada generates these life tables for every province and territory (available on CANSIM), separately for males and females. These tables are available by single year of age for all Canadian provinces but one; an abridged five-year life table is available for Prince Edward Island as well as for the three territories combined.

It is possible to distinguish between two basic types of life tables: (1) period life tables, and (2) cohort (or generational) life tables. The period life table is constructed from information on mortality relating to a relatively short period of time (for example, one or perhaps a few calendar years), whereas cohort life tables use information that corresponds to the full lifespan of actual birth cohorts (for example, in summarizing the mortality experience of all persons who were born in

1900). While the 2009–11 life tables (Tables A.1 and A.2) are an example of period life tables, summarizing the 2009–11 mortality experience of Canadians, several cohort or generational life tables have been produced for past cohorts born in the nineteenth century and early twentieth century (Bourbeau et al., 1997). For cohorts born more recently, it is not possible to calculate a full generational life table unless one projects mortality to predict what mortality rates might look like for these cohorts as they move through whatever years remain in their lifespan.

While cohort life tables are useful for historical research and in the study of mortality trends, most of the life tables currently in the public domain are in fact period life tables. These provide snapshots of the mortality experience of specific populations, or summary measures of mortality not affected by differences in age structure. In creating these period life tables, it is useful to think of what demographers refer to as *hypothetical birth cohorts*. More specifically, it is useful to think of a hypothetical situation, in which a birth cohort has 100,000 newly born persons (i.e., born at the same time). This cohort is subjected throughout its lifespan to a given set of age-specific mortality rates (documented for the period of interest). If we create a period life table for 2009–11, this cohort experiences the mortality rates documented over this three-year period. As life tables are normally calculated for males and females separately, Tables A.1 and A.2 involves two distinct hypothetical cohorts of 100,000 males and 100,000 females who experience the corresponding mortality schedules from the 2009–11 period.

Input of Empirical Data

The empirical basis for the conventional life table (including Tables A.1 and A.2) are age-specific death rates (M_x), which are calculated on the basis of registered deaths and population estimates, both delimited by age and sex. While there are several different procedures possible in calculating M_x (including Statistics Canada's practice of averaging the number of deaths for three consecutive years), the most common practice is merely to divide the total number of deaths in a population at age x in a given year (D_x) by its mid-year population at age x (P_x):

$$M_x = D_x/P_x$$

Since this rate assumes that deaths are uniformly distributed across each year of age, it is considered a reasonable approximation of what demographers refer to as the *central death rate of the life table* (m_x): the number of deaths occurring in a specified period of time (commonly one year) and in a specific age–sex category divided by the average population at risk over this period (that is, for the appropriate age–sex category). Whereas Statistics Canada's life table required an assortment of more complex procedures to obtain these rates—particularly in the modelling of the mortality experience of Canadians at very advanced ages—the results obtained across most age groups are very similar to what would be obtained if one used this relatively simple procedure (for further details on these modelling procedures, see Martel et al., 2013).

Assuming that these age-specific death rates serve as a good approximation of the central death rates of the life table (that is, $M_x \approx m_x$), it is possible to convert them into the basic input necessary for the construction of a life table. More specifically, it is possible to convert these rates into age-specific probabilities of death (conventionally denoted as q_x). With the probability of death, the complete life table begins with information on the likelihood of dying between exact ages x and $x+1$. Assuming that deaths occur evenly throughout an age interval, it is possible to estimate this probability as

$$q_x = 2m_x/(2 + m_x)$$

To the extent that deaths do not occur equally through the age interval (i.e., if they are more common in the first few months of life or among the very aged), variants of this equation are possible (Hinde, 1998; Martel et al., 2013). With this probability of dying calculated across all ages, it is possible to generate, separately by sex, all of the necessary functions of the life table, as follows in the next section.

The Complete Life Table Functions

In Table A.1, we have

(x) exact age, stated in years.
(l_x) the number of persons still alive at exact age x (that is, the number of survivors at exact age x).

The first value of this, l_0, is termed the radix of the life table and is meant to designate the size of the hypothetical cohort at its origin. To facilitate interpretation, this value is usually set at 100,000.

(q_x) the probability of dying over the interval (between exact ages x and $x+1$).

In Table A.1, for example, the probability that a male child will die in his first year of life is $(q_0) = 0.00522$. This translates into 522 deaths out of 100,000 persons. As indicated above, this can be approximated on the basis of age-specific mortality rates.

(p_x) the probability of survival over the interval (between exact ages x and $x+1$). This is obtained merely as $1 - q_x$.

(d_x) the number of persons dying in each interval (between exact ages x and $x+1$), given as $d_x = l_x \cdot q_x$.

In Table A.1, for example, the number of males dying between exact ages 40 and 41 is given as

$$d_{40} = l_{40} \cdot q_{40} = (97,399)(.00132) = 129$$

Beginning with a radix of 100,000 and the values of q_x, it is possible to calculate the age distribution of deaths (d_x) and the number of survivors (l_x) by recognizing that:

$$l_{x+1} = l_x - d_x.$$

In applying this formulae, it is possible to calculate both d_x and l_x across all ages through to that age in which the hypothetical cohort dies out.

(L_x) expresses the *total number of person years lived* by the hypothetical cohort between the exact ages x and $x+1$.

In the absence of more detailed information, L_x is typically obtained merely as an average, based on the assumption that deaths are evenly distributed throughout the year.

$$L_x = (l_x + l_{x+1}) \, / \, 2.$$

For example, for men aged 30:

$$l_{30} = (l_{30} + l_{31}) \, / \, 2 = (98,333 + 98,261) \, / \, 2 = 98,297.$$

For the first year of life, L_x is usually not obtained in this manner, as mortality is far from being evenly distributed throughout early infancy (for details on the distribution of infant deaths and the estimation of L_0, see Martel et al., 2013).

(T_x) indicates the total number of person years lived after exact age x.

Values of (T_x) are obtained by summing the entries in the L_x column from the bottom of the life table upwards, noting the accumulation to each exact age x.

(e_x) shows the average number of years of life remaining to persons at each exact age x (e_0 designates life expectancy at birth, e_{20} designates life expectancy at age 20, and so on). It is obtained merely by dividing each value of T_x by the corresponding number of survivors l_x.

At age 50, for example, life expectancy for men is estimated as

$$e_{50} = T_{50} \, / \, l_{50} = 3,014,926 \, /95,536 = 31.56 \text{ years (or}$$
81.56 years in total)

With the above information, available by age and sex, all sorts of meaningful inferences are possible as to the impact of mortality when comparing different populations.

Survival Rates

Among the most commonly used life-table functions are survival rates. These rates ordinarily do not appear in the life table proper, but they can be derived from it, using either the l_x or the L_x vectors. For some examples, consider the following as based on Tables A.1 and A.2.

The probability of surviving from exact age x to exact age $x + a$ (i.e., from one birthday to another) is possible, calculated as:

$$S_x^{x+a} = l_{x+a} \, / \, l_x$$

For example, the probability of surviving from one's birth through to one's seventieth birthday is calculated as follows:

For males: $S_0^{70} = l_{70} \, / \, l_0 = 80,301 \, / \, 100,000 = 0.803$

For females: $S_0^{70} = l_{70} \, / \, l_0 = 87,202 \, / \, 100,000 = 0.872$

Given the age- and sex-specific mortality rates, observed in 2009–11, of an initial cohort of about 100,000 males, 80,301 would still be alive on their seventieth birthday, which compares to 87,202 women out of an initial cohort of 100,000 females. In other words, a male baby born today would have an 80 per cent chance of living to age 70 if his mortality risks throughout his lifetime were exactly those experienced by the male population of Canada in 2009–11, whereas the comparable statistic for females is 87 per cent. This same statistic can be calculated, from birth through to any age, or, for that matter, between any two birthdays.

Between two ages: the probability of surviving from one's seventieth birthday until one's eightieth is calculated as follows:

For males: $S_{70}^{10} = l_{80} \, / \, l_{70} = 57,515 \, / \, 80,301 = 0.716$

For females: $S_{70}^{10} = l_{80} \, / \, l_{70} = 70,253 \, / \, 87,202 = 0.806$

In other words, given current mortality rates, the percentage of men who reach their seventieth birthday and then survive until their eightieth is 71.6 per cent, whereas 80.6 per cent of women do so.

As an alternative to working with birthdays (or exact ages), it is also possible to calculate the probabilities of survival over time for specific age groups. For example, the probability of a person currently aged x still being alive 10 years hence is calculated as L_{x+10} / L_x.

In working with the *person years lived* column, the probability that persons aged 50–54 will still be alive in 30 years, is given as

$$\frac{L_{80-84}}{L_{50-54}} = \frac{(L_{80} + L_{81} + L_{82} + L_{83} + L_{84})}{(L_{50} + L_{51} + L_{52} + L_{53} + L_{54})}.$$

For males it equals

$$\frac{(55,967+52,804+49,514+46,114+42,622)}{(95,392+95,090+94,759+94,397+94,000)} = 0.522$$

For females, that equals

$$\frac{(68,969+66,307+63,453+60,405+57,165)}{(97,094+96,893+96,675+96,438+96,179)} = 0.654$$

This survival rate indicates that if mortality remains constant over time as observed for the 1995–1997 period, 52.2 per cent of men aged 50–54 will be alive in 30 years (aged 80–84) and about 65.4 per cent of women aged 50–54 will be alive. Other applications include the inversion of the above to obtain reverse survival rates, which allow for all sorts of reverse survival techniques.

Table A.1 ▦ Complete Life Table, Canada, 2009–2011: Males

Exact Age	l_x	d_x	p_x	q_x	L_x	T_x	e_x
0	100,000	522	0.99478	0.00522	99,531	7,933,442	79.33
1	99,478	30	0.99970	0.00030	99,463	7,833,911	78.75
2	99,449	22	0.99978	0.00022	99,438	7,734,448	77.77
3	99,427	16	0.99983	0.00017	99,418	7,635,010	76.79
4	99,411	13	0.99987	0.00013	99,405	7,535,591	75.80
5	99,398	11	0.99989	0.00011	99,392	7,436,187	74.81
6	99,387	10	0.99990	0.00010	99,382	7,336,795	73.82
7	99,377	9	0.99991	0.00009	99,373	7,237,413	72.83
8	99,369	8	0.99992	0.00008	99,364	7,138,040	71.83
9	99,360	8	0.99992	0.00008	99,356	7,038,675	70.84
10	99,352	9	0.99991	0.00009	99,348	6,939,319	69.85
11	99,343	10	0.99990	0.00010	99,339	6,839,971	68.85
12	99,334	12	0.99988	0.00012	99,328	6,740,633	67.86
13	99,322	15	0.99985	0.00015	99,315	6,641,305	66.87
14	99,308	20	0.99980	0.00020	99,298	6,541,990	65.88
15	99,288	28	0.99972	0.00028	99,274	6,442,692	64.89
16	99,260	39	0.99961	0.00039	99,241	6,343,418	63.91
17	99,221	50	0.99949	0.00051	99,196	6,244,177	62.93
18	99,171	59	0.99941	0.00059	99,141	6,144,982	61.96
19	99,112	65	0.99934	0.00066	99,079	6,045,840	61.00
20	99,047	70	0.99929	0.00071	99,011	5,946,761	60.04
21	98,976	74	0.99925	0.00075	98,939	5,847,750	59.08
22	98,902	76	0.99924	0.00076	98,864	5,748,810	58.13
23	98,827	75	0.99924	0.00076	98,789	5,649,946	57.17
24	98,752	73	0.99926	0.00074	98,715	5,551,157	56.21
25	98,679	70	0.99929	0.00071	98,644	5,452,442	55.25
26	98,609	69	0.99930	0.00070	98,574	5,353,798	54.29
27	98,540	68	0.99931	0.00069	98,506	5,255,223	53.33
28	98,472	69	0.99930	0.00070	98,438	5,156,717	52.37
29	98,404	70	0.99929	0.00071	98,369	5,058,279	51.40
30	98,333	73	0.99926	0.00074	98,297	4,959,911	50.44
31	98,261	76	0.99922	0.00078	98,223	4,861,614	49.48
32	98,184	80	0.99918	0.00082	98,144	4,763,391	48.51
33	98,104	84	0.99914	0.00086	98,062	4,665,247	47.55
34	98,020	89	0.99909	0.00091	97,976	4,567,184	46.59
35	97,931	94	0.99904	0.00096	97,884	4,469,209	45.64
36	97,837	100	0.99898	0.00102	97,788	4,371,324	44.68
37	97,738	106	0.99892	0.00108	97,685	4,273,537	43.72
38	97,632	113	0.99885	0.00115	97,576	4,175,852	42.77
39	97,519	120	0.99877	0.00123	97,459	4,078,276	41.82
40	97,399	129	0.99868	0.00132	97,335	3,980,817	40.87
41	97,270	138	0.99858	0.00142	97,201	3,883,482	39.92
42	97,132	148	0.99847	0.00153	97,058	3,786,281	38.98
43	96,984	160	0.99835	0.00165	96,904	3,689,223	38.04
44	96,824	173	0.99821	0.00179	96,737	3,592,320	37.10
45	96,651	187	0.99806	0.00194	96,557	3,495,582	36.17
46	96,464	203	0.99789	0.00211	96,362	3,399,025	35.24
47	96,261	221	0.99771	0.00229	96,150	3,302,663	34.31
48	96,040	241	0.99749	0.00251	95,919	3,206,513	33.39
49	95,799	263	0.99725	0.00275	95,667	3,110,594	32.47
50	95,536	288	0.99699	0.00301	95,392	3,014,926	31.56
51	95,248	316	0.99669	0.00331	95,090	2,919,535	30.65
52	94,932	346	0.99636	0.00364	94,759	2,824,445	29.75
53	94,586	379	0.99599	0.00401	94,397	2,729,685	28.86
54	94,207	415	0.99559	0.00441	94,000	2,635,288	27.97
55	93,792	454	0.99516	0.00484	93,565	2,541,289	27.09

Table A.1 ▣ Continued

Exact Age	l_x	d_x	p_x	q_x	L_x	T_x	e_x
56	93,338	497	0.99467	0.00533	93,089	2,447,723	26.22
57	92,841	544	0.99414	0.00586	92,569	2,354,634	25.36
58	92,297	595	0.99355	0.00645	91,999	2,262,065	24.51
59	91,701	650	0.99291	0.00709	91,376	2,170,066	23.66
60	91,051	711	0.99220	0.00780	90,696	2,078,690	22.83
61	90,340	776	0.99141	0.00859	89,952	1,987,995	22.01
62	89,565	846	0.99055	0.00945	89,141	1,898,042	21.19
63	88,718	923	0.98960	0.01040	88,257	1,808,901	20.39
64	87,795	1,005	0.98855	0.01145	87,293	1,720,644	19.60
65	86,790	1,094	0.98740	0.01260	86,243	1,633,351	18.82
66	85,696	1,189	0.98613	0.01387	85,102	1,547,108	18.05
67	84,507	1,291	0.98472	0.01528	83,862	1,462,006	17.30
68	83,217	1,400	0.98318	0.01682	82,517	1,378,144	16.56
69	81,817	1,515	0.98148	0.01852	81,059	1,295,627	15.84
70	80,301	1,638	0.97960	0.02040	79,482	1,214,568	15.13
71	78,663	1,767	0.97753	0.02247	77,780	1,135,086	14.43
72	76,896	1,903	0.97525	0.02475	75,944	1,057,306	13.75
73	74,993	2,045	0.97274	0.02726	73,971	981,362	13.09
74	72,948	2,191	0.96996	0.03004	71,853	907,391	12.44
75	70,757	2,342	0.96690	0.03310	69,586	835,539	11.81
76	68,415	2,495	0.96353	0.03647	67,167	765,953	11.20
77	65,920	2,650	0.95981	0.04019	64,595	698,785	10.60
78	63,270	2,803	0.95570	0.04430	61,869	634,190	10.02
79	60,467	2,953	0.95117	0.04883	58,991	572,321	9.46
80	57,515	3,096	0.94617	0.05383	55,967	513,330	8.93
81	54,419	3,230	0.94065	0.05935	52,804	457,364	8.40
82	51,189	3,349	0.93457	0.06543	49,514	404,560	7.90
83	47,840	3,452	0.92785	0.07215	46,114	355,045	7.42
84	44,388	3,532	0.92043	0.07957	42,622	308,931	6.96
85	40,856	3,585	0.91224	0.08776	39,063	266,309	6.52
86	37,271	3,608	0.90320	0.09680	35,467	227,246	6.10
87	33,663	3,594	0.89322	0.10678	31,866	191,779	5.70
88	30,068	3,542	0.88220	0.11780	28,297	159,914	5.32
89	26,526	3,448	0.87003	0.12997	24,803	131,616	4.96
90	23,079	3,310	0.85659	0.14341	21,424	106,813	4.63
91	19,769	3,122	0.84206	0.15794	18,208	85,389	4.32
92	16,647	2,884	0.82674	0.17326	15,205	67,182	4.04
93	13,763	2,605	0.81069	0.18931	12,460	51,977	3.78
94	11,157	2,299	0.79396	0.20604	10,008	39,517	3.54
95	8,858	1,935	0.78161	0.21839	7,891	29,509	3.33
96	6,924	1,630	0.76464	0.23536	6,109	21,618	3.12
97	5,294	1,339	0.74710	0.25290	4,625	15,509	2.93
98	3,955	1,072	0.72908	0.27092	3,420	10,884	2.75
99	2,884	834	0.71067	0.28933	2,467	7,465	2.59
100	2,049	631	0.69198	0.30802	1,734	4,998	2.44
101	1,418	464	0.67313	0.32687	1,186	3,264	2.30
102	955	330	0.65424	0.34576	790	2,078	2.18
103	625	228	0.63543	0.36457	511	1,288	2.06
104	397	152	0.61681	0.38319	321	778	1.96
105	245	98	0.59851	0.40149	196	457	1.87
106	147	61	0.58063	0.41937	116	261	1.78
107	85	37	0.56327	0.43673	66	145	1.71
108	48	22	0.54650	0.45350	37	79	1.64
109	26	12	0.53040	0.46960	20	42	1.59
110+	14	14	0.00000	1.00000	22	22	1.56

Source: Statistics Canada, 2013, Demography Division. "Life tables, Canada, provinces, and territories" (84-537-X).

Table A.2 ◻ Complete Life Table, Canada, 2009–2011: Females

Exact Age	l_x	d_x	p_x	q_x	L_x	T_x	e_x
0	100,000	449	0.99551	0.00449	99,596	8,359,982	83.60
1	99,551	21	0.99979	0.00021	99,541	8,260,386	82.98
2	99,531	16	0.99984	0.00016	99,523	8,160,846	81.99
3	99,515	13	0.99987	0.00013	99,509	8,061,323	81.01
4	99,502	10	0.99990	0.00010	99,497	7,961,814	80.02
5	99,492	9	0.99991	0.00009	99,488	7,862,316	79.02
6	99,483	8	0.99992	0.00008	99,479	7,762,829	78.03
7	99,475	7	0.99993	0.00007	99,471	7,663,350	77.04
8	99,468	7	0.99993	0.00007	99,464	7,563,878	76.04
9	99,461	7	0.99993	0.00007	99,457	7,464,414	75.05
10	99,453	8	0.99992	0.00008	99,450	7,364,957	74.05
11	99,446	8	0.99992	0.00008	99,442	7,265,507	73.06
12	99,438	9	0.99991	0.00009	99,433	7,166,066	72.07
13	99,428	11	0.99989	0.00011	99,423	7,066,633	71.07
14	99,417	14	0.99986	0.00014	99,410	6,967,210	70.08
15	99,404	17	0.99982	0.00018	99,395	6,867,800	69.09
16	99,386	22	0.99978	0.00022	99,375	6,768,405	68.10
17	99,364	26	0.99974	0.00026	99,351	6,669,030	67.12
18	99,339	28	0.99972	0.00028	99,325	6,569,679	66.13
19	99,311	29	0.99971	0.00029	99,296	6,470,354	65.15
20	99,282	30	0.99970	0.00030	99,267	6,371,057	64.17
21	99,252	30	0.99970	0.00030	99,237	6,271,790	63.19
22	99,222	30	0.99969	0.00031	99,207	6,172,553	62.21
23	99,192	30	0.99969	0.00031	99,177	6,073,346	61.23
24	99,161	30	0.99970	0.00030	99,146	5,974,169	60.25
25	99,131	30	0.99970	0.00030	99,117	5,875,023	59.26
26	99,102	30	0.99970	0.00030	99,087	5,775,906	58.28
27	99,072	31	0.99969	0.00031	99,056	5,676,819	57.30
28	99,041	32	0.99968	0.00032	99,025	5,577,763	56.32
29	99,009	34	0.99966	0.00034	98,992	5,478,738	55.34
30	98,975	36	0.99963	0.00037	98,957	5,379,746	54.35
31	98,939	39	0.99960	0.00040	98,919	5,280,789	53.37
32	98,899	43	0.99957	0.00043	98,878	5,181,870	52.40
33	98,857	47	0.99953	0.00047	98,833	5,082,992	51.42
34	98,810	50	0.99949	0.00051	98,785	4,984,158	50.44
35	98,759	55	0.99944	0.00056	98,732	4,885,374	49.47
36	98,705	60	0.99940	0.00060	98,675	4,786,642	48.49
37	98,645	65	0.99934	0.00066	98,613	4,687,967	47.52
38	98,580	70	0.99929	0.00071	98,545	4,589,354	46.55
39	98,510	76	0.99923	0.00077	98,472	4,490,809	45.59
40	98,434	83	0.99916	0.00084	98,392	4,392,337	44.62
41	98,351	90	0.99908	0.00092	98,306	4,293,944	43.66
42	98,261	98	0.99900	0.00100	98,212	4,195,639	42.70
43	98,163	107	0.99891	0.00109	98,109	4,097,427	41.74
44	98,056	116	0.99882	0.00118	97,998	3,999,317	40.79
45	97,940	126	0.99871	0.00129	97,877	3,901,319	39.83
46	97,814	137	0.99860	0.00140	97,746	3,803,442	38.88
47	97,677	149	0.99847	0.00153	97,603	3,705,696	37.94
48	97,528	162	0.99834	0.00166	97,447	3,608,094	37.00
49	97,366	176	0.99819	0.00181	97,278	3,510,646	36.06

Table A.2 ▣ Continued

Exact Age	l_x	d_x	p_x	q_x	L_x	T_x	e_x
50	97,190	192	0.99803	0.00197	97,094	3,413,369	35.12
51	96,998	209	0.99785	0.00215	96,893	3,316,275	34.19
52	96,789	227	0.99765	0.00235	96,675	3,219,382	33.26
53	96,561	248	0.99743	0.00257	96,438	3,122,707	32.34
54	96,314	270	0.99720	0.00280	96,179	3,026,269	31.42
55	96,043	295	0.99693	0.00307	95,896	2,930,090	30.51
56	95,749	321	0.99664	0.00336	95,588	2,834,194	28.70
57	95,427	351	0.99632	0.00368	95,252	2,738,606	27.80
58	95,077	383	0.99597	0.00403	94,885	2,643,354	26.91
59	94,693	419	0.99558	0.00442	94,484	2,548,469	26.03
60	94,275	458	0.99515	0.00485	94,046	2,453,985	25.15
61	93,817	500	0.99467	0.00533	93,567	2,359,939	24.29
62	93,317	547	0.99414	0.00586	93,044	2,266,372	23.43
63	92,770	598	0.99355	0.00645	92,471	2,173,329	22.58
64	92,172	654	0.99290	0.00710	91,845	2,080,857	21.73
65	91,518	716	0.99218	0.00782	91,160	1,989,013	20.90
66	90,802	783	0.99138	0.00862	90,411	1,897,853	20.08
67	90,019	856	0.99049	0.00951	89,591	1,807,442	19.27
68	89,163	937	0.98949	0.01051	88,694	1,717,851	18.47
69	88,226	1,024	0.98839	0.01161	87,714	1,629,157	17.68
70	87,202	1,119	0.98716	0.01284	86,642	1,541,443	16.90
71	86,083	1,223	0.98580	0.01420	85,471	1,454,801	16.14
72	84,860	1,335	0.98427	0.01573	84,192	1,369,330	15.39
73	83,525	1,456	0.98257	0.01743	82,797	1,285,137	14.65
74	82,069	1,587	0.98066	0.01934	81,275	1,202,341	13.93
75	80,482	1,727	0.97854	0.02146	79,618	1,121,065	13.22
76	78,755	1,877	0.97616	0.02384	77,816	1,041,447	12.53
77	76,878	2,037	0.97351	0.02649	75,859	9,63,631	11.86
78	74,841	2,206	0.97053	0.02947	73,738	8,87,772	11.21
79	72,635	2,383	0.96720	0.03280	71,444	8,14,034	10.57
80	70,253	2,567	0.96346	0.03654	68,969	7,42,590	9.95
81	67,685	2,757	0.95926	0.04074	66,307	6,73,621	9.35
82	64,928	2,951	0.95455	0.04545	63,453	6,07,314	8.78
83	61,977	3,145	0.94926	0.05074	60,405	5,43,861	8.22
84	58,833	3,335	0.94331	0.05669	57,165	4,83,456	7.68
85	55,498	3,517	0.93662	0.06338	53,739	4,26,291	7.17
86	51,981	3,686	0.92909	0.07091	50,138	3,72,551	6.68
87	48,294	3,835	0.92060	0.07940	46,377	3,22,414	6.21
88	44,460	3,956	0.91103	0.08897	42,482	2,76,037	5.77
89	40,504	4,041	0.90023	0.09977	38,484	2,33,555	5.35
90	36,463	4,082	0.88804	0.11196	34,422	1,95,071	4.96
91	32,381	4,061	0.87458	0.12542	30,350	1,60,649	4.60
92	28,319	3,962	0.86009	0.13991	26,338	1,30,299	4.27
93	24,357	3,785	0.84459	0.15541	22,465	1,03,961	3.96
94	20,572	3,536	0.82810	0.17190	18,804	81,496	3.68
95	17,036	3,211	0.81151	0.18849	15,430	62,692	3.42
96	13,825	2,855	0.79347	0.20653	12,397	47,262	3.18
97	10,969	2,473	0.77451	0.22549	9,733	34,865	2.96
98	8,496	2,084	0.75474	0.24526	7,454	25,133	2.76
99	6,412	1,704	0.73429	0.26571	5,560	17,679	2.57

(Continued)

Table A.2 ▦ Continued

Exact Age	l_x	d_x	p_x	q_x	L_x	T_x	e_x
100	4,708	1,350	0.71329	0.28671	4,033	12,118	2.41
101	3,358	1,035	0.69190	0.30810	2,841	8,085	2.26
102	2,324	766	0.67030	0.32970	1,941	5,244	2.12
103	1,558	547	0.64868	0.35132	1,284	3,303	2.00
104	1,010	377	0.62720	0.37280	822	2,019	1.89
105	634	250	0.60605	0.39395	509	1,197	1.79
106	384	159	0.58539	0.41461	304	688	1.71
107	225	98	0.56538	0.43462	176	384	1.63
108	127	58	0.54614	0.45386	98	208	1.58
109	69	33	0.52778	0.47222	53	110	1.54
110+	37	37	0.00000	1.00000	57	57	

Source: Statistics Canada, 2013, Demography Division. "Life tables, Canada, provinces, and territories" (84-537-X).

Appendix B: Crude Rates, the Total Fertility Rate, and Standardization

Crude Rates

A commonly employed measure in summarizing the prevalence of a given type of demographic event in a population is the *crude rate*. This rate consists of the ratio of the total number of events occurring over a specified period (usually a year) to the average total population in that period (normally the mid-year population). Demographers commonly refer to the *crude death rate* (CDR) and the *crude birth rate* (CBR), as well as the difference between the two, the crude rate of natural increase (r_n). Analogous crude rates have also been developed in neighbouring social sciences, such as criminology, in which a commonly cited statistic is the total crime rate, which merely expresses the total number of crimes reported in a given year relative to the mid-year population. In other words, a crude rate can be calculated in the study of a wide assortment of both demographic and non-demographic processes.

The crude death rate in Canada in 2011 (expressed per 1,000) can be obtained as

$$CDR_{Canada} = \frac{\text{total deaths in 2011}}{\text{mid-year population}} \times 1,000$$
$$= 242,074/34,342,780 \times 1,000$$
$$= 7.05 \text{ deaths per 1,000}$$

This rate is lower than Canada's crude birth rate, obtained as

$$CBR_{Canada} = \frac{\text{total births in 2011}}{\text{mid-year population}} \times 1,000$$
$$= 377,636/34,342,780 \times 1,000 = 11.0$$
$$\text{births per 1,000}$$

Overall, the difference between the two provides Canada's crude rate of natural increase (documented at r_n = 3.95 per 1,000 in 2011). This corresponds to less than half of Canada's overall population growth in 2011, with the remainder a by-product of international migration (Statistics Canada, CANSIM Tables 051-0001 and 053-0001).

While these rates are among the most elementary demographic measures available, they are not without their limitations. The CDR, for example, is a poor indicator of comparative mortality experiences across populations because it is strongly influenced by the age–sex structure of different populations. Similarly, the CBR is not a very refined measure of fertility, as the denominator includes a large number of persons (including children as well as older women not of reproductive age) who are not capable of child-bearing. Consequently, demographers have developed more refined techniques in the study of demographic processes across populations. By calculating age-specific rates, for example, it is possible to study the age pattern of fertility and mortality and, on this basis, calculate more meaningful summary indicators.

Total Fertility Rate

The *total fertility rate* (TFR) is among the most commonly cited measures of fertility. By working with age-specific fertility rates, the TFR summarizes the fertility experience of women of reproductive age, usually for a specific calendar year. As a period measure of fertility, the TFR requires information on all births in a given year, organized by reported age of mothers. A first step in calculating the TFR is to obtain the age-specific fertility rate at each age a (f_a), obtained as

$$fa = \frac{\text{total number of births to women aged } a}{\text{total mid-year population of women aged } a}$$

Alternatively, for five-year age groups, it is possible to calculate rates with births added up across ages. For example, for women aged 20–24,

$$F_{20,24} = \frac{\text{total number of births to women aged 20–24}}{\text{total mid-year population of women aged 20–24}}$$

Table B.1 ▦ Example of Calculating the Total Fertility Rate, 2011

	$f_{a, a+4}$	$5 \times f_{a, a+4}$
15 to 19	0.013	0.063
20 to 24	0.046	0.229
25 to 29	0.095	0.476
30 to 34	0.106	0.530
35 to 39	0.052	0.262
40 to 44	0.010	0.052
45 to 49	0.001	0.003
	sum	1.61

Source: Statistics Canada, 2011, table 102-4505.

With these age-specific rates, it is possible to calculate the TFR by merely summing them up across reproductive ages.

In working with fertility rates f_a,

$$\text{TFR} = \sum_{a=15}^{49} f_a$$

or with five-year age groups one multiplies by 5 (because each woman spends five years in these age groups):

$$\text{TFR} = 5\sum_{a=15-19}^{45-49} f_a$$

As the sum of the age-specific rates, the TFR can be interpreted as "the number of children that a woman would have, on average, if she experienced throughout her reproductive years the age-specific rates as observed in a given year." In international comparisons, this measure is more meaningful than the crude birth rate, as it controls for differences in the relative number of women of reproductive age. While it does not correspond to the experience of any actual cohort of women, it does provide a useful summary indicator of overall fertility at a given point in time. Table B.1 provides an example of how this rate is calculated from 2011 age-specific rates for Canada, with a resultant TFR of 1.61 births.

Standardization

Owing to some of the shortcomings of crude rates, demographers routinely employ *standardization techniques*. These techniques have been developed in order to adjust crude rates for compositional differences across populations. Standardization was first developed in recognition of the simple fact that since demographic rates usually vary in an important manner across different parts of a population, compositional differences can lead to all sorts of difficulties when crude rates are compared. It is well known, for example, that the incidence of mortality varies strongly by age and that differences among populations in age structure can have a considerable influence on the number of deaths reported.

For this reason, some rather counterintuitive statistics are available; for example, the CDR throughout much of Central and South America is currently lower than the CDR for Canada (Population Reference Bureau, 2014). While Canada is a relatively prosperous country and has high standards of population health, its CDR is actually higher than in much of the developing world. When one is working with standardization, the question surfaces as to how much of these overall differences in crude rates are attributable to compositional differences and how much is actually due to differences in the demographic process itself. For example, most Latin American countries continue to have a disproportionate share of their populations at relatively young ages—that is, at ages where the risk of death is relatively low. As a specific example of the sorts of questions addressed through standardization, one might ask, *What level of overall mortality would Latin America experience if it had the same sort of age structure as in Canada?*

Standardization can be used to decompose the prevalence of events, in considering (1) differences in population composition and/or (2) differences in the rates of subparts of the population. This is true both when comparing populations across political boundaries, just as it is true in comparing the same population over time. Briefly, it is possible to distinguish between two fundamental types of standardization, including (1) direct standardization, and (2) indirect standardization. Direct standardization involves the use of some sort of *standard population* (e.g., a standard age structure), whereas indirect standardization involves the use of some *standard set of rates*. The decision to use one standardization technique rather than the other usually depends upon the data as available, although in general, direct standardization is more common.

As with the use of life tables, more meaningful comparisons are possible beyond the use of crude rates. Merely for illustrative purposes, Table B.2 demonstrates the utility of direct standardization by focusing on the mortality difference between Canada and Mexico. While standardization can be used to take into consideration any number of compositional factors (e.g., differences in education, marital status, regional distribution), Table B.2 demonstrates its utility while continuing to focus exclusively on age structure. For more detailed examples of standardization, including *indirect standardization* as well as the development of more complex procedures that simultaneously consider more than one compositional factor and/or more than two populations, see Das Gupta (1993).

Table B.2 ▦ Example of Direct Standardization in Comparing Mortality of Both Sexes in Canada and Mexico Using Canadian Population as a Standard, 2011

	Population		Deaths by age		Death Rate	Expected Deaths
	(1)	(2)	(3)	(4)	(5 = 4 / 2)	(6 = 1 × 5)
	Canada	Mexico	Canada	Mexico	Mexico	(standard)
0 to 4	1,899,064	10,528,322	2,064	34,710	0.0033	6,261
5 to 9	1,810,433	11,047,537	159	2,833	0.0003	464
10 to 14	1,918,164	10,939,937	228	3,445	0.0003	604
15 to 19	2,238,952	11,026,112	794	9,953	0.0009	2,021
20 to 24	2,354,354	9,892,271	1,244	13,325	0.0013	3,171
25 to 29	2,369,841	8,788,177	1,233	14,306	0.0016	3,858
30 to 34	2,327,955	8,470,798	1,428	15,401	0.0018	4,233
35 to 39	2,273,087	8,292,987	1,772	18,151	0.0022	4,975
40 to 44	2,385,918	7,009,226	2,892	20,078	0.0029	6,834
45 to 49	2,719,909	5,928,730	5,204	24,371	0.0041	11,181
50 to 54	2,691,260	5,064,291	8,270	30,528	0.0060	16,223
55 to 59	2,353,090	3,895,365	11,377	35,947	0.0092	21,715
60 to 64	2,050,443	3,116,466	15,237	41,691	0.0134	27,430
65 to 69	1,532,940	2,317,265	18,129	47,196	0.0204	31,222
70 to 74	1,153,822	1,873,934	21,869	54,210	0.0289	33,378
75 to 79	919,338	1,245,483	28,852	59,429	0.0477	43,867
80 to 84	701,140	798,936	37,809	60,308	0.0755	52,926
85 to 89	426,739	454,164	40,903	52,079	0.1147	48,934
90 to 94	171,916	164,924	28,308	30,417	0.1844	31,707
95 to 99	39,147	65,732	11,826	4,983	0.0758	2,968
100 and older	5,268	18,475	2,476	1,598	0.0865	456
Total	34,342,780	110,939,132	242,074	574,959		354,427
			CDR	CDR		Standardized Death Rate
			7.05	5.18		10.3

Sources: Authors' calculations; Statistics Canada CANSIM Tables 102-0503 and 051-0001; United Nations Statistics Division On-Line Date, 2014.

Table B.2 shows Canada's population by age (column 1), Mexico's population by age (column 2), and the corresponding distribution of deaths for each country (columns 3 and 4, respectively). Table B.2 also shows the CDRs for Canada (7.05 deaths per 1,000) and Mexico (5.18 deaths per 1,000), each obtained by dividing the relevant column totals. For example, Mexico's CDR is obtained by dividing the total number of deaths (574,959) by its total population (110,939,132), multiplied by 1,000. As direct standardization involves the selection of a *population standard*, Table B.2 arbitrarily selects the Canadian population as its standard (either population could have been selected in this context). Age-specific rates from Mexico (column 5) are then applied to this standard.

In this example, the simple question is asked: *What level of overall mortality would Mexico experience if it had the same age structure as Canada?* Alternatively, it could have just as easily been asked (by selecting Mexico as the standard), *What mortality would Canada experience if it had the same age structure as Mexico?* Regardless of which standard is selected, the overall conclusion would be much the same; that is, the fact that Mexico's CDR is lower than Canada's is entirely attributable to its younger age structure.

The number of events (deaths for the standard) are calculated separately for each age and then summed across ages (column 6). The resulting crude rate when one is working with this sum is referred to as the *standardized death rate*. After reminding ourselves that the initial crude death rate for Mexico was lower than Canada's (only 5.18 compared to 7.05), the standardized death rate (10.3 deaths per 1,000) is greater than both the initial CDRs. The fact that the standardized death rate is so high clearly indicates that the initial difference in the CDR between the two countries is entirely attributable to Mexico's younger age structure. More specifically, the fact that the standardized death rate (when Canada is used as the standard) is even higher than Canada's CDR demonstrates the clear mortality advantage of Canada. Although not reported in Table B.2, the age-specific death rates in Canada are lower across age categories than in Mexico.

Appendix C: 2014 World Population Data Sheet

Table C.1 ▣ Demographic Data and Estimates for Countries and Regions of the World

	Population Mid-2014	Projection 2030	Projection 2050	Births per 1,000 pop	Deaths per 1,000 pop	Natural Increase (%)
World	7,238,183,566	8,443,711,884	9,683,476,862	20	8	1.2
More Developed	1,248,958,069	1,291,815,446	1,308,512,404	11	10	0.1
Less Developed	5,989,225,497	7,151,896,438	8,374,964,458	22	7	1.4
Less Developed (Excl. China)	4,625,153,497	5,751,805,438	7,063,182,458	24	7	1.7
Least Developed	915,817,323	1,289,851,000	1,854,951,000	33	9	2.4
Africa	1,136,446,104	1,637,378,870	2,428,153,480	36	10	2.5
Africa - Sub-Saharan	920,000,000	1,360,000,000	2,081,000,000	37	11	2.6
Africa - Northern	216,910,509	276,981,870	346,994,880	28	7	2.2
Algeria	39,106,000	49,887,000	60,284,000	25	6	1.9
Egypt	87,900,000	113,190,000	145,968,000	32	6	2.6
Libya	6,253,000	7,459,000	8,350,000	21	4	1.7
Morocco	33,304,000	38,170,000	41,360,000	22	6	1.5
Sudan	38,764,000	55,078,000	77,138,000	34	8	2.5
Tunisia	10,998,000	12,426,870	13,050,880	19	6	1.3
Western Sahara	585,509	771,000	844,000	21	6	1.5
Africa - Western	339,043,206	507,291,000	783,606,000	39	12	2.7
Benin	10,279,000	15,038,000	21,467,000	37	10	2.7
Burkina Faso	17,886,000	28,353,000	46,574,000	43	11	3.1
Cape Verde	508,000	614,000	738,000	22	5	1.7
Cote d'Ivoire	20,805,000	29,227,000	42,339,000	37	14	2.3
Gambia	1,909,000	3,056,000	4,866,000	41	10	3.1
Ghana	27,045,000	37,728,000	52,596,000	34	9	2.5
Guinea	11,579,000	16,913,000	23,888,000	38	12	2.7
Guinea-Bissau	1,746,000	2,473,000	3,504,000	38	13	2.5
Liberia	4,397,000	6,395,000	9,392,000	35	9	2.6
Mali	15,932,000	26,305,000	45,639,000	42	13	2.9
Mauritania	3,984,000	5,640,000	7,921,000	34	9	2.6
Niger	18,156,000	33,806,000	67,989,000	50	11	3.9
Nigeria	177,542,000	261,671,000	396,509,000	39	13	2.5
Senegal	13,933,000	21,813,000	35,131,000	40	8	3.2
Sierra Leone	6,344,000	8,239,000	10,527,000	38	17	2.1
Togo	6,993,000	10,015,000	14,521,000	37	11	2.6
Africa - Eastern	377,599,389	560,560,000	850,737,600	36	9	2.7
Burundi	10,483,000	16,392,000	26,691,000	45	13	3.2
Comoros	748,000	1,006,000	1,332,000	34	9	2.5
Djibouti	886,000	1,075,000	1,244,000	28	9	1.9
Eritrea	6,536,000	9,782,000	14,314,000	33	7	2.6
Ethiopia	95,933,000	130,524,000	165,075,000	28	8	2.1
Kenya	43,210,000	60,029,000	81,281,000	34	9	2.6
Madagascar	22,445,000	34,279,000	52,845,000	34	7	2.7
Malawi	16,829,000	25,960,000	41,203,000	40	12	2.9
Mayotte	224,389	331,000	466,000	31	3	2.8

Total Fertility Rate	Infant Mortality Rate	Life expectancy			GNI (PPP) per capita US $	% Urban	% of population	
		Total	Male	Female			<15	65+
2.5	38	71	69	73	14,210	53	26	8
1.6	5	79	75	82	37,470	77	16	17
2.6	42	69	67	71	8,920	48	29	6
3.0	46	67	65	69	8,060	46	32	5
4.3	64	61	60	62	1,970	28	40	4
4.7	62	59	58	60	4,470	40	41	4
5.1	67	57	56	58	3,220	37	43	3
3.4	33	69	68	71	9,600	51	32	5
2.9	26	71	69	73	12,990	73	28	6
3.5	29	71	69	72	10,850	43	32	6
2.4	14	75	73	77	28,110	78	29	5
2.6	29	71	69	73	7,000	59	28	5
5.2	55	62	60	64	2,370	33	41	3
2.2	16	75	73	77	10,960	66	24	7
2.4	37	68	66	70	-	82	27	3
5.4	66	55	54	55	3,930	45	44	3
4.9	69	59	58	61	1,780	45	43	3
5.9	70	56	56	57	1,560	27	46	2
2.6	24	75	71	79	6,220	62	30	5
4.9	75	51	50	51	2,900	53	41	3
5.6	55	59	57	60	1,620	57	46	2
4.3	53	61	60	62	3,880	51	38	5
5.1	67	56	55	57	1,160	36	42	3
5.0	94	54	53	56	1,240	44	41	3
4.7	54	60	59	61	790	47	43	3
6.1	58	55	55	54	1,540	35	48	3
4.1	72	62	60	63	2,850	41	40	3
7.6	54	58	58	58	910	22	50	3
5.6	69	52	52	53	5,600	50	44	3
5.3	43	63	62	65	2,240	47	44	3
4.9	92	45	45	46	1,750	41	42	3
4.7	66	56	56	57	1,180	38	42	3
4.9	57	60	59	62	1,570	24	44	3
6.1	87	54	52	56	820	10	45	2
4.3	36	61	59	61	1,560	28	42	3
3.4	55	62	60	63	2,190	77	34	4
4.7	42	63	60	65	1,180	21	43	2
4.1	50	63	62	65	1,350	17	43	3
4.3	47	62	60	64	2,250	24	42	3
4.4	42	65	63	66	1,350	33	42	3
5.5	66	55	55	55	760	16	45	3
4.1	4	79	76	82	-	50	45	2

(Continued)

Table C.1 ▣ Continued

	Population Mid-2014	Projection 2030	Projection 2050	Births per 1,000 pop	Deaths per 1,000 pop	Natural Increase (%)
Mozambique	25,059,000	38,385,000	63,517,000	43	13	2.9
Reunion	850,000	1,028,000	1,223,000	17	5	1.2
Rwanda	11,080,000	15,832,000	20,972,000	31	8	2.3
Seychelles	90,000	100,000	99,600	19	7	1.1
Somalia	10,806,000	16,880,000	27,076,000	44	12	3.2
South Sudan	11,739,000	17,297,000	39,267,000	36	12	2.4
Tanzania	50,757,000	79,354,000	129,417,000	40	9	3.1
Uganda	38,845,000	63,388,000	104,078,000	43	9	3.4
Zambia	15,111,000	26,090,000	49,178,000	45	11	3.4
Zimbabwe	14,707,000	21,521,000	30,244,000	33	9	2.4
Africa - Middle	**141,622,000**	**224,784,000**	**371,753,000**	**45**	**15**	**3.0**
Angola	22,364,000	36,389,000	60,836,000	46	14	3.2
Cameroon	22,789,000	34,472,000	54,268,000	39	12	2.7
Central African Republic	4,779,000	6,705,000	9,730,000	47	15	3.2
Chad	13,285,000	21,810,000	37,351,000	48	15	3.3
Congo	4,559,000	6,754,000	10,577,000	38	10	2.8
Congo, Dem. Rep. of	71,167,000	114,853,000	193,644,000	46	16	3.0
Equatorial Guinea	778,000	1,139,000	1,623,000	36	13	2.2
Gabon	1,711,000	2,382,000	3,302,000	32	9	2.3
Sao Tome and Principe	190,000	280,000	422,000	36	7	2.9
Africa - Southern	**61,271,000**	**67,762,000**	**75,062,000**	**21**	**11**	**1.0**
Botswana	2,039,000	2,348,000	2,780,000	24	17	0.7
Lesotho	1,917,000	2,149,000	2,651,000	30	21	0.9
Namibia	2,348,000	3,042,000	3,744,000	30	7	2.2
South Africa	53,699,000	58,707,000	64,072,000	20	11	1.0
Swaziland	1,268,000	1,516,000	1,815,000	30	14	1.6
Americas	**971,504,203**	**1,105,663,284**	**1,217,169,626**	**16**	**7**	**0.9**
America - Northern	**353,405,199**	**396,089,000**	**443,782,000**	**12**	**8**	**0.4**
Canada	35,549,000	41,549,000	48,384,000	11	7	0.4
United States	317,731,000	354,419,000	395,284,000	13	8	0.4
America - Latin America & Caribbean	**618,099,004**	**709,574,284**	**773,387,626**	**18**	**6**	**1.2**
America - Central	**165,429,000**	**195,436,000**	**221,528,596**	**21**	**6**	**1.5**
Belize	358,000	486,000	621,000	23	4	1.9
Costa Rica	4,773,000	5,564,000	6,093,068	15	4	1.1
El Salvador	6,384,000	6,875,000	6,912,000	20	7	1.4
Guatemala	15,860,000	22,566,000	31,345,528	31	5	2.6
Honduras	8,200,000	10,168,000	11,659,000	24	5	2.0
Mexico	119,713,000	137,481,000	150,838,000	19	6	1.4
Nicaragua	6,226,000	7,459,000	8,432,000	23	5	1.9
Panama	3,915,000	4,837,000	5,628,000	20	5	1.5
America - Caribbean	**42,613,977**	**46,666,190**	**48,956,599**	**18**	**8**	**1.1**
Antigua and Barbuda	89,000	107,000	121,000	14	5	0.8

Total Fertility Rate	Infant Mortality Rate	Life expectancy			GNI (PPP) per capita US $	% Urban	% of population	
		Total	Male	Female			<15	65+
5.7	85	53	51	55	1,040	31	45	3
2.4	7	80	77	83	-	94	24	9
4.0	49	65	63	66	1,430	17	41	3
2.4	11.4	73	69	78	23,270	54	22	8
6.6	80	55	53	57	-	38	48	3
7.0	78	55	54	56	2,190	17	42	3
5.3	49	61	60	63	1,750	30	45	3
5.9	57	59	58	60	1,370	18	48	2
6.0	66	58	56	60	3,070	40	47	3
3.8	37	60	59	61	1,560	33	40	3
6.1	97	52	50	53	2,540	42	46	3
6.2	96	52	50	53	6,770	59	48	2
5.1	62	55	54	56	2,660	52	43	3
6.2	116	50	48	51	600	39	40	4
6.6	96	51	50	52	2,000	22	49	2
5.0	64	59	57	60	4,720	64	42	3
6.6	109	50	48	52	680	34	46	3
4.9	89	53	52	55	23,240	39	39	3
4.1	43	63	62	64	17,220	86	38	5
4.3	44	66	64	68	2,950	67	42	4
2.4	44	59	57	60	11,840	59	30	5
2.6	32	47	48	47	15,500	62	34	4
3.3	82	44	42	45	3,320	26	36	6
3.6	39	64	62	67	9,590	38	36	4
2.3	42	60	58	61	12,240	62	29	5
3.4	65	49	50	49	6,220	21	38	3
2.1	15	76	73	79	27,420	79	24	10
1.8	5	79	77	81	52,810	81	19	14
1.6	4.8	81	79	84	42,590	80	16	15
1.9	5.4	79	76	81	53,960	81	19	14
2.2	18	75	71	78	12,900	78	27	7
2.4	16	74	71	77	13,880	72	30	6
2.6	14	74	71	77	8,160	45	36	4
1.8	8.7	80	77	82	13,570	73	24	7
2.2	17	73	68	77	7,490	65	30	7
3.8	23	72	68	76	7,130	50	40	5
2.8	24	74	71	76	4,270	52	35	4
2.2	13	74	71	77	16,110	78	28	6
2.5	17	75	72	78	4,440	56	33	5
2.5	14	76	74	79	19,290	75	28	7
2.3	33	73	70	75	11,740	66	26	9
1.8	16	77	74	80	20,070	30	24	7

(Continued)

Table C.1 ▣ Continued

	Population Mid-2014	Projection 2030	Projection 2050	Births per 1,000 pop	Deaths per 1,000 pop	Natural Increase (%)
Bahamas	373,000	436,000	481,000	16	5	1.1
Barbados	300,000	320,000	333,000	12	8	0.4
Cuba	11,150,000	10,742,700	9,301,420	11	8	0.3
Curacao	154,714	178,000	191,000	13	8	0.5
Dominica	70,625	72,000	63,000	13	8	0.5
Dominican Republic	10,378,000	12,010,000	13,177,000	21	6	1.5
Grenada	111,582	113,000	100,612	16	7	0.8
Guadeloupe	406,277	409,000	399,000	13	7	0.6
Haiti	10,753,000	13,515,000	16,822,000	28	9	1.9
Jamaica	2,721,000	2,868,000	2,730,000	18	7	1.1
Martinique	384,000	423,000	413,000	12	7	0.4
Puerto Rico	3,579,000	3,375,000	2,950,000	11	8	0.3
St. Kitts-Nevis	54,744	63,000	67,000	13	7	0.6
St. Lucia	173,000	180,000	169,000	13	8	0.6
St. Vincent & the Grenadines	106,000	107,000	108,000	17	8	0.9
Trinidad and Tobago	1,343,000	1,248,000	993,000	13	10	0.3
America - South	**410,056,027**	**467,472,094**	**502,902,431**	**17**	**6**	**1.1**
Argentina	42,669,000	50,206,000	59,421,000	19	7	1.1
Bolivia	10,305,000	12,981,000	15,789,000	26	7	1.9
Brazil	202,800,000	223,100,000	226,300,000	15	6	0.9
Chile	17,711,000	19,587,000	20,205,000	14	6	0.9
Colombia	47,662,000	55,736,000	61,311,000	19	6	1.3
Ecuador	16,027,000	19,815,000	23,377,412	23	5	1.8
French Guiana	260,000	421,000	623,000	27	3	2.4
Guyana	745,000	790,000	755,000	20	7	1.3
Paraguay	6,902,000	8,556,000	10,077,000	23	6	1.7
Peru	30,814,000	35,898,000	40,111,000	20	5	1.5
Suriname	564,000	659,000	740,000	20	7	1.3
Uruguay	3,419,000	3,581,000	3,641,000	14	9	0.5
Venezuela	30,206,000	36,112,000	40,501,000	20	5	1.5
Asia	**4,350,937,593**	**4,907,175,950**	**5,252,473,797**	**18**	**7**	**1.1**
Asia (excl. China)	**2,986,865,593**	**3,507,084,950**	**3,940,691,797**	**21**	**7**	**1.4**
Asia - Western	**255,446,000**	**322,481,000**	**387,318,000**	**22**	**5**	**1.7**
Andorra	76,000	75,000	66,000	8	3	0.5
Armenia	3,013,000	2,999,000	2,809,000	14	9	0.5
Azerbaijan	9,538,000	11,080,000	12,081,000	18	6	1.3
Cyprus	1,157,000	1,310,000	1,360,000	13	7	0.6
Georgia	4,785,000	4,796,000	4,647,000	13	11	0.2
Iraq	35,111,000	53,805,000	80,547,000	31	5	2.6
Israel	8,208,000	10,526,000	13,940,000	21	5	1.6
Jordan	7,558,000	9,874,000	13,078,000	28	4	2.4
Kuwait	3,656,000	5,051,000	6,628,000	18	2	1.7

Total Fertility Rate	Infant Mortality Rate	Life expectancy			GNI (PPP) per capita US $	% Urban	% of population	
		Total	Male	Female			<15	65+
2.0	17	75	72	77	21,540	84	26	6
1.8	10	75	73	78	15,080	44	20	13
1.7	4.6	78	76	80	18,520	77	17	13
2.2	9.8	78	74	81	-	-	19	15
2.0	21	73	71	76	9,800	67	22	10
2.5	25	73	70	76	11,150	67	31	6
2.0	9	70	67	73	11,120	39	27	7
2.2	8.1	81	77	84	-	98	21	15
3.4	59	63	61	65	1,710	53	35	4
2.3	21	74	71	76	8,480	54	27	8
1.9	8	82	79	85	-	89	19	17
1.6	8.1	79	75	83	22,730	99	19	16
1.6	17	75	73	78	20,400	32	22	8
1.5	20	75	72	77	10,350	18	23	9
2.2	20	71	70	74	10,610	49	25	7
1.6	24	70	66	74	26,210	14	20	9
2.1	18	75	72	78	12,620	82	26	8
2.3	11.7	77	73	80	-	92	25	10
3.2	39	67	65	69	5,750	67	35	5
1.8	20	75	71	79	14,750	85	24	7
1.9	7.7	79	76	82	21,030	87	22	10
2.3	18	75	72	79	11,890	76	28	7
2.8	17	75	72	78	10,310	63	31	7
3.5	10	79	76	83	-	76	34	5
2.5	29	66	64	69	6,550	28	36	3
2.8	29	73	71	75	7,640	59	33	5
2.4	16	75	72	77	11,360	75	29	6
2.6	20	71	69	74	15,860	70	28	6
2.0	9.3	77	74	81	18,930	94	22	14
2.4	14.4	75	72	78	17,890	89	29	6
2.2	34	71	69	73	10,380	46	25	7
2.5	40	69	67	71	9,700	43	29	6
2.9	25	73	71	76	22,920	70	30	5
1.1	3.4	-	-	-	-	90	15	13
1.6	10	74	71	78	8,140	63	19	11
2.2	11	74	71	77	16,180	53	22	6
1.5	6	79	77	81	29,570	67	17	12
1.7	11	75	70	79	7,040	54	17	14
4.1	29	69	66	73	15,220	71	40	3
3.0	3	82	80	84	32,140	91	28	10
3.5	17	73	72	74	11,660	83	34	4
2.4	8	74	73	75	88,170	98	23	2

(Continued)

Table C.1 ▣ Continued

	Population Mid-2014	Projection 2030	Projection 2050	Births per 1,000 pop	Deaths per 1,000 pop	Natural Increase (%)
Lebanon	4,966,000	5,172,000	5,316,000	13	4	0.9
Oman	4,071,000	5,381,000	6,318,000	20	2	1.8
Palestinian Territory	4,400,000	6,577,000	9,138,000	31	4	2.7
Qatar	2,268,000	2,760,000	2,985,000	11	1	1.0
Saudi Arabia	30,814,000	37,388,000	42,376,000	22	4	1.8
Syria	21,987,000	29,934,000	36,706,000	24	4	2.1
Turkey	77,193,000	88,278,000	93,318,000	16	5	1.1
United Arab Emirates	9,446,000	12,330,000	15,479,000	15	1	1.4
Yemen	25,956,000	33,609,000	38,792,000	36	8	2.8
Asia - South-Central	**1,873,744,900**	**2,219,832,856**	**2,515,806,797**	**22**	**7**	**1.6**
Asia - Central	**67,431,000**	**80,980,470**	**93,436,900**	**24**	**6**	**1.8**
Kazakhstan	17,285,000	20,335,000	24,510,000	23	8	1.5
Kyrgyzstan	5,834,000	7,480,000	9,440,000	28	7	2.1
Tajikistan	8,266,000	11,212,000	14,835,000	34	7	2.7
Turkmenistan	5,307,000	6,160,000	6,570,000	22	8	1.4
Uzbekistan	30,739,000	35,793,470	38,081,900	22	5	1.8
Asia - South	**1,806,313,900**	**2,138,852,386**	**2,422,369,897**	**22**	**7**	**1.5**
Afghanistan	31,281,000	43,500,000	56,511,000	35	8	2.7
Bangladesh	158,513,000	185,064,000	201,948,000	20	6	1.5
Bhutan	746,000	924,000	1,091,000	22	6	1.5
India	1,296,245,000	1,509,976,000	1,656,919,000	22	7	1.5
Iran	77,356,000	90,039,000	99,170,000	19	5	1.4
Maldives	369,900	458,200	529,690	23	3	1.9
Nepal	27,140,000	31,707,000	35,206,000	22	7	1.5
Pakistan	193,979,000	254,729,000	348,007,000	28	8	2.0
Sri Lanka	20,684,000	22,455,186	22,988,207	18	6	1.2
Asia - Southeast	**621,228,400**	**733,411,700**	**830,734,000**	**19**	**7**	**1.3**
Brunei	419,000	495,000	541,000	16	3	1.3
Cambodia	14,804,000	18,393,000	21,684,000	24	6	1.8
Indonesia	251,452,000	306,689,000	365,323,000	20	6	1.4
Laos	6,843,000	8,257,000	9,068,000	26	6	2.0
Malaysia	30,098,000	35,965,700	41,107,000	17	5	1.3
Myanmar	53,719,000	58,698,000	58,645,000	17	9	0.9
Philippines	100,096,000	127,797,000	157,118,000	24	6	1.8
Singapore	5,487,400	6,543,000	7,027,000	9	5	0.5
Thailand	66,443,000	66,771,000	61,024,000	12	8	0.4
Timor-Leste	1,212,000	1,849,000	2,852,000	37	10	2.7
Vietnam	90,655,000	101,954,000	106,345,000	17	7	1.0
Asia - East	**1,600,518,293**	**1,631,450,394**	**1,518,615,000**	**12**	**7**	**0.4**
China	1,364,072,000	1,400,091,000	1,311,782,000	12	7	0.5
Hong Kong, SAR	7,241,000	8,121,000	8,646,000	8	6	0.2
Japan	127,060,000	116,618,000	97,076,000	8	10	-0.2

Total Fertility Rate	Infant Mortality Rate	Life expectancy			GNI (PPP) per capita US $	% Urban	% of population	
		Total	Male	Female			<15	65+
1.5	9	80	78	82	17,390	87	20	9
2.8	9	76	75	78	52,170	75	22	3
4.1	20	73	71	74	4,900	83	40	3
2.1	7	78	78	79	123,860	100	14	1
2.9	16	74	73	75	53,780	81	30	3
3.0	17	74	72	78	-	54	35	4
2.1	10	75	71	78	18,760	77	25	8
1.8	6	77	76	78	58,090	83	16	0
4.4	68	63	62	64	3,820	29	42	3
2.5	47	67	65	68	5,600	33	31	5
2.7	41	68	65	72	9,300	47	29	5
2.7	28	70	65	74	20,570	55	25	7
3.2	27	70	66	74	3,070	34	31	4
3.8	57	67	64	71	2,500	26	36	3
2.4	47	65	61	70	12,920	47	28	4
2.4	44	68	65	72	5,340	51	28	4
2.5	47	67	65	68	5,460	32	31	5
5.1	74	61	59	62	2,000	24	46	2
2.2	33	70	70	71	2,810	26	29	5
2.5	47	68	67	68	7,210	36	30	5
2.4	44	66	65	68	5,350	31	31	5
1.8	16	74	72	76	15,600	71	24	5
2.3	9	74	73	75	9,890	41	26	5
2.4	46	68	67	69	2,260	17	34	5
3.8	74	65	63	66	4,920	35	38	4
2.1	9	74	71	77	9,470	15	26	8
2.4	28	71	68	73	9,130	48	27	6
1.6	4	78	77	80	68,090	76	25	5
2.8	45	63	61	66	2,890	20	31	6
2.6	32	71	69	73	9,260	50	29	5
3.2	68	68	66	69	4,570	34	35	4
2.1	7	75	73	77	22,460	71	26	6
2.0	49	65	63	67	-	31	25	5
3.0	23	69	65	72	7,820	63	34	4
1.2	2	83	80	85	76,850	100	16	11
1.8	11	75	71	78	13,510	47	18	10
5.7	63	62	61	62	6,410	30	42	5
2.1	15	73	70	76	5,030	32	24	7
1.5	14	76	75	78	14,440	58	16	11
1.6	15	75	74	77	11,850	54	16	10
1.1	1.6	84	81	87	54,260	100	11	15
1.4	1.9	83	80	86	37,630	91	13	26

(Continued)

Table C.1 ◙ Continued

	Population Mid-2014	Projection 2030	Projection 2050	Births per 1,000 pop	Deaths per 1,000 pop	Natural Increase (%)
Korea, North	24,851,627	26,688,394	26,969,000	15	9	0.5
Korea, South	50,424,000	52,160,000	48,121,000	9	5	0.3
Macao, SAR	620,666	728,000	797,000	11	3	0.8
Mongolia	2,857,000	3,530,000	4,261,000	28	6	2.3
Taiwan	23,392,000	23,514,000	20,963,000	8	7	0.1
Europe	**740,680,870**	**745,599,446**	**725,823,404**	**11**	**11**	**0.0**
Europe - European Union	**506,708,000**	**516,748,493**	**514,365,650**	**10**	**10**	**0.0**
Europe - Northern	**101,930,728**	**111,139,834**	**118,933,879**	**12**	**9**	**0.3**
Channel Islands	162,000	173,500	177,070	11	8	0.3
Denmark	5,639,000	5,923,334	6,135,809	10	9	0.1
Estonia	1,308,000	1,238,000	1,231,000	11	12	-0.1
Finland	5,463,000	5,831,000	6,078,000	11	9	0.1
Iceland	328,000	372,000	416,000	13	7	0.7
Ireland	4,607,000	5,188,000	5,684,000	15	7	0.9
Latvia	1,990,000	1,627,000	1,447,000	10	14	-0.4
Lithuania	2,930,000	2,744,000	2,491,000	10	14	-0.4
Norway	5,138,000	6,037,000	6,681,000	12	8	0.4
Sweden	9,689,000	10,788,000	11,444,000	12	9	0.2
United Kingdom	64,542,000	71,072,000	76,999,000	12	9	0.3
Europe - Western	**190,213,000**	**196,366,183**	**197,922,196**	**10**	**10**	**0.0**
Austria	8,531,000	9,015,000	9,353,000	9	9	0.0
Belgium	11,200,000	11,910,000	12,588,000	11	10	0.2
France	64,064,000	68,328,000	72,060,000	12	9	0.3
Germany	80,900,000	80,023,000	76,222,000	8	11	-0.2
Liechtenstein	37,000	42,183	44,196	10	6	0.4
Luxembourg	556,000	668,000	741,000	11	7	0.4
Monaco	37,000	43,000	52,000	6	7	-0.1
Netherlands	16,852,000	17,623,000	17,883,000	10	8	0.2
Switzerland	8,187,000	8,714,000	8,979,000	10	8	0.2
Europe - Eastern	**294,048,000**	**284,823,159**	**261,512,841**	**12**	**13**	**-0.1**
Belarus	9,470,000	9,253,000	9,036,000	13	13	-0.1
Bulgaria	7,226,000	6,519,000	5,748,000	9	14	-0.5
Czech Republic	10,511,000	10,778,000	11,073,000	10	10	0.0
Hungary	9,893,000	9,679,356	9,350,112	9	13	-0.4
Moldova	4,110,000	3,443,000	2,080,000	11	11	0.0
Poland	38,479,000	37,504,000	34,821,000	10	10	-0.1
Romania	20,015,000	18,713,000	16,472,000	10	12	-0.3
Russia	143,747,000	143,521,000	134,139,000	13	13	0.0
Slovakia	5,400,000	5,450,000	5,000,000	10	10	0.1
Ukraine	42,900,000	40,050,000	33,834,000	11	15	-0.4

Total Fertility Rate	Infant Mortality Rate	Life expectancy			GNI (PPP) per capita US $	% Urban	% of population	
		Total	Male	Female			<15	65+
2.0	26	69	65	73	-	60	22	9
1.2	2.9	81	78	85	33,440	81	15	12
1.2	3	82	79	86	112,180	100	11	8
2.9	26	67	64	72	8,810	68	28	4
1.1	3.7	80	76	83	-	73	14	12
1.6	6	78	74	81	30,010	72	16	17
1.5	4	80	77	83	34,220	72	16	18
1.8	3	80	78	83	37,860	79	18	17
1.7	2.9	82	79	84	-	31	15	16
1.7	3	80	78	82	44,440	87	17	18
1.5	2.1	76	71	81	24,230	68	16	18
1.8	1.8	81	78	84	38,480	85	16	19
1.9	1.8	82	81	84	38,870	95	21	13
2.0	3.3	81	78	83	35,090	60	22	12
1.5	3.6	74	69	79	21,390	68	14	19
1.6	3.6	74	68	79	23,080	67	15	18
1.8	2.5	82	80	84	66,520	80	18	16
1.9	2.3	82	80	84	44,660	84	17	19
1.9	3.9	81	79	83	35,760	80	18	17
1.7	3	81	78	84	42,220	75	16	19
1.4	3.1	81	79	83	43,810	67	14	18
1.8	3.8	81	78	83	40,280	99	17	18
2.0	3.6	82	79	85	37,580	78	18	18
1.4	3.3	80	78	83	44,540	73	13	21
1.5	3.3	82	79	84	-	15	16	15
1.6	3.5	82	80	84	59,750	83	17	14
1.4	-	-	-	-	-	100	13	24
1.7	3.8	81	79	83	43,210	67	17	17
1.5	3.6	83	81	85	53,920	74	15	18
1.5	8	72	68	77	19,930	69	15	14
1.7	4.3	72	67	78	16,940	76	15	14
1.5	7.3	74	71	78	15,200	73	14	20
1.5	2.5	78	75	81	25,530	74	15	17
1.3	5.1	75	71	78	20,930	69	14	17
1.2	14	71	67	75	5,190	42	16	10
1.2	4.6	77	73	81	22,300	61	15	14
1.3	8.5	74	70	78	18,060	54	16	16
1.7	10.3	71	65	76	23,200	74	16	13
1.3	5.5	76	72	79	24,930	54	15	14
1.5	7	71	66	76	8,960	69	15	15

(Continued)

Table C.1 ▦ Continued

	Population Mid-2014	Projection 2030	Projection 2050	Births per 1,000 pop	Deaths per 1,000 pop	Natural Increase (%)
Europe - Southern	154,489,142	153,270,270	147,454,488	9	10	-0.1
Albania	2,981,000	3,099,000	2,896,000	12	7	0.5
Andorra						
Bosnia-Herzegovina	3,828,000	3,703,000	3,335,000	8	9	-0.1
Bahrain	1,319,000	1,611,000	1,800,000	15	2	1.3
Croatia	4,238,000	3,983,000	3,576,000	10	13	-0.3
Greece	10,972,000	10,663,000	9,382,000	9	11	-0.1
Italy	61,339,000	63,402,000	63,465,000	9	10	-0.1
Kosovo	1,841,000	1,957,000	1,893,000	15	4	1.1
Macedonia	2,066,000	2,028,000	1,844,000	11	9	0.2
Malta	427,000	425,000	371,000	10	8	0.2
Montenegro	619,000	700,520	770,200	12	10	0.3
Portugal	10,396,000	9,854,000	9,108,000	8	10	-0.2
San Marino	33,000	36,000	35,178	10	7	0.3
Serbia	7,129,000	6,734,750	6,359,110	9	14	-0.5
Slovenia	2,061,000	2,088,000	2,070,000	10	9	0.1
Spain	46,453,000	44,489,000	42,253,000	9	8	0.1
Oceania	38,614,796	47,894,334	59,856,555	18	7	1.1
Australia	23,520,000	28,601,000	36,365,000	13	6	0.7
Federated States of Micronesia	103,000	98,000	97,000	24	5	1.9
Fiji	864,000	936,000	1,027,000	21	8	1.4
French Polynesia	271,000	308,000	326,000	17	6	1.1
Guam	161,000	211,000	259,000	22	5	1.7
Kiribati	111,000	150,000	208,000	30	9	2.1
Marshall Islands	55,000	59,000	71,000	30	4	2.5
Nauru	10,560	14,000	17,000	36	8	2.9
New Caledonia	267,000	311,000	347,000	17	5	1.2
New Zealand	4,292,000	4,908,000	5,466,000	13	7	0.7
Palau	18,000	19,000	18,000	14	9	0.5
Papua New Guinea	7,571,000	10,492,000	14,212,000	33	10	2.3
Samoa	192,000	196,000	244,000	29	5	2.4
Solomon Islands	626,000	912,000	354,000	31	5	2.6
Tonga	103,369	106,000	127,000	27	7	2.0
Tuvalu	11,323	14,000	20,000	25	9	1.6

Source: Population Reference Bureau, 2014. *World Population Data Sheet*. Washington, DC: Population Reference Bureau.

Total Fertility Rate	Infant Mortality Rate	Life expectancy			GNI (PPP) per capita US $	% Urban	% of population	
		Total	Male	Female			<15	65+
1.3	4	81	78	83	28,960	68	15	19
1.8	14.4	77	75	80	10,520	54	19	12
1.3	5	76	74	79	9,820	46	16	16
2.1	8	76	75	78	36,140	100	21	2
1.6	3.6	77	74	80	20,370	56	15	19
1.3	2.9	81	78	83	25,630	73	15	20
1.4	3.2	82	80	84	34,100	68	14	21
2.0	11	69	67	71	8,940	38	28	7
1.5	10	75	73	77	11,520	65	17	12
1.4	5.7	80	78	82	26,400	100	15	16
1.7	5.2	74	72	77	14,600	64	19	13
1.2	3	80	77	83	25,350	61	15	19
1.5	6.4	84	82	86	-	94	15	18
1.4	5.4	75	72	77	12,020	59	14	18
1.5	2.9	80	77	83	27,680	50	15	17
1.3	3.1	82	79	85	31,850	77	15	18
2.4	21	77	75	79	30,100	70	24	11
1.9	3.3	82	80	84	42,540	89	19	14
3.5	29	70	69	72	3,840	22	34	4
2.5	15	70	67	73	7,610	51	29	5
2.1	5.1	76	73	78	-	51	25	6
3.1	13.4	78	75	81	-	93	27	7
3.8	45	62	58	66	2,780	54	35	4
4.1	26	70	67	73	4,620	74	40	2
4.3	39	60	58	63	-	100	37	1
2.2	5	77	74	81	-	62	24	8
2.0	4.4	81	80	83	30,750	86	20	14
1.7	11	72	69	75	14,540	84	20	6
4.3	48	62	60	65	2,430	13	39	3
4.7	16	74	73	76	4,840	20	39	5
4.1	26	70	67	74	1,810	20	39	3
3.9	17	71	69	73	5,450	23	37	6
3.2	10	70	67	72	5,990	51	33	5

Appendix D: Population Estimates and Demographic Accounts

While censuses can provide wealth of information on the size, distribution, and characteristics of a population, they are not without their limitations. The Canadian Census for example, which is conducted once every five years, does not provide information on the size and distribution of Canada's population between censuses, nor does it provide information on the years that have passed since the previous census. In addition, population counts based on a census are inaccurate because of *census coverage error*. That is, some people are completely missed in the census, just as some are counted more than once. These two errors are known respectively as *census undercount* and *census overcount*. The coverage error in combination is referred to as *net undercount* (undercount minus overcount).

In light of these problems with the census, most countries generate population estimates that not only correct for coverage error but also produce population data for non-census years. This is true of Canada, the United States, Australia, and Britain, and most other OECD countries. Beginning with the 1971 Census reasonably precise estimates of coverage error are available, the net undercount usually being between 2 and 3 per cent at the national level. With the availability of these estimates, a time series of population data (fully adjusted for census coverage error) has been generated. In reference to these estimates, it is possible to distinguish between *intercensal population estimates* and *post-censal population estimates*. Intercensal estimates apply to the years between censuses, whereas post-censal estimates apply to non-census years after the most recent census. When one is working with these demographic data, post-censal estimates are more timely, as there is no need to wait until the release of the next census, although less accurate. On the other hand,

intercensal estimates involve the retroactive adjustment of past figures with new census data.

Table D.1 provides the provincial/territorial series of intercensal population estimates (1971–2011) as well as the most current set of post-censal estimates (2011–14). At the time of writing, the 2016 Census (and coverage studies) had yet to be completed—a necessary step before the creation of the 2011–16 intercensal estimates. Similarly, Table D.2 includes this same set of estimates (2001–2013) for Canada's 33 census metropolitan areas, whereas Table D.3 does the same for all 293 census divisions, and Table D.4 provides estimates for Canada's 76 economic regions. Briefly, a census division refers to a geographic area established by provincial or territorial law (e.g., county, regional district, regional municipality), whereas an economic region merely refers to a grouping of these census divisions created as a standard geographic unit for analysis of regional economic activity (for further detail on the census geography, see the *2011 Census Dictionary*, catalogue number 98-301-X2011001). In addition (although not included here), Statistics Canada also provides for *all of the above population estimates* a detailed disaggregation by both sex and single years of age (all free and easily downloadable from Statistics Canada's website via CANSIM).

Both types of estimates (intercensal and post-censal) involve data on all relevant components of demographic change, including births, deaths, immigration, and emigration, as well as interprovincial and intraprovincial migration. In keeping with Canada's system of demographic accounts, all of those components are either documented directly on the basis of vital statistics and/or administrative data or estimated indirectly on the basis of administrative data sets. While not included in this text, CANSIM Table 051-004 includes all of the components currently available, for the provincial/territorial estimates, for the full time series of 1971–2014. The demographic data that generally enter into Canada's system of demographic accounts vary considerably in quality, from the information available on births and deaths, which is highly accurate owing to mandatory registration, to the data on emigration, which are less than precise because there is no border registration system in Canada. Statistics Canada does not currently release component data at lower levels of geography (for example, for metropolitan areas or economic regions), yet at the national/provincial/territorial levels, it does release this data for detailed age (single year) and sex groups.

In documenting international migration, the Canadian state has a vested interest in keeping track of, and maintaining accurate data on, all new immigrants and non-permanent residents (NPRs) who enter into Canada. The term NPR refers to persons who do not have the right to live in Canada permanently but who are not simply visitors (i.e., people with work permits or student visas, refugee claimants, and other temporary residents). Internal migration and interprovincial migration are estimated on the basis of a *change of address file* that is regularly updated and maintained by Canada Customs and Revenue, with adjustments made for the incompleteness of this dataset. For further detail on the administrative datasets that underlie Canada's system of demographic accounts, including issues relating to data quality, check various methodological overviews (see Statistics Canada, 2012e).

In developing post-censal population estimates (by province and territory), Statistics Canada uses the following equation, which is a slightly revised version of the basic demographic balancing equation presented in Chapter 1. For each province and territory, it is possible to estimate total population by accounting for all relevant demographic change since the most current census (using the component data summarized earlier). As most of the population figures in Table D.1 are intercensal (1971–2011), the following equation applies directly only to those years that follow the most recent census (2011):

$$P_{(t+a)} = P_t + B_{(t,t+a)} - D_{(t,t+a)} + I_{(t,t+a)} - E_{(t,t+a)} + NPR_{(t,t+a)} + In_{(t,t+a)} - Out_{(t,t+a)}$$

where

$P_{(t+a)}$ = post-censual estimate of the population at time t+a

P_t = base population at time t (most recent census adjusted for coverage error)

$B_{(t,t+a)}$ = number of births between time t and time t+a

$D_{(t,t+a)}$ = number of deaths between time t and time t+a

$I_{(t,t+a)}$ = number of immigrants between time t and time t+a

$E_{(t,t+a)}$ = number of emigrants between time t and time t+a

$NPR_{(t,t+a)}$ = net change in the number of non-permanent residents between time t and time t+a

$In_{(t,t+a)}$ = number of in-migrants (from other provinces) between time t and time t+a

$Out_{(t,t+a)}$ = number of out-migrants (to other provinces) between time t and time t+a

As an initial step, the base population P_t is adjusted to reflect Canada's population on 1 July rather than census day (in mid-May) and is also adjusted for coverage error. All component data are for the reference year 1 July 30 to June 30 rather than specific calendar years. When population estimates are developed by age and sex, the same basic equation is applied to each age and sex cohort; the component data used are organized by birth cohort and sex. With regard to its population estimates for *census metropolitan areas* (CMAs), *census divisions* (CDs), and *economic regions* (ERs), Statistics Canada further refines this component data to correspond to specific urban areas and regions and by including an additional component (intraprovincial migration—that is, migration into and out of specific CMAs or regions). In addition, while not specified in the above equation, the emigration component is the sum of three more specific components (emigrants, returning emigrants, and net change in the number of persons temporarily abroad).

Shortly after each census, intercensal estimates are published in an effort to reconcile previous estimates with the new census-based information. The production of intercensal estimates involves two further steps beyond the generation of post-censal estimates: (1) the calculation of the error of closure; and (2) the distribution of the error of closure by intercensal year. The *error of closure* can be defined as "the difference between the enumerated population of the most recent census (after adjustments for census coverage error) and the most current set of post-censual population estimates for this same date (i.e., census day)." On the assumption that the coverage studies that follow

each enumeration are unbiased, the adjusted census figures are accepted as true. Assuming that this error of closure can then be distributed uniformly over the corresponding intercensal period, some relatively simple arithmetic functions can be used to adjust the previous post-censal estimates.

CANSIM Table 051-004 (not included in this text) also includes the full-time series of these adjustments (in the form of a residual component) relevant in the generation of corrected intercensal estimates (1971–2011). As Statistics Canada is not in the habit of revising past component data because of closure error, it is necessary to also consider this *residual component* in the full accounting of demographic change across censuses. This generation of intercensal estimates by age and sex is analogous to the above, in first identifying the respective closure errors and then revising past estimates accordingly to correct for closure error. Similarly, analogous adjustments are made at the national level for provinces and territories, just as they are made for census metropolitan areas.

Table D.1 Annual Population Estimates, July 1971 to July 2014, Canada, Provinces, and Territories

Year	Canada	NL	PEI	NS	NB	QC	ON	MB	SK	AB	BC	YT	NWT	NWT	NU
1971	21,962,032	530,854	112,591	797,294	642,471	6,137,305	7,849,027	998,876	932,038	1,665,717	2,240,470	18,991	36,398		
1972	22,218,463	539,124	113,460	802,255	648,769	6,174,216	7,963,117	1,001,652	920,780	1,694,090	2,302,086	20,143	38,771		
1973	22,491,777	545,561	114,620	812,386	656,720	6,213,149	8,075,547	1,007,358	911,937	1,725,327	2,367,271	21,148	40,753		
1974	22,807,969	549,604	115,962	818,751	664,744	6,268,571	8,204,275	1,018,206	908,457	1,754,621	2,442,578	21,069	41,131		
1975	23,143,275	556,496	117,724	826,549	677,008	6,330,303	8,319,795	1,024,975	917,415	1,808,689	2,499,564	21,908	42,849		
1976	23,449,808	562,639	118,648	835,166	689,494	6,396,761	8,413,779	1,031,758	931,612	1,869,287	2,533,899	22,441	44,324		
1977	23,725,843	565,348	119,902	840,028	695,843	6,433,133	8,504,080	1,037,369	944,621	1,948,263	2,570,315	22,462	44,479		
1978	23,963,203	567,639	121,684	844,628	699,514	6,440,459	8,590,144	1,040,881	952,430	2,022,241	2,615,162	23,157	45,264		
1979	24,201,544	570,075	122,885	849,396	703,158	6,445,996	8,662,088	1,037,272	959,735	2,096,966	2,665,238	22,972	45,763		
1980	24,515,667	572,759	123,735	852,659	706,219	6,505,997	8,746,013	1,034,435	967,548	2,191,029	2,745,861	23,019	46,393		
1981	24,819,915	575,302	123,551	854,871	706,438	6,547,207	8,812,286	1,035,545	975,759	2,291,104	2,826,558	23,880	47,414		
1982	25,116,942	573,795	123,588	859,038	707,457	6,580,631	8,920,288	1,045,224	986,582	2,369,827	2,876,513	24,668	49,331		
1983	25,366,451	579,164	125,102	868,289	714,842	6,602,976	9,039,564	1,059,752	1,001,249	2,393,587	2,907,502	23,664	50,760		
1984	25,607,053	580,065	126,563	877,471	720,488	6,631,220	9,167,484	1,071,810	1,014,615	2,393,907	2,947,181	23,921	52,328		
1985	25,842,116	579,275	127,619	885,848	723,287	6,665,802	9,294,657	1,082,495	1,024,928	2,404,490	2,975,131	24,375	54,209		
1986	26,100,278	576,306	128,436	889,087	725,019	6,708,170	9,437,359	1,091,552	1,028,717	2,432,930	3,003,621	24,430	54,651		
1987	26,446,601	575,242	128,641	893,606	727,768	6,781,984	9,637,945	1,098,373	1,032,799	2,440,877	3,048,651	25,706	55,009		
1988	26,791,747	574,982	129,289	897,216	730,349	6,837,077	9,838,620	1,102,152	1,028,225	2,456,614	3,114,761	26,653	55,809		
1989	27,276,781	576,551	130,153	903,841	735,129	6,925,128	10,103,305	1,103,792	1,019,439	2,498,325	3,196,725	27,167	57,226		
1990	27,691,138	577,368	130,404	910,451	740,156	6,996,986	10,295,832	1,105,421	1,007,727	2,547,788	3,292,111	27,957	58,937		
1991	28,037,420	579,644	130,369	914,969	745,567	7,067,396	10,431,316	1,109,604	1,002,713	2,592,306	3,373,787	28,871		38,724	22,154
1992	28,371,264	580,109	130,827	919,451	748,121	7,110,010	10,572,205	1,112,689	1,003,995	2,632,672	3,468,802	30,084		39,416	22,883
1993	28,684,764	579,977	132,177	923,925	748,812	7,156,537	10,690,038	1,117,618	1,006,900	2,667,292	3,567,772	30,337		39,820	23,559
1994	29,000,663	574,466	133,437	926,871	750,185	7,192,403	10,819,146	1,123,230	1,009,575	2,700,606	3,676,075	29,684		40,578	24,407
1995	29,302,311	567,397	134,415	928,120	750,943	7,219,219	10,950,119	1,129,150	1,014,187	2,734,519	3,777,390	30,442		41,432	24,978
1996	29,610,218	559,698	135,737	931,327	752,268	7,246,897	11,082,903	1,134,136	1,018,945	2,775,133	3,874,317	31,387		41,741	25,669
1997	29,905,948	550,911	136,095	932,402	752,511	7,274,611	11,227,651	1,136,128	1,017,902	2,829,848	3,948,583	31,797		41,625	25,884
1998	30,155,173	539,843	135,804	931,836	750,530	7,295,935	11,365,901	1,137,489	1,017,332	2,899,066	3,983,113	31,149		40,802	26,373
1999	30,401,286	533,329	136,281	933,784	750,601	7,323,250	11,504,759	1,142,448	1,014,524	2,952,692	4,011,375	30,785		40,638	26,820
2000	30,685,730	527,966	136,470	933,821	750,517	7,356,951	11,683,290	1,147,313	1,007,565	3,004,198	4,039,230	30,431		40,480	27,498
2001	31,020,596	522,046	136,665	932,491	749,819	7,396,415	11,897,370	1,151,450	1,000,239	3,058,084	4,076,881	30,157		40,845	28,134
2002	31,358,418	519,483	136,876	935,155	749,379	7,441,498	12,093,299	1,156,636	996,816	3,128,262	4,100,161	30,337		41,694	28,822
2003	31,641,630	518,445	137,221	937,676	749,434	7,485,491	12,243,758	1,163,528	996,431	3,182,852	4,123,937	30,940		42,595	29,322
2004	31,938,004	517,402	137,681	939,612	749,408	7,535,278	12,390,068	1,173,223	997,312	3,238,387	4,155,017	31,454		43,305	29,857
2005	32,242,364	514,315	138,064	937,899	748,044	7,581,192	12,527,990	1,178,296	993,523	3,321,638	4,195,764	31,899		43,401	30,339
2006	32,570,505	510,584	137,865	937,869	745,609	7,631,873	12,661,566	1,183,524	992,302	3,421,361	4,241,691	32,271		43,178	30,812
2007	32,887,928	509,039	137,721	935,071	745,407	7,692,736	12,764,195	1,189,366	1,002,048	3,514,031	4,290,988	32,557		43,374	31,395
2008	33,245,773	511,529	138,764	935,865	746,855	7,761,504	12,882,625	1,197,774	1,017,346	3,595,755	4,349,412	33,088		43,350	31,892
2009	33,628,571	516,729	139,909	938,194	749,954	7,843,475	12,997,687	1,208,589	1,034,782	3,679,092	4,410,679	33,732		43,149	32,600
2010	34,005,274	521,972	141,678	942,073	753,044	7,929,365	13,135,063	1,220,930	1,051,425	3,732,573	4,465,924	34,596		43,278	33,353
2011	34,342,780	525,037	144,038	944,469	755,530	8,007,656	13,263,544	1,233,728	1,066,349	3,790,191	4,499,139	35,402		43,501	34,196
2012	34,752,128	526,874	145,258	944,835	756,816	8,084,754	13,410,082	1,250,499	1,087,336	3,888,632	4,542,508	35,166		43,374	34,729
2013	35,154,279	528,194	145,505	942,930	755,635	8,153,971	13,550,929	1,265,405	1,106,247	4,007,199	4,582,625	36,364		43,841	35,434
2014	35,540,419	526,977	146,283	942,668	753,914	8,214,672	13,678,740	1,282,043	1,125,410	4,121,692	4,631,302	36,510		43,623	36,585

Notes:

[1] NWT before the creation of Nunavut.

[2] Estimates are final intercensal up to 2011. Beyond 2011, the post-censal estimates (2012–2014) will eventually be revised and updated on the basis of the 2016 Census.

[3] These estimates are also available in the below listed CANSIM Table by single years of age and sex.

Source: Statistics Canada, CANSIM Table 051-0001, accessed 4 December 2014.

Table D.2 Annual Canadian Population Estimates by Census Metropolitan Area, 1 July 2001 to 1 July 2013

Geography	2001	2002	2003	2004	2005	2006	2007	2008	2009	2010	2011	2012	2013
St. John's, NL	176,443	177,795	179,403	181,632	182,522	183,777	186,067	189,771	193,867	198,436	202,533	205,891	208,372
Halifax, NS	369,265	374,410	378,005	380,623	381,795	384,585	386,498	390,005	393,692	398,259	402,433	406,903	408,702
Moncton, NB	122,270	123,797	125,396	127,048	128,244	129,707	131,123	132,752	135,293	137,655	140,228	142,797	144,941
Saint John, NB	126,074	125,866	125,817	125,786	125,411	124,951	125,550	126,315	127,432	128,020	128,605	128,528	127,883
Saguenay, QC	162,351	160,973	159,864	158,875	157,778	157,264	157,213	157,698	158,064	158,651	159,383	159,978	160,229
Québec, QC	703,960	708,734	712,571	718,110	721,871	728,221	736,993	746,711	756,499	766,563	776,821	785,191	791,934
Sherbrooke, QC	184,084	185,846	187,810	189,681	191,614	193,283	195,028	196,724	199,113	201,657	204,709	207,477	210,031
Trois-Rivières, QC	143,313	143,210	143,500	144,260	144,813	145,664	147,023	148,731	150,245	151,895	153,247	154,391	155,011
Montréal, QC	3,532,719	3,570,528	3,600,252	3,628,543	3,654,948	3,684,084	3,714,846	3,750,744	3,797,117	3,842,786	3,885,709	3,936,875	3,981,802
Ottawa–Gatineau, ON/QC	1,110,344	1,126,332	1,140,080	1,150,021	1,160,448	1,172,106	1,188,073	1,207,376	1,228,635	1,250,553	1,270,232	1,288,720	1,305,210
Kingston, ON	152,774	154,925	156,551	157,513	157,866	158,117	158,664	159,838	161,375	162,913	164,492	165,987	167,151
Peterborough, ON	115,323	116,737	117,925	118,913	120,042	120,610	120,560	120,895	120,988	121,865	122,197	122,738	123,105
Oshawa, ON	308,599	315,101	322,777	330,304	337,398	344,262	348,280	352,630	357,061	362,255	367,266	373,818	379,995
Toronto, ON	4,882,782	5,003,947	5,084,427	5,166,803	5,248,352	5,334,812	5,418,207	5,504,836	5,591,195	5,681,721	5,769,759	5,869,950	5,959,505
Hamilton, ON	689,072	697,025	703,998	710,139	715,083	719,434	722,102	725,297	729,247	736,141	742,498	750,802	758,073
St Catharines–Niagara, ON	391,875	394,770	397,351	400,507	402,871	403,959	402,581	401,456	401,337	401,957	402,563	404,073	404,971
Kitchener–Cambridge–Waterloo, ON	431,559	439,944	446,842	455,643	463,552	470,597	474,219	478,759	482,586	487,186	492,961	498,978	504,258
Brantford, ON	128,504	129,629	131,100	132,612	134,391	135,417	136,330	136,972	137,741	138,465	139,388	140,435	141,296
Guelph, ON	129,198	131,207	133,154	135,337	137,658	139,329	140,035	141,399	142,587	144,204	145,637	148,060	150,305
London, ON	453,092	458,647	462,738	467,622	471,711	475,903	478,492	481,249	483,045	486,129	489,461	494,511	498,623
Windsor, ON	320,946	326,628	330,232	333,182	335,178	336,009	333,507	330,475	328,335	328,173	328,321	330,954	333,082
Barrie, ON	155,337	161,654	167,951	173,873	179,572	184,411	186,064	187,831	189,307	190,813	192,777	195,421	197,821
Greater Sudbury, ON	161,493	161,197	161,706	162,221	162,998	164,214	164,808	165,515	165,684	165,200	165,253	165,508	165,534
Thunder Bay, ON	126,698	126,822	127,462	127,763	127,769	127,066	126,024	125,463	125,087	125,098	124,952	125,132	125,093
Winnipeg, MB	695,868	700,033	704,341	710,292	713,063	715,928	719,065	723,251	729,333	736,368	746,059	759,311	771,221
Regina, SK	197,031	196,959	198,062	199,142	199,434	200,142	202,481	205,240	209,590	213,482	217,710	225,038	232,090
Saskatoon, SK	231,077	232,829	234,445	236,780	238,297	240,548	244,193	249,745	256,355	262,929	270,226	281,493	292,597
Calgary, AB	977,834	1,007,510	1,029,552	1,053,232	1,087,941	1,124,388	1,153,769	1,185,812	1,219,194	1,240,158	1,264,460	1,307,854	1,364,827
Edmonton, AB	962,323	984,538	1,000,866	1,017,054	1,041,966	1,074,111	1,104,557	1,131,156	1,161,950	1,183,047	1,206,040	1,241,723	1,289,554
Kelowna, BD	154,188	155,950	158,370	161,066	163,577	167,110	170,987	175,041	178,220	181,366	183,524	185,665	186,345
Abbotsford–Mission, B	153,934	155,364	157,057	159,710	161,930	164,310	165,676	168,000	170,566	172,720	174,321	176,679	177,508
Vancouver, BC	2,074,543	2,098,155	2,115,570	2,133,234	2,159,016	2,188,844	2,218,134	2,254,269	2,301,492	2,344,347	2,373,045	2,408,653	2,443,277
Victoria, BC	325,765	328,300	330,844	333,331	336,856	339,711	341,571	344,085	348,070	351,210	352,072	355,222	357,327

Notes:

[1] Based on Standard Geographic Classification, 2011.

[2] Estimates are final intercensal up to 2011. Beyond 2011, the post-censal estimates (2012–2013) will eventually be revised and updated on the basis of the 2016 Census.

[3] These estimates are also available in the cited CANSIM Table (see the source line), by single years of age and sex.

Source: Statistics Canada, CANSIM Table 051-0056, accessed 4 December 2014.

Table D.3 Annual Canadian Population Estimates by Census Division, 1 July 2001 to 1 July 2013

	2001	2002	2003	2004	2005	2006	2007	2008	2009	2010	2011	2012	2013	% change 2001–2013
Newfoundland and Labrador														
Division No. 1	247,406	248,162	249,252	251,119	251,092	251,663	253,094	256,381	260,682	265,442	268,890	271,522	273,091	10.4
Division No. 2	24,761	24,251	23,880	23,465	23,099	22,416	21,912	21,789	21,979	21,914	21,649	21,455	21,187	−14.4
Division No. 3	19,663	19,221	18,960	18,589	18,202	17,782	17,317	17,020	16,833	16,689	16,522	16,300	16,042	−18.4
Division No. 4	22,542	22,428	22,207	21,990	21,661	21,274	21,043	20,960	21,058	21,183	21,145	20,997	20,737	−8.0
Division No. 5	41,184	40,990	41,040	41,169	41,367	41,167	41,062	40,966	41,219	41,472	41,731	41,740	41,601	1.0
Division No. 6	36,864	36,902	37,047	36,936	36,672	36,546	36,517	36,734	37,185	37,621	37,952	38,292	38,520	4.5
Division No. 7	37,961	37,556	37,302	36,904	36,297	35,697	35,224	35,100	35,201	35,243	35,178	34,964	34,650	−8.7
Division No. 8	42,867	42,139	41,714	40,967	40,165	39,131	38,363	38,106	38,113	37,993	37,537	37,078	36,498	−14.9
Division No. 9	20,420	19,939	19,515	19,060	18,682	18,169	17,768	17,527	17,361	17,271	16,983	16,756	16,467	−19.4
Division No. 10	25,692	25,278	24,963	24,682	24,581	24,282	24,240	24,409	24,487	24,500	24,753	25,043	25,222	−1.8
Division No. 11	2,686	2,617	2,565	2,521	2,497	2,457	2,499	2,551	2,611	2,644	2,697	2,694	2,687	0.0
Prince Edward Island														
Kings	19,365	19,242	19,182	19,123	19,136	18,837	18,577	18,506	18,529	18,475	18,387	18,021	17,568	−9.3
Prince	44,933	45,035	45,133	45,261	45,257	45,142	45,173	45,336	45,197	45,324	45,346	45,250	45,037	0.2
Queens	72,367	72,599	72,906	73,297	73,671	73,886	73,971	74,922	76,183	77,879	80,305	81,894	82,632	14.2
Nova Scotia														
Annapolis	22,332	22,190	22,104	22,001	21,993	21,856	21,648	21,454	21,283	21,219	21,113	21,070	20,945	−6.2
Antigonish	20,082	19,904	19,688	19,576	19,498	19,360	19,395	19,524	19,688	19,946	20,047	19,954	19,761	−1.6
Cape Breton	112,088	111,017	110,489	110,556	109,226	108,317	107,023	106,119	105,353	104,621	103,586	102,448	100,823	−10.1
Colchester	50,629	50,892	51,191	51,350	51,331	51,253	51,344	51,556	51,915	51,955	52,103	51,921	51,550	1.8
Cumberland	33,440	33,291	33,115	33,000	32,892	32,756	32,533	32,431	32,310	32,084	31,933	31,575	31,089	−7.0
Digby	20,071	19,923	19,929	19,776	19,653	19,388	19,051	18,770	18,573	18,474	18,346	17,981	17,545	−12.6
Guysborough	10,061	9,838	9,696	9,529	9,368	9,220	8,928	8,712	8,576	8,382	8,254	8,102	7,936	−21.1
Halifax	369,274	374,407	377,981	380,574	381,724	384,584	386,490	389,975	393,668	398,250	402,441	406,907	408,714	10.7
Hants	41,647	41,689	41,827	42,033	42,071	42,310	42,357	42,425	42,622	43,044	43,259	43,384	43,359	4.1
Inverness	20,444	20,304	20,119	20,015	19,745	19,427	18,892	18,610	18,423	18,427	18,260	17,943	17,546	−14.2
Kings	60,433	60,570	60,902	61,161	61,386	61,621	61,350	61,366	61,591	61,829	61,957	61,657	61,043	1.0
Lunenburg	48,885	48,737	48,675	48,586	48,472	48,202	48,043	48,055	47,986	48,060	48,217	48,074	47,773	−2.3
Pictou	48,226	47,982	47,993	47,948	47,816	47,610	47,056	46,691	46,687	46,691	46,595	46,395	45,997	−4.6
Queens	12,019	11,909	11,780	11,711	11,589	11,447	11,356	11,310	11,230	11,240	11,140	11,131	11,091	−7.7
Richmond	10,489	10,312	10,187	10,110	10,035	9,942	9,761	9,667	9,620	9,591	9,438	9,384	9,304	−11.3
Shelburne	16,655	16,581	16,443	16,296	16,114	15,901	15,497	15,265	15,036	14,938	14,772	14,545	14,271	−14.3
Victoria	8,167	8,122	8,083	7,978	7,883	7,757	7,630	7,508	7,406	7,335	7,237	7,067	6,863	−16.0
Yarmouth	27,549	27,487	27,474	27,412	27,103	26,918	26,717	26,427	26,227	25,987	25,771	25,523	25,179	−8.6
New Brunswick														
Albert	27,524	27,585	27,812	27,901	28,042	28,137	28,253	28,396	28,694	28,940	28,983	29,151	29,266	6.3
Carleton	27,921	27,900	27,729	27,598	27,407	27,169	27,132	27,241	27,273	27,154	27,128	26,990	26,735	−4.2
Charlotte	28,131	28,073	27,981	27,941	27,848	27,558	27,379	27,094	26,982	26,809	26,622	26,518	26,328	−6.4
Gloucester	85,156	84,002	83,012	82,098	81,301	80,366	79,745	79,168	78,810	78,468	77,850	77,284	76,583	−10.1

Table D.3 ▦ Continued

	2001	2002	2003	2004	2005	2006	2007	2008	2009	2010	2011	2012	2013	% change 2001–2013
Kent	32,257	32,273	32,259	32,219	32,155	32,009	31,754	31,638	31,313	31,176	30,858	30,788	30,665	-4.9
Kings	65,984	66,294	66,502	66,763	67,039	67,164	67,711	68,198	68,966	69,548	70,005	69,943	69,670	5.6
Madawaska	36,558	36,286	35,873	35,547	35,139	34,715	34,437	34,089	33,873	33,709	33,491	33,369	33,202	-9.2
Northumberland	53,053	52,562	52,172	51,812	51,392	50,612	50,064	49,513	49,055	48,841	48,411	48,166	47,834	-9.8
Queens	12,184	12,151	12,134	12,138	12,081	11,855	11,620	11,444	11,249	11,174	11,065	10,971	10,860	-10.9
Restigouche	37,072	36,358	36,017	35,408	34,936	34,396	33,926	33,576	33,163	32,767	32,594	32,226	31,779	-14.3
Saint John	78,499	78,018	77,770	77,488	76,823	76,199	76,199	76,415	76,860	76,969	77,119	77,036	77,548	-2.5
Sunbury	26,513	26,523	26,551	26,624	26,455	26,187	26,280	26,527	26,774	27,207	27,530	27,813	27,944	5.4
Victoria	21,741	21,485	21,419	21,157	21,065	20,698	20,514	20,313	20,146	20,032	19,957	19,747	19,494	-10.3
Westmorland	128,317	130,070	131,733	133,605	134,751	136,243	137,363	139,024	141,098	143,299	145,715	148,030	149,921	16.8
York	88,909	89,799	90,470	91,109	91,610	92,301	93,030	94,219	95,698	96,951	98,202	98,965	99,221	11.6
Quebec														
Abitibi	25,033	24,693	24,569	24,394	24,478	24,433	24,432	24,500	24,446	24,562	24,551	24,670	24,820	-0.9
Abitibi-Ouest	22,327	21,919	21,495	21,193	21,012	20,902	20,897	20,991	21,036	21,062	21,131	21,072	21,048	-5.7
Acton	15,457	15,385	15,343	15,404	15,375	15,414	15,427	15,454	15,414	15,440	15,486	15,492	15,538	0.5
Antoine-Labelle	34,131	34,504	34,817	35,173	35,384	35,629	35,512	35,397	35,276	35,344	35,347	35,383	35,235	3.2
Argenteuil	29,501	29,581	29,744	29,948	30,098	30,210	30,686	31,056	31,492	31,934	32,353	32,447	32,650	10.7
Arthabaska	65,335	65,593	65,757	66,007	66,336	66,778	67,505	67,945	68,684	69,173	69,841	70,242	70,789	8.3
Avignon	15,544	15,454	15,410	15,357	15,308	15,256	15,244	15,252	15,320	15,280	15,318	15,220	15,220	-2.1
Beauce-Sartigan	48,837	48,950	49,235	49,448	49,784	50,095	50,281	50,517	50,827	51,117	51,505	51,848	52,156	6.8
Beauharnois-Salaberry	60,296	60,407	60,533	60,830	61,068	61,171	61,388	61,503	61,801	62,117	62,485	62,883	63,456	5.2
Bécancour	19,429	19,228	19,089	19,096	18,933	18,926	19,227	19,504	19,695	19,989	20,241	20,317	20,472	5.4
Bellechasse	33,991	34,000	34,004	33,979	33,861	33,700	33,900	34,135	34,515	35,108	35,627	35,903	36,373	7.0
Bonaventure	18,597	18,352	18,205	18,272	18,164	17,997	18,012	17,917	18,006	18,067	18,068	18,081	17,932	-3.6
Brome-Missisquoi	52,741	52,759	52,842	52,933	52,963	53,099	53,612	54,154	54,554	55,381	55,985	56,289	56,934	8.0
Charlevoix	13,419	13,403	13,349	13,328	13,277	13,225	13,175	13,217	13,318	13,380	13,400	13,354	13,322	-0.7
Charlevoix-Est	16,929	16,787	16,778	16,634	16,530	16,443	16,351	16,334	16,318	16,357	16,337	16,327	16,280	-3.8
Coaticooke	18,773	18,758	18,713	18,616	18,634	18,592	18,786	18,840	18,875	18,915	18,949	18,928	18,890	0.6
D'Autray	39,177	39,417	39,457	39,719	40,166	40,662	41,285	41,568	41,790	41,952	41,941	41,836	41,995	7.2
Deux-Montagnes	84,409	85,069	85,978	87,127	88,211	89,759	91,337	93,672	95,491	96,980	98,219	99,134	99,891	18.3
Drummond	89,591	90,280	91,063	92,089	93,074	93,885	94,967	96,110	97,333	98,467	99,674	100,415	101,316	13.1
Francheville	142,219	142,090	142,335	142,981	143,532	144,331	145,549	146,911	148,193	149,533	150,590	151,505	152,228	7.0
Gatineau	231,356	234,139	237,328	240,615	243,169	244,868	249,196	253,893	259,455	263,555	268,838	271,846	274,367	18.6
Joliette	55,277	55,492	56,317	57,268	58,226	58,831	59,730	60,737	61,758	63,137	64,174	65,120	66,262	19.9
Kamouraska	22,913	22,630	22,468	22,374	22,304	22,175	22,008	21,833	21,787	21,751	21,570	21,341	21,364	-6.8
La Côte-de-Beaupré	21,413	21,635	22,015	22,283	22,721	23,263	23,835	24,615	25,262	25,864	26,408	26,572	26,994	26.1
La Côte-de-Gaspé	18,854	18,539	18,173	18,014	17,944	17,953	17,981	18,071	18,042	18,120	18,076	18,054	17,921	-4.9
La Haute-Côte-Nord	13,133	12,936	12,802	12,659	12,506	12,352	12,198	11,932	11,741	11,657	11,607	11,458	11,382	-13.3
La Haute-Gaspésie	12,934	12,746	12,592	12,528	12,454	12,361	12,290	12,200	12,195	12,138	12,130	12,011	11,902	-8.0
La Haute-Yamaska	75,064	75,817	76,682	77,737	78,894	80,180	81,575	82,727	83,716	84,983	85,839	86,567	87,411	16.4
La Jacques-Cartier	27,016	27,578	28,158	28,798	29,468	30,254	31,440	32,856	34,415	35,962	37,494	38,400	39,905	47.7
La Matapédia	20,271	19,980	19,706	19,587	19,459	19,257	19,172	19,002	18,880	18,746	18,653	18,496	18,371	-9.4

La Mitis	19,669	19,577	19,491	19,415	19,418	19,383	19,365	19,297	19,206	19,143	19,032	18,943	18,907	-3.9
La Nouvelle-Beauce	31,296	31,244	31,291	31,419	31,538	31,799	32,498	33,211	33,849	34,629	35,473	35,845	36,501	16.6
La Rivière-du-Nord	92,337	93,627	95,833	98,381	100,696	102,741	105,446	108,643	111,048	113,829	116,626	119,488	122,436	32.6
La Tuque	16,144	15,862	15,766	15,699	15,631	15,529	15,445	15,348	15,301	15,285	15,214	15,215	15,195	-5.9
La Vallée-de-la-Gatineau	19,980	20,085	20,375	20,593	20,777	20,933	20,839	20,847	20,820	20,961	20,935	20,888	20,914	4.7
La Vallée-de-l'Or	43,068	42,575	42,503	42,481	42,275	42,207	42,532	42,792	42,877	43,061	43,283	43,620	43,813	1.7
La Vallée-du-Richelieu	98,100	99,243	101,097	103,217	105,525	107,981	109,602	112,010	114,036	116,237	117,877	119,385	121,043	23.4
Lac-Saint-Jean-Est	52,700	52,375	51,949	51,870	51,590	51,512	51,690	51,949	52,284	52,574	52,939	53,040	53,223	1.0
Lajemmerais	65,368	66,501	67,294	68,397	69,673	70,676	71,037	71,760	72,594	74,046	75,124	75,763	76,455	17.0
L'Assomption	105,969	105,995	106,392	107,237	108,689	110,832	113,903	116,188	117,770	119,471	120,983	121,924	123,494	16.5
Laval	350,332	354,874	359,194	363,388	367,928	372,495	378,873	385,430	392,608	399,559	406,098	412,131	417,304	19.1
Le Domaine-du-Roy	33,442	33,021	32,674	32,383	32,261	32,151	32,218	32,177	32,134	32,042	32,063	31,964	31,763	-5.0
Le Granit	22,199	22,314	22,355	22,263	22,383	22,481	22,419	22,458	22,449	22,398	22,305	22,328	22,294	0.4
Le Haut-Richelieu	102,786	103,745	105,111	106,992	108,679	109,942	111,271	112,705	113,831	114,745	115,375	115,755	116,603	13.4
Le Haut-Saint-François	21,815	21,778	21,822	21,914	21,910	21,724	21,814	22,105	22,098	22,184	22,194	22,085	22,113	1.4
Le Haut-Saint-Laurent	24,926	24,884	25,035	25,050	25,077	25,026	24,828	24,614	24,560	24,488	24,486	24,512	24,611	-1.3
Le Rocher-Percé	19,605	19,269	19,033	18,842	18,651	18,474	18,370	18,251	18,139	18,126	18,037	17,821	17,690	-9.8
Le Saguenay-et-son-Fjord	169,788	168,417	167,310	166,319	165,211	164,695	164,525	165,013	165,419	166,116	166,852	167,421	167,775	-1.2
Le Val-Saint-François	28,920	28,977	28,988	29,161	29,208	29,240	29,455	29,482	29,612	29,788	29,838	29,919	30,118	4.1
L'Érable	24,459	24,264	24,108	23,947	23,505	23,265	23,129	23,233	23,296	23,500	23,499	23,506	23,613	-3.5
Les Appalaches	44,045	43,841	43,643	43,630	43,661	43,527	43,473	43,200	43,244	43,330	43,342	43,131	42,846	-2.7
Les Basques	10,003	9,903	9,798	9,682	9,598	9,481	9,420	9,311	9,270	9,232	9,155	9,094	9,019	-9.8
Les Collines-de-l'Outaouais	36,012	37,358	38,620	39,399	41,068	42,470	42,878	43,612	44,037	46,142	46,910	47,875	48,717	35.3
Les Etchemins	18,069	17,994	17,969	17,889	17,779	17,676	17,638	17,547	17,434	17,354	17,338	17,182	17,100	-5.4
Les Îles-de-la-Madeleine	13,055	13,026	13,042	13,040	13,089	13,165	13,103	13,029	12,960	12,939	12,844	12,751	12,619	-3.3
Les Jardins-de-Napierville	23,279	23,452	23,549	23,806	23,946	24,421	25,151	25,645	25,988	26,254	26,496	26,571	26,964	15.8
Les Laurentides	39,445	39,958	40,670	41,496	42,477	43,215	43,612	44,163	44,572	45,183	45,441	45,540	45,804	16.1
Les Maskoutains	80,487	80,491	80,795	80,960	81,049	81,403	81,973	82,752	83,536	84,472	85,012	85,581	86,003	6.9
Les Moulins	112,393	114,492	117,612	121,834	126,386	130,530	135,169	139,613	143,984	147,294	150,711	153,517	155,551	38.4
Les Pays-d'en-Haut	31,656	32,889	33,916	34,968	35,982	36,791	37,800	38,595	39,231	40,076	40,547	41,096	41,415	30.8
Les Sources	14,813	14,773	14,720	14,548	14,605	14,499	14,518	14,607	14,622	14,796	14,822	14,636	14,639	-1.2
Lévis	124,524	125,586	126,531	127,904	129,474	131,498	133,716	135,457	137,153	138,591	140,137	141,173	141,911	14.0
L'Île-d'Orléans	6,904	6,907	6,961	6,940	6,908	6,869	6,920	6,849	6,844	6,770	6,743	6,699	6,649	-3.7
L'Islet	19,726	19,521	19,374	19,360	19,130	18,956	18,979	18,793	18,698	18,602	18,609	18,560	18,474	-6.3
Longueuil	379,401	381,141	383,282	385,161	386,391	388,756	391,318	392,971	395,964	399,399	403,342	408,090	412,467	8.7
Lotbinière	27,357	27,229	27,307	27,378	27,553	27,651	28,002	28,385	28,760	29,407	29,922	30,403	30,912	13.0
Manicouagan	34,191	33,840	33,703	33,671	33,474	33,250	32,927	32,592	32,576	32,465	32,339	32,297	32,189	-5.9
Maria-Chapdelaine	27,374	26,972	26,610	26,251	26,013	25,928	25,764	25,688	25,623	25,516	25,395	25,298	25,308	-7.5
Maskinongé	35,644	35,530	35,504	35,613	35,796	35,799	36,088	36,162	36,207	36,510	36,528	36,493	36,550	2.5
Matane	22,905	22,650	22,421	22,363	22,294	22,344	22,253	22,212	22,118	21,979	21,891	21,883	21,791	-4.9
Matawinie	44,042	45,301	46,761	47,985	49,023	49,911	49,703	49,765	49,860	50,058	50,210	50,795	50,917	15.6
Mékinac	13,044	12,999	12,816	12,792	12,795	12,698	12,775	12,859	12,864	12,911	12,962	12,890	12,817	-1.7
Memphrémagog	43,185	43,551	44,172	44,821	45,276	45,570	46,177	46,898	47,493	48,189	48,715	48,840	49,551	14.7
Minganie–Le Golfe	12,538	12,427	12,271	12,129	12,103	11,959	11,829	11,727	11,714	11,827	11,816	11,750	11,772	-6.1

(Continued)

Table D.3 ▫ Continued

	2001	2002	2003	2004	2005	2006	2007	2008	2009	2010	2011	2012	2013	% change 2001–2013
Mirabel	27,992	29,287	30,886	32,250	33,681	35,342	36,778	38,290	39,585	41,065	42,607	43,970	45,888	63.9
Montcalm	39,520	39,714	39,874	40,695	42,042	43,135	44,440	45,539	46,749	47,934	48,918	49,798	50,708	28.3
Montmagny	23,864	23,730	23,611	23,420	23,362	23,296	23,124	23,071	23,111	23,178	23,052	22,909	22,841	-4.3
Montréal	1,850,357	1,866,906	1,872,378	1,873,695	1,872,626	1,872,136	1,869,896	1,873,181	1,887,599	1,902,049	1,915,617	1,940,289	1,959,987	5.9
Nicolet-Yamaska	23,932	23,625	23,407	23,398	23,190	23,117	23,085	22,960	22,964	22,980	22,929	22,955	23,055	-3.7
Nord-du-Québec	39,327	39,506	39,736	40,004	40,251	40,291	40,902	41,349	41,900	42,535	43,023	43,523	43,999	11.9
Papineau	20,797	20,919	21,194	21,553	21,717	21,987	22,207	22,249	22,592	22,703	22,756	22,726	22,871	10.0
Pierre-De Saurel	50,982	50,585	50,528	50,412	50,355	50,165	50,436	50,758	50,985	50,958	51,244	51,044	51,077	0.2
Pontiac	14,822	14,707	14,707	14,739	14,757	14,769	14,687	14,683	14,635	14,503	14,466	14,390	14,331	-3.3
Portneuf	45,830	46,012	46,140	46,469	46,563	46,792	47,146	47,648	48,336	49,137	49,820	50,620	51,566	12.5
Québec	520,072	522,935	524,739	527,985	529,069	532,102	536,524	542,210	547,953	554,333	560,659	566,618	570,379	9.7
Rimouski-Neigette	53,288	53,096	53,323	53,434	53,462	53,539	53,957	54,238	54,618	55,062	55,593	56,169	56,484	6.0
Rivière-du-Loup	32,434	32,511	32,666	33,040	33,258	33,578	33,763	33,979	34,290	34,464	34,664	34,484	34,715	7.0
Robert-Cliché	19,147	19,072	19,080	19,029	18,991	18,935	19,101	19,053	19,183	19,384	19,422	19,441	19,590	2.3
Roussillon	149,413	151,202	153,426	156,202	158,337	161,170	163,202	165,833	168,660	171,351	173,856	176,174	178,430	19.4
Rouville	30,555	30,560	30,675	30,946	31,178	31,743	32,672	33,530	34,578	35,472	36,079	36,344	36,582	19.7
Rouyn-Noranda	40,323	40,049	39,770	39,715	39,841	40,264	40,382	40,590	40,876	41,115	41,439	41,630	41,904	3.9
Sept-Rivières-Caniapiscau	39,622	38,902	38,623	38,728	38,754	39,008	39,049	39,217	39,460	39,564	39,926	40,092	40,209	1.5
Shawinigan	52,997	52,494	52,311	52,192	52,136	52,050	51,630	51,385	50,955	50,634	50,263	49,884	49,752	-6.1
Sherbrooke	141,684	143,171	144,707	146,088	147,604	148,952	149,643	150,827	152,599	154,311	156,759	159,275	160,745	13.5
Témiscamingue	17,813	17,647	17,433	17,304	17,152	17,081	16,833	16,587	16,483	16,404	16,279	16,328	16,346	-8.2
Témiscouata	22,813	22,509	22,349	22,056	21,987	21,843	21,614	21,382	21,208	20,945	20,626	20,643	20,440	-10.4
Thérèse-De Blainville	133,461	136,483	139,028	141,019	143,101	144,977	147,767	149,434	151,638	153,900	155,543	156,717	157,647	18.1
Vaudreuil-Soulanges	104,408	107,297	110,275	113,926	117,950	122,147	126,455	130,721	134,195	137,835	140,819	143,127	145,514	39.4
Ontario														
Algoma	123,763	122,624	122,052	121,663	121,567	121,188	121,027	120,791	120,076	119,808	119,344	118,553	117,600	-5.0
Brant	128,922	130,070	131,560	133,090	134,887	135,937	136,466	137,254	138,136	138,972	139,939	140,906	141,686	9.9
Bruce	66,367	67,000	67,412	67,697	67,404	67,427	67,369	67,297	67,222	67,541	67,764	67,834	67,841	2.2
Chatham–Kent	111,897	111,531	111,638	111,554	112,160	112,353	111,162	109,953	108,799	107,490	106,682	106,266	105,722	-5.5
Cochrane	89,509	88,386	87,682	87,450	87,259	86,920	86,181	85,245	84,475	83,800	83,276	82,840	82,289	-8.1
Dufferin	53,087	53,930	54,826	55,737	56,426	56,467	57,013	57,325	57,489	58,014	58,528	58,764	58,913	11.0
Durham	527,623	538,113	550,527	562,573	573,688	584,255	593,870	602,621	610,018	619,053	626,765	636,208	645,043	22.3
Elgin	84,721	85,199	85,738	86,718	87,439	88,616	89,141	89,340	89,236	89,592	89,843	90,173	90,392	6.7
Essex	390,778	397,657	401,968	405,465	407,807	408,799	406,010	402,929	400,311	399,887	399,665	401,264	402,060	2.9
Frontenac	144,157	146,315	147,941	148,850	149,109	149,262	149,436	150,463	151,863	153,126	154,322	154,989	155,318	7.7
Greater Sudbury	161,146	160,860	161,376	161,894	162,664	163,847	164,388	165,122	165,266	164,823	164,853	165,086	165,087	2.4
Grey	92,560	93,201	94,069	94,597	95,017	95,353	95,205	95,201	94,994	95,016	94,769	94,923	94,981	2.6
Haldimand–Norfolk	109,535	110,178	110,731	111,399	111,811	112,407	112,084	112,285	112,110	111,992	111,848	111,451	110,940	1.3
Haliburton	15,683	15,956	16,271	16,377	16,498	16,577	16,731	16,963	17,006	17,167	17,385	17,735	18,071	15.2
Halton	390,937	403,255	415,781	430,369	444,218	457,721	468,143	479,998	493,623	506,718	517,159	528,610	539,423	38.0
Hamilton	510,089	514,877	518,751	520,992	522,469	523,629	524,002	525,599	527,652	531,663	535,602	541,013	545,585	7.0
Hastings	132,227	133,446	133,930	135,068	135,938	136,642	137,399	137,744	137,849	138,074	138,351	138,319	138,050	4.4
Huron	61,975	61,855	61,699	61,500	61,347	61,285	61,032	60,962	60,909	60,677	60,522	59,525	58,477	-5.6

Kawartha Lakes	72,004	72,921	74,282	75,320	76,357	76,861	76,178	75,893	75,276	75,018	74,942	75,472	75,918	5.4
Kenora	66,526	66,985	67,749	68,174	68,401	68,590	68,053	68,138	68,711	69,003	69,639	69,903	70,002	5.2
Lambton	131,808	132,308	132,429	132,500	132,519	132,563	132,413	132,220	132,080	131,783	131,356	130,942	130,297	-1.1
Lanark	64,997	65,486	65,801	66,004	66,097	65,937	66,088	66,064	66,287	66,990	67,274	67,363	67,356	3.6
Leeds and Grenville	100,400	100,922	101,654	101,972	102,317	102,425	102,308	102,113	101,702	101,874	101,752	101,867	101,873	1.5
Lennox and Addington	40,947	41,132	41,376	41,590	41,832	41,920	42,006	42,279	42,345	42,786	42,872	43,624	44,351	8.3
Manitoulin	12,713	12,783	12,814	12,914	12,926	13,025	13,064	13,193	13,213	13,306	13,336	13,443	13,538	6.5
Middlesex	421,979	426,851	430,203	434,116	437,441	440,685	442,471	445,122	446,874	449,928	452,845	457,734	461,737	9.4
Muskoka	55,496	56,424	57,539	58,286	59,057	59,625	59,859	60,216	60,618	60,927	61,095	61,529	61,859	11.5
Niagara	426,845	430,444	433,698	437,610	440,687	442,407	441,312	440,702	440,802	441,842	442,803	444,399	445,351	4.3
Nipissing	86,313	86,570	86,679	86,754	87,289	87,413	87,161	87,054	87,030	87,364	87,551	87,518	87,362	1.2
Northumberland	80,513	81,096	81,946	82,639	83,187	83,497	83,505	83,608	83,732	83,823	84,060	84,615	85,084	5.7
Ottawa	806,928	818,212	826,821	832,147	837,877	845,922	855,530	869,015	883,741	899,016	912,248	924,404	934,300	15.8
Oxford	103,206	103,650	104,479	105,081	106,056	106,546	106,355	106,691	106,997	107,826	108,674	109,747	110,725	7.3
Parry Sound	41,201	41,493	41,829	41,980	42,191	42,375	42,540	42,870	42,814	43,086	43,154	43,149	43,077	4.6
Peel	1,032,170	1,073,664	1,109,027	1,144,822	1,179,752	1,212,811	1,244,118	1,272,021	1,293,927	1,318,153	1,340,528	1,365,030	1,387,869	34.5
Perth	76,538	76,876	77,335	77,396	77,230	77,054	77,021	76,980	77,163	77,105	77,127	77,559	77,919	1.8
Peterborough	130,859	132,685	134,216	135,494	136,897	137,560	137,363	137,606	137,517	138,315	138,494	138,841	138,992	6.2
Prescott and Russell	79,496	80,372	81,484	82,248	82,785	83,228	83,854	84,782	85,402	86,743	87,780	88,608	89,323	12.4
Prince Edward	25,850	26,126	26,189	26,271	26,351	26,170	25,943	25,837	25,846	25,855	25,804	25,593	25,352	-1.9
Rainy River	22,943	22,709	22,579	22,466	22,362	22,263	21,948	21,622	21,198	20,988	20,877	20,554	20,166	-12.1
Renfrew	98,848	99,182	99,841	100,442	100,589	101,075	101,884	102,521	103,021	103,489	104,078	104,147	104,013	5.2
Simcoe	392,825	403,551	414,112	423,457	431,984	438,349	441,904	446,046	449,419	454,109	458,930	465,880	472,208	20.2
Stormont, Dundas, and Glengarry	115,321	115,678	116,333	116,447	116,024	115,639	115,427	115,375	115,245	115,468	115,557	115,543	115,419	0.1
Sudbury	24,202	23,865	23,498	23,116	22,654	22,510	22,378	22,317	22,189	22,026	21,633	21,370	21,086	-12.9
Thunder Bay	157,034	156,491	156,556	156,253	155,572	154,125	152,281	151,308	150,611	150,242	150,016	149,938	149,604	-4.7
Timiskaming	35,700	35,117	34,754	34,777	34,561	34,336	34,330	34,197	33,958	33,945	33,929	33,740	33,509	-6.1
Toronto	2,584,246	2,604,609	2,597,099	2,593,523	2,597,295	2,609,207	2,617,600	2,632,349	2,654,359	2,676,148	2,704,622	2,741,775	2,771,770	7.3
Waterloo	456,707	465,653	473,032	482,460	490,939	498,511	502,876	508,325	512,438	517,720	523,753	529,646	534,762	17.1
Wellington	194,982	197,633	200,147	203,097	206,297	208,419	209,012	210,312	211,384	213,187	214,694	217,267	219,598	12.6
York	762,797	807,358	844,305	877,719	904,756	931,833	960,754	988,757	1,014,754	1,043,585	1,065,504	1,086,335	1,106,096	45.0
Manitoba														
Division 1	16,942	17,202	17,529	17,764	17,879	17,844	17,798	17,792	17,743	17,686	17,469	17,201	16,925	-0.1
Division 2	52,354	53,099	53,860	55,112	56,484	57,838	60,059	61,704	63,442	65,252	66,777	68,670	70,583	34.8
Division 3	43,459	43,724	44,228	44,862	45,549	46,348	47,598	48,991	50,804	51,538	52,367	53,406	54,388	25.1
Division 4	10,194	10,055	9,881	9,804	9,736	9,593	9,491	9,420	9,409	9,441	9,431	9,476	9,521	-6.6
Division 5	14,212	13,988	13,921	13,783	13,671	13,572	13,308	13,267	13,205	13,020	13,094	13,271	13,497	-5.0
Division 6	10,388	10,296	10,220	10,159	10,104	10,052	10,034	10,023	10,043	10,085	10,188	10,316	10,460	0.7
Division 7	58,722	58,791	59,297	60,110	60,795	61,024	61,551	62,209	63,264	64,523	65,672	66,441	67,183	14.4
Division 8	14,979	14,914	14,788	14,627	14,494	14,410	14,301	14,363	14,361	14,358	14,354	14,414	14,482	-3.3
Division 9	24,077	24,029	24,207	24,659	24,141	23,968	23,903	23,912	23,799	23,906	23,837	23,697	23,558	-2.2
Division 10	9,711	9,739	9,886	10,007	10,132	10,189	10,288	10,432	10,567	10,686	10,886	10,961	11,041	13.7
Division 11	639,154	642,863	646,468	651,452	653,394	655,786	657,628	660,826	666,062	672,641	681,114	692,613	702,715	9.9
Division 12	19,773	19,799	19,989	20,169	20,147	20,293	20,737	21,213	21,546	21,842	22,200	22,601	23,005	16.3
Division 13	43,441	43,835	44,222	44,995	45,680	46,022	46,294	46,857	47,252	47,673	48,157	48,812	49,471	13.9

(Continued)

Table D.3 ▣ Continued

	2001	2002	2003	2004	2005	2006	2007	2008	2009	2010	2011	2012	2013	% change 2001–2013
Division 14	18,070	18,027	18,132	18,370	18,549	18,657	18,703	18,642	18,712	18,765	18,806	18,916	19,024	5.3
Division 15	22,493	22,383	22,328	22,251	22,102	21,920	21,788	21,742	21,762	21,910	21,873	21,614	21,386	-4.9
Division 16	10,605	10,546	10,536	10,425	10,208	10,186	10,196	10,148	10,070	10,053	10,055	10,053	10,055	-5.2
Division 17	23,521	23,321	23,144	23,055	23,001	22,870	22,704	22,668	22,701	22,637	22,434	22,181	21,932	-6.8
Division 18	23,268	23,510	24,000	24,053	24,340	24,400	24,318	23,958	23,808	23,893	23,711	23,644	23,583	1.4
Division 19	16,240	16,326	16,554	16,545	16,569	16,854	16,902	17,475	17,558	17,803	17,849	17,944	18,039	11.1
Division 20	11,296	11,232	10,937	10,899	10,759	10,641	10,541	10,377	10,225	10,187	10,051	9,901	9,753	-13.7
Division 21	23,179	23,018	23,017	22,780	22,411	22,220	21,872	21,873	22,011	22,047	21,977	21,983	22,011	-5.0
Division 22	36,170	36,948	37,814	38,817	39,615	40,298	40,809	41,222	41,511	42,165	42,393	42,669	42,929	18.7
Division 23	9,202	8,991	8,570	8,525	8,536	8,539	8,543	8,660	8,734	8,819	9,033	9,248	9,474	3.0
Saskatchewan														
Division 1	30,852	30,539	30,386	30,031	29,851	29,885	30,435	30,883	31,346	31,917	32,342	32,721	33,185	7.6
Division 2	22,057	21,789	21,574	21,267	20,992	20,794	20,989	21,420	21,923	22,434	22,848	23,258	23,708	7.5
Division 3	15,115	14,805	14,390	14,071	13,677	13,348	13,247	13,192	13,072	13,028	12,941	12,789	12,640	-16.4
Division 4	11,946	11,744	11,672	11,498	11,467	11,276	11,353	11,322	11,335	11,262	11,177	11,201	11,210	-6.2
Division 5	33,140	32,676	32,350	31,902	31,479	31,089	31,245	31,694	32,118	32,494	32,753	32,435	32,129	-3.1
Division 6	223,882	223,607	224,664	225,646	225,753	226,405	228,865	232,222	236,866	241,211	245,526	253,064	260,348	16.3
Division 7	47,940	47,549	47,639	47,587	46,944	46,463	46,560	47,000	47,444	47,611	47,912	48,193	48,440	1.0
Division 8	31,305	30,777	30,551	30,436	30,054	29,818	29,790	30,114	30,464	30,672	30,672	30,678	30,628	-2.2
Division 9	37,631	37,209	36,665	36,371	35,697	35,393	35,433	35,703	35,954	36,114	36,077	36,505	36,952	-1.8
Division 10	19,737	19,426	19,028	18,751	18,343	17,964	17,904	17,970	18,150	18,009	17,908	17,457	17,009	-13.8
Division 11	242,895	244,424	245,722	247,791	249,018	251,103	254,765	260,252	266,953	273,795	280,987	291,930	302,703	24.6
Division 12	24,202	23,811	23,591	23,448	22,944	22,908	23,123	23,202	23,383	23,687	23,795	23,849	23,912	-1.2
Division 13	24,528	24,123	23,557	23,403	23,125	22,847	23,172	23,483	23,551	23,731	23,665	23,760	23,847	-2.8
Division 14	40,265	39,580	39,171	38,673	38,023	37,170	37,109	37,432	37,701	38,002	38,033	37,829	37,593	-6.6
Division 15	82,360	82,038	81,817	81,826	81,332	80,729	81,630	82,887	84,067	85,192	86,089	86,774	87,429	6.2
Division 16	38,502	38,523	38,490	38,341	38,103	37,910	37,941	38,353	38,663	38,872	38,846	39,044	39,217	1.9
Division 17	41,057	40,968	41,469	42,021	42,216	42,214	43,126	44,005	44,818	45,544	46,449	47,408	48,354	17.8
Division 18	32,825	33,228	33,695	34,249	34,505	34,986	35,361	36,212	36,974	37,751	38,329	38,651	38,999	18.8
Alberta														
Division 1	69,151	70,363	71,503	73,137	75,103	77,083	78,953	80,300	81,210	81,266	81,288	82,294	83,935	21.4
Division 2	137,372	139,159	140,739	142,314	144,456	147,527	152,071	155,478	158,215	160,572	162,120	164,376	167,784	22.1
Division 3	38,493	38,269	38,331	38,123	38,373	38,907	39,396	39,645	39,757	39,684	39,612	39,970	40,507	5.2
Division 4	11,535	11,399	11,126	11,076	10,948	10,884	10,927	10,804	10,730	10,598	10,338	10,090	9,879	-14.4
Division 5	48,823	49,562	50,140	50,511	51,346	52,778	53,986	54,572	55,033	54,977	54,922	55,469	56,317	15.3
Division 6	1,049,059	1,081,450	1,105,613	1,131,524	1,169,252	1,208,763	1,242,201	1,277,147	1,313,916	1,338,030	1,363,607	1,409,076	1,468,701	40.0
Division 7	41,359	40,948	40,672	40,598	40,874	41,097	41,490	41,796	41,912	41,673	41,408	41,589	42,029	1.6
Division 8	157,153	161,235	165,158	169,372	175,478	182,008	186,631	189,646	192,774	194,215	196,240	201,475	208,327	32.6
Division 9	20,063	20,243	20,357	20,429	20,557	21,049	21,579	21,846	21,967	21,905	21,960	21,528	21,188	5.6
Division 10	85,111	86,043	86,873	87,225	88,058	89,495	91,981	93,248	94,440	95,097	95,947	96,943	98,751	16.0
Division 11	1,002,458	1,025,092	1,041,586	1,057,949	1,083,442	1,116,742	1,147,440	1,175,560	1,206,476	1,227,761	1,250,519	1,285,083	1,331,893	32.9
Division 12	62,753	63,248	63,862	64,172	65,098	66,135	67,263	68,319	68,817	69,338	69,767	70,838	72,551	15.6

	2001	2002	2003	2004	2005	2006	2007	2008	2009	2010	2011	2012	2013	2001-2013
Division 13	65,527	66,253	67,115	67,154	67,759	69,053	70,287	70,939	71,170	71,089	70,922	70,830	71,090	8.5
Division 14	27,482	27,606	27,649	27,836	28,268	28,840	29,177	29,436	29,546	29,353	29,577	29,886	30,534	11.1
Division 15	34,896	35,066	35,221	35,219	35,198	35,574	36,489	37,374	38,000	38,081	37,908	38,568	39,831	14.1
Division 16	44,244	47,141	49,733	51,809	53,343	55,519	59,373	62,103	65,249	68,074	71,226	74,079	79,107	78.8
Division 17	59,302	59,873	60,322	60,826	61,075	61,743	62,803	63,629	63,950	63,805	63,594	63,971	64,766	9.2
Division 18	14,666	14,583	14,448	14,290	14,377	14,835	14,988	14,913	14,944	15,029	15,038	15,200	15,542	6.0
Division 19	88,637	90,729	92,404	94,823	98,633	103,329	106,996	109,000	110,977	112,026	114,198	117,474	122,342	38.0
British Columbia														
Alberni–Clayoquot	31,597	31,238	31,260	31,278	31,512	31,474	31,442	31,588	31,718	31,767	31,581	31,262	30,882	-2.3
Bulkley-Nechako	42,473	41,446	40,807	40,509	39,746	39,377	39,542	39,762	39,748	39,998	39,905	39,726	39,637	-6.7
Capital	340,112	342,865	345,623	348,326	352,069	355,033	356,471	359,318	363,427	366,729	367,632	370,725	372,927	9.6
Cariboo	68,231	66,701	65,472	64,547	64,009	63,864	64,281	64,684	64,213	63,835	63,314	62,691	62,516	-8.4
Central Coast	3,918	3,782	3,535	3,464	3,374	3,274	3,254	3,232	3,239	3,257	3,277	3,252	3,202	-18.3
Central Kootenay	59,377	58,461	57,853	57,575	57,362	57,204	57,786	58,534	58,970	59,243	59,297	58,827	58,507	-1.5
Central Okanagan	154,190	155,977	158,401	161,086	163,596	167,113	171,016	175,086	178,261	181,388	183,521	185,659	186,352	20.9
Columbia–Shuswap	50,202	50,165	50,345	50,393	50,827	51,346	51,774	51,968	51,819	51,677	51,234	50,768	50,461	0.5
Comox Valley	58,646	58,455	58,813	59,629	60,392	61,027	61,932	62,949	63,449	63,974	64,417	64,664	64,565	10.1
Cowichan Valley	75,052	75,249	76,102	77,134	77,974	78,856	79,361	80,253	80,881	81,367	81,485	81,368	81,294	8.3
East Kootenay	58,625	58,175	57,699	57,195	56,919	56,918	57,419	58,053	58,199	58,059	57,679	57,953	57,690	-1.6
Fraser Valley	247,831	250,342	253,345	257,855	261,601	265,459	269,310	273,693	277,663	281,412	283,905	287,460	289,430	16.8
Fraser–Fort George	99,134	97,348	95,676	95,001	95,030	95,213	95,775	95,468	94,323	93,979	93,887	93,823	94,111	-5.1
Greater Vancouver	2,074,527	2,098,126	2,115,523	2,133,151	2,158,904	2,188,859	2,218,191	2,254,307	2,301,494	2,344,337	2,373,037	2,408,627	2,443,248	17.8
Kitimat-Stikine	43,080	41,943	41,204	40,568	39,951	39,458	39,174	39,190	39,060	38,601	38,066	37,990	37,917	-12.0
Kootenay Boundary	33,128	32,424	31,931	31,447	31,449	31,419	31,576	31,684	31,666	31,695	31,494	31,500	30,849	-6.9
Mount Waddington	13,641	13,171	12,695	12,426	12,237	11,940	11,996	12,023	11,848	11,808	11,716	11,469	11,563	-15.2
Nanaimo	132,480	133,879	135,673	138,245	140,433	142,079	143,687	145,515	146,744	148,178	148,770	149,756	150,545	13.6
North Okanagan	76,337	76,531	77,122	77,817	78,905	79,264	80,200	81,344	82,042	82,418	82,391	82,590	82,285	7.8
Northern Rockies	5,986	6,045	6,198	6,390	6,426	6,387	6,216	6,002	5,994	6,053	6,054	5,998	6,039	0.9
Okanagan-Similkameen	79,898	80,210	80,473	81,040	81,176	81,079	81,591	82,083	81,790	81,596	81,639	80,509	79,358	-0.7
Peace River	57,406	57,637	58,121	58,603	59,160	60,372	61,137	61,226	61,478	61,285	61,768	62,560	63,847	11.2
Powell River	20,571	20,210	19,992	19,903	19,930	20,018	20,245	20,338	20,287	20,273	20,106	19,979	20,379	-0.9
Skeena–Queen Charlotte	22,537	21,921	21,359	20,900	20,527	20,171	19,936	19,874	19,681	19,449	19,135	19,023	18,635	-17.3
Squamish–Lillooet	34,600	35,119	35,594	36,070	36,198	36,552	37,016	37,864	38,466	38,981	39,513	41,069	41,078	18.7
Stikine	788	788	731	698	670	651	635	639	636	644	638	609	612	-22.3
Strathcona	41,529	41,391	41,641	42,218	42,765	43,176	43,439	43,785	43,796	43,853	43,928	43,840	43,907	5.7
Sunshine Coast	26,685	27,049	27,313	27,728	28,111	28,313	28,591	28,949	29,046	29,041	28,918	28,827	28,730	7.7
Thompson-Nicola	124,300	123,513	123,436	123,821	124,511	125,795	127,995	129,940	130,741	131,027	130,832	130,784	131,412	5.7
Yukon Territory	30,157	30,337	30,940	31,454	31,899	32,271	32,557	33,088	33,732	34,596	35,402	36,247	36,700	21.7
Northwest Territories														
Region 1	6,815	6,929	6,907	7,020	7,068	6,984	7,002	6,964	6,999	7,010	6,949	6,898	6,811	-0.1
Region 2	2,507	2,547	2,547	2,589	2,602	2,570	2,562	2,532	2,511	2,492	2,427	2,470	2,509	0.1
Region 3	2,705	2,762	2,842	2,888	2,894	2,885	2,875	2,852	2,826	2,844	2,919	2,898	2,873	6.2
Region 4	3,252	3,328	3,415	3,477	3,482	3,464	3,464	3,444	3,400	3,373	3,377	3,390	3,388	4.2
Region 5	6,795	6,949	7,142	7,262	7,274	7,247	7,277	7,286	7,236	7,244	7,282	7,295	7,263	6.9
Region 6	18,771	19,179	19,742	20,069	20,081	20,028	20,194	20,272	20,177	20,315	20,547	20,669	20,693	10.2

(Continued)

Table D.3 ▣ Continued

	2001	2002	2003	2004	2005	2006	2007	2008	2009	2010	2011	2012	2013	% change 2001–2013
Nunavut														
Baffin	15,130	15,557	15,746	16,062	16,307	16,502	16,768	17,014	17,353	17,767	18,090	18,284	18,720	23.7
Keewatin	7,942	8,061	8,216	8,413	8,559	8,722	8,911	9,050	9,215	9,434	9,779	10,011	10,320	29.9
Kitikmeot	5,062	5,204	5,360	5,382	5,473	5,588	5,716	5,828	6,032	6,152	6,327	6,408	6,551	29.4

Notes:

[1] Based on Standard Geographic Classification, 2011.

[2] Estimates are final intercensal up to 2011. Beyond 2011, the post-censal estimates (2012–2013) will eventually be revised and updated on the basis of the 2016 Census.

[3] These estimates are also available in the cited CANSIM Table (see the source line), by single years of age and sex.

[4] In NL, MB, SK, AB, YT, NWT, and NU, provincial law does not provide for these administrative areas. CDs have been created by Statistics Canada in collaboration with provincial governments.

Source: Statistics Canada, CANSIM Table 051-0062, accessed 4 December 2014.

Table D.4 ■ Annual Canadian Population Estimates by Economic Region, 1 July 2001 to 1 July 2013

	2001	2002	2003	2004	2005	2006	2007	2008	2009	2010	2011	2012	2013	2001–2013% change
Newfoundland and Labrador														
Avalon Peninsula	247,407	248,168	249,256	251,123	251,091	251,663	253,097	256,381	260,680	265,439	268,890	271,522	273,091	10.4
South Coast–Burin Peninsula	44,424	43,472	42,838	42,052	41,301	40,195	39,228	38,809	38,812	38,604	38,171	37,755	37,229	−16.2
West Coast–Northern Peninsula–Labrador	112,526	111,253	110,293	109,419	108,795	107,350	106,608	106,414	106,738	107,074	107,309	107,230	106,714	−5.2
Notre Dame–Central Bonavista Bay	117,689	116,590	116,058	114,808	113,128	111,376	110,106	109,939	110,499	110,855	110,667	110,334	109,668	−6.8
Prince Edward Island	136,665	136,876	137,221	137,681	138,064	137,865	137,721	138,764	139,909	141,678	144,038	145,165	145,237	6.3
Nova Scotia														
Cape Breton	151,192	149,766	148,885	148,664	146,887	145,446	143,312	141,910	140,805	139,974	138,520	136,841	134,535	−11.0
North Shore	162,439	161,908	161,686	161,404	160,904	160,196	159,254	158,910	159,171	159,060	158,932	157,947	156,333	−3.8
Annapolis	124,415	124,450	124,835	125,196	125,449	125,789	125,353	125,242	125,495	126,087	126,326	126,108	125,344	0.7
Southern	125,178	124,635	124,302	123,779	122,933	121,852	120,662	119,825	119,052	118,700	118,246	117,254	115,859	−7.4
Halifax	369,267	374,396	377,968	380,569	381,726	384,586	386,490	389,978	393,671	398,252	402,445	406,911	408,718	10.7
New Brunswick														
Campbellton-Miramichi	175,281	172,918	171,197	169,316	167,627	165,371	163,735	162,253	161,025	160,073	158,857	157,678	156,198	−10.9
Moncton–Richibucto	188,097	189,932	191,807	193,729	194,947	196,390	197,367	199,069	201,103	203,422	205,549	207,962	209,845	11.6
Saint John–St Stephen	172,615	172,384	172,252	172,188	171,708	170,920	171,289	171,708	172,808	173,324	173,747	173,498	172,547	0.0
Fredericton–Oromocto	127,605	128,474	129,157	129,873	130,150	130,348	130,932	132,183	133,727	135,331	136,801	137,753	138,029	8.2
Edmundston–Woodstock	86,221	85,671	85,021	84,302	83,612	82,580	82,084	81,642	81,291	80,894	80,576	80,106	79,431	−7.9
Québec														
Gaspésie-Îles-de-la-Madeleine	98,592	97,387	96,455	96,052	95,607	95,206	94,998	94,721	94,659	94,669	94,473	93,938	93,284	−5.4
Bas-Saint-Laurent	204,297	202,859	202,222	201,951	201,781	201,599	201,553	201,255	201,378	201,323	201,185	201,054	201,091	−1.6
Capitale-Nationale	651,594	655,251	658,141	662,433	664,547	668,960	675,391	683,732	692,448	701,799	710,864	718,593	725,095	11.3
Chaudière–Appalaches	390,855	391,169	392,043	393,457	395,134	397,131	400,713	403,369	406,774	410,703	414,428	416,396	418,704	7.1
Estrie	291,389	293,321	295,476	297,410	299,620	301,057	302,812	305,217	307,752	310,579	313,581	316,010	318,350	9.3
Centre-du-Québec	222,747	222,992	223,425	224,537	225,037	225,970	227,913	229,753	231,973	234,109	236,185	237,436	239,245	7.4
Montérégie	1,313,255	1,323,473	1,336,477	1,351,976	1,366,458	1,383,293	1,399,946	1,417,137	1,434,404	1,453,178	1,469,506	1,483,578	1,499,088	14.2
Montreal	1,850,357	1,866,896	1,872,359	1,873,706	1,872,647	1,872,128	1,869,882	1,873,176	1,887,598	1,902,046	1,915,614	1,940,286	1,959,987	5.9
Laval	350,325	354,874	359,196	363,380	367,919	372,496	378,875	385,431	392,607	399,554	406,095	412,128	417,304	19.1
Lanaudière	396,378	400,410	406,413	414,736	424,528	433,900	444,230	453,407	461,909	469,844	476,936	482,989	488,927	23.3
Laurentides	472,932	481,396	490,871	500,360	509,627	518,662	528,938	539,250	548,333	558,312	566,685	573,777	580,966	22.8
Outaouais	322,964	327,212	332,225	336,904	341,484	345,031	349,815	355,285	361,549	367,873	373,905	377,725	381,200	18.0
Abitibi–Témiscamingue	148,565	146,884	145,772	145,089	144,760	144,886	145,074	145,458	145,715	146,202	146,682	147,319	147,931	−0.4
Mauricie	260,048	258,975	258,733	259,278	259,889	260,408	261,488	262,666	263,522	264,874	265,556	265,986	266,542	2.5
Saguenay-Lac-Saint-Jean	283,306	280,789	278,547	276,819	275,067	274,287	274,203	274,829	275,464	276,251	277,250	277,724	278,069	−1.8

Region														% Change
Côte-Nord	99,484	98,104	97,400	97,186	96,836	96,568	96,003	95,469	95,490	95,514	95,688	95,597	95,552	-4.0
Nord-du-Québec	39,327	39,506	39,736	40,004	40,251	40,291	40,902	41,349	41,900	42,535	43,023	43,523	43,999	11.9
Ontario														
Ottawa	1,167,147	1,180,665	1,192,088	1,198,815	1,205,096	1,213,153	1,223,209	1,237,349	1,252,377	1,270,084	1,284,614	1,297,788	1,308,274	12.1
Kingston–Pembroke	442,029	446,203	449,278	452,222	453,822	455,072	456,670	458,845	460,926	463,330	465,426	466,671	467,083	5.7
Muskoka–Kawarthas	354,553	359,081	364,252	368,114	371,996	374,123	373,637	374,289	374,150	375,251	375,978	378,194	379,926	7.2
Toronto	5,160,789	5,285,710	5,371,096	5,458,249	5,544,080	5,635,460	5,720,468	5,807,554	5,893,725	5,986,128	6,073,365	6,172,728	6,261,167	21.3
Kitchener–Waterloo–Barrie	1,097,603	1,120,768	1,142,117	1,164,752	1,185,647	1,201,741	1,210,804	1,222,007	1,230,727	1,243,030	1,255,905	1,271,557	1,285,481	17.1
Hamilton–Niagara Peninsula	1,312,372	1,326,858	1,340,386	1,353,847	1,365,486	1,374,746	1,377,877	1,384,026	1,391,653	1,402,004	1,411,402	1,422,996	1,432,593	9.2
London	609,906	615,701	620,421	625,916	630,936	635,846	637,966	641,152	643,109	647,347	651,362	657,654	662,854	8.7
Windsor–Sarnia	634,482	641,497	646,035	649,520	652,485	653,714	649,586	645,103	641,190	639,160	637,702	638,471	638,078	0.6
Stratford–Bruce Peninsula	297,440	298,935	300,191	301,191	300,998	300,625	300,441	300,287	300,338	300,182	299,841	299,218	299,218	0.6
Northeast	574,547	571,696	570,684	570,547	571,108	571,614	571,069	570,790	569,023	568,158	567,075	565,698	563,547	-1.9
Northwest	246,502	246,185	246,884	246,895	246,336	244,979	242,284	241,069	240,520	240,233	240,533	240,396	239,773	-2.7
Manitoba														
Southeast	89,068	90,098	91,379	93,048	94,513	95,974	98,591	100,706	102,735	104,786	106,442	108,468	110,509	24.1
South Central	53,652	53,777	54,107	54,665	55,286	55,941	57,089	58,412	60,213	60,979	61,799	62,883	63,910	19.1
Southwest	105,816	105,463	105,767	106,305	106,681	106,565	106,681	107,243	108,272	109,534	110,831	111,646	112,530	6.3
North Central	48,767	48,682	48,880	49,291	48,766	48,568	48,492	48,707	48,728	48,950	49,077	49,072	49,081	0.6
Winnipeg	639,154	642,864	646,470	651,454	653,383	655,791	657,634	660,825	666,059	672,638	681,113	692,612	702,714	9.9
Interlake	84,778	85,372	86,355	87,415	88,568	89,078	89,314	89,457	89,770	90,329	90,674	91,372	92,078	8.6
Parklands	45,422	45,099	44,616	44,378	43,968	43,695	43,440	43,195	42,998	42,879	42,540	42,135	41,740	-8.1
North	84,793	85,281	85,954	86,667	87,131	87,912	88,125	89,229	89,814	90,835	91,252	91,844	92,453	9.0
Saskatchewan														
Regina–Moose Mountain	276,791	275,941	276,629	276,954	276,596	277,079	280,284	284,525	290,142	295,560	300,721	309,048	317,246	14.6
Swift Current–Moose Jaw	106,308	104,876	104,253	103,592	102,140	100,903	100,950	101,628	102,317	102,672	102,701	102,860	102,917	-3.2
Saskatoon–Biggar	291,630	292,354	292,867	294,630	295,087	296,865	301,065	306,931	313,876	321,216	328,442	339,534	350,457	20.2
Yorkton–Melville	90,505	89,310	88,043	87,023	85,519	84,448	84,581	85,367	86,223	86,617	86,739	86,398	86,091	-4.9
Prince Albert	202,180	201,107	200,944	200,864	199,676	198,021	199,807	202,683	205,250	207,609	209,417	211,055	212,593	5.2
Northern	32,825	33,228	33,695	34,249	34,505	34,986	35,361	36,212	36,974	37,751	38,329	38,651	38,999	18.8
Alberta														
Lethbridge–Medicine Hat	245,016	247,792	250,573	253,575	257,934	263,521	270,420	275,422	279,180	281,522	283,020	286,640	292,226	19.3
Camrose–Drumheller	186,827	187,952	188,810	189,411	191,227	194,257	198,385	200,419	202,116	202,345	202,613	204,089	206,974	10.8
Calgary	1,049,063	1,081,455	1,105,611	1,131,519	1,169,239	1,208,755	1,242,198	1,277,137	1,313,919	1,338,010	1,363,595	1,409,064	1,468,689	40.0
Banff–Jasper–Rocky Mountain House	82,442	82,914	83,226	83,485	84,022	85,462	87,244	88,653	89,521	89,339	89,446	89,983	91,554	11.1
Red Deer	157,156	161,236	165,161	169,371	175,481	182,007	186,626	189,649	192,776	194,222	196,243	201,478	208,330	32.6
Edmonton	1,002,449	1,025,083	1,041,586	1,057,952	1,083,449	1,116,745	1,147,449	1,175,571	1,206,474	1,227,774	1,250,529	1,285,093	1,331,903	32.9
Athabasca–Grande Prairie–Peace River	228,135	231,441	234,291	237,094	241,844	248,959	255,073	258,482	261,039	261,948	263,754	267,477	273,742	20.0
Wood Buffalo–Cold Lake	106,996	110,389	113,594	115,980	118,442	121,655	126,636	130,422	134,067	137,413	140,991	144,915	151,656	41.7
British Columbia														
Vancouver Island and Coast	717,545	720,238	725,340	732,619	740,678	746,883	751,828	759,055	765,385	771,211	772,917	776,320	779,264	8.6
Lower Mainland–Southwest	2,383,648	2,410,640	2,431,769	2,454,808	2,484,820	2,519,180	2,553,113	2,594,823	2,646,673	2,693,765	2,725,368	2,765,978	2,802,486	17.6
Thompson–Okanagan	484,929	486,396	489,777	494,156	499,016	504,597	512,574	520,420	524,653	528,105	529,617	530,310	529,868	9.3

(Continued)

Table D.4 ■ Continued

Kootenay	151,127	149,060	147,483	146,216	145,730	145,539	146,781	148,271	148,835	148,999	148,470	148,280	147,046	-2.7
Cariboo	167,363	164,047	161,146	159,547	159,038	159,076	160,054	160,150	158,535	157,813	157,201	156,514	156,627	-6.4
North Coast	65,617	63,864	62,564	61,469	60,480	59,628	59,110	59,064	58,741	58,050	57,201	57,013	56,552	-13.8
Nechako	43,260	42,234	41,538	41,208	40,416	40,029	40,175	40,401	40,385	40,642	40,544	40,336	40,249	-7.0
Northeast	63,392	63,682	64,320	64,994	65,586	66,759	67,353	67,228	67,472	67,339	67,821	68,557	69,886	10.2
Yukon Territory	30,157	30,337	30,940	31,454	31,899	32,271	32,557	33,088	33,732	34,596	35,402	36,247	36,700	21.7
Northwest Territories	40,845	41,694	42,595	43,305	43,401	43,178	43,374	43,350	43,149	43,278	43,501	43,620	43,537	6.6
Nunavut	28,134	28,822	29,322	29,857	30,339	30,812	31,395	31,892	32,600	33,353	34,196	34,703	35,591	26.5

Notes:

[1] Based on Standard Geographic Classification, 2011.

[2] Estimates are final intercensal up to 2011. Beyond 2011, the post-censal estimates (2012–2013) will eventually be revised and updated on the basis of the 2016 Census.

[3] These estimates are also available in the CANSIM Table cited in the source line, by single years of age and sex.

Source: Statistics Canada, CANSIM Table 051-0059, accessed 4 December 2014.

Glossary

Aboriginal Canadian Person whose ancestors were indigenous to Canada before the arrival of Europeans in North America. Can sometimes be referred to as a First Nations person (see *status Indian*), but other Aboriginal groups are the Métis and Inuit.

age-specific birth rate The number of live births occurring in a given age group per 1,000 women in that age group.

age-specific death rate The number of deaths occurring in a given age group per 1,000 persons in that age group.

aging index Defined by the United Nations as the number of people aged 65 years and over per 100 persons under 15 years of age.

allophone In Canada, a person with a mother tongue that is neither English nor French.

anglophone A person whose mother tongue is English.

carrying capacity The carrying capacity of an environment is the maximum population size that can be sustained, given the available technology plus food, habitat, water, and other necessities available in the environment.

cause-specific death rate The number of deaths due to a specified cause per 100,000 population in a given year.

census The enumeration of all persons in a country, involving the total process of collecting, compiling, evaluating, analyzing, and disseminating population data. In Canada there is a census every five years of all Canadian citizens, landed immigrants, and non-permanent residents.

census coverage error Errors made in documenting the size of a country's population through a census; inevitably, a small proportion is either completely missed (resulting in undercount) or counted more than once (resulting in overcount).

census metropolitan area (CMA) A very large urban area (known as the urban core), together with adjacent urban and rural areas that have a high degree of social and economic integration with the urban core. A CMA must have an urban core of at least 100,000 (as measured in the previous census).

census family A married or common-law couple living together, with or without sons or daughters who have never been married, or a lone parent living with at least one married son or daughter who has never been married.

chain migration The practice by which families and ethnic groups that have already migrated attract and sponsor migration from the same place of origin.

cohort-component method A method of population projection or estimation that relies on age- and sex-specific data on fertility, mortality, and migration. Population data for a base year are followed through time, by adding on all births and in-migrants and subtracting all deaths and out-migrants.

cohort completed fertility The average births per women, for women of given birth cohorts who have completed their child-bearing years.

cohort A group of people, observed through time, who share a common temporal demographic experience. For example, a group of people born in 1960 can serve as a cohort. There can also be marriage cohorts, university-admission-year cohorts, and so on.

component A component of demographic change, including births, deaths, immigrants, and emigrants (among others).

crude birth rate The number of live births per 1,000 population in a given year.

crude death rate The number of deaths per 1,000 population in a given year.

decomposition Determining the extent to which the different prevalence of events in the whole population is a function of (1) changes in the structure or composition of the population, and (2) changes in the rates within categories of this structure or composition.

demographic-transition theory The theory that the rate of population growth passes through three stages, from stable high rates of mortality and fertility, through declining rates, to a third stage of stable low rates of fertility and mortality. There is little population growth in the first and third stages, but much growth in the second stage as mortality declines faster than fertility.

demography The study of populations, their size, distribution, and composition, changes in them, and the components of such changes—that is, births, deaths, migration, and social mobility (change of status).

dependency ratio The ratio of people deemed dependent to those who are in the active labour force. Traditionally, people aged 0–14 and 65+ are treated as dependants of persons at labour-force ages (15–64).

dwelling, private A dwelling that has a separate set of living quarters with a private entrance either from outside the building or from a common hall, lobby, vestibule, or stairway inside the building.

dwelling, collective A dwelling used for commercial, institutional, or communal purposes, such as a hotel, a hospital, or work camp.

ecological footprint an estimate of the total amount of (productive) land required to support an individual or population, including providing all of their resources and assimilating all of their various waste.

economic family A group of two or more persons who live in the same dwelling and are related to each other by blood, marriage, common-law relationship, or adoption.

emigration The number of people leaving a country over a given period of time.

employment rate The number of persons employed (full- or part-time), expressed as a percentage of the total population 15 years of age and over.

epidemiological transition A transition that accompanies the demographic transition and that entails the gradual shift in health and disease patterns from the high mortality of the past to relatively low mortality.

ethnicity A multidimensional concept that includes things such as race, origin or ancestry, identity, language, and religion.

ethnic ancestry The ethnicity or nationality of one's ancestors on first arriving in North America (with the exception of Aboriginal persons).

ethnic identity The culture(s) or ethnic background(s) to which one self-identifies.

fecundity The physical capacity to have children.

fertility The reproductive performance of a population.

first-generation Canadian A person who is an immigrant to Canada and was born in another country to non-Canadian parents.

francophone A person whose mother tongue is French.

general fertility rate The number of live births in a given year per 1,000 women aged between 15 and 49.

general marital fertility rate The number of live births in a given year per 1,000 married women aged between 15 and 49.

global warming Increasing average temperatures over time due to the build-up of greenhouse gases in the atmosphere. Usually refers to the modern, human-produced trend.

greenhouse gases (GHGs) Gases in the atmosphere that warm the earth by "trapping" radiated heat from the sun, rather than allowing it to escape. Carbon dioxide and methane are two examples.

head tax A tax levied per person, in particular to persons of Chinese origin under the Chinese Immigration Act.

health-adjusted life expectancy A measure of life expectancy that takes into account a person's state of health and hence quality of life. To calculate this life expectancy, a series of categories of less-than-optimal health are first assigned on the basis of a survey that asks respondents to rank their various health conditions. Being near-sighted, for instance, but otherwise fully healthy receives a score of 95 per cent, whereas a life spent in completely disabling pain might be evaluated as not worth living. These scores are then multiplied by the years of life that someone would be expected to live under various conditions, to obtain a life expectancy that is adjusted for the health status of the population.

heritage language In Canada, a mother tongue other than English and French.

home language The language spoken most often or regularly at home.

household A person or group of persons occupying the same private dwelling.

human ecology The study of how human populations interact with their sustaining environments.

immigrant classes The different categories of immigrant as defined by the Immigration Act. The independent class consists of those who are selected through the points system, together with their families. The family class consists of those admitted by virtue of a close family relationship with someone who is already in the country. The refugee class consists of those who are admitted because their lives or safety were in danger in their homeland. The business class and the investment class, which are treated as part of the independent class, consist of people who are admitted because they have undertaken to start a business in Canada or make a large investment.

immigration The number of people moving into a country over a given period of time.

impact equation (IPAT) Developed by Paul Erlich and colleagues, it is a formula that suggests a relationship between a population's size (P), its affluence (A) and its level and type of technology (T) in explaining the scope of a particular environmental impact (I), such as concentrations of atmospheric greenhouse gases ($I = P \times A \times T$).

index of continuity An index that compares the persons who are of a given mother tongue (taken as the denominator) to those who are currently using that same language at home.

infant mortality rate The number of deaths of infants under one year of age per 1,000 live births in the same year.

in-migration Movement into a specified area from a different part of the same country, as a component of internal migration.

internal migration The movement of people within a given country. Generally, only movement across municipal boundaries is counted as internal migration; interprovincial migration is one kind of internal migration.

Inuit An Aboriginal population indigenous to Canada's Far North. Currently, most Inuit live in Nunavut, the Northwest Territories, Labrador, or northern Quebec.

knowledge of languages The ability to conduct a conversation in a specified language.

knowledge of official languages The ability to conduct a conversation in English or French or both.

labour force Civilian non-institutional population 15 years of age and over who are either employed or unemployed during a specified reference week. To count as unemployed, a person must either be on temporary lay-off or be actively seeking work.

labour-force participation rate The proportion of the population 15 years of age and over that is in the labour force (i.e., either employed or looking for work) in a specified reference period.

lactational infecundity The temporary reduction in fecundity common in nursing mothers.

life expectancy Unless otherwise indicated, life expectancy at birth. It is an estimate of the average number of additional years a person can expect to live, based on the age-specific death rates of a given year.

lifetime migration Migration that compares place of birth and place of residence at time of census.

lone-parent family One parent with one or more children who have never married, living in the same dwelling.

low income cut-offs (LICOs) Income levels at which families or unattached individuals are considered to be living in "straitened circumstances." Statistics Canada currently produces LICOs before and after tax, which are periodically revised on the basis of changes in the average standard of living of Canadians. These are essentially "relative measures" of low income that vary by family size and degree of urbanization.

matrilineal Descent through the female line.

mean income The average income of a specified income unit (individuals, families, or households).

median income That point in the income distribution at which one half of income units (individuals, families, or households) fall above and one half fall below.

Métis People of mixed Aboriginal and European ancestry, who have a distinct ancestry and history in Canada.

migration The movement of people from one area of a country to another, or between countries.

morbidity The state of illness and disability in a population.

mortality Actual deaths in a population, as one of the three basic demographic processes.

mother tongue The language first learned in the home as a child and still understood by the individual.

multiple-family household A household consisting of two or more families.

natural fertility The fertility that a population would experience in the complete absence of deliberate fertility control.

natural increase (or natural decrease) The difference between the number of births and the number of deaths in a population over a given period. Can be given in absolute numbers or as a percentage of the mid-year population.

neo-natal death rate The number of deaths of infants under four weeks of age per 1,000 live births in a given year.

net migration The difference between the number of immigrants and the number of emigrants in a population over a given period. Net migration can also refer to the net balance of internal migration (in-migration minus out-migration to a particular area).

net internal migration The net effect of migration on the population of an area in a given period. For a specific province, equal to the difference between the total number of in-migrants from other provinces and territories minus the total number of losses to other parts of the country.

net international migration The total number of immigrants entering Canada over a given period minus the total number of emigrants leaving Canada.

net reproduction rate The average number of daughters who would be born to a woman, if throughout her life she conformed to the age-specific fertility and mortality rates of a given year.

net undercount The difference between the total number of people missed in a census (gross undercount) and the total number counted more than once or included erroneously (gross overcount).

non-family household A household whose members do not include a family.

non-permanent residents People with a usual place of residence in Canada yet without the right to live permanently in the country. This includes people with student visas or work permits as well as refugee claimants who are awaiting a decision on their case.

onward migration The movement of migrants from the place of origin to a destination other than the place of origin.

out-migration The process of leaving an administrative subdivision of a country to take up residence in another subdivision of the same country.

parity The number of children previously born to a woman.

parity progression ratio The proportion of women of a given parity who go on to have an additional birth.

patrilineal Descending through the male line.

perinatal death rate The number of fetal deaths from 28 weeks' gestation to 1 week after birth per 1,000 live births in a given year.

population estimate Information about population not directly available from a census, usually based on administrative datasets and various approximation techniques. Commonly made between censuses (intercensal estimates) or after the most recent census (post-censal estimates).

population growth The change in population size over a specific period of time. A function of natural increase (births minus deaths) plus net migration (immigration minus emigration).

population momentum The tendency of a population, owing to a high proportion of people of child-bearing age, to experience natural increase even when the total fertility rate is fewer than 2.1 births per woman.

population processes The three ways in which populations change from one time to another—namely, births, deaths, and migration.

population projection A calculation of the number of people expected in the future, given a current population size and stated assumptions about future fertility, mortality, and migration.

population state The size, distribution, and composition of the population at a given time.

population structure (or composition) The distribution of a population into various components (such as age groups or types of families) that add up to the whole population under investigation.

post-neonatal death rate The number of deaths of infants between 4 weeks and 1 year of age per 1,000 live births.

predominant language A measure of which of the official languages is predominant for a given person. Based on which of the official languages is known or is spoken at home.

primary migration Migration from one's place of birth.

pronatalism An attitude or doctrine that favours a high level of fertility.

rate The relative frequency of a particular event within a population or subpopulation. Thus, the numerator of a rate is the event under consideration (such as births, labour-force participation, or child poverty) and the denominator is the relevant population or subpopulation (such as age groups or type of family).

replacement migration The use of migration to replace a deficiency of fertility.

replacement fertility A level of fertility that, if continued over a long period, would ensure the replacement of one generation of women by another generation of daughters who are themselves able to reach reproductive ages. Given that some deaths occur before women reach reproductive age, the total fertility rate of 2.1 is generally considered to be replacement fertility.

return migration Migration that involves a return to the place of origin or place of birth.

returning Canadians People who previously emigrated from Canada and who return to live permanently in Canada.

rural Used to describes all territory lying outside urban Canada. Includes small towns, villages, other populated places with less than 1,000 population, rural fringes of metropolitan areas, agricultural lands (rural farm), as well as remote and wilderness areas.

rural non-farm All non-agricultural lands classified as rural in Canada.

second-generation Canadian A person born to immigrant parents in Canada.

sex ratio The number of males per 100 females in a population

sex ratio at birth The number of male births per 100 female births for a population; has been documented at about 105 male births per 100 female births throughout the twentieth century in Canada.

standard population A population structure (or composition) which is applied to alternative sets of rates when one is standardizing a set of rates.

standardization Applying the rates for two or more periods, or two or more populations, to a standard population structure or composition.

status Indian People who have legal status as North American Indians. Eligibility for status is defined by the Indian Act. Status Indians are often referred to as First Nations people.

total fertility rate The average number of children that would be born to a woman during her lifetime if she were to pass through all her child-bearing years conforming to the age-specific fertility rates of a given year. An indicator of the level of child-bearing in a population, measured in terms of births per woman.

urban area An area that has a minimum population of 1,000 and a population density of at least 400 persons per square kilometre, based on the most recent census.

visible minority As defined in Canada's Employment Equity Act, people, other than Aboriginal persons, who are not white in race or colour.

vital statistics Data on the vital events of birth and death, and also including such events as abortions, marriages, and divorces, cause of death, birth weight, and so on.

References

AANDC (Aboriginal Affairs and Northern Development Canada). 2013. "Registered Indian population by sex and residence, 2012." Statistics and Measurement Directorate. Ottawa: Department of Aboriginal Affairs and Northern Development Canada.

Abada, Teresa, Feng Hou, and Bali Ram. 2009. "Ethnic differences in educational attainment among the second generation of immigrants." *Canadian Journal of Sociology* 34: 1–28.

———, and Sylvia Lin. 2014. "The labour market outcomes of the children of immigrants in Ontario." *Canadian Studies in Population* 41: 78–96.

Abella, Irving, and Harold Troper. 1982. *None Is Too Many: Canada and the Jews of Europe, 1933–1948*. Toronto: Lester and Orpen Dennys.

Abella, Rosalie. 1984. *Equality in Employment: Report of the Commission on Equality in Employment*. Ottawa: Minister of Supply and Services.

Achilles, Rona. 1986. *The Social Implications of Artificial Reproductive Technologies*. Report for Review of Demography. Ottawa: Health and Welfare Canada.

Adams, Owen B, and D.N. Nagnur. 1988. *Marriage, Divorce and Mortality*. Ottawa: Statistics Canada cat. no. 84-536.

Adamuti-Trache, Maria, Paul Anisef, and Robert Sweet. 2013. "Impact of Canadian postsecondary education on occupational prestige of highly educated immigrants." *Canadian Review of Sociology* 50(2): 178–202.

Adsera, Alicia, Ana M. Ferrer, Wendy Sigle-Rushton, and Ben Wilson. 2012. "Fertility patterns of child migrants: Age at migration and ancestry in comparative perspective." *Annals of the American Academy of Political Science and Social Science* 643: 160–239.

———, and Ana M. Ferrer. 2014. "Factors influencing the fertility choices of child immigrants in Canada." *Population Studies* 68(1): 65–79.

AFN (Assembly of First Nations). 2008. "Annual General Assembly Resolution No. 31/2008. Quebec City." Lisa Dillon, ed. *Cahier québécois de démographie* 34(2): 193–350.

Alasia, Alessandro, and Neil Rothwell. 2003. "The rural–urban divide is not changing: Income disparities persist." *Rural and Small Town Canada Analysis Bulletin* 4(4).

Alba, Franciso, Jean-Pierre Garson, and El Mouhoub Mouhoud. 1998. "Migration policies in a free trade area: The issue of convergence with the economic integration process." In *Migration, Free Trade and Regional Integration in North America*. Paris: Organisation for Economic Co-operation and Development, pp. 261–78.

Alberta Treasury Board and Finance. 2012. "Alberta population projections." Economics, Demography and Public Finance. Edmonton: Government of Alberta.

Alder, George. 1992. "Theories of fertility decline: A non-specialist's guide to the current debate." In *The European Experience of Fertility Decline, 1850–1970*, John R. Gillis, Louise A. Tilly, and David Levine, eds. Cambridge, UK: Blackwell.

Allard, Yvon, Russell Wilkins, and Jean-Marie Berthelot. 2001. "Potential years of life lost among health regions with a high proportion of Aboriginal residents." Paper presented at the meetings of the Federation of Canadian Demographers, Ottawa, December.

Ambert, Anne-Marie, and Maureen Baker. 1988. "Marriage dissolution." In *Family Bonds and Gender Divisions*, B. Fox, ed. Toronto: Canadian Scholars' Press.

Anderson, Alan, and James Frideres. 1981. *Ethnicity in Canada: Theoretical Perspectives*. Toronto: Butterworths.

Andersson, Gunnar. 1996. "The impact of children on divorce risks of Swedish women." Stockholm Research Reports in Demography, no. 102. Stockholm: Stockholm University, Demographic Unit.

Angel, L. 1984. "Health as a crucial factor in the changes from hunting to developed farming in the eastern Mediterranean." In *Paleopathology at the Origins of Agriculture*, M.N. Cohen and G.J. Armelagos, eds. Orlando: Academic Press, pp. 51–73.

Angus, H.F. 1946. "The future of immigration into Canada." *Canadian Journal of Economics and Political Science* 12: 379–86.

Ariès, Philippe. 1980. "Two successive motivations for the declining birth rate in the West." *Population and Development Review* 6: 645–50.

Armstrong, Pat, Barbara Clow, Karen Grant, Margaret Haworth-Brockman, Beth Jackson, and Ann Pederson, eds. 2012. *Thinking Women and Health Care Reform in Canada*. Toronto: Women's Press.

Avery, Don. 1979. *Dangerous Foreigners: European Immigrant Workers and Labour Radicalism in Canada, 1896–1932*. Toronto: McClelland & Stewart.

Aydemir, Abdurrahman. 2003. "Effects of business cycles on the labour market participation and employment rate assimilation of immigrants." In Charles Beach, Alan G.

Green, and Jeffrey Reitz, eds. *Canadian Immigration Policy of the 21st Century.* Montreal and Kingston: McGill-Queen's University Press, pp. 373–412.

———, Wen-Hao Chen, and Miles Corak. 2005. *Intergenerational Earnings Mobility among the Children of Canadian Immigrants.* Statistics Canada Analytical Studies Branch Research Paper, Ottawa: Statistics Canada cat. no. 11F0019MIE- No. 267.

———, and Chris Robinson. 2006. "Return and onward migration among working age men." Analytical Studies Branch Research Paper Series—No. 273. Ottawa: Statistics Canada.

Badets, Jane, and Tina Chui, 1994. *Canada's Changing Immigrant Population.* Ottawa: Statistics Canada cat. no. 96-311.

———, and Linda Howatson-Leo. 1999. "Recent immigrants in the workforce." *Canadian Social Trends* 52: 16–22.

Badgley, Robin F., and Catherine A. Charles. 1978. "Health and inequality: Unresolved policy issues." In *Canadian Social Policy,* S.A. Yelaja, ed. Waterloo, ON: Wilfrid Laurier University Press, pp. 71–86.

Bah, Sulaiman, and Fernando Rajulton. 1991. "Has Canadian mortality entered the fourth stage of the epidemiologic transition?" *Canadian Studies in Population* 18(2): 18–41.

Baizan, Pau. 2007. "The impact of labour market status on second and higher-order births." In *Family Formation and Family Dilemmas in Contemporary Europe,* G. Esping-Andersen, ed. Bilbao: Fundacion bbva, pp. 93–127.

Balakrishnan, T.R. 1987. "Therapeutic abortions in Canada and their impact on fertility." In *Contributions to Demography.* Edmonton: Population Research Laboratory.

———. 1989. "Changing nuptiality patterns and their fertility implications in Canada." In *The Family in Crisis: A Population Crisis?,* J. Légaré, T.R. Balakrishnan, and R. Beaujot, eds. Ottawa: Royal Society of Canada

———, and Carl Grindstaff. 1988. *Early Adulthood Behaviour and Later Life Course Paths.* Report for Review of Demography. Ottawa: Health and Welfare Canada.

———, and Gyimah, Stephen. 2003. "Spatial residential patterns of selected ethnic groups: Significance and policy implications." *Canadian Ethnic Studies* 35: 113–34.

———, K.J. Krotki, and E. Lapierre-Adamcyk. 1985. "Contraceptive use in Canada, 1984." *Family Planning Perspectives* 17: 209–15.

———, Evelyne Lapierre-Adamcyk, and Karol J. Krotki. 1993. *Family and Childbearing in Canada.* Toronto: University of Toronto Press.

———, and Fernando Rajulton. 1992. "Infertility among Canadians: An analysis of data from the Canadian Fertility Survey (1984) and General Social Survey (1990)." Prepared for *Royal Commission on New Reproductive Technologies,* May.

Bankston, Carl L., and Min Zhou. 2003. "Social capital and immigrant children's achievement." *Sociology of Education* 13: 13–39.

Barber, Clarence. 1978. "On the origins of the Great Depression." *Southern Economic Journal* 44: 432–56.

———. 1979. "Some implications of declining birth rates in developed countries." Paper presented to the Royal Society of Canada, Saskatoon, May.

Barker, Paul. 1990. "An assessment of Ontario's health strategy." *Canadian Public Policy* 16: 432–44.

Barkham, S. 1989. *The Basque Coast of Newfoundland.* Plum Point: Great Northern.

Basavarajappa, K.G., and Bali Ram. 1983. *Population and Migration in Historical Statistics of Canada.* Ottawa: Statistics Canada cat. no. 11-516-X.

Battle, Ken. 1997. *The 1997 Budget's Child Benefits Package.* Ottawa: Caledon Institute of Social Policy.

———. 2009. *Beneath the Budget of 2009: Taxes and Benefits.* Ottawa: Caledon Institute of Social Policy.

Beach, Charles M. 2008. "Canada's aging workforce: Participation, productivity, and living standards." In *A Festschrift in Honour of David Dodge,* Bank of Canada, pp. 197–217.

———, Alan G. Green, and Christopher Worswick. 2011. *Toward Improving Canada's Skilled Immigration Policy and Evaluation Approach.* Toronto: C.D. Howe Institute.

Beaujot, Roderic. 1985. "Population policy development in Canadian demography." *Canadian Studies in Population* 12: 203–19.

———. 1988. Attitudes among Tunisians toward family formation. *International Family Planning Perspectives* 14(2): 54–61.

———. 1991. *Population Change in Canada: The Challenges of Policy Adaptation.* Toronto: McClelland & Stewart.

———. 1995. "Family patterns at mid-life (marriage, parenting and working)." In *Family over the Life Course,* R. Beaujot, Ellen M. Gee, Fernando Rajulton, and Zenaida Ravanera, eds. Ottawa: Statistics Canada cat. no. 91–543.

———. 1998. "Demographic Considerations in Canadian Language Policy." In *Language and Politics in the United States and Canada: Myths and Realities,* ed. Thomas Ricento and Barbara Burnaby. London: Lawrence Erlbaum, pp. 71–84.

———. 1999. "Immigration and demographic structures." In *Immigrant Canada: Demographic, Economic and Social Challenges,* Shiva S. Halli and Leo Driedger, eds. Toronto: University of Toronto Press, pp. 93–115.

———. 2000a. *Earning and Caring in Canadian Families.* Peterborough, ON: Broadview Press.

———. 2000b. "Les deux transitions démographiques du Québec, 1860–1996." *Cahiers québécois de démographie* 29: 201–30.

———. 2002a. "Projecting the future of Canada's population: Assumptions, implications, and policy." Presidential address presented at the meetings of the Canadian Population Society, Toronto, May. See www.ssc.uwo.ca/sociology/popstudies/dp/dp02-06.pdf.

———. 2002b. "Earning and caring: Demographic change and policy implications." *Canadian Studies in Population* 29: 195–225.

———. 2004. "Delayed life transitions: Trends and implications." Contemporary Family Trends series. Ottawa: Vanier Institute of the Family.

———. 2006. "Delayed life transitions: Trends and implications." In K. McQuillan and Z. Ravanera, eds., *Canada's Changing Families: Implications for Individuals and Society.* Toronto: University of Toronto Press, pp. 105–32.

———, and Kevin McQuillan. 1982. *Growth and Dualism: The Demographic Development of Canadian Society.* Toronto: Gage.

———, and J. Peter Rappak. 1989. "The link between immigration and emigration in Canada, 1945–1986." *Canadian Studies in Population* 16, no. 2: 201–16.

———, and J. Peter Rappak. 1990. "The evolution of immigrant cohorts." In *Ethnic Demography*, Shiva S. Halli et al., eds. Ottawa: Carleton University Press, pp. 111–39.

———, and Deborah Matthews. 2000. "Immigration and the future of Canada's population," Discussion Paper No. 2000-1. London, ON: University of Western Ontario, Population Studies Centre.

———, and Alain Bélanger. 2001. "Perspectives on below replacement fertility in Canada: Trends, desires, and accommodations." Paper presented at the International Union for the Scientific Study of Population Workshop, International Perspectives on Low Fertility, Tokyo, March.

———, and Ali Muhammad. 2006. "Transformed families and the basis for childbearing." In *Canada's Changing Families: Implications for Individuals and Society.* K. McQuillan and Z. Ravanera, eds. Toronto: University of Toronto Press, pp. 15–48.

———, and Zenaida Ravanera. 2008. "Family change and implications for family solidarity and social cohesion." *Canadian Studies in Population* 35(1): 73–101.

———, and Zenaida Ravanera. 2009. "Family models for earning and caring: Implications for child care and for family policy." *Canadian Studies in Population* 36: 145–66.

———, and Juyan Wang. 2010. "Low fertility in Canada: The Nordic model in Quebec and the U.S. model in Alberta." *Canadian Studies in Population* 37(3–4): 411–43.

———, Jianye Liu, and Don Kerr. 2011. "Low income status by population groups, 1961–2001." In *The Changing Canadian Population*, Barry Edmonston and Eric Fong, eds. Montreal and Kingston: McGill-Queen's University Press, pp. 99–117.

———, Ching Jiangqin Du, and Zenaida Ravanera. 2013a. "Family policies in Quebec and the rest of Canada." *Canadian Public Policy* 39(2): 221–39.

———, Jianye Liu, and Zenaida Ravanera. 2013b. "Family diversity and inequality: The Canadian case." *Population Change and Lifecourse Discussion Paper Series* 1(1): 7. See http://ir.lib.uwo.ca/pclc/vol1/iss1/7.

———, and Muhammad Munib Raza. 2013. "Population and immigration policy." In *Canadian Studies in the New Millennium*, P. James and M. Kasoff, eds. Toronto: University of Toronto Press, pp. 129–62.

Beaupré, Pascale, Pierre Turcotte, and Anne Milan. 2006. "Junior comes back home: Trends and predictors of returning to the parental home." *Canadian Social Trends* 82: 28–34.

———, Michael Wendt, and Heather Dryburgh. 2010. "Making fathers 'count.'" *Canadian Social Trends* 90: 26–34.

Begall, Katia. 2013. "How do educational and occupational resources relate to the timing of family formation? A couple analysis of the Netherlands." *Demographic Research* 29: 907–34.

Bégin, Monique. 1987. "Demographic change and social policy: Implications and possible alternatives." Pp. 209–30 in *The Future of Social Welfare Systems in Canada and the United Kingdom*, S. Seward, ed. Ottawa: Institute for Research on Public Policy.

Béland, Daniel and John Myles. 2012. "Varieties of federalism, institutional legacies, and social policy: Comparing old-age and unemployment insurance reform in Canada." *International Journal of Social Welfare* 21: S75–S87.

Bélanger, Alain. 1998. "Trends in contraceptive sterilization." *Canadian Social Trends* 50: 16–19.

———. 1999. *Report on the Demographic Situation in Canada, 1998–1999.* Ottawa: Statistics Canada cat. no. 91–209.

———. 2002. *Report on the Demographic Situation in Canada 2001.* Ottawa: Statistics Canada cat no. 91–209.

———. 2013. "The impact of Canadian immigrant selection policy on future imbalances in labour force supply by broad skill levels." Paper presented at Conference on

Income, Health, and Social Programs in an Aging Population, sponsored by Cluster on Population Change and Lifecourse, Ottawa, 27 March.

——, and Jean Dumas. 1998. *Report on the Demographic Situation in Canada 1997*. Ottawa: Statistics Canada cat. no. 91-209.

——, and Pierre Turcotte. 1999. "L'influence des caractéristiques sociodémographiques sur le début de la vie conjugale des Québécoises." *Cahier québécois de démographie* 27: 173–97.

——, Laurent Martel, Jean-Marie Berthelot, and Russell Wilkins. 2002. "Gender differences in disability-free life expectancies for selected risk factors and chronic conditions in Canada." *Journal of Women and Aging* 14(2): 61–83.

——, and S. Gilbert. 2003. "The fertility of immigrant women and their Canadian-born daughters." *Report on the Demographic Situation in Canada, 2002*. Ottawa: Statistics Canada.

Belshaw, J.D. 2009. *Becoming British Columbia: A Population History*. Vancouver: University of British Columbia Press.

Benac, Nancy. 2010. "United States shifts focus to food marketing in battle to reduce childhood obesity." *Canadian Medical Association Journal* 182(1).

Beneteau, Renée. 1988. "Trends in suicide." *Canadian Social Trends* 11: 22–4.

Bengtsson, Tommy, and Alain Gagnon, eds. 2011. "Revisiting mortality crises of the past: Introduction." *Genus: A Population Journal* 67(2): 1–7.

Berkes, F. 2002. "Cross-scale institutional linkages: Perspectives from the bottom up." Pp. 293-321 in *The Drama of the Commons*, E. Ostrom, T. Dietz, N. Dolsak, P.C. Stern, S. Stonich, and E.U. Weber, eds. Washington, DC: National Academy Press.

Bernard, André, Ross Finnie, and Benoît St-Jean. 2008. "Interprovincial mobility and earnings." In *Perspectives 2008*. Ottawa: Statistics Canada cat. no. 75-001-X.

——, Martin Bell, and Elin Charles-Edwards. 2014. "Life-course transitions and the age profile of internal migration." *Population and Development Review* 40(2): 213–39.

Bernardi, Fabrizio, and Jonas Radl. 2014. "The long-term consequences of parental divorce for children's educational attainment." *Demographic Research* 30: 1653–80.

Bernhardt, Eva. 2005. "No, we should not worry about the future of Europe's population." Presented at European Population Day Debate, Congress of the International Union for the Scientific Study of Population, Tours, France, 18–23 July.

Bianchi, Suzanne, Laurent Lesnard, Tiziana Nazio, and Sara Raley. 2014. "Gender and time allocation of cohabiting and married women and men in France, Italy, and the United States." *Demographic Research* 31: 183–216.

Bibby, Reginald, and D.C. Posterski. 1985. *The Emerging Generation*. Toronto: Irving.

Bigham, B.L., E. Bull, M. Morrison, R. Burgess, J. Maher, S.C. Brooks, and L.J. Morrison. 2011. "Patient safety in emergency medical services: Executive summary and recommendations from the Niagara summit." *Canadian Journal of Emergency Medicine* 13(1): 13–18.

Bignami-Van Assche, Simona, and Visseho Adjiwanou. 2009. "Dynamiques familiales et activité sexuelle précoce au Canada." *Cahiers québécois de démographie* 38(1): 41–69.

Bijak, Jakub, Dorata Kupiszewska, Marek Kupiszewsk, Katarzyna Saczuk, and Anna Kicinger. 2007. "Population and labour force projections for 27 countries, 2002–2052: Impact of international migration on population ageing." *European Journal of Population* 23: 1–31.

Billari, Francesco, 2008. "The happiness commonality: Fertility decisions in low-fertility settings." Paper presented at the Conference on How Generations and Gender Shape Demographic Change: Toward Policies Based on Better Knowledge, Geneva: UNECE, 14–16 May.

Bingoly-Liworo, Germain. 2007. *La constitution de la descendance au Canada: Le rôle de l'allongement des études, du premier emploi et des conditions d'emploi*. Ph.D. thesis, Université de Montréal.

——, and Evelyne Lapierre-Adamcyk. 2006. "Devenir parent au Canada: L'effet de l'allongement des études." *Cahiers québécois de démographie* 35(2): 103–40.

Bjorkland, A. 2006. "Does family policy affect fertility? Lessons from Sweden." *Journal of Population Economics* 19: 3–24.

Blake, Raymond. 2009. *From Rights to Needs: A History of Family Allowances in Canada*. Vancouver: University of British Columbia Press.

Blanchet, Didier. 2002. "Évolution: Démographiques et retraites: quinze ans de débats." *Population et Sociétés* 383: 1–4.

Blayo, Y. 1975. "La mortalitié en France en 1740 à 1829." *Population* 30: 123–42.

Bloom, David E. 2010. *Global Demographic Change and Its Macroeconomic Consequences*. Boston: Harvard University.

——, D. Canning, and J. Sevilla. 2003. *The Demographic Dividend: A New Perspective on the Economic Consequences of Population Change*. Santa Monica: RAND.

———, David Canning, and Günther Fink. 2011. *Implications of Population Aging for Economic Growth*. PGDA Working Paper No. 64. Cambridge: Harvard University

Bloskie, Cyndi, and Guy Gellatly. 2012. *Recent Developments in the Canadian Economy*. Analysis Branch: Economic Insights. Ottawa: Statistics Canada cat. no. 11-626-X — No. 019.

Bohnert, Nora. 2011. "Examining the determinants of union dissolution among married and common-law unions in Canada." *Canadian Studies in Population* 38(3–4): 93–104.

———, and Patrice Dion. 2014. "Projection of international immigration." In *Population Projections for Canada (2013 to 2063), Provinces and Territories (2013 to 2038): Technical Report on Methodology and Assumptions*, Nora Bohnert, Jonathan Chagnon, Simon Coulombe, Patrice Dion, and Laurent Martel, eds. Ottawa: Statistics Canada.

———, Jonathan Chagnon, Simon Coulombe, Patrice Dion, and Laurent Martel, eds. 2014. *Population Projections for Canada (2013 to 2063), Provinces and Territories (2013 to 2038): Technical Report on Methodology and Assumptions*. Ottawa: Statistics Canada.

———, Anne Milan, and Heather Lathe. 2014a. "Living arrangements of children in Canada: A century of change." *Insights on Canadian Society*. Ottawa: Statistics Canada cat. no. 75-006-X.

———, Anne Milan, and Heather Lathe. 2014b. "Enduring diversity: Living arrangements of children in Canada over 100 years of the Census." *Demographic Documents*. Ottawa: Statistics Canada cat. no. 91F0015M – No. 11.

Boily, Nicole. 1987. "Dénatalité, immigration et politique familiale: Le point de vue des femmes." Paper presented at the meetings of the Association des Démographes du Québec, Ottawa, May.

Boling, Patricia. 2008. "Demography, culture, and policy: Understanding Japan's low fertility." *Population and Development Review* 34(2): 307–26.

Bone, R.M. 2011. *The Regional Geography of Canada*, Fifth Edition. Don Mills, ON: Oxford University Press.

Bongaarts, John. 2011. "Opinion: 7 billion and counting." *Newsday*. 28 October.

Borjas, George J. 1999. *Heaven's Door: Immigration Policy and the American Economy*. Princeton, NJ: Princeton University Press.

Boroditsky, Richard, William Fisher, and Michael Sand. 1996. "The 1995 Canadian Contraception Study." *Journal SOGC*, December: 1–31.

Boserup, Ester. 1965. *The Conditions of Agricultural Growth: The Economics of Agrarian Change under Population Pressure*. London: Allen & Unwin.

———. 1981. *Population and Technology*. Chicago: University of Chicago Press.

———. 1986. "Comment." *Population and Development Review* 12 (suppl.): 238–42.

———. 1988. 'Some Demographic Properties of Transfer Schemes: How to Achieve Equity between Generations'. Pp. 92–105 in *Economics of Changing Age Distributions in Developed Countries*, ed. R. Lee. Oxford: Clarendon Press.

———. 1999. *My Professional Life and Publications, 1929–1998*. Copenhagen: Museum Tusculanum Press.

Boswell, John. 1988. *The Kindness of Strangers: The Abandonment of Children in Western Europe from Late Antiquity to the Renaissance*. New York: Pantheon.

Boudarbat, Brahim, and Lee Grenon. 2013. "Sample attrition in the Canadian survey of labor and income dynamics." Forschungsinstitut zur Zukunft der / Arbeit Institute for the Study of Labor, discussion paper no. 7295. Bonn, Germany.

Bourbeau, Robert. 2002. "Canadian mortality in perspective: A comparison with the United States and other developed countries." *Canadian Studies in Population* 29: 313–69.

———, and Jacques Légaré. 1982. *Évolution de la mortalité au Canada et au Québec, 1831–1931*. Montreal: Les Presses de l'Université de Montréal.

———, Jacques Légaré, and Valérie Émond 1997. *New Birth Cohort Life Tables for Canada and Quebec, 1801–1991*. Ottawa: Statistics Canada, cat. no. 91F0015MPE1997003.

Bouvier, Leon F. 2001. "Replacement migration: Is it a solution to declining and aging populations?" *Population and Environment* 22: 377–81.

Boxhill, W. 1984. "Limitations of the use of ethnic origin data to quantify visible minorities in Canada." Working paper prepared for Statistics Canada, Housing, Family and Social Statistics Division.

Boyd, Monica. 1984. *Canadian Attitudes towards Women: Thirty Years of Change*. Ottawa: Supply and Services Canada.

———. 1989. "Family and personal networks in international migration: Recent developments and new agendas." *International Migration Review* 23: 638–70.

———. 1999. "Canadian, Eh? Ethnic Origin Shifts in the Canadian Census." *Canadian Ethnic Studies* 31: 1–19.

———. 2002. "Educational attainments of immigrant offspring: Success or segmented assimilation?" *International Migration Review* 36: 1037–60.

———. 2005. "Immigration, international migration and the redistribution of Canada's population." Population Change and Public Policy SSHRC Cluster Workshop, 2005.

———. 2009. "Social origins and the educational and occupational achievements of the 1.5 and second generations." *Canadian Review of Sociology* 46: 339–69.

———, and Doug Norris. 1995. "Leaving the nest? Impact of family structure." *Canadian Social Trends* 38: 14–17.

———, and Doug Norris. 2001. "Who are the 'Canadians'? Changing Census Responses, 1986–1996." *Canadian Ethnic Studies* 33(1): 1–25.

———, and Derrick Thomas. 2001. "Match or mismatch? The labour market performances of foreign-born engineers." *Population Research & Policy Review* 20: 107–33.

———, and Joanne Nowak. 2011. "Social networks and international migration." In *International Migration and Immigrant Incorporation: The Dynamics of Globalization and Ethnic Diversity in European Life*, Jan Rath and Marco Martiniello, eds. Amsterdam: University of Amsterdam Press.

Boyd, R. 1990. "Demographic history, 1774–1874." In *Handbook of North American Indians: Northwest Coast*, vol. 7, W. Suttles, ed. Washington, DC: Smithsonian Institution, pp. 135–48.

———. 1992. "Population decline from two epidemics on the northwest coast." In *Disease and Demography in the Americas*, J.W. Verano and D.H. Ubelaker, eds. Washington, DC: Smithsonian Institution, pp. 249–55.

Bras, Hilde. 2014. "Structural and diffusion effects in the Dutch fertility transition, 1870–1940." *Demographic Research* 30: 151–86.

Brennan, Richard J. 2010. "Conservatives relied on a few complaints to scrap the census." *Toronto Star*, 7 January.

Brockington, Riley. 2010. *Summary: Public School Indicators for Canada, the Provinces, and Territories, 2002/2003 to 2008/2009*. Ottawa: Statistics Canada.

Broderick, Carlfred. 1979. *Marriage and the Family*. Englewood Cliffs, NJ: Prentice Hall.

Brown, Robert. 2012. "More health care does not mean better health: Balance between health care spending and social supports crucial." *The Globe and Mail*, 5 September.

Bureau de l'actuaire en chef. 2008. "Rapport sur le portrait de la clientèle du régime québécois d'assurance parentale 2006." Quebec: Bureau de l'actuaire en chef.

Burgess, E.W., H. Locke, and M. Thomas. 1963. *The Family: From Institution to Companionship*. New York: American.

Burton, Peter, Shelley Phipps, and Lihui Zhang. 2014. "The prince and the pauper: Movement of children up and down the Canadian income distribution." *Canadian Public Policy* 40(2): 111–125.

Bushnik, Tracey, Jocelynn Cook, Edward Hughes, and Suzanne Tough. 2012. "Seeking medical help to conceive." *Health Reports* 23(4): 3–9.

Buttner, Thomas, and Wolfgang Lutz. 1989. "Measuring fertility responses to policy measures in the German Democratic Republic." Working Paper 89–37. Vienna: IIASA.

Caldwell, Gary. 1988. "L'avenir de la communauté anglophone du Québec." *L'Action Nationale* 78L359-365.

———, and Daniel Fournier. 1987. "The Quebec question: A matter of population." *Canadian Journal of Sociology* 12: 16–41.

Caldwell, John C. 1997. "The global fertility transition: The need for a unifying theory." *Population and Development Review* 23(4): 803–12.

Canadian Cancer Society. 2012. *Canadian Cancer Statistics, 2012*. Toronto: Canadian Cancer Society (in collaboration with Statistics Canada, Public Health Agency of Canada, Provincial/Territorial Cancer Registries).

Canadian Council for Refugees. 2013. *Year in Review: Changes in 2012 for Refugees and Other Newcomers to Canada*. Montreal: Canadian Council for Refugees.

Canadian Human Mortality Database. 2012. Department of Demography, Université de Montréal. Available at www.demo.umontreal.ca/chmd.

Capeluck, Evan. 2014. *Convergence across Provincial Economies in Canada: Trends, Drivers and Implications*. Ottawa: Centre for the Study of Living Standards Research Report, March.

Carment, David, and David J. Bercuson. 2008. *The World in Canada: Diaspora, Demography, and Domestic Politics*. Montreal and Kingston: McGill Queen's University Press.

Caron Malenfant, Éric, and Alain Bélanger. 2006. "The fertility of visible minority women in Canada." In *Report on the Demographic Situation in Canada, 2003 and 2004*. Ottawa: Statistics Canada, pp. 35–64.

Carrière, Yves, and Jacques Légaré. 2000. "Unmet needs for assistance with ADLs and IADLs: A measure of healthy life expectancy." *Social Indicators Research* 51: 107–23.

———, and Diane Galarneau. 2011. "Delayed retirement: A new trend?" *Perspectives on Labour and Income* 23(4).

———, Janice Keefe, Jacques Légaré, Xiaofen Lin, Geoff Rowe, Laurent Martel and Sameer Rajbhandary. 2008. *Projecting the Future Availability of the Informal Support Network of the Elderly Population and Assessing Its Impact on Home Care Services*. Demographic Documents Research Paper No. 009. Ottawa: Statistics Canada.

Cartwright, Steven. 1941. *Population: Canada's Problem*. Toronto: Ryerson Press.

Cassils, J. Anthony, and Madeline Weld. 2001. *Why Canada Needs a Population Policy.* A paper submitted to the Standing Committee on Citizenship and Immigration, House of Commons, Parliament of Canada.

Castles, Stephen, and Mark Miller. 2009. *The Age of Migration: International Population Movements in the Modern World.* London: Palgrave Macmillan.

Castonguay, Charles. 1979. "Exogamie et anglicisation chez les minorités canadiennes-français." *Canadian Review of Sociology and Anthropology* 16: 21–31.

Cavanagh, J., A.J. Carson, M. Sharpe, and S.M. Lawrie. 2003. "Psychological autopsy studies of suicide: A systematic review." *Psychological Medicine* 33(3): 395–405.

CCME. 2009. *Canada-Wide Strategy for the Management of Municipal Wastewater Effluent.* Winnipeg, MB: Canadian Council of Ministers of the Environment.

Certified General Accountants Association of Canada. 2012. *Youth Unemployment in Canada: Challenging Conventional Thinking?* Ottawa: CGA-Canada.

Ceobanu, Alin M., and Tanya Koropeckyj-Cox. 2012. "Should international migration be encouraged to offset population aging? A cross-country analysis of public attitudes in Europe." *Population Research and Policy Review* 31: 261–84.

Chackiel, Juan, and Alexia Peyser. 1993. "Indigenous population from Latin American national censuses." Presented at the International Union for Scientific Study of Population Conference, Montreal, August.

Chafetz, Janet Saltzman, and Jacqueline Hagan. 1996. "The gender division of labour and family change in industrial societies." *Journal of Comparative Family Studies* 27: 187–219.

Chappell, Neena L., Lynn McDonald, and Michael Stones. 2008. *Aging in Contemporary Canada,* Second Edition. Don Mills, ON: Pearson Canada.

——, and Marcus J. Hollander. 2013. *Aging in Canada.* Don Mills, ON: Oxford University Press.

Charbonneau, H. 1975. *Vie et Mort de nos Ancêtres.* Montreal: Les Presses de l'Université de Montréal.

——. 1980. "Jeunes femmes et vieux maris: La fécundité des mariages précoces." *Population* 35: 1101–22.

——. 1981. "Remariage et fécondité en Nouvelle-France." In *Mariages et Remariages dans tes Populations du Passé,* J. Dupaquier, E. Hélin, P. Laslett, M. Livi-Bacci, and S. Sogner, eds. London: Academic Press, pp. 561–71.

——. 1984. "Trois siècles de dépopulation amérindienne." In *Les Populations Amérindiennes et Inuit du Canada,* ed. Normandeau and V. Piché. Montreal: Les Presses de l'Université de Montréal, pp. 28–48.

——, and A. Larose. 1979. *The Great Mortalities: Methodological Studies of Demographic Crises in the Past.* Liège: Ordina.

——, A. Guillemette, J. Légaré, B. Desjardins, Y. Landry, and F. Nault. 1987. *Naissance d'une population : Les Français établis au Canada au XVIIᵉ siècle.* Montreal: Les Presses de l'Université de Montréal.

——, A. Guillemette, J. Légaré, B. Desjardins, Y. Landry, and F. Nault. 1993. *The First French Canadians: Pioneers in the St Lawrence Valley.* Newark, NJ: University of Delaware Press.

——, D. Desjardins, J. Légaré, and Hubert Denis. 2000. "The population of the St. Lawrence Valley, 1608–1760." In *A Population History of North America,* ed. M. Haines and R. Steckel. Cambridge, UK: Cambridge University Press, pp. 99–142.

Charles, Enid. 1936. *The Menace of Under-Population.* London: Watts.

——. 1948. *The Changing Size of the Family in Canada.* Ottawa: Dominion Bureau of Statistics, Eighth Census of Canada, 1941.

——, N. Keyfitz, and H. Roseborough. 1946. *The Future Population of Canada.* Ottawa: Dominion Bureau of Statistics, Bulletin No. FB4.

Cheal, David. 1996. "Stories about step-families." In *Growing Up in Canada.* Ottawa: Statistics Canada cat. no. 89–550.

——. 1999. *New Poverty : Families in Postmodern Society.* Westport, CT: Greenwood Press.

Chen, Greg. 2005. "Safety and economic impacts of photo radar program." *Traffic Injury Prevention* 6: 299–307.

Chen, J., D. Beavon, and R. Wilkins. 1997. "Mortality of retired public servants in Canada." *Proceedings of the Social Statistics Section, American Statistical Association.* Alexandria, VA, pp. 86–91.

——, Edward Ng, and Russel Wilkins. 1996. "The health of Canada's immigrants in 1994–95." *Health Reports* 7(4): 33–45.

——, and Wayne J. Millar. 1998. "Age of smoking initiation: Implications for quitting." *Health Reports* 9(4): 39–46.

——, and Wayne J. Millar. 2000. "Are recent cohorts healthier than their predecessors?" *Health Reports* 11: 9–23.

Chesnais, Jean-Claude. 1985. "The prevention of deaths from violence." In *Health Policy, Social Policy and Mortality Prospects,* J. Vallin and A.D. Lopez, eds. Liège, Belgium: Ordina, pp. 261–79.

——. 1987. "Population trends in the European community, 1968–1986." *European Journal of Population* 3: 281–96.

———. 1989. "L'inversion de la pyramide des âges en Europe: Perspectives et problèmes." In *International Population Conference*, vol 3: 53–68. Liège, Belgium: IUSSP.

———. 1996. "Fertility, family, and social policy in contemporary Western Europe." *Population and Development Review* 22: 729–40.

Childcare Resource and Research Unit. 2009. *Early Childhood Education and Care in Canada, 2008*. Toronto: Childcare Resource and Research Unit.

Choinière, Robert. 1993. "Les inégalités socio-économiques et culturelles de la mortalité à Montréal à la fin des années 1989." *Cahiers québécois de démographie* 22: 339–61.

Choudhry, S. and M. Pal. 2007. "Is every ballot equal? Visible vote dilution in Canada." *IRPP Choices* 13: 1.

Chui, Tina W.L., James Curtis, and Ronald D. Lambert. 1991. "Immigrant background and political participation: Examining generational patterns." *Canadian Journal of Sociology* 16(4): 375–97.

Chung, Lucy. 2006. "Education and earnings." *Perspectives on Labour and Income* 7(6). Ottawa: Statistics Canada cat. no. 75-001-XIE, online edition.

Cicchino, Stefania, and K. Bruce Newbold. 2007. "Interregional return and onwards migration in Canada: Evidence based on a micro-regional analysis." *Canadian Journal of Regional Science* 30: 211–40.

CIHI (Canadian Institute for Health Information). 2008. *Reducing Gaps in Health: A Focus on Socio-Economic Status in Urban Canada*. Ottawa: Canadian Institute for Health Information.

———. 2011. *Health Indicators, 2011*. Ottawa: Canadian Institute for Health Information.

———. 2012a. *Health Indicators, 2012*. Ottawa: Canadian Institute for Health Information.

———. 2012b. *Hospital Mental Health Services in Canada*. Ottawa: Canadian Institute for Health Information.

———. 2012c. *Health Care Cost Drivers: Physician Expenditure*. Ottawa: Canadian Institute for Health Information.

———. 2013a. *National Health Expenditure Trends, 1975 to 2013*. Ottawa: Canadian Institute for Health Information.

———. 2014a. *Induced Abortions Reported in Canada, 2011*. Ottawa: Canadian Institute for Health Information.

———. 2014b. *National Health Expenditure Trends, 1975–2014*. Ottawa: Canadian Institute for Health Information.

Citizenship and Immigration Canada. 1999. *Citizenship and Immigration Statistics, 1996*. Ottawa: Citizenship and Immigration Canada.

———. 2000. *Facts and Figures 2000: Statistical Overview of the Temporary Resident and Refugee Claimant Population*. Ottawa: Citizenship and Immigration.

———. 2001. *Annual Report to Parliament on Immigration*. Ottawa: Citizenship and Immigration Canada.

———. 2008. *Citizenship and Immigration Canada's Mandate, Mission and Vision*. Ottawa: Citizenship and Immigration Canada.

———. 2012. *Canada: Facts and Figures: Immigration Overview, Permanent and Temporary Residents*. Ottawa: Research and Evaluation Branch. Citizenship and Immigration Canada.

———. 2014. *Annual Report to Parliament on Immigration*. Ottawa: Citizenship and Immigration Canada.

Clark, A.H. 1968. *Acadia: The Geography of Early Nova Scotia*. Madison, WI: University of Wisconsin Press.

Clark, Warren. 2000. "100 years of education." *Canadian Social Trends* 59: 3–9.

———. 2007. "Delayed transitions of young adults." *Canadian Social Trends* 84: 14–22.

Clathworthy, S.J. 2003. "Re-assessing the population impacts of Bill C–31 section 6." In *The Aboriginal Condition: Research Foundations for Public Policy*, Jerry White, Paul Maxim, Paul Whitehead, and Dan Deavon, eds. Vancouver: University of British Columbia Press.

———. 2009. *Recent Trends in the Demographic Characteristics of First Nations Populations in Canada*. Ottawa: Strategic Research, Indian and Northern Affairs Canada.

Coale, Ansley J. 1973. "The demographic transition." *International Population Conference*, vol. 1: 53–72. Liège, Belgium: IUSSP.

———, and S. Watkins. 1986. *The Decline of Fertility in Europe*. Princeton, NJ: Princeton University Press.

Coates, Ken, and Bill Morrison. 2013. *Campus Confidential: 100 Startling Things You Don't Know About Canadian Universities*. Toronto: James Lorimer.

Cohen, Joel. E. 1995. *How Many People Can the Earth Support?* New York: W.W. Norton.

———. 2010. *Beyond Population: Everyone Counts in Development*. CGD Working Paper 220. Washington, DC: Center for Global Development.

Coleman, David, 2000. "Who's afraid of low support ratios? A UK response to the UN Population Division report on 'replacement migration.'" Paper presented at meeting of United Nations Expert Group, New York, October.

———. 2005. "Population prospects and problems in Europe." *Genus* 61(3–4): 413–64.

———. 2006. "Immigration and ethnic change in low-fertility countries: A third demographic transition." *Population and Development Review* 32: 401–46.

———. 2008. "The demographic effects of international migration in Europe." *Oxford Review of Economic Policy* 24: 453–77.

———. 2009. "Migration and its consequences in 21st century Europe." *Vienna Yearbook of Population Research* 29: 1–18.

Coleman, James S. 1988. "Social capital in the creation of human capital." *American Journal of Sociology* 94: S95–S120.

Colgan, Charles, and Stephen Tomblin, eds. 2003. *Regionalism in a Global Society: Persistence and Change in Atlantic Canada and New England*. Toronto: University of Toronto Press.

Coltrane, Scott. 1995. "The future of fatherhood." In *Fatherhood*, William Marsiglio, ed. Thousand Oaks, CA: Sage.

———. 1998. *Gender and Families*. Thousand Oaks, CA: Pine Forge Press.

Conference Board of Canada. 2013. *How Canada Performs: A Report Card on Canada. Income Inequality*. Ottawa: Conference Board of Canada.

Connidis, Ingrid Arnet. 1989. "Contact between siblings in later life." *Canadian Journal of Sociology* 14: 429–42.

———. 2010. *Family Ties and Aging*. Thousand Oaks, CA: Pine Forge Press/Sage.

———, and Andrea Willson, 2007. "Aging." In *Introduction to Sociology: A Canadian Focus*, W.E. Hewitt, Jerry White, and James T. Teevan, eds. Don Mills, ON: Pearson Canada, pp. 120–42.

Conservation Council of Ontario and Family Planning Federation of Canada. 1973. *A Population Policy for Canada?* Toronto: Conservation Council of Ontario and Family Planning Federation of Canada.

Constant, A., S. Petersen, C.D. Mallory, and J. Major. 2011. *Research Synthesis on Cost Drivers in the Health Sector and Proposed Policy Options*. CHSRF series of reports on cost drivers and health system efficiency: Paper 1. Ottawa: CHSRF.

Cooke, Martin, and Dan Beavon. 2007. "The Registered Indian Human Development Index, 1981–2001." In *Aboriginal Well-Being: Canada's Continuing Challenge*. Jerry White, Dan Beavon, and Nicholas Spence, eds. Toronto: Thompson Educational Publishers.

———, and Éric Guimond 2009. "Measuring changing human development in First Nations populations: Preliminary results of the 1981–2006 Registered Indian Human Development Index." *Canadian Diversity* 7: 53–72.

———, P. Wilk, K. Paul, and S. Gonneville. 2013. "Predictors of obesity among Métis children: Socio-economic, behavioural and cultural factors." *Canadian Journal of Public Health* 104, no. 4.

Copp, Terry. 1974. *The Anatomy of Poverty: The Condition of the Working Class in Montreal, 1897–1929*. Toronto: McClelland & Stewart.

Corak, Miles. 2010. *Chasing the Same Dream, Climbing Different Ladders: Economic Mobility in the United States and Canada*. Washington, DC: Economic Mobility Project, PEW Charitable Trusts.

———, W.H. Chen, A. Demanti, and D. Batten. 2002. "Social cohesion and the dynamics of income in four countries." Presented at the 27th General Conference of the International Association for Research in Income and Wealth (IARIW), Stockholm, 18–24 August.

Corbett, D.C. 1957. *Canada's Immigration Policy: A Critique*. Toronto: University of Toronto Press.

Corscadden, Lisa, Michael Wolfson, Michel Grignon, Sara Allin. 2013. "Who uses and pays for healthcare over a lifetime—And how does this impact income inequality?" Ottawa: Canadian Institute for Health Information.

Côté, James E., and Anton L. Allahar. 1994. *Generation on Hold: Coming of Age in the Late Twentieth Century*. Toronto: Stoddart.

Coulombe, Serge, and Jean-François Tremblay. 2006. *Migration, Human Capital and Skills Redistribution Across the Canadian Provinces*. Human Resources and Social Development Canada-Industry Canada-Social Sciences and Humanities Research Council (HRSDC-IC-SSHRC) Skills Research Initiative. Working Paper 2006 D-07. Ottawa: HRSDC.

Courchene, Thomas J. 1981. "A market perspective on regional disparities." *Canadian Public Policy* 7: 506–18.

Cowan, H. 1968. *British Immigration before Confederation*. Canadian Historical Booklet No. 22. Ottawa: Canadian Historical Association.

Cranswick, Kelly, and Donna Dosman. 2008. "Eldercare: What we know today." *Canadian Social Trends* 86: 48–56.

Crawford, Cameron. 2013. *Looking into Poverty: Income Sources of Poor People with Disabilities in Canada*. Toronto: Institute for Research and Development on Inclusion and Society (IRIS) and Council of Canadians with Disabilities.

Crompton, Susan. 2000. "100 years of health." *Canadian Social Trends* 59: 12–17.

———, and Michael Vickers. 2000. "One hundred years of labour force." *Canadian Social Trends* 52: 2–14.

Crossley, Thomas F., and Lori J. Curtis. 2006. "Child poverty in Canada." *Review of Income and Wealth* 52(2): 237–60.

Crouch, Mirn, and Lenore Manderson. 1993. *New Motherhood*. Newark, NJ: Gordon and Breach.

Cybulski, J.S. 1994. "Culture change, demographic history, and health and disease on the northwest coast." In *In the Wake of Contact, Biological Responses to Conquest*, C.S. Larsen and G.R. Milner, eds. New York: Wiley-Liss, pp. 75–85.

Dagenais, Daniel. 2000. *La fin de la famille moderne.* Quebec City: Les Presses de l'Université Laval.

Daly, Herman E. 2007. *Ecological Economics and Sustainable Development: Selected Essays of Herman Daly.* Northampton, MA: Edward Elgar Publisher.

Dandy, Kimberley, and Ray Bollman. 2008. "Seniors in rural Canada." *Rural and Small Town Canada Analysis Bulletin* 7(8).

Daniels, J. 1992. "The Indian population of North America in 1492." *William and Mary Quarterly* 49: 298–320.

Das Gupta, P. 1993. *Standardization and Decomposition of Rates: A User's Manual.* Washington, DC: Current Population Reports. U.S. Bureau of the Census, Series P–23, No 186.

David, Paul A. 1986. "Comment." *Population and Development Review* 12 (Suppl.): 77–86.

Davis, Kingsley. 1949. *Human Society.* New York: Macmillan.

———. 1984. "Wives and work: Consequences of the sex role revolution." *Population and Development Review* 10: 397–417.

———. 1986. "Low fertility in evolutionary perspective." *Population and Development Review* 12 (Suppl.): 48–65.

Day, Kathleen M., and Stanley L. Winer. 2012. *Interregional Migration and Public Policy in Canada: An Empirical Study.* Montreal and Kingston: McGill-Queen's University Press.

Deaton, Richard Lee. 1989. *The Political Economy of Pensions: Power, Politics and Social Change in Canada, Britain and the United States.* Vancouver: University of British Columbia Press.

de Broucker, Patrice. 2005. *Without a Paddle: What to Do About Canada's Young Drop-Outs.* Ottawa: Canadian Policy Research Networks.

Demeny, Paul. 1986. "Population and the invisible hand." *Demography* 23: 473–88.

———. 2011. "Population policy and the demographic transition: Performance, prospects, and options." *Population and Development Review* 37(S): 249–74.

Denton, Frank T., Christine Feaver, and Byron Spencer. 1997. *Immigration, Labour Force and the Age Structure of the Population.* QSEP Research Report No. 335. Hamilton, ON: McMaster University, Research Institute for Quantitative Studies in Economics and Population.

———, Christine H. Feaver, and Byron G. Spencer. 2001. "Alternative pasts, possible futures: A 'what if' study of the effects of fertility on the Canadian population and labour force." Paper presented at the meetings of the Federation of Canadian Demographers, Ottawa, December.

———, and Byron G. Spencer. 2000. "Population aging and its economic costs: A survey of the issues and evidence." *Canadian Journal on Aging* 19: 25–43.

———, and Byron G. Spencer. 2002. "Some demographic consequences of revising the definition of 'old age' to reflect future changes in life table probabilities." *Canadian Journal on Aging* 21: 349–56.

———, and Byron G. Spencer. 2010. *Age of Pension Eligibility, Gains in Life Expectancy, and Social Policy.* Quantitative Studies in Economics and Population Research Reports 442. Hamilton, ON: McMaster University.

Department of Finance. 2012. *Equalization Program.* Ottawa: Department of Finance. See www.fin.gc.ca. fedprov/eqp-eng.asp.

Department of Health and Social Services, Nunavut. 2004. *Nunavut Report of Comparable Health Indicators.* Nunavut Health and Social Services. Iqaluit: Government of Nunavut.

Desrosiers, Hélène, and Céline Le Bourdais. 1991. "The impact of age at marriage and timing of first birth on marriage dissolution in Canada." *Canadian Studies in Population* 18: 29–51.

Dickason, Olive Patricia. 1992. *Canada's First Nations: A History of Founding Peoples from Earliest Times.* Toronto: Oxford University Press.

———, and William Newbigging. 2010. *A Concise History of Canada's First Nations*, Second Edition. New York: Oxford University Press.

Dickinson, James, and Bob Russell. 1986. "The structure of reproduction in capitalist society." In *Family, Economy and State*, J. Dickinson and B. Russell, eds. Toronto: Garamond.

Dietz, Thomas, and Eugene A. Rosa. 1997. "Environmental impacts of population and consumption." In *Environmentally Significant Consumption: Research Directions*, P.C Stern, T. Dietz, V. Ruttan, R.H. Socolow, and J. Sweeney, eds. Washington, DC: National Academy Press, pp. 92–99.

Dion, Patrice and Simon Coulombe. 2008. "Portrait of the mobility of Canadians in 2006: Trajectories and characteristics of migrants." In *Report on the Demographic Situation in Canada, 2005 and 2006*, Alain Bélanger, ed. Ottawa: Statistics Canada cat. no. 91-209-X, pp. 78–98.

———, Jonathan Chagnon, and Jean-Dominique Morency. 2010. *Population Projections for Canada, Provinces and*

Territories, 2009 to 2036. Ottawa: Statistics Canada cat. no. 91-520-X.

Dionne, Claude. 1989. "Le choix d'avoir un enfant." Paper presented to the ASDEQ Conference, Montreal, April.

Dobyns, H. 1983. *Their Number Become Thinned: Native American Population Dynamics in Eastern North America.* Knoxville, TN: University of Tennessee Press.

Doucet, Andrea. 2009. "Gender equality and gender differences: Parenting, habitus and embodiment." *Canadian Review of Sociology* 46(2): 103–21.

Douglas, F.R., R. Jones, and D.B. Smith. 2006. *Journeys: A History of Canada.* Don Mills, ON: Nelson.

Dribe, Martin, and Francesco Scalone. 2014. "Social class and net fertility before, during, and after the demographic transition: A micro-level analysis of Sweden 1880–1970." *Demographic Research* 30: 429–64.

Drummond, Don. 2014. *Wanted: Good Canadian Labour Market Information.* Montreal: Institute for Research on Public Policy.

Dryburgh, Heather. 2000. "Teenage pregnancy." *Health Reports* 12(1): 9–19.

Duchesne, Louis. 1997. "Naître au naturel: Les naissances hors mariage." *Statistiques* 1: 1–4.

Dufour, Desmond, and Yves Péron. 1979. *Vingt ans de mortalité au Québec.* Montreal: Les Presses de l'Université de Montréal.

———. 1990a. *Report on the Demographic Situation in Canada, 1988.* Ottawa: Statistics Canada cat. no. 91–209.

———. 1990b. *Report on the Demographic Situation in Canada, 1990.* Ottawa: Statistics Canada cat. no. 91–209.

———, and Alain Bélanger. 1997. *Report on the Demographic Situation in Canada, 1996.* Ottawa: Statistics Canada cat. no. 91–209.

Dumas, Jean. 1990. *Report on the Demographic Situation in Canada, 1990.* Ottawa: Statistics Canada cat. no. 91–209.

———, and Alain Bélanger. 1997. *Report on the Demographic Situation in Canada, 1996.* Ottawa: Statistics Canada cat. no. 91–209.

Dumont, J.C., and G. Lemaitre. 2005. *Counting Migrants and Expatriates: A New Perspective. Social, Employment and Migration Statistics.* OECD Working Papers No. 25. Paris: Organisation for Economic Cooperation and Development.

Dungan, Peter, Tony Fang, and Morley Gunderson. 2010. *The Macroeconomic Impacts of Canadian Immigration: An Empirical Study Using the Focus Mode.* Toronto: University of Toronto Press.

Easterlin, Richard. 1980. *Birth and Fortune: The Impact of Numbers on Personal Welfare.* New York: Basic Books.

———, and Eileen Crimmins. 1985. *The Fertility Revolution:*

A Supply–Demand Analysis. Chicago: University of Chicago Press.

Economic Council of Canada. 1991. *Economic and Social Impacts of Immigration.* Ottawa: Economic Council of Canada, Study no. 22, 171.

Edmonston, Barry. 1996. "Interprovincial migration of Canadian immigrants." Presented at the meetings of the Population Association of America, New Orleans, May.

———. 2002. "Interprovincial migration of Canadian immigrants." Presented at the meetings of the Canadian Population Society, Toronto, June.

———. 2011. "Internal migration." In *The Changing Canadian Population,* Barry Edmonston and Eric Fong, eds. Montreal and Kingston: McGill-Queen's University Press, pp. 190–206.

———. 2014. "Two centuries of demographic change in Canada." *Canadian Studies in Population* 41(1–2): 1–37.

———, Sharon M. Lee, and Zheng Wu. 2010. "Fertility intentions in Canada: Change or no change?" *Canadian Studies in Population* 37(3–4): 297–337.

Ehrlich, Paul. 1968. *The Population Bomb.* New York: Ballantine Books.

———, and John P. Holdren. 1971. "Impact of population growth." *Science* 26: 1212–17.

———, and Anne H. Ehrlich, 1990. *The Population Explosion.* New York: Simon & Schuster.

———, and Anne H. Ehrlich. 2004. *One with Nineveh: Politics, Consumption and the Human Future.* Washington, DC: Island Press.

———, and Anne H. Ehrlich, 2012. "Can a collapse of global civilization be avoided?" Proceedings of the Royal Society. B280: 20122845.

EIA (US Energy Information Administration). 2012. Washington: US Department of Energy.

———. 2013. *Total Carbon Dioxide Emissions from the Consumption of Energy in Million Metric Tons.* Independent Statistics and Analysis. Washington, DC: United States Energy Administration Information.

———. 2014. "Canada: Overview." Washington, DC: US Department of Energy, United States Energy Information Administration.

Ellison, F. Larry, and Kathryn Wilkins. 2012. "Canadian trends in cancer prevalence." *Health Reports* 23(1).

Emond, Andrew. 2009. "Montreal's wastewater treatment, Part I—A history of problems." *Spacing Magazine: Canadian Urbanism Uncovered* 15(1).

Employment and Immigration. 1989. *Success in the Works.* Ottawa: Employment and Immigration.

Engelman, Robert. 2007. "Northern numbers, northern nature: Thoughts on the potential for studying the population and environment in Canada." Paper presented at the workshop on Demographics and the Environment. Policy Research Initiative. Ottawa: PRI, March.

Environment Canada. 2006. *Canada's Fourth National Report on Climate Change: Actions to Meet Commitments under the United Nations Framework Convention on Climate Change*. Ottawa: Environment Canada.

——. 2011a. *National Inventory Report, 1990–2009: Greenhouse Gas Sources and Sinks in Canada*. Catalogue No. En81-4//1-2009E.

——. 2011b. *Municipal Water Use Report* cat. no.: En11-2/2009E.

——. 2012. *Climate Trends and Variations Bulletin— Annual*. Ottawa: Environment Canada.

——. 2013a. *Climate Trends and Variations Bulletin*. Ottawa: Environment Canada.

——. 2013b. *Water*. Ottawa: Environment Canada Publications.

——. 2014. *National Inventory Report 1990–2013: The Canadian Government's Submission to the UN Framework Convention on Climate Change*. Ottawa: Environment Canada Publications.

Eschbach, Karl. 1995. "The enduring and vanishing American Indian: American Indian population growth and intermarriage in 1990." *Ethnic and Racial Studies* 18: 89–108.

Esping-Andersen, G. 1990. *The Three Worlds of Welfare Capitalism*. Cambridge: Policy Press.

European Environment Agency. 2012. "Environmental indicator report, 2012: Ecosystem resilience and resource efficiency in a green economy in Europe." Copenhagen: European Environment Agency.

Evans, Robert G. 1987. "Hang together or hang separately: The viability of a universal health care system in an aging society." *Canadian Public Policy* 13: 165–80.

——, K.M. McGrail, S.G. Morgan, M.L. Barer, and C. Hertzman. 2001. "Apocalypse no: Population aging and the future of health care systems." SEDAP Research Paper No. 59. Hamilton: McMaster University, SEDAP.

Ewing B., D. Moore, S. Goldfinger, A. Oursler, A. Reed, and M. Wackernagel. 2010. *The Ecological Footprint Atlas*. Oakland, CA: Global Footprint Network.

Farber, Bernard. 1964. *Family Organization and Interaction*. San Francisco: Chandler.

Fassbender, K., R. Fainsinger, and M. Carson. 2009. "Cost trajectories at the end of life: The Canadian experience," *Journal of Pain and Symptom Management* 38(1): 75–80.

Federation of Canadian Municipalities. 2012. "Proposed federal wastewater regulations: Backgrounder." Federation of Canadian Municipalities Briefing Note on Wastewater Regulations, 18 July.

——. 2013. "100 municipal leaders in Ottawa to tackle national issues facing cities and communities." Press Release, 26 November.

Fellegi, Ivan P. 1988. "Can we afford an aging society?" *Canadian Economic Observer* 1: 4.1–4.34.

——. 1997. *On Poverty and Low Income*. Ottawa: Statistics Canada.

——. 2010. "The organization of statistical methodology and methodological research in National Statistical Offices." *Survey Methodology* 36: 123–30.

Ferguson, Michael. 2014. *Report of the Auditor General of Canada* (spring report). Ottawa: Office of the Auditor General of Canada.

Finance Canada. 2012. *Equalization Program*. Ottawa: Department of Finance Canada.

Findlay, Leanne, and Dafna Kohen. 2012. "Leave practices of parents after the birth or adoption of young children." *Canadian Social Trends*. Statistics Canada cat no. 11-008-X, online edition.

Flaherty, James M. 2012. *Jobs, Growth and Long-Term Prosperity: The Economic Action Plan*. Minister of Finance, 29 March.

Flato, Gregory, and Jochem Marotzke. 2013. "Evaluation of climate models." In the *Working Group 1 Contribution to the Intergovernmental Panel on Climate Change Fifth Assessment Report*, IPCC, pp. 741–865.

Florida, Richard. 2002. *The Rise of the Creative Class*. New York: Basic Books.

FOA (Food and Agriculture Organization of the United Nations). 2002. *A Note on Unsustainable Fisheries and Trends in World Fish Catches*. Report and Documentation of the International Workshop on Factors of Unsustainability and Overexploitation in Fisheries. Bangkok, Thailand, 4–8 February.

Fong, Eric, ed. 2006. *Inside the Mosaic*. Toronto: University of Toronto Press.

——, and Feng Hou. 2013. "Effects of ethnic enclosure of neighborhoods, workplace, and industrial sectors on earning." *Social Science Research* 42: 1061–76.

——, Nora Chiang, and Nancy A. Denton, eds. 2013. *Immigrant Adaptation in Multi-Ethnic Societies: Canada, Taiwan, and the United States*. New York: Routledge.

Foot, David (with Daniel Stoffman). 2000. *Boom, Bust & Echo 2000: Profiting from the Demographic Shift in the New Millennium*. Toronto: Macfarlane Walter & Ross.

——. 2001. *Boom, Bust & Echo: Profiting from the Demographic Shift in the 21st Century*. Toronto: Stoddart.

Foster, Jason. 2013. "Making temporary permanent: The silent transformation of the temporary foreign worker program." *Just Labour: A Canadian Journal of Work and Society* 19: 22–46.

Fox, Bonnie, and Meg Luxton. 1991. "Conceptualizing a family." Paper prepared for Health and Welfare Canada, Review of Demography.

Frederick, Judith, and Jason Hamel. 1998. "Canadian attitudes to divorce." *Canadian Social Trends* 48: 6–11.

Frenette, Marc. 2014. *An Investment of a Lifetime? The Long-Term Labour Market Premiums Associated with a Post-secondary Education.* Analytical Studies Branch Research Paper Series, no. 359. Ottawa: Statistics Canada.

Frenette, Marc and Rene Morrissette. 2003. Will They Ever Converge? Earnings of Immigrants and Canadian-born Workers Over the Last Two Decades. *Statistics Canada Analytical Studies Branch Research Series 11F0019MIE, Working Paper No. 215.*

Frideres, James S. 1998. *Aboriginal Peoples in Canada: Contemporary Conflicts.* Scarborough, ON: Prentice Hall and Allyn and Bacon Canada.

———, and Rene Gadacz. 2012. *Aboriginal Peoples in Canada, Ninth Edition.* Don Mills, ON: Pearson Prentice Hall.

Friedan, Betty. 1963. *The Feminine Mystique.* New York: Norton.

Friedman, Debra, Michael Hechter, and Satoshi Kanazawa. 1994. "A theory of the value of children." *Demography* 31: 375–401.

Friesen, Joe. 2012. "Rethinking immigration: The case for the 400,000 solution." *The Globe and Mail,* 4 May.

Furstenberg, Frank, Sabino Kornrich, and Juan March. 2013. "Investing in children: Changes in parental spending on children, 1972–2007." *Demography* 50(1): 1–23.

Fyfe, J.C., K. von Salzen, N.P. Gillett, V.K. Arora, G.M. Flato, and J.R. McConnell. 2013. "One hundred years of arctic surface temperature variation due to anthropogenic influence." *Nature,* 3: 26–45.

Galarneau, Diane, and René Morrissette. 2008. "Immigrants' education and required job skills." *Perspectives* 6: 5–18. Ottawa: Statistics Canada.

———, and Marian Radulescu. 2009. "Employment among the disabled." *Perspectives on Labour and Income* 10: 5–15.

Garloff, Alfred, Carsten Pohl, and Norbert Schanne. 2013. "Do small labor market entry cohorts reduce unemployment?" *Demographic Research* 27: 379–406.

Gaudet, Stéphanie, Martin Cooke, and Joanna Jacob. 2011. "Working after childbirth: A lifecourse transition analysis of Canadian women from the 1970s to the 2000s." *Canadian Review of Sociology* 48(2): 153–80.

Gauthier, Anne Hélène. 1987. "Nouvelles estimations du coût de l'enfant au Canada." *Cahiers québécois de démographie* 16: 187–208.

———. 1991. "The economics of childhood." In *Childhood as a Social Phenomenon,* A.R. Pence, ed. Vienna: European Centre for Social Welfare Policy and Research.

———. 1996. *The State and the Family.* Oxford: Clarendon.

———. 2007. "The impact of family policies on fertility in industrialized countries: A review of the literature." *Population Research and Policy Review* 26: 323–46.

———. 2008. "Some theoretical and methodological comments on the impact of policies on fertility." *Vienna Yearbook of Population Research, 2008*: 25–8.

———, Timothy Smeeding, and Frank Furstenberg. 2004. "Are parents in industrialized countries investing less time in children?" *Population and Development Review* 30(4): 647–71.

———, and Dimiter Philipov. 2008. "Can policies enhance fertility in Europe?" *Vienna Yearbook of Population Research 2008*: 1–16.

Gauvreau, Danielle. 2001. "Rats des villes et rats des champs: Populations urbaines et populations rurales du Québec au recensement de 1901." *Cahiers québécois de démographie* 30: 171–90.

———, Diane Gervais, and Peter Gossage. 2007. *La fécondité des Québécoises, 1870–1970: d'une exception à l'autre.* Montréal: Les Editions du Boréal.

———, and Peter Gossage. 2001. "Canadian fertility transitions: Quebec and Ontario at the turn of the twentieth century." *Journal of Family History* 26: 162–88.

Gee, Ellen M. 1986. "The life course of Canadian women: An historical and demographic analysis." *Social Indicators Research* 18: 263–83.

———. 1990. "Demographic change and intergenerational relations in Canadian families: Findings and social policy implications." *Canadian Public Policy* 16: 191–9.

———, and Gloria Gutman. 2000. *Overselling Population Aging: Apocalyptic Demography, Intergenerational Challenges, and Social Policy.* Don Mills, ON: Oxford University Press.

———, Barbara A. Mitchell, and Andrew Wister. 1995. "Returning to the parental nest: Exploring a changing Canadian life course." *Canadian Studies in Population* 22: 121–44.

———, and Jean E. Veevers. 1983. "Accelerating sex differences in mortality: An analysis of contributing factors." *Social Biology* 30: 75–85.

Gemery, H. 2000. "The white population of the colonial United States, 1607–1790." Pp. 143–90 in *A Population History of North America,* ed. M. Haines and H. Steckel. Cambridge, UK: Cambridge University Press.

George, M.V., A. Romaniuc, and F. Nault. 1990. "Effects of fertility and international migration on the changing age composition in Canada." Paper presented at the Conference of European Statisticians, Ottawa.

———, Shirley Loh, and Ravi Verma. 1997. "Impact of varying the component assumptions of projected total population and age structure in Canada." *Canadian Studies in Population* 24: 67–86.

Germain, Marie-France, Claude Grenier, and Gilles Montigny. 2001. "Demographic profiles of Canada, the United States and Mexico, 1950–2050." In the Federation of Canadian Demographers' *Demographic Futures in the Context of Globalization: Public Policy Issues*, pp. 35–63.

Giddens, Anthony. 1991. *Modernity and Self-Identity: Self and Society in the Late Modern Age*. Cambridge, UK: Polity Press.

Giese, Rachel. 2011. "Arrival of the fittest." *The Walrus* 8: 15–20.

Gil Alonso, Fernando. 2005. "The uneven distribution of family responsibilities among women and men and its link with low fertility: Some evidence for European Union countries from Eurobarometer data." Paper presented at the Conference of the International Union for the Scientific Study of Population, Tours, France, 18–23 July.

Gilbert, Stéphane, Alain Bélanger, and Jacques Ledent. 2001. "Immigration, migration interne et croissance urbaine au Canada pour le période de 1976 à 1996." Presented at the meetings of the Association des Démographes du Québec, Sherbrooke, May.

Glossop, Robert. 1994. "The Canadian family." *Canadian Social Trends* 35: 2–10.

Goddard, I. 1996. *Languages: Handbook of North American Indians*. Washington, DC: Smithsonian Institution.

Goldmann, Gustave. 1998. "Shifts in ethnic origins among the offspring of immigrants: Is ethnic mobility a measureable phenomenon?" *Canadian Ethnic Studies* 30: 121–48.

———, and Andy Siggner. 1995. "Statistical concepts of Aboriginal people and factors affecting the counts in the Aboriginal Peoples Survey." In *Towards the Twenty-First Century: Emerging Demographic Trends and Policy Issues in Canada*. Ottawa: Federation of Canadian Demography, pp. 265–90.

Goldscheider, Calvin. 1971. *Population, Modernization and Social Structure*. Boston: Little, Brown.

Goldscheider, Frances, and Linda J. Waite. 1986. "Sex differences in the entry into marriage." *American Journal of Sociology* 92: 91–109.

Goldstein, Joshua, Deniz Dilan, Karaman Orsal, Michaela Kreyenfeld, and Aiva Jasilioniene. 2013. "Fertility reactions to the 'Great Recession' in Europe: Recent evidence from order-specific data." *Demographic Research* 29: 85–104.

———, Tomas Sobotka, and Aiva Jasilioniene. 2009. "The end of 'lowest-low fertility'?" *Population and Development Review* 35(4): 663–99.

Golini, Antonio. 1996. "International population movements: Imbalances and integration." In *Resources and Population: Natural, Institutional, and Demographic Dimensions of Development*, B. Colombo, P. Demeny, and M.F. Perutz, eds. Oxford, UK: Oxford University Press, pp. 287–301.

Gomez, Rafael, and David Foot. 2013. "The destiny of demographic change." *Policy Options* 34: 55–7.

Goodwin, N., and G. Institute. 2011. "Externality." *The Encyclopedia of Earth*. See www.eoearth.org/view/article/152717.

Gordon, Raymond, ed. 2005. *Ethnologue: Languages of the World*. Dallas. SIL International.

Gossage, Peter. 1999. *Families in Transition: Industry and Population in Nineteenth-Century Saint-Hyacinthe*. Montreal and Kingston: McGill-Queen's University Press.

———, and Danielle Gauvreau. 2000. "Demography and discourse in transition: Quebec fertility at the turn of the twentieth century." *The History of the Family* 4: 375–95.

Gougeon, Philippe. 2009. "Shifting pensions." *Perspectives on Labour and Income* 10: 16–23.

Government of Alberta. 2008. *Alberta's Oil Sands: Opportunities, Balance*. Edmonton: Government of Alberta

Grady, Patrick. 2013. "Clement Gignac is wrong on immigration." Immigration Papers. Ottawa: Global Economics Commentaries.

Grant, Hugh, and David Wolf. 2006. *Staples and Beyond: Selected Writings of Mel Watkins*. Montreal and Kingston: McGill-Queen's University Press.

Green, Alan. 2002. "What is the Role of Immigration in Canada's future?" Presented at the Conference on Canadian Immigration Policy for the 21st Century, Kingston, Ontario, October.

———, and David Green. 2004. "The goals of Canada's immigration policy: A historical perspective." *Canadian Journal of Urban Research* 13: 102–39.

Green, David, and Christopher Worswick. 2004. *Entry Earnings of Immigrant Men in Canada: The Roles of Labour Market Entry Effects and Returns to Foreign Experience*. Strategic Policy, Planning and Research Branch. Ottawa: Citizenship and Immigration Canada.

Greenberg, L., and C. Normandin. 2012. "Disparities in life expectancy at birth." Statistics Canada cat. no. 82-624-X.

Grenier, Gilles, and Réjean Lachapelle. 1988. "Apects linguistiques de l'évolution démographique." Report for Review of Demography. Ottawa: Health and Welfare Canada.

Grimes, B.F. 2000. *Ethnologue: Languages of the World*, 14th edition. Dallas: SIL International.

Gross, D.M., and N. Schmitt, 2012. "Temporary foreign workers and regional labour market disparities in Canada." *Canadian Public Policy* 38: 233–63.

Grubel, Herbert, ed. 2009. *The Effects of Mass Immigration on Canadian Living Standards and Society.* Vancouver: Fraser Institute.

Guillemette, Y., and B.P. Robson. 2006. *No Elixir of Youth: Immigration Cannot Keep Canada Young.* Backgrounder no. 96. Toronto: C.D. Howe Institute.

Guimond, Eric. 2003. "Fuzzy definitions and population explosion: Changing identities of Aboriginal groups in Canada." In *Not Strangers in These Parts: Aboriginal People in Cities*, David Newhouse and Evelyn Peters, eds. Ottawa: Public Radio International, pp. 35–50.

Guo, S., C. Zeller, W. Chumlea, and R. Siervogel. 1999. "Aging, body composition and lifestyle." *American Journal of Clinical Nutrition* 70: 405–11.

Guralnik, Jack, and Edward Schneider. 1987. "Prospects and expectations of extending life expectancy." Pp. 125–45 in *Technological Prospects and Population Trends*, T.J. Espenshade and G.T. Stolnitz, eds. Boulder, CO: Westview Press.

Habtu, Roman. 2002 "Men 55 and older: Work or retire?" *Perspectives on Labour and Income* 3: 27–34.

Haines, M.R. 2001. "The urban mortality transition in the United States, 1800–1940." NBER Historical Paper No. 134.

Haines, Michael, and Richard Steckel. 2000. *A Population History of North America.* Cambridge, UK: Cambridge University Press.

Hall, David. 2002. "Risk society and the second demographic transition." *Canadian Studies in Population* 29, no. 2: 173–93.

Halli, Shiva, Frank Trovato, and Leo Driedger, eds. 1990. *Ethnic Demography.* Ottawa: Carleton University Press.

Hamilton, L.C., and O. Otterstad. 1998. "Sex ratio and community size: Notes from the northern Atlantic." *Population and Environment* 20(1):11–22.

Hamplova, Dana, and Céline Le Bourdais. 2008. "Educational homogamy of married and unmarried couples in English and French Canada." *Canadian Journal of Sociology* 33(4): 845–72.

Handa, Jagdish. 1986. *Wage and Occupational Structure in an Economy with an Aging Population: The Canadian Case in the Years Ahead.* Ottawa: Health and Welfare Canada, Report for Review of Demography.

Hango, Darcy, and Céline Le Bourdais. 2009. "The effect of education on early parenthood among young Canadian adults." *Canadian Studies in Population* 36(3–4): 237–65.

Hardin, Garrett. 1968. "The tragedy of the commons." *Science* 162: 1243–8.

Hareven, Tamara K. 1983. "American families in transition: Historical perspective on change." In *Family in Transition*, A.S. Skolnick and J.H. Skolnick, eds. Boston: Little, Brown.

Harper, Charles L., and Thomas H. Fletcher. 2010. *Environment and Society: Human Perspectives on Environmental Issues*, Canadian Edition. Don Mills, ON: Pearson Canada.

Harris, C.C. 1983. *The Family and Industrial Society.* London: George Allen and Unwin.

Harris, M., and E. Ross. 1987. *Death, Sex and Fertility: Population Regulation in Pre-industrial and Developing Societies.* New York: Columbia University Press.

Harrison, Brian. 1997. "Language integration: Results of an intergenerational analysis." *Statistical Journal of the United Nations Economic Commission for Europe* 14: 289–303.

——. 2000. "Passing on the language: Heritage language diversity in Canada." *Canadian Social Trends* 58: 14–19.

——, and Louise Marmen. 1994. *Languages in Canada.* Scarborough, ON: Prentice Hall.

Hatton, T., and J. Williamson. 2003. "Demographic and economic pressure on emigration out of Africa." *Scandinavian Journal of Economics* 105: 465–86.

Hawkins, Freda. 1972. *Canada and Immigration: Public Policy and Public Concern.* Montreal and Kingston: McGill-Queen's University Press.

Hawkley, L.C., and J.T. Cacioppo. 2011. "Loneliness and health." Pp. 1172–76 in *Encyclopedia of behavioural medicine*, M. Gellman and J.R. Turner, eds. New York: Springer.

Health Canada. 2003. *Statistic Profile on the Health of First Nations in Canada.* Ottawa: First Nations and Inuit Health Branch, Health Canada.

——. 2009. *Drinking Water Advisories in First Nations Communities in Canada: A National Overview.* Catalogue H34-208/2009E.

——. 2010. *Report on the Findings of the Oral Health Component of the Canadian Health Measures Survey.* Retrieved from www.fptdwg.ca/English/e-documents.html.

Heibert, Daniel. 2007. "Migration and the demographic transformation of Canadian cities: The social geography of Canada's major metropolitan centres in 2017." In *The Changing Face of Canada*, Roderic Beaujot and Don Kerr, eds. Toronto: Canadian Scholars' Press, pp. 220–56.

Heintz-Martin, Valerie, Céline Le Bourdais, and Dana Hamplova. 2014. "Childbearing among Canadian stepfamilies." *Canadian Studies in Population* 41(1–2): 61–77.

Hengeveld, Rob. 2012. *Wasted World: How Our Consumption Challenges the Planet.* Chicago: University of Chicago Press.

Henripin, Jacques. 1954. *La population canadienne au début du XVIIIᵉ siècle.* Paris: Universitaires de France.

———. 1957. "From acceptance of nature to control: The demography of the French Canadians since the seventeenth century." *Canadian Journal of Economics and Political Science* 23: 10–19.

———. 1968. *Tendances et facteurs de la fécondité au Canada.* Ottawa: Dominion Bureau of Statistics.

———. 1989. *Naître ou ne pas être.* Québec: Institut Québécois de recherché sur la culture.

———, and Evelyne Lapierre-Adamcyk. 1974. *La fin de la revanche des berceaux: qu'en pensent les Québécoises?* Montreal: Les Presses de l'Université de Montréal.

———, and Evelyne Lapierre-Adamcyk. 1986. *Essai d'évaluation du coût de l'enfant.* Report submitted to Bureau de la statistique du Québec.

———, Paul-Marie Huot, Evelyne Lapierre-Adamcyk, and Nicole Marcil-Gratton. 1981. *Les enfants qu'on n'a plus au Québec.* Montreal: Les Presses de l'Université de Montréal.

———, and Y. Péron. 1972. "The demographic transition of the province of Quebec." Pp. 213–31 in *Population and Social Change*, D. Glass and R. Revelle, eds. London: Edward Arnold.

Henry, L. 1961. "Some data on natural fertility." *Eugenics Quarterly* 8: 81–91.

Héran, François. 2013a. "Politique familiale et fécondité: Quelles leçons retenir des expériences européennes?" Paper presented at the International Union for the Scientific Study of Population Conference, Busan, South Korea, 26 August.

———. 2013b. "Fertility and family-support policies: What can we learn from the European experience?" Keynote speech, opening ceremony of the 27th International Population Conference IUSSP, Busan, South Korea, 26 August.

Herbert-Copley, Brent. 2013. "Why thirty-somethings are still in entry-level jobs." Special to *The Globe and Mail*, August 12.

Higgins, Jenny. 2008. *Depopulation Impacts.* St John's, NL: Newfoundland and Labrador Heritage.

Hiller, Harry H. 2009. *Second Promised Land Migration to Alberta and the Transformation of Canadian Society.* Montreal and Kingston: McGill-Queen's University Press.

Hinde, A. 1998. *Demographic Methods.* London: Arnold Publishers.

Hodge, Gerald. 2008. *The Geography of Aging: Preparing Communities for the Surge in Seniors.* Montreal and Kingston: McGill-Queen's University Press.

Hodgson, Dennis. 2009. "Abortion, family planning, and population policy: Prospects for the common-ground approach." *Population and Development Review* 35: 479–518

———, and Susan Cotts Watkins. 1997. "Feminist and neo-Malthusians: Past and present alliances." *Population and Development Review* 23(3): 469–523.

Hoem, Britta, and Jan Hoem. 1996. "Sweden's family policies and roller-coaster fertility." *Journal of Population Problems* 52: 1–22.

Hoem, Jan. 1995. *Educational Capital and Divorce Risk in Sweden in the 1970s and '80s.* Stockholm Research Reports in Demography no. 95. Stockholm, Sweden: Stockholm University, Demographic Unit.

Hofferth, Sandra, and Frances Goldscheider. 2010. "Family structure and the transition to early parenthood." *Demography* 47(2): 415–37.

Hogan, S., and J. Lise. 2003. "Life expectancy, health expectancy and the life cycle." *Horizons* 6: 2–9.

Hohn, Charlotte. 1987. "Population policies in advanced societies: Pronatalist and migration strategies." *European Journal of Population* 3: 459–81.

Homer-Dixon, Thomas. 2006. *The Upside of Down: Catastrophe, Creativity and the Renewal of Civilization.* Toronto: Alfred A. Knopf.

Hou, Feng, and T.R. Balakrishnan. 1996. "The integration of visible minorities in contemporary Canadian society." *Canadian Journal Of Sociology* 21: 307–26.

———, and Simon Coulombe. 2010. "Earnings gaps for Canadian-born visible minorities in the public and private sectors." *Canadian Public Policy* 36: 29–43.

———, and John Myles. 2008. "The changing role of education in the marriage market: Assortative marriage in Canada and the United States since the 1970s." *Canadian Journal of Sociology* 33(2): 337–66.

———, and Garnett Picot. 2013. "Annual levels of immigration and immigrant earnings." Paper presented at the meetings of the Canadian Population Society, Victoria, 5-7 June.

Houle, René. 2013. "2011 census data on language: Different questionnaires, different results." Paper presented at the Canadian Population Society Meetings, University of Victoria, June.

Hout, Michael, and Joshua Goldstein. 1994. "How 4.5 million Irish immigrants became 40 million Irish Americans: Demographic and subjective aspects of ethnic composition of white Americans." *American Sociological Review* 59: 64–82.

Hum, Derek, and Wayne Simpson. 1999. "Wage opportunities for visible minorities in Canada." *Canadian Public Policy* 25: 379–94.

Hurd, W.B. 1939. "Some implications of prospective population changes in Canada." *Canadian Journal of Economics and Political Science* 5: 492–503.

Hutchings, J.A., and J.D. Reynolds. 2004. "Marine fish population collapses: Consequences for recovery and extinction risk." *BioScience* 54: 297–309.

Hutchinson, Michael. 2002. "Baby boom bust." *Aboriginal Times* 6(5): 30–3.

IEA (International Energy Association). 2014. Data Services. See www.iea.org/stats.

Ibbott, Peter, Don Kerr, and Roderic Beaujot. 2006. "Probing the future of mandatory retirement in Canada." *Canadian Journal on Aging* 25: 161–78.

Imgur. 2014. "Share of young people in EU, aged 25–34, who are still living with their parents." Available at http://imgur.com/r/MapPorn/6ZFTC0V.

Immigration and Refugee Protection Act n S.C. 2001, c. 27. Assented to 1 November 2001. Ottawa: Government of Canada.

INAC. 1999. *Basic Departmental Data 1998*. Ottawa: Department of Indian Affairs and Northern Development.

———. 2000. *Registered Indian Population Projections for Canada and Regions, 1998–2008*. Ottawa: Indian and Northern Affairs Canada.

———. 2005. *Basic Departmental Data, 2004*. Ottawa: Indian and Northern Affairs Canada.

———. 2009. *Discussion Paper on Needed Changes to the Indian Act Affecting Indian Registration and Band Membership, McIvor v. Canada*. Ottawa: Minister of Indian Affairs and Northern Development and Federal Interlocutor for Métis and Non-status Indians.

Ingstad, H. 2001. *The Viking Discovery of America: The Excavation of a Norse Settlement in L'Anse aux Meadows, Newfoundland*. New York: Checkmark Books.

Innis, Harold. 1980. *The Idea File of Harold Adams Innis*, William Christian, ed. Toronto: University of Toronto Press.

Institut de la statistique du Québec. 2013. *Le bilan démographique du Québec*. Québec: Institut de la statistique du Québec.

IPCC. 2013. *Climate Change 2013: The Physical Science Basis*. Working Group I. Geneva: International Panel on Climate Change.

Ipsos. 2011. "Nearly half (45 percent) of world citizens believe immigration has had a negative impact on their country." Press release, Paris: Ipsos, 4 August.

Jain, A., and J. Bongaarts. 1981. "Breastfeeding: Patterns, correlates and fertility effects." *Studies in Family Planning* 12: 79–99.

James, P., R. Wilkins, A. Detsky, P. Tugwell, and Douglas Manuel. 2007. "Avoidable mortality by neighbourhood income in Canada: 25 years after the establishment of universal health insurance." *Journal of Epidemiology and Community Health* 61: 287–96.

Jenness, D. 1932 [1977]. *The Indians of Canada*. Toronto: University of Toronto Press.

Johnson, B., and L. Blackwell. 2007. "Review of methods for estimating life expectancy by social class using the ONS Longitudinal Study." *Health Statistics Quarterly* 35: 28–36.

Jones, Landon. 1980. *Great Expectations: America and the Baby Boom Generation*. New York: Coward, McCann & Geoghegan.

Jos, G.J., Greet Olivier, Jeroen Janssens-Maenhout, and A.H. Peter. 2012. *Trends in Global CO_2 Emissions: 2012 Report*. PBL Netherlands Environmental Assessment Agency. The Hague/Bilthoven.

Kalbach, Madeline, and Warren Kalbach. 1999. "Persistence of ethnicity and inequality among Canadian immigrants." *Canadian Studies in Population* 25: 83–105.

Kalbach, Warren E, and W.W. McVey. 1979. *The Demographic Bases of Canadian Society*. Toronto: McGraw-Hill.

Kalmijn, Matthijs. 2013. "The Educational Gradient in Marriage: A Comparison of 25 European Countries." *Demography* 50(4): 1499–1520.

Kaplan, Hillard S., Jane B. Lancaster, and Kermyt G. Anderson. 1998. "Human parental investment and fertility: The life histories of men in Albuquerque." In *Men in Families: When Do They Get Involved? What Difference Does It Make?* A. Booth and A.C. Crouter, eds. Mahwah, NJ: Lawrence Erlbaum, pp. 55–109.

Kapsalis, C., René Morissette, and Garnett Picot. 1999. "The returns to education, and the increasing wage gap between younger and older workers." Statistics Canada: Analytical Studies Branch Research Paper Series cat. no. 11F0019MIE, No. 131.

Katzenberg, M. Anne. 1992. "Changing diet and health in pre- and proto-historic Ontario." *MASCA Research Papers in Science and Archaeology* 9: 23–31.

Keefe, Janice, Jacques Légaré and Yves Carrière. 2005. *Developing New Strategies to Support Future Caregivers of the Aged in Canada: Projections of Need and their Policy Implications*. SEDAP Research Program, Research Paper No. 140. Hamilton: McMaster University.

Keeley, B. 2007. *Human Capital: How What You Know Shapes Your Life*. Paris: Organisation for Economic Co-operation and Development.

Kelley, Ninette, and Michael J. Trebilcock. 2010. *The Making of the Mosaic: A History of Canadian Immigration Policy.* Toronto: University of Toronto Press.

Kennedy, Mark. 2012. "Budget 2012: Canadians expect bad news, opposed to OAS trims, poll shows." Postmedia News, 16 March.

Kennedy, Sheela., J. McDonald, and N. Biddle. 2006. *The Healthy Immigrant Effect and Immigrant Selection: Evidence from Four Countries.* Hamilton: SEDAP research paper No.164.

———, and Elizabeth Thomson. 2010. "Children's experiences of family disruption in Sweden: Differentials by parent education over three decades." *Demographic Research* 23(17): 479–508.

Kenney, Jason. 2009. "Helping newcomers to enter the workforce." Speaking notes for the minister of citizenship, immigration and multiculturalism to the 2009 Top Employer Summit, Royal York Hotel. Toronto: 19 November.

———. 2012. Address to the Competition for Global Talent Immigration Conference. Calgary: 28 June.

Kerr, Don, and Roderic Beaujot. 2003. "Child poverty and family structure in Canada, 1981–1997." *Journal of Comparative Family Studies* 34(3): 321–35.

———, and Hugh Mellon. 2010. "Demographic change and representation by population in the Canadian House of Commons." *Canadian Studies in Population* 37(1): 53–75.

———, and Hugh Mellon. 2012. "Energy, population and the environment: Exploring Canada's record on CO2 emissions and energy use relative to other OECD countries." *Population and Environment* 34: 257–78.

Keyfitz, Nathan. 1950. "The growth of the Canadian population." *Population Studies* 4: 47–63.

———. 1982. *Population Change and Social Policy.* Cambridge: Abt Books.

———. 1986. "The family that does not reproduce itself." *Population and Development Review* 12 (Suppl.): 139–54.

———. 1988. "Some Demographic Properties of Transfer Schemes: How to Achieve Equity between Generations." Pp. 92–105 in *Economics of Changing Age Distributions in Developed Countries*, ed. R. Lee. Oxford: Clarendon Press.

———. 1989. "On future mortality." IIASA Working Paper 89–59. Laxenburg, Austria: International Institute for Applied Systems Analysis.

———. 1990. "Effect of mortality uncertainty on population projections." Presented at the meeting of the Population Association of America, Toronto, May.

Kiernan, Katherine. 2001. "Cohabitation in Western Europe: Trends, issues and implications." In *Just Living Together: Implications of Cohabitation on Families, Children, and Social Policy*, A. Booth and A.C. Crouter, eds. Mahwah, NJ: Erlbaum, pp. 3–31.

———. 2002. "Demography and disadvantage: Chicken and egg?" In *Understanding Social Exclusion*, J. Hills, J. Le Grand, and D. Piachaud, eds. Oxford, UK: Oxford University Press.

King, Karen M. 2009. "The geography of immigration in Canada: Settlement, education, labour activity and occupation profiles." Working Paper Series, Ontario in the Creative Age. Toronto: Rotman School of Management.

Kneale, Dylan. 2008. "Postponement and childlessness: Evidence from two British cohorts." *Demographic Research* 19: 1935–68.

Krahn, Harvey, J. Graham, S. Lowe, and Karen Hughes. 2011. *Work, Industry and Canadian Society*, Fifth Edition. Scarborough, ON: Nelson.

Krotki, Karol J. 1990. "International migration and Canada's ethnic/linguistic composition: Language policy, multiculturalism." In *Facing the Demographic Future*, R. Beaujot, ed. Ottawa: Royal Society of Canada, pp. 23–4.

———, and Dave Odynak. 1988. "The emergence of multiethnicities in 1981 and 1986: Their sociological significance." Discussion Paper no. 63. Edmonton: Population Research Laboratory.

Krugman, Paul. 2009. *The Conscience of a Liberal.* New York: W.W. Norton and Company.

Kustec, Stan. 2012. *The Role of Migrant Labour Supply in the Canadian Labour Market.* CIC Ref. No.: RR20120705. Ottawa: Citizenship and Immigration Canada.

Kyriazis, Natalie. 1982. "A parity-specific analysis of completed fertility in Canada." *Canadian Review of Sociology and Anthropology* 19: 29–43.

Lachapelle, Réjean. 1988. 'Quelques tendances démolinguistiques au Canada et au Québec'. *L'Action Nationale* 78: 329–43.

———. 1989. "Evolution of language groups and the official languages situation of Canada." In *Demolinguistic Trends and the Evolution of Canadian Institutions.* Special Issue, Canadian Issues series of the Association for Canadian Studies. Ottawa: Secretary of State, pp. 7–33.

———. 2001. "La notion de migration de remplacement: Sa portée, ses limites et ses prolongements." Paper presented at meetings of the Association des Démographes du Québec, Sherbrooke, May.

———. 2009. *The Diversity of the Canadian Francophonie: Rendez-vous de la Francophonie Presentation.* Ottawa: Statistics Canada.

——, and Jacques Henripin. 1982. *The Demolinguistic Situation in Canada: Past Trends and Future Prosepects.* Montreal: Institute for Research on Public Policy.

——, and Jean-François Lepage. 2010. *Languages in Canada: 2006 Census.* Ottawa: Canadian Heritage/Statistics Canada.

Laffont, J.J. 2008. "Externalities." In *New Palgrave Dictionary of Economics,* Second Edition, Steven N. Durlauf and Lawrence E. Blume, eds. Basingstoke, UK: Palgrave Macmillan.

Laflamme, Valérie. 2001. "Familles et modes de résidence en milieu urbain québécois au début du XXe siècle: L'example de la ville de Québec, 1901." *Cahiers québécois de démographie* 30: 261–88.

Lalonde, Marc. 1974. *A New Perspective on the Health of Canadians.* Ottawa: Health and Welfare Canada.

Landry, Y. 1993. "Fertility in France and New France: The distinguishing characteristics of Canadian behaviour in the seventeenth and eighteenth centuries." *Social Science History* 17: 577–92.

Lapierre-Adamcyk, Évelyne. 2010. "L'évolution de la fécondité et la politique familiale québécoise." *Santé, Société et Solidarité* 2010 (2): 63–73.

——, and Marie Hélène Lussier. 2003. "De la forte fécondité à la fécondité désirée." In *La démographie québécoise: enjeux du XXIe siècle.* V. Piché and C. Le Bourdais, eds. Montreal: Les Presses de l'Université de Montréal, pp. 66–109.

Laplante, Benoît, Jean-Dominique Morency, and Maria Constanza Street. 2010. "L'action politique et la fécondité: Aperçu d'une étude empirique du processus qui régit la première naissance au Canada." *Santé, Société et Solidarité* (2): 75–84.

——, Jean-Dominique Morency, and Maria Constanza Street. 2011. "Policy and fertility: An empirical study of childbearing behaviour in Canada." Manuscript.

Lappegard, Trude, Marit Ronsen, and Kari Skrede. 2009. "Socioeconomic differentials in multi-partner fertility among fathers." Paper presented at the International Population Conference of the International Union for the Scientific Study of Population, Marrakesh, 27 September to 2 October.

Laroque, G. and B. Salanie. 2004. "Fertility and financial incentives in France." *CESifo Economic Studies* 50: 423–50.

Lavoie, Yollande. 1972. *L'émigration des canadiens aux États-Unis avant 1930.* Montreal: Les Presses du l'Université de Montréal.

Le Bourdais, Céline, and Evelyne Lapierre-Adamcyk. 2004. "Changes in conjugal life in Canada: Is cohabitation progressively replacing marriage?" *Journal of Marriage and the Family* 66: 929–42.

——, and Nicole Marcil-Gratton. 1998. "The impact of family disruption in childhood on demographic outcomes in young adulthood." In *Labour Markets, Social Institutions, and the Future of Canada's Children,* M. Corak, ed. Ottawa: Statistics Canada Cat. No. 89-553-XPB, pp. 91–105.

Le Bras, Hervé. 1988. "The demographic impact of post-war migration in selected OECD countries." Presented at OECD Working Party on Migration, Paris.

Leclerc, Annette, Jean-Francois Chastang, Gwenn Menvielle, and Daniele Luce. 2006. "Socioeconomic inequalities in premature mortality in France: Have they widened in recent decades?" *Social Science and Medicine* 62(8): 2035–45.

Ledent, J., and P. Rees. 1986. "Life tables." In *Migration and Settlement: A Multiregional Comparative Study,* A. Rogers and F. Willekens, eds. Dordrecht, Netherlands, and Boston: D. Reidel Publishing, pp. 385–418.

Légaré, Jacques. 1988. "A population register for Canada under the French regime: Context, scope, content and applications." *Canadian Studies in Population* 15: 1–16.

——. 1990. "Une meilleure santé plutôt qu'une vie prolongée: Plaidoyer pour une réorientation d'une politique de santé pour les personnes âgées." Unpublished manuscript.

Legoff, Jacques. 1989. "Les conséquences économiques et sociales des évolutions démographiques en Europe." *Population et Avenir* 593/594: 6–9.

LeGrand, Thomas. 1998. "Croissance de la population mondiale et environnement: Les enjeux." *Cahiers québécois de démographie* 27: 221–52.

Leridon, Henri, and Catherine Villeneuve-Gokalp. 1994. *Constances et Inconstances de la famille.* Paris: Presses Universitaires de la France.

Lemmen, D.S., F.J. Warren, J. Lacroix, and E. Bush, eds. 2008. *From Impacts to Adaptation: Canada in a Changing Climate, 2007.* Ottawa: Government of Canada.

Lesthaeghe, Ronald. 1989. *Demographic Recruitment in Europe: An Exploration of Alternative Scenarios and Policies.* Interuniversity Papers in Demography Working Paper 1985-5. Brussels: Vrije Universiteit Brussels.

——. 1995. "The second demographic transition in western countries: An interpretation." In *Gender and Family Change in Industrialized Countries,* K. Oppenheim Mason and A-M. Jensen, eds. Oxford: Clarendon Press.

——. 2010. "The unfolding story of the second demographic transition." *Population and Development Review* 36(2): 211–51.

———, and Antonio Lopez-Gay. 2013. "Spatial continuities and discontinuities in two successive demographic transitions: Spain and Belgium, 1880–2010." *Demographic Research* 28: 77–136.

———, and Guy Moors. 2000. "Life course transitions and value orientations: Selection and adaptation." Interuniversity Papers in Demography, Working Paper No. 2000–7. Brussels: Vrije Universiteit Brussel.

———, and C. Vanderhoeft. 1997. "Ready, willing and able: A conceptualization of transitions to new behavioral forms." Interuniversity Papers in Demography, Working Paper No. 1997–8. Brussels: Vrije Universiteit Brussel.

Lewin, Roger. 2005. *Human Evolution: An Illustrated Introduction.* Malden, MA: Blackwell.

Li, Nam, and Zheng Wu. 2001. "The long term effects of immigrant fertility on the age structure of the population." Presented at the meetings of the Canadian Population Society, Quebec City, May.

Li, Peter. 1996. *The Making of Post-War Canada.* Toronto: Oxford University Press.

Liaw, Kao-Lee. 1986. *Review of Research on Interregional Migration in Canada.* Ottawa: Report for Health and Welfare Canada, Review of Demography.

Lichter, Daniel T. 2006. "Family structure and poverty." Pp. 342–46 in *Encyclopedia of Sociology*, ed. George Ritzer. Oxford: Blackwell.

Lieberson, Stanley, and Mary C. Waters. 1993. "The ethnic responses of whites: What causes their instability, simplification and inconsistency." *Social Forces* 72: 421–50.

Livi-Bacci, Massimo. 2000. "An additional person: Increasing or diminishing returns?" Presented at the meetings of the Population Association of America, Los Angeles, March.

———. 2012. *A Concise History of World Population*, Fifth Edition. Cambridge, UK: Blackwell.

Loh, S., and M.V. George. 2007. "Projected population and age structure for Canada and provinces: With and without international migration." *Canadian Studies in Population* 34: 103–27.

———, Verma, E. Ng, M.J. Norris, M.V. George, and J. Perreault. 1998. *Population Projections of Registered Indians, 1996–2021.* Working paper. Ottawa: Statistics Canada.

Long, David, and Olive Patricia Dickason, eds. 2011. *Visions of the Heart: Canadian Aboriginal Issues.* Don Mills, ON: Oxford University Press.

Lundstrom, Karin E., and Gunnar Andersson. 2012. "Labor-market status, migrant status and first childbearing in Sweden." *Demographic Research* 27: 719–42.

Luong, May. 2010. "The financial impact of student loans." *Perspectives on Labour and Income* 11: 5–18.

Lupri, Eugen, and James Frideres. 1981. "The quality of marriage and the passage of time: Marital satisfaction over the life cycle." *Canadian Journal of Sociology* 6: 283–306.

Lutz, Wolfgang, Brian C. O'Neill, and Sergei Scerbov. 2003. "Europe's population at a turning point." *Science* 299: 1991–92.

MacDonald, Michael. 2012. "Cod making a comeback in Newfoundland, research shows." *The Globe and Mail*, July 2.

MacDonald, N. 1939. *Canada, 1763–1841: Immigration and Settlement.* London: Longmans.

Malenfant, Éric Caron, André Lebel, and Laurent Martel. 2010. *Projections of the Diversity of the Canadian Population, 2006 to 2031.* Ottawa: Statistics Canada cat. no. 91-551-X.

———, and Jean-Dominique Morency. 2011. *Population Projections by Aboriginal Identity in Canada, 2006 to 2031.* Statistics Canada cat. no. 91-552-X.

Maloney, J.H., N. De Jong, and D. Boylan. 1973. "The first centuries." Pp. 1–36 in *Canada's Smallest Province: A History of Prince Edward Island.* W. Bolger, ed. Charlottetown: Prince Edward Island Centennial Commission.

Malthus, T.R. [1798] 1965. *An Essay on the Principle of Population as It Affects the Future Improvement of Society.* New York: Augustus Kelley.

Manpower and Immigration Canada. 1974. *Immigration Policy Perspectives.* Ottawa: Information Canada.

Manton, Kenneth G. 1987. "The population implications of breakthroughs in biomedical technologies for controlling mortality and fertility." Pp. 147–93 in *Technological Prospects and Population Trends*, T.J. Espenshade and G.T. Stolnitz, eds. Boulder, CO: Westview Press.

Manuel, D. G., and J. Hockin. 2000. "Recent trends in provincial life expectancy." *Canadian Journal of Public Health* 91(2): 118–19.

Manzoli, Lamberto, Paolo Villari, Giovanni M. Pirone, and Antonio Boccia. 2007. "Marital status and mortality in the elderly: A systematic review and meta-analysis." *Social Science and Medicine* 64(1): 77–94.

Marcil-Gratton, Nicole. 1988. *Les modes de vie nouveaux des adultes et leur impact sur les enfants au Canada.* Ottawa: Report for Health and Welfare Canada, Review of Demography.

Marmot, M. 2005. *Status Syndrome: How Your Social Standing Directly Affects Your Health and Life Expectancy.* London: Bloomsbury Publishing.

———, and R. Wilkinson. 2005. *Social Determinants of Health.* Don Mills, ON: Oxford University Press.

Marr, William L. 1987. "Canadian population policy: Some constraints and parameters." In *Contributions to Demography*. Edmonton: Population Research Laboratory, pp. 505–25.

Marsden, Lorna R. 1972. *Population Probe*. Toronto: Copp Clark.

Marshall, Katherine. 1996. "A job to die for." *Perspectives on Labour and Income* 8: 26–31.

———. 2006. "Converging gender roles." *Perspectives on Labour and Income* 18(3): 7–19.

———. 2008. "Fathers' use of paid parental leave." *Perspectives on Labour and Income*. Ottawa: Statistics Canada Cat No. 75-001-X (online edition).

———. 2010. "Employer top-ups." *Perspectives on Labour and Income* 11(2).

———. 2011. "Generational change in paid and unpaid work." *Canadian Social Trends* 92: 13–24.

Martel, Laurent. 2013. "Mortality overview." In *Report on the Demographic Situation in Canada*. Ottawa: Statistics Canada, cat. no. 91-209-X.

———, and Alain Bélanger. 1999. "An analysis of the change in dependence-free life expectancy in Canada between 1986 and 1996." Pp. 164–86 in *Report on the Demographic Situation in Canada 1998–1999*. Ottawa: Statistics Canada cat. no. 91–209.

———, Éric Caron Malenfant, Jean-Dominique Morency, André Lebel, Alain Bélanger, and Nicolas Bastien. 2011. "Projected trends to 2031 for the Canadian labour force." *Canadian Economic Observer* 24(12).

———, Martin Provost, André Lebel, Simon Coulombe and Adam Sherk. 2013. *Methods for Constructing Life Tables for Canada, Provinces and Territories*. Ottawa: Statistics Canada cat. no. 84-538-X.

Martin, Laetitia, and Feng Hou. 2010. "Sharing their lives: Women, marital trends and education." *Canadian Social Trends* 90: 68–72.

Marx, K. [1890] 1906. *Capital: A Critique of Political Economy*. Samuel Moore and Edward Aveling, trans. Frederick Engels, ed. New York: Modern Library.

Massey, Douglas, Joaquin Arango, Graeme Hugo, Ali Kouaouch, Adela Pellegrino, and J. Edward Taylor. 1994. "An evaluation of international migration theory: The North American case." *Population and Development Review* 20(4): 699–751.

Matthews, Beverly. 1999. "The gender system and fertility: An exploration of the hidden links." *Canadian Studies in Population* 26: 21–38.

———, and Roderic Beaujot. 1997. "Gender orientations and family strategies." *Canadian Review of Sociology and Anthropology* 34: 415–28.

Matthews, Deborah. 2006. "Can immigration compensate for below-replacement fertility? The consequences of the unbalanced settlement of immigrants in Canadian cities, 2001–2051. London, ON: Ph.D. dissertation, Faculty of Graduate Studies, University of Western Ontario.

———. 2012. *Ontario's Action Plan for Health Care*. Queens Park: Newsroom.

Matthews, Georges. 1988. "Le vieillissement démographique et son impact sur la situation des personnes âgées et les service qui leur sont offerts." Montreal: INRS-Urbanization.

Matysiak, Anna, Martha Styrc, and Daniele Vignoli. 2014. "The educational gradient in marital disruption: A meta-analysis of European research findings." *Population Studies* 68(2): 197–215.

Maynard, Donna, and Don Kerr. 2010. "British Columbia's longevity advantage." *Canadian Journal of Regional Science* 32(3): 361–76.

McDaniel, Susan A. 1986. *Canada's Aging Population*. Toronto: Butterworths

———. 2008a. "The conundrum of demographic aging and policy challenges: A comparative case study of Canada, Japan and Korea." Paper presented at the meetings of the Canadian Population Society, Vancouver, June.

———. 2008b. "Demographic ageing as a guiding paradigm in Canada's welfare state." In *Ageing: Key Issues for the 21st Century*, Susan A. McDaniel, ed. London: Sage, pp. 5–25.

———. 2009. "The conundrum of demographic aging and policy challenges: A comparative case study of Canada, Japan and Korea." *Canadian Studies in Population* 36: 37–62.

———, and Zachary Zimmer, eds. 2013. *Global Ageing in the Twenty-First Century: Challenges, Opportunities and Implications*. London: Ashgate.

McDonald, James, and Christopher Worswick. 1997. "Unemployment incidence of immigrant men in Canada." *Canadian Public Policy* 23: 353–73.

McDonald, Lynn, and Peter Donahue. 2000. "Poor health and retirement income: The Canadian case." *Aging and Society* 20: 493–522.

———, Peter Donahue, and Victor Marshall. 2000. "The economic consequences of unexpected early retirement." In *Independence and Economic Security in Old Age*, Frank Denton, Deborah Fretz, and Bryon Spencer, eds. Vancouver: University of British Columbia Press, pp. 101–30.

McDonald, Peter. 1997. "Gender equity, social institutions and the future of fertility." Working Papers in Demography No. 69. Canberra: Australian National University, Research School of Social Science.

———. 2000. "Gender equality in theories of fertility." *Population and Development Review* 26: 427–39.

——. 2002. "Low fertility: Unifying the theory and the demography." Presented at the meetings of the Population Association of America, May, Atlanta.

——. 2006. "Low fertility and the state: The efficacy of policy." *Population and Development Review* 32(3): 485–510.

——, and R. Kippen. 2001. "Labour supply prospects in 16 developed countries, 2000–2050." *Population and Development Review* 27(1), 1–32.

McDougall, Barbara. 1990. "Speech to Opinion Forum on immigration," Toronto, 15 February.

McInnis, E. 1969. *Canada: A Social and Political History.* Toronto: Holt, Rinehart and Winston.

McInnis, R. Marvin. 1980. "A functional view of Canadian immigration." Presented at the annual meetings of the Population Association of America, Denver, April.

——. 2000a. "The population of Canada in the nineteenth century." In *A Population History of North America,* M.R. Haines and R.H. Steckel, eds. Cambridge, UK: Cambridge University Press, pp. 371–432.

——. 2000b. "Canada's population in the twentieth century." In *A Population History of North America,* M.R. Haines and R.H. Steckel, eds. Cambridge, UK: Cambridge University Press, pp. 529–99.

McKeown, K., R.G. Brown, and R.G. Record. 1972. "An interpretation of the modern rise of population in Europe." *Population Studies* 26: 345–82.

McLanahan, S. 2004. "Diverging destinies: How children are faring under the second demographic transition." *Demography* 41(4): 607–27.

McLaren, Angus, and Arlene Tiger McLaren. 1986. *The Bedroom and the State: The Changing Practices and Politics of Contraception and Abortion in Canada, 1880–1980.* Toronto: Oxford University Press.

McNeill, William. 1984. "Human migration in historical perspective." *Population and Development Review* 10: 1–18.

McNicoll, Geoffrey. 1986. "Economic growth with below-replacement fertility." *Population and Development Review* 12 (suppl.): 217–37.

——. 1995. "Institutional impediments to population policy in Australia." *Journal of the Australian Population Association* 12: 97–112.

McQuillan, Kevin. 2011. *All the Workers We Need: Debunking Canada's Labour Shortage Fallacy.* Calgary: School of Public Policy Research Paper 16.

——. 2013. "All the workers we need: Debunking Canada's labour shortage fallacy." The School of Public Policy, SPP Research Series (www.policyschool.ucalgary.ca).

McSkimmings, Judie. 1990. "The farm community." *Canadian Social Trends* 16: 20–3.

McVey, W., and W. Kalbach 1995. *Canadian Population.* Don Mills, ON: Nelson Canada.

Meadows, Donella, H. Gary Meadows, Jorgen Randers, and William W. Behrens. 1972. *The Limits to Growth.* New York: Universe Books.

Meek, Ronald L., ed. 1971. *Marx and Engels on the Population Bomb: Selections from the Writings of Marx and Engels Dealing with the Theories of Thomas Robert Malthus,* Dorothea L. Meek and Ronald L. Meek, trans. Berkeley, CA: Ramparts Press.

Mellon, Hugh, and Don Kerr. 2012. "The Fair Representation Act of 2012 fully explained." *Journal of Parliamentary and Political Law* 6: 545–55.

Ménard, Jean-Claude. 2009. Statement on 3 November addressed to Parliament. Office of the Chief Actuary, Office of the Superintendent of Financial Institutions Canada at the Status of Women Committee. Ottawa: Government of Canada.

Mercenier, J., M. Mérette, and M. Fougère. 2005. *Population Ageing in Canada: A Sectoral and Occupational Analysis.* Skills Research Initiative Working Paper No. 2005 A06.

Mercredi, Ovide. 1997. "Written transcript of conversation, subject: Royal Commission on Aboriginal Peoples." National Press Theatre, 30 April.

Meuvret, J. 1965. "Demographic crisis in France from the sixteenth to the eighteenth century." In *Population in History,* eds. D. Glass and D. Eversley. London: Edward Arnold.

Michalowski, Margaret. 2013. "2011 National Household Survey: Estimates' coverage and quality." Paper presented at the Canadian Population Society Meetings, University of Victoria, June.

——, and Kelly Tran. 2008. "Canadians abroad." *Canadian Social Trends* 18: 31–8.

Michaud, Jean-François, M.V. George, and S. Loh. 1996. *Projections of Persons with Disabilities.* Ottawa: Statistics Canada cat. no. 91-538.

Michaud, Sylvie. 2014. "2011 National Household Survey: Design and quality." Presented at Meetings of the centre interuniversitaire québécois de statistiques sociales, Montreal.

Mikkonen, J., and D. Raphael. 2010. *Social Determinants of Health: The Canadian Facts.* Downsview, ON: York University School of Health Policy and Management.

Milan, Anne. 2011a. "Migration: International, 2009." In *Report on the Demographic Situation in Canada.* Ottawa: Statistics Canada cat. no. 91-209-X.

——. 2011b. "Mortality: Causes of death." In *Report on the Demographic Situation.* Ottawa: Statistics Canada cat. no. 91-209-X.

———. 2013a. "Fertility: Overview, 2009 to 2011." *Report on the Demographic Situation in Canada*. Ottawa: Statistics Canada cat. no. 91-209-X.

———. 2013b. "Marital status: Overview, 2011." In *Report on the Demographic Situation in Canada*. Ottawa: Statistics Canada, cat. no. 91-209-X.

———, and Nora Bohnert, 2012. "Fifty years of families in Canada: 1961 to 2011." *Families, Households and Marital Status, 2011 Census of Population*. Ottawa: Statistics Canada, cat. no. 98-312-X2011003.

Millar, Wayne J., and John M. Last. 1988. "Motor vehicle traffic accident mortality in Canada, 1921–1984." *American Journal of Preventative Medicine* 4: 220–30.

———, and Thomas Stephens. 1992. "Social Status and Health Risks in Canadian Adults: 1985 and 1991." *Health Reports* 5: 143–56.

Milligan, Kevin. 2008. *Canadian Tax and Credit Simulator: CtaCS, User Guide, Version 2008-1*. Vancouver: University of British Columbia, Department of Economics.

Mintz, S. 2012. "Childbirth in early America." *Digital History*. Retrieved 15 May.

MKJA. 2005. *National Circumstances Affecting Canada's Greenhouse Gas Emissions: Technical Report*. Vancouver: MK Jaccard and Associates.

Mooney, J. 1928. *The Aboriginal Population of America North of Mexico*. Washington, DC: Smithsonian Miscellaneous Collections 80: 1–40.

Moore, Stephen, and Julian Simon. 2000. *Its Getting Better All the Time*. Washington, DC: The Cato Institute.

Moreau, Claudia, Hélène Vézina, Vania Yotova, Robert Hamon, Peter de Knijff, Daniel Sinnett, and Damian Labuda. 2009. "Genetic heterogeneity in regional populations of Quebec: parental lineages in the Gaspé Peninsula." *American Journal of Physical Anthropology* 139(4): 512–22.

Morency, Jean-Dominique, and Benoît Laplante. 2010. "L'action publique et la première naissance au Canada." *Cahiers québécois de démographie* 39(2): 201–41.

Morgan, S. Philip. 2003. "Is low fertility a twenty-first-century demographic crisis?" *Demography* 40(4): 589–603.

Morissette, René. 1998. "The declining labour market status of young men." In *Labour Markets, Social Institutions and the Future of Canada's Children*. Miles Corak, ed. Statistics Canada cat. no. 89-553-XPB, pp. 31–50.

———. 2008. "Earnings in the last decade." *Perspectives on Labour and Income* 20(1): 57–69.

———, and Marc Frenette. 2014. *Wages and Full-Time Employment Rates of Young High School Graduates and Bachelor Degree Holders, 1997 to 2012*. Analytical Studies Branch Research Paper Series 2014360e. Ottawa: Statistics Canada.

———, and Yuri Ostrovsky. 2007. "Pensions and retirement savings of families." *Perspectives on Labour and Income* 8: 5–18.

———, and Garnett Picot. 2005. *Low-Paid Work and Economically Vulnerable Families Over the Last Two Decades*. Analytical Studies Branch Research Paper Series no. 248. Ottawa: Statistics Canada.

———, Xuelin Zhang, and Marie Drolet. 2002. "Are families getting richer?" *Canadian Social Trends* 66: 15–19.

Morrison, W. 1984. *Under One Flag: Canadian Sovereignty and the Native Peoples of Northern Canada*. Ottawa: Treaties and Historical Research Centre.

Moseley, Christopher, ed. 2010. *Atlas of the World's Languages in Danger. Memory of Peoples*, 3rd ed. Paris: UNESCO Publishing.

Moseley, W.G., and E. Jerme. 2010. "Desertification." Pp. 715–19 in *Encyclopedia of Geography*, B. Warf, ed. Thousand Oaks, CA: Sage Publications.

Muckle, R.J. 2007. *The First Nations of British Columbia*. 2nd ed. Vancouver: University of British Columbia Press.

Muhsam, Helmut V. 1979. "The demographic transition: From wastage to conservation of human life." In *Population Science in the Service of Mankind*. Liège, Belgium: Ordina, pp. 143–63.

Mulcair, Thomas. 2012. "NDP government would restore retirement age to 65." Interview on CTV News, 26 October.

Munro, Anne, Alessandro Alasia, and Ray D. Bollman. 2011. "Self-contained labour areas: A proposed delineation and classification by degree of rurality." *Rural and Small Town Canada Analysis Bulletin* 8(8). Ottawa: Statistics Canada.

Muntaner, Carles, Paul Sorlie, Patricia O'Campo, Norman Johnson, Eric Backlund. 2001. "Occupational hierarchy, economic sector, and mortality from cardiovascular disease among men and women: Findings from the National Longitudinal Mortality Study." *Annals of Epidemiology* 11(3): 194–201.

Murphy, Brian, Paul Roberts, and Michael Wolfson. 2007. "High-income Canadians." *Perspectives on Labour and Income* 8(9).

———, X. Zhang, and C. Dionne. 2012. *Low Income in Canada: a Multi-line and Multi-index Perspective*. Income Research Paper Series. Ottawa: Statistics Canada cat. no. 75F0002M.

Myers, Ransom. 2003. "A note on unsustainable fisheries." Report and Documentation of the International Workshop on Factors of Unsustainability and Overexploitation in Fisheries. Bangkok, Thailand, 4–8 February 2002.

Myles, John. 2000. "The maturation of Canada's retirement income system: Income levels, income inequality and low-income among the elderly." Research Paper Series, no. 147. Ottawa: Statistics Canada.

———. 2010. "The inequality surge." *Inroads: The Canadian Journal of Opinion* 26: 66–73.

———, and Garnett Picot. 1993. "Does post-industrialism matter? The Canadian experience." In *Changing Classes*, G. Esping-Anderson, ed. Newbury Park, CA: Sage Publishers, pp. 171–94.

———, Feng Hou, Garnett Picot, and Karen Myers. 2007. "Employment and earnings among lone mothers during the 1980s and 1990s." *Canadian Public Policy* 33(2): 147–72.

———, and Paul Pierson. 2001. "The comparative political economy of pension reform." Pp. 305–33 in *The New Politics of the Welfare State*, Paul Pierson, ed. Oxford, UK: Oxford University Press.

Myrskyla, Mikko, Joshua R. Goldstein, and Yen-hsin Alice Cheng. 2013. "New cohort fertility forecasts for the developed world: Rises, falls, and reversals." *Population and Development Review* 39: 31–56.

Nabalamba, A., and W.J. Millar. 2007. "Going to the doctor." *Health Reports* 18(1): 23–35.

Nadeau, Serge. 2011. "The economic contribution of immigration in Canada—Recent developments. What do we know? What does it mean for policy?" Research Group on the Economics of Immigration. Ottawa: University of Ottawa.

Nagnur, Dhruva. 1986. *Longevity and Historical Life Tables.* Ottawa: Statistics Canada cat. no. 89-506.

Nam, Charles. 1994. *Understanding Population Change.* Itasca, MN: F.E. Peacock.

Nash, Alan. 1989. "International refugee pressures and Canadian public policy response." Discussion Paper 89.B.1. Ottawa: Institute for Research on Public Policy.

Nathanson, Constance, and Alan Lopez. 1987. "The future of sex mortality differentials in industrialized countries: A structural hypothesis." *Population Research and Policy Review* 6: 123–36.

National Center for Health Statistics. 2014. *Health, United States, 2013: With Special Feature on Prescription Drugs.* Hyattsville, MD. Library of Congress cat. no. 76–641496.

National Council of Welfare. 2012. *A Snapshot of Racialized Poverty in Canada.* Poverty Profile: Special Edition. Ottawa: National Council of Welfare.

National Energy Board. 2006. *Canada's Oil Sands, Opportunities and Challenges to 2015: An Update.* Ottawa: National Energy Board cat. no. NE23-116/2006E.

Natural Resources Canada. 2010. *Energy Efficiency Trends in Canada.* Ottawa: Natural Resources Canada, Office of Energy Efficiency.

Nault, François. 1997. "Narrowing mortality gaps, 1978 to 1995." *Health Reports* 9: 35–41.

———, J. Chen, M.V. George, and M.J. Norris. 1993. *Population Projections of Registered Indians, 1991–2016.* Ottawa: Statistics Canada.

———, and Alain Bélanger. 1996. *The Decline of Marriage in Canada, 1981 to 1991.* Ottawa: Statistics Canada cat. no. 84-536.

———, Roger Roberge, and Jean-Marie Berthelot. 1997. "Ésperance de vie et espérance de vie en santé selon le sexe, l'état matrimonial et le statut socio-économique au Canada." *Cahiers québecois de démographie* 25: 241–59.

Navaneelan, Tanya. 2012. "Suicide rates: An overview." In *Health at a Glance.* Ottawa: Statistics Canada, pp. 3–11.

Needleman, Lionel. 1986. "Canadian fertility trends in perspective." *Journal of Biosocial Science* 18: 43–56.

Never, Gerda. 2008. "Moving toward gender equality." Paper presented at the Conference on How Generations and Gender Shape Demographic Change: Toward Policies Based on Better Knowledge. Geneva: UNECE, 14–16 May.

Nevitte, Neil. 1996. *The Decline of Deference.* Peterborough, ON: Broadview Press.

Newacheck, Paul W., and A.E. Benjamin. 2004. "Intergenerational equity and public spending." *Health Affairs* 23: 142–46.

Newbold, K. Bruce. 1996. "The ghettoization of Quebec: Interprovincial migration and its demographic effects." *Canadian Studies in Population* 23: 1–21.

Ng, Edward. 2011. *Insights into the Healthy Immigrant Effect: Mortality by Period of Immigration and Birthplace.* Health Research Working Paper Series no. 82-622-X No.008. Health Analysis Division. Ottawa: Statistics Canada.

———, and François Nault. 1996. "Census based estimates of fertility by mother's socio-economic characteristics in Canada, 1991." Presented to the Canadian Population Society meetings, St Catharines, ON, June.

Ni Bhrolchain, Maire. 1993. "Women's and men's life strategies in developed societies." Presented at meetings of the International Union for the Scientific Study of Population, Montreal, August.

Nolan, Stephen. 2007. *Leaving Newfoundland: A History of Out-Migration.* St John's, NL: Flanker Press.

Norman, Ross M.G. 1986. "The nature and correlates of health behaviour." *Health Promotion Studies,* Series No. 2. Ottawa: Health and Welfare Canada.

Norris, Mary Jane. 2000. "Contemporary demography of Aboriginal peoples in Canada." In *Visions of the Heart:*

Canadian Aboriginal Issues, David Long and Olive Patricia Dickason, eds. Toronto: Harcourt Canada.

———. 2011. "Aboriginal languages in Canada: Generational perspectives on language maintenance, loss, and revitalization." In *Visions of the Heart: Canadian Aboriginal Issues*, 3rd edition, David Long and Olive Patricia Dickason, eds. Toronto: Oxford University Press, pp. 113–45.

———, Don Kerr, and François Nault. 1995. *Technical Report on Projections of the Population with Aboriginal Identity, Canada, 1991–2016*. Report prepared by the Population Projections Section, Demography Division, Statistics Canada, for the Royal Commission on Aboriginal Peoples. Ottawa: Statistics Canada.

Odynak, Dave. 1994. "Age at first intercourse in Canada." *Canadian Studies in Population* 21: 51–70.

OECD (Organisation for Economic Co-operation and Development). 2001a. "Fiscal implications of aging: Projections of age-related spending." Pp. 145–67 in *OECD Economic Output 69*. Paris: OECD.

———. 2001b. *Reforms for an Ageing Society: Social Issues*. Paris: OECD.

———. 2006. *Live Longer, Work Longer: A Synthesis Report*. Paris: OECD.

———. 2010. *Factbook: Economic, Environmental and Social Statistics*. Paris: OECD.

———. 2011. *Doing Better for Families*. Paris: OECD.

———. 2013. *Education at a Glance, 2013: OECD Indicators*. Paris: OECD.

———. 2014a. "Population and migration, international migration, immigrant and foreign population." In *Factbook 2014: Economic, Environmental and Social Statistics*. Paris: OECD.

———. 2014b. *Economic Surveys: Canada*. Paris: OECD.

Oeppen, Jim, and James Vaupel. 2002. "Demography: Broken limits to life expectancy." *Science* 296: 1029–31.

———, and James Vaupel. 2004. "The linear rise in the number of our days." In *Perspectives on Mortality Forecasting: the Linear Rise in Life Expectancy: History and Prospects*, T. Bengtsson, ed. Stockholm: Swedish Social Insurance Agency, pp. 9–18.

Office of the Chief Actuary of Canada. 2010. *25th Actuarial Report on the CPP as at 31 December 2009*. Ottawa: Minister of Public Works and Government Services cat. no. IN3-16-1-2010.

———. 2011. *Mortality Projections of the 25th CPP Actuarial Report*. Presented at the 2011 Annual Meeting of the Canadian Institute of Actuaries, Ottawa.

———. 2012. *Actuarial Reports on the CPP and OAS Programs*. Ottawa: Office of the Superintendent of Financial Institutions.

Office of the Privacy Commissioner of Canada. 2011. *Annual Report to Parliament 2010–2011—Report on the Privacy Act*. Gatineau: Government of Canada.

Okonny-Myers, Ima. 2010. *The Interprovincial Mobility of Immigrants in Canada*. Research and Evaluation: Citizenship and Immigration Canada. Ottawa: CIC.

Olah, Livia. 2003. "Gendering fertility: Second births in Sweden and Hungary." *Population Research and Policy Review* 22: 171–200.

Olshansky, S.J., and B. Ault. 1986. "The fourth state of the epidemiological transition." *Milbank Quarterly* 64: 355–91.

———, D. Goldman, Y. Zheng, and J.W. Rowe. 2009. "Aging in America in the twenty-first century: Demographic forecasts from the MacArthur Research Network on an aging society." *The Milbank Quarterly* 87(4): 842–62.

———, D. Passaro, R. Hershow, J. Layden, B.A. Carnes, J. Brody, L. Hayflick, R.N. Butler, D.B. Allison, and D.S. Ludwig. 2005. "A Possible decline in life expectancy in the United States in the 21st century." *New England Journal of Medicine* 352: 1103–10.

Olson, Sherry, and Patricia Thornton. 2011. *Peopling the North American City: Montreal 1840–1900*. Montreal and Kingston: McGill-Queen's University Press.

Omran, A. 1971. "The epidemiological transition: A theory of the epidemiology of population change." *Milbank Memorial Fund Quarterly* 49: 509–38.

Ontario Hospital Association. 2010. *Ideas and Opportunities for Bending the Health Care Cost Curve*. Toronto: Ontario Hospital Association (in collaboration with the Ontario Association of Community Care Access Centres and the Ontario Federation of Community Mental Health and Addiction Programs).

Ontario Ministry of Finance. 2010. *Ontario's Long-Term Report on the Economy*. Toronto: Queen's Printer for Ontario.

Oppenheimer, Valerie K. 1987. "A theory of marriage timing: Assortive mating under varying degrees of uncertainty." Unpublished manuscript.

———. 1988. "A theory of marriage timing." *American Journal of Sociology* 94(3): 563–91.

Orpana, H., J-M Berthelot, M. Kaplan, D. Feeny, B. McFarland, and N. Ross. 2010. "BMI and mortality: results from a national longitudinal study of Canadian adults." *Obesity* 18: 214–18.

Osberg, Lars. 1988. *Is It Retirement or Unemployment? The Constrained Labour Supply of Older Canadians*. Ottawa: Report for Health and Welfare Canada, Review of Demography, Health and Welfare.

Ostrom, E. 1990. *Governing the Commons: The Evolution of Institutions for Collective Action.* Cambridge, UK: Cambridge University Press.

Ostrovsky, Yuri, Feng Hou, and Garnett Picot. 2008. *Internal Migration of Immigrants: Do Immigrants Respond to Regional Labour Demand Shocks?* Analytical Studies Branch Research Paper Series. Ottawa: Statistics Canada cat. no. 11F0019M - No. 318.

Pacaut, Philippe. 2010. "Les ajustements de la vie professionnelle des Canadiennes en fonction de leur vie familiale." Ph.D. thesis, INRS and Université de Montréal.

———, Céline Le Bourdais, and Benoît Laplante. 2007. "Dynamiques et déterminants de la participation des femmes au marché du travail après la naissance d'un enfant au Canada." *Cahiers québécois de démographie* 36(2): 249–79.

Pailhé, Ariane. 2008. "Walking the tightrope of career and family." Paper presented at the Conference on How Generations and Gender Shape Demographic Change: Toward Policies Based on Better Knowledge, UNECE. Geneva. 14–16 May.

———, and Anne Solaz. 2012. "The influence of employment uncertainty on childbearing in France: A tempo or quantum effect?" *Demographic Research* 26: 1–40.

Pal, Leslie. 2013. *Beyond Policy Analysis: Public Issue Management in Turbulent Times.* Scarborough, ON: Nelson Canada.

Palameta, Boris. 2004. "Low income among immigrants and visible minorities." *Perspectives on Labour and Income* 5(4).

———. 2007. "Economic integration of immigrants' children." *Perspectives on Labour and Income* 8(10): 5–16.

Park, Robert, and Ernest W. Burgess. 1925. *The City.* Chicago: University of Chicago Press.

Passel, Jeffrey. 1997. "The growing American Indian population, 1960–1990: Beyond demography." *Population Research and Policy Review* 16: 11–31.

Paterson, Stephanie, Karine Levasseur and Tatyana Teplova. 2004. "I spy with my little eye: Canada's child policy framework." In *How Ottawa Spends, 2004–2005: Mandate Change and Continuity in the Paul Martin Era*, Bruce Doern, ed. Montreal and Kingston: McGill-Queen's University Press, pp. 131–50.

Pati, S., R. Keren, E.A. Alessandrini, and D.F. Schwarz. 2004. "Generational differences in public spending, 1980–2000." *Health Affairs* 23: 131–42.

Pelletier, F., J. Légaré, and R. Bourbeau. 1997. "Mortality in Quebec during the nineteenth century: From the state to the cities." *Population Studies* 51: 93–103.

Pendakur, Krishna, and Ravi Pendakur. 2011. "Colour by numbers: Minority earnings in Canada, 1995–2005." *Journal of International Migration and Integration* 12: 305–29.

Penney, Christopher. 2013. "Aboriginal data as a result of changes to the 2011 Census of population." Strategic Research Directorate with the collaboration of Statistics Canada and the Statistics and Measurement Directorate of AANDC.

Pérez, Claudio. 2002. "Health status and health behaviour among immigrants." *Health Reports* 13 (supplement): 89–100.

Péron, Hélène Desrosiers, Heather Juby, Evelyne Lapierre-Adamcyk, Céline Le Bourdais, Nicole Marcil-Gratton, and Jael Mongeau. 1999. *Canadian Families at the Approach of the Year 2000.* Ottawa: Statistics Canada cat. no. 96-321, no. 4.

———, E. Lapierre-Adamcyk, and Denis Morissette. 1987. "Les répercussions des nouveaux comportements démographiques sur la vie familiale: La situation canadienne." *International Review of Community Development* 18: 57–66.

———, and Jacques Légaré. 1988. "L'histoire matrimoniale et parentale des générations atteignant le seuil de la vieillesse d'ici l'an 2000." Ottawa: Report for Health and Welfare Canada, Review of Demography.

Péron, Yves. 1999. "L'Évolution des familles de recensement de 1971 à 1991." Pp. 74–101 in Y. Péron et al., eds., *Les familles canadiennes à l'approche de l'an 2000.* Ottawa.

———, Hélène Desrosiers, Heather Juby, Evelyne Lapierrre-Adamcyk, Céline Le Bourdais, Nicole Marcil-Gratton, and Jael Mongeau. 1999. *Canadian Families at the Approach of the Year 2000.* Ottawa: Statistics Canada cat. no. 96-321, no. 4.

———, and Claude Strohmenger. 1985. *Demographic and Health Indicators.* Ottawa: Statistics Canada cat. no. 82-543.

Peters, Paul A. 2013. "An age and cause decomposition of differences in life expectancy between residents of Inuit Nunangat and residents of the rest of Canada, 1989 to 2008." *Health Reports* 24: 3–9.

Pew Research Center. 2010. *The Decline of Marriage and Rise of New Families.* A Social & Demographic Trends Report. Pew Research Center.

Picker, Les. 2013. *The Effects of Education on Health.* National Bureau of Economic Research. Retrieved from www.nber.org/digest/mar07/w12352.html.

Picot, Garnett, and Feng Hou. 2010. "Seeking success in Canada and the United States, labour market outcomes among the children of immigrants." Pp. 79–114 in *Equal Opportunities? The Labour Market Integration of the*

Children of Immigrants. Paris: Organization for Economic Cooperation and Development.

——, and Feng Hou. 2011. *Seeking Success in Canada and the United States: The Determinants of Labour Market Outcomes among the Children of Immigrants.* Analytical Studies Branch Research Paper Series. Ottawa: Statistics Canada.

——, Feng Hou, and Simon Coulombe. 2007. *Chronic Low Income and Low-Income Dynamics among Recent Immigrants.* Business and Labour Market Analysis Division. Analytical Studies Branch Research Paper Series, No. 294. Ottawa: Statistics Canada.

——, Feng Hou, and Simon Coulombe. 2008. "Poverty dynamics among recent immigrants to Canada." *International Migration Review* 42: 393–424.

———, Yuqian Lu, and Feng Hou. 2009. "Immigrant low-income rates: The role of market income and government transfers." *Perspectives on Labour and Income* 13: 13–27.

——, John Myles, and Wendy Pyper. 1998. "Markets, families and social transfers: Trends in low income among the young and old, 1973–1993." In *Labour Markets, Social Institutions and the Future of Canada's Children,* 3rd Edition, pp. 11–30.

——, and Arthur Sweetman. 2012. *Making It in Canada: Immigration Outcomes and Policies.* IRPP Study No. 29. Montreal: Institute for Research on Public Policy.

Pike, Robert. 1988. "Education and the schools." In *Understanding Canadian Society,* J. Curtis and L. Tepperman, eds. Toronto: McGraw-Hill.

Pimm, S.L., G.J. Russell, J.L. Gittleman, and T.M. Brooks. 1995. "The future of biodiversity." *Science* 269: 347–50.

Pinnelli, A., 2001. "Les déterminants de la fécondité en Europe: Nouvelles formes de familles, facteurs contextuels et individuels." In *Fécondité et nouveaux types de ménages et de formation de la famille en Europe.* A. Pinnelli, H. Hoffomann-Nowtny, and F. Beat. Strasbourg, eds. Conseil de l'Europe, Etudes démographiques, vol. 35.

Polèse, Mario. 1987. "Patterns of regional economic development in Canada: Long-term trends and issues." In *Still Living Together,* W.J. Coffey and M. Polèse, eds. Ottawa: Institute for Research on Public Policy, pp. 13–32.

Policy Research Initiative. 2007. "Population at 2017." *Horizons* 9(4).

Pollard, John H. 1979. "Factors affecting mortality and the length of life." In *Population Science in the Service of Mankind.* Liège, Belgium: Ordina, pp. 53–80.

Ponting, Rick. 1997. *First Nations in Canada: Perspectives on Opportunity, Empowerment and Self-Determination.* Toronto: McGraw-Hill.

Population Reference Bureau (PRB). 2011. *Population Handbook.* Washington, DC: Population Reference Bureau.

——. 2014. *World Population Data Sheet.* Washington, DC: Population Reference Bureau.

Portes, Alejandro, and Min Zhou. 1993. "The new second generation: Segmented assimilation and its variants." *Annals of the American Academy of Political and Social Sciences* 530: 74–96.

Prescott-Allan, Robert. 2001. *Well Being of Nations: A Country by Country Index of Quality of Life and the Environment.* Co-published by Canada's International Development Research Centre (IDRC) and Island Press, with the support of the World Conservation Union (IUCN) and the International Institute for Environment and Development (IIED).

Preston, Samuel H. 1984. "Children and the elderly: Divergent paths for America's dependents." *Demography* 21: 435–58.

—— 1986. "Changing values and falling birth rates." *Population and Development Review* 12 (Suppl.): 176–95.

——, and Michael R. Haines. 1991. *Fatal Years: Child Mortality in Late Nineteenth-Century America.* Princeton, NJ: Princeton University Press.

——, Christine Himes, and Mitchell Eggers. 1989. "Demographic conditions responsible for population aging." *Demography* 26: 691–709.

——, and E. Van de Walle. 1978. "Urban French mortality in the nineteenth century." *Population Studies* 32: 275–97.

Public Health Agency of Canada. 2013. *Health-Adjusted Life Expectancy (HALE) in 2012.* Ottawa: PHAC.

Purr, Allan, Livia Olah, Mariam Tazi-Preve, and Jorgen Dorbritz. 2009. "Men's childbearing desires and views of the male role in Europe at the dawn of the 21st century." *Demographic Research.* Online journal available at demographic-research.org.

Pyper, Wendy. 2008. "RRSP investments." *Perspectives on Labour and Income* 9: 5–11.

——, and Philip Giles. 2002. "Approaching retirement." *Perspectives on Labour and Income* 14: 9–16.

Radke, Doug. 2006. *The Radke Report: Investing in Our Future: Responding to the Rapid Growth of Oil Sands Development, Final Report.* Edmonton: Government of Alberta.

Ram, Bali. 2004. "New estimates of Aboriginal fertility, 1966–1971 to 1996–2001." *Canadian Studies in Population* 31: 179–96.

——, and Y. Edward Shin. 1999. "Internal migration of immigrants." In *Immigrant Canada: Demographic, Economic, and Social Challenges,* Shiva Halli and Leo Driedger, eds. Toronto: University of Toronto Press, pp. 148–62.

Ramage-Morin, Pamela L. 2008. "Motor vehicle accident deaths." *Health Reports* 19(3): 1–7.

———, Margot Shields, and Laurent Martel. 2010. "Health-promoting factors and good health among Canadians in mid- to late life." *Health Reports* 21 (3): 1–9.

Ranson, Gillian. 1998. "Education, work and family decision making: Finding the 'right time' to have a baby." *Canadian Review of Sociology and Anthropology* 35: 517–33.

Rao, G. Lakshmana, Anthony H. Richmond, and Jerzy Zubrzycki. 1984. "Immigrants in Canada and Australia." In *Demographic Aspects and Education*, vol. 1. Downsview, ON: York University, Institute for Behavioural Research.

Raphael, D. 2009. *Social Determinants of Health: Canadian Perspectives*. Toronto: Canadian Scholars' Press.

Ravanera, Zenaida. 1995. "A portrait of the family life of young adults." In *Family over the Life Course*, R. Beaujot, Ellen M. Gee, Fernando Rajulton, and Zenaida R. Ravanera, eds. Ottawa: Statistics Canada, cat. no. 91-543, pp. 7–35.

———, and Roderic Beaujot. 2010. "Childlessness and socio-economic characteristics: What does the Canadian 2006 General Social Survey tell us?" Paper presented at the meetings of the Canadian Sociological Association, Montreal, June.

———, Roderic Beaujot and Jianye Liu. 2009. "Models of earning and caring: Determinants of the division of work." *Canadian Review of Sociology* 46(4): 319–37.

———, and Fernando Rajulton. 1996. "Stability and crisis in the family life course: Findings from the 1990 General Social Survey, Canada." *Canadian Studies in Population* 23: 165–84.

———, and Fernando Rajulton. 2007. "Changes in economic status and timing of marriage of young Canadians." *Canadian Studies in Population* 34(1): 49–67.

———, Fernando Rajulton, and Thomas Burch. 1998a. "Trends and variations in the early life courses of Canadian men." Discussion Paper no. 98-7. London, ON: University of Western Ontario, Population Centre.

———, Fernando Rajulton, and Thomas Burch. 1998b. "Early life transitions of Canadian women: A cohort analysis of timing, sequences, and variations." *European Journal of Population* 14: 179–204.

Raymond, Mélanie. 2008. *High School Dropouts Returning to School*. Culture, Tourism and the Centre for Education Statistics Research Papers. Ottawa: Statistics Canada.

Rees, William E. 1992. "Ecological footprints and appropriated carrying capacity: What urban economics leaves out." *Environment and Urbanization* 4(2):121–30.

———. 2007. "Eco-footprint analysis: Tracking (un)sustainability." Paper presented at the Workshop on Demographics and the Environment, Policy Research Initiative, Ottawa, March.

———. 2008. "Science, cognition and public policy." *Academic Matters*. 9–12 April.

———. 2013. "Ecofootnotes." See http://williamrees.org.

Reitz, Jeffrey. 2001. "Immigrant success in the knowledge economy: Institutional change and the immigrant experience in Canada, 1970–1995." *Journal of Social Issues*, 57(3): 579–613.

———. 2011. *Pro-immigration Canada: Social and Economic Roots of Popular Views*. Research Study 20. Montreal: Institute for Research on Public Policy.

———, Heather Zhang, and Naoko Hawkins. 2011. "Comparisons of the success of racial minority immigrant offspring in the United States, Canada and Australia." *Social Science Research* 40: 1051–66.

Review of Demography and Its Implications for Economic and Social Policy. 1989. *Charting Canada's Future*. Ottawa: Health and Welfare Canada.

Richards, John. 2010. "Reducing lone-parent poverty." *C.D. Howe Institute Commentary* no. 305 (www.cdhowe.org).

Richmond, Anthony H. 1988. *Immigration and Ethnic Conflict*. New York: St Martin's Press.

———. 1989. "Immigrants in multicultural Canada." Unpublished manuscript.

———, and Warren Kalbach. 1980. *Factors in the Adjustment of Immigrants and their Descendants*. Ottawa: Statistics Canada cat. no. 99-761E.

Riley, J. 1989. *Sickness, Recovery and Death: A History and Forecast of Ill Health*. Iowa City, IA: Macmillan and University of Iowa Press.

Rindfuss, Ronald, and Audrey VandenHeuvel. 1990. "Cohabitation: Precursor to marriage or an alternative to being single." *Population and Development Review* 16: 703–26.

Robbins, Paul, John Hintz, and Sarah A. Moore. 2014. *Environment and Society: A Critical Introduction*. Oxford, UK: Wiley Blackwell.

Roberts, K.C., M. Shields, M.D. Groh, A. Aziz, J.A. Gilbert. "Overweight and obesity in children and adolescents: Results from the 2009 to 2011 Canadian Health Measures Survey." *Health Reports* 23, 3: 1–5.

Robitaille, N., and R. Choinière. 1985. *An Overview of Demographic and Socioeconomic Conditions of the Inuit in Canada*. Ottawa: Department of Indian and Northern Affairs.

Rogers, A. 1980. "Introduction to multistate mathematical demography." *Environment and Planning* A12, pp. 489–98.

Rogers, Richard G. and Robert Hackenberg. 1987. "Extending Epidemiologic Transition Theory." *Social Biology* 34: 234–43.

Romaniuc, Anatole. 1981. "Increase in natural fertility during the early stages of modernization: Canadian Indian case study." *Demography* 18: 157–72.

———. 1984. *Fertility in Canada: From Baby-Boom to Baby-Bust.* Ottawa: Statistics Canada cat. no. 91-524.

———. 2000. "Aboriginal population of Canada: Growth dynamics under conditions of encounter of civilizations." *The Canadian Journal of Native Studies* 20: 95–137.

Romanow, Roy. 2002. *Building on Values: The Future of Health Care in Canada.* Final report of the Royal Commission on the Future of Health Care in Canada. Ottawa: Canadian Government Publishing.

Ronsen, Marit. 2001. "Fertility and family policy in Norway: Is there a connection?" Presented at the International Union for the Scientific Study of Population Conference—International Perspectives on Low Fertility: Trends, Theories and Policies, Tokyo, March.

Roos, Noralou P., Patrick Montgomery, and Leslie L. Roos. 1987. "Health care utilization in years prior to death." *Milbank Quarterly* 65: 231–54.

Rose, R. 2010. La politique familiale au Québec: La recherche d'un équilibre entre différents objectifs. *Santé, Société et Solidarité* (2): 31–42.

Ross, N., S. Tremblay, S. Khan, D. Crouse, M. Tremblay, and J-M Berthelot. 2007. "Body mass index in urban Canada: Neighborhood and metropolitan area effects." *American Journal of Public Health* 97: 500–08.

Roussel, Louis. 1979. "Générations nouvelles et mariage traditionnel." *Population* 34: 141–62.

———. 1989. *La famille incertaine.* Paris: Odile Jacob.

Rovny, Allison E. 2011. "Welfare state policy determinants of fertility level." *Journal of European Social Policy* 21: 335–47

Rowe, Geoff. 1989. "Union dissolution in a changing social context." In *The Family in Crisis: A Population Crisis?* J. Légaré, T.R. Balakrishnan, and R. Beaujot, eds. Ottawa: Royal Society of Canada, pp. 141–63.

———, and Huan Nguyen. 2003. *Early Retirement in Perspective: Insights from the LifePaths Microsimulation Model.* Report prepared for Human Resources Development Canada. Ottawa: HRDC.

Roy, Francine. 2005. "Canada's trade and investment with China." *Canadian Economic Observer* 18(6).

Roy, Laurent, and Jean Bernier. 2006. "La politique familiale, les tendances sociales et la fécondité au Québec: Une expérimentation du modèle nordique?" Quebec: Ministère de la Famille, des Aînés et de la Condition féminine.

Roy, R., and H. Charbonneau. 1978. "La nuptialité en situation de déséquilibre des sexes: Le Canada du XVIIe Siècle." In *Annals de Démographie Historique, 1978; la mortalité du passé.* Société de Démographie Historique. La Haye, New York, Mouton: 285–94.

Royal Commission on Aboriginal Peoples (RCAP). 1995. *People to People, Nation to Nation: Highlights from the Report of the Royal Commission on Aboriginal Peoples.* Ottawa: Indian and Northern Affairs Canada cat. no. Z1-1991/1-6E.

Royal Commission on New Reproductive Technologies. 1993. *Proceed with Care.* Ottawa: Minister of Government Services.

Royal Commission on the Economic Union and Development Prospects for Canada. 1985. *Report.* 3 vols. Ottawa: Supply and Services Canada.

Ruddick, Elizabeth. 2001. "Recent trends in international labour flows to Canada." Presented at the meetings of the Federation of Canadian Demographers, Ottawa, December.

———. 1997. "Migration and population replacement." *Canadian Studies in Population* 24: 1–26.

Rutstein, D.D., W. Berenberg, T.C. Chalmers, C.G. Child, A.P. Fishman, and E.B. Perrin. 1976. "Measuring the quality of medical care." *New England Journal of Medicine* 1976 (294): 582–88.

Ryder, Norman. 1959. "The cohort as a concept in the study of social change." *American Sociological Review* 30(1965): 843–61.

———. 1985. *A Population Policy for Canada.* Toronto: University of Toronto.

———. 1997. "Migration and population replacement." *Canadian Studies in Population* 24: 1–26.

Sager, Eric W., and Peter Baskerville, eds. 2007. *Household Counts: Canadian Households and Families in 1901.* Toronto: University of Toronto Press.

Samuel, T. John. 1984. "Economic adaptation of refugees in Canada: Experience of a quarter century." *International Migration* 22: 45–55.

———. 1987. *Visible Minorities in Canada: Contributions to Demography.* Edmonton: Population Research Laboratory.

Sanz, Ismael, and Francisco J. Velázquez. 2007. "The role of ageing in the growth of government and social welfare spending in the OECD." *European Journal of Political Economy* 23: 917–31.

Sarlo, Christopher A. 2013. *The Cost of Raising Children.* Vancouver: The Fraser Institute.

Satzewich, Vic, and Nikolaos Liodakis. 2013. *Race & Ethnicity in Canada: A Critical Introduction.* Don Mills, ON: Oxford University Press.

Saunders, Doug. 2012. "What would a Canada of 100 million look like?" *The Globe and Mail*, May 17.

Saunders, S., P. Ramsden, and D. Herring. 1992. "Transformation and disease: Precontact Ontario Iroquoians." In *Disease and Demography in the Americas*, J. Verano and D. Ubelaker, eds. Washington, DC: Smithsonian Institution Press.

Saurette, P. 2010. "When smart parties make stupid decisions." *The Mark News*, 23 July.

Savard, R., and J. Proulx. 1982. *Canada: Derrière l'épopée, les autochtones*. Montreal: L'Hexagone.

Sawyer, Robert. 2000. "The next century." *The Globe and Mail*, 1 January.

Scanzoni, Letha, and John Scanzoni. 1976. *Men, Women and Change: A Sociology of Marriage and the Family*. New York: McGraw-Hill.

Schellenberg, Grant. 2004. *The Retirement Plans and Expectations of Non-retired Canadians Aged 45 to 59*. Analytical Studies Branch research paper series. Ottawa: Statistics Canada.

———, and Cynthia Silver. 2004. "You can't always get what you want: Retirement preference and experiences." *Canadian Social Trends* 75: 2–7.

Schoen, Robert, Young J. Kim, Constance A. Nathanson, Jason Fields, and Nan Marie Astone. 1997. "Why do Americans want children?" *Population and Development Review* 23: 333–58.

Schwartz, Christine R. 2010. "Earnings inequality and the changing association between spouses' earnings." *American Journal of Sociology* 115(5): 1524–57.

Schwartz, Saul, and Ross Finnie. 2002. "Student loans in Canada: An analysis of borrowing and repayment." *Economics of Education Review* 21: 497–512.

Scoffield, Heather. 2012. "Government targets young Canadians with pension reform pitch." Canadian Press. 21 February.

Service Canada. 2013. "Taxi and limousine drivers and chauffeurs analytical text 7413—Taxi and limousine drivers and chauffeurs." Ottawa: Service Canada.

Settersten, Richard A., and Jacqueline L. Angel, eds. 2011. *Handbook of Sociology of Aging*. New York: Springer.

Sharpe, Andrew, and Jill Hardt. 2006. "Five deaths a day: Workplace fatalities in Canada, 1993–2005." Canadian Centre for Living Standards Research Paper 2006, 4 December 2006.

Sheikh, Munir A. 2010. Queen's Lecture on the Census. School of Policy Studies, Kingston, Queens University.

———. 2013. "Good government and Statistics Canada: The need for true independence." *Academic Matters* (2), 18–22.

Shields, Margot, Margaret D. Carroll, and Cynthia L. Ogden. 2011. *NCHS Data Brief* no. 56 (March 2011).

———, and Stéphane Tremblay. 2002. "The health of Canada's communities." *Supplement to Health Reports* 13. Ottawa: Statistics Canada cat. no. 82-003.

Shorter, Edward.1975. *The Making of the Modern Family*. New York: Basic Books.

Siegel, Jacob S. 2002. *Applied Demography: Applications to Business, Government Law and Public Policy*. Orlando: Academic Press.

Siegfried, A. 1937. *Le Canada, puissance international*. Paris: Librairie Armand Colin.

Sierra Club of Canada. 2013. "Population policy." See www.sierraclub.ca/en/node/590.

Siggner, Andy, Annette Vermaeten, Chris Durham, Jeremy Hull, Eric Guimond, and Mary Jane Norris. 2001. "New developments in Aboriginal definitions and measures." Presented at the Canadian Population Society Meetings, Quebec City, June.

Simmons, Alan. 2010. *Immigration and Canada: Global and Transnational Perspectives*. Toronto: Canadian Scholars' Press.

Simon, Julian L. 1981. *The Ultimate Resource*. Princeton: Princeton University Press.

———. 1996 *The Ultimate Resource II*. Princeton, NJ: Princeton University Press.

———. 1999. *Hoodwinking the Nation*. New Brunswick: Transaction Publishers.

Simpson, Jeffrey. 2010. "PM's census policy senseless but great for party." *The Globe and Mail*, 17 July.

———. 2012. *Chronic Condition: Why Canada's Health Care System Needs to be Dragged into the 21st Century*. Toronto: Penguin/Allen Lane.

———, Mark Jaccard, and Nic Rivers. 2007. *Hot Air: Meeting Canada's Climate Change Challenge*. Toronto: McClelland & Stewart.

Sinding, Steven. 1993. "Panel Presentation to the Plenary Session on the contribution of IUSSP to the 1994 UN International Conference on Population and Development." Presented at the General Conference of the International Union for the Scientific Study of Population, Montreal, August.

———. 2009. "Population, poverty and economic development." *Philosophical Transactions of the Royal Society* 364(1532): 3023–30.

Singman, Jeffrey L. 1999. *Daily Life in Medieval Europe*. Westport, CT: Greenwood Press.

Sironi, Maria, and Frank F. Furstenberg. 2012. "Trends in the economic independence of young adults in the United States: 1973–2007." *Population and Development Review* 38(4): 609–30.

Sisco, Ashley, and Carole Stonebridge. 2010. *Toward Thriving Northern Communities*. Ottawa: Conference Board of Canada.

Skeldon, Ron. 2000. "Asia." In *International Organization on Migration, Trafficking of Migrants*. Geneva: International Organization on Migration, pp. 7–30.

Skolnick, Arlene. 1987. *The Intimate Environment*. Boston: Little, Brown.

Skills Research Initiative. 2008. *The Labour Market and Skills Implications of Population Aging in Canada: A Synthesis of Key Findings and Policy Implications*. Ottawa: Human Resources and Social Development Canada.

Smil, Vaclav. 2012. *Global Catastrophes and Trends: The Next Fifty Years*. Cambridge, MA: The MIT Press.

———. 2013. *Harvesting the Biosphere: What We Have Taken from Nature*. Cambridge, MA: The MIT Press.

Smith, Dorothy. 1997. "Sociology of everyday life." Presented at the Department of Sociology, University of Western Ontario, 17 January, London, Ontario.

Smith, P.C., A. Anell, R. Busse, L. Crivelli, J. Healy, A.K. Lindahl, G. Westert, and T. Kene. 2012. "Leadership and governance in seven developed health systems." *Health Policy* 106: 37–49.

Snyman, H.A., and G.N. Smit. 2007. "Cattle-rangeland management practices and perceptions of pastoralists towards rangeland degradation in the Borana zone of southern Ethiopia." *Journal of Environmental Management* 82: 481–94.

Soneji, Samir, and Gary King. 2012. "Statistical security for social security." *Demography* 49: 1037–60.

Stafford, James. 1987. "The Political economic context of post-war fertility patterns in Canada." In *Contributions to Demography*. Edmonton: Population Research Laboratory.

———. 1990. "Regions and Migration." In *Comments on "Charting Canada's Future."* London, ON: Federation of Canadian Demographers, pp. 27–36.

Statistics Canada. 1974. *Population Projections for Canada and the Provinces and Territories, 1972–2001*. Ottawa: Statistics Canada cat. no. 91-514.

———. 1979. *Population Projections for Canada and the Provinces and Territories, 1976–2001*. Ottawa: Statistics Canada, cat. no. 91-520.

———. 1985. *Population Projections for Canada, Provinces and Territories, 1984–2006*. Ottawa: Statistics Canada cat. no. 91-520-X.

———. 1987. *Health and Social Support 1985*. Ottawa: Statistics Canada cat. no. 11-612.

———. 1989. *Births and Deaths*. Ottawa: Statistics Canada cat. no. 82-204.

———. 1990. *Population Projections for Canada, Provinces and Territories, 1989–2011*. Ottawa: Statistics Canada cat. no. 91-520-X.

———. 1994. *Population Projections for Canada, Provinces and Territories, 1993–2016*. Ottawa: Statistics Canada cat. no. 91-520-X.

———. 1995. *Life Tables, Canada and Provinces, 1990–1992*. Ottawa: Statistics Canada cat. no. 84-537.

———. 1997. "1996 Census Marital status, common-law unions and families." *The Daily*, 14 October.

———. 1999. "Life expectancy." *Health Reports* 11(3): 9–24.

———. 2000. *Income in Canada*. Ottawa: Statistics Canada cat. no. 75-202-XIE.

———. 2001. *Population Projections for Canada, Provinces and Territories, 2000–2026*. Ottawa: Statistics Canada cat. no. 91-520-X.

———. 2002. "Changing conjugal life in Canada." *The Daily* 11 July: 3–6.

———. 2005. *Population Projections for Canada, Provinces and Territories, 2005–2031*. Ottawa: Statistics Canada cat. no. 91-520-X.

———. 2008a. *Earnings and Incomes of Canadians over the Past Quarter Century, 2006 Census*. Ottawa: Statistics Canada cat. no. 97-563-X.

———. 2008b. *Aboriginal Peoples in Canada in 2006: Inuit, Métis and First Nations, 2006 Census*. Ottawa: Statistics Canada cat. no. 97-558-XIE.

———. 2008c. CANSIM Table 051-0004.

———. 2009a. *Labour Force Survey Estimates, Monthly*. Ottawa: Statistics Canada. CANSIM 282-0003.

———. 2009b. *Persons Registered under the Indian Act, by Province and Territory*. Special Table. Census of Population Special Table.

———. 2009c. *Population Projections for Canada, Provinces and Territories, 2009–2036*. Ottawa: Statistics Canada cat. no. 91-520-X.

———. 2010a. *Participation and Activity Limitation Survey 2006*. Analytical Paper: Health Statistics Division. Ottawa: Statistics Canada cat. no. 89-628-X-No.015.

———. 2010b. *Summary Elementary and Secondary School Indicators for Canada, the Provinces and Territories, 2006–2007 to 2008–2009*. Tourism and Centre for Education Statistics Division. Ottawa: Statistics Canada cat. no. 81-595-M - No. 099.

———. 2010c. *Population Projections for Canada, Provinces and Territories, 2009 to 2036*. Ottawa: Statistics Canada cat. no. 91-520-X.

———. 2010d. *Canadian Cancer Registry Database (July)*. CANSIM, Table 103-0553 and cat. no. 82-231-X.

———. 2012a. *The Canadian Population in 2011: Age and Sex*. Analytical Document: Census. Ottawa: Statistics Canada cat. no. 98-311-X2011001.

———. 2012b. *Changes in Smoking between 1994/1995 and 2004/2005, 2006/2007, 2008/2009, by Sex*. Ottawa: Statistics Canada CANSIM 104-7006.

———. 2012c. *Labour Force Survey Estimates, Annual*. Ottawa: Statistics Canada CANSIM 282-0001.

———. 2012d. *Deaths, by Cause: External Causes, Age Group and Sex, Canada*. Ottawa: Statistics Canada CANSIM 102-0540.

———. 2012e. *Population and Family Estimation Methods at Statistics Canada*. Ottawa: Statistics Canada cat. 91-528-X.

———. 2012f. *Linguistic Characteristics of Canadians*. 2011 Census of Population Analytical Product. Ottawa: Statistics Canada.

———. 2012g. *The Canadian Population in 2011: Population Counts and Growth*. Census Analytical Document. Ottawa: Statistics Canada cat. no. 98-310-X2011001.

———. 2012h. *Population and Dwelling Counts, for Canada and Census Subdivisions (municipalities), 2011 and 2006 Censuses*. Population and Dwelling Count Highlight Tables. Ottawa: Statistics Canada cat. no. 98-310-XWE2011002.

———. 2012i. *Population Growth in Canada: From 1851 to 2061*. Census in Brief: Population and Dwelling Counts, 2011 Census.

———. 2012j. *Government Sector Revenue and Expenditure*. CANSIM 380-0506.

———. 2012k. *Living Arrangements of Young Adults Aged 20 to 29. Families, Households and Marital Status, 2011 Census of Population*. Ottawa: Statistics Canada Cat. No. 98-312-X2011003.

———. 2012l. *Portrait of Families and Living Arrangements in Canada. Families, Households and Marital Status, 2011 Census of Population*. Ottawa: Statistics Canada cat. no. 98-312-X2011001.

———. 2012m. *Components of Population Growth, Canada, Provinces and Territories, 1971/1972 to 2013/2014*. CANSIM 051-0004.

———. 2012n. *Aboriginal Languages in Canada: Language, 2011 Census of Population*. Catalogue 98-314-X2011003.

———. 2012o. *Final Report on 2016 Census Options: Proposed Content Determination Framework and Methodology Options*. Census Management Office, 2016 Census Strategy Project.

———. 2012p. *Living Arrangements of Young Adults Aged 20 to 29*. Ottawa: Statistics Canada cat. no. 98-312-X-2011003.

———. 2012q. "2011 Census of Population: Families, households, marital status, structural type of dwelling, collectives." *The Daily* 19 September.

———. 2013a. *Life Tables, Canada, Provinces and Territories, 2009–2011*. Ottawa: Statistics Canada.

———. 2013b. *Infant Mortality Rates*. CANSIM, Table 102-0504.

———. 2013c. *Components of Demographic Change*. CANSIM 051-0009.

———. 2013d. *Number of Non-permanent Residents, Canada, Provinces and Territories*. CANSIM 051-0020.

———. 2013e. *Components of Population Growth by Census Metropolitan Area, Sex and Age Group for the Period from July 1 to June 30*. CANSIM 051-0047.

———. 2013f. *Annual Demographic Estimates: Canada, Provinces and Territories*. Ottawa: Statistics Canada cat. no. 91-215-X.

———. 2013g. *Labour Force Survey*. CANSIM 28-0086.

———. 2013h. *Aboriginal Peoples in Canada: First Nations People, Métis and Inuit*. Ottawa: Statistics Canada Catalogue no. 99-011-X2011001.

———. 2013i. *Estimates of Population, by Age Group and Sex for July 1, Canada, Provinces and Territories*. CANSIM Table 051-0001.

———. 2013j. *Get to Know Canadian Farmers and their Families*. 2011 Census of Agriculture. Ottawa: Statistics Canada CANSIM 004-0100 to 004-0129.

———. 2013k. *Mobility and Migration*. National Household Survey 2011. Ottawa: Statistics Canada Catalogue 99-013-X.

———. 2013l. *Interprovincial In-,Out-, and Net-Migrants, Canada, Provinces, and Territories*. Ottawa: Statistics Canada CANSIM 051-0018.

———. 2013m. *The Report on the Demographic Situation in Canada*. Ottawa: Statistics Canada cat. no. 91-209-X.

———. 2013n. *Income of Individuals, by Sex, Age Group and Income Source, 2011 Constant Dollars*. Ottawa: Statistics Canada CANSIM 202-0407.

———. 2013o. *Labour Force Survey Estimates (LFS), by Usual Hours Worked, Main or All Jobs, Sex and Age Groups*. CANSIM 282-0016.

———. 2013p. *Labour Force Survey Estimates by Sex and Detailed Age Group*. CANSIM 282-0002.

———. 2013q. *Immigration and Ethnocultural Diversity in Canada*. Analytical Document, National Household Survey. Ottawa: Statistics Canada.

———. 2013r. *Population Estimates, by Age and Sex, by Province/territory*. CANSIM 051-0001.

———. 2013s. *Population Estimates, by age and sex, CMAs*. CANSIM 051-0056.

————. 2013t. *Life Tables, Canada, Provinces and Territories 2007–2009.* Ottawa: Statistics Canada.

————. 2013u. *Persons in Low Income Families, LICOs 1992 Base, After-Tax.* CANSIM 202-0802.

————. 2013v. *Births 2011.* Statistics Canada: CANSIM Table 102-4508.

————. 2013w. *Immigration and Ethnocultural Diversity in Canada.* Analytical Product NHS. Ottawa: Statistics Canada.

————. 2013x. *Labour Force Status, Visible Minority, Immigrant Status and Period of Immigration, Highest Certificate, Diploma or Degree, Age Groups and Sex for the Population Aged 15 Years and Over, in Private Households of Canada, Provinces, Territories, Census Metropolitan Areas and Census Agglomerations.* 2011 National Household Survey.

————. 2013y. *Education Indicators in Canada 2012: An International Perspective.* Catalogue no. 81-604-X. Ottawa: Tourism and the Centre for Education Statistics Division.

————. 2013z. *Public and Private Elementary and Secondary Education Expenditures*—annual. CANSIM 478-0014.

————. 2013aa. *Summary Elementary and Secondary School Indicators for Canada, the Provinces and Territories, 2006/2007 to 2010/2011.* Tourism and the Centre for Education Statistics. Catalogue 81-595-M No. 99.

————. 2013ab. *Estimates of Population, by Age Group and Sex for July 1, Canada, Provinces and Territories.* CANSIM 051-0001.

————. 2013ac. *Postsecondary Enrolments, by Program Type, Credential Type, Classification of Instructional Programs, Primary Grouping, Registration Status and Sex.* CANSIM 477-0029.

————. 2013ad. *Low Income Lines, 2011–2012.* Income Research Paper Series Issue: 2013002.

————. 2013ae. *Births.* Catalogue no. 84F0210X.

————. 2013af. *National Household Survey (NHS) Aboriginal Population: Data Tables Aboriginal Ancestry.* Ottawa: Statistics Canada cat. no. 99-011-X2011029.

————. 2013ag. *National Household Survey (NHS) Aboriginal Peoples in Canada: First Nations People, Métis and Inuit.* Ottawa: Statistics Canada cat. no. 99-011-X2011001.

————. 2013ah. *Annual Demographic Estimates: Canada, Provinces and Territories.* Ottawa: cat. no. 91-215-X.

————. 2014a. *Population Projections for Canada (2013 to 2063), Provinces and Territories (2013 to 2038).* Ottawa: Statistics Canada cat. no. 91-620-X.

————. 2014b. *Leading Causes of Death.* CANSIM Table 102-0561.

————. 2014c. *Health in Canada.* See www.statcan.gc.ca/eng/health/index.

————. 2014d. "Deaths and mortality rates, by age group and sex, Canada, provinces and territories." Table 102-0504.

————. 2014e. "Deaths and mortality rate, by selected grouped causes and sex, Canada, provinces and territories." Table 102-0552.

————. 2014f. *Population Projections for Canada, Provinces and Territories.* Ottawa: Statistics Canada.

————. 2014g. "Couple families by presence of children in private households, 2011 counts, children (all ages), for Canada, provinces and territories." Available at www12.statcan.gc.ca/census-recensement/2011/dp-pd/hlt-fst/fam/Pages/highlight.cfm?TabID=1&Lang=E&Asc=1&PRCode=01&OrderBy=999&View=1&tableID=301&queryID=1&Children=1.

————. 2014h. *Education Indicators in Canada: An International Perspective, 2013.* Catalogue 81-604-X. Ottawa: Tourism and the Centre for Education Statistics Division.

————. 2014i. *Labour Force Survey Estimates, by Educational Attainment, Sex and Age Group, Unadjusted for Seasonality.* CANSIM 282-0003.

————. 2014j. *Distribution of Total Income, by Economic Family Type, 2011 Constant Dollars.* CANSIM 202-0401.

————. 2014k. *Gini Coefficients of Market, Total and After-Tax Income of Individuals, Where Each Individual is Represented by their Adjusted Household Income, by Economic Family Type, 1976 to 2011.* CANSIM 202-0709.

————. 2014l. *Persons in Low Income Families, 1976 to 2011.* CANSIM 202-0802.

————. 2014m. *Population Estimates, by Age and Sex, CMAs.* CANSIM 051-0056.

————. 2014n. *Components of Demographic Change.* CANSIM 051-0009.

————. 2014o. *Report on the Demographic Situation in Canada.* Ottawa: Statistics Canada cat. no. 91-209-X.

————. 2014p. *Annual Demographic Estimates: Canada, Provinces and Territories.* Ottawa: Statistics Canada cat. no. 91-215-X.

Stavely, M. 1977. "Population dynamics in Newfoundland: The regional patterns." Pp. 49–76 in *The Peopling of Newfoundland*, J. Mannion, ed. St John's, NL: Memorial University, Institute for Social and Economic Research.

Stechbart, Meredith, and Jeffrey Wilson. 2010. *Province of Ontario Ecological Footprint and Biocapacity Analysis.* Oakland, CA. Global Footprint Network.

Steckle, Richard, and Jerome Rose. 2002. *The Backbone of History: Health and Nutrition in the Western Hemisphere.* Cambridge, UK: Cambridge University Press.

Stevenson, D., and R. Gilbert. 2005. "Coping with Canadian federalism: The case of the Federation of Canadian Municipalities." *Canadian Public Administration* 48(4): 528–51.

Stewart, T. 1973. *The People of America*. New York: Scribner's.

Sticht, Thomas G. 2010. "Educated parents, educated children: Toward a multiple life cycles education policy." *Education Canada* 50(4).

Stoffman, Daniel. 2002. *Who Gets In: What's Wrong with Canada's Immigration Program and How to Fix It.* Toronto: Macfarlane Walter & Ross.

Stolnitz, George J. 1987. "Conclusions." In *Technological Prospects and Population Trends*, T.J. Espenshade and G.T. Stolnitz, eds. Boulder, CO: Westview Press, pp. 195–211.

Stone, Lawrence. 1977. *The Family, Sex and Marriage in England 1500–1800*. London: Weidenfeld and Nicolson.

Stone, Leroy. 2006. *New Frontiers of Research on Retirement*. Ottawa: Statistics Canada.

———, and S. Fletcher. 1986. *The Seniors Boom: Dramatic Increases in Longevity and Prospects for Better Health*. Ottawa: Statistics Canada.

———. 1988. *Family and Friendship Ties among Canada's Seniors*. Ottawa: Statistics Canada.

Strain, Laurel A. 1990. "Receiving and providing care: The experiences of never-married elderly Canadians." Presented at the Twelfth World Congress of Sociology, Madrid, July.

Sturtevant, William C., ed. 2006. *Handbook of North American Indians*. Washington, DC: Smithsonian Institution.

Sullivan, Matthew S., and Ian R. Swingland. 2006. "Extinction risk: Predicting and redressing the threat." *Biodiversity and Conservation* 15(6): 2009–16.

Suzuki, David. 2011. "Is seven billion people too many?" Vancouver: The Suzuki Foundation.

———. 2013. "Le réchauffement climatique rend le Canada vulnérable." *L'Express*. Propos recueillis par Jean-Michel Demetz, publié le 01/07/2013.

Sweeney, Megan. 1997. "Women, men and changing families: The shifting economic foundations of marriage." Working Paper No. 97-14. Madison, WI: University of Wisconsin, Center for Demography and Ecology.

———. 2002. "Two decades of family change: The shifting economic foundations of marriage." *American Sociological Review* 67: 132–47.

Szreter, Simon. 1995. *Fertility, Class and Gender in Britain, 1860–1940*. Cambridge, UK: Cambridge University Press.

Tabah, Léon. 1988. "The demographic and social consequences of population aging." In *Economic and Social Implications of Population Aging*. New York: United Nations, pp. 121–44.

Tach, Laura, Ronald Mincy, and Kathryn Edin. 2010. "Parenting as a 'package deal': Relationships, fertility, and nonresident father involvement among unmarried parents." *Demography* 47(1): 181–204.

Tal, Benjamin. 2012. "Productive conversations: Long-term immigration approach needed to maximize newcomers' employability. *Financial Post*, 24 July.

Taylor, Christopher. 1987. *Demography and Immigration in Canada: Challenge and Opportunity*. Ottawa: Employment and Immigration Canada.

Teillet, Jean. 2010. *Métis Law in Canada, 2010*. Toronto: Pape Salter Teillet LLP.

Termote, Marc, Frédéric Payeur, and Normand Thibault. 2011. *Portrait démolinguistique. Perspectives démolinguistiques du Québec et de la region de Montréal (2006–2056)*. Québec: Gouvernement du Québec.

Testa, Maria Rita, and Laurent Toulemon. 2006. "Family formation in France: Individual preferences and subsequent outcomes." *Vienna Yearbook of Population Research, 2006*: 41–75

Thériault, J. Yvon. 1989. "Lourdeur ou légèreté du devenir de la francophonie hors Québec." In *Demolinguistic Trends and the Evolution of Canadian Institutions*. Ottawa: Secretary of State.

Thévenon, Olivier. 2008. "Les politiques familiales des pays développés: Des modèles contrastés." *Population et Sociétés* 448: 1–4.

———. 2011. "Family policies in OECD countries: A comparative analysis." *Population and Development Review* 37(1): 57–87.

———, and Anne Gauthier. 2010. "L'influence des politiques d'aide aux familles sur la fécondité dans les pays développés." *Santé, Société et Solidarité* 2010(2): 53–62.

Thompson, Debra. 2010. "The politics of the census: Lessons from abroad." *Canadian Public Policy* 36(4): 377–82.

Thompson, Linda, and Alexis Walker. 1989. "Gender in families: Women and men in marriage, work, and parenthood." *Journal of Marriage and the Family* 51: 845–71.

Thornton, Patricia, and Sherry Olson. 2011. "Mortality in late nineteenth-century Montreal: Geographic pathways of contagion." *Population Studies* 65(2): 157–181.

Thornton, Russell. 1987. *American Indian Holocaust and Survival: A Population History Since 1492*. Norman, OK: University of Oklahoma Press.

———. 2000. "Population history of Native North Americans." In *A Population History of North America*, Michael R. Haines and Richard H. Steckel, eds. New York: Cambridge University Press.

Timlin, M.F. 1951. *Does Canada Need More People?* Toronto: Oxford University Press.

Tina W.L., James Curtis, and Ronald Lambert. 1991. "Immigrant background and political participation: Examining generational patterns." *Canadian Journal of Sociology* 16: 375–97.

Tjepkema, Michael. 2002. "The health of the off-reserve Aboriginal population." *Health Reports* 13 (suppl.): 73–88.

——, and Russell Wilkins. 2011. "Remaining life expectancy at age 25 and probability of survival to age 75, by socio-economic status and Aboriginal ancestry." *Health Reports* 22: 31–6.

——, Russell Wilkins, Sacha Senécal, Éric Guimond, and Christopher Penney. 2009. "Mortality of Métis and registered Indian adults in Canada: An 11-year follow-up study." Statistics Canada, *Health Reports* 20: 1–21.

Torrey, Barbara Boyle, and Carl Haub. 2004. "A comparison of US and Canadian mortality in 1998." *Population and Development Review* 30(3): 519–30.

Tossou, Ayéko. 2002. "Fécondité différentielle des immigrants et des natifs: Québec, 1976–1996." *Cahiers québécois de démographie* 31: 95–112.

Transport Canada, 2011. *Canadian Motor Vehicle Traffic Collision Statistics 2011.* Ottawa: Transport Canada (in cooperation with the Canadian Council of Motor Transport Administrators).

Tremblay, Marc, and Hélène Vézina. 2010. "Genealogical analysis of maternal and paternal lineages in the Quebec population." *Human Biology* 82(2): 179–98.

Trost, Jan. 1986. "What holds marriage together." In *Continuity and Change in Marriage and Family*, J. Veevers, ed. Toronto: Holt, Rinehart and Winston.

——. 1996. "Family Structure and Relationships: The Dyadic Approach." *Journal of Comparative Family Studies* 27: 395–408.

Trovato, Frank. 1992. "Mortality differentials in Canada by marital status." *Canadian Studies in Population* 19: 111–43.

——. 1998. "Nativity, Marital Status and Mortality in Canada." *Canadian Review of Sociology and Anthropology* 35: 65–91.

——. 2000. "Canadian Indian mortality during the 1980s." *Social Biology* 47: 135–45.

——. 2001. "Aboriginal mortality in Canada, the United States and New Zealand." *Journal of Biosocial Science* 33: 67–86.

——. 2007. "Narrowing sex differential in life expectancy in Canada." In Rod Beaujot and Don Kerr, eds., *The Changing Face of Canada: Essential Readings in Population.* Toronto: Canadian Scholars' Press, pp. 127–140.

——. 2009. *Canada's Population in a Global Context: An Introduction to Social Demography.* Don Mills, ON: Oxford University Press.

——. 2010. "Fertility in Alberta in a context of rapid economic growth, 1997–2007." *Canadian Studies in Population* 37: 497–524.

——, and N.M. Lalu. 1996. "Causes of death responsible for the changing sex differential in life expectancy between 1970 and 1990 in thirty industrialized nations." *Canadian Studies in Population* 23: 99–126.

——, and N.M. Lalu. 2012. "Narrowing sex differentials in life expectancy in the industrialized world: Early 1970s to early 1990s." In Frank Trovato, ed. *Population and Society: Essential Readings*, Second Edition. Don Mills, ON: Oxford University Press.

——, and D. Odynak. 2011. "Sex differences in life expectancy in Canada: Immigrant and native-born populations." *Journal of Biosocial Science* 43: 353–67.

——, and Anatole Romaniuc, eds. 2014. *Aboriginal Populations: Social Demographic and Epidemiological Perspectives.* Edmonton, AB: University of Alberta Press.

Turcotte, Martin. 2011. "Intergenerational education mobility: University completion in relation to parents' education level." *Canadian Social Trends* 92: 37–43.

——, and Grant Schellenberg. 2007. *A Portrait of Seniors in Canada.* Ottawa: Statistics Canada cat. no. 89-519-XIE.

Turcotte, Pierre, and Alain Bélanger. 1997. "Moving in together." *Canadian Social Trends* 47: 7–9.

Ubelaker, D.H. 1976. "Prehistoric New World population size: Historical review and current appraisal of North American estimates." *American Journal of Physical Anthropology* 45: 661–6.

——. 2000. "Patterns of disease in early North American populations." In *A Population History of North America*, M. Haines and R. Steckel, eds. Cambridge, UK: Cambridge University Press, pp. 51–98.

United Nations. 1989. *World Population at the Turn of the Century.* New York: United Nations Population Studies No. 111.

——. 1994. Population and Development: Programme of Action Adopted at the International Conference on Population and Development, Cairo, 5–13 September 1994. A/SB21/5/Add.1, New York: United Nations.

———. 1995. Population and Development: Programme of Action Adopted at the International Conference on Population and Development, Cairo, 5–13 September 1994. United Nations ST/ESA/Ser. A/149. New York: United Nations.

———. 2000. *Replacement Migration: Is It a Solution to Declining and Aging Populations?* New York: United Nations, Population Division.

———. 2004. *World Population in 2300.* New York: United Nations.

———. 2006. *International Migration.* Department of Economic and Social Affairs. New York: United Nations, Population Division.

———. 2011a. *International Migration and Development: A Review in Light of the Crisis.* CDP Background Paper No. 11. Population Division. New York: United Nations.

———. 2011b. *Actions in the Follow-Up to the Recommendations of the International Conference on Population and Development: Fertility Reproductive Health and Development.* Report of the Secretary-General, Commission on Population and Development.

———. 2011c. *Population Facts: World Population Prospects.* New York: United Nations, Population Division, Department of Economic and Social Affairs.

———. 2011d. *World Population Prospects, the 2010 Revision.* New York: United Nations, Population Division, Department of Economic and Social Affairs.

———. 2012. *UN Data: A World of Data: Child Dependency Ratio.* New York: United Nations, Population Division.

———. 2013a. *World Population Prospects: The 2012 Revision, Highlights and Advance Tables.* Working Paper No. ESA/P/WP.228. New York: United Nations, Population Division, Department of Economic and Social Affairs.

———. 2013b. Report of the UNECE Regional Conference on ICPD beyond 2014 "Enabling choices: Population priorities for the 21st Century." United Nations, Economic and Social Council, Economic Commission for Europe ECE/AC.27/2013/2.

———. 2013c. "Enabling choices: Population priorities for the 21st Century." *Report of the UNECE Regional conference on ICPD beyond 2014.* United Nations: Economic and Social Council. Geneva: ECE/AC.27/2013/2.

———. 2013d. *World Population Prospects: The 2012 Revision, Highlights and Advance Tables,* Working Paper No. ESA/P/WP.228. Department of Economic and Social Affairs, Population Division.

———. 2014. *The UNHCR, Environment and Climate Change: an Overview.* Geneva: The United Nations High Commissioner for Refugees.

UNDP. 2012. *United Nations Development Report.* New York: United Nations Development Programme.

United Nations Framework Convention on Climate Change. 1992. New York: United Nations. FCCC/INFORMAL/84 GE.05-62220.

UNFCCC. 2009. United Nations Framework Convention on Climate Change (UNFCCC) Secretariat (see http://unfccc.int).

UNFPA. 2011. "World population to reach 7 billion on 31 October." Press release. New York: United Nations Population Fund.

UNHCR. 2014. *Global Trends: The Costs of War.* Geneva: United Nations High Commissioner for Refugees.

United States Bureau of the Census. 2013. "Population estimates: Annual estimates of the resident population for selected age groups by sex for the United States." Washington: US Census Bureau.

Uppal, Sharanjit, and Sébastien LaRochelle-Côté. 2014. "Overqualification among recent university graduates in Canada." *Insights on Canadian Society* 8: 1–12.

Ursel, Jane. 1986. "The state and the maintenance of patriarchy: A case study of family, labour and welfare legislation in Canada." In *Family, Economy and State,* James Dickinson and Bob Russell, eds. Toronto: Garamond Press.

Usalcas, Jeannine. 2009. "The labour market in 2008." *Perspectives on Labour and Income* 21(1): 47–52.

Vancouver, Central Area Planning Report. 2007. *Report for the City of Vancouver.* Vancouver: Municipal Government.

Van de Kaa, Dirk. 1987. "Europe's second demographic transition." *Population Bulletin* 42: 1–58.

———. 2008. "Demographic transitions." The Hague: Netherlands Interdisciplinary Demographic Institute.

Vanderkamp, John. 1988. "Canadian post-secondary enrolment: Causes, consequences and policy issues." Ottawa: Report for Review of Demography, Health and Welfare.

Van de Walle, Étienne, and John Knodel. 1980. "Europe's fertility transition: New evidence and lessons for today's developing world." *Population Bulletin* 34: 1–34.

Van Lerberghe, Wim, and Vincent De Brouwere. 2001. "Of blind alleys and things that have worked: History's lessons on reducing maternal mortality." In *Safe motherhood strategies: a review of the evidence,* V. De Brouwere, W. Van Lerberghe, eds. Antwerp: ITG Press, pp. 7–33.

Vaupel, J.W., A. Baudisch, M. Dolling, D. Roach, and J Gampe. 2004. "The case for negative senescence." *Theoretical Population Biology* 65: 339–51.

Veall, Michael R. 2012. "Top income shares in Canada: Recent trends and policy implications." *Canadian Journal of Economics* 45: 1247–72.

Veevers, Jean E. 1980. *Childless by Choice.* Toronto: Butterworths.

Verano, J., and D. Ubelaker. 1992. *Disease and Demography in the Americas*. Washington, DC: Smithsonian Institution Press.

Veugelers, John W.P., and Thomas R. Klassen. 1994. "Continuity and change in Canada's unemployment–immigration linkage (1946–1993)." *Canadian Journal of Sociology* 19: 351–70.

Vézina, Hélène, Danielle Gauvreau, and Alain Gagnon. 2014. "Socioeconomic fertility differentials in a late transition setting: A micro-level analysis of the Saguenay region of Quebec." *Demographic Research* 38: 1097–128.

Vézina, Mireille. 2012. *General Social Survey: Overview of Families in Canada—Being a Parent in a Stepfamily: A Profile*. Ottawa: Statistics Canada cat. no. 89-650-X—No. 002.

———, and Susan Crompton. 2012. "Volunteering in Canada." *Canadian Social Trends* 69: 37–55.

Vignoli, Daniele, Sven Drefahl, and Gustavo De Santis. 2012. "Whose job instability affects the likelihood of becoming a parent in Italy? A tale of two partners." *Demographic Research* 26 41–62.

Visco, I. 2000. "Welfare systems, ageing and work: An OECD perspective." *Banca Nazionale del Lavoro Quarterly Review* 53: 3–29.

Wackernagel, Mathis, and William Rees. 1996. *Our Ecological Footprint: Reducing Human Impact on the Earth*. Gabriola Island, BC: New Society Publishers.

———, Chad Monfreda, Dan Moran, Paul Wermer, Steve Goldfinger, Diana Deumling, and Michael Murray. 2005. *National Footprint and Biocapacity Accounts 2005: The Underlying Calculation Method*. Oakland, CA: Global Footprint Network.

Wadhera, Surinder. 1990. "Therapeutic abortions, Canada." *Health Reports* 1: 229–45.

Waite, Linda J., and Lee A. Lillard. 1991. "Children and marital disruption." *American Journal of Sociology* 96: 930–53.

Waldram, J.B., D.A. Herring, and T.K. Young. 2006. *Aboriginal Health in Canada: Historical, Cultural and Epidemiological Perspectives*. Toronto: University of Toronto Press.

Walsh, L. 2000. "The African American population of the colonial United States." Pp. 191–240 in *A Population History of North America*, M. Haines and H. Steckel, eds. Cambridge, UK: Cambridge University Press.

Wanner, Richard. 2003. "Entry class and the earnings of immigrants to Canada, 1980–1995." *Canadian Public Policy* 29: 53–71.

Ware, Roger, Pierre Fortin, and Pierre Emmanuel Paradis. 2010. *The Economic Impact of the Immigrant Investor Program in Canada*. Montreal: The Analysis Group.

Wargon, Sylvia T. 2002. *Demography in Canada in the Twentieth Century*. Vancouver: University of British Columbia Press.

Weeks, John R. 2012. *Population: An Introduction to Concepts and Issues*, 11th edition. Belmont, MA. Wadsworth.

Weiss, K.H. 1973. "Demographic models for anthropology." *American Antiquity* 38: 1–18.

Wells, R. 1975. *The Population of the British Colonies in America before 1776: A Survey of Census Data*. Princeton, NJ: Princeton University Press.

Wells, Spencer. 2010. *Pandora's Seed: The Unforeseen Cost of Civilization*. New York: Random House.

Wente, Margaret. 2012. "Go west, young Canadians." *The Globe and Mail*, 9 February.

Westoff, Charles F. 1986. "Perspectives on nuptiality and fertility." *Population and Development Review* 12 (Suppl.): 155–70.

Wheeler, Mark. 2008. "Braving the no-go zone: Canada's sub-replacement fertility rate." *Transition* 38(4): 3–8.

White, J.P., J. Peters, P. Dinsdale, and D. Beavon, eds. 2010. *Aboriginal Policy Research*, vol 1-9. Toronto: Thompson Educational Publishing.

White, Phillip M. 2006. *American Indian Chronology: Chronologies of the American Mosaic*. Santa Barbara, CA: Greenwood Publishing Group.

Wilkins, K., N.R. Campbell, M.R. Joffres, F.A. McAlister, M. Nichol, S. Quach, H.L. Johansen, and M.S. Tremblay. 2010. "Blood pressure in Canadian adults." *Health Reports* 20(1): 1–10.

Wilkins, Russell. 1980. *Health Status in Canada*. Montreal: Institute for Research on Public Policy.

———, Jean-Marie Berthelot, and Edward Ng. 2002. "Trends in mortality by neighbourhood income in urban Canada from 1971 to 1996." *Health Reports* 13 (supplement): 45–71.

———, Michael Tjepkema, Cameron Mustard, and Robert Choinière. 2008a. "The Canadian Census Mortality Follow-up Study 1991 through 2001." *Health Reports* 19: 25–43.

———, Sharanjit Uppal, Philippe Finès, Sacha Senécal, Éric Guimond, and Rene Dion. 2008b. "Life expectancy in the Inuit-inhabited areas of Canada, 1989 to 2003." *Health Reports* 19(1): 7–19.

Wilkinson, Bruce. 1986. "Elementary and secondary education policy in Canada: A survey." *Canadian Public Policy* 12: 535–72.

Williamson, R.F., and S. Pfeiffer, eds. 2003. *Bones of Our Ancestors: The Archaeological and Osteobiography of the Moatfield Ossuary*. Mercury Series Archaeology Paper 163. Gatineau, QC: Canadian Museum of Civilization.

Wilson, Chris. 1985. *The Dictionary of Demography*. Oxford: Blackwell Reference.

——. 2013. "Thinking about post-transitional demographic regimes: A reflection." *Demographic Research* 28(46): 1373–88.

Wilson, Jeffrey. 2001. *The Alberta GPI Accounts: Ecological Footprint*. Report # 28. Alberta Drayton Valley, AB: Pembina Institute.

——, and Mark Anielski. 2005. *Ecological Footprints of Canadian Municipalities and Regions*. Edmonton, AB: The Canadian Federation of Canadian Municipalities.

Woldemicael, Gebremariam, and Roderic Beaujot. 2012. "Fertility behavior of immigrants in Canada: Converging trends." *Journal of International Migration and Integration* 13: 325–341.

Wolfson, Michael. 1990. "Perceptions, facts and expectations on the standard of living." In *Facing the Demographic Future*, R. Beaujot, ed. Ottawa: Royal Society of Canada, pp. 15–17.

——, G. Rowe, J.F. Gentleman, and M. Tomiak. 1993. "Career earnings and death: a longitudinal analysis of older Canadian men." *Journal of Gerontology* 48(4): S167–S179.

Woolley, Francis. 2013. "Visible minority: A misleading concept that ought to be retired." Special to *The Globe and Mail*, 10 June.

World Commission on Environment and Development. 1987. *Our Common Future*. New York: Oxford University Press.

World Health Organization. 2010. *Global Status Report on Non-communicable Diseases*. Geneva: WHO.

Wright, Robert. 1988. "The impact of income redistribution on fertility in Canada." *Genus* 44: 139–56.

——, and Paul Maxim. 1987. "Canadian fertility trends: A further test of the Easterlin Hypothesis." *Canadian Review of Sociology and Anthropology* 24: 339–57.

Wu, Zheng. 1995. "Childbearing in cohabiting relationships." Presented at Canadian Population Society meetings, June, Victoria.

——. 1997. "Third birth intentions and uncertainty in Canada." Presented at Canadian Population Society Meetings, St John's, Newfoundland and Labrador, June.

——, and Christoph M. Schimmele. 2009. "Divorce and repartnering." In *Families: Changing Trends in Canada*, Sixth Edition, Maureen Baker, ed. Whitby, ON: McGraw-Hill Ryerson, pp. 154–78.

Xu, Li. 2012. *Who Drives a Taxi in Canada?* Ottawa: Citizenship and Immigration Canada, Research and Evaluation.

Yale Center for Environmental Law and Policy. 2005. *Environmental Sustainability Index Benchmarking National Environmental Stewardship*. New Haven, CT: Yale Center for Environmental Law and Policy.

Yalnizyan, Armine. 2010. *The Rise of Canada's Richest 1%*. Ottawa: Canadian Centre for Policy Alternatives.

Yan, Xiaoyi. 2001. "Understanding personal savings and wealth accumulation." Paper presented at the 2001 Economic Conference: Economic and Social Trends in a Dynamic Economy, Ottawa.

Young, K.T. 1994. *The Health of Native Americans: Towards a Biocultural Epidemiology*. New York: Oxford University Press.

Yssaad, Lahouaria. 2012. *The Canadian Immigrant Labour Market, 2008–2011*. The Immigrant Labour Force Analysis Series. Ottawa: Statistics Canada cat. no. 71-606-X.

Yukon Bureau of Statistics. 2010. *Life Expectancy in the Yukon 2010*. Culture, Tourism and the Centre for Education Statistics.

Zawilski, Valerie, ed. 2009. *Inequality in Canada: A Reader on the Intersections of Gender, Race, and Class*. Don Mills, ON: Oxford University Press.

Zelinsky, Wilbur. 1971. "The hypothesis of the mobility transition." *Geographical Review* 61(2): 219–49.

Zhang, Xuelin. 2009. "Earnings of women with and without children." *Perspectives on Labour and Income* 10(3). Statistics Canada cat. no. 75-001-XWE.

Zhao, John, Doug Drew, and T. Scott Murray. 2000. "Knowledge workers on the move." *Perspectives* 2: 32–46.

Zhou, Min. 2009. *Contemporary Chinese America: Immigration, Ethnicity, and Community Transformation*. Philadelphia, PA: Temple University Press.

Ziegler, E. 1988. *Refugee Movements and Policy in Canada*. Report for Review of Demography. Ottawa: Health and Welfare Canada.

Zsigmond, Zoltan, Garnett Picot, Warren Clark, and Mary Sue Devereau. 1978. *Out of School—Into the Labour Force*. Ottawa: Statistics Canada cat. no. 81-570.

Index

approaches, 66–7; elderly, 42, 56–7, 67; ethics, 67–8; and gender, 3, 59–60; immigrants, 62–4; and income, 219; and life expectancy, 41–2, 43–4; and mortality, 66, 170; in northern regions, 62; policy, 64, 65–7; and population change, 3; pre-contact period, 19–20; and work, 211; young people, 42, 46–7

Health Act (1985), 42

health-care system, treatment and mortality, 170

health costs: and aging, 206–7, 217–19, 221; of children, 83; factors, 66; and last days of life, 66; lifetime costs, 218, 219; preventive *vs.* curative models, 67; provinces and territories, 217–18; public and private, 64, 65–6; worldwide, 66

health regions, indicators of health, 56

Health Status in Canada, 55

heart disease, 44, 46–7, 49–50. *see also* cardiovascular diseases

higher education. *see* university

high schools, 263–4

history of Canadian population: pre-contact period, 16–21; Aboriginal peoples and contact, 21–3; European settlement, 23–31; nineteenth century, 31–6

home language, 250–1, 252, 285

home leaving, 231–2

homogamy, educational, 235–6

Hospital Insurance Diagnostic Services Act (1957), 64

hospitals, costs, 66

household units: composition and diversity, 242–3; definition, 242; growth, 225–6; and inequality, 243–4, 245; one-person households, 242

housework, 89

Human Development Index, Canada in, 277–8

human ecology and footprint, 311–15

Immigration Act (1953), 103–4

Immigration Act (1976), 105–6

Immigration Acts (1910 and 1916), 103–4

immigration and immigrants: age and aging, 116–18, 122, 198–200; ancestry and ethnicity, 254–7; annual migration 1920–2010, 102; assimilation, 261–2; assumptions for projections, 167, 170–1; attitudes toward, 134–5, 172, 184–5; benefits, 186; births to immigrants, 111, 112–13; to British North America, 31–2, 33; classes, 129; demographic impact, 111–15; disease, 32; and distribution of population, 142–3; economic adjustment by class, 129–30; and economy, 106, 108, 109, 121–5, 129–30; and education, 125–6, 127, 130–1; exclusions and restrictions, 102–3, 104; fertility, 81, 113; and gender, 63; geographic distribution, 118–21; and globalization, 110, 136; health, 62–4; history and trends,

100–8, 116, 333–4, 335; impact on population, 2, 29, 333–4; income, 126–31; integration, 109, 135, 152–3; 261; and language, 133–4, 250, 252–3, 254; and mortality, 32, 62–4; mortality rates, 63; to New France, 24–5, 27–8, 30; nineteenth century, 101; 1989–present, 106–8; non-permanent residents, 115–16; patterns and forms, 109–10; place of origin, 132–3; planned and actual levels, 107–8; points system, 104–5, 106, 122, 129; policy, 99–108, 116, 123, 184–5, 186; and politics, 134–5, 185; and population growth, 111–15, 116, 117, 199–200; postwar, 103–8; projections, 170–1, 172, 175–6, 178–9, 199–200; provinces and territories, 153; in redistribution of population, 152–3; refugees, 100, 104–5; as replacement migration, 178–9; second generation, 131; skills and productivity, 122–4; sociocultural aspects, 109, 125, 131–5; socioeconomic status and profiles, 125–31, 259–62; tax and dependency, 122; theorical understandings, 108–11; unemployment, 123–4, 128; from US, 31; visible minorities (*see* visible minorities); and work, 100, 108, 121–2, 123–6, 127, 131, 179–81, 337. *see also* foreign-born population

Immigration and Refugee Protection Act (2001), 106, 115, 328

income: age and aging, 213–14; distribution, 266–7, 270–5; and education, 265–6; and family, 243–4, 246, 270–1, 273–4; fertility and children, 85, 86; Gini coefficient, 272–3; and health, 219; immigrants, 126–31; inequality, 272–3; low (*see* low income); mean and median, 270–1; provinces and regions, 141; visible minorities, 259, 260–1; young people, 213–14

independent immigrants, 129

Indian Act (1867), 281, 295–6

Indian Register, 282–3, 287, 295

indigenous peoples. *see* Aboriginal peoples

inequality, 158–60, 243–4, 245, 272–3

infant mortality: Aboriginal peoples, 288, 289; decline, 56–7; and life expectancy, 43; New France, 26; nineteenth and twentieth centuries, 35, 43; pre-contact period, 20–1

infectious diseases. *see* disease

infertility, 83

injuries, in traffic accidents, 54

internal migration: across provinces, 150–1, 153–5; and age, 156–7; dynamics, 149–52; factors, 150–1; municipalities, 156–7; net movement, 153–5; political implications, 157–8; rates, 151, 336–7; in redistribution of population, 153–5; and work, 159–60

international migration. *see* immigration and immigrants

International Panel on Climate Change (IPCC), 324

interprovincial migration, 150–1, 153–5